KEY SOCIOLOGICAL THINKERS

Also by Rob Stones:

Structuration Theory (2005)
Sociological Reasoning: Towards a Past-Modern Sociology (1996)

Rob Stones is also the series editor of
Traditions in Social Theories

and the forthcoming series editor of
Themes in Social Theory

Key Sociological Thinkers

Second Edition

Edited by
Rob Stones

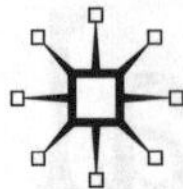

First edition published 1998
Second edition published 2008 by
PALGRAVE MACMILLAN
Houndmills, Basingstoke, Hampshire RG21 6XS and
175 Fifth Avenue, New York, N. Y. 10010
Companies and representatives throughout the world

PALGRAVE MACMILLAN is the global academic imprint of the Palgrave Macmillan division of St. Martin's Press, LLC and of Palgrave Macmillan Ltd. Macmillan® is a registered trademark in the United States, United Kingdom and other countries. Palgrave is a registered trademark in the European Union and other countries.

ISBN-13: 978–0–230–00157–2 (paperback)
ISBN-10: 0–230–00157–2 (paperback)
ISBN-13: 978–0–230–00156–5 (hardback)
ISBN-10: 0–230–00156–4 (hardback)

This book is printed on paper suitable for recycling and made from fully managed and sustained forest sources. Logging, pulping and manufacturing processes are expected to conform to the environmental regulations of the country of origin.

A catalogue record for this book is available from the British Library.

A catalog record for this book is available from the Library of Congress.

10 9 8 7 6 5 4 3 2 1
17 16 15 14 13 12 11 10 09 08

Printed in China

In memory of my mother and father

Patricia Charlton Wilson 1935–2006
James Gordon Stones 1927–2002

Contents

Notes on Contributors

Michèle Barrett is Professor of Modern Literary and Cultural Theory in the School of English and Drama at Queen Mary, University of London. Her books include *Virginia Woolf: Women and Writing* (2003), *Women's Oppression Today: Problems in Marxist Feminist Analysis* (1988), with Mary McIntosh *The Anti-Social Family* (1988), *The Politics of Truth: From Marx to Foucault* (1991), with Anne Phillips *Destabilizing Theory: Contemporary Feminist Debates* (1992), *Imagination in Theory: Essays on Writing and Culture* (1999), and with Duncan Barrett *Star Trek: The Human Frontier* (2000). She is currently working on literary, cultural, biographical and theoretical issues related to shell shock and the First World War.

Lawrence Barth is a Senior Lecturer at the Graduate School of the Architectural Association, London. His teaching and research interests centre on the intersection of politics, critical theory and urbanism. He has written on the implications of Jean Francois Lyotard's philosophy for urban social theory in 'Immemorial visibilities: seeing the city's difference', *Environment and Planning A* (1996), on Henri Lefebvre and romanticism, in *Daidalos, 75* (1999), and on a Foucauldian approach to the diagram and urban governmental reason in 'Diagram, dispersal, region', in C. Najle and M. Mostafavi (eds) *Landscape Urbanism* (2003).

Ted Benton is Professor of Sociology, University of Essex. His current interests are in environmental issues and modern social theory, especially in links between socialist and 'green' perspectives. Publications include *Philosophical Foundations of the Three Sociologies* (1977), '"Objective" interests and the sociology of power', *Sociology* (1981), *The Rise and Fall of Structural Marxism* (1984), 'Biology and social science: why the return of the repressed should be given a (cautious) welcome', *Sociology* (1991), *Natural Relations: Ecology, Animal Rights and Social Justice* (1993), with M. Redclift (eds) *Social Theory and the Global Environment* (1994), (ed.) *The Greening of Marxism* (1996), with Ian Craib *The Philosophy of Social Science* (2001) in Palgrave's Traditions in Social Theory series, and most recently the single-authored volume *Bumblebees* (2006) for the prestigious Collins New Naturalist series, combining 15 years of his own field studies of the species with all the latest research and findings, and framing this with his pioneering critical approach to grasping the interactions between the natural and social worlds. Ted is also one of the co-authors of the *Handbook of Environment and Society* (2007).

Tony Blackshaw is a Senior Lecturer in the Social and Cultural Studies of Sport at Sheffield Hallam University. He teaches and researches in a range of areas related to community, sport and social exclusion. His unshakable interest is the interface between theory and practice and this is reflected in his two major studies in the sociology of sport and leisure: *Leisure Life: Myth, Masculinity and Modernity* (2003), and *New Perspectives on Sport and 'Deviance': Consumption, Performativity and Social Control* with Tim Crabbe (2004). The first of these, based on his own extensive fieldwork, is drawn on in the 'Seeing Things Differently' section of his chapter here. His book-length account of the work of *Zygmunt Bauman* (2005) was described enthusiastically by Peter Beilharz as 'Bauman unplugged'.

Ira J. Cohen is Professor of Sociology, teaching social theory as a member of the Graduate Faculty in Sociology at Rutgers University in New Brunswick and in the Department of Sociology, Rutgers University in Newark. He has published works on a broad range of themes in classical and contemporary social theory, including 'The underemphasis on democracy in Marx and Weber', in R.J. Antonio and R.M. Glassman (eds) *A Weber–Marx Dialogue* (1985), *Structuration Theory: Anthony Giddens and the Constitution of Social Life* (1989), 'Structuration theory and social order: five issues in brief', in J. Clarke, C. Modgil and S. Modgil (eds) *Anthony Giddens: Consensus and Controversy* (1990), 'Theories of action and praxis', in B. Turner (ed.) *The Blackwell Companion to Social Theory* (1996), and with Mary F. Rogers 'Autonomy and credibility: voice as method', *Sociological Theory* (1994), and 'Structuration', extended entry in G. Ritzer (ed.) *Sage Encyclopedia of Social Theory* (2004). Ira is general editor of the *Modernity and Society* series, a group of text-readers edited by distinguished theorists for Basil Blackwell including Robert Antonio's volume on Marx, Mustafa Emirbayer's on Durkheim and Steven Kalberg's on Weber. He is currently working on a single-authored volume, *Disengaged Involvement: On the Sociology of Solitude*.

John Heritage is Professor of Sociology at the University of California, Los Angeles. He has published extensively in the fields of ethnomethodology and conversation analysis, including *Garfinkel and Ethnomethodology* (1984), *Structures of Social Action: Studies in Conversation Analysis* co-edited with Max Atkinson (1984), *Talk at Work* co-edited with Paul Drew (1992), *The News Interview: Journalists and Public Figures on the Air* with Steven Clayman (1992) and *Communication in Medical Care* co-edited with Douglas Maynard (2006).

Robert Holton is Professor of Sociology at Trinity College, Dublin. He is the author of numerous books and articles on globalization, social theory, historical sociology, immigration and ethnicity, including *Cities, Capitalism, and Civilisation* (1986), *Talcott Parsons on Economy and Society* (1986) and *Max Weber on Economy and Society* (1989) (both with B.S. Turner), *Economy and Society* (1992), 'Classical social theory', in *The Blackwell Companion to Social Theory* (1996), *Globalization and the Nation-State* (1998), and *Making Globalization* (2005).

Jason Hughes is a Lecturer in Business and Management at Brunel University and teaches in the area of human resources. A book based on his Ph.D. thesis, *Learning* *to Smoke: Tobacco Use in the West*, was published in 2003 and was the recipient of the European Norbert Elias prize in 2006. Other publications are *Sociology and its Discontents: Norbert Elias and Contemporary Social Theory* (ed., with Eric Dunning, forthcoming 2007), *Communities of Practice: Critical Perspectives* with N. Jewson and L. Unwin (2007), 'Smoking', in G. Ritzer, (ed.) *The Blackwell Encyclopedia of Sociology* (2006), 'Bringing emotion to work: emotional intelligence, resistance, and the reinvention of character', *Work, Employment and Society* (2005). He has recently edited a special edition of the *Journal of Workplace Learning*, and is a member of the editorial board for the journal *Work, Employment and Society*. You can hear him being interviewed about his award winning book on Radio 4's Thinking Allowed programme here: http://www.bbc.co.uk/radio4/factual/thinkingallowed_20030219.shtml.

Bob Jessop is Director of the Institute for Advanced Studies and Professor of Sociology at the University of Lancaster. He has written extensively on Marxism, theories of the state, political sociology and political economy. His publications include *The Capitalist State: Marxist Theories and Methods* (1982), *Nicos Poulantzas: Marxist Theory and Political Strategy* (1985), *State Theory: Putting Capitalist States in their Place* (1990), and *The Future of the Capitalist State* (2002). He is also the co-author of *Thatcherism: A Tale of Two Nations* (1988), *Strategic Dilemmas and Path Dependency in Post Socialism* (1995), and *Beyond the Regulation Approach: Putting Capitalist Economies in their Place* (2006).

Karin A. Martin is an Associate Professor of Sociology and Women's Studies at the University of Michigan. Her Ph.D. was from the University of California at Berkeley where Nancy Chodorow was her adviser. She is the author of *Puberty, Sexuality and the Self: Girls and Boys at Adolescence* (1996). She does research on gender, sexuality, bodies and childhood. Her work has appeared, *inter alia*, in *The American Sociological Review* and *Gender & Society*.

Nicos Mouzelis is Professor Emeritus of Sociology at the London School of Economics. He has written widely on issues of sociological theory, theories of underdevelopment and organization theory. His most recent publications include *Post-Marxist Alternatives: The Construction of Social Orders* (1990), *Back to Sociological Theory: The Construction of Social Orders* (1991), *Sociological Theory: What Went Wrong?* (1995), 'Social and system integration: Lockwood, Habermas, Giddens', *Sociology* (Feb. 1997), 'The subjectivist–objectivist divide: against transcendence', *Sociology* (34(4), 2000), 'Reflexive modernisation and the third way: the impasses of Giddens' social democratic politics', *Sociological Review* (49(3), 2001), and *Bridges: Between Modern and Late/Post-Modern Social Theorising* (forthcoming).

Maggie O'Neill is Senior Lecturer in the Department of Social Sciences, Loughborough University. She describes her scholarly endeavours as 'critical theory in praxis' drawing upon the influences of Adorno, Benjamin, feminisms and participatory action research (especially the work of William Foot Whyte and Orlando Fals Borda). Maggie has written extensively on Adorno and feminisms, participatory and visual methodologies, the sex industry, gender and organizations, asylum, migration, humiliation and human dignity. She has a long-standing interest in the sociology of art, cultural criminology and the transformative role of art and aesthetics. Maggie is a board member of the Human Dignity and Humiliation Studies network. Her books include *Adorno, Culture and Feminism* (1999), *Prostitution and Feminism: Towards a Politics of Feeling* (2001), *Prostitution: A Reader* with Roger Matthews (2002), *Dilemmas in Managing Professionalism and Gender in the Public Sector* with Jim Barry and Mike Dent (2002), and *Sex Work Now* with Rosie Campbell (2006).

William Outhwaite is Professor of Sociology at the University of Newcastle upon Tyne. His research interests include the philosophy of the social sciences (especially realism), social theory (especially critical theory and contemporary European social theory), political sociology, contemporary Europe and the sociology of knowledge. He is the author of *Understanding Social Life: The Method Called Verstehen* (1986), *Concept Formation in Social Science* (1983), *New Philosophies of Social Science: Realism, Hermeneutics and Critical Theory* (1987), *Jürgen Habermas: A Critical Introduction* (1994), *The Future of Society* (2006), and with Larry Ray *Social Theory and Postcommunism* (2005). Edited books include *The Habermas Reader* (1996), with Tom Bottomore *The Blackwell Dictionary of Twentieth-century Social Thought* (1993), with Luke Martell *The Sociology of Politics* (1998), and with Stephen Turner *The Sage Handbook of Social Science Methodology* (2007).

Ken Plummer is Emeritus Professor of Sociology at the University of Essex and has been a regular visiting professor at the University of California, Santa Barbara. In addition to a long-standing interest in the teaching of introductory sociology, his major research interests lie in the fields of sexuality, stigma, methodology and symbolic interactionist theory He is the author of *Sexual Stigma* (1975), *Documents of Life* (1983), and *Telling Sexual Stories* (1995), *Documents of Life 2: An Invitation to a Critical Humanism* (2001); and *Intimate Citizenship* (2003). He is also the editor of *Symbolic Interactionism*, vols I and II (1991), *The Making of the Modern Homosexual* (ed. 1981), *Modern Homosexualities* (ed. 1992) and *The Chicago School* (1997, 4 vols). His most recent articles include 'Intimate citizenship in an unjust world', in M. Romero and E. Margolis (eds) *The Blackwell Companion to Social Inequalities* (2005), and 'Rights work: constructing lesbian, gay and sexual rights in modern times', in L. Morris (ed.) *Rights: Sociological Perspectives* (2006). Ten years ago he founded the Sage journal *Sexualities* and he continues to edit this from the Department of Sociology at Essex.

Whitney Pope is Emeritus Professor of Sociology at Indiana University, Bloomington. In addition to publishing articles on sociological theory and suicide, he is the author of what is widely regarded as the finest book-length examination of Emile Durkheim's study of suicide, *Durkheim's 'Suicide': A Classic Analysed* (1976), and of

Alexis de Tocqueville: His Social and Political Theory (1986). His subsequent research interests included Tocqueville's theory of freedom, assessing the asserted trade-off between economic growth and equality, and relations between the state and the market in the USA from colonial times to the present. Whitney retired in 1999 and, together with his wife, now runs a bed and breakfast in Sedona, Arizona (see final section of introduction).

Lawrence A. Scaff is Professor of Political Science and Sociology at Wayne State University and recently served as Dean of the College of Liberal Arts. He is the author of the classic study *Fleeing the Iron Cage: Culture, Politics and Modernity in the Thought of Max Weber* (1989), and has written extensively on topics in modern social theory and German social thought. Recent articles include 'Civil society and its discontents: reflections on the North American experience', in *Building Democracy and Civil Society East of the Elbe*, ed. Sven Eliaeson (2006), 'The creation of the sacred text: Talcott Parsons translates *The Protestant Ethic and the Spirit of Capitalism*', *Max Weber Studies* (5(2/6), 2005/6), 'Weber, art, and social theory', *Etica & Politica (Ethics & Politics)* (6(2), 2005) at http://www.univ.trieste.it/~etica, 'Remnants of romanticism: Max Weber in Oklahoma and Indian territory', *Journal of Classical Sociology* (5(1), 2005), 'The mind of the modernist: Simmel on time', *Time & Society* (14(1), 2005), 'Rationalization', in G. Ritzer (ed.) *Encyclopedia of Social Theory* (2005), 'Max Weber and the social sciences in America', *European Journal of Political Theory* (3(2), 2004), 'Neo-Weberian approaches', in R.J.B. Jones (ed.) *Routledge Encyclopedia of International Political Economy* vol. 2 (2001), and 'Weber on the cultural situation of the modern age', in S. Turner (ed.) *The Cambridge Companion to Max Weber* (2000).

Ralph Schroeder is James Martin Research Fellow at the Oxford Internet Institute. Before coming to Oxford University, he was Professor in the School of Technology Management and Economics at Chalmers University in Gothenburg. His publications include *Rethinking Science, Technology and Social Change* (2007), *An Anatomy of Power: the Social Theory of Michael Mann* with John A. Hall (eds 2006), *Max Weber, Democracy and Modernization* (ed. 1998), *Possible Worlds: The Social Dynamic of Virtual Reality Technology* (1996), and *Max Weber and the Sociology of Culture* (1992). His current research includes work on e-science.

Alan Sica is Professor of Sociology and Founding Director of the Social Thought Program at Pennsylvania State University. He edited the American Sociology Association journal, *Sociological Theory* (1989–94) and has been associate editor of the *American Journal of Sociology* and the *American Sociological Review*. Among his books are *Hermeneutics: Questions and Prospects* (1984), *Weber, Irrationality, and Social Order* (1988), *What is Social Theory?* (ed. 1998), *The Unknown Max Weber* (2000), *Max Weber and the New Century* (2004), *Max Weber: A Comprehensive Bibliography* (2004), *Social Thought: From the Enlightenment to the Present* (2004), *The Disobedient Generation* with Stephen Turner (2005), and *Comparative Methods in the Social Sciences* (2006).

Rob Stones is Professor in Sociology at the University of Essex, and served as head of department from 2004 to 2007. His recent publications include *Structuration Theory* (2005), with Sung Kyung Kim, 'Film, postmodernism and the sociological imagination', in J. Powell and T. Owen (eds) *Reconstructing Postmodernism* (2007), 'Rights, social theory and political philosophy: a framework for case study research', in L. Morris (ed.) *Rights: Sociological Perspectives* (2006), 'Anthony Giddens', in G. Ritzer (ed.) *Encyclopaedia of Social Theory* (2004), 'Social theory, the civic imagination and documentary film: a past-modern critique of the "Bloody Bosnia" season's *The Roots of War*', *Sociology* (2002), 'Social theory, documentary film and distant others: simplicity and subversion in *The Good Woman of Bangkok*', *European Journal of Cultural Studies* (2002), 'Refusing the realism–structuration divide', *European Journal of Social Theory* (2000). He is the editor of two book series for Palgrave Macmillan, *Traditions in Social Theory* and *Themes in Social Theory*.

Loïc Wacquant is Professor of Sociology at the University of California, Berkeley and Researcher at the Centre de sociologie européenne, Paris. A student and close collaborator of Pierre Bourdieu for two decades, he has been a visiting professor in Los Angeles, New York, Rio de Janeiro and Paris. A MacArthur Foundation Fellow, he is the author of over one hundred scholarly articles and his books dealing with comparative urban marginality, embodiment, the penal state, ethnoracial domination and social theory have been translated into a dozen languages. They include *Body and Soul: Notebooks of An Apprentice Boxer* (2004), *The Mystery of Ministry: Pierre Bourdieu and Democratic Politics* (2005), *Das Janusgesicht des Ghettos und andere Essays* (2006), and *Urban Outcasts: A Comparative Sociology of Advanced Marginality* (2007). He is a co-founder and editor of the interdisciplinary journal *Ethnography*. For more information, see http://sociology.berkeley.edu/faculty/wacquant/.

Patrick Watier is Professor of Sociology at the University of Strasbourg and Director of the Institute of War Studies, associated with the Centre for the Sociology of European Culture, CNRS, Strasbourg. His publications include 'Les resources de l'interprétation sociologique', *L'Année Sociologique* (2007), 'Compréhension et savoir ordinaire', in M. Maffesoli and D. Jeffrey (eds) *La sociologie compréhensive* (2005), 'Puissance sociale et connaissance ordinaire', in *Dérive autour de l'œuvre de Michel Maffesoli* (2005), 'G. Simmel', in M. Dorai (ed.) *Histoire de la Psychologie Sociale* (2002), 'Trust and psychosociological feelings: socialization and totalitarianism', with I. Markhova, in I. Markhova (ed.) *Trust and Democratic Transition in Post-Communist Europe, Proceedings of the British Academy*, vol. 119 (2004), *Une introduction à la sociologie compréhensive* (2002), *Simmel sociologue* (2003), *Le savoir sociologique* (2000), and 'The war writings of Georg Simmel', *Theory, Culture and Society* (1991).

Karin Widerberg is Professor of Sociology at the Department of Sociology and Human Geography, University of Oslo, Norway. Her main research fields – on which she has published extensively – are theory of science and methodology, understandings of gender (in general) and, more specifically, time, work, the body, sexual violence and law from within a gender perspective. Among her books (published in both Norwegian and Swedish) are *The Gender of Knowledge* (1995), *The History of a Qualitative Research Project* (2001), *The Times of Tiredness* (2001) and *Writing Social Science* (2003). Methodology is a key issue in all her writings, no matter what the theme, and exploring and developing qualitative methods is a main concern and activity. Her recent major research project was on 'The sociality of tiredness: the handling of tiredness in gender, generation and class perspectives'. She is currently involved in the EU project 'Changing knowledge and disciplinary boundaries through integrative research methods in the social sciences and humanities'.

Robin Williams is Reader in the School of Applied Social Sciences at the University of Durham. His interests are in the sociology of interaction and forensic science. He is the author of a number of publications on the sociology of Erving Goffman, the interpretative tradition in sociology and the police uses of forensic science and technology. These include *The Handbook of Forensic Science* with J. Fraser (2008, forthcoming), *Using DNA in Crime Investigation* with P. Johnson (2007), 'Sociology, ethics, and the priority of the particular: learning from a case study of genetic deliberations' with E. Haimes, *British Journal of Sociology* (2007), entries on 'DNA profiling' and 'Fingerprints', in T. Newburn, and P. Neyroud, *Dictionary of Policing* (2007), 'Inclusiveness, effectiveness and intrusiveness: issues in the developing uses of DNA profiling in support of criminal investigations' with P. Johnson, *Journal of Law, Medicine and Ethics* (2005), 'Residual categories and disciplinary knowledge: personal identity in sociological and forensic investigations', *Symbolic Interaction* (2003), *Making Identity Matter* (2000), 'Understanding Goffman's methods', in P. Drew and A. Wooton (eds) *Erving Goffman: Exploring the Interaction Order*, and 'Goffman's sociology of talk', in J. Ditton (ed.) *The View from Goffman* (1980).

Simon Williams is Professor of Sociology at the University of Warwick. He has long-standing research interests in the sociology of health and illness, the body, and emotions, areas in which he has published widely. His books include *The Lived Body* (1998), *Emotions and Social Theory* (2001) and *Medicine and the Body* (2003). His most recent research has focused on sleep as a neglected sociological issue, including a new book *Sleep and Society: Sociological Ventures into the (Un)Known* (2005). He also has newly emerging research interests in the pharmaceutical industry and is currently co-editing a monograph for the journal *Sociology of Health and Illness* on 'Pharmaceuticals and Society', which will be published in 2008.

Acknowledgements

The first acknowledgement must, of course, go to the authors of the chapters that make up this volume. The achievement of the book is theirs and I would like to express my gratitude to them for contributing such a fine collection of papers. Then, at the publishers, Palgrave Macmillan, I would like to thank Emily Salz for her enthusiasm and editorial advice, Catherine Gray for initiating the idea of a second edition and taking this forward in the early stages, and to Anna Reeve and Sheree Keep for keeping me informed and involved at key moments in the publication process. I'm also indebted to Sue Aylott, who like Catherine was also closely involved in the first edition, for her invaluable administrative assistance and her always cheerful dedication to the task. Aardvark Editorial, in the guise of Linda Norris and Maggie Lythgoe, continue to combine skill and lightning efficiency nine years on, making the copy editing and proof stages as painless as possible.

I am also extremely grateful to my colleagues, past and present, in the formidable Department of Sociology at the University of Essex for providing such a stimulating and inspiring environment in which to research and teach. Finally, the book is dedicated, with deep appreciation, to my parents who were wise enough to understand the importance of values and obligations in a life well lived, and loving enough to ensure they passed this on to their children.

Introduction: Continuity and Change in the Preoccupations of Key Sociological Thinkers

Rob Stones

In the main part of this introduction to the second edition of *Key Sociological Thinkers*, I want to provide a frame within which to situate the chapters that follow. I will do this by highlighting some of the key continuities and changes in the themes that have preoccupied sociological thought in the past 150 years or so. Among other things, I hope to show the importance of understanding the past preoccupations of sociological theory for grasping sociology's relationship to the present. I will focus upon a limited number of salient themes: modernity; consciousness and identity; values and value relevant critique; and political commitments and their philosophical justification. I will follow this with discussions of: the necessity of combining different themes when addressing particular problems; sociology's civic mission; and the role of sociological thought in the formulation of political strategy. In the final part of the chapter, I will outline the structure of the book, what it hopes to achieve, and the changes that have been made since the first edition.

I will start by mentioning a critique of sociological theory that runs counter to what I will argue. Thus, in the wake of the poststructuralist and postmodernist turns in social theory – turns, I should add, which I have much sympathy with on many other scores – the classical sociologists who appear in Part I of this volume, with particular, but not exclusive, reference to **Karl Marx, Max Weber** and **Emile Durkheim**, are often referred to disparagingly as the dead white males (DWMs), pithily reversing the order of the initial capitals of the three surnames of the trinity. The insidious suggestion is partly, of course, the rather glib one that, as the three writers are dead, their work is somehow naturally and *necessarily obsolete*, but also that their colour and sex necessarily reflect both *social privilege and a narrowness of outlook* that seriously compromise their writings.

The critique of the DWMs is, of course, partly hyperbole, but it is hyperbole that is taken seriously by many and has real consequences. I don't want to disparage or underestimate the passion and the anger provoked when groups – women, ethnic, indigenous, racial and sexually marginalized, to name just some – confront their own or others' absence from the pages of serious social reflection. These responses are authentic, vital and deadly serious. However, such responses are entirely compatible with an equally serious, systematic and responsible approach to righting the balance, to finding a new, sophisticated equilibrium; one that embraces all the thinkers that can help to do justice to the complexity and subtlety of social relations. There is too much to be lost by a quick and easy dismissal of the DWMs whose works form the first three chapters of Part I of *Key Sociological Thinkers*. It is important to understand how seminal their contributions were at the time, and also to grasp which aspects of their work – as they stand or appropriately adapted – are still relevant and critically powerful when applied to contemporary social life. None of this prevents us from also looking carefully at what has indeed changed since the middle of the nineteenth century, both in terms of the major defining characteristics of social relations *and* in the concerns of the key sociological thinkers of today compared with those of yesteryear. In fact, the more we can truly appreciate the continuities, the more we will be able to accurately identify the changes, and the quality of our understanding will be that much greater.

Social Privilege, Narrowness of Outlook and Obsolescence

It would be difficult to deny that the work of the early sociological thinkers was affected by the social privileges and related narrowness of outlook associated with being white and male in the late nineteenth and early twentieth centuries. The same could be said, and often is, about many of the white male social theorists writing today. To acknowledge this, however, is not necessarily to invalidate the work of those authors, certainly not in their entirety. Points about relative narrowness of perspective can be made about any writer, privileged and underprivileged, of any colour, ethnicity, gender, class, sexuality, historical period and so on. While it is important to be aware that social privilege means that some voices will be heard more often than others, the appropriate response is to foster a greater plurality of voices, not to condemn the voices that have been heard irrespective of the value of what they have been saying. To judge the latter, it is necessary to read their work carefully for what it has to offer, for the insights about society and the analysis of society it presents, as well as to pinpoint its blind spots and prejudices.

Poststructuralism and postmodernism, trading on and growing from a series of other intellectual and cultural developments in the latter half of the twentieth century, including feminism, structuralism and internal critiques of Marxism, have often concentrated on the blind spots and prejudices of earlier theories at the expense of the insights they have to offer. Thus, they rightly emphasize the many differences of race, ethnicity, sex, gender, sexual preferences, identity and so on that have a profound effect on the quality of people's lives and the way they are treated by others, and which were neglected and marginalized by earlier thinkers. They emphasize what they see as the neglected plurality of different social positions beyond the white and the male. Some of these writers would see an additional failing in a writer such as Marx as being his excessive concern with class at the expense of the many other social dimensions central to a postmodern outlook. All this is positive as long as it is also remembered that Marx's concern with class was determinedly from the perspective of the oppressed and the exploited, was politically engaged, and was part of a sophisticated and multilayered analysis of social relations and their dynamics, albeit a corrigible one. Despite being privileged in terms of being white, male and relatively well cared for materially – while also being an immigrant, an exile and a member of an ethnic minority – Marx, like other key theorists who grappled with the social fabric of modernity and capitalism, has many insights to offer that can still be fruitfully adopted and, in some cases, where necessary, partially reconceptualized as a result of later social developments and the writings of later authors. As with other authors, his writing should not be dismissed as of no consequence simply because it has limitations. And what is true for social privilege and narrowness of outlook is also true with respect to the implicit charge of obsolescence.

The assumption of the obsolescence of earlier writers is a serious oversimplification of issues that require more careful thought. In part, the assumption is based on a radical overestimation of the differences between the era of modernity, on the one hand, and that of late, post- or liquid modernity on the other. There are certainly differences but there are also significant continuities, both in the structural forces and patterns of organization and in the forms of consciousness and identity that characterize both. The political and critical dimensions of the writings of sociological theorists in both earlier and later periods also contain many intriguing continuities alongside equally absorbing developments and differences.

Six Themes of Continuity and Change

In discussing the topics outlined above – modernity, consciousness and identity, values and critique, and political commitments; with the latter three all framed by the overarching concept of modernity – I suggest that it is illuminating to be guided by six analytical themes that can help to highlight contours and degrees of continuity and change in sociological thought over the past 150 years. The first three themes directly concern what theorists have said about the very *nature of societies* themselves, social relations as they have existed at different times and places from the mid-nineteenth century to the present day. They simply encourage one to notice and reflect upon:

1. The deeper continuities in social relations that mark both the modernity of the nineteenth and early twentieth centuries and the late or liquid modernity of the latter decades of the twentieth century and the beginning of the twenty first. Contemporary societies clearly continue to be marked by forms and degrees of capitalism, industrialism, urbanization, a specialized division of labour, bureaucracy, forms of surveillance, inequalities, poverty and warfare, to name just some.
2. The specific aspects of contemporary social relations that are truly novel. These include: the variety of forms of information and communication technologies, increasingly rapid forms of transportation of people and goods; the speed and intensity of scientific, economic and cultural innovation; the mass media saturation of the public sphere; the rapidity of cycles of production and consumption; the ways in which identity markers of class, gender, ethnicity and so on are, as theorists such as **Zygmunt Bauman** insist, now much more likely to be unsettled, contingent and liquid, to 'flow into each other';[1] and the move from production-centred to service-centred activities in highly significant parts of the global economy.
3. The uneven combinations of the old and the new, of the elements of modernity and those of late/post-/liquid modernity within contemporary social relations.

By way of contrast, the fourth and fifth themes do not directly concern the nature of social relations themselves, but instead invite a focus on the continuities and changes in the *nature of the theories* used to think about societies. They encourage awareness of:

4. The history and the contours of concept development and refinement in different areas of sociological thought, through contestation and rejoinder over time, with the social scientific community adapting its voluntary codes and standards of critical analysis, debate and evidence[2] in response both to the power of argument and to changing social conditions.
5. Those aspects of different theoretical approaches that – taking into account the developments and refinements suggested by 4 above – have the potential to be fruitfully combined, and those instances when there is a need to clarify irreconcilable differences – the latter being a much less common occurrence than is often assumed, once rigorous standards of argumentation and assessment are applied. The perspectives of the DWMs may well be narrow taken on their own, but so are most approaches. A combination

of theoretical and conceptual approaches – selected according to the question at hand – will often be the most appropriate and fruitful response.

The sixth and final theme uses and builds upon the distinction between accounts of the nature of societies themselves and accounts of theoretical and conceptual tools used to examine those societies. It uses this distinction to insist upon another logically correlative distinction between *new societal features* (included in the domain of 1, 2 and 3) – such as globalization and the information society, including, for example, the speed of communication and the implications for command over distance – and *new ways of seeing*, conceptually and theoretically, things that were there from the onset of modernity but which were either generally neglected, as with race, ethnicity and the position of women, or were previously seen in very different ways in sociological thought. Aspects of the older theories can, for example, be very helpful in the analysis of new societal features, just as new ways of seeing things can provide fresh insights not only into new societal features but also into long-standing and/or historical societal features. One example of the latter can be found in the writings of **Michel Foucault** on regimes of regulation and governance, both of whole populations and within particular sets of institutions and discourses such as those of prisons, clinics, mental asylums, sexual practices and so on. It is salutary to recognize that recent thinkers, like Foucault, have managed to engage the imagination and passion of readers while writing about subjects that are at least contemporaneous with the writings of the original DWMs. **Nancy Chodorow**, in combining the psychoanalytic techniques of object relations theorists with the insights of feminism, sheds new light and insight on practices – women's mothering – that are pressing now; many of her insights would, of course, also have been illuminating for the inhabitants of late nineteenth-century modernity had they been available then. Similar points could be made about **Dorothy Smith**'s astute insistence on the insights to be gained through a sustained emphasis on the pivotal role played by printed (and now electronic) texts in the organization and mediation of social relations.

These points will inform the commentary that follows, and as their relevance should be readily apparent to the attentive reader, I won't overlabour the analysis by remarking on them explicitly at each juncture. Rather, I will do this only when I feel it to be particularly useful.

Modernity 1: From Tradition to Modernity

'Modernity' is the label often used to characterize the stage in the history of social relations, dating roughly from the end of the eighteenth century, that is characterized by the democratic and industrial revolutions. Strong arguments can be made to the effect that sociology as a discipline developed as a response to the advent and challenges of modernity. A more specific argument was made by Bob Jessop in his original chapter on Marx that:

> In developing his critique of capitalism, Marx also helped to trigger the development of sociology. The latter provided an alternative account of modern industrial societies as the basis for economic, social and political reforms that might prevent the revolution Marx predicted and for which a growing working-class movement was mobilizing.[3]

We will return to this general domain later in addressing the relationship between sociology, political values and political strategy, and in looking at the recent renewal of 'public sociology'.

Modernity is typically contrasted with traditional forms of society along lines parallel to Ferdinand Tönnies' distinction between *Gemeinschaft* and *Gesellschaft*, or Durkheim's contrast between mechanical and organic solidarity.[4] More recently, the comparison has been with: postmodernity, which is argued to have superseded modernity; late modernity, which is said to entail a radical intensification of tendencies already embedded within modernity; or Zygmunt Bauman's liquid modernity, which works with the late modernity arguments but only to take them to a new, almost apocalyptic level, emphasising fluids, flows and the transition from a 'heavy' and 'solid' hardware-focused modernity to a 'light' and 'liquid', software-based modernity'.[5] It is the contrast between modernity and these latter characterizations of contemporary society that I want to concentrate on here, but it can first be helpful to recognize just how radical the change was from traditional to modern societies in order to appreciate, by way of contrast, the relative continuities within the different stages of modernity.

Thus, in the traditional forms of society, relations had been built primarily upon small-scale, homogeneous and closely regulated communities. Strongly held beliefs, values and norms existed alongside repressive laws and severe punishments for nonconformist transgressions. Close, face-to-face ties with familiar others predominated, as did relatively unquestioning acceptance of ascribed social status. The transition from tradition to modernity involved a mass migration from the countryside to newly expanding cities, a rapid growth in production for exchange and the rise of the money economy, and the development of a specialized division of labour. All these emergent phenomena clearly remain as dominant fixtures within late or postmodern societies, albeit transmuting and adapting in the specific forms they take. The differentiation and specialization of functional tasks meant that connections between people in this modern type of society were increasingly based on an impersonal and rule-guided mutual interdependence between strangers rather than on an emotional involvement based on personalized forms of face-to-face interaction. Correspondingly, the basis of solidarity became weaker and more abstract, allowing for the growth of individuality and freedom. Peter Wagner's *A Sociology of Modernity*[6] suggests an enduring tension within modernity between the structures and values that encouraged this extension of liberty and the partly contradictory structures and values of discipline and order. Ralph Schroeder's chapter on **Michael Mann**'s work in the current volume notes a parallel tension between the extension of the democratic rights of individuals – with the state providing, for example, more education, health benefits or family services – and the tendency towards excessive state power as it is granted the necessary access to and control over personal information, which automatically also increased its capacity for surveillance.[7] Surveillance has grown along with modernity, as is powerfully evidenced in the work of Michel Foucault, although its reach and its forms have undergone radical changes from the latter part of the twentieth century. This is something emphasized by both Mann and **Anthony Giddens** among the thinkers represented in this volume.

Other dimensions of modernity included the consolidation of the nation-state as the locus of political organization and symbolic allegiance, and the rapid expansion of bureaucracy as a technically efficient, calculable and predictable means of organizing the many administrative tasks required to impose order on modernity's complexity. In *Modernity and the Holocaust*, Bauman focused attention on the huge destructive potential within the apparent 'civilizing process' of modernity. The Nazis' destruction of the Jews and others in the gas chambers of central Europe during the Second World War was not the result of a regression to pre-modern ways but was a direct product of modernity, one that is ever-present. It was a consequence of the modernist impulse to engineer and control the social environment together with a combination of the modern state's unprecedented centralization of power and the modern bureaucratic mode of administration. More recently, there has been much debate about the continuing significance of the nation-state in the contemporary era of globalization, with Giddens and Mann, for example, representing different positions on this. Giddens is more globalist, arguing that many of the nation-state's former powers have either been lifted outwards to the supranational level and/or downwards to the local level. Mann, on the other hand, argues 'that the state is not generally losing power: our primary social cages nowadays are nation-states'.[8] There are significant differences here, with implications when it comes to strategy, but it is important not to overlook the extent to which there is also much agreement between them on the sociological salience of both the nation-state and the international state system, and on the need for sociologists to restructure their conceptual apparatus so that they are able to think beyond and across borders.[9] Both also emphasize the importance of adequately conceptualizing, and giving due significance to, military power, something that has been generally neglected in sociological theory.

Modernity 2: Late, Post- and Liquid Modernity

The term 'late modernity' has been used by writers who don't accept that there has been a transition to a new societal stage of 'postmodernity', but who do wish to acknowledge that there has been a radical intensification of some of the tendencies of modernity. Emphases differ but the general position is associated most prominently with the works of Giddens, Frederic Jameson, David Harvey and **Jürgen Habermas**. Whereas postmodernists such as Jean-François Lyotard and Jean Baudrillard[10] tend to emphasize the *novelty* and intensity of disruptions and dislocations of meaning, and fragmentation and centrifugal forces at the cultural level, theorists of late modernity focus on the heightening and extension of a range of *pre-existing* institutional features that are said to underlie these cultural changes. They also emphasize the continued significance both of centripetal, ordering forces, and the possibility for emancipatory politics. For Harvey and Jameson, the fluidities, disjunctions, simulations and forms of nihilism that postmodernism detects and promotes in the cultural sphere are the product of deeper structural changes brought about in the postindustrial, globally networked period of late capitalism; the era of post-Fordism.[11] Giddens, likewise, emphasizes the intensification and reconfiguration of global capitalism, but in conjunction also with parallel transformations in other aspects of modernity (see below). Both Giddens and Harvey place issues of time and space at the centre of their analyses. Information, media and transportation technologies mean that the world has radically shrunk in terms of communication, identity and the coordination of activities.

Some Marxists have argued that the resurgence of concerns with modernity in the context of the debates about post- or late modernity serves an ideological function in deflecting attention away from the centrality of capitalism to social relations. Theorists of late modernity discussed above – to whom we could add Michael Mann with his fourfold IEMP (ideology, economics, military and politics) model of power (see Chapter 21) – reject this argument, arguing for a more pluralistic understanding in which the role of capitalism is not neglected or underplayed, but is nevertheless treated as just one among several of the defining systemic features of modern society. Marxist theorists such as **Louis Althusser** and Nicos Poulantzas, writing in the 1960s and 70s, went some way to acknowledging this complexity of current social formations, stressing the relative autonomy, distinctive institutional bases and internal dynamics of the political, ideological and legal levels of society from the economic. However, these theorists tended to retain a conceptualization of society that was rooted in, and bounded by, the nation-state rather than in a more complex network of connections and relations, which also either transcended individual states or crosscut them at a number of different levels and social spheres. Having said this, there were embryonic signs of a reconceptualization, which may have been developed had his life not been cut short, in Poulantzas's analysis of the overthrow of three European military regimes, *Crisis of the Dictatorships*.[12] Here there is a clear appreciation of the way in which international political and economic factors entered into the very constitution of the balance of power within the national political arenas of Portugal, Greece and Spain during decisive conjunctures in the 1970s. **Stuart Hall**, who has remained a major intellectual presence within Anglo-American social and cultural theory and British left-wing politics from the late 1950s to the present day, and who is both Marxist inspired and resolutely non-economistic – being influenced heavily by the cultural turn that left its mark on much of twentieth-century Marxism – has also done much to reconceptualize social relations beyond national societies (to paraphrase John Urry).[13] Hall has done this both in his writings on global and diasporic cultures and on colonialism and post-colonialism,[14] all of which he has not been reluctant to render in frameworks shot through with references to both capitalism *and* modernity.

Critical theorists of later modernity thus recognize the continuing centrality of the dynamics of capitalism, bearing both continuities and changes from those analysed by Marx a century or so ago, but they see capitalism alongside, and as interweaving with, other features of modernity such as colonialism, industrialism, surveillance and administrative control, and the centralization of the means of violence. In Giddens' work, each of the latter four features is connected to a parallel institutional dimension of globalization: the world capitalist economy, the international division of labour, the nation-state system, and the world military order. Ulrich Beck, in *Risk Society: Towards a New Modernity*, argues that the unintended 'risk' consequences of industrialism, from the dangers of the nuclear and chemical age, through the corruption of food chains and the pollution of the seas, to the effects of global warming, are at least as important as the dynamics of capitalism *per se*. Giddens draws on Beck's notion of 'reflexive modernization' to emphasize the double-bind in which, in an age of heightened complexity, diverse perspectives and an unprecedented access to knowledge about the conditions of activity, the latter information is inevitably and chronically employed to reorder and redefine these conditions, despite awareness that the effects will often be perverse.

Bauman, for his part, also emphasizes the continuing power of capital to break down borders, 'fences, barriers, fortified borders and checkpoints',[15] but argues that the form in which it does this, and the implications for human life, have been radically transformed by the final triumph of time over space. His most telling metaphors are those of speed and impersonality as he speaks of the 'light' and 'liquid' nature of power in the age of instant communication and command, and the tendency of the flows of finance, capital, information, military power and so on to see all kinds of territorially rooted social bonds and networks simply as 'an obstacle to be cleared out of the way'.[16] Bauman often writes in a way that seems to self-consciously exaggerate existing tendencies and potentials, conjuring powerful insights about the present and poetic prophecies about the future in a way that seems to cut through to the essence of things, and Tony Blackshaw's chapter conveys extremely well the excitement and the profusion of insights generated by this (although I am much less inclined than Blackshaw is to elevate Bauman above all others, as remarkable as he undoubtedly is). But in adopting this style and strategy, Bauman tends, at times, to court forms of **reductionism** (see the meaning given on p. 233 in the chapter on Althusser) in which countervailing factors are ignored. For example, his conviction that the deployment of US military force (paraphrasing Clausewitz's famous formula) 'looks increasingly like a "promotion of global free trade by other means"'[17] is one example of his tendency to believe that the capitalist system renders 'irrelevant and ineffective'[18] all other power structures. This seems to be an instance of straight disagreement with Mann's contention, derived from his more systematic conceptualization of different power structures, that it is military power and not just economic interests that are central to America's role in the world today, and to the war in Iraq in particular.[19] Neither Bauman nor Mann can be judged to be right or wrong without a close engagement with the available empirical evidence on the basis of their respective conceptual frameworks. However, the analytical and conceptual advances made by contemporary social theory suggest that a more fine-grained and adequate assessment of the relative significance of economic influences would be gained by following Mann in also looking at military, ideological and political forms of power.

Consciousness and Identity

At the level of practical relations and consciousness, Weber wrote of the way in which the dominance within modernity of rational calculation – what he called 'rationalization' – over more emotional, affective or spiritual forms of apprehension led to a progressive disenchantment of the social world. A related development concerning identity arising from the transition from traditional to modern society, generating a profound sense of ambivalence within the modern individual, was a feeling of rootlessness and nostalgia for more communal forms of solidarity, something that has, if anything, intensified within late and liquid forms of modernity.[20] **Georg Simmel** emphasized the role played by monetary exchange in consolidating the impersonal and calculative nature of the relations between people in conditions of modernity, and also the similar role played by the encroachment of the pressures of clock time into everyday being. He also highlighted the relentless assailing of the senses and the disjointed, fragmentary nature of experience in modernity's cities, and the cold and blasé attitudes that individuals adopted in response as a means of subjective self-protection. In similar vein, **Talcott Parsons** formalized the effects of modernity on forms of social interaction in his celebrated **pattern variables** (see glossary box on p. 141). Interaction within modernity was said to be characterized by: generalized criteria (universalism rather than particularism); the criteria of performance and related credentials (achievement rather than ascription); attention to only limited aspects of a person (specificity rather than diffuseness or holism); and an instrumental, means-end rationality that distances itself from emotional involvement (neutrality rather than affectivity).

These trends have intensified in the era of postmodernity, as advances in multiple forms of technology – including information, communication, organizational and visual technologies – allied to enduring modernist attempts at control and the perpetuation of profits have led to the dislocation, restructuring and reconstitution of geographies, populations and, accordingly, consciousness and identity. Taken together, all these developments have contributed to what Frederic Jameson, a major commentator on postmodernism, has labelled 'schizophrenic identities'.[21] These indicate states of mind in which people struggle to maintain their bearings, purpose and sense of coherence and meaning as they are confronted by the speed and the seemingly perpetual nature of change. Typically for postmodern views of the subject – reacting, not least, to the overwhelming media saturation of society in the form of the internet, myriad other forms of communication and information, countless television channels, the free availability and general ubiquity of narrative and music-based film, videos and DVDs, a plurality of celebrity-focused and other magazines, specialized and general, and so on – there is an emphasis on the threat of a fragmented consciousness and disorientation in the face of flux, speed, flows and the implosion of meanings and purpose, as words, images and sounds are consumed for the pleasures of the moment, in and for themselves, with little thought for their connection to their wider social, historical and cultural context, such that, fatefully, **signifiers** become increasingly unhinged from **signifieds** (see the glossary box on signification on p. 294). Jameson is pessimistic about the implications of this state of being for the fate of the self:

> schizophrenic experience is an experience of isolated, disconnected, discontinuous, material signifiers which fail to link up into a coherent sequence. The

schizophrenic thus does not know personal identity in our sense, since our feeling of identity depends on our sense of the persistence of the 'I' and the 'me' over time.[22]

It is more than possible that Jameson exaggerates what is going on at the level of identity, at least for many people in the world. A legion of empirical, localized studies in diverse places would be required to properly examine the extent to which the picture he paints is a reality. The results would certainly be uneven, but there is little doubt that there is something we need to take seriously in what he says.

Not only have there been shifts in consciousness and identity themselves through the twentieth century and into the new millennium, there have also been significant shifts in the way in which sociologists have thought about consciousness and identity. Jameson's characterization of schizophrenic identities owes much to developments in cultural theory and in structuralist and poststructuralist thought, which slowly undermined too easy a notion of subjectivity and identity as being located and bounded within individuals and/or as being ineluctably linked to, and defined by, just one social category such as class, race or gender. These approaches encouraged us to see that the consciousness of individuals was always shot through with the multilayered linguistic and visual discourses, values and norms of their social context. Instead of bounded individuals, they drew attention, at one end of a continuum, to the porosity of borders between the individual and the meanings and significations of the social world in which they are embedded. At the other extreme, as in Jameson's characterization, they suggested that there were no borders at all; that the plurality of discourses out there in a semiotically saturated world had entirely overrun and destroyed the boundaries and thus the autonomy of the individual. While, again, the reality is certainly uneven, this way of seeing, which decentres the individual subject (who may be more or less capable of autonomy – of maintaining their own separate sense of identity and making up their own mind with respect to the plethora of discourses that inhabit them), has the corresponding effect of moving discourses and other dimensions of context nearer to the centre of the stage.

The recognition of the importance of social context in producing hybrid or mixed forms of consciousness has profound implications for the way sociology approaches the consciousness of various categories of groups, including those of class, gender, ethnicity, religion and so on, as well as the identity of individuals from these groupings with respect to their situated roles (see Chapter 8 on Merton), within institutional complexes of work, civic involvement and so on. Thus, Michèle Barrett's chapter on Stuart Hall recounts the poststructuralist critique of that Marxist conception of class in which, for example, working-class subjects were seen as having bounded, unitary and essentialized class interests. Post-Marxists such as Ernesto Laclau and Chantal Mouffe,[23] major influences on Hall's work, drew on a combination of Antonio Gramsci's cultural Marxism, Louis Althusser's structural Marxism, and the poststructuralist insights of Derrida and Foucault to re-envisage the way of seeing and conceptualizing the consciousness of social groups in terms of overlapping and competing discourses rather than essentialized identities. The phenomenology, perceptions and consciousness of people belonging to a particular class are in this way of seeing, constructed and contested through discourses rather than simply given by their class location. There is more to fight over and establish in this way of seeing. It is also an approach more suited to the age of postmodernity/late modernity that is saturated with information and semiotics, which is characterized by hybridity, flux, crossovers and bricolage and a plurality – again, more or less depending on place – of language games, cultures and subcultures, structures of feeling and so on. One should not forget, however, the huge caveat insisted upon by the proponents of 'late modernity', which is that very little of all this cultural flux lacks grounding of one kind or another in the weight of definable institutional influences, structural inequalities, roles, practices and organizational mechanisms. Thus, we should expect differing social locations to be linked to variations in identity and consciousness, but we should expect the nature of this link to be much more complex than that suggested by orthodox Marxist conceptions of class.

The relationship between the structural forms of modernity and the consciousness of its human inhabitants, brought out by Simmel, with respect to the organization of the city, and by Parsons in a more generalized and formalized manner, is given a moral dimension in Bauman's account of the Holocaust. He argues with power and force that the functional division of labour and **instrumental rationality** (reasoning narrowly restricted to the best means of achieving preordained goals – see glossary box (**instrumental reason**) on p. 252) and below for further discussion of Weber's emphasis on rationalization and instrumental reasoning as central features of modernity) structurally embedded within modern bureaucracies routinely produces a distance from the victims of political and administrative decisions that is both spatial and moral, and its correlates are moral invisibility and indifference. This is a point reinforced in Jason Hughes' chapter on **Norbert Elias**, in which he not only concurs with Bauman that the very long chains of interdependence and the division of social functions that play such a part in the 'civilizing process' greatly facilitated the Holocaust, but also that controls associated with civilization, particularly the pushing of 'distasteful' aspects of human behaviour behind the scenes of everyday life, themselves made possible the silence and acquiescence that allowed the long chains of organized and coordinated activities to proceed without protest.[24] This is a theme that is continued and elaborated upon by Jürgen Habermas. He details how the forms of prescriptive instrumental reasoning promoted by the systems of money and bureaucracy slowly but surely colonize the consciousness and truly communicative competences of individuals, impoverishing their moral sensibilities and deliberative capacities.

Values and Critical Theory

The Critique of Instrumental Reasoning and Reification

In this section, I want to explore two forms of tension within the *critical* positions taken up by certain key thinkers. In both cases I will start from the work of Weber. The first case involves an unresolved ambivalence in Weber's work that is central to the tradition of critical theory. It is between what he sees as the positive goods of order, efficiency and predictability that can be provided by bureaucracy, and his counter-fear that modernity's insistence upon the specialization of tasks threatened to trap men and women within a 'steel hard casing'[25] binding them to hard, unremitting and relentlessly methodical work. Weber was profoundly concerned that narrow technique and instrumental reasoning were subjugating the 'ultimate and most sublime values'[26] of humankind. Fritz Ringer writes that Weber was plagued by the 'dreadful' thought that individual freedom, equality and cultural vitality would all be subjugated by human beings who had been turned by bureaucracy into 'nervous and cowardly'[27] creatures whose need for 'order' was placed above all else. He feared that the world might some day be inhabited only 'by those little cogwheels', those human beings 'glued to a little post and striving for a little better one'.[28] In his chapter on Weber's work, Lawrence Scaff quotes the famous lines from the final page of *The Protestant Ethic and the Spirit of Capitalism* in which its author sees a process in train whereby the old enchanted ideas and ideals are replaced by 'mechanized petrification':

> For of the last stage of this cultural development, it might well be truly said: 'Specialists without spirit, sensualists without heart; this nullity imagines that it has attained a level of civilization never before achieved.'[29]

This critical aspect of Weber's thought presages that of major theorists in the tradition of critical theory. **Theodor Adorno**'s critique of the **reification** (see glossary box, p. 205) of thought around instrumental reasoning parallels Weber's critique and both also resonate with Jürgen Habermas's critique of one-sided modernity, just alluded to, in which narrow technocratic ways of thinking are linked to the decline of a thriving public sphere with the capability to underpin free and independent communication and critical judgement. Narrowly focused rationalization and instrumental reasoning, in search of capitalist profits and/or scientific, technical and administrative control, are seen to have led to a serious skewing of society's evolution. That is, the obsessive concern with bringing about order and control, with instrumental reasoning, has led to society's neglect and/or subjugation and impoverishment of many other dimensions central to being truly human. The exploration of these other dimensions and their fate have increasingly preoccupied critical contemporary perspectives and include: the *value spheres* of formal morality and ethics – of issues of justice and rights, for example, and of what it means to live a good or virtuous life; of art and aesthetics; of culture; of erotics; of devotion – religious or otherwise (see Patrick Watier's chapter on Simmel); and of the issues of existential being and empathy with others, including the significance of value commitments,[30] emotions and psychological and bodily suffering. **Arlie Russell Hochschild**'s *The Managed Heart: The Commercialization of Human Feeling*,[31] for example, did much to inspire a burgeoning literature on the emotions that has emphasized their manipulation and management in the service of profit, power and bureaucracy, as well as the profound inequalities of emotional experience that have resulted from this. Combining the influences of Goffman, feminism, Darwin, anthropology and Freud with her own creative imagination and empirical research, Hochschild's analysis is an illustration of a new way of seeing a phenomenon that has long been there, at the same time as it draws attention to its newly intensified dimensions, as the commodification of emotion work is coupled with more codified and regulated forms of monitoring and surveillance.

Similar hybrids of newly theorized perspectives on long-standing phenomena and newly emergent, late-modern manifestations of those phenomena are also strikingly apparent in Simon Williams' research into the sociology of sleep[32] and Karin Widerberg's studies in the sociology of tiredness.[33] In both, an intriguing background theme of struggle can be discerned between these irrevocable aspects of being human and the demands of impersonal and intrusive systems of power. Hochschild's most recent work on migration and international care chains focuses on, among other things, the phenomenon of relatively poor mothers from countries such as the Philippines or Guatemala, who feel impelled for economic reasons to leave their own children in the care of others, perhaps elderly relatives or siblings, in order to travel overseas to take on the role of nanny to the children of middle-class, often white families in the US, Hong Kong or elsewhere. This is a good example of the systematic reallocation of conditions of emotional and psychological well-being embedded within intensified processes of globalization. This is a deeply structured and powerful set of relational interdependencies that raises potent questions about justice, rights and the space afforded to individual autonomy.

Many of the writers who criticize the narrow destructiveness of instrumental reasoning and the part it has played in the excesses, sometimes murderous, of attempts at social engineering believe that there should be a cultivation of degrees of autonomy for at least some of the various different spheres of social life, one that respects their specific concerns and their inner logic as well as their potential for informing the other spheres. Adorno writes on behalf of a richer subjectivity than that allowed for by the reification of thought and values, by commodity fetishism, the forces of capitalism and by what he sees as the mystifications and deceptions of mass culture. He denounces the commodification of culture, expresses a loss of hope in history as progress, but hangs on to a belief in the transformative potential of art, especially, as Maggie O'Neill emphasizes, art that is not explicitly political but which emerges from the 'sedimented stuff of society', which is autonomous and abstract, which shakes rigid ways of thinking through paradox and ambiguity, art from the likes of Kafka, Beckett, Schoenberg, with its potential to reveal the 'unintentional truths of the social world and preserve independent thinking'.[34]

The critical dimensions of Adorno's writings are underpinned by his idea of negative dialectics or **non-identity thinking** (see glossary box, p. 122), which, in effect, enable the critique and subversion of easy prejudicial and dehumanizing labels and of the manipulation of needs. They do this by revealing the non-identity, the lack of fit, between the dehumanizing claim and the social reality, as in Maggie O'Neill's examples of the invidious equivalence created between 'junk' and refugees and asylum seekers, and also of the inflated and misleading claims for the powers of consumer commodities. The resources available for this kind of critique can be enhanced by borrowing from the writings of Alfred Schutz on phenomenology in the social world, and from the fruits of their integration into **Harold Garfinkel**'s writings on ethnomethodology (see Chapter 12). Thus, as Patrick Watier explains in his chapter on Simmel (Chapter 4), we all routinely take up what seems to us a 'natural attitude' in our relationships with various others – intimates, strangers, friends and enemies – in which we construct the other as a personality, a psychological unity, by drawing on '*a priori* representations that consist in attributing an assembly of fragmentary perceptions to one person'.[35] The one person can turn into a group of people, or a class or a race. We develop these seemingly natural *a prioris* – these routine assumptions – from past experiences, which include the typical representations of others from conversations and media representations, and they are useful to us in forging our routine expectations of what stances to take towards others and what to expect of them in social interaction. As group typifications are convenient shorthand substitutes for really knowing a person, for assembling their attributes from first-hand knowledge and being open to new information about them, they can easily turn into prejudicial stereotypes, distant from actual social realities. This is brought out in Ken Plummer's discussion of **Herbert Blumer**'s dismissal of biological accounts of race and his alternative emphasis on the social processes of relationships and categorizations, where race prejudice existed as an attitude towards an abstract categorization such as the Jew, the Oriental or the Negro. The appropriate reaction to such categorizations is to direct attention precisely to the manners in which they are constructed, and the resultant 'defining systems surrounding groups'.[36] Writing about these issues in the late 1930s, Blumer believed that the challenging of such categories in public debates had a major role to play in resisting and weakening segregation and discrimination.

Adorno's non-identity thinking, designed to attack the corrupting power of reification, offers an incisive critical framework to enlist in the critique and challenge demanded by the public contestation of such issues, as much today as when Blumer and Adorno themselves were writing. Non-identity thinking requires an ability to look beyond received messages, beyond the socially induced natural attitude, as well as a spirit of openness towards alternative, more appropriate typifications and previously unnoticed sense data. Such openness is what Garfinkel advocated for the appropriate use of the 'documentary method of interpretation' (Heritage, Chapter 12), and it is also implicit in **Erving Goffman**'s discussion of the need for apologies and 'repair work' when initial assessments of social situations turn out to have been mistaken. Poststructuralism – as discussed above and represented in this book by the work of Stuart Hall – can also be useful here, as it too sets out to subvert typified binary oppositions, such as man/woman, black/white, able bodied/ disabled and so on, in an effort to appreciate the greater range of differences and complex hybridities that exist in the social world. All these potentially reinforcing tools and motivations of critique threaten the power of reification, a goal which lies at the heart of Adorno's critical theory. I choose to interpret in this light Michèle Barrett's observation in Chapter 18 that Stuart Hall, along with other sociological thinkers, has turned away from social and cultural theory. That is, I don't interpret it as a turning away from the sociological enterprise and the sociological imagination but as a plea for the radical integration of a wider range of imaginations and approaches into a broadly defined critical theory. In Hall's case, this has meant an exploration of the visual arts. Hall's interest in cultural diversity, postcolonialism and diaspora arts is a logical extension of critical theory's desire to subvert reification. It is a contemporary take on the determination not to allow the relative autonomy of the different spheres of life, in this case the realm of aesthetics (resolutely linked to other spheres), to be dominated by a narrow and reified version of the social. On the contrary, it is to turn to art as a source of disruption and spirit.

The urgency with which investment in authentic critical theory is required is thus closely linked to the precise ways in which the relatively differentiated spheres – for example (as above), the aesthetic, the political, the moral, the erotic and the devotional – are themselves often under siege from other spheres such as the economic, the bureaucratic and, we should add, the militaristic. It is important to be able to excavate and specify the uneven processes to which the former set of spheres is subject, as Habermas has long pointed out, to degrees of colonization and impoverishment by capitalist and bureaucratic modes of calculation. As theorists of postmodernity have observed, there is often also a process of 'de-differentiation' going on, in which some key areas of the cultural sphere are invaded by other realms from *within* culture, such that the 'aesthetic realm begins to colonize both theoretical and moral-political spheres' at the same time as that aesthetic realm is itself increasingly pervaded by commercial institutions in the area of cultural economy, so that 'one is hard put to say where the commercial institution stops and where the cultural product starts'.[37] Thus, critical theory (and its close companion, public sociology, which we shall come to below) needs to combat a situation in which individuals and groups inhabit increasingly superficial and mechanical spheres of life, the character of which undermines social and human capacities and sensibilities; a context in which the remaining distinctiveness of spheres and what is valuable and meaningful in their residues is in danger, in another crank of the ratchet, of being further constricted or distorted by commercial, bureaucratic and other modes of narrow calculation. The consequence is that people increasingly find themselves in the midst of those sensations, provocations and 'schizophrenic' experiences recounted by theorists of late and postmodernity, without those enduring social, historical, cultural and other anchors and coordinates formerly provided by vibrant and complex values spheres. They are condemned, thus, to live more and more in a series of discontinuous and relatively meaningless presents, detached from the past and from the future. A strong and creative critical theory in the era of late or liquid modernity consequently needs to be both dogged and subtle. It should strive to retrieve and recover a reflexive appreciation of what is of value in each of the spheres, maintaining a grasp of the distinctive qualities, accumulated learning and capacities germane to each, being able to locate them historically and in terms of social structure. It should at the same time, however, be open, in a Janus-faced manner that is attentive not only to forms of distortion and narrowing of the spheres through infiltration and colonization, but also to the subversive, liberating potential of disruptive, fluid, cross-cutting combinations between spheres as expressed in the writings of Adorno, Chodorow, Hall, Bauman and others.

Value Freedom, Value Relevance and Political Commitment in Sociology

The second tension in Weber's work is with respect to the relationship between value freedom (or value neutrality) and value relevance in social science. This is a distinction that it is important to scrutinize with some care as it has important implications, as we shall see below, for all kinds of critical theory.

Value freedom (Wertfreiheit) expressed Weber's belief that social science could not be used to choose between different values. The aim of social science, he insisted, should be to aim at objectivity without allowing political and ethical values and preferences to interfere with this. Richard Swedberg notes how Weber:

> argued forcefully against academic teachers engaging in political and other propaganda when they were lecturing: 'the prophet and the demagogue do not belong on the academic platform'. He also was against introducing political action into the classroom.[38]

I find it easy to accept the importance of striving to keep prejudice and bias out of the dialogue between concepts and evidence, for this is one of the bases of social science's claims for objectivity. The key point here as far as I am concerned is the one made simply and directly by Weber in his seminal lecture 'Science as a vocation':

> Anybody who is a reasonable teacher has as his first duty to teach his students to acknowledge 'inconvenient' facts. I mean facts which are inconvenient for this party opinion. And there are extremely inconvenient facts for every party opinion – for mine as well. I believe that if the academic teacher forces his audience to get used to this, he achieves a more than merely intellectual achievement. I would even be so immodest as to use the expression 'moral achievement' if that does not sound too elevated for something that is so obvious.[39]

This defensible notion of objectivity does, however, have to be combined carefully with Weber's commitment to *value relevance (Wertbeziehung)*, which insists that a researcher's own values, influenced by what is significant in the social and cultural milieu in which she or he lives, will inevitably play a role in the choice of subjects to study and in how they are conceptualized.[40] It is more difficult than is usually acknowledged to reconcile Weber's insistence that academics should separate politics from their social science with his commitment to value relevance. His recognition that a person inevitably imports her or his own values into their choice and conceptualization of topic surely means that it is impossible to eradicate politics from social science in the way suggested in the first of the two quotations above. Thus, while the sociologist clearly should place objectivity and the revelation of inconvenient facts on a pedestal (value neutrality), this does not mean that politics has no place in the classroom or within the domain of social science (value relevance). This is a tension with direct implications for all kinds of critical theory, as the insights and observations of critical theories will, by definition, be value relevant, meaning that they will be closely related to their proponents' normative commitments. These commitments, values, have a direct effect on which phenomena thinkers choose to study, how they look at them, and how they teach them, as well as to the related but not identical issue of what they think should be done about them (that is, their prescriptive politics).

In his seminal account of *Science, Technology and Society in Seventeenth Century England*, **Robert K. Merton**, in extending Weber's argument about the Protestant ethic to the sphere of science, explicitly introduced the notion of value relevance in deriving scientists' selection of problems from the dominant values and interests of the day.[41] In a move that is highly reminiscent of feminist standpoint theorists, **Pierre Bourdieu** and other theorists of structuration, and variants of postmodernism in both sociology and anthropology, Merton goes on to note that value relevance also 'suggests that differing social locations, with their distinctive interests and values, will affect the selection of problems for investigation'.[42] Values necessarily enter into the selection of topics for investigation (and Weber[43] himself was also clear that this was inevitable) and, as feminists insist, these are political values in the widest sense, even if answering the question of 'what to do now' cannot be entirely derived from either (see below). For example, the idea of value relevance is central to the work of Dorothy Smith, who, combining this with a version of the narrowness of outlook thesis, sharply criticizes the conceptual apparatus of sociology for its reflection of the position of men as rulers. The adequate conceptualization of women's practices, she argues, should take women's own activities and experiences as a starting point. As Karin Widerberg puts it in her chapter on Smith, we are to start where women are situated and to look up and around at the structure and functioning of society from this position. This should not be a sociology from above looking down at daily life, but one from 'where the subject is located in her body and is active in her work in relation to particular others'.[44] It is from here that the 'relations of ruling' will come into view.

It seems clear to me that political values and social science cannot be easily separated, and that this need not interfere with objectivity in the dialogue between (politically informed) value relevant positions and empirical evidence, in the methodologically informed discipline and honesty with which one confronts 'inconvenient' facts. Both in the classroom and when social science is brought into public debate, the recognition of these points can, and should, however, be accompanied by a recognition that, as one of Europe's leading sociologists, John Scott, has recently put it, there is a 'diversity of standpoints from which knowledge can be constructed, and [a] variety of legitimate political preferences that citizens can advocate'.[45] Drawing these conclusions on the basis of Weber's distinction, one is left with a position that is the same as that vigorously advocated by Michael Burawoy, not least in his presidential address to the American Sociological Association in 2004, for the revival of 'public sociology'.[46] Scott, himself a recent president of the British Sociological Association, supports this move, praising the clear virtues of speaking to audiences as equals by making clear the preferences of the sociologist him or herself, while also emphasizing that sociology is a 'technical and difficult discipline and that its value to public discussion lies precisely in its complexity and difficulty'.[47]

> The key task for public sociology, then, is to establish the means through which publics are motivated to take seriously and to engage with its academic products. This is a slow, incremental process in which people must be persuaded and enticed into reading sociology and, most importantly, thinking sociologically. A great deal can be achieved through the public that we encounter every day – our students – but there is a more difficult task of building a dialogue with the publics outside the universities.
>
> The advocacy of public sociology is a claim for autonomy combined with a claim for engagement – and that is its challenge. The public role of the sociologist, as Max Weber might have said, is not to participate in policy research (although he or she may, of course, do that) but to speak autonomously as a citizen from the standpoint of a well-grounded base of sociological knowledge.[48]

The Political Value Commitments of Sociologists and their Philosophical Justification

In reading the chapters of this book, it will be readily apparent that the majority of sociological thinkers have indeed been political, and the reasoning of the last section is that this has been entirely justified. I would add that it is also essential if sociology is to continue to fulfil the same role in the self-understanding of the age that it has so far played for most of its relatively short historical life. One can see a significant degree of continuity in the *political engagement*, often direct, of key sociological thinkers. Much of this engagement has involved, as Burawoy puts it, the analysis of the 'social preconditions of politics and the politicization of the social'[49] but it has also entailed direct involvement in the formal political process itself, investigating this too with the theoretical and conceptual tools of sociological analysis. This political engagement is an enduring legacy inherited from the thinkers covered in Part I: from Marx and Engels' revolutionary Communist identification with the working classes, uprooted and dispossessed by capitalism, with nothing to lose but their chains; and Weber's 'combative and indefatigable' engagement with German politics, condemning, among others, 'Bismarck for crushing all independent leadership; the German monarchy for blatant incompetence and dilettantism; the bourgeoisie for its weak class consciousness and unwillingness to struggle for political power against the state bureaucracy';[50] through Durkheim's intervention in the Dreyfus affair[51] and profound concern with France's moral crisis, which, he argued, was reflected in a discernible individual malaise and fundamental divisions between conservatives, liberals and radicals during the Third Republic (1871–1940); to the creative 'public philosophy' of Herbert Blumer, exemplified in his seminal 1937 paper on the nature of racial prejudice; and Adorno's critique of the growing commodification of culture and ideological mystification, and the promotion of the transformative role of art and critical thought. The choices made by these theorists to study particular social phenomena were value relevant choices, as were the concepts they chose to study them with. This is readily apparent in Marx's work, for example, whether we are talking about the vagaries of capitalism, alienation, the revolutionary potential of the working classes, or false consciousness.

Fewer of the thinkers covered in Part II of this volume are explicitly political in their value orientations. While it is important to grant a certain degree of autonomy to internal trajectories within sociological thought itself, it seems plausible to suggest that this is closely related to what was happening within society, to the postwar state of affluence and the relatively consensual mode of civic and political engagement that accompanied it. This was the kind of environment that led **David Lockwood** and his co-authors to research and test the so-called *embourgeoisement* thesis, popular in the UK in the late 1950s and early 1960s, which argued that 'the affluent working class was increasingly becoming middle class' (Mouzelis, Chapter 11) and to emerge with their 'privatization thesis':

> A type of home-centred existence where the joys of consumption or newly acquired gadgets, and of private family life become more important than class struggles and the expression of collective sentiments and interests in the public domain. (Mouzelis, Chapter 11)

Althusser and Chodorow stand out among the thinkers of this part as theorists whose value relevance stances are explicitly political. In Althusser's case, as Ted Benton points out (Chapter 13), it is significant that he was writing within a social milieu that had seen the French Communists play a crucial role in the resistance against the Nazis during the occupation of France in the course of the war. The ensuing influence of the Communist Party in the French postwar world, in large part a consequence of this, was palpable, and developments in the nation's intellectual life over the next twenty or thirty years, expressed not least in the struggle between existentialist humanism and structuralist currents of thought, were closely linked to struggles in the Soviet Union, Communist China, and the uneasy position of Communist parties within the liberal democracies of Western Europe. Chodorow's politics can perhaps be located in a period of transition as the postwar consensus gave way to a variety of societal conflicts in the 1960s and 70s. Karin Martin notes (in Chapter 14) that they were part of the grand theorizing of the second wave of feminism in Europe and the US, which examined, criticized and strove to change 'all aspects of gender inequality in social life' (Martin, Chapter 14). Dorothy Smith was also an energetic and influential part of this movement. She was born before Chodorow but wrote her most influential work in the 1980s and 90s, and engaged less in grand theorizing and more, as we have seen, in the theorization of the phenomenologies, practices and encounters of women's everyday life.

All the theorists of the final period, without exception, have taken overtly political stances of one kind or another, and all have written directly about politics. This, with little doubt, reflects something about the times we have moved into, times in which elements of continuity are rarely left untouched by forces of rapid change in which the increasing complexity, instrumentality, impersonality and fluidity of social interdependencies, are all shot through with the varied inflexions of new technologies and their mutational effects on forms of risk, inequalities, exploitation, marginalization, scapegoating and stigma at local, national, international and global levels. Responding to these times, most theorists have felt compelled to engage directly in civil society interventions, prominent political debates and/or formal political activism. These are activities that include: Habermas's engagement with the student protests of 1968 and his high-profile contribution to the 'historians' dispute' *(Historikerstreit)* on the nature of the Holocaust (see Outhwaite, Chapter 15); Bourdieu's establishment of the collective 'Raisons d'agir', 'bringing together researchers, artists, labour officials, journalists and militants of the unorthodox Left (with branches in several European countries)' (Wacquant, Chapter 16), and his strident critiques of the hegemony of neoliberalism; Foucault's journalistic activism on the death penalty, abortion and suicide, and his 'intervention(s) on behalf of prisoners and prison reform, his concern for those who have been socially marginalized such as immigrants, mental patients, and homosexuals, his sympathy for the plight of conscripted soldiers, and his unwavering support for Eastern European dissidents and the Solidarity union in Poland';[52]

Hochschild's explicit critique of the class and gender inequalities in emotion work and, later, of the exploitation and human suffering embedded in the international chains of care; Giddens' involvement in the formal sphere of politics, advocating Third Way politics to Tony Blair and the Clintons, and, in focusing on globalization in the BBC's 1999 Reith Lectures, three of whose five broadcasts were delivered from Delhi, Hong Kong and Washington, taking further his arguments about the outmoded nature of the old 'Left' and 'Right' distinction through an appeal to the recently minted sociological concepts of risk and reflexivity; Mann's intervention in the debates over the 'war on terror' through the publication of *Incoherent Empire* in 2003, which drew on his IEMP model to carefully scrutinize the very uneven capacities of the US, and to argue for an abandonment of its current global policies that were said to be simply increasing world disorder and danger; and, among many other things, Hall's influential dissection of Thatcherism and his iconic and illuminating characterization of it as 'authoritarian populism',[53] and the articulate and incisive critiques of racism, colonialism and postcolonialism that have marked the whole of his intellectual career.

The pervasiveness of political commitment among key thinkers gives a particular salience and urgency to the further question of how to *justify* one's value relevant stance in a way that takes it beyond the purely subjective or arbitrary. This is a different question than that of asking whether it is inevitable and/or right that sociologists introduce values, including political values, into their work, questions that we have answered in the affirmative. For this is not about whether it is appropriate to introduce values into sociology but, rather, is about how one justifies, philosophically and morally, the values that one does introduce. This is a pressing question, as political commitment and/or social and artistic critique have given many social theorists their most profound motivation. If they were called on to do so, then how would different key thinkers justify their stance on the political commitments outlined above? Most theorists have been content just to commit to their values, reinforcing them with a theoretical and empirical grounding, the best of them being open to those inconvenient facts of which Weber spoke, but without the intellectual resources at hand to bring their sociology into philosophical engagement with the relevant literatures and debates necessary to justify their positions in terms of advanced moral argument. Wacquant's chapter on Bourdieu, to take one example, emphasizes Bourdieu's conviction that the intellectual has a civic mission that necessarily combines both 'autonomy and engagement' and in which 'she is invested with a specific authority, granted by virtue of the hard-won independence of the intellectual field from economic and political powers; and she puts this specific authority at the service of the collectivity by investing it in political debates.'[54] Having said this, and in spite of his militant and energetic political engagement,

Bourdieu still accepted Weber's position that 'social science cannot stipulate the political goals and moral standards we should pursue'.[55] He knew that his authority came from the objectivity of the social science produced by himself and his colleagues, but that the moral and political value commitments which drove this science – those accounts of how things were and how they came about, including, in *The Weight of the World*, the forms of inequality and misery that were rendered invisible by the authorities and the established media – were ultimately beyond the competence of social science taken on its own. So, what to do about the relative weakness of social science when it gets to the border between its value relevant critiques of existing social relations and the justification of its own critical values? This is an enduring question that, I believe, will rightly be placed at the centre of the sociological stage in the coming years.

While the politically related values of key theorists informed the topics they chose to study and the way they conceptualized these topics, the extent to which their values reflected the social and cultural values of the societies in which they were embedded, and thus could be legitimized at least in this respect, would presumably vary from case to case. This question about values is, however, something that could be approached through sociological analysis. Here research into the extent to which the value commitments of a given theorist are shared by the population at large would begin by trying to establish what the de facto popular conception of values was in relation to a particular issue in a given time and place. One would need to separate out, within general popular conceptions, those instances of truly normative commitments to existing sets of social arrangements from other instances of fatalistic acceptance of, or pragmatic acquiescence in, what people actually considered to be morally distasteful states of affairs. Attention would thus be paid to the sociological exploration of empirical specificities, including an excavation of the relevant explicit and tacit normative rules, injunctions and sanctions at play among the members of given societies or societal groups. This would allow us to see whether a theorist's values, and the pursuit of certain kinds of political goals, would be normatively approved of and supported within a given society.

The possibility and desirability of this kind of exploration, of the extent to which theorists' value relevant positions are consistent with the normative ideals of a particular society, is consistent with the incisive notion of 'internal social criticism' coined by Mark Cladis in *A Communitarian Defense of Liberalism*,[56] a self-consciously Durkheimian exploration of contemporary political philosophy. Cladis places great emphasis on grasping the 'historically situated ideals, customs, beliefs, institutions, and practices'[57] of given societies as a basis for understanding what would be acceptable and unacceptable morally within those societies. Durkheim believed that 'organic solidarity' within modern societies rested both on economic interdependencies and cooperation per se, and a shared morality that closely regulates it. The latter is said to have two components. One of these is what he called 'moral polymorphism', which consists in plural spheres and secondary groups that 'provide local environments that envelop individuals and that sustain them with intimate ties and specialized moral education'.[58] These diverse pockets of modern moral life 'supplant the strong collective conscience of traditional societies'.[59] The second component is a more broadly shared set of pervasive social beliefs and practices. Durkheim believed that here the cult of the human person, the individual, and his or her dignity, worth, rights and liberties was at the centre of this and that, in this domain, the collective consciousness had, if anything, become stronger. This 'moral individualism' was tempered by an acceptance that some forms of constraint and subordination to a just democratic state were necessary, and this acceptance of some kind of reflective balance was underpinned by more broadly shared values and beliefs. Clearly influenced by the political theorists John Rawls and Michael Walzer, Cladis thus interprets Durkheim as arguing that the shared principles that underlie just democratic societies should combine respect for the plurality of beliefs and practices of secondary groups – such as churches, synagogues, mosques, clubs and political organizations – or spheres of life – such as the economic or the social, and the various institutional clusters within these – with concern for 'the common good of the political community'.

Keeping both these levels in mind, it is fruitful to ask whether the value relevant principles of any given theoretical tradition or key sociological theorist is in harmony with, or at odds with, a society's 'historically fashioned social inheritance',[60] its own dominant moral ideals. Similarly, however, a deep understanding of those historically situated moral values and normative *ideals* could also act as the basis of 'internal criticism' of existing *practices* that are at odds with this sociologically excavated and articulated ideal self-image. A grasp of the historically fashioned inheritance would, in this case, form the basis of criticism that sought to reform dominant social practices – perhaps instrumentally, pragmatically or fearfully adhered to – which fell short of the society's own ideal moral and political standards of behaviour.

This space for internal critique is opened up in the conditions of plurality that characterize non-traditional societies, through a self-conscious comparison of our deep-rooted beliefs and views about social norms, on the one hand, with the behaviour that we see is actually fostered and supported by our social institutions and arrangements, on the other.

The critical or political advocacy of many sociological theorists has, in fact, implicitly appealed to, and attempted to foster, greater awareness of this kind of discrepancy. A lucid example of this can be found in the chapter in this volume on Adorno in which attention is drawn to the discrepancies in so-called free societies between the societal ideals of freedom and the inequalities of social power that restrict and restrain the actualization of freedom in that society's practices (see glossary box, **Identity and non-identity thinking**, p. 122). The possibility of internal critiques means, among other things, that one needn't just always accept the simple majority views and surface opinions of a society. An example of this would be where a popular majority is either indifferent to, or even positively supportive of, the erosion of minority rights, whether these be those of the poor, the homeless, immigrants, asylum seekers, indigenous peoples, or those based on factors such as sexuality, gender, race, class or ethnicity. An example related to sexuality taken from the work of the liberal political philosopher Ronald Dworkin can make this point clear. Dworkin relates how Lord Devlin, in a lecture delivered to the British Academy in 1958, expressed the view that if the majority of the British people found homosexuality an 'abominable vice' then they should be free to 'eradicate it' from society.[61] Dworkin subverts this argument precisely by showing that such intolerance would transgress society's deeper ideals which insist there is more to morality than simple surface practices or expressions of taste and distaste. The deeper moral ideals of a society – the background set of understandings about norms, standards and thinking about social justice and ethics, we share as part of our forms of life – must be distinguished from such things as unjustifiable emotional reactions, manifestations of personal aversion or taste, arbitrary stands and so on. A *moral ideal* at the heart of liberal societies, for example, is that the restriction of another's freedom and autonomy cannot be justified on the basis of forms of prejudice and rationalization. The restriction of another's freedom should only be countenanced where its exercise would fall foul of standard substantive liberal tests such as the demand that practices shouldn't harm self or others, or restrict the autonomy of others to live their lives in accordance with their own beliefs about what gives value to a life.[62] Such ideals can form the basis of an internal critique.

The justification of alternative or radical value relevant political positions can also be prompted by discrepancies within the cluster of social beliefs adhered to by a societal member, such that the different beliefs they hold seem to contradict each other. Such discrepancies can be brought to light in the course of practical activity or through the subjection of beliefs to critical analysis. Transformative art or critical theory of the kind valorized by Adorno, Hall and others can serve this kind of internal critique of dominant values by means of subverting reified and complacent acquiescence in moral practices that offend deeper sensibilities. An internal critique is thus one that respects the socially embedded nature of value commitments, and sees the need to develop critiques of dominant value positions from a vantage point that has a serious grasp of how things look from within those social relations, but it is equally one that is able to accommodate a deeply critical condemnation of those very same relations.[63]

I have argued there is a need for the sociological exploration of values, and the internal critique of these, in order to ground any kind of value relevant theoretical and political position, radical or conservative. However, we have also begun to see that this only takes us so far in challenging Weber's insistence that social science does not possess the resources to enable us to choose between different values. Thus, once we have investigated the sociological truths about a particular society's dominant surface beliefs, deep-rooted moral beliefs, or deeper sensibilities about how we should behave, that is, once we have dealt with extant sociological realities we then also have to engage directly and explicitly with moral arguments and the philosophical justification for moral positions, such as one finds in the value spheres of moral and political philosophy, spheres which have their own relative autonomy and degree of specialization. It is at this point, armed with a grasp of the relationship between the political commitments of a key thinker and its relationship to sociological realities at different depths, that we can then also fruitfully enlist the aid of moral and political philosophy.[64] The defence of value relevant commitments with respect to a particular issue would here require three interrelated moments:

1. A *sociological* investigation of the de facto popular conceptions of values in relation both to secondary groups and in relation to the shared values, principles, projects and goals of the public and/or political sphere; of any pertinent social divisions within these; of popular support for instances of internal critiques of existing social arrangements (possibly theorist or activist inspired); and of the potential for opening up further critiques of existing practices on the basis of the values investigated and illuminated.
2. A decision about the particular aspects of abstract *moral or political philosophy* – aspects such as justice, authenticity, equality, liberty, autonomy, virtue, notions of the public interest, democracy, sovereignty, obligation, rights, community, identity and the nature of belonging[65] – that might be the most fruitful, and appropriate, to draw upon to address a specific issue about normative values. The value relevant positions of the key thinkers can stand in here as significant markers of the kinds of critiques of existing social arrangements that are possible from within (internal to) a given society. I want to argue that the variety of internal critiques represented by the variety of key thinkers each needs to engage with relevant concepts and notions from moral and political philosophy in order to be able to offer explicitly normative justifications for their positions. An explicit engagement with the concept of justice, for example, would surely be pertinent to the examination of possible justifications for Foucault's value relevant concern for prisoners, and this could be placed alongside notions of the public interest; profound interrogations of conceptions of liberty, virtue and equality are all germane to the texture of his concern with the social position of homosex-

uals; and the issues of autonomy and rights are pertinent to his approach to mental patients. The tension between liberty of expression and respect for community lies at the heart of Habermas's value relevant position on the nature of the Holocaust and how it should be collectively remembered; while ethical issues around equality, identity and the nature of belonging need to be invoked in order to debate Hochschild's value relevant condemnation of the inequalities of international chains of care. This is to name just a few examples, and it is barely to scratch the surface of the many issues that social and moral theories need to address further. But it should nevertheless be clear that a theorist's value relevant critique, or a popular, normative value relevant position, needs to be brought into direct confrontation with the accumulated wisdom and nuanced debates of normative political philosophy in order to explore the grounds of their claims for legitimacy.

3. The *combination of the sociological and the moral,* or a return to dig deeper and with more focus into the findings of 1 now armed with the fruits of 2. This means going beyond just 1 taken on its own; that is, beyond a critique based just on a discrepancy between one's own de facto values and/or value relevant position *and* existing practices. Explicit moral argumentation is now introduced. This means combining 1 and 2 together in order to focus back on sociological realities with a view on the development of methodological and political strategies. Thus, sociological realities, including the de facto popular conception of values and orientations, can now be returned to and engaged with on the basis of a more refined, philosophically and morally elaborated and informed value relevant position. This explicitly defensible value relevant political position can be used to guide further analysis, informing the selection of areas of investigation and the precise empirical foci of interest, including those relevant to an assessment of the likelihood of popular support for the chosen form of critique. An exploration of the extent to which the more defensible value relevant positions, explored in relation to chosen aspects of moral or political philosophy (in 2, above), actually or potentially hold some cultural currency in the social relations at hand would allow one to go beyond both sociological critique denuded of moral justification and moral argumentation cut off from any sense of its likely social effectiveness.

This is clearly difficult, although exciting and challenging, terrain, terrain that will be explored slowly, bit by bit, over the coming years. My basic conclusion here, however, is straightforward: it is neither desirable nor possible to keep political, value relevant commitments out of sociological theory, but the defence of such value commitments is no easy matter, and it is a matter that cannot be left to social theory alone.

The Sociological Imagination and Civic Ethnomethods

In this section, I will stress that it is important to bring together knowledge and understanding of different substantive sociological themes into single case study explorations. These include the four we have focused on in this chapter – modernity, consciousness and identity, values and critique, and political commitment – but also other themes that figure in the chapters of this book such as: the relationship between religion and economics; between individualism and community; types of social solidarity; the changing nature of the state and also its role in welfare citizenship; the rise of the professions and affluent workers; the categorization and stigmatization of groups of people; the changing role of technology in social relations; changes in gendered and sexual identities; the reproduction of mothering; emotion work; modes of disciplinary control and governance; colonialism and cultural difference; globalization; and the politics of risk. While I have treated the four main themes of the introduction relatively discretely, separately, the investigation and exploration of particular sociological problems often involves a combination of overlapping and interlocking themes integrated together within an event, experience, life history, institutional development, cycle of policy-making or period of national or global change. The skills of being able to draw on an appreciation of the great sociological themes, and to combine them appropriately when addressing a particular situation, can provide much, not only to the academic sociologists who push back the boundaries of knowledge and teach and inspire the new generations, but also to decision-makers, whether these are power elites or individual citizens, as they go about their business on the large stage, perhaps in high politics, or on a more limited local stage, often no less political. In order for citizens of all kinds to be able to look beyond surface appearances, to understand the deeper mechanisms and causal influences that worked and combined to create the surface events in the here and now, sociologists, and their colleagues in adjacent and complementary disciplines, must – and, as we have seen, often do – pursue a civic mission to turn substantive themes from the key theorists into popular currency. Central to each of these themes is the conceptual and methodological skill of being able to combine different themes within the explanation of a single case, and then also to compare across cases.

In considering the development of greater general sociological awareness, the notion of *civic ethnomethods*, as a composite from the writings of Garfinkel and Bourdieu, is usefully suggestive of the basic background knowledge, skills and dispositions required to approach social and political questions in a sociologically literate fashion. There are sections explicitly focused on methods and methodology in many of the chapters of this book (see the lists of Key Issues at the beginning of Parts I, II and III), and these are all useful in thinking about the nature of these transposable skills. The skills should never be simply and solely confined to methodology but should be combined with theories and concepts directed towards the substantive and the empirical. Perhaps the most fruitful overarching notion of orientation to adopt here is what C. Wright Mills labelled *The Sociological Imagination*.[66] Mills' perceptive and enduring observations on the sociological imagination can be extended and deepened in many ways through continuing dialogue with the work of the key thinkers. In his conception of the sociological imagination, surface biographical experiences or events, as personally experienced, observed or captured on the TV news, for example, or in documentary or newsreel footage, can only be properly and profoundly understood once they are located at the junction of larger social structures and historical forces. Likewise, the full significance of the forms taken by macro-social structures, such as those of capitalism in its changing forms, and of modernity and late modernity, only really come alive once their impact on human lives and experiences can be grasped. We see history and the large structures of society in individual experiences and we understand individual fulfilment and suffering through those large forces. In a related expression, it is through the sociological imagination that we are able to make meaningful links between public issues and private troubles.

The cultivation of adequate civic ethnomethods requires, among other things, the development of the facility to understand the combination of different social forces and influences on lives and events, and this, *inter alia*, requires the ability to move backwards and forwards between the large-scale, middle-scale and micro-scale of society. Sometimes key thinkers concentrate on the large structures of whole epochs of society and at others, as in the case of Goffman or Garfinkel, they focus on micro-interactions. Perhaps the scale in sociological theory most urgently in need of both further recognition and elaboration is that of the middle scale, or meso-level, in which individuals and groups are situated in their various roles, interdependencies and social and organizational relations with respect to situated others, each of which is embedded in their own set of roles, interdependencies and social and organizational relations. This is the terrain on which the large social structures and historical forces meet individual lives, not as society versus the individual in some David and Goliath encounter writ large, but in the midst of the ongoing processes of particular subsets of social relationships. These have been given various names by various theorists, with: Weber and Habermas speaking of value spheres; Merton talking of role-sets, status-sets and their various accompanying relationships; Blumer and symbolic interactionists couching things in terms of 'interactive webs of people "doing things"';[67] Elias talking about figurations of mutual interdependencies; Bourdieu conceptualizing them in terms of different fields such as education, politics, the juridical, religion, the intellectual, journalism, art and sport; Mann speaking of networks of intersecting power structures; and Ira J. Cohen, a prominent American proponent of structuration theory, developing the work of Giddens to coin the notion of position-practice relations, relations that contain vertical and horizontal sets of power relationships and interdependencies.

The long list of thinkers who have mentioned this level indicates that it has not been entirely neglected thus far, but there is much work left to be done. A good starting point would be the investigation and elaboration of overlaps and areas of potentially productive synthesis of the various already existing conceptualizations at this level. Another arm of the strategy could be a heightened sensitivity to the presence and influence of various micro- and macro-influences on the workings and processes of this meso-level. As an illustration of what might be involved here one could ask about the macro-influence of the balance of power within the international state system and the micro-influences of particular officials, politicians and diplomats – drawing on their interactional skills, motivations and principles, and background knowledge – on the decisions made within the meso-level figurations of mutual dependencies and position-practices of the US State Department, the British Foreign Office and the UN Security Council to mount air attacks against Serbia in March 1999, ostensibly, at the very least, on humanitarian grounds, in the face of the persecution of the Muslim majority in Kosovo by Serbian forces led by the president of the rump of the former Yugoslavia, Slobodan Milošević. The nature of the causal impact of the meso-structures themselves on individuals, institutions and events will vary according to the specific instance, but it is fairly safe ground to assume that most of the time a plurality of different causal processes, mediated through the different levels, combine to create a particular event, with some of the processes and levels being more important than others. There is further conceptual work to be done here, but this is, nevertheless, classic theoretical ground. Sociologists have long seen one of their primary objectives as the task of isolating and identifying particularly salient causes and to trace over time their trajectory, their interaction with other causes, and their impact.

Within an analysis of the meso-level, one is likely to find powerful traces of those larger forces of history and social structure discussed above in characterizing modernity and late modernity. Thus, for example, continuities and changes in the global organization of social relations, from modernity to late or liquid modernity, will combine, in differing ways in different places, to help structure the meso-networks of life that pertain for the various people we encounter in the Seeing Things Differently section of each key thinker in the chapters to come. The trajectories and vicissitudes of macro-forces impinge equally, but naturally, in a range of different, specific ways: on the structuring of the lives of the Bosnian and Afghan refugees and asylum seekers who represented their lived experience in artistic form in the Global Refugees project discussed by Maggie O'Neill in her chapter on Adorno; through the national and international economic policies, labour market conditions, and modes of stock market and financial governance, which helped to create the context of life for the 'working poor' discussed by Karin Widerberg in her chapter on Dorothy Smith – as they trawl through the low-paid job advertisements, take routine employment and drug tests, and scratch around for transportation costs for their often unsuccessful interviews; on the global context encompassing the small group within the US government that initiated the 2003 Iraq War, discussed by Ralph Schroeder in his chapter on Michael Mann; and on the post-national identities taken up by the individual subscribers to Habermas's 'constitutional patriotism' – 'in which citizens move beyond the simple loyalties of "my country right or wrong" to a more reflective rational identification with "their" states'.[68] The effects of these large, macro-structures, however, will inevitably be mediated by meso-locales and networks that provide the more imminent context of forces and pressures, threats and inducements, constraints and opportunities, which impinge upon the experiences and judgements of the people involved. Both macro- and meso-structures will have their impacts on the micro-level formation of individual biographies, selves, values and dispositions, and character. These will be more or less related to very imminent moments, but will layer themselves over the experiences of a lifetime and, as Pierre Bourdieu conveys with his concept of habitus, are often transmitted in a process of routine osmosis rather than by conscious and reflective adoption.

The Sociological Imagination and Political Strategy

We have seen that the relationship between politics and the key sociological thinkers is both a salient and a complex one, and I will briefly sketch the main lessons drawn so far before going on to say something about those points where a sociological grasp of the conjuncture meets the formulation of political strategy. The lessons drawn so far are:

1. To accept value relevance and the related political stances of theorists as legitimate, intrinsic dimensions of their activity.
2. The caveat that one should strive to bring oneself and others face to face with uncomfortable and inconvenient facts, including the existence and nature of any gaps between one's own value relevant position and those of dominant and/or minority groups within a society.
3. The need to justify value relevant positions on both sociological and moral/philosophical levels, and to be prepared to debate with alternative positions. This is a logical extension of the position of 'public sociology'.

Taking these things as given, we should now note that the development of political strategy in any conjuncture will benefit hugely from the skills and ethnomethods outlined in the previous section. One needs to have a sense of the various forces and pressures – from the macro through the meso to the micro – at work within the relevant conjuncture in order to adequately weigh up the possibilities for, and probable consequences of, alternative courses of action within the strategic terrain. In any moral and ethical justification for political strategy that goes beyond just the statement of abstract principles to be applied universally (pure *deontological* approaches), one always needs to consider what the consequences would be of taking a particular course of action. This is the case in pure *consequentialist* or teleological approaches, but the same also applies to those more subtle approaches that combine consequentialist and deontological approaches, as in, for example, the two possibly most influential works of political theory of the latter half of the twentieth century, John Rawls's *Theory of Justice* and his partially revisionist volume *Political Liberalism*. In so addressing the issue of possibilities and their probable consequences, it is necessary to be systematic, hard-headed and honest, and there are many lessons to be learned here from 2 above, which counsels ruthless candour and discipline with respect to the 'facts of the situation'. Marx, Weber and Merton are the theorists who have perhaps paid the keenest attention to issues of the probable consequences of possible actions. Marx railed against the dangerous **voluntarism** (see glossary box on p. 231) of Hegelian idealists and would-be political activists who failed to understand the exigencies of the subjective and objective circumstances for action,[69] while Weber observed, for example, that a teacher should be able to 'tell you that if you want such-and-such an end, then you must also accept such-and-such secondary results, which experience shows to occur'.[70] Merton, for his part, famously explored the distinction between the *manifest* consequences of an action and those *latent*, functionally related consequences of an action, which could be benign or disastrous for a social system, and which may or may not have been intended, but which were not typically the immediate point of the action for the actor concerned.[71] This is a complex of distinctions that is central to recent developments around reflexive modernity and the systematically produced unintended social and environmental consequences, including side-effects, of industrialism.

One central dimension of the strategic terrain, and one that is too often downplayed or overlooked, is that there are hermeneutic processes going on within it. To grasp the terrain consequently requires a corresponding phenomenological grasp of such processes. The ability to empathize with other people, whether they be unidentified strangers in the city, distant others caught up in tragic world events on the TV screen in the corner of the room, anonymous forces in a battle of corporate wills or ethnic conflict, or personal intimates, is central to the spirit of the sociological imagination. It is a theme that has been explored by key thinkers from Weber's notion of *verstehen (understanding)*, through the absolutely central role given to phenomenology and hermeneutics in the writings of Schutz, Garfinkel, Habermas, Giddens and others, through to Bauman's moral injunction to cultivate a 'being-for' the Other. The latter adds a moral dimension to even a phenomenologically informed strategic reasoning that could still otherwise be pursued in a narrow instrumental fashion. Bauman explains that what he means by 'being-for' the Other is something that provides the very precondition for responses of 'empathy, commiseration or compassion'.[72] It means 'that the Other is cast as a target for emotion'.[73] The emotionality of the encounter is primary for Bauman who, invoking Levinas's notion of 'the face', refers to the 'sudden opening up to the Other, the unplanned explosion of non-indifference, the abrupt closing of distance'.[74] The essential point is that the self is no longer satisfied with the 'being-aside'[75] relationship to the Other that is marked by indifference, reification and regulation by external norms; there is an awakening to the 'inaudible call for assistance ... which the vulnerability and weakness of the Other, revealed in the nakedness of the face, issues without speaking'.[76] Bauman is clear that 'opening up' should precede any thoughts or decisions about taking a specific course of action in relation to the Other, about what decisions we must make as citizens. Decisions should not be made in an externalist, cold, 'being aside' manner. 'Being tied to the Other by emotion' means that: 'I am responsible for her/him, and most of all for what my action or inaction may do to her/him'.[77] On the other hand, these ties do also, ultimately, involve determining what 'needs to be done' in order to exercise my responsibility to her/him.[78]

In current times, Bauman's points resonate poignantly with Weber's specific insistence, derived from his comparative studies of the world religions, on the importance of understanding different and sometimes fundamentally divergent world-views from the inside, on the basis of *verstehen*. Scaff comments here on the profound discrepancies between different action orientations towards the world, as in the opposing forms of asceticism and mysticism, and how the 'extension of western forms into other contexts has typically provoked a clash – both rejection and emulation of these forms – in all kinds of traditional orders'.[79] Such power-imbued cultural clashes, it is probably superfluous to say, are chronic in the current era of globalization, with the extension of western forms of rationalization and profit maximization into multiple areas of the life of distinct types of society, from the reconstitution of economic and material infrastructures, through the consumption of all kinds of electronically mediated cultural and media images and messages, to the subversion and reconfiguration of forms of community solidarity. A profound identification with the individuals and groups caught up in the webs of these and other social forces of varying magnitudes and scales would provide the motivation for, and a more reasonable basis than most, engaging with further questions of political strategy, of 'What needs to be done?' Remaining sensitive to Cladis's warnings about the need to engage in criticism that 'seeks to reform society by self-consciously working within its historically fashioned social inheritance', one can see that phenomenology, hermeneutics and the moral impulse are all intimately involved in the relationship between the sociological imagination and political strategy.

It is important not to forget the structural dimensions of the strategic terrain as one gives adequate due to the phenomenological, interpretive state of things. In truth, the structural and the phenomenological are always, also, intimately related, even within what is often portrayed as the structural. In any event, the sociological contours of the circumstances in which the Other finds him or herself will profoundly affect not only his or her aspirations, desires, hopes and fears, but also the objective possibilities for, and constraints on, his or her actions. The latter will be affected by all the scales appreciated by the sociological imagination, intermeshing with each other to constitute the immediate set of local networked relationships in which a person finds him or herself. Here, concepts around the themes of structure, agency, habitus, field, strategy and so on, developed by recent social theorists such as Bourdieu, Giddens, Jeffrey Alexander, Mustafa Emirbayer and Ann Mische, Margaret Archer, Nicos Mouzelis, Andrew Sayer and others,[80] allow increasingly more complex and fine-grained apprehensions of the relations between social circumstances and actors at this immediate level at which political strategy has to operate. The concepts allow a greater critical purchase through their ability to focus with more precision on the detailed nature of the strategic terrain on which immediate events are produced.

Debates have raged, and continue to rage, about the precise relationship between social structure, agency consciousness, constraints and strategic possibilities, but from within the key thinkers represented in this book there is little dissent from the view that all these are closely related in ways that should, in principle, be open to identification with analytical precision. Much headway has been made here, with fruitful conceptual refinements increasingly being brought into an engagement with the varying demands of different empirical contexts. The debates between theorists over these topics have also become increasingly interesting as attempts at greater empirical refinement generate conceptual conflict and contestation.[81] Another area where work remains to be done is in the conceptual linking of the different levels of the macro-, meso- and micro-scales as they impinge upon those broader conditions and consequences of action discussed by Marx, Weber and Merton. This is to switch the focus away from just the area of imminent sanctions and rewards attached to various immediate possibilities and to focus also on the likely meso- and macro-level consequences of political strategy in specific circumstances, the consequences that begin to stretch away in time and space, and whose reverberations can be immense.

Having said this, sociological theory has made some progress here as elsewhere and already possesses a formidable stock of internally related insights and methods, whose greater diffusion among the great, the good and the ordinary beyond the ranks of professional sociologists and social theorists could immeasurably enrich the current state of civic and political understanding of the social. Bourdieu, beyond all doubt, was right to stress the vital significance of an ongoing civic mission. Burawoy, in turn, is equally right to want to take things one step further, to a public sociology in which the recognition that there is a variety of legitimate political preferences means that the civic missions of competing groups, each expected to 'combine scientific objectivity and academic autonomy',[82] should, all things being equal, be listened to respectfully as equal participants. The 'all things being equal' clause here is an allusion to the final piece of the jigsaw, the need to expose all political preferences, all value relevant positions, to the glare, also, of explicit moral and ethical debate and justification of the kind outlined above.

How to Use This Book

The aim of *Key Sociological Thinkers* is to introduce readers to the riches of sociological thought by providing a clear, accessible and manageable overview of key developments from Marx to Bauman. The aim is to do this in a way that will create a thirst to read and study more sociology, and to be able to make connections between its lessons and everyday lives. The relative brevity of the individual chapters should make it easier for readers new to the field, or new to particular thinkers, to stay the course, while also allowing them to develop a clear idea of the particular significance of each theorist. While the chapters are written clearly enough, and have been kept short enough, to be accessible to the sociological beginner, there is also much here for more advanced students of the subject, a point highlighted in reviews of the first edition. Readers are also encouraged to dig deeper and a reading list is provided at the end of each chapter in order to facilitate this. The common format for the chapters that contributors were asked to follow was structured with an eye more on capturing the imagination of readers rather than on any attempt at exhaustive coverage of topics. It was felt that if the former is achieved, readers will naturally go on to find out more in their own ways, following their own interests. It was also hoped that dispensing with any injunction to be exhaustive would enable contributors to have more fun while writing the individual chapters.

Twenty-one chapters were specially commissioned for the original volume. All but two – those on **Sigmund Freud** and **Simone de Beauvoir** – remain in the present edition. After listening to feedback on the first edition, after much reflection and with constraints on the length of the book, it was decided to introduce four new key thinkers' chapters and to make some space by cutting Freud and de Beauvoir. I do have regrets here as it is clear that an understanding of Freud, for example, is necessary to fully follow key aspects of the work of Habermas, Chodorow and Hochschild, while de Beauvoir was a seminal influence on second wave feminism. For these reasons, I hope that readers will still return to the first edition to consult the excellent introductions to these thinkers provided by the late Ian Craib on Freud, and by Mary Evans on de Beauvoir. The four newly commissioned chapters are on Theodor Adorno, Dorothy Smith, Michael Mann and Zygmunt Bauman.

All the chapters were commissioned from authors with a close knowledge of their subject. Many are themselves routinely counted as among the most innovative and influential sociological theorists of their generation, and those who are not yet in this bracket are on their way to being so. The list of contributors also bears the mark of a conscious editorial decision to approach only those writers who had an enthusiasm for their key thinker, in the hope that this would be conveyed to the reader and, conversely, that one would avoid the almost inevitable problem of single-authored textbooks in which the author is at best lukewarm towards, and at worst dismissive of, thinkers with whom he or she differs. I feel that it is good to run along with the excitement of a new perspective as far as is possible and for as long as is possible until one begins to sense for oneself the obstacles and limitations that it can not overcome, at least by itself. Then is a good time to read the critiques to see if they can tell you something about your own growing problems with aspects of that key thinker's work. The book also wishes to convey a spirit of openness within the sociological enterprise, whereby one does not necessarily always have to make a choice between different theories. Most of these theories have been developed out of a spectrum of concerns with a rich and varied range of quite disparate questions and problematics. They very rarely have an identical focus, but can quite often, as we have seen, be interestingly and fruitfully combined.

Four Types of Contents Page

In addition to the standard contents page giving the names of the 23 key thinkers and the authors of the individual chapters, there are also three other types of contents list. The first is of the Seeing Things Differently sections of each chapter (see section 3, below), providing another point of entry into chapters, one that immediately gives an impression of how the more abstract and conceptual thinking of that key thinker can be applied to real-world situations, informing and illuminating the way in which these are apprehended. The second is a list of the glossary boxes that appear at various points in many of the chapters. With the agreement of the contributors, I have introduced these in order either to clarify central concepts that may be unfamiliar or difficult for readers new to a field, or to provide important background material. The glossary words or phrases are highlighted in **bold type** in the text and their page numbers are emboldened in the index at the back of the book. Finally, there are separate, more extended contents pages at the beginning of Parts I, II and III respectively. These include a list of all the headings and subheadings within each chapter so that readers can see at a glance the issues that are covered. The three broad sections provide a rough sense of chronology and historical orientation, one that mirrors the pathways I have followed in the present chapter in exploring the continuities and changes in the preoccupations of the key thinkers. The ordering is a rough and ready attempt to combine the bare facts of the years when the key theorist was writing, or still is writing, with a sense of the timing of their most significant impact on sociological thought. Finally, within each chapter, the names of key thinkers other than the thinker who is the subject of that chapter are highlighted in bold the first time an author makes reference to them; this is in the same way that the first reference to any of the key thinkers has been highlighted in this introduction. The purpose of this is simply to highlight points of influence and/or connection between thinkers. References to Freud and de Beauvoir continue to receive this treatment in the current edition.

Outline of the Common Format for the Individual Chapters

Contributors were asked to follow the common format outlined below as far as this was possible and where it was not possible (or desirable) to follow it to the letter, then to adhere to its spirit. In most cases, contributors were happy to follow this format very closely.

Section 1: Driving Impulses

This section asks: What were the driving impulses and influences – both intellectual influences and those of social milieu (society, politics, culture) – that motivated the thinker to spend so much time and energy attempting to come to terms with a given range of issues? Where did the simmering passion come from, the obsessive inquisitiveness necessary to fuel the discipline of thought and writing over decades? This section is not a generalized review of the intellectual and social climate within which the theorist was writing but, rather, a more focused exploration of the intellectual and social influences on those preoccupations of the theorist singled out for elaboration in the next section.

Section 2: Key Issues

Authors present four or five issues that were central to the work of their theorist. These are philosophical, methodological or substantive. There is usually a mixture of these, with the majority being substantive. The restriction to five is obviously arbitrary but has the advantage of deflecting the emphasis away from an exhaustive coverage of topics and towards providing a manageable nucleus of information designed to be more inspiring than daunting.

Section 3: Seeing Things Differently

Authors provide a graphic sense of how their key thinker has illuminated their own view of society. They do this by providing a substantive example/illustration taken from either the wider sociological literature (that is, not an example from this thinker's own work, as this could come in Section 2), or from another source such as a novel, a movie, a documentary, the world of politics, or from everyday life. This section allows the reader to think more closely about the relation between abstract theory and empirical realities; encouraging an awareness of how the best theory does indeed lead us to see the empirical world in new and often surprising ways.

Section 4: Legacies and Unfinished Business

This section addresses such questions as: What are the major intellectual and social legacies of this thinker? Which later thinkers/schools of thought has he or she influenced? Which parts of the intellectual legacy are still being investigated, still bearing fruit, or have still to be fully investigated? Are there themes that have been criticized, reworked and reformulated by later thinkers in such a way that they shed more light on the problematic that motivated the original thinker? Which later thinkers have taken up themes and issues explored by this theorist and have carried them further?

Section 5: Further Reading

This is a short reading list of books and journal articles that enables the reader to take his or her interest further.

Variations on the Guidelines and Changes since the First Edition

A small number of the contributors felt that they could best treat their thinker by departing somewhat from the letter of the guidelines, while remaining faithful to the spirit of their objectives. Thus, for example, Alan Sica's elegantly written chapter on Robert K. Merton departs quite substantially from the general format. Sica finds his own compelling way to convey his enthusiasm and respect for this subject, a way that politely eschews the path of elaboration and exemplification of key concepts, and instead lures the reader deeper into the Merton universe (on the fringes of which, Sica tells us, many of us have already been for many years, albeit unwittingly) by dangling delicious promises of what we will find there. He directs us, for example, to books or articles of Merton's that analyse the American society of the 1930s and 40s and asks us to compare what we find there with what we see around us today. He invokes comparisons of Merton with magicians and jugglers, speaks of the regal elegance of his 'many enduring expressions', and sums him up with the word 'quality', his most enduring characteristic being his 'sheer intelligence and energetic application, over 60 years, of mindfulness to the disentangling of social phenomena'. He succeeds in making us want to 'read further'. In this second edition, I have introduced an extended glossary box into this chapter – on theories of the middle range and on open-ended functionalism – to provide more conceptual background for the uninitiated reader.

For the second edition, authors were asked to update sections 4 and 5, Legacies and Unfinished Business and Further Reading and anything else they felt should be addressed, given the time that has passed since the first edition. All this, together with the four new chapters, the substantial new introductory essay and the addition of further glossary boxes, amounts to a significantly altered volume from the first edition. Some authors have made very substantial additions to their original chapters and a particular mention should be made in this respect to Michèle Barrett's introduction of original and fascinating material in her extensive new Afterword to the chapter on Stuart Hall, which it is a privilege to be able to include here. In one or two cases, the authors of the original chapters were unable, for various reasons, to update the chapters themselves. In these cases I have made the changes myself, and have noted this in the text. One of the authors who was otherwise indisposed is Whitney Pope, the author of the chapter on Durkheim, of a highly esteemed book on Durkheim's *Suicide*, and also an authority on the social and political thought of Alexis de Tocqueville. He has retired from academic life and, together with his wife, now runs The Penrose Bed and Breakfast, 250 Red Butte Dr. Sedona, Arizona 86351. For those wanting to spend some time on vacation talking sociology and Durkheimian rituals over early morning eggs and coffee, bookings can be taken on: email: WPope@ThePenrose.com; website: ThePenrose.com.

The success of the first edition exceeded what could have been hoped for; it is still a core text for many sociological and social theory courses, and is still selling well nearly a decade after publication. The changes and additions that have been made in this second edition have brought the coverage up to date and have also provided a good deal that is substantially new. My hope is that you enjoy this new edition of *Key Sociological Thinkers* and that it plays its own limited part in what proves in the coming years to be a significant renewal of sociology's civic mission, a major rejuvenation of public sociology.

Seeing Things Differently

This is an alternative contents list, focusing just on the section 'Seeing Things Differently' that appears within most chapters. In this section, authors relate how the perspective of their key thinker has made them see the social world in a new and illuminating way, drawing their attention to aspects of the world that otherwise would have passed them by. They do not draw directly on examples given in the work of their thinker, but use examples from everyday life, literature and film, or from the subsequent work of sociologists working within the tradition of that thinker. The examples tend to be graphic and colourful. Readers may wish to get an initial feel for a thinker new to them (or even to those not so new to them) by going first to this section before returning later to read the chapter from the beginning. I have taken the liberty of providing my own individual titles for the sections. In one or two cases, authors did not include a section explicitly entitled 'Seeing Things Differently'; where this is the case I have selected an analogously colourful or illustrative section of their chapters towards which to direct the reader, inventing an appropriate heading. In these cases, I have followed my heading with the author's own section heading in brackets. The page numbers given are to the 'Seeing Things Differently' sections within the relevant chapter.

List of Glossary Boxes

PART I

CONTENTS

CHAPTER 1

Karl Marx

BOB JESSOP

Driving Impulses

It is paradoxical to begin a book on key sociological thinkers with Marx. He had two career ambitions as a student: journalism or university teaching. After disruptions due to censorship, suppression and political activism, he did eventually eke a living from economic and political reporting. He never secured an academic post and, had he succeeded, he would not have taught sociology. He dismissed it as 'rubbish' on reading the sociological treatise of its founding father, Auguste Comte; and, in any case, its intellectual 'take-off' as a distinct discipline occurred after his death.[1] More generally, his work is best described as *pre*-disciplinary rather than mono- or even multi-disciplinary (whether economics, history, sociology, anthropology, politics, international relations, philosophy, literary criticism and so forth). Furthermore, contrary to what the later history of Marxism suggests, Marx had little theoretical or political impact outside socialist circles during his lifetime. Even *The Communist Manifesto* (1848), intended as a popular account of scientific socialism, was largely ignored for several decades. In addition, of its two authors, Engels was the better known in the 1840s and 50s – especially for his damning account of the condition of the English working class; and, even after the first volume of *Das Kapital* was published in 1867 (in English in 1887), it was Engels' popularizing works on historical materialism that stimulated study and debate in the international working-class movement. In short, as a key sociologist, Marx was a largely neglected apostate.

Yet Marx is often heralded as a founder of sociology and his studies (or influential, if often distorted, accounts of them) provide the main critical foil for much in sociological theory and sociological research. For example, **Max Weber** and **Emile Durkheim** often debated with Marx's ghost (as mediated in part through Engels) in developing their ideas, offering bourgeois ripostes to his historical materialism. And, although Marxism is frequently declared moribund, it has equally often been revived and integrated into current sociological thinking. Thus Marx should certainly count as a 'key sociological thinker', if we redefine this term as a key influence in the development of sociology.

Marx was born in 1818 in the Westphalian town of Trier, close to France. He studied humanities at Bonn University and then law and philosophy in Berlin. There he joined a Young Hegelian club devoted to literary and philosophical issues and aiming to develop the radical potential of Hegel's philosophy against the conservative cast inherited from its master. The initial battleground against Right Hegelianism was the nature of religion; later, influenced by Feuerbach, it was the differences between idealism and materialism. Marx's writings in this period mainly concerned philosophy, law and politics and expressed radical democratic and republican opinions. Only in the mid-1840s did he first study political economy, develop his version of 'scientific socialism' and advocate Communism.

This shift depended on political and theoretical factors. Disillusioned with other philosophers for merely interpreting the world, instead of changing it, Marx became increasingly active politically in Germany and France. He also lost faith in a simple radical extension of democracy and social equality and became convinced of the revolutionary potential of the working masses. Marx saw them as uprooted and dispossessed by industrialization and urbanization and condemned to a life of poverty, oppression and alienation. Lacking any stake in society and subject to all its ills, they would sooner or later combine to overthrow it. While Marx initially saw in this 'proletariat' – literally those whose children were their sole property – only the massed ranks of suffering humanity, his later research on English economists (notably Smith and Ricardo) and the English economy (then the most advanced in capitalist terms) led him to see it as a distinct class with distinct interests exploited by the dominant capitalist class in an expanding but contradictory capitalist mode of production. Thus he came to emphasize the world-transforming revolutionary dynamic of capitalism *and* its creation of an expanding, worldwide class of dispossessed waged labour that, sooner or later, would overthrow it.

This brief account may explain why Marxism is said to have three sources: German philosophy, French politics (especially French socialism), and English economics. But Marx's capacity to combine them into Marxism arose from his close identification with the proletariat and its struggles. The resulting theoretical and political analyses in turn stimulated sociological responses that provided an alternative account of industrial societies and suggested reforms that might integrate the working class and prevent the revolution predicted by Marx.[2]

Key Issues

The first central issue in Marx's work for our purposes concerns the nature of the social world and is expressed in the philosophical dispute between idealism and materialism. The second concerns the methodological lessons he drew from his version of materialism (sometimes called 'historical materialism') and its implications for social analysis. More substantive aspects of Marxist 'sociology' can be explored in terms of the historical specificity of capitalism; class relations and class struggle; and the relative autonomy of the state in class societies.

A Materialist Social Ontology

Philosophy and the social sciences both involve long-running debates over the relation of mind and matter. These debates are organized around two poles (idealism and materialism) but have many permutations. It is sufficient here to contrast Hegelian idealism and Marxian materialism.

Hegel's ideas are hard to grasp on first encounter but a general sense of his position is needed. He treated the self-consciousness of the mind as a substantive, really existing, disembodied entity and regarded individual minds as fragments of the one true mind (or Absolute Spirit). In separating spirit, ideas and values from the natural world, he could treat the latter as the result of the self-realization of the Absolute Spirit. He could also claim that 'the real is rational'. This claim was rejected by the Young Hegelians, who condemned poverty, misery and political oppression. In true idealist fashion, however, they attributed these evils to the grip of unsound ideas – especially mystification and illusions produced by religion. Thus human emancipation would depend on overcoming such false consciousness.

Marx soon broke with the Young Hegelians and would later claim to have turned Hegel, whom he saw as standing on his head, right side up. Marx started from real human activity, arguing that consciousness is a product of that activity. He argued that 'it is not the consciousness of men that determines their existence, but their social existence that determines their consciousness'.[3] The essence of human beings was their social nature – people could only develop their capacities and realize their full potential in a free society. If poverty, misery and political oppression existed, the pathological organization of society was to blame rather than aberrant ideas. Human emancipation required the material transformation of society rather than a mere change in consciousness. Marx also argued that the key feature of societies was how they organized material production. He analysed this in different ways. But, in general, he studied the material world in terms of a materialist **ontology** of labour, that is, humans were social animals who produced themselves and society through active social labour (sometimes interpreted to include all social practices). Thus, whereas Hegel viewed the intellectual world of reason, ideas and spirit as the ultimate determinant of history, Marx looked to the material world for the key to understanding and transforming historical development.[4]

> ***Ontology***
>
> *A philosophical or abstract view about the sorts of entities that are in the world, that the world is made up of. Ontologies are typically very general, referring to all times and all places or, at least, to vast periods of history when the sorts of things that are in the world are held to have stayed the same. Examples are the nature of human beings, the nature of the most basic aspects of human life and human societies, the nature of structure and agency, time and space, or the human body.*

Historical Materialism

Marx developed a distinctive method for analysing this development. This has been identified as historical materialism but its precise meaning and content are controversial. For some, it simply inverts Hegelian idealism by explaining history in terms of the discontinuous development of material production. For others, it involves applying Hegelian dialectics to the internal relations and contradictions of capitalism. The first view holds more for the young Marx and his later wide-ranging historical analyses, the second applies more to the mature Marx and his abstract critique of capitalism. Marx also tried different ways of presenting his version of materialism. The popular view in *The Communist Manifesto*, for example, contrasts with Marx's more abstract critique on capitalism. Engels would later reject extreme interpretations of their work that overemphasized the determining role of technology and/or the economy more generally.

The *Manifesto* argues forcefully that 'the history of all hitherto existing societies is the history of class struggle'. Class struggle is the motor of history. To understand the course of history, one must explore the class relations that typify different historical epochs, the antagonisms and forms of class struggle embodied in such class relations, the development of class consciousness and revolutionary movements to challenge the dominant class(es), and the role of successful revolutions in developing new **modes of production** and forms of social organization. It provides a prophetic account of the future development and dynamic of capitalism in an increasingly integrated world market and global society.

> ***Mode of production***
>
> *This is a complex concept that refers to a specific form of organization of material production and distribution and their social preconditions that can be reproduced for an extended period. From the viewpoint of production, it includes two main elements: the forces of production; and the social relations of production. The former comprise all those material and social factors used or drawn upon by workers and/or owners in the production, distribution and circulation of goods and services. These factors include: instruments of production (such as tools and machinery); raw materials; labour power (physical strength, skills, cooperation, information) and infrastructure (such as roads, canals, or, more recently, the information superhighway). Social relations of production are the way that production is organized in a particular society, including, most importantly, the ownership of the means of production and control over the labour process (for example lord and serf/peasant; capitalist owners and proletarian labour; Communist state ownership).*

> ***Economic base and political and ideological superstructure***
>
> *Marx's 1859 Preface to the* Contribution to the Critique of Political Economy *claims a strong relationship between the dominant mode of production and the political and ideological aspects of a given social formation. It is much debated how and how far the dominant mode of production (often described as the 'economic base') determines and moulds politics and ideas. Some commentators suggest that Marx implied a one-sided, quasi-mechanical and complete determination; others argue that he saw it in terms of a fundamental asymmetry in which the political and ideological enjoy a certain 'relative autonomy' vis-à-vis the dominant material base.*

An alternative account of historical development, more obviously indebted to the Hegelian dialectic (as reinterpreted and applied by Marx), emphasized the self-destructive contradictions and 'laws of motion' of specific modes of production. Marx advanced two versions of this approach: one in the form of a grand historical narrative in the 1859 Preface, the other more specific to capitalism in *Capital*. The Preface argues that society's economic organization (its mode of production) comprises a distinctive pattern of forces and relations of production; this is the foundation (or **economic base**) on which arises a complex **political and ideological superstructure** and definite forms of social consciousness; initially, for each mode of production, the relations of production help to develop the productive forces; later, they act as a fetter on development; this initiates an era of social revolution in which the dominant relations of production (and their legal expression in property rights) are challenged; any resulting changes in the economic basis sooner or later lead to superstructural changes. This pattern holds for all societies from primitive Communism through antiquity and feudalism to contemporary capitalism –

which is described as the last antagonistic mode of production. *Capital* was more concerned with the genesis and dynamic of capitalism and made fewer grand transhistorical claims. It discussed the class struggle mainly in terms of the struggle between capital and labour within capitalism rather than its role in the revolutionary defeat of capitalism. Thus it comprises a critical political economy of the capitalist system and its antagonisms more than a popular political sociology of revolutionary class struggle. In contrast to the *Manifesto*, both texts focus on the unfolding logic of a system rather than class struggle.

The Critique of Capitalism

Capital was less concerned to forecast how and when capitalism would collapse or be overthrown (although Marx expected this) than to examine its genesis, functioning and crisis tendencies. Much of his illustrative material came from England. But he predicted other countries would develop in similar fashion because capitalism had an inherent logic transcending its specific instantiations. The key to understanding this logic was the 'commodity' form of social relations – a form that developed fully only in capitalism.

Marx analysed capitalism as a mode of production that had two key features. First, goods and services are produced as commodities, that is, are produced for sale with a view to monetary profit rather than for the immediate consumption of the producers. Second, more importantly, the individual's labour-power (capacity to work) acquires the form of a commodity bought and sold in the labour market. The commodification of labour-power is the distinguishing feature of capitalism. Slaves can certainly be bought and sold; but slave-owners use force to extract surplus from their slaves and must maintain them regardless of their output. Wage-labourers retain their personal liberty and are free, in principle, to choose for whom they work; hence capitalism involves free exchange rather than coercion. Without alternative means of subsistence, however, workers must sell their labour-power to some capitalist to survive. In this sense they are 'wage-slaves'.

Marx claimed that 'value added' in capitalism as a whole (and hence the total profit for reinvestment or redistribution) is entirely due to labour-power. Machines, tools, buildings and so on merely transfer part of their value as they are used up in production. Individual capitalists may gain above-average profits through innovation or market fluctuations or by reducing their turnover time. But these mechanisms simply reallocate the surplus value produced by the working class. As innovations are adopted by all producers and/or as supply and demand are re-equilibrated, these advantages disappear and workers' productivity and wage costs once again become crucial. In short, taking capitalism as a whole, only labour-power can add value.

Whether or not labour-power actually does so, however, depends on capital's ability to control workers in the labour process. It is not so much the hours that workers spend at work but their productivity that matters. Thus the struggle between capital and labour to increase productivity (by extending the working day, intensifying effort during this time, or boosting output by cost-effective, labour-saving techniques) is the fundamental basis of the economic class struggle in capitalism. Class struggle is not simply about relative shares of the capitalist cake. It is rooted in the organization of production (control over the labour process) as well as in market relations (including struggles over wages) or distribution (including redistribution through the state). It concerns not only the accumulation of money as capital but also the overall reproduction of capital's capacity to dominate wage-labour in the economy and, through the importance of the extra-economic conditions of existence of capitalism and the tendency for workers to extend their resistance outside the factory gates and labour market, in the wider society as well.

Marx analysed many different aspects of capitalism from this viewpoint: commodities, money, capital, wages, competition, prices, profits, ground rent and so on. But these were all related to the organization of the labour process as a process of valorization or 'value-adding'. He also defined some fundamental laws rooted in the generalization of the commodity form to labour-power and competition for surplus profits between different capitals. These laws do not operate with iron necessity as an external force. Instead they are tendencies realized in and through the class struggle in specific conjunctures.[5]

Class as a Social Relation

Marx returned many times to the analysis of class relations and struggles, not only in the economy but also in politics, religion, the family, morality and so on. Yet Marx never completed a text devoted to class as such and, although his theoretical work and political action were explicitly developed from a proletarian viewpoint, he wrote little directly about this class in contrast to the bourgeoisie, landowners, petty bourgeoisie, peasants and lumpenproletariat. Moreover, when *Capital III* was about to discuss classes in capitalism, Engels, his posthumous editor, records simply that 'here the manuscript breaks off'.[6]

Marx denied he had discovered classes or class struggle. He did claim credit for showing that 'the existence of classes is merely linked to particular historical phases in the development of production'.[7] In particular, Marx identified the secret of capitalist economic exploitation and why it produced specific forms of class struggle. Only in capitalism are classes demarcated in terms of relations of production that are disembedded from broader institutional forms (such as the family or kinship, political bonds, or religion). In introducing market relations and the cash nexus into all spheres of society and throughout the world, it overturned the traditional social bonds among society's members. Thus social relations in capitalist societies are largely shaped by the capital–labour relation and the dynamic of accumulation.

This is most clearly stated in the *Manifesto*. It claims that capitalism creates its own gravediggers by creating the industrial proletariat. As capitalism tightens its grip around the globe, non-capitalist classes are eliminated and the proletariat expands. It is also concentrated in ever-larger numbers as factories and industrial cities grow in size. As individuals, then groups of workers in a factory or trade and, eventually, all workers in a nation-state (even the world economy) mobilize to resist capitalist exploitation, they grow more conscious of their shared class position and common interest in overthrowing capitalism. Their economic struggles are resisted by the state as well as capitalists. The working classes then move on from trade unionism to party political organization and more revolutionary consciousness. Communists should provide intellectual and political leadership here without regard to immediate party advantage or national differences. As economic conditions worsen and the proletariat gain strength, revolution will eventually occur. The proletariat will then use state power to dispossess capital of the means of production and subject the economy to social control.

The *Manifesto* has influenced sociological theories of class formation, class consciousness and political action. It was already said to have been falsified within 50 years (for example in the work of Bernstein, a German social democrat).[8] But Marx himself modified this approach in his more scientific works as well as his more detailed historical analyses. Thus the *Grundrisse* (1857–61) and *Capital* qualified earlier arguments about the polarization of class relations, suggesting that, as capitalism developed, it would require a growing middle class of clerks, engineers, managers, accountants and so on.[9] Marx's historical studies also described several significant classes or class fractions as well as non-class movements that could play major historical roles in making or breaking revolutions. Later observation of democratic experiences in the USA, Britain and Germany led Marx to suggest that a parliamentary road to socialism was feasible. Conversely, his studies of Russia inspired a belief that a peasant-based revolution might establish a different form of Communism rooted in surviving social patterns of rural community life.

The State and Politics

Marx's work on the state and politics is equally fragmented, incomplete and inconsistent. Neither he nor Engels provided coherent theories of the state as an organ of class domination, of political parties as an organizational form, of nations, nationalism and national states, of the strategy and tactics of revolution (especially whether it is inevitably violent or could assume a more parliamentary form), or of the nature of the 'dictatorship of the proletariat' and 'withering away of the state' that would supersede the capitalist type of state. Given that their project was as much political as theoretical, these are surprising and serious omissions.

In radically simplified terms, Marx and Engels developed two broad views of the state. One sees it as an instrument of class rule wielded more or less successfully by the economically dominant class to secure continuing economic exploitation and political control. The other sees the state as a potentially autonomous authority that could regulate the class struggle in the public interest or even manipulate it to the private advantage of the political stratum. The former view is clearly expressed in the *Manifesto*, the latter appears most famously in Marx's analyses of France under Louis Bonaparte.[10] Building on this twofold division, some commentators suggest the first view typifies more normal periods of class struggle, the latter characterizes 'exceptional' periods when class struggles are stalemated and/or can be depicted as threatening social catastrophe. This interpretation has since been applied by Marxists to Fascism, military dictatorships and the Soviet Union. A third view of the state should be added. Rooted in Marx's earliest critiques of Hegel, it was reworked during subsequent studies and most clearly restated in his remarks on the Paris Commune in 1870. Here the state is seen as an alienated form of political organization because it is based on a separation of rulers and ruled. Only when this separation is abolished through the self-organization of society will political alienation disappear.[11]

Seeing Things Differently

This section contrasts two approaches to the future of capitalism: the classical Marxist emphasis on the relations of production and sociological analyses of the changing forces of production. The latter analyses distinguish the stages of social development in terms of their material basis of production rather than changing class relations. Two key transitions are identified: from agrarian to industrial societies; and then to postindustrialism. Such theorists also argue that, whereas industrial societies depended on the exploitation of waged labour, postindustrial growth relies on the production and utilization of knowledge. Classical Marxists see this as deeply misleading. An interesting test case is provided by the contrasting 1970s' predictions of a Belgian Marxist, Ernest Mandel, and an American sociologist, Daniel Bell, about social futures.[12] Whereas Mandel forecast that 'late capitalism' would develop on a global scale with increased inequalities and instabilities, Bell expected the demise of industrial society based on economic exploitation, and narrow concern with private profit and loss in favour of a knowledge-based, postindustrial society oriented to cooperation and the public interest. A similar contrast occurs in the work of David Harvey, a British Marxist geographer, and Manuel Castells, a Spanish sociologist and, like Bell, an ex-Marxist, who now examines informationalism rather than postindustrialism.[13]

Bell predicted that the economy would change from one largely producing goods to one in which services such as health, education, research and government became increasingly important activities. The university would replace the business firm as the core institution. In occupational terms, there would be a decisive shift towards the professional and technical class – especially scientists and engineers. Organizing material production would become less important than mastery of theoretical knowledge for purposive innovation and social control. As such knowledge developed, postindustrial society would assess its technological needs and plan and control its technological growth. Market forces would decline in favour of public planning based on a new 'intellectual technology' for rational decision-making. Knowledge would be freely accessible and could be used to expand leisure for all.

Bell got many predictions wrong. This is partly because he extrapolated from the USA as the leading capitalist nation,[14] ignoring the effects of US hegemony in an increasingly integrated world market. Just because industrial production is transferred abroad to exploit lower costs and/or new markets while headquarters' functions and other advanced services are retained at home, national economies and societies do not stop being subordinate to the logic of capital. Instead, this logic is generalized to the global level and reimposes itself at the national scale. Indeed, contemporary developments confirm Marx's predictions that capitalism entails the destruction of pre-capitalist relations, increasing polarization, a growing reserve army of labour, and recurrent crises. Bell also erred in believing that technological development enabled a choice between economic exploitation under capitalism and social emancipation in a planned, learning society. He ignored capital's capacity to exploit new technologies to reinforce its economic, political and social control and deprive people of such a choice. In this sense, his views are reminiscent of the Young Hegelians, who believed that a change in social consciousness would be enough to effect the material transformation of the world.

Castells drew on Bell in his analysis of informationalism, a mode of development based on the self-reflexive application of knowledge to the production of knowledge as the critical factor of production. But he rejected Bell's prediction that postindustrialism would lead to democratically controlled social engineering. Instead, he argued that, whereas industrialism could prosper under either statism or capitalism, capitalism alone could realize the full potential of informationalism. Castells thereby confirmed its capacity to use informationalism to overcome its crisis, reinforce control over the labour process, and develop a reinvigorated 'networked' capitalism that can operate around the globe in real time. While his hard-nosed *post hoc* assessment is superior to Bell's utopian vision, he shares Bell's neglect of the inherent contradictions of postindustrialism in capitalist conditions. Both theorists regard knowledge as a simple factor of production rather than as a potentially conflictual field of social relations. I explore the implications of this latter approach below.

Some of Mandel's predictions also erred. But he did show how profit-seeking rather than social planning drives technological development and how the logic of accumulation shapes the wider society. Mandel saw multinational firms (not universities) as the core institution of late capitalism and believed they would be the vehicles through which antagonisms would intensify between American, Japanese and European capitalists. While there are certainly elements of such an antagonism (now including China, India and Russia too), there is also evidence for an increasingly powerful transnational class and international regimes organized under US hegemony. Moreover, whereas Bell took technological innovation for granted, Mandel employed Marxism to explain its wave-like development over long periods. This was linked in late capitalism to a great increase in research and development, the expansion of skilled and intellectual labour, the growth of producer services as well as the commodification of working-class leisure and so on. Mandel also suggested that technological progress would become a major theme in late capitalist ideology (a prediction reflected ideologically in Bell's own work as well as in the dominance of the 'knowledge-based economy' in current accounts of capitalism). He also argued that new forms of the global expansion of capitalism would require new forms of state intervention as national economies became more open and competition grew more intense. If his analyses erred in some respects, it is because he was too committed to the Marxist view that the logic of capitalism could explain most changes in economic, political and sociocultural organization.

Harvey's recent analyses of the 'new imperialism' and neoliberalism are firmly grounded in classical Marxism in contrast to Castell's retreat from such positions. He argues that these new trends are grounded in the crisis of the postwar mode of growth and reflect the search for new spatial and social fixes to restore the dynamic of capital accumulation at the expense of greatly increased uneven development and the roll-back of the gains achieved by the working class in postwar welfare states. He also notes the increased importance for accumulation and class domination of 'accumulation by dispossession', including the privatization of public assets, the role of intellectual property rights in appropriating the intellectual commons, and a renewed resort to military power. While there is much to debate in his work, which increasingly combines careful theoretically informed empirical analysis with forceful but oversimplified class rhetoric, it does indicate the continuing heuristic and explanatory power of key Marxian categories in exploring capital accumulation.[15]

A more balanced Marxist analysis should demonstrate where both Bell and Mandel erred and also how Harvey, but not Castells, has been able to integrate some key insights from Marx into his more recent analysis of contemporary capitalism. It would reveal that the contradiction between the information society and information economy is a particular form of that between the forces and relations of production. Bell believed that, once knowledge becomes the principal factor in economic expansion, it could become the property of all and a basis for democratic control. But capital seems bent on asserting property rights in all forms of information and knowledge. Thus intellectual property rights are now a key stake in international conflicts – with the USA, Bell's paradigmatic postindustrial society, in the lead. Likewise, there is a growing struggle by capital to extend property rights (and hence the right to private profit) to include the human genome, wild plants, animals, tribal medicines, outer space, the oceans and so on. An interesting case relevant to the arguments of all four theorists is the commodification of the internet – an anarchic cyberspace originally free from government and capitalist control and now a key site of surveillance and an important marketing channel.

Legacies and Unfinished Business

Issues raised by Marx have long shaped sociological enquiry into the nature, history, overall logic and future development of capitalism. In this sense, his writings have the status of 'classic' texts, that is, texts whose questions are still considered important but whose answers are no longer always accepted as valid. But reception of his work is often ambivalent and politicized and involves positive and negative phases. Intellectually, this is due to its richness, complexity and discontinuities as well as to the incompleteness of some texts and posthumous appearance of others. Politically, it is due in part to Marx's critique of capitalism, his support for Communism, and his confusing advocacy of both democracy and the 'dictatorship of the proletariat'; in part, to the appropriation of his name (if not always his ideas) by Marxism-Leninism and its association with Stalinism; and, most recently, to the collapse of the Soviet bloc, which some see as a deathblow to Marxism and others as the long-awaited opportunity to revive Marx without getting entangled with the failed Soviet experiment. However, even where Marx's actual or alleged ideas provoke disagreement, they still provide major reference points in many kinds of social analyses.

Marx's standing as a 'key sociological thinker' is best linked to his work on the political economy of capitalism rather than his commitment to the grave-digging role of the proletariat. In particular, his analysis of the commodity form (especially its generalization to wage-labour) is still essential to understanding the dynamic of capitalism. Problems arise when this critique is applied to society as a whole. The centrality of labour-power and the labour process in capitalism does not entail that capitalism (even broadly defined) is equally central for explaining the development of entire societies. This is an issue for empirical investigation. Indeed, social scientists increasingly argue that no system (whether the economy, the state, law, religion or another system) can determine the overall logic of societal development or become so powerful that it can overcome all forms of resistance. This should provide an interesting basis to explore the nature and limits of any domination of societal development by the logic of capital accumulation.

After 150 years of debate on Marx's work, much unfinished business still remains. If we regard Marx primarily as a theorist of the capitalist mode of production, at least two issues remain contentious. The first involves difficult and often esoteric debates about the 'labour theory of value', that is, the view that the value of any commodity is the sum of the values of the commodities that enter into its production. This allegedly holds for labour-power itself so that its value depends on the value of the commodities needed to renew its capacity to labour. This view has few defenders today, in part because of the increased importance of the 'moral and historical component' in wage formation, in part because it ignores the role of unpaid (and typically female) domestic labour in reproducing labour-power, and in part because it takes little account of so-called unproductive labour paid for by the state to provide (until recently) non-commodified educational, health and other services. There is a more general theoretical problem too. It does not follow from the existence of a market for living labour-power that it has the same commodity character as an inert machine. Indeed, most of Marx's conclusions about the labour process, capitalist exploitation, class conflict and the overall logic of capital could be derived from exploring, as he did, the consequences of treating labour-power as if it were a commodity like any other. In this sense, it is not Marx who defines labour-power as a simple commodity but capitalism that treats it like a commodity.

Second, there is increasing recognition that, while capitalism may have a distinctive dynamic, its future remains open. Marx's detailed analyses of capitalist development implied nothing inevitable about its rise or demise and the 1859 Preface stressed that no mode of production ever ended before its full potential had been exhausted. Capitalism is not moving inexorably towards some predetermined revolutionary crisis (even if its growth clearly has fundamental ecological limits) but has instead shown remarkable regenerative capacities. This is reflected in recent debates about the competitiveness of different varieties of capitalism. Marx himself also discussed different paths of development and emphasized the mediating role of class struggle.

As a theorist of society rather than capitalism, Marx is sometimes accused of seeking to explain everything in terms of class relations or, worse still, of technological development; or else of being so vague about base–superstructure relations that his views can be read in many ways. There is still scope for discussing the importance in different contexts of class consciousness relative to gender, ethnic, national or other identities and of class struggles compared to other social movements. Likewise, there is much scope for debating the relative importance of the capital relation as opposed to technology, the inter-state system, patriarchy, struggles in civil society and so on for the future of contemporary society. In these respects, Marx has left a rich research agenda to be explored on many levels and across many domains.

FURTHER READING

The following are excellent commentaries either on Marx's work as a whole or central specialized aspects of his work.

Antonio, R.J. (ed.) (2003) *Marx and Modernity: Key Readings and Commentary*, Oxford: Blackwell.

Burkett, P. (1999) *Marx and Nature: A Red and Green Perspective*, New York: St Martin's Press.

Fine, B. and Saad-Filho, A. (2004) *Marx's 'Capital'* (4th edn), London: Pluto.

Graham, K. (1992) *Karl Marx: Our Contemporary*, Toronto: University of Toronto Press.

Lebowitz, M.A. (2003) *Beyond Capital: Marx's Political Economy of the Working Class* (2nd edn), Basingstoke: Palgrave Macmillan.

McLellan, D. (1977) *Karl Marx: His Life and Thought*, Basingstoke: Macmillan – now Palgrave Macmillan.

CHAPTER 2

Max Weber

LAWRENCE A. SCAFF

Driving Impulses: Life and Orientation

Max Weber is one of the Promethean figures of social thought. Born in 1864 into a Protestant upper-middle-class family, his ancestors included German merchants and businessmen on his father's side of the family and French Huguenots on his mother's side. A successful lawyer and National Liberal politician in Berlin, Weber's father, Max Weber senior, introduced his son to the exhilarating world of European politics and statesmanship in the age of Bismarck. An educated woman with strong religious beliefs and commitments to social welfare, his mother, Helene, encouraged his intellectual and spiritual development. The poles of young Max's existence were thus clearly marked: either pursuit of power and a life of public affairs, or devotion to *Geist* and the life of the mind. These alternatives shaped the entire course of Weber's life and work, culminating in his brilliant last testimonial: the speeches on politics and science as vocations.

Completing his dissertation and habilitation in 1889 and 1891 on topics in economic history at the Humboldt University of Berlin, Weber reluctantly entered the university world of teaching and scholarship, while expressing a longing for a life of political engagement. But hopes for either career were dashed in his thirties, when he suffered a psychological collapse in 1898, brought on by overwork and family strife *and* having the outward characteristics of a classic **Freudian** oedipal conflict, as his colleague, Friedrich Meinecke, later pointed out. Weber's convalescence was painfully slow, and after a dazzling start at the universities of Freiburg and Heidelberg, he eventually returned to teaching at Vienna and Munich only during the last two years of his life. All the major work for which he is known today, from *The Protestant Ethic and the 'Spirit' of Capitalism* (1904–5) to the unfinished text of *Economy and Society* (published posthumously in 1922), was written in the diaspora, so to speak, of two decades outside the protected environment of academia. This mature work can be seen as a labour of recovery and a triumph of self-mastery.

Weber's social and cultural world was marked by deep conflicts and irreconcilable tensions, as if to mirror his personal turmoil. It is well known that the Industrial Revolution hit the continent full force after Germany's unification in 1871, leading to massive social dislocations, rapid urbanization, incipient class conflict, and the formation of revolutionary political movements. But we often need to be reminded that by the turn of the century new cultural movements were underway as well – in art and architecture, literature and drama, and in the conventions concerning sex and gender. Weber felt these tensions deeply and observed them at close range. Because of his temperament, interests and personal relationships, he found himself placed at the centre of the raging cross-currents, often attempting to understand them, respond to them, or resist them. Why do people conduct their lives as they do, often in such different ways? What material forces restrict or enlarge their life opportunities? What moral powers do they call upon in facing up to the demands of the world? Even his comparative and historical scholarship that may seem most remote from the present, such as the studies of society and religion in China and India, radiates an intense curiosity about these questions, which ultimately concern the fate of civilizations.

During the last year of his life in 1920, following a heated student-sponsored debate with Oswald Spengler, who expounded his 'decline of the West' thesis, Weber remarked that the intellectual world of his time had been formed in large measure by the writings of **Marx** and Nietzsche. They had defined the major themes for the twentieth century: the question of social justice, the nature of the capitalist economy, the fate of western civilization, the problem of our relationship to history and knowledge, modernity and its discontents. Weber read their work, addressed their themes, and sustained a dialogue with their followers. Like Marx, he identified himself throughout his life as a political economist. Much of his discussion of the relationship between economics and religion can be seen as a sustained inquiry into the validity of the 'materialistic conception of history' popularized by the man he called 'the great thinker'.[1] And like Nietzsche, Weber was fascinated with the expressions and problems of culture, both traditional and modern, and particularly its effects on our personalities and the way we conduct our lives. Much of his cultural science and sociology thus took the form of a critical response to what he called Nietzsche's 'brilliant' constructions.[2]

Had Weber added **Freud** to his citation, then his remark on the occasion of the Spengler debate would have encompassed our own times as well. Indeed, Weber read some of Freud's essays, and he knew the work of the experimental psychologists, such as Wundt and William James. But he had little patience with the 'talking cure' and other new therapies. Instead, what he took from the debates about subjectivity and the psyche was the problem of rationalism, that 'superficially simple concept' he once said[3] – its nature, varieties and consequences. Weber's life-work was an effort to map this contested terrain.

Key Issues

Weber thought deeply about an unusually wide range of subjects, covering the sweep of world civilization and the nature of human inquiry. The leading question of his three-volume study of the world religions – Why is it that we have capitalism in the West? – served as a focal point for a comparative *tour de force* of the relationship between religion and economics. Weber then used these studies to probe the nature of what he called the 'disenchantment of the world' and the 'rationalization' of life, that is, in general the tendency of our activities and practices to become intellectualized, calculable, defined by technique, and subjected to means–ends tests. In the course of these investigations, he also sought clarity about the character of work and vocation in the modern world, just as he puzzled over the nature of authority and power, and the problem of knowledge and the knowledge-seeker in the human sciences.

On the Relationship between Religion and Economics

Weber's reputation is owed above all to his studies of *The Protestant Ethic and the 'Spirit' of Capitalism*. Provoking an instant debate and numerous follow-up investigations, which show little sign of diminishing, Weber proposed a thesis that connected the dynamic 'capitalist' system of production and exchange with a religiously inspired *ethos* of work and self-control. Weber called the latter a kind of asceticism oriented towards acting in the here and now, which he found especially characteristic of members of the Protestant sects. With respect to the hypothetical connection between this particular economic system and a particular religion, Weber claimed only to have unearthed an 'elective affinity' that helped to identify one reason for the emergence and success of modern capitalism. Making a point that is often overlooked, he denied proposing a causal connection or a specification of necessary and sufficient conditions for the rise of capitalism. But he did contend that one of the important factors favouring the kind of dynamic, market-oriented economies typical of the West resided in the Reformation and the creation of anti-traditional belief systems that sanctioned work, savings, investment, entrepreneurial success, or in short, the systematic creation of wealth *as a calling*. Commitment to a 'calling' or 'vocation' was an unconditional duty, a matter of attempting to fulfil the demands of a practical ethic and way of life. Originating in the search for religious salvation, the idea of the calling came to be extended over time to the search for worldly achievement and recognition.

Of course, Weber understood that concealed beneath the banner of 'capitalism', that 'most fateful force in our modern life',[4] as he called it, are a variety of quite different characteristics. Like most abstract nouns in the lexicon of science, capitalism (and feudalism, mercantilism, socialism and so on) can only be a pure or 'ideal' type, not a real entity, that the investigator constructs from complex events for analytic purposes. As production for a market, capitalism had appeared elsewhere in history – in ancient Rome, for example. As entrepreneurial activity aimed at amassing savings, it achieved prominence in the Italian city-states of the Renaissance. Or as the forcible seizure of booty, it could be found throughout world history. But Weber's point was that this particular modern configuration of forces – production for a market, separation of the enterprise from the household, the rational organization of formally 'free' labour, technical means of book-keeping, rational calculation of profits for reinvestment – amounted to a new, dynamic *system*, which once set in motion would transform traditional societies everywhere around the globe. He saw that an important starting point for this transformation (although not the only one) was located in changes in the moral order – specifically, the predominance of asceticism oriented towards action in this world and mundane achievement. This orientation towards action, or *ethos*, formed the groundwork for the distinctive character of western culture as a whole – its 'specific and peculiar rationalism' in Weber's words.[5] Thus, the ethos affected not only western culture's modes of production and exchange, but also its science and technology, legal and political orders, administrative systems, and its cultural life as a whole.

Weber's comparative studies of the world religions – religion in China and India, in ancient Judaism, and a planned study of Islam that remained unfinished – were carried out with the aim of showing exactly why and how conditions for the indigenous emergence of modern capitalism were missing in these contrasting settings. The combinations there of mysticism and asceticism focused on another world, a heaven or nirvana, were associated with different consequences for civilization. Indeed, Weber considered asceticism and mysticism to be radically opposed practices for achieving the goals of life, just as he perceived a principled opposition between action oriented towards the world in which we live and towards another imagined world beyond human experience and time. The consequences of such different orientations have been far-reaching, to say the least, for as we have seen repeatedly, the extension of western forms into other contexts has typically provoked a clash – both rejection and emulation of these forms – in all kinds of traditional orders.

The Disenchantment of the World and the Rationalization of Life

From Weber's perspective, his inquiry into the capitalist world order elaborated primarily a historical thesis, although he was alert to its implications for the present and future: What does such a thesis mean for us today, living centuries after the Reformation and the scientific revolution of the Enlightenment? The answer to this question opens on to one of Weber's great themes, announced on the famous concluding pages of *The Protestant Ethic and the 'Spirit' of Capitalism*. For there he noted that 'Limitation to specialized work, with a renunciation of the Faustian universality of man which it involves, is a condition of any valuable work in the modern world.' In a previous age the 'Puritan wanted to work in a calling; we are forced to do so'. Today the modern economic order is 'bound to the technical and economic conditions of machine production' that determine our lives with the power of an unavoidable fate, a fatality that threatens to confine us within an 'iron cage'. Gazing further into our century, Weber intoned in phrases recalling Nietzsche:

> No one knows who will live in this cage in the future, or whether at the end of this tremendous development entirely new prophets will arise, or there will be a great rebirth of old ideas and ideals, or, if neither, mechanized petrification, embellished with a sort of convulsive self-importance. For of the last stage of this cultural development, it might well be truly said: 'Specialists without spirit, sensualists without heart; this nullity imagines that it has attained a level of civilization never before achieved.'[6]

The metaphor of the 'iron cage' or 'casing as hard as steel' is one of Weber's most arresting images for describing the condition of humankind in a bureaucratized world, or, more abstractly stated, the constriction of opportunities and possibilities in a world dominated by 'purposive' or 'instrumental rationality' *(Zweckrationalität)*, a type of rationality oriented exclusively towards the efficient maximization of practical goals. Such a prospect suggests the depth to the problem of work and calling in the modern age, and indeed, much of Weber's attention was given to reflection on the conditions of vocational activity and the internal demands on the character or personality placed upon representative figures like the scientist, teacher, scholar, cleric, politician, official, administrator, lawyer, journalist, artist, intellectual or entrepreneur. In 'Science as a Vocation' and 'Politics as a Vocation', Weber pronounced his last words on this theme, issuing in both texts an eloquent appeal for personal moral engagement – a call to integrity and an 'ethic of responsibility' – and for the contributions of knowledge to 'self-clarification'.[7]

If this response to the 'iron cage' sounds unsurprising and uncomplicated, then it is important to recognize that Weber raised the stakes for an answer considerably higher than previous social theorists. Unlike either Marx or **Durkheim**, for example, he understood the practice of science or the pursuit of knowledge as both a progressive, beneficial activity, but also a 'disenchanting' activity – in his words, 'the most important fraction of the process of intellectualization which we have been undergoing for thousands of years'.[8]

Just as politics had to face up to the 'diabolical' consequences of the use of power, so science had to confront the disenchanting consequences of 'intellectualist rationalization'.

Weber chose dramatic and theologically weighted language to state his case for his commitment to a 'disenchanting' science and against a naive belief in progress:

> The fate of an epoch which has eaten of the tree of knowledge is that it must know that we cannot learn the *meaning* of the world from the results of its analysis, be it ever so perfect; it must rather be in a position to create this meaning itself. It must recognize that a *Weltanschauung* can never be the product of advancing empirical knowledge, and that therefore the highest ideals, which move us most powerfully, are formed for all time only in the struggle with other ideals which are just as sacred to others as ours are to us.[9]

In this view, one consequence of disenchantment was the dominion of technique, the certainty that the human mind could master nature by calculation. But the hubris of world mastery also meant, as he said, that 'the bearing of humankind has been disenchanted and denuded of its mystical and inwardly genuine plasticity', and that 'the ultimate and most sublime values have retreated from public life either into the transcendental realm of mystic life or into the brotherliness of direct and personal human relations'.[10] The dilemma is that science is only one of the orders of life, and although it is uniquely qualified to gain knowledge about nature and the human world, its competence *qua science* does not extend to answering our most urgent questions: What should we believe in? How should we conduct ourselves? What kinds of lives should we lead? The vital, but disenchanting order of science cannot answer our questions about the 'meaning' of life and the world. Other orders and spheres of value have a powerful say in these matters, according to Weber, and the different answers they give are joined in an irreconcilable, endless struggle with each other.

Method and the Philosophy of Science

What conclusions can be drawn from this position? In his writings on method and the philosophy of science, Weber developed a complex, nuanced answer that unfortunately is often misconstrued. Briefly put, on the one hand, he articulated the notion that science should aim for 'objectivity', in the sense of creating a conversation in which personal bias and ideological distortion are held in check. This was a prescriptive ideal for *disinterested* inquiry. But, on the other hand, he acknowledged that western experimental science as practised in the modern age is historically and culturally determined. It is an all too human activity and a product of a particular concatenation of circumstances, not a quest rooted in the nature of things. Nevertheless, arrayed against alternatives, science still offers the best possible means for searching for the 'truth' about ourselves, our history, and our possible future.

Stated abstractly, then, the body of knowledge known as 'science' was provisional in the sense of being conditioned by cultural values, social interests and historical developments. But it was also 'valid' because it was formulated through critical and self-corrective methods and rational standards of inquiry, subjected to the controlling debates of the scientific community. 'For scientific truth is precisely what is *valid* for all who *seek* the truth' is Weber's shorthand way of stating the idea.[11] This position should underscore the **voluntarist**, rather than the **relativist** consequences of science in the Weberian mould. Emphasizing the significance of conscious choosing, Weber surely would have agreed with J.S. Mill's assertion that 'The human faculties of perception, judgement, discriminative feeling, mental activity, and even moral preference, are exercised only in making a choice'.[12]

Voluntarist and relativist

Weber's attitude to the status of knowledge claims was voluntarist *because he believed that the most adequate forms of knowledge were produced by means of the social scientific community applying their own voluntary codes and standards of critical analysis, debate and evidence. Such standards were always the result of hard-fought, and ongoing, battles between differing positions. The voluntarism refers to the clear choices that have to be made within such a process. While Weber would readily concede that such standards were culturally and historically situated, his position still differs from* relativism *because the latter attitude to knowledge is simply that any claim is as good as any other. A relativist does not believe that some knowledge claims are more adequate than others. She or he does not recognize the qualitative difference between an unsubstantiated opinion, on the one hand, and a belief that has been subjected to critical and self-corrective methods and rational standards of inquiry, on the other. Weber certainly did recognize this difference.*

Notwithstanding the intense effort Weber expended on these topics, he remained an extraordinarily sceptical philosopher of science, believing that no important scientific problem is ever solved by purely methodological or philosophical interventions alone. It is fitting to emphasize, therefore, that his substantive work recorded a passion for historical knowledge and an understanding of social action and institutional forms – as he liked to remark, the clear-sighted investigation of 'what is' that is the substance of his essays in the sociology of religion and his later sociology and social economics in *Economy and Society*.

Authority or 'Legitimate Domination'

One of the most important aspects of Weber's later work was the analysis of authority or 'legitimate domination' – *Herrschaft* in the original terminology. The centrepiece of this widely cited contribution – the threefold typology of **legal-rational, traditional and charismatic authority** – was used by Weber as a general scheme for analysing specific configurations of power. It was also the general framework for much that he had to say in the different areas of sociological investigation that he helped to found: studies of bureaucracy, law, leadership, the state, social stratification, and the city as a political community. Although simplified and overly schematic, the categories in Table 2.1 indicate something about the scope of these efforts and the kind of terminology Weber employed.

> ***Legal-rational, traditional and charismatic authority***
>
> *In the section entitled 'The Three Pure Types of Authority' in* Economy and Society, *Weber writes: 'There are three pure types of legitimate domination. The validity of the claims to legitimacy may be based on:*
>
> 1. *Rational grounds – resting on a belief in the legality of enacted rules and the rights of those elevated to authority under such rules to issue commands (legal authority).*
> 2. *Traditional grounds – resting on an established belief in the sanctity of immemorial traditions and the legitimacy of those exercising authority under them (traditional authority); or finally,*
> 3. *Charismatic grounds – resting on devotion to the exceptional sanctity, heroism or exemplary character of an individual person, and of the normative patterns of order revealed or ordained by him (charismatic authority).' (Economy and Society,* Berkeley, University of California Press, 1978, p. 215)

Weber was fascinated by the tensions and contradictions among the different bases for legitimation and power in social life, and he thought it important to take account of the different ways in which these bases could be rationalized:

> Bureaucratic authority is specifically rational in the sense of being bound to intellectually analysable rules; while charismatic authority is specifically irrational in the sense of being foreign to all rules. Traditional authority is bound to the precedents handed down from the past ... [whereas] within the sphere of its claims, charismatic authority repudiates the past, and is in this sense a specifically revolutionary force.[13]

Table 2.1 Basic characteristics of the three pure types of authority or 'legitimate domination' (adapted from Weber, *Economy and Society*)

	Organization	*Membership*	*Law*	*Responsibility*	*Leadership*
I. LEGALITY					
Instrumental rationality	Bureaucratic	Specialized	Legal formalism	Impersonal	Monocratic
Value rationality	Professional	Rational competence	Promulgation of natural law	Public service	Collegial democratic
II. TRADITION					
Patriarchy/ patrimony	None/ gerontocracy/ personal staff	Birth, honour	Prescription, precedent	Personalistic	Monocratic/ collegial
Estates	Personal staff	Fealty, personal loyalty	Prescription	Personalistic	Collegial (estate collegiality)
III. CHARISMA	Voluntaristic devotion	Personal	Substantive legal principles	Commitment to a cause	Monocratic/ democatic

Every society contained a complex mixture of the three types, and yet there was also a dynamic relationship among them that could be observed: ordinary tradition and legal forms challenged by extraordinary charisma, but then charisma itself transformed into 'rational' rule-governed routines. Social change came about in part because of such clashes between competing structures of power, expressed on the surface of social reality by competing claims to legitimation. From Weber's perspective, to trace the dynamic relationships and process in different spheres of action was the point of the specialized sociologies of bureaucracy, the law, or the state.

Unlike Durkheim or Marx, Weber fathered no coterie of disciples or specific school of thought. But even so, aspects of his political sociology have achieved a powerful grip on the modern imagination: instrumental rationality as a potent agent of change, bureaucracy as an immensely effective mechanism of control, professionalism as a standard of conduct, and 'charisma' as a mythic quality of personality and leadership. From worries about 'bureaucracy' to the quest for 'charisma' we have learned to speak in Weberian formulae. One reason is that despite the way the present overshadows the past and dominates our vision, the early twenty-first century still shares important resemblances with its nineteenth-century points of origin.

Seeing Things Differently

Resemblances are not difficult to locate. To take one example, applications and evidence of Weber's insights are commonplace because of the managed environments we experience daily. The lessons of the tendencies and characteristics Weber discussed under the heading of rationalization seem to be everywhere – in popular culture and entertainment, in the economic trends associated with 'globalization', in the marketing of everything from political candidates to spiritual beliefs, and in the workings of modern organizations of all kinds.

Consider a typical experience: recently one of my students accepted a well-paid position in a prominent firm in the burgeoning 'service' economy. Shortly after her arrival, the firm moved into new corporate headquarters equipped with the latest electronic paraphernalia and design features. One management innovation was the use of the open-plan office, that is, a large space, sealed off and soundproofed against the outside world, occupied by numerous employees and partitioned only by cubicles separating open work areas, rather than floor-to-ceiling walls with windows and connecting passageways. The expressed aim, of course, was improved communication, better consultation and higher levels of productivity. But in practice employees experienced the environment as a sterile and noisy capsule, paradoxically creating a feeling of isolation, yet without a sense of privacy. To regain a sense of freedom and equilibrium required flight into other spaces. The corporate response was not to humanize the means or reassess the appropriate ends for the work environment, but rather to employ more sophisticated instrumentalities: background 'white noise' was piped into the office space to simulate a 'normal' human environment, which otherwise had been suppressed. Weeks of 'fine-tuning' ensued, in which painfully shrill static was modulated into something less recognizable and more tolerable. 'In a world now devoid of meaning', as Jacques Attali remarks, 'background noise [is] increasingly necessary to give people a sense of security; it is a means of silencing, a concrete example of commodities speaking in place of people, of the monologue of institutions.'[14]

What is striking about such cases is the irrationalism associated with instrumental rationality, the way in which human requirements are contravened by the rationalization of activity as a goal-oriented enterprise. Consider the situation that sometimes prevails in the contemporary university. It was not so long ago that universities were institutions in which at least some of the time 'collegial' principles prevailed, using Weber's category. That is, authoritative decision-making depended in some important ways and in some settings on discussion, deliberation and often rather messy efforts to form or approximate a consensus. Governance could have been interpreted using the model of 'communicative action' that **Jürgen Habermas** has promoted in his work.

Moreover, there were some areas of scholarly activity and student life that had little to do with rational ends, such as 'efficiency' or 'effectiveness'. But as the imperatives of 'planning', 'productivity' and 'efficiency' have taken hold, the modern university has come to resemble any enterprise subjected to means–ends rationalization. In Weber's terminology, this kind of rationalization signifies the deployment of instrumental rationality in the service of bureaucratic domination. In the marketplace of university policies, it means the deployment of 'total quality management' teams to eliminate inefficiencies, the use of productivity metrics for the evaluation of scholarship, the assignment of targets and quotas for future accomplishments, the application of 'algorithms' to yield judgements about policy, the treatment of students as 'consumers' of a product or 'customers' shopping for goods and services, the understanding of teachers as service 'providers' or facilitators, and the measurement of learning 'outcomes' to justify continued financial support.

Humans are inventive creatures and thus respond with an impressive array of efforts to adapt, exploit, subvert or outwit these languages and mechanisms of control. Knowledge and its application offer the only way out in such circumstances. Before intelligence arrives, however, the institutional lives we lead may end up still more impoverished than before, and the tensions between life and vocation, of which Weber was acutely aware, may be left in an even more severe state of crisis.

Weberian Legacies

Weber's work has grown in stature over the decades, affecting studies in the sociology of religion, political and historical sociology, sociology of law and the state, the methodology and philosophy of the social sciences, the theory of social action (from **Parsons** to Habermas), and moral and political philosophy. Weber's thinking about disenchantment, rationalization, and the relationship between ideas and material interests also influenced discussions within the Frankfurt School and in some branches of revisionist Marxism, as represented by Lukács and the early Michels. Today some scholars even refer to a Weberian 'paradigm' in social theory and social science. Weberian social theory has a distinctive imprimatur, and it is commonly thought to refer to multicausal, comparative analyses that give special attention to the interaction between structural factors and subjective beliefs and intentions. Stated in this manner, it is important to see that the older disputes pitting materialism against idealism, positivism against historicism, or formal theory against empirical history have ended in the victory of neo-Weberian approaches. Work that focuses on large-scale comparative historical questions dealing with institutional change, political and economic transformation, the global expansion of modern capitalism, or the dynamic relationship between state and civil society rests implicitly on Weberian foundations. The effort 'to bring the state back in' follows in the footsteps of Weber's thought, as does the 'new institutionalism', work on state–society relationships, or developments in the field of economic sociology that Weber helped to define.[15] Working with explicit models of rationality and different kinds of explanatory hypotheses, contemporary scholarship has continued along the path set forth by Weber.

It is also the case, however, that some aspects of Weber's work have been either poorly understood or neglected. As someone who emerged as a political economist at the intersection between historicism and positivism, rejecting both and attempting to find a new synthesis, Weber staked out independent positions that were often difficult to grasp, even for his contemporaries.

Today there are two relatively new areas of inquiry in which Weber's work may prove useful and thought-provoking: economic sociology or social economics, and cultural sociology. With regard to the former, it is usually overlooked that Weber devoted considerable effort in *Economy and Society* to specifying the 'categories of economic action' which would guide our understanding of rational action that is both social and economic, and thus serve as a bridge between the two disciplines. Interest in types and models of rational action has been a central preoccupation in the social sciences generally, as it was in Weber's work. The Weberian view always embedded economic rationality in its social context, as evidenced in Weber's own early studies of the stock exchange and commodity markets.[16] His assumption of 'embeddedness' is shared with contemporary economic sociology. Now, at a time when some sociologists and economists are looking for ways to escape from the relatively narrow idea of rationality found in classical economic theory and theories of choice, the Weberian categories and standpoint offer an instructive alternative worth revisiting.[17]

Similarly, much of Weber's actual writing and most innovative thinking, such as his unfinished essay on music,[18] addressed themes and issues in cultural sociology. There has been a tendency, however, either to ignore this work or to restrict it to specialized topics in sociology, instead of connecting it with larger cultural themes and contemporary problems. But the current discussions across the human sciences of a more broadly configured interest in 'culture', as found importantly in the work of **Foucault** and **Bourdieu**, provide an opportunity to extend this aspect of the Weberian perspective into areas of cultural production and expression, such as painting, architecture or literature, that Weber himself only began to consider.[19] To explore the emergence, development and rationalization of a particular sphere of culture, as well as the cultural revolts against the rationalization process itself, is to address those grand civilizational themes that represent the most challenging extension of the Weberian legacy in the twenty-first century.

FURTHER READING

There is an extensive and growing literature in English on Weber's life and work, compiled in Alan Sica, *Max Weber: A Comprehensive Bibliography* (2004). Richard Swedberg has issued a comprehensive Weberian lexicon, *The Max Weber Dictionary* (2005). A good brief introduction is Dirk Käsler, *Max Weber* (tr. 1988). Randall Collins, *Weberian Sociological Theory* (1986), surveys Weber's sociological interests. Lawrence Scaff, *Fleeing the Iron Cage* (1989), addresses the theme of culture and modernity, as do the essays in Sam Whimster (ed.), *Max Weber and the Culture of Anarchy* (1999). Peter Breiner, *Max Weber and Democratic Politics* (1996), and Sung-Ho Kim, *Max Weber's Politics of Civil Society* (2004), probe political topics. Stephen Kalberg, *Max Weber's Comparative-Historical Sociology* (1994), systematizes Weber's contribution to comparative studies; Wolfgang Schluchter, *Paradoxes of Modernity* (1996), does the same for the sociology of modernity; and Richard Swedberg, *Max Weber and the Idea of Economic Sociology* (1998), states the case for Weber as an economic sociologist. Nicholas Gane, *Max Weber and Postmodern Theory* (2002), explores Weber's relationship to postmodernism and ideas about re-enchantment. Essays in two recent collections discuss two of Weber's most important texts: Charles Camic et al. (eds), *Max Weber's Economy and Society* (2005), and William Swatos and Lutz Kaelber (eds) *The Protestant Ethic Turns 100* (2005).

CHAPTER 3

Emile Durkheim

WHITNEY POPE

Driving Impulses

Emile Durkheim sought to establish a new, scientific sociology capable of helping France overcome its moral crisis, a crisis reflected in the turmoil, violence and discontent pervading French society. Ever since the French Revolution, the nation had been wracked by conflict between monarchists and antimonarchists, Catholics and their secular opponents, and capital and labour. Intellectuals debated the nature of the crisis and possible cures. Conservatives longed for a return to the religion, authority, hierarchy and community of a more stable past; liberals believed in individual freedom and rights and the use of peaceful means to achieve a free, secular, democratic republic; and radicals felt that a revolutionary transformation was necessary to achieve social justice. The lower orders of society demanded greater equality even as the upper orders sought to retain or regain their power and privileges. Different kinds of governments succeeded one another: the First Republic, the First Empire, the Houses of Bourbon and then Orléans, the Second Republic, the Second Empire and finally the Third Republic (1871–1940). Defeated by Germany in the war of 1870 and torn by the Dreyfus scandal at the end of the century, which exacerbated social fissures to the extent of bringing the country to the brink of civil war, France was devastated by the First World War in which six of the eight million men mobilized for military service became war casualties.[1] At the individual level, rising suicide rates reflected a growing sense of malaise. Durkheim's goal was to develop a sociology that would help France to overcome its continuing moral crisis.

In doing so he incorporated many themes of his predecessors, often acknowledging his intellectual debt to them. Auguste Comte recognized the *sui generis* nature of society, which he defined as a living organism, and championed the development of a scientific sociology using the same methods employed in the natural sciences. Charles Montesquieu analysed the way in which customs vary from society to society. Alexis de Tocqueville advocated the proliferation of secondary groups as sources of community and the strengthening of local power that would promote freedom by counterbalancing the power of the national government. Even though Durkheim emphasized these and other French origins of sociology, he was also influenced by German thinkers. He was impressed by the empirical foundations of experimental German psychology and felt that those German scholars who emphasized the importance of the collective moral life – who understood that rules, customs and morality, and not reason and individual interests, are the bases of social life – were on the right track.[2] The English philosopher and sociologist, Herbert Spencer, whose thought was a powerful intellectual current of the times both in Europe and the USA, helped to pioneer the structural-functional approach to sociology that Durkheim further developed.

Even while building on other disciplines, Durkheim sought to differentiate sociology by eliminating their shortcomings. He thought that philosophy was too abstract and lost in endless metaphysical speculations, with philosophers too prone to counter one speculation with another and to deductively derive the conclusions implied in their general premises rather than beginning with the facts and then proceeding inductively. Although sociologists should emulate those psychologists who based their work on empirical evidence, psychology's focus on the individual failed to recognize that social phenomena must be explained in terms of other social phenomena. The economists also suffered from beginning and ending their explanations with individuals, thereby incorrectly seeking to derive the social from the individual. In employing a far too general conception of an abstract, universal, profit-seeking individual, the economists also failed to recognize that individuals vary, depending on the society and their place within it.[3] Durkheim's intellectual passion, then, was to develop a new science of sociology, which, shorn of the shortcomings of competing approaches to social life, would help France overcome its version of the general European crisis that he boldly defined as history's greatest moral crisis.[4]

Key Issues

Legitimating the Discipline: Sociology, Science and Emergence

Establishing sociology as a legitimate scientific discipline required, first, that sociology have its own distinctive subject matter and, second, that it be studied scientifically, a powerful combination that would differentiate sociology from the other academic disciplines with which it was most likely to be confused and establish it as a legitimate science worthy of taking its place alongside such established sciences as physics and chemistry.

Durkheim's definition of sociology's distinctive province is based on the doctrine of emergence, which distinguishes levels of reality. The interaction, organization, structural relations and interconnectedness of phenomena at one level of reality give rise to new, emergent phenomena at the next higher level: most importantly, the physical to the chemical, chemical to biological, biological to psychological, and psychological to sociological. Emergent phenomena must be explained in terms of causes at their own level of reality and cannot be explained in terms of, that is, reduced to, causes at some lower level. Just as water cannot be explained in terms of the characteristics of oxygen and hydrogen taken separately, social phenomena cannot be explained in terms of the characteristics of individuals. Rather, both water and society are emergent phenomena relative to the characteristics of the parts (individuals) whose interactions and relations constitute them.

He viewed social phenomena as natural phenomena, parts of nature. As such, they should be studied using the same scientific methods that have proven to be so powerful in the disciplines that study other aspects of nature such as physics, chemistry and biology. Science explains effects in terms of their respective causes in an effort to discover the laws and theories governing these cause-and-effect relationships. Scientists should not proceed deductively, applying preconceived conceptions and conclusions to the facts. Rather, they must begin with the natural world itself, with empirical reality, by carefully observing, defining, gathering, comparing and classifying facts and only then proceeding inductively to identify the cause-and-effect relationships these facts reveal.

The Relationship Between the Individual and Society: Images of Society

Durkheim made effective use of two images of society, one of which, using the language and imagery of the natural sciences of his day, views the individual and the social as opposed forces. This opposition provides a basic source of conflict, tension and energy in Durkheim's theory. The more powerful the given systems of causes and effects, the greater the importance of the science that studies them. Accordingly, in showing how social forces overcome individual forces and direct, coerce, contain, control and socialize the individual, Durkheim demonstrated not only sociology's independence from psychology but also the power of social, relative to individual, forces and therefore sociology's scientific legitimacy.

The 'individual' in this formulation is a theoretical construct quite different from the individuals actually encountered in society. It refers to the unsocialized component of the individual's personality, the individual divorced from social life and, sometimes, to the individual in pursuit of egoistic interests. In contrast, the individuals who populate any society are eminently social beings guided by moral rules. Indeed, Durkheim felt that we acquired all the best in ourselves, and all the things that distinguish us from other animals, from our social existence. Thought, language, world-views, rationality, morality, aspirations, in short, culture, derive from society. Thus, the unsocialized 'individual', the 'individual' divorced from society, the beast within us, is a poor approximation of the highly socialized beings who constitute societies.

Durkheim's second image of society is borrowed, not from the physical sciences, but from biology: like the human body, society is a structural-functional system of interacting, exchanging, mutually adjusting and supportive parts that make necessary contributions towards the survival of the whole. Structures (parts) are analysed in terms of their effects or functions, that is, the services they perform for the system. The family gives birth to, legitimates and socializes children; religion integrates society; the state enforces laws, adjudicates disputes and makes decisions binding on the entire society; and the economy provides the goods and services necessary for survival.

Three Studies of Social Solidarity

The Division of Labour in Society

In a number of studies of social solidarity developing these perspectives, Durkheim pursued his goal of establishing a useful scientific sociology. His first major book, *The Division of Labor in Society*[5] employs his evolutionary functionalism to examine the changing bases of social solidarity as primitive societies integrated by the similarities underlying mechanical solidarity evolve into advanced societies integrated by the differences underlying organic solidarity. Primitive societies are composed of a small number of similar individuals who constitute a homogeneous, undifferentiated mass. The strong emotional reactions to infractions of the strict, unforgiving moral code embodied in the collective conscience – that is, shared, strongly held beliefs, values and sentiments – and the repressive law at its core underlie the harsh justice and severe punishments that perpetuate the similarities underlying mechanical solidarity.

Over time, societies may grow in size, heightening pressure on increasingly scarce resources. Durkheim felt that this intensified struggle for existence produced the specialization and division of labour that permit the same resources to support more people. Society undergoes structural and functional differentiation, as different individual activities are grouped into different institutions specializing in their respective functions. Individuals and institutions relate to one another on the basis of the complementary differences that make them mutually dependent on one another. The collective conscience becomes weaker and more abstract, permitting the development of greater individuality and freedom. Mechanical solidarity based on likenesses and a powerful collective conscience is increasingly supplanted by a division of labour producing an organic solidarity based on the mutual interdependence of individuals and groups. Repressive law is largely replaced by restitutive law, which calls not for revenge but rather for the return of things to the conditions that would have prevailed had the legal offences not occurred. In sum, the course of social evolution is marked by a transition from small, simple, homogeneous tribal societies integrated by likenesses and a powerful, concrete collective conscience to large, modern, differentiated industrial societies integrated by the interdependence of individuals and structures created by the division of labour.

The contrasts between mechanical and organic solidarity coexist with some basic similarities, as shown in Figure 3.1.

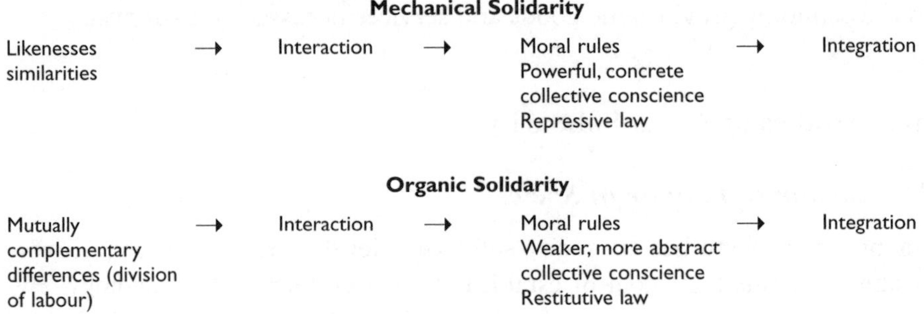

Figure 3.1

One difference between mechanical and organic solidarity lies in the impetus to interaction: similarities versus differences. Another is the change in morality embodied in the changing nature of the collective conscience and the transition from repressive to restitutive law. Beyond these differences, the causal chains are the same, and both mechanical and organic solidarity are proportional to rates of interaction and therefore the strength of the moral rules that integrate society.

Suicide

Durkheim's most famous work, *Suicide*,[6] pursues the study of social solidarity. The choice of suicide was brilliant because studying it permitted him to meet psychology on its own ground. People have their own individual reasons for killing themselves, making suicide a pre-eminently personal act. To prove that this was nonetheless a social phenomenon with social causes would be a powerful demonstration of the importance of social factors and another feather in sociology's hat. Above all, then, Durkheim sought to develop a sociological theory of suicide, which meant that suicide had to be explained in terms of social causes. Durkheim did not seek to explain individual instances of suicide. He did not appeal to individual differences in motivation, personality, depression or mental health to explain why one person committed suicide but another did not. Rather, he sought to explain variation in suicide rates, for example why rates were lower in one group than another, why a given group's rates changed over time, or why rates for people in one social condition were higher than those for another.

Durkheim explains suicide in terms of two independent variables, integration and regulation. Too much or too little of either causes suicide. Thus, both high levels of integration (altruism) and low levels of integration (egoism) cause suicide (see Figure 3.2), just as do high levels of regulation (fatalism) and low levels of regulation (anomie) (see Figure 3.3).

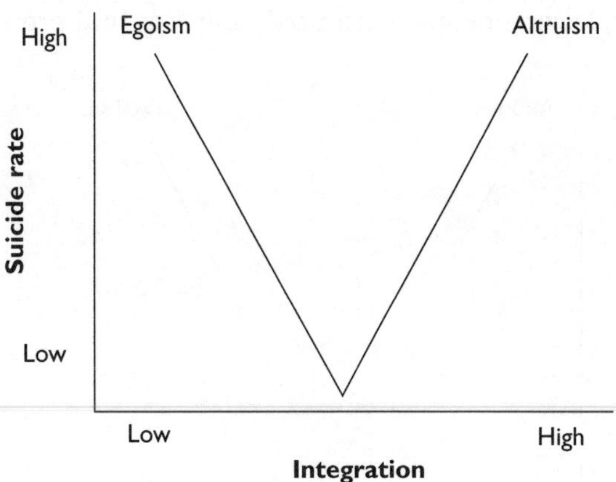

Figure 3.2

Egoism and anomie are the main causes of suicide in the modern world. Applying his theory of egoism to religious, familial and political 'society', Durkheim argued that each instance revealed the same relationship: the greater the egoism, the higher the suicide rate. Compared to more integrated groups, egoistic groups have lower rates of interaction, people think about themselves more than others and are less bound to one another, there is less community, and social control is weaker. *Anomie* is weak regulation or normlessness. Chronic anomie is produced by a gradual weakening of social control, in contrast to acute anomie, which is caused by sudden changes either in the situation of a given individual, for example divorce or widowhood, or in social institutions, for example economic booms and busts. Applying his theory of chronic anomie to marriage and to economic institutions, Durkheim argues that the gradual diminution of social control in each had produced higher suicide rates. Applying his theory of acute anomie to the widowed and divorced and to times of rapid economic change, Durkheim asserts that these sudden changes weaken social control, because, given the new circumstances, the old rules no longer apply and new ones have not had time to develop, thereby leading to higher suicide rates for both widowed and divorced persons, compared to the still married, and to higher suicide rates during both economic busts *and* booms, compared to times of economic stability. To explain how anomie leads to higher suicide rates, Durkheim pointed to uncontrolled appetites and aspirations. As social beings, humans acquire desires and goals. But these are inherently expandable and their attainment simply stimulates the desire for more. The only thing that can restrain inherently insatiable desires is social regulation. Hence, when social regulation is weak, desires outstrip attainment, leaving people frustrated, unhappy and prone to suicide.

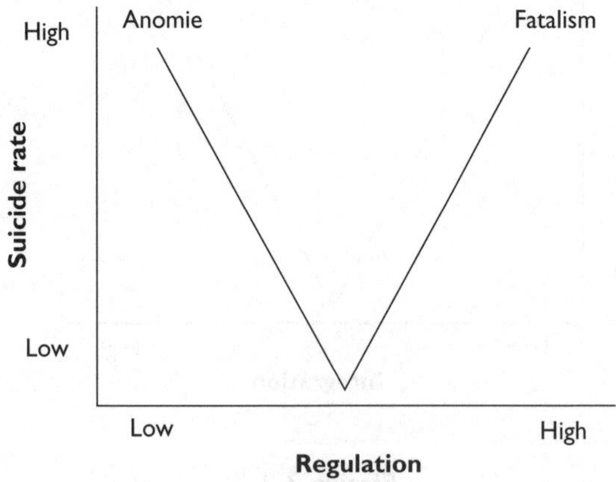

Figure 3.3

More than one hundred years after its publication in 1897, *Suicide* remains a landmark: it is widely regarded as sociology's exemplary piece of research, because it skilfully interrelates theory and data, using data to test and develop theory and using theory to explain the data, an approach that allowed Durkheim to reject competing biological and psychological theories while validating his sociological theory of variation in suicide rates. Numerous later studies have repeatedly confirmed most of Durkheim's basic findings; and, indeed, sociology has found it difficult to move substantially beyond the theory and findings so persuasively presented in *Suicide*.

The Elementary Forms of the Religious Life

Durkheim's final major work, *The Elementary Forms of the Religious Life*,[7] one of the greatest works of the twentieth century, deepens his account of interaction as the source of integration by extending his analysis of emotions and, more importantly, by demonstrating the importance of symbols. Durkheim assumed that religion's essential nature would be most visible in the simplest religion which would be found in the simplest societies. Accordingly, he made extensive use of studies of a tribe of primitive Australian aborigines, the Arunta. Durkheim observes that religion cannot be defined in terms of the supernatural, the idea of which is a late development in human thought, or of conceptions about gods and spirits, because such beliefs are secondary or absent in some great religions such as Buddhism and Jainism. Rather, he defined religion in terms of what he regarded as the most basic distinction known to humans, that between the sacred and the profane. Religious symbols are sacred objects; religious beliefs are about sacred objects; and religious practices are oriented towards sacred objects.

Identifying religion as the basic source of moral rules and social integration among the Arunta, Durkheim analysed it as a cyclical process. As people pursue their secular lives, religious sentiments weaken and would die without periodic renewal. Reminded by religious symbols of their beliefs and obligations, people gather to perform religious ceremonies. During these ceremonies, with high rates of interaction and common focus, participants publicly engage in ceremonial behaviour symbolizing their religious beliefs. This common affirmation strengthens these beliefs by bringing them to the forefront of consciousness. Collective rituals also generate intense emotion that, in becoming attached to the beliefs symbolized in the ceremonies and to their participants, strengthens them, while bonding the participants to each other. Religious ceremonies, then, integrate society, both by strengthening collective beliefs and morals and by mutually bonding their participants. The function of religion is to integrate society.

Religion is a system of mutually reinforcing beliefs, rites (behaviour) and symbols (which include both objects and the rites themselves). Beliefs cause the rites by reminding people of their religious duties. As visible physical enactments (symbols) of beliefs, the rites reinforce beliefs. Within a wide range of beliefs, content is secondary; rather, what is essential is that they cause believers to enact the rites, which strengthen the common beliefs and sentiments that integrate society. Symbolic objects are important because, while society cannot be continuously gathered in the performance of rites, such objects can serve as constant reminders of religious beliefs and obligations.

Durkheim's perspectives explain both the extrinsic sacredness of religious symbols and the intimate link between groups and symbols. The Arunta are organized into clans (kinship groups), each represented by its own sacred religious symbol or totem (emblem). But what is the source of the totem's sacredness, the feelings of respect and awe it inspires? Durkheim rejects the argument that the inherent qualities of what the totems ostensibly represent inspire these feelings, because the totems represent not awesome forces of nature, such as thunder and lightning, but the most ordinary, mundane objects of everyday existence, such as plants or, more typically, animals like kangaroos or crows. Furthermore, these things themselves are not sacred; only their symbolic representation, the totem, is. Clearly, the totem's sacredness is not intrinsic but superimposed. But by what? Participants feel the power and emotion generated by religious ceremonies. Unable to explain the origin of that power, they attribute it to some object in their presence, which thereby becomes sacred. Furthermore, Durkheim argued, if the totem stands for the clan, is that not because the clan and the totem are ultimately the same thing, because the totem represents the power of society that is especially manifest during collective religious ceremonies? Durkheim concluded that religion is simply society worshipping itself. Durkheim's first book, *The Division of Labor*, emphasizes the role of interaction in creating social solidarity; his last book, *The Elementary Forms*, emphasizes how a particularly intense form of interaction, religious or ritual interaction, creates an especially powerful form of integration.

Seeing Things Differently

We may use Durkheim's perspectives to analyse sports as a system of mutually reinforcing beliefs, rites, symbols and emotions bonding people into communities. Doing so will help us to understand the importance of sports, why people talk so much and feel so strongly about them, the depth of attachment to favourite teams, the emotional impact of attending the game, and why fans who do not know each other often find it easier to talk about sports than anything else. Although our example is American collegiate football, Durkheim's perspectives suggest the more general importance of what is ostensibly simply an entertaining pastime.

As the big event approaches, there is increasing talk about the game, with ever-more heartfelt expressions of support for the home team. Friday night's pep rally fires up fans and team alike. Saturday morning, university banners appear on homes and lawns throughout the area and on the parade of vehicles heading towards the stadium, as people publicly remind themselves and others of their loyalties. Tailboard parties reinforce these shared commitments. Fans experience a further rise in excitement as the expectant crowd fills the stadium, grouping themselves into two opposing factions, which, although unequal in size, are nonetheless equally enthusiastic and outfitted in team colours and hats, symbolizing their loyalties. The home crowd is pleased to see its team logo emblazoned on the field itself, with the university's name prominently written in both end zones. Each group roars as its team returns to the field shortly before kickoff, dressed in distinctive uniforms with helmets featuring the team's logo. After booing or chanting 'Who cares?' after the introduction of each member of the visiting team's starting line-up, the home crowd roars its support for the home team's line-up. Immediately before the game, everyone participates in another ritual, honouring the country's flag and singing the national anthem. As this temporary interruption reinforcing their common commitment to the larger national community ends, the crowd yells in happy anticipation of the game and collectively produces the characteristic crescendo accompanying kickoffs. During the game, fans energetically take advantage of numerous opportunities to collectively participate in the common activities demonstrating their shared beliefs, emotions and togetherness: cheering their team, standing to cheer after scores and for especially important plays, yelling at referees, waving team banners as they participate in cheers led by cheerleaders dressed in team colours, booing opponents, and cheering still more, as cheerleaders race around the stadium carrying a large university flag waving in the breeze. Half-time performances by the two university bands, dressed in school colours, include opportunities for supporters to sing school songs. After the game, the crowd files out, supporters of the losing team unhappy and subdued, supporters of the winning team talking boisterously and perhaps lingering to prolong the moment.

In short, sporting events exemplify the conditions of religious ritual: high rates of group interaction, focus on sacred symbols, and collective ritual behaviour symbolizing group membership and strengthening shared beliefs, values, aspirations and emotions. People experience the general excitement that builds in anticipation of the game, the stimulation and sheer joy of being surrounded by others sharing their enthusiasm, and the ebb and flow of emotions following the waxing and waning fortunes of their team. Regardless of whether they have just shared the thrill of victory or the agony of defeat, fans continue to assert their common hopes for their team and experience a reinforced emotional commitment to it and the sport itself.

Just as Durkheim analysed the waxing and waning strength of religion among the Arunta as a function of the cycle of religious life, so the intensity of commitment to spectator sports is a function of cycles. The weekly cycles begin with concern about the upcoming game, which peaks during the game itself. The seasonal cycle finds fans increasingly involved, as games cumulate, influencing chances for winning the league championship and for post-season play. Additionally, interest grows in the annual 'big game' with a traditional, especially reviled, rival, the winner of which keeps the game's symbol – an axe, an old oak bucket or some other trophy – for a year until the next big game. Finally, there is the yearly cycle with interest diminishing in the off season.

If sporting events are very much what they seem to be – entertainment for millions of followers – they are also much more. They create groups and subgroups. Fans support their team against all rivals but will then support another league team in its post-season play against a non-league team and support any national team in international competition. Although divided into partisans of different teams, fans also constitute a larger group of people who follow the sport and enjoy talking about it. Game crowds constitute emotional groups with common sentiments who bond together as they relish the spectacle and their many shared activities in the presence of sacred symbols. In sum, like other sporting events, football games unite believers into a community of fans.

Legacies and Unfinished Business

Durkheim had his greatest immediate influence in France, where he offered the first French university course in social science and was the driving force behind institutionalizing sociology within the academy. Through the force of his personality, the power of his ideas, the persuasiveness of his arguments, the range and originality of his writings, the charisma of his teaching, the influence of his students, and the extensiveness of his contacts both within and outside the academy, his influence extended well beyond sociology into numerous related disciplines, especially anthropology, history and linguistics. In England, his greatest influence was on British social anthropology, notably the works of A.R. Radcliffe-Brown, an influence suggested in the title of a collection of his essays, *Structure and Function in Primitive Society*.[8] Durkheim also had great influence on American sociology both before and especially after the Second World War. His initial influence was on functionalism and its leading theorists, **Talcott Parsons** and **Robert K. Merton**. Parsons' first major work, *The Structure of Social Action*,[9] sought to synthesize the works of Durkheim and **Weber** (and several others) into a theory of action. Later, Parsons greatly expanded this theory by synthesizing it with a structural-functional image of society, addressing a basic Durkheimian question: How do social institutions do all those things necessary for society to survive? Parsons' most famous student, Merton, built on Durkheim's theory of anomie to develop his own theory of anomie and deviance. Whereas Durkheim's general concepts of the collective conscience and solidarity *(Division)*, integration and regulation *(Suicide)* and collective representations *(The Elementary Forms)* fail to differentiate between norms and goals, making this distinction allowed Merton to identify four kinds of deviance – innovation, ritualism, retreatism and rebellion – in what remains one of sociology's most influential theories of conformity and deviance.[10]

Perpetuating Durkheim's focus on interaction, another American sociologist, **Erving Goffman** asks: What selves, motivations and strategies do people bring to interaction; how do these affect the interaction itself; and how are they reinforced or altered by interaction? Goffman's analysis of deference and demeanour builds on Durkheim's insight that in the modern world the individual is sacred.[11] On the one hand, as sacred beings we are entitled to the deference demanded by all sacred objects; on the other, since we must be so treated, we also experience the pressure to display demeanour worthy of such respect. Goffman extends his analysis by showing how what appear to be simply everyday encounters can be analysed as sacred ceremonies. When two people meet, each experiences the pressure to appropriately acknowledge the other. Both ask, 'How are you?' not because they necessarily care but to fulfil the requirements of the greeting ceremony. After marking the end of the ceremony with 'goodbyes', each finds it awkward to quickly re-encounter the other. Having gone through and appropriately ended the greeting ceremony, repeating it seems unnecessary but ignoring the other person also seems inappropriate. Similarly, after having thanked the host and said their 'goodbyes', people find it awkward to return to a party to retrieve something left behind. Defining these everyday encounters as sacred ceremonies helps Goffman to penetrate beneath the surface to expose their underlying dynamics.

Perhaps the most influential American sociological theorist of his generation, Randall Collins extends Durkheim's and Goffman's analyses of ritual interaction. Distinguishing a vertical and horizontal dimension of social interaction, Collins uses the first to build his theory of social stratification. Giving orders makes people proud and self-confident and encourages them to identify with the organization in the name of which they give orders and which supports them. In contrast, taking orders makes people less self-confident, more passive and more cynical about and alienated from the organizations in which they take orders. Order-givers share the upper-class culture structured by their place in the social hierarchy just as order-takers share their working-class culture. This vertical dimension of social interaction is crosscut by the horizontal dimension, ritual density, which itself includes two components: first, how much of the time is the individual in the presence of other people and, second, are these other people the same or different people? High rates of interaction with the same people create robust group solidarity with high levels of conformity and a strong sense of insiders versus outsiders (Durkheim's mechanical solidarity). In contrast, where people spend less time with others, giving them more privacy, and interact with a variety of people, there is less solidarity and conformity, greater individuality and people think more relativistically and abstractly. Collins, then, uses two dimensions of interaction, vertical and horizontal, to explain group solidarity, how interaction affects world-views, and how individuals with similar world-views perpetuate distinctive class structures. In this way, Collins develops the perspectives of a classic consensus, functionalist theorist (Durkheim), which he then introduces into the heart of his contemporary conflict theory.[12]

Even such a brief overview of Durkheim's legacy in American sociology suggests the range of his influence, which extends from functionalists like Parsons to conflict theorists like Collins, who emphatically reject functionalism. We can see the application and extension of his ideas to society as in Parsons; to conformity and deviance as in Merton's theory of anomie and deviance; to ritual interaction as in Goffman; and to beliefs, rituals, emotions, bonding, class cultures and stratification as in Collins. Durkheim's deep, multifaceted theory retains its power to inspire successive generations of sociologists as they theorize about everything from social structure to human agency to the relationship between the two.

FURTHER READING

Collins, R. and Makowsky, R. (1993) *The Discovery of Society* (5th edn) New York: McGraw-Hill, pp. 272–9.

Durkheim, E. (1973) 'The dualism of human nature and its social conditions', in *Emile Durkheim on Morality and Society*, Chicago: University of Chicago Press, pp. 149–63.

Goffman, E. (1967) *Interaction Ritual*, Garden City, NY: Anchor Books.

Lukes, S. (1972) *Emile Durkheim: His Life and Work*, New York: Harper & Row.

Merton, R. (1957) 'Social structure and anomie', in *Social Theory and Social Structure*, rev. and enl. edn, Glencoe, IL: The Free Press, pp. 131–60.

Pope, W. (1976) *Durkheim's 'Suicide'*, Chicago: University of Chicago Press.

ADDITIONAL FURTHER READING (SECOND EDITION) – ROB STONES

A very useful selection of Durkheim's own writings organized thematically has been brought together by Mustafa Emirbayer in his *Emile Durkheim: Sociologist of Modernity* (Oxford, Blackwell, 2003). The ten chapters of this book are divided into four parts dealing with: (i) methodology; (ii) the topology of modernity, itself divided into the themes of social structure, culture and symbolic classification, collective emotions, and individual and collective agency; (iii) the institutional order of modern societies; and (iv) the forms and fate of morality in modernity. Each of the ten chapters includes at least two 'Modern Selections', which reveal the enduring influence of Durkheim's work on more recent writing, including selections from Bourdieu, Foucault, Goffman, James C. Scott, bell hooks and Viviana Zelizer. Emirbayer provides a thoughtful and stimulating introductory chapter reflecting on the approach he has used to organize the volume, one of the virtues of which is a focus on 'the continuities in Durkheim's thought that nonetheless spanned the various phases of his development' (Emirbayer, 2003, p. 25).

In this the Emirbayer volume can be contrasted, as he points out, with the work of Jeffrey C. Alexander who has consistently highlighted what he believes to be a number of discontinuities and tensions in Durkheim's work. There are tensions, according to Alexander, between idealism and materialism, between positivism and interpretivism, and normatively between liberalism and conservatism (for example Alexander, *Theoretical Logic in the Social Sciences*, Vol. 2. *The Antinomies of Classical Thought: Marx and Durkheim* (Berkeley, CA, University of California Press, 1982). Alexander also argues for a distinctive cultural turn in Durkheim's work from the mid-1890s, based on a new-found appreciation of religion, ritual and the symbolic realm. The major reference point here is Alexander's collection *Durkheimian Sociology: Cultural Studies* (Cambridge, Cambridge University Press, 1988).

Alexander and Philip Smith's edited *Cambridge Companion to Durkheim* (Cambridge, Cambridge University Press, 2005) is an excellent collection of articles by distinguished scholars in the field who explore the historical context of Durkheim's ideas, the significance of his work for cultural theory, and the implications of his work for the relationship between sociology and moral philosophy. One of the authors included who deals with the latter domain is Mark Cladis ('Beyond Solidarity? Durkheim and twenty-first century democracy in a global age') who a decade earlier was the author of an imaginative and influential work, *A Communitarian Defense of Liberalism: Emile Durkheim and Contemporary Social Theory* (Stanford, CA, Stanford University Press, 1992), which brought Durkheim's moral sociology into an engagement with seminal contributions in contemporary moral and political philosophy such as Rawls, Dworkin, Walzer, MacIntyre and Rorty. This engagement is drawn on in my introductory chapter to this second edition of *Key Sociological Thinkers*. Another significant chapter in the *Cambridge Companion*, revealing the enduring power of Durkheim's work for the analysis of contemporary events, is Edward A. Tiryakian's 'Durkheim, Solidarity, and September 11'. Jonathan S. Fish's *Defending the Durkheimian Tradition: Religion, Emotion and Morality* (Aldershot, Ashgate, 2005), also brings out some remarkably contemporary resonances. It starts with a close rereading of the work of Durkheim and Parsons on religion, which is extended into perceptive insights on related strands of Durkheimian thought that are argued to be central to postmodern social theory. Finally, Willie Watts Miller's *A Durkheimian Quest: Solidarity and the Sacred* (Basingstoke: Palgrave Macmillan, forthcoming), part of the *Traditions in Social Theory* series, will be an invaluable single volume account of the conceptual contours and development of the major themes in Durkheimian sociology.

CHAPTER 4

Georg Simmel

PATRICK WATIER*

Driving Impulses

Georg Simmel has always occupied a special place in the pantheon of the founders of sociology. Lewis Coser's characterization of him as a stranger, an outsider within the academy, seems appropriate only if one looks just to his formal position within academia. It does not, however, take into account the position of Simmel in the wider intellectual domain, nor his role in the institutional consolidation of sociological research: he occupied an ambiguous position, at one and the same time marginal from the point of view of academic standing and central within the intellectual milieu. Many factors, including no doubt the apparent eclecticism of his work – ranging from historiography through psychology and sociology to aesthetics – contributed to this and to the reception of his work. Simmel's *Soziologie* (1992) ran to over 700 pages but he never for a second believed, as did Comte, that sociology should be the queen of the sciences, the pinnacle of the intellectual enterprise. Paradoxically, those things that assured Simmel a central place in the history of ideas in the early years of the twentieth century, his imaginative, bold and exploratory journeys back and forth across the borders of sociology, philosophy and aesthetics, together with his reflections on culture, are what contributed, at least in part, to his lack of recognition in the academic world.

Born of upper-middle-class parents in Berlin in 1858 in a house that stood at the intersection of two of the city's busiest thoroughfares, Friedrichstrasse and Leipzigerstrasse, Simmel converted from Judaism to Christianity and was educated at the Werder Gymnasium and then at the university from which he graduated in 1885. It was while in Berlin that he laid the foundations for his subsequent career. He was appointed *Privatdozent* in 1895, and *Ausserordentlicher* Professor in 1901, but he had to wait until 1914 to be appointed as a full professor at the University of Strasbourg, which at that time was part of

* Translation by Phil Brew and Rob Stones © Phil Brew and Rob Stones

Germany, Alsace having been annexed at the end of the 1870 Franco–Prussian War. Simmel spent the last years of his life here, regretting that Strasbourg did not possess an intellectual milieu comparable with that of Berlin. It is important to note that his academic career met with considerable resistance. Some of his colleagues believed that his teaching would have a destructive effect on his students, and he would certainly have encountered recurrent anti-Semitism. His life in Berlin, one of the world's great cities, was clearly instrumental in developing his interest in the new social relations that individuals of necessity evolve when the majority of their dealings are with people they do not know, strangers in the broadest sense, people who were not part of one's circle of acquaintances.

Key Issues

A Plurality of Approaches, a Plurality of Forms

From as early as his 1894 volume, *The Problem of Sociology*, Simmel insisted on the necessity of drawing boundaries around the domain of the new discipline. But it would be simplistic to see Simmel as just a sociologist, confining himself within these boundaries, and an examination of his work as a whole, and of the range of themes that he dealt with, reveals that he covered much more than the sociological domain. His *oeuvre* included erudite discussions on values, money, culture, the individual, the artistic personality and fashion. It raised questions about the transformation of large cities and the implications of this for the lives of individuals, and explored the new relations between the sexes arising out of modern forms of association. Simmel, through all his probings into social and cultural questions, attempted to capture the spirit of the times, to describe the transformation of the soul of modern society. He was sensitive to the question of women and to the feminist movement, and speculated on the possibility of a specifically feminist culture, and on the relations between the claims of women and the struggles of workers. Noting the arrival and institutionalization of a social world brought increasingly under the aegis of the calculable and the intellectual, he made a connection between this and the lifestyles of modern man, and wondered what new relations might emerge between the **objective and subjective cultures**. He began to sketch out a sociology of feelings and insisted on the recognition that psychosocial categories such as loyalty and gratitude were essential supports of sociation. In short, he attempted to describe the liaisons that individuals construct within forms of **sociation**. It is also worth emphasizing that from 1890 to 1918 Simmel attempted to envisage both the possibilities for liberation and emancipation and the limitations placed on the development of individuals, at least in part, by the ever-growing significance assumed by technology, and by the attendant interminable focus on a succession of technical means whose ends were no longer clear.

Sociation

Sociation is a translation of the German Vergesellschaftung *used by Simmel and the French term* socialization *used in the original version of this chapter by Patrick Watier. It is the translation used in the classical translations of Simmel's work by Kurt Wolff and Donald Levine,*[1] *respectively. It is meant to denote any type of coming together of people in social interaction, from, for example, a formal association in an enterprise, a club or a meeting, through the interactions of invited guests at a party, to a chance meeting of two or more friends or strangers in a busy street, on a crowded beach, or in a launderette. Sociation combines within it: the animating social interests, wishes and emotions brought to the interaction (that is, the* contents*) on the one hand; and the elementary or institutionalized shapes, configurations and densities created by the social and material positioning of the actors involved in relation to each other (that is, the* forms*), on the other hand. Birgitta Nedelmann*[2] *has noted how the dynamic aspects of the process of sociation also involve individuals in 'externalising' activity, productively creating social effects, and 'internalising' activity, taking up selective attitudes to the social pressures they experience* (erleben)*, pressures that emerge from previous interaction sequences.*

Objective and subjective cultures

As an example of the internalizing activity involved in sociation, Nedelmann cites Simmel's famous account of The Metropolis and Mental Life*, and specifically the* blasé *or aloof attitude taken up by inhabitants of the teeming modern city as they are exposed to a 'permanent overstimulation' of their senses. Individuals 'receive' and 'suffer' these societal experiences but the* blasé *attitude they take up is a result of them more or less consciously looking for ways to prevent their individuality being crushed by this 'overwhelming objective power of modern urban life'. The city is a massive, imposing, externalized product of past interactions, past processes of sociation within modernity's complex division of labour. This is just one example of the increasing density, weight, and sophistication of the external world, of what Simmel calls 'objective' or material culture. As objective culture increases, it threatens to swamp the subjective life of the individual, eliciting all kinds of more or less desperate coping strategies. The great irony is precisely that as objective culture increases it does become overwhelming, which in turn means that the subjectivity of any one individual can have access only to fragments of it. Objective culture comes to stand against the vital life force of individual creativity as something with its own rigidity and autonomous existence, but, more positively, it can also provide the cultural basis for subjective attempts at self-cultivation and growth where these can embrace the paradoxes between objective and subjective culture.*[3]

The modes of relations between individuals and society, the relations between the subjective culture and the objective culture, emerged more and more distinctly to Simmel as posing the central questions of social development. He attempted to capture this in his coining of the expression 'the tragedy of culture': life and creativity seek expression but can find it only within forms characterized by a distancing from these very wellsprings.

The rich and varied quality of Simmel's work can be better understood if one accepts his view that the social world and its reality can be envisaged from a number of different angles of attack. Distinct forms of investigation can be applied to it, as he points out in *The Philosophy of Money*, where he developed a number of fundamental epistemological categories. The tentative and fragmented character of some of his work, his always nuanced and hypothetical pronouncements, his relativist conceptions, and his interest in seemingly trivial phenomena are all easily explained once one grasps the spirit of this central idea of a plurality of forms of investigation. There was a close relationship between the forms of investigation and sociohistorical forms. It was a sociohistorical form, for example, that cleared a pathway for the emergence of what Simmel refers to as a 'pure form', money, whose impact on modern society and styles of living he was able to theorize in these terms. Also, just on the level of sociohistorical forms, different forms coexisted with each other, conditioning and influencing each other. Money was itself the condition of the transformation of forms of association, but, seen from another angle, it was the transformation of these social forms that allowed the development of a money economy.

The changes are analysed by a chain of elegant and plausible reasoning that can be seen as hypothetical, and it is understandable that many more conventional sociologists should have found themselves confused by his idiosyncratic artistry. The variety of topics studied, combined with the confusion created by the conception of a plurality of forms of investigation, mentioned above, was liable to puzzle, and indeed certainly did puzzle, many readers. Within this plurality of forms, Simmel came to place greater and greater importance on art and religion. The centre of his problematic shifted towards a cultural analysis of the modern world and the contradictions that cut across it.

Before going on to present Simmel's sociology in more detail, I would first like to dispose of a familiar accusation often levelled at it, which is that it is unbridled speculation, and a hopelessly vague and woolly conception of sociology. This accusation has come primarily from professional sociologists, most notably from **Durkheim**. It took a good deal of courage for Célestin Bouglé to end his review of *Soziologie for L'Année Sociologique* with the words: 'these observations and unsubstantiated jottings, they too have their place within the domain of sociology in the broadest sense'. But in saying this did not Bouglé stray into the terrain of Simmel's opponents, surrendering to them far too much ground in terms of the importance of proof, which the Simmelian perspective precisely did not concern itself with? Was not the domain of sociology in this broader sense a reference to that very specific kind of social philosophy that always had such a bad press within the Durkheimian school? Is it not accurate to say that this was in fact outside the scope of Simmel's ambition, given that he aimed at the creation of a 'pure sociology' that he clearly distinguished from the more speculative domain of socio-philosophical questions? In attempting to justify a place for Simmel within sociology, it seems to me that Bouglé has consigned him to quarters that failed to encompass the formal sociology that constituted the very core of what Simmel sought to establish.

The Sociological Point of View

From his first works Simmel tried to establish a new type of analysis that rested on a determinate point of view, a specific perspective on the facts. If it proved possible to isolate such a level of abstraction, then sociology would rest on an analysis of the forms of sociation seen from such a perspective (letter of 22.11.1896 from Simmel to Bouglé, in which he speaks of the acquisition of a sociological point of view); and on a particular abstraction of social reality that consists of separating the form of sociation from its content, and that views society from a certain distance, which enables one to recognize association and reciprocal action as the fundamental constituents of that within society which is pure society and nothing more.

These three terms – the 'sociological point of view', 'abstraction' and 'variable distance' – indicate the intellectual activity of configuring social reality, and thus of constituting a sociological object that does not pre-exist. Simmel believed that, in order to constitute itself as a science of social reality, sociology must reject all notions of realism. To develop this point he drew upon respected arguments concerning the constitution of historical knowledge. Indeed, *The Problems of the Philosophy of History* directly addresses the question of realism in its first chapter, which deals with the 'intrinsic conditions of historical research'. Simmel argues here that 'all knowledge is the translation of the immediate givens of experience into a new language, a language with its own inherent forms, categories and rules'.[4] The problem of sociology is precisely that of constituting a language, of creating categories through which reality – both facts and social experience – acquires the status of knowledge. In this sense, knowledge is always a second-order construction, it is not a mirror image nor a carbon copy of the real, which realism had always claimed it to be. Sociology must, then, forge those *a priori* instruments that all areas of knowledge require to enable them to organize their subject matter, since it is clear that 'in the last resort, the content of any science doesn't rest on simple objective facts, but always involves an interpretation *(Deutung)* and a shaping *(Formung)* of them according to categories and rules that are the *a priori* of the science concerned'.[5]

Form and Content

Taking as his starting point previous sociological scholarship, the results of epistemological studies carried out in relation to historical knowledge, and the relativist theory of knowledge developed in *The Philosophy of Money*, Simmel returns in his great *Soziologie* to the questioning of sociology itself and the determination of its field of study. The procedures of abstraction that Simmel's 'pure sociology' applies to those elements within society that are purely societal and nothing more involve the separation of the form from the content of sociation. Sociation is the configuration from within which a number of individuals engage in reciprocal action, and the reciprocal action can only have its source in the expression of certain instincts or the desire to achieve certain goals. The social level that Simmel endeavoured to make intelligible is necessarily the result of interactions between individuals, but it develops specific properties and consequences of its own into which no research had been carried out. Such a project would require clear distinctions to be made between, on the one hand, the instincts, interests, tendencies and targets or goals manifested by individuals, which are the *content* or the material of sociation, and, on the other hand, the *forms* in which individuals, in order to realize this content, come to socialize. Time and again Simmel emphasized the heuristic character of the form–content distinction. It is a distinction that belongs to the group of categories designed to help the human intellect to organize what is given in immediate experience:

> Just as the forms of sociology are formulated on the basis of an unlimited number of contents, in the same way the forms themselves develop out of the most general and the most profoundly rooted fundamental psychic functions. Everywhere, form and content are *relative* concepts, categories of knowledge developed in order to cope with phenomena and to organise them intellectually. Thus a feature seen as it were from above as form in one relationship, will in another, seen from below, need to be described as content.[6]

Contents, motives and dispositions, such as hunger, love, work, religion or the impulse to sociability, are not in themselves social. They exist in society because they are to be found in individuals, and in this sense they provide the conditions for all sociation, but they become really social only through the forms of reciprocal action through which, and within which, individuals associate with and influence one another. The notion of 'liaison' is fundamental, because sociology studies the forms that come into being when individuals reciprocally influence each other through interaction and form social unities. Not hesitating to play with the elasticity of the word 'liaison', especially pronounced in popular German, and the range of the activities that it can include, Simmel writes:

> The more decisive a purely sociological concept is (which is not to say a substantive or particularistic concept, but rather one referring to a simple form of relationship), the more readily it will define linguistically its own content and realisations. ... Such is the character of that most purely sociological word: 'liaison'. In its general use in popular language where it has the meaning of an erotic relationship, the word's ability to be stretched this way and that has been exploited to the maximum. Lovers 'have' a liaison, they 'are', as a sociological unit, a liaison, and finally, he is 'her liaison' and she his.[7]

Simmel takes as his starting point the existence of dispositions, which have a flexibility that enables them to enter into different forms of sociation. To take some examples: devotion is one of those dispositions that is seen within family relationships, in the relationships that individuals may have with a group, or workers with their party, or again, that individuals have with their native country. These dispositions can be present in numerous relations but in many ways only reach complete fulfilment when they constitute the principal basis of the sociation currently active. The same goes for sociability. It is present in numerous relations but will only acquire its full accomplishment within the interplay of pure sociality, in the way that devotion will only acquire its ultimate fulfilment when it takes on religious expression. The sociology of meals shows how such sociation takes for granted that the content, the hunger that needs to be satisfied, becomes to some degree secondary, passing into the background, compared with the links that are formed reciprocally between fellow guests or within the family. Hunger becomes form within the configuration of the meal, the particular orientation of the participants towards one another. The individuals are thus linked together by this form, which then, as the currently dominant mode of reciprocal orientation, serves to guide the mutual activities that take place within it.

Sociation in the broadest sense, whatever the content involved, corresponds to a form 'that manifests itself in a thousand different ways, and within which individuals, because of their interests – sensual or ideal, transient or enduring, conscious or unconscious, causally or teleologically driven – become a unit within which these interests are realised'.[8] The relevance of this analytical distinction between content and form (which cannot of course be separated in social reality) is demonstrated to the extent that it is possible to show that different contents can be socialized by and within the same form, and, conversely, that the same content can give rise to very different forms of sociation. Love or economic advantage, for example, can be used to illustrate that this is possible. These contents can indeed give rise to diverse forms of reciprocal action, such as in a range of different commercial or family relationships. But as exchanges they are also liable to be exemplars of some general overarching form. On the other hand, formal relationships such as imitation or competition can be instrumental in the direction of individuals towards a range of goals and interests within associations as varied as those that characterize political parties or religious communities. Similarly, the religious impulse as content can give rise to non-religious forms of sociation, just as, in its purest form, it can express itself as religion.

Reciprocal action is the realization of a unit, a society, or of a sociation. Simmel suggested that it would therefore be more appropriate to speak of the process of sociation, the 'pure forms of sociation', rather than of society. It is to be noted from the outset that sociation can have varying degrees of intensity according to the type and depth of intimacy of reciprocal action, and also that it is not possible to think of even the most minimal of relations between humans as being of no importance.

Micro-relations

One of Simmel's central contributions is undoubtedly the following: that the sociological point of view reveals sociation as process, a web of relationships between individuals that forms, dissolves and reforms anew, allowing us to glimpse the 'microscopic molecular processes' that connect us to each other. Célestin Bouglé, in his critical review of *Soziologie*, saw very clearly that sociology for Simmel

> must encompass more than simply ... collective practices and habits. It finds its subject matter whenever any relation whatsoever is formed between people, anywhere where a reciprocal action takes place between one person and another. In sum, the analysis of interactions is, for Monsieur Simmel, as for Tarde (one recognises just how many similarities there are between the styles and sensibilities of these two thinkers), the very essence of sociology. It must of course concern itself with the great institutions – churches, political powers, commercial organisations – that dominate individuals and which, once established, seem to take on a life of their own. But even more fruitful is the study of what Monsieur Simmel calls association 'in its incipient state', that is, relations between individuals, the effect they exert upon each other.[9]

The discipline of sociology had until then, in his view, concentrated its attention exclusively on those massive sociations that crystallized in the largest social forms, whereas the very smallest liaisons between individuals run right through all these large social forms.

Seemingly insignificant micro-forms are the focus of Simmel's attention because they give society its flexibility, its viscosity. Through all these processes – a meal taken together, a walk, an exchange of glances, a pavement conversation – society becomes increasingly 'society', and social beings are thereby fortified. A Durkheimian would recognize that the number and the intensity of the relationships contribute to the moral density of society. What Simmel clearly added was the possibility of personal development and fulfilment for the individual.

He also added a micro-exploration of process. Forms of sociation are society in process, and it follows that one can study the varying degrees to which people create social units, how through the multiple associations that form it socially the 'same group becomes more "society" than it was before'.[10] So, for example, a group will strengthen its own societal character through the reciprocal socializing action of struggle with another group, and this same consolidation can also be achieved by forms of secret sociation, just as it can through fashion or by taking a meal together. If a secret society is a form of sociation, it is because 'the secret determines the reciprocal relations of those that share it'.[11] Sharing a secret leads to specific relations with neighbouring groups, of self-protection for example, as well as affecting the relations within the group. These examples illustrate the gradual character that Simmel attributes to sociation, that is, different sociations bind the members of groups to varying degrees, create differing degrees of cohesion between individuals. Furthermore, the degree to which the members of the group are conscious of the forms themselves will also vary. The content of a sociation activity can become so deeply embedded within the consciousness of the members of a group that the individuals actually forget the formal fact and the nature of the sociation. According to Simmel, the content of the activity in which members of a group engage often makes them forget the form of sociation within which it takes place. This, he claims, is a very general phenomenon. On the other hand, any group formed within a wider circle, particularly where there is a clearly defined boundary, as with the sharing of a secret or a creed, strengthens the boundary and accentuates the awareness of the members as to the fact of their forming a society. Most sociations, nevertheless, come about through processes based on *implicit* knowledge, and the attention devoted to the goals of the activity masks the sociation within which it takes place. Forms of sociation can therefore be differentiated according to the degree of consciousness of the formal ties that unite participants. The higher the degree, the more the accent placed on the reciprocal ties will be explicitly valued compared with the pure content, that is, the material activity of the association.

Forms of sociation are based on contents that are not in themselves social, but part of the psychophysical constitution of human beings. They presuppose the possibility of psychic relations that enable people to collaborate or to act against one another, and in so doing form associations, unions and societies. One of the most fruitful aspects of Simmel's sociology is his detailing of the presuppositions on which associations are founded and his emphasis on the role played within forms of sociation by psychosocial drives such as trust, loyalty, gratitude, devotion and belief in human nature. Microsociology allows us to get very close to everyday life, to perceive both the dense web of reciprocal obligations, and the importance of certain forces and dispositions that make society possible. Without speaking about the power of rules or norms, one can see that individuals interact with one another according to certain dispositions, imbuing their relations with goodwill, trust and confidence. The absence of these social sentiments would make social relations impossible.

Such dispositions are not, however, immutable and it must be noted that the increasing objectivization of culture is modifying the ways in which trust is given and this, in turn, modifies what is known and not known by individuals about one another. 'The modern shop keeper who enters into a business relation with another shop keeper; the researcher who embarks on a research project in collaboration with another researcher; the leader of a political party who makes a pact with another party leader over electoral issues or legislative proposals – all know, with the exception of a few minor gaps, just what they need to know about their partner in order to set up the relationship they wish to establish.'[12] This shift in the distribution of knowledge and non-knowledge results from the qualitative and quantitative evolution of relations and often we know only very little of the individuals with whom we are in relation.

The greater the number of liaisons, the more a psychologically differentiated individual can realize the multiple potentialities inscribed within a multifaceted personality. In his earliest writings on social differentiation, Simmel examined the ways in which modern society differs from traditional societies, and he emphasized the proliferation of possible affiliations and new interconnections between social circles. The interlacing of social circles is a model of social differentiation that leads us to a description of society characterized by more flexible memberships, no longer structured in a pattern of concentric circles, but crisscrossing, intersecting and overlapping with each other, out of which each individual is assumed to be able to construct his or her individuality. Such a model widens the margins of individual liberty, but also produces new moral complications, for, being less subject to the close surveillance of any single group, the individual is confronted with potential contradictions resulting from these multiple memberships. This type of model that draws our attention so clearly to both gains and losses is very common in Simmel's work. He is thus neither purely and simply an apologist for, nor a one-sided critic of, modernity.

The Simmelian perspective differs from classic approaches in that he focuses his attention on forms of sociation in their incipient state. The study of society is therefore that of all forms of sociation and cannot be confined to the analysis of large institutions that orchestrate social relations. This is because the large institutions themselves are shot through with mutual ties and reciprocal actions, with the seemingly insignificant forms of liaison through which individuals socialized forming societies whose existence is more or less ephemeral, more or less durable.

Such an objective necessitates the prior analysis of the potentiality conditions of society – society's conditions of possibility – and, in a digression in Chapter 1 of *Soziologie*, Simmel makes a notable contribution to the analysis of this problem of the constitution of society.

The *A Priori* of Sociation

A priori

An a priori *is a basic belief about something that is derived from philosophical or abstract reflection rather than from direct experience or from some kind of direct contact with the empirical world. Few people now believe that we can have any direct unmediated experience of the empirical world because, following the philosopher Immanuel Kant, it is generally believed that all experience is at least partly structured by pre-existing beliefs or presuppositions we have about the world (we know that the ball is a long way off and that it will take some time to retrieve it because, not least, we implicitly work with conceptions of time and space). Time and space are two* a priori *categories by which we make sense of sense experience, that are fundamental preconditions for the very possibility of sense experience as we know it. Another basic category is that of substance. It would be impossible for us to experience the ball as something of substance unless we first understood the general concept or category of substance. Analogously, Simmel wants to investigate the preconditions for sociation. If sociation happens, then what preconditions must be in place in order to allow it to happen? These preconditions are the* a priori *of sociation. Thus there are* a priori *or preconditions for being able to gain knowledge about society, and also for being able to practically reproduce or constitute society.*

The digression that forms part of Chapter 1 of *Soziologie* summarizes those ***a priori*** that underpin the study of the forms of sociation. It is based on the distinction formulated by the sociological point of view between the form and content of sociation, but in order to properly execute this stage, it is necessary first to satisfy a requirement that is at once both ontological and epistemological: that is, to analyse those specific relations between the conditions for the constitution of society and the conditions for gaining knowledge of it. The purpose of the 'Digression on the question: How is society possible?' is precisely to show that the answer to such a question requires a type of investigation different from that required to answer the question 'How is nature possible?' Society's existence presupposes that those elements that constitute it have knowledge of it and recognize it, but not in the sense of knowing it from the outside, as an observer of the physical world might gain knowledge of its phenomena, but from the inside, as members of society itself. In fact, Simmel specified that he preferred to speak of ability or practical skill *(savoir)* rather than knowledge in a passive sense *(connaissance)*, for the constitution of society presupposes at the very least a practical ability (a knowing 'how to') that individual subjects use to establish relations with one another. The analysis of the conditions for the constitution of any society must examine both the modes of knowledge and the modes of actualization of society. The *a priori* involved relate not only to knowledge of society but also touch, fundamentally, on the very existence of society itself. More precisely, they concern the modes of formation of social liaisons. The existence of societies presupposes the activation by its potential members of their abilities and skills, feelings and perceptions of reciprocal relations, in other words, of their sociation skills.

In addition, one must bear in mind the very special position that these constituent elements occupy in sociation, that is, that liaisons at one and the same time include and embrace individuals and yet never include them totally, nor perfectly. For social relations to exist supposes a minimum hermeneutic threshold in a general sense, at least the tacit practical ability of individuals to interpret the actions and reactions of other individuals. The status of this type of interpretation and the bases from which it derives must be the focus of investigation. Society as the sum of reciprocal actions is possible only through the incessant socializing activities of individuals. In interpreting Simmel's work, and in steering it a little towards ethnomethodological conceptions (cf. **Garfinkel**, Chapter 12), one can say that society is only made possible by the reciprocal activities of individuals *(Verbindungen)*, who have to understand one another, activate a particular knowledge of those activities, and make use of the practical abilities through which they know, recognize and produce society. All social liaison, as reciprocal action, on the one hand consists of a process of people influencing each other, of orienting themselves towards one another – a theme that social psychology was to develop, and Simmel can in this sense be considered as one of the founders of that discipline – and on the other, comes into being through a self-awareness of the social unit being formed, a consciousness of sociation as process.

Indeed, the unit is produced through the 'multiplicity of specific relations, and through the feeling and the knowledge that one determines others and is determined by them'.[13]

The content of *Soziologie*, Simmel tells us, still within the 'Digression on the question: How is society possible?' is an investigation into the modes and processes of sociation. The forms of sociation are at once the setting and the outcome of the socializing activities of individuals. Sociation itself actualizes social energy and this is why Simmel defines society as a becoming and not simply as a state. Society is in this sense always in the process of being created and re-created. People are social beings by definition and therefore engage in reciprocal activities from the start with certain inbuilt dispositions, but it is those particular reciprocal orientations peculiar to sociation that create society. What we normally refer to as 'society' is therefore the result, precarious and in a perpetually unstable equilibrium, of all forms of sociation. Sociology within Simmel's perspective concentrates on the processes at work in the creation of societies, on the totality of social liaisons that we, abstractly, constitute into society. He seeks to prove their importance by the simple means of a thought experiment: if you were to try to imagine them not existing, what is revealed is the disappearance of society in any normal sense of the word.

One can say, using the admittedly different vocabulary and perspective of Alfred Schutz (cf. Garfinkel, Chapter 12), that Simmel sets himself the objective of describing the implicit presuppositions of people's comprehension of one another on the basis of 'the natural attitude', for without the latter, reciprocal actions could not occur. He explains that we are led to construct the other as a personality, as a psychological unity, and that in doing so we draw on *a priori* representations that consist in attributing an assembly of fragmentary perceptions to one person. Such a procedure we call 'comprehension'. Comprehension and attribution are connected since the personality that we understand and to which we attribute such and such an intention is an ideal type construction, or, to use Schutz's term, a typification. The understanding of the other through typification is an *a priori* of sociation, whose value lies in its usefulness for gaining knowledge and undertaking action, above all of course, in our routine day-to-day lives. All forms of sociation presume mutual anticipations and norms of conduct. The processes of reciprocal influence or action thus pass necessarily through the psychology of persons. Sociation is a psychic unit that is produced by separate spatial elements forming a new unit but, more importantly, having an awareness of forming this new unit. It is this which differentiates social units from natural phenomena. For the latter, spatial coexistence is not accompanied by an awareness of coexistence as a unit, or of at least the possibility of such. Once this difference is accepted, it leads to the conclusion that for its interpretation and comprehension, society requires a psychological knowledge that is nevertheless not a psychology. Unless the psychic dimension of sociation is taken into account, society 'would be a mere puppet theatre, no more meaningful than the merging of one cloud into another or the entanglement of the branches of a tree. So psychological motivations – feelings, thoughts, needs – must be recognized, not simply as the underpinning of any sociation, but as its very essence and as the only form of knowledge which really interests us.'[14] All sociation presumes psychological knowledge and interactive skills, an exchange between I and you, 'an exchange alternating between the me and the you', and just as reciprocal action characterizes sociation, the latter can only be created on the basis of the construction of psychological skills. Social life would not be as we know it if individuals did not orientate themselves on the basis of expectations, suppositions, anticipations and typifications that are the mental representations of their mutual behaviour.

All sociation brings into play mechanisms for the interpretation of others and of situations, mechanisms that are tied to the functioning of the mind and that produce, beyond the individual units, a social form that serves as a kind of mould for the orientation of individuals. Pursuing a comparison with the themes of **Erving Goffman**, sociation consists in the agreement on a common line of conduct. This agreement may be achieved with varying degrees of familiarity, varying degrees of novelty, but it always demands attention and mutuality. Sociation between strangers clearly requires more adjustments, a greater sensitivity and more versatile practical skills than that between an old married couple where a long shared past provides a framework for current typifications. The establishment of a relation between strangers involves each tentatively advancing towards the other seeking the reassurance of a shared framework; whereas between acquaintances and, *a fortiori*, between intimates, this is taken for granted. Typification proceeds according to the requirements of the activity or the objective being pursued, drawing on a knowledge of background assumptions or, again, that which **Max Weber** referred to as a 'nomological' knowledge of habitual ways of behaving within typical situations.

It follows from these remarks that comprehension plays a central role in social life. In this respect, Simmel is interested in comprehension in the social sciences not simply as a method, but takes as his theme what Schutz later developed in his phenomenological sociology. When we speak here of comprehension, we are led towards the ordinary, everyday level of understanding and knowledge we all have of one another, based on typifications. Comprehension as the practical actualization of a synthesis of typifications, prior to being a method of the social sciences, is a mode of thinking by which individuals become aware of their relations and, *a fortiori*, of social reality.

Simmel did not produce a systematic sociology but the sociological perspective that he brought to bear on reciprocal relations between individuals has proved extremely fruitful, and for some time now he has once more been recognized as a thinker whose contribution is still insightful and fresh enough to inspire research into today's contemporary world.

Some Recent Developments: Trust, Confidence and Religion

It is possible to identify two sets of Simmelian themes that in recent years have taken on powerful resonances both in the contemporary sociohistorical landscape and in the perspectives of theorists who have attempted to come to terms with it. These two themes, of trust and confidence, on the one hand, and of religion, on the other, illustrate the heuristic relevance of the abstraction between *contents* – trust, confidence and piety – and *forms* of sociation, as these contents can be seen to give rise to, but also to be powerfully shaped by, significantly discrepant forms of sociation.

In a world of increasing complexity, where contingency and uncertainty are increasingly central to experience, social forms of trust and confidence have taken on a special significance. These forms contain within them their own plurality, for to speak about trust is to speak about a host of associated social experiences and topics: belief, risk, uncertainty, doubt, insurance, credibility, credit, anticipation, familiarity, inductive knowledge and Bayesian principles of common sense. All these play important roles in the establishment and maintenance of social relations, and trust and confidence are central to them all. Simmel's remarks on these topics have, most prominently, been taken up, developed and extended by **Anthony Giddens**[15] and Niklas Luhmann[16] in their attempt to theorize the unstable relations of what the former has labelled 'reflexive modernization'.

The Simmelian conception of religion makes if possible to capture both its grounds and its persistence beyond any illumination of a transcendental urge to believe. Simmel's perspective on religion allows a comprehension of all the phenomena that involve emotional relations of piety between individuals. These relations of piety take on plural forms of sociation. Simmel sees pure religious devotion as simply the most perfect expression, the *entéléchie*, of these kinds of contents, which in varying levels of intensity manage to irrigate a whole variety of other relations. The concept of piety makes it possible to capture not only the diffuse forms of formal religiosity that inhabit today's global cultures, but also the dashes of religion that survive disaffection with the transmitted religions. Beyond those contents that are crystallized in formal doctrines and a range of conventional forms of religious sociation, the intrinsic breadth of Simmel's conception of religious forms also allows one to see the myriad of contents whose motivations and inspirations are a more immanent religiosity that is both a fact and a function of the human spirit.[17]

FURTHER READING

Kurt Wolff's collection, *The Sociology of Georg Simmel* (Glencoe: Free Press, 1950), and Donald Levine's *Georg Simmel: On Individuality and Social Forms* (Chicago: Chicago University Press, 1971) remain the classic English-language sources for Simmel's writing. Mike Featherstone and David Frisby's more recent collection *Simmel on Culture* (London, Sage, 1997) brings together for the first time a wide range of essays on culture, aesthetics and style, some previously untranslated, while also containing some familiar classics such as 'Metropolis and mental life' that are also included in Wolff. Also see G. Simmel, *Conflict and the Web of Group Affiliations* (Glencoe, IL: The Free Press, 1955). For insightful commentaries and investigations into specific topics see: Gary Oakes, *Essays on Interpretation in the Social Sciences* (Totawa, NJ: Rowman & Littlefield, 1980); Jules Wanderer, 'Adventure in a theme park', in *Georg Simmel between Modernity and Postmodernity*, in F. Doerr-Backes and L. Nieder (Wurzburg: Konigshausen & Neumann, 1995, pp. 171–88); Simona Draghici, *The Pauper/Georg Simmel* (Washington DC: Plutarch, 2001); Patrick Watier and Ivanava Markhova, 'Trust and psycho-sociological feelings: socialization and totalitarianism', in I. Markhova (ed.) *Trust and Democratic Transitions in Post-Communist Europe, Proceedings of the British Academy*, vol. 119, pp. 25–46 (Oxford, Oxford University Press, 2004); and Patrick Watier, 'Les resources de l'interprétation sociologique. Dans les traces de G. Simmel et M. Weber', *L'Année Sociologique*, vol. 57, no. 1, 2007. Specifically on the Simmelian conception of religion used in the final section, see Patrick Watier, 'Les sentiments psychosociaux dans la sociologie de G. Simmel', in L. Deroche and P. Watier (eds) *La sociologie de G. Simmel* (1908). *Essais de modélisation sociale* (Paris, PUF, 2002). Recent invaluable attempts to give a brief systematic overview of Simmel's writing that complement the present chapter are Birgitta Nedelmann, 'The continuing relevance of Georg Simmel: staking out anew the field of sociology', in George Ritzer and Barry Smart (eds) *Handbook of Social Theory* (Thousand Oaks, CA: Sage, 2001, pp. 66–78), and Lawrence Scaff, 'Georg Simmel', in George Ritzer (ed.) *The Blackwell Companion to Major Classical Social Theorists* (Oxford: Blackwell, 2003, pp. 239–66).

CHAPTER 5

Herbert Blumer

KEN PLUMMER

Driving Impulses

The Trouble with Sociology

'Herbert Blumer's work was lodged in the tradition of American Pragmatism, of James, Dewey and Mead. Indeed, it could be said that Herbert Blumer was the last sonorous voice of that tradition in this century.'[1] Troy Duster's comment hints at the quietness of the revolution in sociological thought ushered in by Blumer and those whose work he developed and continued. As Howard Becker has put it: 'Though we seldom recognise his enormous impact, few sociologists are untouched by his thought.'[2] When discussing Blumer we are thus confronted by a paradox. On the one hand, he was 'an inspiring teacher, engaging writer, talented administrator, charismatic personality, and forceful intellectual'.[3] On the other hand, he is probably the sociologist who is least known by the students who read this book. Yet he is the carrier of a very distinctive sociological tradition – symbolic interactionism; with a very specific set of practical concerns – to do sociology 'naturalistically'. This brief article aims to introduce some of his ideas.

Throughout much of the twentieth century, Blumer was driven by an irritation with many of the sociological orthodoxies of his day, and sought to develop his own humanistic, pragmatist approach – now popularly known as 'symbolic interactionism' (a term he coined in 1937). Blumer was a perpetual and ardent critic of all the major traditions of sociological reasoning from the start of his career to the end of it. At one extreme, he stood opposed to the trivial and quite misleading reduction of social life to surveys and measurements as if they actually told us anything; and at the other extreme, he questioned the superimposition of abstract and reified concepts like culture, structure, attitude or industrialization on to social life, as if they somehow explained something. For him, the appropriate stance for sociology was to look closely and carefully at human group life and collective behaviour through 'action': 'action must be the starting point (and the point of return) for any scheme that purports to treat and analyse human society empirically'.[4]

In one discussion he put it like this:

> More and more over the years, as I have had occasion to reflect on what is going on in sociology, the more convinced I have become of the inescapable need ... of recognising that a human group consists of people who are living. Oddly enough this is not the picture which underlies the dominant imagery in the field of sociology today. They think of a society or group as something that is there in the form of a regularised structure in which people are placed. And they act on the basis of the influence of the structure on them. This is a complete inversion of what is involved ... [instead] there are people who engaged in living, in having to cope with situations that arise in their experience, organising their behaviour and their conduct in the light of those situations they encounter, coming to develop all kinds of arrangements which are ongoing affairs ... The metaphor I like to use is just 'lifting the veil' to see what is happening.[5]

Here we have the kernel of his thought, still relevant today. Most sociology cuts out the living lives in process and turns instead to grander schemes of analysis: from structures and variables to discourse and advanced methodologies. Blumer wants to bring back the huffing and puffing human being in action.

This is not a fashionable view today, and we must be careful not to misread Blumer. As Becker says, 'he was never anti-theoretical, anti-empirical, or anti-measurement'.[6] And he always saw the importance of social organization, power and history. But his concern was that theories and observations had to be about real things in the world: 'Empirical research [should] pay attention to the nature of what was being studied; and ... we [should] measure real quantities.'[7] This was his abiding concern: he urged sociologists to talk about 'real' things with 'real' evidence. If you wanted to understand drug user activity, for example, you had to explore and inspect these worlds closely and carefully from every angle you could, building your understanding out of this. It was hopelessly misconceived to cut short the work of intimately familiarizing yourself with 'drugs' by constructing abstract theoretical schemas about it; likewise it was a gross error to think you could simply 'measure' drug life from abstracted interviews and questionnaires conducted aloofly. One of his students, Howard S. Becker, produced the classic study of marijuana use, in his *Outsiders* (1963), precisely because of this first-hand involvement in a social world, followed by his subsequent close attention to conceptual building (a litany of powerful theories and concepts are developed in his book:

labelling, 'motives', 'culture', 'moral crusaders', 'becoming and careers').[8] And the same was true of race relations, or trade union activity, or the industrialization process in Latin America – all areas he worked on. His passion was to improve sociology and to do this he adopted the perpetual mantle of critic. He was against thoughtless measurement and obscure abstract theory equally. And insofar as he was, he was opposed to the two major strands of doing sociology. It remains the case today that sociology can largely be divided into those who theorize with little empirical content and those who produce elaborate data-sets with very little theory. What he complained about for 60 years has still not been rectified.

On Background and Style

To understand Herbert Blumer's work, he should be seen as the mantle bearer of two important, connected, North American intellectual traditions, which he found at the University of Chicago, the foremost sociological centre for much of the earlier part of the twentieth century.[9]

One source of Blumer's passion clearly lay in his admiration for his great teacher, the Chicago philosophical pragmatist George Herbert Mead. Blumer attended his lectures, assisted in their posthumous publication, and became the major sociological proselytizer on Mead's behalf for many years after Mead's death (most notably, in three key publications).[10] For Blumer, Mead was probably 'the only "true genius" he had ever met, and he clearly had a profound impact upon him. He was teaching his ideas throughout his life.'[11] For both Mead and Blumer, 'science' was the major form of thought for the modern world, a science grounded in the pragmatic attitude.

Another source of his passion lay more generally in being part of the Chicago School of Sociology. He was trained there, gained his Ph.D. there in 1928, taught there from 1931 and, when he left in 1953 to chair the Department of Sociology at the University of California at Berkeley, he took this inheritance with him. The core concerns of Chicago sociology – in the work of W.I. Thomas, Robert Park and others – was to study the city as a mosaic of social worlds; to get away from the library and to do real research in the city, and to build out of this a conceptually and theoretically grounded view of the social world. The philosophical strain of Mead and the empirical obsessions of 'Chicago' left a marked impact on Blumer.

I think this dual background generated tensions in Blumer's work, for the Meadian influence was not always compatible with the fieldwork Chicago inheritance. The former, after all, highlighted a philosophical issue, the latter an empirical one.[12] One paradox concerns his advocacy for empirical work yet his general failure to do it. From his earliest doctoral work on method in social psychology to his last ruminations, he was obsessively concerned with finding out the best way to study everyday collective behaviour and group experience – doing it as scientifically as possible, yet at the same time he often seemed reluctant to actually do it himself. There are some studies of media, fashion, race and industrialization but in the main doing empirical work was not his strength – even though he advocated it all the time. As a critic said to him in the early 1950s: 'you seem to advocate a lingering intellectual hypochondria in which we dwell upon all the dire things which may go wrong if we do attempt research'.[13] It may indeed well be that he saw the doing of sociology as so difficult, as so fraught with problems in 'getting it right' that he incapacitated himself.[14] While, ironically, he is something of a 'scientific absolutist'[15] and his work reeks of a sureness about what sociology most surely is and indeed surely should be, he also advocates a deep scepticism and a critical approach to all things. He is, if you like, sure about being unsure.

He was also against systematizing and synthesizing. Much of his work reads like scattered fragments; his most famous book, *Symbolic Interactionism* (1969), was only written under duress, encouraged by his students. He was against providing coda, recipes, models. Others have tried to do this for him – but it is clear he did not personally like it. Codification and abstraction strain against pragmatism.[16] But Becker, for example, one of his foremost students, remarked after his death that Blumer's work in fact harboured a deductive axiomatic theory – one organized around the idea of the collective act: 'any human event can be understood as the result of the people involved continually adjusting what they do in the light of what others do, so that each individual's line of activity "fits" into what the others do'.[17]

Key Issues – Theorizing in the Empirical World: Sampling Blumer's Work

While Blumer is probably best known for his writings on George Herbert Mead and his development of the theory of symbolic interactionism (SI), there is so much more to him than this. A full-length appraisal of his work must still be awaited. Among his accomplishments were the development of a distinctive methodological style; the exploration of key areas of social life – industrial relations, race and racism, the mass media, collective behaviour, social movements and social problems; as well as a concern with industrialization, social structure, social change and comparative sociology, especially within Latin America. (Some of these latter interests are not commonly recognized.)[18] Although he personally never swerved from the position of interactionism that he championed, his chairmanship at Berkeley was characterized by a wide-ranging support for a variety of styles of doing sociology. In a short review I can only briefly highlight a few of his contributions.

Creating Symbolic Interactionism and Developing a Theory of the Self

For Blumer:

> Human group life consists of the fitting together of the lines of action of the participants; such aligning of actions takes place predominantly by the participants indicating to one another what to do and in turn interpreting such indications made by the others; out of such interaction people form the objects that constitute their worlds; people are prepared to act towards their objects on the basis of the meaning these objects have for them; human beings face their world as organisms with selves, thus allowing each other to make indications to himself; human action constructed by the actor on the basis of what he notes, interprets and assesses; and the interlinking of such ongoing action constitutes organisations, institutions, and vast complexes of interdependent relations. To test the validity of these premises one must go to a direct examination of actual human group life.[19]

Here we have a litany of sensitizing concepts: selves, joint actions, objects, interactions, interpretations, organizations, interdependencies.[20] What lies at the heart of SI is an image of the world that says:

- always look for the processes, the changes, how lives, groups and whole societies emerge. Nothing is ever fixed and static: social life is always emergent. 'The empirical world is continuously recast'[21]
- always look for the meanings, the symbols, the languages in which social life gets done. It is this which makes human life truly distinctive, and why it needs special kinds of methods to 'dig out' these shifting meanings
- always look for the interactions and interconnections. There is no such thing as an individual in this view, as individuals are always in interaction with others. Societies are interactive webs of people 'doing things together'.[22]

One key concept that binds much of this together is the concept of the self, developed from Mead. What makes human beings distinctive is that they develop reflective and reflexive ideas of who they are through communication with themselves and others. People are able to indicate who they are; they are able to see themselves through the eyes of others; they are able to indicate to others who they are; they are able to make, present, transform and work on 'selves'. Selves, for Blumer and Mead, are processes contingent upon language, communications, role taking and interaction with others.

It is crucial to see that Blumer's work neither ignores nor minimizes the importance of wider social forces, power, history or the economic. He is certainly opposed to grand theory in the abstract and had he lived he would have been no friend at all to the current whirl of discourse analysis that so often becomes cut off from empirically observable language. But he is not opposed to a wider sense of social structure insofar as a society is constituted through symbolic interaction: 'Human society is to be seen as consisting of acting people, and the life of a society is to be seen as consisting of their actions.'[23]

For Blumer, society is 'the framework inside of which social action takes place and is not a determinant of that society'.[24] Collective actions are the concern. Blumer always stresses the 'group setting' in which all of social life is conducted.

Building a Methodological Stance of 'Naturalistic Rigour'

Closely allied is his work on methods. Blumer developed the 'pragmatic turn' that highlighted the importance of grounding analysis in concrete sets of experience. Pragmatism is a general philosophical position that shuns grand abstractions, dualisms and split thinking in favour of directly and practically looking at the limited and local truths as they emerge in concrete experience.[25] The much heralded self, for example, was one major way around the classic dualist split of subject and object, individual and society. Neither should be given priority; both were always present and in dialectical tension with each other. By looking at the self in concrete situations, it was manifest that self was both subject and object: only abstract philosophy could say otherwise.

For Blumer, then, it becomes a *sine qua non* that 'an empirical world exists as something available for observation, study and analysis'. Moreover, 'it *stands over against* the scientific observer with a character that has to be dug out'. 'Reality for empirical science exists only in the empirical world, can be sought only there, and can be verified only there.'[26] The obdurate empirical world has to be the focus of study.

This leads to much of Blumer's work being about methods.[27] One of his most famous contributions to such debates comes in his (book-length) review of a sociological classic in 1939. At this time in the USA, there was an evaluation of the state of USA sociology, and the study by W.I. Thomas and F. Znaniecki, *The Polish Peasant in Europe and America*, had been adjudicated the best example of good sociological work. Some 2,000 pages long, it charted the migration of Polish peasants from the old communities to the new cities in the USA. It used life histories, letters and documents of many kinds as a way of collecting data. And Blumer was asked by the Social Science Research Council to provide a review of it. While he was, as usual, very critical of this study, he also praised the range of methods, the concern with detail and the importance given to subjective factors. This is never to suggest that he denied 'objective factors'; but he is concerned with any sociology that does not take seriously the fact that humans 'always act in social situations', 'actors are always oriented and guided in situations by subjective dispositions'.[28] Sympathetically drawing from Thomas and Znaniecki, he says:

> (1) Group life consists *always* of the action of human actors; (2) such action always takes place as an adjustment of human actors to social situations; and (3) action in situations is always in the form of actors expressing their dispositions. Ergo, sociological research has to ferret out the play of subjective dispositions, and sociological propositions have to incorporate the record of that play.[29]

Human documents, naturalistic study, life histories: these are the tools Blumer favoured to get at these subjective dispositions. And this agreed, they then need their own methodological logic: much of the standard talk about representativeness, data adequacy, reliability and decisive theoretical validation leads up wrong paths once 'subjective dispositions' become the issue. For instance, representativeness is usually seen to raise the problem of sampling. But, for Blumer, modern sampling theory usually overlooks the fact that

> not all people who are involved in the given area of social action under study are equally involved, nor are they equally knowledgeable about what is taking place; hence they cannot be regarded as equally capable of supplying information on the form of social action under study. Some of the people ... are in the periphery; others ... may be in the mainstream ... [but] poor observers. To include them ... may weaken the study.[30]

If grasping subjectivity is the issue, representativeness changes its character. For example, in his research on labour arbitration, Blumer suggests not a random sample of workers but rather the need to listen closely to the 'key informants' who know much better what is going on. Not everyone does. All this means that standard views on 'representative samples' need challenging.

Studying the Empirical World: An Example – Going to the Movies

Blumer researched a number of areas, but he was one of the first to conduct audience research on the movies, and as such he anticipated the much later development of 'audience ethnography' found in such works as Janice Radway's *Reading the Romance.*[31] As part of a widespread concern about the impact of movies on young people, a series of investigations were set up in the late 1920s and early 1930s (popularly known as the Payne Studies, they were initiated by a pro-movie censorship group, the Motion Picture Research Council). Blumer was involved with one of these that looked at young people. Straightforwardly, he asked some 1,500 young people to write 'motion-picture autobiographies', backed up with more selective interviews, group discussions and observations. In all this, he demonstrated his commitment to the empirical world – effectively to know what impact media had on young people's lives, it is best to simply ask them. And following on from this, much of his ensuing book *Movies and Conduct* (1933) is given over to young people's first-hand accounts of the films they have seen – how they provide the basis of imitation, play, daydreams, emotional development and 'schemes of life'. For Blumer, the task is not to impose some preordained theoretical framework on his subjects (as so much contemporary audience ethnography chooses to do – usually from a psychoanalytic frame), but rather to let the people speak for themselves. One entry – dealing with stereotypes – reads:

> *Female, 19, white college senior:* One thing these pictures did was to establish a permanent fear of Chinamen in my mind. To this day I do not see a Chinese person but what I think of him as being mixed up in some evil affair. I always pass them as quickly as possible if I meet them in the street, and refuse to go into a Chinese restaurant or laundry.[32]

Quite rightly, others more recently have been critical of his straightforward naivety of approach. Just ask people. Denzin, for example, has recently been very critical of Blumer's work in this area, suggesting that, while progressive in method, it is shrouded with Blumer's assumptions ('pro-middle class and anti-film'),[33] was open to being used to crusade against movie content, and viewed texts unproblematically.[34] True, Blumer's initial studies in the 1930s now look somewhat simple: but he was the first to take audience responses seriously.

Creating a Public Philosophy: An Example – the Problem of Race Relations

Lyman and Vidich, in their analysis of the work of Herbert Blumer, suggest his work should be seen as the embodiment of an emerging new creative 'public philosophy' in North America during the course of the twentieth century. Suggesting the bankruptcy of past ideas, and especially those of social science, and drawing from the pragmatic mode of Chicago philosophers, Blumer saw the need for the systematic investigation of problems in American public life: from race to industrial relations; from the media to the consequences of industrialization. This work is less well known than his account of the Meadian self, but it is all part of a coordinated, seamless approach.[35] His was not a counsel of despair in the face of so many social problems, and neither was it a plea for revolutionary change. Instead, a public philosophy – pragmatic, populist, democratic – had to be forged that recognized the empirical world and opened debates around it. As Lyman and Vidich comment:

> His approach emphasizes the collective construction of meaning that imparts definitions to the various schemes of social reality, repudiates the allegedly irrevocable effects of structural arrangements, and allows for – indeed, expects and encourages – opposition, individuality and idiosyncrasy within the social order.[36]

An example of all this can be found in his abiding concern with race relations – the big issue of North American sociology. From some of his earliest writings, and under the influence of Robert E. Park, Blumer took an active interest in the study of race relations (although contemporary studies more or less systematically ignore all his work). For him, 'race prejudice has a history, and the history is collective'.[37] 'The defining process must be seen as central in the career of race relations.'[38] Starting with a paper in 1937 on 'the Nature of Race Prejudice' and ending with a summary paper in 1980 on 'Theories of Race and Social Action' (co-authored with Troy Duster), Blumer evolved a comprehensive theory of race relations. It was a fully social theory – he dismissed biological accounts of race, saw the whole process as a social one involving relationships and categorizations, and urged public debates to change and weaken segregation and discrimination. Using Blumer's own words, the following could be taken as a summary of his position:

1. Race prejudice is fundamentally a matter of relationships between racial groups (and not as a set of feelings that members of one racial group have towards the members of another racial group) … this directs us immediately to a sociological level and not a personal one.

2. Race prejudice is directed towards a 'conceptualised group' or abstract category; it exists as an attitude towards what is logically an abstraction (the Jew, the Oriental, the Negro) ... this directs us to a concern with the abstraction, categorizations and defining systems surrounding groups.
3. Race prejudice is a highly variable, changing and complex phenomenon; it differs a great deal from time to time and from place to place ... this directs us to its changing historical nature, its variability amongst different groups and times, to the fact that nothing is permanent about it. One group like 'the Jew' may appear at one time for one group; another like 'the Negro' may appear at other times for other groups; and others like the 'Arab' or the 'Moslem' may appear at yet another.
4. Race prejudice is a collective process though which racial groups form images of themselves and of others; it is a process in which two groups define their position in relation to each other; it is the sense of social position emerging for this collective process of characterization that provides the basis of racial prejudice ... this directs us to concerns with labelling, racialization and the creation of 'others'.
5. Race prejudice is a collective process that involves four patterns in the dominant group: (1) a feeling of superiority; (2) a feeling that the subordinate race is intrinsically different and alien; (3) a feeling of proprietary claim to certain areas of privilege and advantage; and (4) a fear and suspicion that the subordinate race harbours designs on the prerogatives of the dominant race ... this directs us to hierarchy, dominance, difference and privilege as bases of race prejudice.
6. The source of race prejudice lies in a felt challenge to this sense of group position. Race prejudice has its origins in many sources. One of them undoubtedly is the general ethnocentrism of groups, but of more importance is a sense of threat where a dominant group feels insecure and has its status, or economic position, threatened ... this directs us to the fact that the conflict is group based not individual based.

This is only a very provisional summary of Blumer's position. But like so much of his work, if followed through, these ideas are highly suggestive for public change.

Seeing Things Differently

Blumer brings to sociology a perspective for seeing the world that has influenced a great many studies: from illness and dying to occupations and classroom interaction; from social movements and collective behaviour to the patterning and organization of social problems; from crime and deviance to labour and industrial relations; from media studies to life history research; from self theory to race relations. Blumer's overarching concern with staying true to the empirical world and providing a rigorous methodology for inspecting and exploring it has guided a great many sociologists. Wittingly or unwittingly, a large corpus of work has flowed from Blumer's seminal ideas.

I read Blumer in 1970, shortly after embarking upon a Ph.D. that was to explore the sociology of sexuality. The major intellectual influences on me at that time had been Howard S. Becker's *Outsiders* and David Matza's *Becoming Deviant*, which had both introduced me to the key ideas of labelling theory; it turns out that both had been strongly shaped by Blumer's ideas. Yet these were both 'substantive' or topic-based studies, and it was only really when I read Blumer's *Symbolic Interactionism* that the full weight of his arguments became clearer. The book itself has major flaws: there is repetition (as one might expect from a series of largely previously published essays); it was dated in parts (much of it draws from the 1930s and 40s – which to a child of the 1960s could have been seen as very old-fashioned); and there is very little in the way of referencing, footnoting or acknowledging to guide the reader any further. But it came to me as a serious exhortation to think about what I was trying to do sociologically. It gave me a series of themes (process, symbols, interaction), an image of society (as a precarious network of interactions) and human beings (as symbolic, active creators of social worlds who inhabit coordinates of repetitive social actions), a view of methodology (which largely reiterated the old Park dictum to 'get off the seat of your pants and see what is going on' but tempered it with a concern for the logic of method), and a sense of required techniques for studying society (those which advocated intimate familiarity with the social world – through field research and life histories in particular). All these themes helped shape my view of sociology, but also of sexuality in general and homosexuality (as it was then called) in particular. And some have suggested more recently that many of its ideas these days implicitly shape much more of sociology than has been generally credited.[39]

There have been several major traditions for the study of sexuality: Kinsey's surveys, Masters and Johnson's therapies, psychodynamic theories turn to the unconscious, anthropological travel notes about patterns of sexual behaviour in remote islands. As a graduate student, I read through these studies assiduously, but felt something was lacking in each. Overwhelmingly, they suggested the importance of biology, the natural and an essentially uncontested notion of sexuality: it was a given and remained untheorized socially. Only the anthropological approach came near to capturing the distinctly human features of sexuality. Blumer's ruminations hence came as a brilliant, even shocking, set of tips for how human sexuality could be studied. In effect, he told me to go and look at sexualities in naturalistic settings (a bit like the anthropologists) and to build up life stories of people's sexualities (while being aware of how hard this was to do). He suggested to me that human sexuality should be approached as a massive symbolic enterprise, as something that emerges in human interactions, and that it is something we effectively piece together as joint actions. It is patterned but creative, symbolic while being biologic, and always social – varying in meaning in time, places and encounters.[40]

I was not alone in these realizations. A little earlier in the ground-breaking work of Gagnon and Simon,[41] they had come to similar conclusions and developed an approach to sexuality that they called a 'sexual scripting' approach. It provided the foundations of what some now call (perhaps inappropriately) the 'constructionist' approach to sexualities.

Legacies and Unfinished Business – Blumer at Century's Turn

Blumer was a sociologist for the twentieth century. His influence – primarily as the founder of symbolic interactionist theory – has been enormous. Not a prolific writer or researcher himself, he seems to have trained whole generations of sociologists in his distinctive view of the world. [42] He gave them all the pragmatist inheritance.

Nevertheless, by the time he died, many of his ideas had been moved on. We had entered a 'Post-Blumerian World'.[43] It is true that symbolic interactionism had become a strong force with its own journal, yearbook, professional body and conferences.[44] Likewise, many of his leads were continuing to be developed. Thus, the theory of action continues to be refined.[45] Mead and Blumer's abiding concern with self and identity as processual and changing has become a widespread concern of more and more scholars (indeed in the 1990s, identity theory became highly fashionable). Ethnographic and life history work continues, and becomes more sophisticated. And some have significantly reworked the theory so that it can now look better at emotions, structures and semiotics. Others have not just developed it, they have pushed it into hitherto unknown territories. For some, it has become the harbinger of postmodern social theory.[46] Feminism,[47] gay activist theory[48] and the politics of race[49] have all recently been linked further to it. Yet although Blumer may not have approved of all these developments, he would certainly not have been surprised. Sociologists come and go, as do sociological 'fashions' – indeed, this was yet another area he studied – and Blumer would have been the last to claim that new generations should stick to old orthodoxies. Since Blumer saw change as rapid and inevitable, he would not have been overly puzzled by them. As he remarked, 'Social change is woven into the very fabric of modern life ... It represents modern society in action.'[50] 'We have to transform our mentality to suit the new world [and] you are hereby enjoined to begin the change.'[51] He has left us a rich legacy with which to further this change.

Postscript Second Edition: Wonderful Directions for Research

Whatever Blumer's legacies have been, I have continued to find his ideas fruitful and the work of the symbolic interactionist tradition continues to infuse and stimulate contemporary research. Blumer and the theory of symbolic interactionism has indeed 'got under my skin', just as it has for Norman Denzin, a prime contemporary exponent.[52] On a number of recent occasions, as I start to think about research areas, I have found that symbolic interactionism always provides some wonderful directions. In looking at stories in social life,[53] at social movements[54] and at human rights,[55] a focus on Blumer has provided me with a myriad of questions to examine. In each one of these areas, I have drawn on the symbolic interactionist image of the world outlined earlier, looking for processes of change, for the meanings by which things get done, and for the major interactants, their interconnections and how they 'do things together'. I also ask what stages are biographies, situations, campaigns or networks moving through? So, in writing about the lesbian and gay movements, I identified definite stages in which rights appeared through 'rights work'.[56] Thus, there was a series of overlapping temporal stages in which an initial imagining of rights then opened out on to a vocalizing of claims to these rights. There were claims to legal equality; claims to acceptance on equal grounds with heterosexuals; claims to equal opportunities at school and work; the claim to be free from homophobic attack; and the claim to behave as heterosexuals might in the street – holding hands, even kissing.[57] The imagining and vocalization of such claims was followed by a stage in which they were fed into the shifting construction of identities and also became a source of empowering storytelling. Gradually, over time, social sub-worlds were related, in which some of these rights came to be respected more of the time, in tandem with the establishment of a public culture of rights that increased their visibility and legitimacy, albeit always in parallel with similar interactional sequences of backlash and resistance.

I have found the symbolic interactionist view of the world fruitful to examine any area of social life. The world-view works best when it is joined to the methodological injunction to get close to the features of social life you wish to study – through observation of self and others, participant or otherwise, and through ethnography, documents and stories. It may not be fully adequate on its own, but it is certainly a valuable pathway to much that is essential in social relations.

FURTHER READING

Atkinson, P. and Housley, W. (2003) *Interactionism*, London: Sage concurs with the observation with which this chapter began, arguing that even though relatively few sociologists explicitly identify themselves as symbolic interactionists the ideas of Mead, Blumer and others in this tradition have permeated sociological research to the point at which they are an often unnoticed but profoundly pervasive influence. Atkinson and Housley are excellent guides and they provide a very good charting of the history of symbolic interactionist thought. They also provide an important and intriguing account of recent British sociology. An important foundational text for symbolic interactionism is G.H. Mead's (1934) *Mind, Self and Society*, Chicago: University of Chicago Press. Works by Blumer himself that it is important to consult directly include:

Blumer, H. (1969) *Symbolic Interactionism: Perspective and Method*, Englewood Cliffs, NJ: Prentice Hall.

Blumer, H. (2004) (edited and introduced by Thomas J. Morrione) *George Herbert Mead and Human Conduct,* Alta Mira, NY: Rowman & Littlefield.

Blumer, H. and Duster, T. (1980) 'Theories of race and social action', in *Sociological Theories: Race and Colonialism*, Paris: UNESCO, pp. 211–38.

Norman Denzin's (1992) *Symbolic Interactionism and Cultural Studies*, Oxford: Blackwell is a good overview of ways in which symbolic interactionism has influenced and been influenced by cultural studies in both its US and British forms.

Gary Fine's (ed.) (1988) Special issue of *Symbolic Interaction,* **11**(1) on Herbert Blumer's legacy is essential reading.

Lyman, S. and Vidich, A. (1988) *Social Order and Public Philosophy: The Analysis and Interpretation of the Work of Herbert Blumer*, Fayetteville, AR: University of Arkansas Press is an excellent source through which to explore the importance to Blumer of creating pragmatic, populist and democratic dialogue and debate about social problems. Such dialogues had to be grounded in engagement with the empirical world. Blumer's work here has many resonances with the contemporary resurgence of Public Sociology.

Maines, D.R. (2001) *The Faultline of Consciousness: A View of Interactionism in Sociology*, New York: Aldine De Gruyter focuses much more closely, as the title indicates, on issues of consciousness and processes of doing and being.

SUPPLEMENTARY READING

Plummer, K. (1995) *Telling Sexual Stories: Power, Change and Social Worlds*, London: Routledge. Symbolic interactionism, with its emphasis on the ubiquity of social change and social becoming, is combined here with narrative analysis and the sociology of sexuality to explore the new domain of 'Intimate Citizenship'. The study focuses on the intersection between storytelling and sex, understanding sexual stories as the product of negotiated networks of collective activity.

Plummer, K. (1998) 'The gay and lesbian movement in Britain, 1965–1995: schism, solidarities and social worlds', in B. Adam, J.W. Duyvendak and A. Krouwel (eds) *The Global Emergence of Gay and Lesbian Politics*, Philadelphia: Temple University Press.

Plummer, K. (2006) 'Rights work: constructing lesbian, gay and sexual rights in modern times', in L. Morris (ed.) *Rights: Sociological Perspectives*, London: Routledge. This is discussed briefly in the postscript, above, to this second edition.

CHAPTER 6

Theodor Adorno

MAGGIE O'NEILL

Driving Impulses

In order to fully grasp the driving impulses and key ideas that underpin the work of Theodor Adorno, we need to understand the sociocultural and historical backdrop to his work. This backdrop includes the creative forces of modernity; the gathering forces of anti-Semitism, Nazism and the Holocaust; and the development of the counterculture movement and postmodernism, or the 'hyper-modern' as Adorno defines it in *Aesthetic Theory* (1997).

Adorno was a sociologist, philosopher and musicologist. He was born an only child in Frankfurt to a Jewish father (a wine merchant) and Catholic mother (an accomplished musician). His work is constituted by the interrelation of aesthetics, phenomenology, western Marxism and musicology. He is described by Martin Jay[1] as 'precocious, musically and intellectually'. He was introduced at the age of fifteen to German classical philosophy by Siegfried Kracauer (a friend of the family). They began by reading Kant's *First Critique* and he learned 'to decode philosophical texts as documents of historical and social truth'.[2]

After graduating from the University of Frankfurt with a doctorate in philosophy at the age of 21, influenced by Marxism, psychoanalysis, Kant, Hegel's dialectics, the phenomenology of Husserl and musicology (all crucial to the development of his thinking), and where he met his friend and collaborator Horkheimer, Adorno was accepted by Alban Berg as a music student in Vienna. Here he met composers such as Schoenberg whose atonal twelve-tone scale was to be immensely important to him. Adorno praised Schoenberg

> for negating the bourgeois principle of tonality and exposing its claims to naturalness in the same way that dialectical thought undermined the pseudo-naturalism of bourgeois economics.[3]

On his return to Frankfurt from Vienna in 1927, he was connected through his intellectual and personal friendships with Horkheimer, Lowenthal and Kracauer to the Institute for Social Research, where he became professor of sociology until his forced migration in 1934. Here he also met the western Marxists Bloch, Brecht, Weill, Lukács and, most importantly, Walter Benjamin. Adorno's work is influenced by and inextricably connected to that of his friend Benjamin.[4] However, Adorno's Hegelian reading of **Marx** differed from the latter group, in that his focus upon developing dialectical critique did *not* accept that committed or political art (such as Brecht's *Mother Courage*) could counter the barbaric forces of capitalism and anti-Semitism. 'When genocide becomes part of the cultural heritage in the themes of committed literature, it becomes easier to continue to play along with the culture that gave birth to murder.'[5] For Brecht and Benjamin, committed art could make a difference. In contrast, Adorno argued that works that were autonomous, that emerged from the sedimented stuff of society (not explicitly politically directed or posited by the artist or author) such as Kafka, Beckett and Schoenberg (so more abstract work) 'could compel the change of attitude which committed works merely demand'.[6]

Adorno's forced migration was spent first of all at Merton College, Oxford (three and a half years) followed by positions at the Institute for Social Research in New York and then at Berkeley in California. After the war, Adorno returned with his colleagues Horkheimer and Pollack to rebuild and reopen the Frankfurt Institute for Social Research. The Institute was officially opened in 1951 and in 1953 Adorno became the director.

It was during his exile in North America that Adorno wrote some of his most powerful and popular texts: *The Authoritarian Personality, Dialectic of Enlightenment* and *Minima Moralia: Reflections from a Damaged Life*. Shierry Nicholsen writes about the importance of *Minima Moralia*, written during and in the aftermath of the Second World War, because in it Adorno explores 'the thinking individual's struggle to retain the capacity to think and experience in the midst of a constellation of power, individual and society that reduces the very idea of the good life to a mere glimmer'.[7] Anyone who has witnessed the pile of shoes and boots in the Holocaust exhibition at the Imperial War Museum, London, or indeed has visited Dachau or Auschwitz will understand what Adorno means here. Moreover, Adorno also said 'I have no wish to soften the saying that to write lyric poetry after Auschwitz is barbaric.'[8]

It was in North America that Adorno applied **Freud**'s work to his analysis of the Holocaust, which in turn led to his involvement in *The Authoritarian Personality*,[9] one of a multivolume series of studies in prejudice. In this influential text, Adorno et al. draw links between anti-Semitism and totalitarian thinking, arguing for an analysis that looks for explanations at the level of the psyche as well as the social sphere.

Dialectics and dialectical thinking are very important to Adorno's critical analysis of the social world. Adorno took dialectics beyond Marx and Hegel, arguing that there was no identity between subject and object, no teleological thinking (remember Marx felt that the proletariat were the subject/object of history and would lead a revolution to squash capitalism and usher in socialism). Indeed, critical theory should not be subject to political goals, nor could history be synonymous with progress as emphasized by Enlightenment thinkers. Instead, Adorno focuses upon the relationship between subjectivity and the social world (influenced by Freud); the growing commodification of culture; the loss of hope in history as progress; and the transformative potential of art – defined as the last vestige of 'truth' in a world overtaken by the forces of capitalism, commodification and reification (influenced by Lukács) as instrumental reason.

The common themes and key ideas that form the core around which Adorno's critical analysis unfolds include three interrelated concepts that I will explain more fully in the next section. The first of these is negative dialectics or **non-identity thinking**, which serves to understand and counter the impact of the increasing commodification of social life. The second is *Kulturkritik* that served to analyse the impact of the culture industry (identified by Adorno as mass deception) involving the analysis of **identity thinking** and instrumental reason. Finally, there is the transformative role of art and critical thought. The task of artist and critical theorist is to reveal the unintentional truths of the social world and preserve independent thinking. Thus, autonomous (not committed) art and critical analysis could be held up like a mirror to society, thus potentially serving a liberating, transformative function.

Identity and non-identity thinking

For Adorno, a real object in the world (anything from capitalism as a whole, through an outbreak of ethnic violence to a TV advertisement) can always outstrip the concepts by means of which a subject, *a* person, *perceives that object. That is, any attempt to fully capture the complexity of a real object in a concept is doomed to failure. It needs to be understood that any object could be approached as if through a prism, through a constellation of different perspectives, and that even then there would always be more. Something about the object would always escape the constellation of concepts designed to capture it. A subject can thus never fully capture the object, there can never be an identity between the subject's concepts and the objects out there. 'Identity thinking' is misleading as it mistakenly assumes away the gap between subjective concepts and their objects. On the other hand,* non-identity thinking *can be a valuable critical tool. Non-identity thinking, or what Adorno sometimes calls* the immanent method, *examines inconsistencies, or 'lack of fit', between the concept of an object and its actual existence. This lack of fit is particularly marked in, for example, racist and sexist stereotypes. Stereotypes of women, for example, tend not only to be obtuse as to the distance between their concept of women and the actual reality of particular women, but they also treat all women as* equivalent*, ignoring any differences between them. While particularly marked in the case of stereotypes, identity thinking inevitably creeps into conceptions of all other social objects. Non-identity thinking provokes the interrogation of all such easy assumptions of identity and equivalence.*

Through a focused determination to unmask 'lack of fit', non-identity thinking can shed new light on the object itself. It can reveal glimpses of the object that have not previously been seen or acknowledged, even if sometimes it can only do this fleetingly. The method can be used to subvert lazy or expedient ways of thinking encouraged by the mass media, from the language used in news bulletins to the messages of commercial advertisements, phenomena discussed later in the chapter. David Held gives an example from political discourse, showing how non-identity thinking can work to question conventional notions of freedom: 'In the so-called free society in which we live the inequality of social power ensures that the claimed identity between concept (freedom) and object (the present state of affairs) is false. The negation of the concept of freedom in practice points to aspects of society which aid, restrict and restrain freedom's actualization'.[10] That is, the dominant concept of freedom in liberal democratic societies, with all its political and ideological persuasiveness, does not fit with the complex reality of power inequalities and their differential impact on people's actual freedom. Non-identity thinking homes in on this and exposes it.

Key Issues

Instrumental Reason and Identity Thinking

I began writing this chapter in New York at a workshop on Humiliation and Human Dignity where, in discussions about the quality of life, conflict and peace, it was argued that there is a need for the kind of growth that can foster social communities and relationships, that this is needed to interrupt pathways of violence in order to build egalization[11] and human dignity and to counter negative social forces such as the impact of humiliation, **instrumental reason** (see glossary box, p. 248), racism, sexism and identity thinking. In reflecting upon this chapter and the workshop, my thoughts turned to ways in which Adorno's work was dedicated to unmasking the false, seeking the truth in life's fictions and working against the forces of totalitarianism that include prejudice, racism and 'othering'.

The quality of life and the impact of destructive forces are expressed for Adorno through the society of domination – an administered society marked by instrumental reason and identity thinking. As Nicholsen states, for Adorno:

> the structure of contemporary society is one of domination, and ... domination has reached into the very fabric of daily life. Even the smallest pleasures of life serve to legitimize a society based on domination and thus to legitimize the suffering beneath the surface ... The individual must be constantly vigilant, and yet is unable to avoid complicity with this pervasive structure of domination. Complicity seems to follow from participation of any kind. Conversation itself, the medium of social life, entangles one in complicity.[12]

As an example, Nicholsen draws upon an excerpt from *Minima Moralia*, 'How nice of you doctor.'[13] Here Adorno describes how through a chance conversation on a train, we might consent to statements that ultimately are abhorrent to us and 'that one knows ultimately to implicate murder'.[14] As Nicholsen states, the 'false appearance of agreement is enough to undermine truth'.[15] Adorno elucidates:

> Sociability itself connives at injustice by pretending in this chill world we can still talk to each other, and the casual amiable remark contributes to perpetuating silence, in that the concessions made to the interlocutor debase him.[16]

To take this further, sociability as affability is described by Adorno as having a screening (denial) effect on class and relationships, allowing both to 'triumph more implacably'.[17] In Nicholsen's reading, affability is malignant, in the sense of being destructive of respect for human beings; thus, we can argue, leading to humiliation (our own and the 'other's'), isolation and loss of human dignity, particularly if we go along with a judgemental statement that runs totally counter to our own values, such as sexist or racist comments.

Nicholsen describes her reaction to the articles in *Minima Moralia* as on the one hand resonating with them, for they seem true and it is a relief to hear someone say them so directly; but, on the other hand, they are so pessimistic that they are literally unbearable for they leave no way out. Quoting Adorno, she says:

> As Adorno describes it, the untruth of ordinary life is so pervasive, and complicity with domination so unavoidable, that we are condemned to solitary suffering. All we can do is hold fast to an awareness of pain, and try to remember that something better might have been, might conceivably still be, possible.[18]

Thus, dominant ideology, instrumental reason and identity thinking increasingly shape both the individual psyche and social structures/processes. The drive for equivalence rooted in the exchange principle reduces the world and subjects to thing-like equivalences. This constitutes *identity thinking*. The non-identical becomes 'commensurable and identical'.[19] In American society (where Adorno was writing), affability and phoniness can easily mask or screen the forces of Fascism. Thus, in Nicholsen's reading, it becomes possible that 'Affability as a mask of tolerance and egalitarianism ... hides impersonal social violence.'[20]

By way of an example, in my college accommodation, I was (being only an occasional TV viewer) surprised by the quantity of commercial breaks in TV programmes and what can only be described as the onslaught of advertising and consumer products that promise to make my life better; products such as: a 'urine guard' that will protect my floors and carpets from cat urine – for only a few dollars; to being offered the possibility of changing my world by 'thinking in line with the word of God' and 'Dr Dollar' by donating every month to 'Change 2006'. All I have to do is set up my account and they do the rest and 'God's kingdom will benefit'. Or, for a monthly fee, I can have clean air in my home and avoid the long-term effects of pollution with a unit that changes the air in my bedroom/house every ten minutes, thus protecting me from dust mites, pollen and viruses.

These examples of product advertising are good examples of identity thinking in operation – seeing/feeling equivalence between my access to clean air and accepting the need to pay for it as the exchange of equivalents. *Instrumental reason* is defined by Adorno as *technological reason* that dominates nature, and *social reason* that leads to the domination of human beings. And the drive for equivalence (money for clean air; money for access to the kingdom of God) rooted in the exchange principle reduces the world (objects) and subjects to thing-like equivalences. The non-identical becomes 'commensurable and identical'.

It is but a short step from the manipulation of needs described above to seeing the equivalence between asylum seekers and 'social junk' as 'swamping' our cities and towns. Newspaper headlines reinforce the equivalence in the public imagination of the scapegoating and 'othering' of people seeking refuge from totalitarian regimes, dire poverty and certain death, as scroungers, tricksters and undeserving. In *What's the Story? Results from Research into Media Coverage of Refugees and Asylum Seekers in the UK*, written by Sarah Buchanan et al., and based on the Article 19 research project conducted by the Cardiff School of Journalism, it was found that:

> Media reporting of the asylum issue is characterised by the inaccurate and provocative use of language to describe those entering the country to seek asylum. 51 different labels were identified as making reference to individuals seeking refuge in Britain and included meaningless and derogatory terms such as 'illegal refugee' and 'asylum cheat'.[21]

For Adorno, the very fabric of social life is constituted by domination, instrumental reason and identity thinking and his critical analysis of society looked to negative dialectics, *Kulturkritik* and the role of art as unintentional truth in offering some semblance of hope in a damaged world.

Negative Dialectics

In *Negative Dialectics*, Adorno argued against the drive for equivalence we see identified above, and for the non-identity between subject and object. Influenced by Nietzsche and Lukács, he argued that concepts as ordinarily used mask the truth – they have become lies. *Negative Dialectics* looked to Marxism as method and dialectical thinking as the core of that method. And it was up to the subject (us) through negative dialectics to access the 'truth' that was largely hidden by the operation of identity thinking, instrumental reason and reification (a version of ideology). Reification – the treatment of people as things, fixed and without critical capacities – is rooted in society *not* the individual psyche and change can only be brought about socially by changing society. However, as we have seen, reification is an outcome of identity thinking at the level of the psyche, and is a fact of consciousness as well as a social category. Gillian Rose interprets identity thinking as the way unlike things appear as like, and she believes that it is this mode of thinking – that considers them as equal – which constitutes reification as both a social phenomenon and as a process of thinking.[22] Our very subjectivity is being 'liquidated' by the power of reification and identity thinking.

In response, non-identity thinking confronts the partial truth of an object with the potential truth and advances the interests of the truth by identifying the false using the form of the constellation. The critical theorist seeks to assemble a response/argument through what Adorno calls 'constellational thought', and in so doing holds up a mirror to society. If we agree with Adorno that domination has reached into the very fabric of social life, into language and subjectivity, then tools for the critical analysis of society must proceed dialectically by identifying the true in the false – in constellational not linear form.

The example in the previous section from *Minima Moralia* is a useful example of non-identity thinking. Affability in the face of statements that we know to 'uphold murder' (that is, dehumanizing, sexist, prejudicial/racist remarks) serves to uphold false conditions and reinforce identity thinking, and ultimately does violence not only to the speaker but to ourselves. For Adorno, any thinking that is determined by a desire to control the world cannot qualify for the status of 'truth'. What constitutes truth is that which hides behind appearance, and unmasking can only come about by changing society, although it is art as well as critical theory that can provide the change-causing gesture;[23]

and, as identified above, *not* in the form of committed art but through unintentional/autonomous art such as that of Becket, Schoenberg, Picasso and Kafka.

> Nowhere in Kafka does there glimmer the aura of the infinite idea; nowhere does the horizon open. Each sentence is literal and each signifies. The two moments are not merged as the symbol would have it, but yawn apart and out of the abyss between them blinds the glaring ray of fascination. Here too, in its striving not for symbol but for allegory, Kafka's prose sides with the outcasts. Each sentence says 'interpret me' and none will permit it ... For more than most writers, it must be said of Kafka that not *verum* but *falsim* is *index sui* [not the truth but the opposite is the truth].[24]

Kafka's fragmentary style[25] denies closed systems and truth can be found in the gaps and contradictions in the text: 'What is enclosed in Kafka's glass ball is even more monotonous, more coherent and hence more horrible than the systems outside.'[26]

Kulturkritik

The development of the administered society, identity thinking and the growth of 'mass culture' were for Adorno synonymous: 'The culture industry perpetually cheats its consumers of what it perpetually promises.'[27] The culture industry is described as the entertainment business: it helps to maintain the hold of reification. No effort is required of us as consumers, our reactions are prescribed (if I have cats, I need a urine guard; I might want to feel I have a stake in the kingdom of heaven but in my chaotic and busy life paying for it may be a step towards living it; clean air is important in the context of risk society and what a relief I have the opportunity to pay for it), capitalism is sustained and instrumental reason is strengthened. In *Adorno: the Stars Down to Earth*, Stephen Crook states that Adorno raises unsettling questions about contemporary culture, and he asks

> how far dependency has become the typical condition of the 'self' in advanced societies, how deeply authoritarian currents run through our superficially pluralistic cultures, and how free our beliefs and opinions are from the pervasive undercurrent of irrationalism?[28]

Adorno and Horkheimer describe the culture industry as 'mass deception' and non-identity thinking or negative dialectics through *Kulturkritik* performs the much-needed task of revealing the truth, uncovering the meaning of objects and preserving independent thinking. Nicholsen believes that Adorno offers a 'non-discursive rationality' as an alternative to 'a dominating systematizing rationality that is the counterpart of an administered world'.[29] This non-discursive rationality is best described through the concept of autonomous art, and its role in uncovering unintentional truth.

The Transformative Role of Art: Art as Unintentional Truth

Adorno describes works of art as rebuses or picture puzzles and shows us that what is contained in them is the sedimented stuff of society. Picasso's *Guernica* is an example he uses in *Aesthetic Theory*:

> by means of inhumane construction, [*Guernica*] achieves a level of expression that sharpens it to social protest beyond all contemplative misunderstanding. The socially critical zones of artworks are those where it hurts; where in their expression, historically determined, the untruth of the social situation comes to light. It is actually against this that the rage of art reacts.[30]

Art as a social product is a cipher of the social; it is formed through the objective demands of the material, the historically given techniques and means of production, the subjective experiences and playfulness of the artist; and at the same time is an independent force in society. Works of art are constitutive – they bring something new into society as well as reflecting what is already there.[31] 'The new' is a blind spot (reminiscent of Benjamin's dialectical images in *Trauerspiel*) on the side of a positive mimesis[32] in tension with the increasingly instrumental and constructive character of reified society.[33]

However, the crisis of modernism, the growing forces of totalitarianism, an increasingly administered society and ideology as reification are represented in the increasingly affirmative nature of art – described by Adorno as *Entkunstung* (desubstantialization). This brings with it the loss of art's capacity to act as a medium of the truth. The related crisis in art includes the commodification of art (the integration of art into life or art viewed as a thing among things), or art viewed as a vehicle for the psychology of the producer or the viewer). The central concept of dissonance of art turns into its opposite as affirmation and commodification.

On the other hand, 'auratic art', art that resists accommodation, remains the last vestige of hope in a damaged world. Auratic art invokes 'frisson', 'shudder', and, in the realm of unfreedom, freedom can only find its representation fleetingly, unintentionally, as 'coming and going' in the unresolved tensions between *mimesis* (sensuousness, spirit, playfulness that animates art works) and the *constructive rationality* (means and social forces, demands of the material and artistic sphere) of production. The socially critical dimensions of auratic art are those that hurt 'where in their expression, historically determined, the untruth of the social situation comes to light'.[34]

The problem is that art's opposition is minimal within the increasing reification and desubstantialization of art. The truth content of art is explained via the dialectic of art – mimesis versus constructive rationality. 'It is through the dialectical combination of mimesis and rationality that art is produced'.[35] Given the growth of identity thinking and instrumental reason and the takeover by the constructive/rational pole of the dialectic, mimesis retreats into abstraction in an attempt to avoid affirmation. Art survives as cultural heritage or affirmative pleasure, as business for profit. Culture as redemption becomes culture as manipulation, save for the few autonomous works where the sedimented aspects of the social, the subjective/collective are contained, and, in the tension between mimesis and constructive rationality, truth unfolds from within the work, rather than being posited intentionally by the artist.

For Adorno, the mystery of art is its demystifying power. And it calls for a twofold reflection 'on the being of itself of art, and its ties with society'.[36] Art 'as a refuge for mimetic behaviour ... represents truth in the twofold sense of preserving the image of an end smothered completely by rationality and of exposing the irrationality and absurdity of the status quo'.[37] The task of the philosopher and critical theorist is to interpret the social world through critical theory; not as 'legislators' degraded to 'propagandists or censors ... for they help to weave the veil'[38] but as interpreters.[39]

Seeing Things Differently

Adorno's work provides both inspiration and a driving force for my own work as a feminist scholar, particularly in relation to the themes of: non-identity thinking; interpretive sociology/ethnography (micrology); and the role of mimesis – again, to be interpreted as sensuous awareness – in producing knowledge that is potentially transformative. I describe this as critical theory in praxis. Indeed, Adorno's writing on the dialectic of art as being formed in the tension between mimesis and constructive rationality has led me to develop a methodology I call *ethno-mimesis*, a renewed methodology influenced by Adorno's account of the dialectic of art, and indeed Adorno's articulation of coming to know the work of art.[40]

A 'force field'[41] (Jay, 1993) develops around theory, experience and praxis (as knowledge for) in the process of my immersion in the lives of sex workers, asylum seekers, refugees and migrants. The research process involves a theory of feeling/involvement/sensuousness in critical tension to reason, rationality, objectification and the triangulation of data. This methodology incorporates ethnography (micrology) and mimesis (as sensuous knowledge) and involves creative methods such as the production of art works by research participants as visual/poetic data to be interpreted alongside more orthodox data such as interviews, surveys and observation.

'The splinter in your eye is the best magnifying glass.'[42] This quotation describes how I feel about this process. The statement encourages us to focus upon what is ordinarily overlooked, the small scale, the minutiae of lived experience. In focusing upon pain and the unsayable – the gap between the appearance and the reality – that can be found within the small scale, we can often reach a better understanding of the broader social picture. Drawing upon Adorno, it is only by trying to say the 'unsayable', the 'outside of language', 'the mimetic' the sensual, the non-conceptual, that we can we approach a 'politics' that undercuts identity thinking, refuses to engage in identity thinking – but rather crisscrosses binary thinking and remains unappropriated. Works of art, as ciphers of the social world, help us to access the sedimented stuff of society, what may be unsayable, and help to reveal the unintentional truths of society.

This kind of politics and praxis strikes resonances with some contemporary feminist theorists,[43] especially when we loosen up the knowledge/ideology axis contained in Adorno's works, for Adorno argued himself into a one-way street, in that only autonomous art could mirror social conditions. If we acknowledge that we do have the resources to look behind appearances and engage critically with our world, society, politics and culture, and that constructive rationality and reification are not quite so embedded as Adorno argued, then we can explore the transformative potential of critical theory, critical praxis. For some people, critical analysis of their society involves being placed outside 'citizenship' and brings the risk of death – as in the case of Nelson Mandela and those asylum seekers who have stood up against totalitarian regimes, have refused to be bystanders or 'affable' amidst the horror of the real.

In my work, I argue that through art works, performing arts, live arts, painting, poetry, literature, photography and architecture, we are able to get in touch with our 'realities', our social worlds and the lived experiences of others, in ways which demand critical reflection. For Nicholsen, the critical potential of art is that it can 'pierce us' and 'help us to grasp reality in its otherness within the context of the image society that attempts to tame and inhibit critical reflection'.[44] Nicholsen looks to photography to help us develop a broader, more compassionate and accurate consciousness.

As an example, see the piece below created by a Bosnian refugee as part of an Arts and Humanities Research Board (AHRB), funded project on 'Global Refugees: Exile, Displacement and Belonging' (a colour version of this picture can be seen at http://www.lboro.ac.uk/departments/ss/global_refugees/index.html).[45]

Figure 6.1 Good neighbour

In the Global Refugees project, representing lived experience in artistic form could be potentially regressive, in that (remembering Adorno's comments on the desubstantialization of art) it may facilitate the transformation of pain into enjoyment, where suffering can simply be consumed or enjoyed and something of its horror is removed. However, our research does not simply memorialize the testimonies of the participants, but through retelling, rewriting, reconstructing and reimagining the loss, displacement and exile faced by the people involved, and in representing their stories or testimonies through art forms to as wide an audience as possible (in community centres as well as galleries), the processes of regeneration and reconstruction emerged and acted as a spur to the processes of community development. Challenging and resisting dominant images and stereotypes of 'refugees' and 'asylum seekers' can also serve to raise awareness, educate and empower individuals and groups.

Through art forms such as Figure 6.1, ethnographic research and artistic representation can inform each other, developing greater knowledge and understanding through the production of texts as 'feeling forms', for they contain 'truths' about the social world. The image represents the artist's feelings towards her Serbian neighbour who saved her life. This work does not support the regressive moment in art – the transformation of pain into joy, but rather serves to increase awareness of emotional pain and acts as a counter to postemotionalism. Moreover, we can acquire a more complex understanding of our similarities and differences through such intertextual feeling forms – in them we glimpse the sedimented stuff of society and, in the process, if we engage, we can be informed, empowered and challenged.

For Nicholsen, the very conjunction of non-discursive rationality and the aesthetic dimension are the key to Adorno's potential usefulness to us as a counter to 'a dominating systematizing rationality that is the counterpart of an administered world'.[46]

Legacies and Unfinished Business

Adorno's central dialectic of mimesis and constructive rationality provides an example of the importance of understanding the critical tension between emotion, feeling, spirit, subjectivity and our 'out there' sense of being in the world – institutions, organizations, bureaucracy and objectification. Given the relationship he outlines between culture, the culture industry and reification, the need is for immanent, dialectical criticism – in order to say the unsayable – the 'unutterable' – to undercut cultural criticism (he defines this as legitimating the status quo) with dialectical criticism.

The major intellectual legacies of Adorno's work on art, society and culture include his work on:

1. Deconstructing identity thinking – the false identity between subject and object marked by instrumental reason – Keith Tester's[47] examination of the 'dialectic of reification' uses Adorno to develop his analysis of the inhuman condition, the fabrication and reification of our social worlds.
2. Understanding the interrelationship between psychic, social and cultural processes and practices. Nicholsen picks this up in her work on aura and subjectivity[48] and utilizes Adorno and Benjamin to push forward both the understanding and practice of environmental consciousness and psychoanalytic psychotherapy.[49]
3. Working at the intersections of philosophy, politics and aesthetics in order to illuminate the contradictory nature of social and sexual oppression. Not by way of an answer or solution to the problems of the modern age, marked by increasing consumption, capitalism and reification of all aspects of life, but rather as tools for the critical analysis of society.

A number of feminists have creatively taken up these themes in their reworking or use of Adorno and I will focus upon some of these in what follows, drawing out just some of the many fruitful avenues of critical thought that Adorno's work continues to inspire. In his writings Adorno develops a relentless attack upon essentializing the feminine, at the same time as proclaiming the utter loss of hope in the Enlightenment as progress. Becker-Schmidt[50] informs us that in German sociology, Adorno's attempts to 'relate societal transformations to restructurings of psychical energies on a collective scale' have not been continued; and that it is feminists who have productively analysed Adorno. However, for Becker-Schmidt, because Adorno's image of femininity is conformist rather than progressive, his ideas must first be transformed into a feminist perspective. She does this by focusing upon theories of equality and difference in gender relations and also by asking in what way differences in the power relations between men and women support social domination above and beyond gender relations. Difference, identitarian logic and the correspondence between gender hierarchies and societal hegemonies are key themes in her work and have far-reaching impactions for feminisms. For example, Becker-Schmidt identifies that, in the women's movement, sociological positions have emerged that emphasize 'the difference between gender groups in order to grant the social group "woman" a voice for asserting her own interests'. On the other hand, 'we come across concepts in the social sciences which postulate "equality" as an absolute demand as well'.[51] Becker-Schmidt goes on to explore why these approaches conceptualize equality and difference as opposites rather than as mediated positions and what effect this has on the formulation of women's policies. The important message here, for me, is that drawing upon Adorno's critique of identitarian logic, we can disrupt binary thinking and explore and analyse the mediations between opposite stances to develop more complex sociological thinking. A good example is the current feminist discourse on prostitution, with one group arguing for sex as work and the other arguing for sex as violence and abuse.

Juliet Flower Macannel produces a brilliant psychoanalytic analysis of Adorno and women, describing herself as ambivalent and resistant to his work. She tells us that in her reading of Adorno, there is little fault to find in his theoretical works as far as women are concerned, 'his aphorisms about women are almost always proto-feminist. Long before the women's movement he assailed women's abuse, archaic as well as contemporary.'[52] Adorno, she says, is clear that 'The feminine character, and the ideal of femininity on which it is modelled, are products of masculine society.'[53] Flower Macannel writes that 'Adorno contrasted the bad equality of today and its demand to eradicate differences, with a potentially "better state" in which people could be different without fear.'[54] In relation to the liberation of woman, he tells us that 'Women's new emancipation has only a mere "appearance" of life.'[55] Identifying that there can be no emancipation for women without that of society, Adorno identifies the battle of the sexes 'in the way a housewife holds her husband's coat for him'. In 'the incongruity between his authoritarian pretensions and his helplessness', his wife helps him on with his coat. 'In demystifying the husband, whose power rests on his money, earning trumped up as human worth, the wife too expresses the falsehood of marriage, in which she seeks her whole worth. No emancipation without that of society.'[56] However, for Flower Macannel, Adorno's concept of 'woman' is limited to a bourgeois definition/understanding: 'If we want to imagine or dream ourselves beyond both the family and capitalist society as women we do not get much help from him.'[57] For Flower Macannel, Adorno's theoretical works take analysis of the woman question only so far, yet we are made aware also of the complexity of the 'woman question' and its relation to sexual and social structures and forces.

Nicholsen's work in the field of psychoanalytic psychotherapy and environmental consciousness is also greatly influenced by Adorno. In a recent paper,[58] she explores passion, psychoanalysis and the postemotional dilemma in order to show the usefulness of Adorno to us in understanding the present. She describes how the concept of 'postemotionalism', coined by Stefan Meštrović in 1990s North America, was explained 'brilliantly' by Adorno in the 1940s. 'Postemotionalism' is a state of being where 'synthetic, quasi-emotions become the basis for the widespread manipulation of self and others, and the culture industry as a whole'. In postemotional society, 'a new hybrid of intellectualized, mechanical, mass-produced emotions have appeared on the world scene'.[59] Drawing upon *Minima Moralia*, Nicholsen draws parallels with Adorno and refers to a section called 'Invitation to the dance'. Here Adorno tells us that part of the mechanism of domination is to 'forbid recognition of the suffering it produces'. Nicholsen draws links to postemotionalism and 'normotic illness', coined by Bollas to describe clients who experience themselves as commodity objects, marked also by mental flatness and lack of human relationships. Nicholsen argues that psychoanalysis could help to increase awareness of emotional pain and decrease the experience of postemotionalism.

FURTHER READING

The following texts will help the reader to take further the themes of this chapter.

Adorno, T.W. (1980 [1977]) 'Commitment', in *Aesthetics and Politics*, translation editor R. Taylor, London: Verso; see also the Afterword by F. Jameson.

Adorno, T.W. (1996) *Minima Moralia*, translated by E.F.N. Jephcott, London: Verso.

Adorno, T.W. (1997) *Aesthetic Theory*, translated by R. Hullot-Kentor, Minneapolis: University of Minnesota Press.

Benjamin, A. (1989) *The Problem of Modernity: Adorno and Benjamin*, London: Verso. A collection of chapters by philosophers; see especially J. Hodge, 'Feminism and postmodernism'.

Buck-Morss, S. (1977) *The Origin of Negative Dialectics*, Brighton: Harvester Press.

Crooks, S. (1994) *Adorno: the Stars down to Earth*, London: Routledge. Read the 'Introduction: Adorno and authoritarian irrationalism'.

Jay, M. (1984) *Adorno*, London: Fontana. A great introduction from the Fontana Modern Masters series.

Nicholsen, S. (1997) *Exact Imagination Late Work: On Adorno's Aesthetics*, Cambridge, MA: MIT Press. A wonderful collection of articles on Adorno's aesthetics by one of Adorno's translators.

O'Neill. M. (ed.) (1999) *Adorno Culture and Feminism*, London: Sage. A collection of chapters by an international group of feminist scholars working with Adorno's theories, including the cited chapters by Becker-Schmidt and Flower Macannel.

O'Neill, M. in association with Giddens, S. Breatnach, P. Bagley, C. Bourne, D. and Judge, T. (2002) 'Renewed methodologies for social research: ethno-mimesis as performative praxis', *Sociological Review*, **50**(1).

O'Neill, M. (2004) 'Global refugees, (human) rights, citizenship and the law', in Cheng, S. (ed.) *Law, Justice and Power*, California: Stanford University Press.

Rose, G. (1978) *The Melancholy Science: an Introduction to the Thoughts of T.W. Adorno*, London: Routledge.

Witkin, R. (1998) *Adorno on Music*, London: Routledge. A detailed account of Adorno's work on music from a sociological perspective.

CHAPTER 7

Talcott Parsons

ROBERT HOLTON

Driving Impulses

Talcott Parsons (1902–1979) is regarded by some as the leading American sociologist of the twentieth century, by others as a theorist whose work is deeply flawed. What few scholars dispute is that Parsons took up the challenge of tackling the central questions posed by nineteenth-century sociology, while at the same time responding to contemporary intellectual and political issues. From the earlier period he took up the problem of social order, striving to find an answer to the question 'How is it that societies hold together?' His search for an answer led him to reject the economists' emphasis on self-interest, and to assert the importance of norms and values in social life. Meanwhile, Parsons was also deeply concerned with political issues faced by the world in which he lived. These included the struggle between capitalism and Communism, the advent of Fascism and world war, racial and ethnic conflict, and the lack of a stable global environment for political security.

Born into a religious milieu,[1] Parsons maintained an interest in the big questions that define the human condition, together with the ambition of bringing such issues within a single overarching framework of theory and explanation. These concerns engendered an abiding concern to construct theories about the social system, amounting to a truly comprehensive mapping of human society. This was designed to include both the social structures within which individuals find themselves, and the actions of individuals and organizations seeking to choose meaningful courses of action in pursuit of their goals. Some sociologists have focused predominantly on the 'macro-', or large-scale phenomena such as markets or bureaucracies, while others have been mostly concerned with 'micro-' or small-scale phenomena, such as intimate interpersonal relations and personality formation. In Parsons' case, he attempted to look at both, bridging what has often been called the 'macro–micro' divide in social thought.

Parsons' mapping of the contours of social life also led him to reject the excessive development of intellectual specialization. This meant that economists were experts on the economy, political scientists on the political system and psychologists on the personality. The problem with this was that it failed to address the interactions and exchanges between the different parts of society, including, for example, the ways in which political and cultural phenomena influenced the economy and vice versa. One key task for sociology was to explain such interconnections. This required syntheses bringing together elements from a range of disciplines, including economics, social psychology, psychiatry and political science as well as sociology, and also a range of thinkers such as **Weber, Durkheim, Freud,** Alfred Marshall and Keynes.[2]

Parsons was a theorist, dealing with big questions at a high level of generality. Yet, this does not mean he never conducted research, or took an interest in particular events around him. On the contrary, his theoretical work was also designed to unravel the mysteries and resolve the puzzles surrounding the practical everyday life of individuals and societies. Situations that Parsons explored included illness and interactions between doctor and patient and divisions of labour and responsibility within the family between men and women. Underlying these concerns was a resolve to understand both the nature of modern society, and the direction of contemporary social changes.

While Parsons' thought is highly relevant to real-world situations, it is clear that his primary significance is as a grand theorist. Most of his work is intentionally written in a highly abstract language, and organized within conceptual frameworks that are complex and often unfamiliar. For some, this renders much of his work unreadable, but those prepared to dig deeper have often been rewarded with profound insights into the nature of social life. The justification for theoretical abstraction as pursued by Parsons, and certain other key thinkers in this volume, is that it may offer pathways of understanding that are unavailable in common sense.

An intellectual passion to comprehend human society as a systematic entity was certainly a driving force in Parsons' sociology. But alongside that was a moral concern for the desirability of social reform. Parsons took a stand for liberal-democratic values against totalitarianism and racism. A key element in this moral vision was that of social inclusion. No individual or social group should be denied full membership of what he called 'the societal community', on the basis of characteristics ascribed to that person or group on account of their social status or race. Similarly, no political authority should so dominate the non-governmental institutions of society, such as business, the professions or the universities, that their capacity to advance personal autonomy, professional ethics and intellectual freedom would be undermined. Parsons' sociological account of how modern society operated was also an account of how social life should be organized so as to realize the values he believed in.

Key Issues

Social Action and Social System

The basic building blocks of Parsons' general theory of social life are very generalized and abstract. Yet they are worth the effort required to understand them because they deal with nearly all the major theoretical questions that sociology has considered hitherto. A useful starting point involves the twin concepts of 'social action' and 'social system'. One of the most fundamental issues in sociology is the so-called structure–agency dilemma. Are the actions of individuals and groups determined by the large structures of social life? Or do actors make voluntary choices according to their own values or objectives? Examples of structural determination include Marx's emphasis on the mode of production, or Durkheim's emphasis on modes of social solidarity. Examples of voluntary choice include economists' emphasis on the market sovereignty of consumers following their preferences.

Parsons' initial approach to this problem was to think in terms of what he called a 'voluntaristic theory of action'.[3] Social action did indeed involve voluntary choices by individuals and groups in pursuit of their objectives. Social action, in this sense, must be meaningful to those involved. Yet the matter could not be left there, because three vital additional elements were necessary to any general mapping of social life.

First, there was the problem of the component parts of voluntaristic action, including its characteristic forms of motivation. The dominant utilitarian model held by economists emphasizes the importance of self-interest in pursuit of personal tastes or preferences, developed outside society. Parsons did not doubt the importance of self-interest, but rejected the proposition that this was at the centre of social action. One of the difficulties here was that self-interest deals only with the means by which actors may seek to realize their ends, rather than with the origins of their ends, by which is meant the things they value. Utilitarianism, in effect, produced an incomplete and excessively narrow account of social action, leaving out the ways that the values and social rules embodied within human interaction influence individual wants and desires. Fashion is a classic case of socially derived wants.

A second, related point arises here. The problem with utilitarianism is not simply its abbreviated account of the cultural richness of human life. Where it also fails is in its inability to account for social order. Parsons here raises what he calls the 'utilitarian dilemma'.[4] If the ends of social action are random and arbitrary, contingent on the biology or psychology of the individual, then how is it possible for such individual actions to be reconciled with each other in an orderly and predictable way? If self-interest rules, then society would be in a constant state of war, as individuals clashed with each other.

One way that utilitarians tried to resolve this difficulty was to portray social action as a rational response to the external environment faced by the actor. Given the constraints of the situation they faced, such as limited natural resources, rational individuals acted in a self-interested way to maximize benefits and minimize costs. For economists, the institution of the market was one means by which the rational pursuit of self-interest would generate order and pattern. Within given external conditions, equilibrium between supply and demand would occur through the price mechanism. Order would eventuate, as if by the operation of a hidden hand, rather than any deliberate construction of regulatory rules or laws.

This kind of reply did not satisfy Parsons. First, he disputed the proposition that rationality and self-interest necessarily resulted in the harmonization of different actions. People made choices for a range of different value-driven reasons, and according to a range of social definitions of the situation they found themselves in. Neither rationality nor self-interest was sufficient to produce integration into a stable pattern of rules. Second, Parsons felt that undue emphasis on the given conditions under which action took place threatened to undermine the voluntaristic approach to action. In other words, once you start to explain individual actions in terms of the surrounding environment, you start to undermine the idea of individual choice or autonomy, and reinstate the importance of structural determination.

The way out of this dilemma for Parsons was to bring social values and rules of conduct (or norms) fully into the picture. This helps sociology to go one better than economics by explaining where the ends of action come from. They derive not from innate individual tastes and desires, but from society. Social order arises from the rules that regulate self-interest, and from the development of shared value systems that provide individuals with meaningful ways of selecting between courses of action.

In emphasizing the normative as well as the self-interested side of social action, Parsons accepted that there were indeed social constraints on social action. A third element was then needed to complete a general mapping of social life, namely some way of systematizing both the types of social action individuals engaged in, and the types of constraint or challenge that all human societies must face. These questions led Parsons to speak of the social system,[5] and not simply social action.

A system may be regarded as any entity that is relatively free-standing in relation to other entities. To say that nations are social systems is to say that they exhibit socially generated patterns in the way they function, and in the way the various component parts, such as the economy, government, the law and so forth, mesh with one another. Parsons' idea of the social system drew on his earlier interest in biology, and in particular the human body. Just as the body comprises a range of different organs (heart, lungs, liver and so on) to perform the vital functions necessary for its survival and growth, so society requires institutions (for example households, firms, government and so on) capable of fulfilling functions necessary for society's equilibrium and development. The attraction of this model was that it emphasized the key importance of differentiation between specialized types of social function and organization. Different institutions perform different functions.

The next step was to identify the basic social functions that social systems must successfully perform if they are to survive. Parsons focused on four. The first involved adaptation (A) to the external or natural environment from which scarce physical resources derive, or, put more simply, the economic function. The second was called goal attainment (G), meaning the political utilization of resources to meet particular ends. The third function of integration (I) refers to the achievement of legitimate rules or norms to regulate the entire system, reflected, for example, in law. The fourth function, latent pattern maintenance (L), is to do with the transformation of values that are personal to the individual into value patterns that are shared and stable within a given system.

This four-function theory is often referred to by the acronym AGIL. Taken as a whole, it is intended as a comprehensive account of the challenges faced by actors in any social system, large or small. Any social entity may then be regarded as a social system, provided it meets the test of being autonomous from the broader environment. Parsons is not talking only of the social system of nation-states, but of more micro-level organizational social systems, as well as the most macro-level system, namely global society.

The patient reader is at this point entitled to ask whether this vast theoretical edifice is really capable of being applied to real-world situations. Parsons, as we shall see below, was convinced it could.

Evolution and Modernity

Like earlier generations of sociologists, Parsons struggled to understand the distinctive character of modern society as it had emerged in Western Europe and North America since the sixteenth century. Most western thinkers until recently have approached this enterprise in evolutionary terms. 'Social evolutionism' refers to the theory that human society contains within it an unfolding potential to develop new institutions and ways of life. This potential is realized insofar as social arrangements emerge that are somehow better able to meet human needs than those which went before. Evolutionary change typically takes place through a series of stages. These are usually regarded as progressive, lending to evolutionism a strongly normative as well as scientific tone. Put more simply, progress is good.

Parsons' sociological predecessors had focused on a wide-ranging set of indicators of modernity, from the dominance of society over nature through technological change, to a greater autonomy for individuals in relation to social rules. Parsons incorporated many of these earlier strands of analysis, but came to the view that a more complex and multidimensional approach to evolutionary change was required.[6] Human history was not simply a matter of one single evolutionary process, such as technological change or economic individualism, but involved a far wider set of elements. At a system level, these encompassed every aspect of the AGIL framework, including economic, political, legal and cultural institutions. At the level of social interaction within the real world, changes were also evident in the challenges and choices faced by individuals in giving meaning to their actions.

Parsons tried to bring 'system' and 'action' together, within four sets of **pattern variables,**[7] namely *universalism/particularism*, *achievement/ascription*, *specificity/diffuseness* and *neutrality/affectivity*. Modernity was defined in terms of contrasts between the former and the latter terms in each of these pairs. It meant universalism rather than particularism, an emphasis on achievement rather than ascription, specificity rather than diffuseness in social roles and greater neutrality rather than affectivity.

Pattern variables

1. Particularism versus universalism: *Actors have to decide whether to judge a person by general criteria (universalism) or criteria unique to that person (particularism).*
2. Achievement versus ascription: *Actors have to decide whether to judge people by performance criteria (such as educational qualifications, professional credentials, business 'success' and so on) or in terms of qualities that are ascribed on the basis of heredity of other forms of endowment (such as age, sex, race, caste and so on) that lack a performance standard.*
3. Specificity versus diffuseness: *Actors have to choose, in any particular situation, whether to engage with others in a holistic way concerned with many aspects of that person's activities or well-being, or only for specific restricted purposes. An example of the latter is the dentist's concern with a patient's teeth to the exclusion of any other aspect of that person's life.*
4. Neutrality versus affectivity: *Actors can either engage in a relationship for instrumental reasons without the involvement of feelings (neutrality) or for emotional reasons (affectivity).*[8]

If this is what modernity comprises, how then may the historical development of modernity be understood? Parsons' argument was that social systems, which developed institutions capable of better performing all four AGIL functions, had an evolutionary advantage over those which did not.

This argument was applied to western history, wherein Parsons located key institutions that gave particular societies an evolutionary advantage over others.[9] Examples included the development of common law in seventeenth-century England, which provided a universal set of norms that helped secure individual rights and property rights free from the arbitrary personal intervention of monarchs. He felt this innovation provided a better solution to society's integration (I) problems than previous forms of law, and gave England an evolutionary advantage over other places where law was less secure. Law and integration, rather than the customary focus on technological change, help explain why the first Industrial Revolution occurred in England.

Professions

A more concrete contemporary interest of Parsons was the evolution of the professions as a key aspect of modernity.[10] It was from a study of the professions that Parsons first developed the 'pattern variables' mentioned above. In line with his general emphasis on the normative basis of social action, Parsons regarded the professions not primarily as self-interested economic actors, but rather as occupations regulated by a normative code of conduct towards clients. The professional relationship with the client was regarded as an example of characteristics such as universalism and neutrality, whereby professional services would be guaranteed to the client on a standardized basis, and in a detached manner, irrespective of the particular ascribed status or social characteristics of the client. What mattered was not which social group the client came from, but rather their exposure to universalistic professional knowledge by a provider motivated by more than self-interest.

This argument, based on evidence gathered in a US context of limited state involvement in healthcare, took the market-based context of health delivery as the norm for its analysis of the professions. This served to highlight Parsons' more general argument about the limits of self-interest as a basis for social order. Markets dominated by individual self-interest could not explain the stable rule-bound patterns of social interaction that we see when we look at the operation of professional–client relations. These depend rather on normative commitments, such as the idea of the service ethic or vocation for their articulation. According to Parsons, the rewards to individual professionals accrue not primarily in terms of money. Nor do they depend on the ascribed social background of the professional, as in the case of members of families of traditional healers. They arise instead from individual achievement measured against professional standards. The compliance of the client in such interactions is dependent upon the professional acting in accordance with these standards.

Parsons applied this model of the professions more generally to modern society. He saw it as one more manifestation of the limits of self-interest and the importance of normative rules of behaviour in generating social order. The hardest challenge he faced in this respect was to apply the model to economic life in general, and the operation of large corporations in particular. Where once the functions of ownership and management had been conducted by family members within the family firm, the modern corporation was now typically a limited liability company, owned by a mass of shareholders, but operated by specialist managers.

For Parsons this had two points of significance. The first was that older forms of divisive class conflict between capitalist owners and a propertyless proletariat would no longer be central to modern society.[11] The old schism between capital and labour was reminiscent of the social and economic divide between lord and peasant. It was being superseded by opportunities for upward social mobility created by mass access to education, and processes of occupational specialization.

The second point of significance for Parsons was that he expected the increasing autonomy of management as a profession to generate the same kinds of normative rules of behaviour that he had found in the medical profession. Self-interest and profit-seeking within the corporation would certainly not be undermined, but they would, in his view, be subjected to a more ethical discipline emanating from managers. This particular argument was, however, based more on expectation than observation, as Parsons was the first to admit.

The Sick Role

A final substantive aspect of Parsons' sociology is his major contribution to the analysis of health and illness. This work is of great significance because it shows Parsons claiming for sociology areas of investigation conventionally allocated to biology and medicine. The principal feature of this claim was his notion of the sick role.[12]

For Parsons, sickness was not only a biological state, but also a matter of social significance. One did not become sick independent of the social system, rather one was socially defined as sick. The social definition of sickness was elaborated in his idea that sickness was a social role with a particular set of features.

Four such features of the sick role were identified. The first was that it justified the withdrawal of the sick person from normal work and family duties.

Second, the person was not seen as responsible for his or her condition, and hence could not become well without outside intervention. Third, there was a responsibility on the sick person to become well, withdrawal only being legitimate if subsequent return was accepted as a duty. Fourth, the person should seek professionally competent healthcare and therapy.

These role expectations were also connected to broader analyses of social order, linking social action at the individual level, with the wider social system. Illness in this sense was regarded by Parsons as a kind of deviancy, where normative controls, such as the obligation to get well through medical therapy, were essential to the restoration of the normal functioning of both the individual and the society. Yet it is a misreading of Parsons to suggest he believed all sick people would take up the obligations of the sick role and seek recovery. On the contrary, he felt that certain kinds of chronic sickness, and much mental illness, were responses to social tensions where individuals felt unable to cope. Sickness in this sense offered a legitimate role, by permitting withdrawal from stressful situations.

In Parsons' discussion of the sick role, we see both his general theoretical ambitions and his concern for concrete interactions of daily life at work. At one and the same time, he is challenging the idea that 'the invading microbe' is the root cause of all sickness, while claiming for sociology a part in the fine-grained analysis of health and illness, within – not outside – society.

Seeing Things Differently

Great social thinkers are noteworthy not only for the array of concepts and theories they develop, but also for their creative capacity to assist us to see things differently. Sometimes we do not become aware of the potential insights contained in their work until faced with a personal experience that we have tried to make sense of. The following autobiographical episode illustrates that sociologists are sometimes the last to apply sociology to themselves, but that a key thinker like Parsons may sometimes belatedly come to the rescue.

University teachers spend a good deal of time in committees, trying to exercise forms of self-government appropriate to their professional autonomy. In the university where I work, we periodically have staff meetings to discuss our teaching and research, and a host of questions to do with resources like rooms and computers. I sometimes feel these meetings are an interruption to my work as a sociologist.

As I sit in these meetings, I hear colleagues debating with each other. Some bring their values to bear in a very open way, declaring this or that teaching philosophy to be good and others to be flawed in some way. They seek a consensus of values, but are often frustrated when value conflict seems irresolvable. Another way of debating is to speak instead of particular policies which it is felt will realize the complex set of goals present among a dozen or so strongly willed individuals. If a majority vote for a particular policy, say to devote more resources to teaching first-year and less to upper-year topics, then this will generally carry legitimacy. It is hard to get very far with this kind of discussion, however, without being aware of the level of human and financial resources that we have at our disposal to meet our policy pronouncements. Morally and politically driven arguments about where the department should go and what it should prioritize are fine, but can we really afford to implement them?

And of course it sometimes gets a bit heated, although no more so than any other body of people who care about what they do. At this point, some attempt is often made to keep things civil and fair, ensuring that the more vocal and opinionated do not drown out others. There is no written set of rules that enshrine such rules of debate and decision-making, but they have a reality nonetheless, some kind of sense of obligation to the department as such that usually puts a rein on excesses of moralizing or political self-interest.

Department meetings are fine, but I am usually pleased when they are over and I can get back to teaching and research. And then one day it hit me. The department was a social system in its own right, inasmuch as it is able to determine within limits the direction it will take. But more than that, it has a range of subsystems in operation, dealing with something like the AGIL functions that any system must successfully perform to survive and develop. If we pursue the G (policy-setting) and L (value-forming) functions too hard without thought of A (resources) or I (the overall integration of the department) functions, then we will get into trouble. This may take the form of an A (resource) crisis, or an I (integration) crisis. When I attend the departmental meeting then, I am not suspending an engagement with sociology for the next two hours. No, the sociological way of seeing things remains relevant all the time, and in all circumstances. Yet it took Parsons' highly abstract AGIL system theory for me to see this reality in my everyday work life.

Legacies and Unfinished Business

There are few fields in which the legacy of Parsons has not been felt. But his most significant impact has been twofold. First, he made major contributions in social theory and system theory. Much of this work drew on Parsons' synthesis of European and American strands of social thought. To assist this work, Parsons translated texts written in other languages into English, such as

Max Weber's *The Protestant Ethic and the 'Spirit' of Capitalism.*[13] Parsons' general theories of action and the social system have influenced other key thinkers in the postwar period, even though they have taken social theory in different directions from Parsons. This applies to the critical theorist **Jürgen Habermas**, who has produced a more radical version of system theory that emphasizes crisis as much as equilibrium.[14] It also applies to the psychoanalytic feminist **Nancy Chodorow**, who has developed a gendered analysis of personality formation, that goes beyond Parsons' very conservative account of child socialization and the nuclear family.[15]

The second kind of impact made by Parsons was in more specific areas such as the sociology of the professions, the family, medical sociology, sociology of education, economic sociology and social stratification. Research in each of these areas has taken Parsons' work as a major reference point, although it would be equally true to say that a good deal of what he wrote has become obsolete in the light of further study. One of the major reasons for this is the weakness of his work in discussing power and inequality. A range of critics across all the areas listed make the same general point.[16] Sociologists of the professions, for example, claim Parsons underestimates professional self-interest and power over clients, while exaggerating the impact of normative rules in regulating professional action. Economic sociologists, meanwhile, argue that Parsons prematurely announced the demise of capitalism, countering his rather benign view of economic life with an emphasis on continuing inequalities of power and personal life chances deriving from economic property rights.

While Parsons became the dominant theoretical figure in American sociology during the 1950s and early 1960s, the rising tide of criticism that greeted his work in the late 1960s and early 1970s led to a rapid process of eclipse.[17] This occurred in the context of radical social upheaval in American society, linked to student protests against the Vietnam War and the military–industrial complex, explosions of black protest in the inner city, and the emergence of feminist movements to challenge the gender division of labour and conventional forms of sexuality. Many similar processes were evident in other western societies. The net effect was to render Parsons' discussion of social order, achieved through value consensus and commitment to normative integration, very shaky. Sociologists returned to what was now called 'conflict theory', in contrast with Parsons' emphasis on order.

Between the mid-1970s and the mid-1990s, however, the USA and western society went a long way towards restabilization. Institutions such as the regulated market, the democratic polity and the rule of law, which Parsons regarded as conferring evolutionary advantage on social systems, experienced a revival in the restabilized West, boosted also by the collapse of Soviet

Communism in Russia and Eastern Europe. These social trends helped to encourage a revival in Parsonian sociology, which has continued apace.[18]

One notable feature of contemporary theory is the attempt to confront and reconcile Parsons with his critics. This involves returning to Parsons' texts to identify previously unperceived strengths as well as weaknesses. One such underappreciated resource is Parsons' nuanced account of socialization. This was previously regarded as an almost automatic effect of the operation of the social system, drawing the criticism that Parsons operated with an oversocialized conception of human actors. Put another way, it was assumed Parsons' theory of the social system left individuals as robots programmed by an all-powerful set of rules.

This interpretation of Parsons is, however, wide of the mark. What he was trying to say was more subtle than his critics supposed. At one level, socialization did operate in systemic ways through the core institutions of society founded on rules and values. Yet Parsons also wanted to leave space for the individual and for individualism, which he saw as such a crucial feature of modern society. He reconciled individual autonomy with the social system by claiming that we learn to be individuals, but this learning process is never automatic nor is it without tensions and conflicts. One reason for this is that one can never be socialized into the social system as such, only into particular patterns of life, within the home, the school and the workplace. The processes operating here do not create robots but rather individuals with particular biographies and trajectories through life. Socialization is never smooth, perfect or trouble free.[19]

Many of the conflicts of the 1960s, for example, were regarded by Parsons as integration (I function) problems, stemming from the continuing exclusion of particular groups (for example blacks or students), from the goal-setting (G function) political process. Democracy was the most satisfactory way of meeting goal-setting (G) functions, but not if significant parts of society were excluded. Insofar as extensions of citizenship rights and new political participation structures achieve greater inclusion of the excluded, so too will reintegration occur.

The net effect of the Parsons revival has been to encourage a more open, less partisan sociology that moves beyond polarized opposites, such as conservative Parsonian versus radical sociology, or order versus conflict sociology. The search for a more persuasive synthesis of different sociological traditions is entirely within the spirit of Parsons' work, and that of the key thinkers before him such as Marx and Weber. Parsons' legacy is therefore rich, stimulating and still highly relevant. It remains a legacy worth embracing.

FURTHER READING

Gerhardt, U. (2002) *Talcott Parsons: an Intellectual Biography*, Cambridge: Cambridge University Press. This study emphasizes the committed social and political project that animated Parsons' work. Gerhardt argues that Parsons was determined that sociological analysis should be geared towards the defence and development of contemporary democratic forms.

Hamilton, P. (1983) *Talcott Parsons*, London/Chichester: Tavistock/Horwood Ellis. This is an excellent guide through the different stages and phases of development within Parsons' work.

Hamilton, P. (ed.) (1992) *Talcott Parsons: Critical Assessments*, 4 vols, London: Routledge. An invaluable collection of many of the most important critical engagements with many different aspects of Parsons' writings.

Holton, R. (1991) 'Talcott Parsons and the integration of economic and sociological theory', *Sociological Inquiry*, **61**(1): 102–14.

Moss, L. and A. Savchenko (eds) (2006) *Talcott Parsons: Economic Sociologist of the Twentieth Century*, Oxford: Blackwell.

Robertson, R. and Turner, B.S. (eds) (1991) *Talcott Parsons: Theorist of Modernity*, London: Sage. A stimulating collection of commissioned chapters that engaged with Parsons' relationship to modernity at the time when the modernity and post-modernity debate was at its height.

Wrong, D. (1961) 'The oversocialised conception of man in modern sociology', *American Sociological Review*, **26**: 183–93. This is a classic critique of Parsons for overemphasizing the extent to which social influences dominate individuals and limit their autonomy.

PART II

CONTENTS

CHAPTER 8

Robert K. Merton

ALAN SICA

Sociology in the Post-Mertonian Mode

When Robert K. Merton died on 23 February, 2003, *The New York Times* ran a one-third-page obituary, with photo, something that seldom happens in honour of a sociologist. Even notable scholars, like Merton's student and colleague, Peter Blau (d. 2002), have received no mention in the *Times* when they expired. It was clear that the Merton obituary had been in the file, waiting, for some time, bearing the strange title, 'Robert K. Merton, Versatile Sociologist and Father of the Focus Group, Dies at 92.' Merton himself would hardly have accredited 'the focus group' as his main achievement, yet perhaps Michael T. Kaufman, the obit's author, was on to something. The other major development regarding Merton during the last few years was the publication of *The Travels and Adventures of Serendipity: A Study in Sociological Semantics and the Sociology of Science* (2004), a unique monograph by Merton and Elinor Barber (d. 1999), finished in 1958, but which he refused to publish in English until moments prior to his own death. Between these apparently disparate facts – that the *Times* judged his lasting achievement to be the invention of the focus group, indispensable tool in market and political survey research, and that his final book dealt with the sociologically quizzical occurrence of happenstance – there lies some insight into Merton's troubling legacy, which, at the height of its influence, embodied the most hopeful, robust and boldest vision of what sociology could accomplish since the days of his spiritual mentor, **Emile Durkheim**, a century ago. That sociology has fallen in self-estimation and external acclaim since those heady days of the 1950s and 60s goes without saying. Merton's role in that rise and fall is something worth considering.

Approaching Merton

The list of entire books and articles principally committed to explaining or elaborating Robert K. Merton's contributions to social science is long and distinguished. His core work, *Social Theory and Social Structure*, has been translated into a dozen languages since 1949, when it first appeared in English, and has required 30 printings to fill the global market's demand.[1] Along with perhaps one other book from the same period – Gerth and Mills' 1946 compilation, *From Max Weber* – this collection of Merton's earlier essays is as close to a bible as one is likely to come when surveying social theories that provided inspiration and conceptual guidelines for the most fruitful social research undertaken since the Second World War.

While this intense veneration was surely gratifying for Merton and his legion of followers, it presents a serious dilemma for the expositor hoping to give a newcomer some sense of the process whereby Merton's name has become synonymous with analytic brilliance, conceptual creativity and intellection at the highest level. Simply put, there is too much Merton to compress within the confines of a brief chapter – too many of his own books, articles, essays, introductions; too many ideas, research strategies, programmes for projects still waiting to be carried out; too many extraordinary students, commentators and researchers who have 'fine-tuned' aspects of Merton's thinking or empirical work. (As only one piece of evidence from among dozens that exist indicating Merton's nonpareil position in the field, consider that in 1990, 52 years after his dissertation saw print, an entire volume was dedicated to analysing its *continuing* significance by means of chapters written by 18 scholars, including by Merton himself, and four reprints, plus one new entry.[2])

Thus, a simplifying choice must be made in order to render an economical presentation of his accomplishments. Such a reduction will necessarily 'privilege' one avenue over a host of possible others, in an effort to offer what some readers might nevertheless regard as an artificially tidy description of Merton's sociological world and, just as interestingly, his world-view. Therefore, this chapter does not purport to present, or even to describe in broad terms, all Merton's achievements in sociology or its theories. Rather, it highlights his special use of theoretical language, the creation of which uniquely marks his work as superior to that of any other American social theorist in the realm of conceptualization qua linguistic innovation.

It should therefore be emphasized that this is not Merton's own preferred mode of exposition in the realm of theory work. As he wrote nearly 50 years ago, 'The *distinctive* intellectual contributions of the sociologist are found primarily in the study of unintended consequences (among which are latent functions) of social practices as well as in the study of anticipated consequences (among which are manifest functions).' Reprinted in 1991 as part of a sourcebook of pregnant sociological quotations that Merton himself co-edited,[3] this could well be taken as his own s'ociological self-image, and bears notably small concurrence with the partial evaluation of his work expressed in what follows.

Theories of the middle range; and open-ended functionalism

At the heart of Merton's approach is a combination of two elements. The first is an interest in analysing the part played by particular social arrangements and practices in the reproduction of, and the capacities of, a social system. This is an interest in analysing the functions *of these arrangements and practices. Where the introduction of certain practices is seen to prevent the reproduction of a social system or to undermine the capacities it possesses, then they are seen as* dysfunctional. *Merton's approach to functional analysis is one that leaves open whether or not any set of social arrangements or mechanisms is indeed functional or dysfunctional. This is always a question for theoretically informed empirical investigation.*

This leads to the second major element in Merton's approach, theories of the middle range. These are theories of delimited scope that are empirically grounded. They are delimited in the sense that they are specialist theories dealing with particular aspects of social reality, rather than being grand theories about whole societies and their historical trajectories. They do, however, have a generalizing quality, thus providing empirical investigations with significance beyond the specifics of the individual case. Middle-range theories typically begin with a conceptual image, much as in the natural sciences Boyle's theory of atmospheric pressure began with the imagery of the atmosphere as a 'sea of air', which in turn led to Pascal's inference that there should be less pressure on a mountain top than on its base. Among the many conceptual images that Merton singles out as forming the basis of fruitful hypotheses and theoretical problems in the social sciences are those of: role-sets and status-sets; institutional interdependence; relative deprivation with respect to reference groups; and anomic behaviour as a consequence of sociostructural constraints frustrating attempts to fulfil culturally encouraged goals.

For such conceptual images to have theoretical worth, they need to generate distinctive problems for sociological enquiry. The theory of reference groups and relative deprivation *does this by questioning the common-sense, 'self-evident', idea that in a mass disaster, for example, the 'magnitude of objective loss is related linearly to the subjective appraisal of the loss and that this appraisal is confined to one's own experience'.*[4] *Empirical investigation of specific instances informed by this theory reveals that 'under specifiable conditions, families suffering serious losses will feel less deprived than those suffering smaller losses if they are in situations leading them to compare themselves to people suffering even more severe losses'.*[5]

Another conceptual image, that of role-sets, *allows one to see the connection between middle-range theory and functional analysis in Merton's work. Instead of seeing a social position, such as a mother, a politician or a sportswoman, as a single role, Merton reserves the term 'status' to denote the social position and insists that all of these positions/statuses contain a number of different roles within them. They each demand from their incumbents not just the enactment of one role but, rather, the enactment of a number of roles, a role-set. The image of the role-set draws attention to the fact that any one status, say that of a teacher, an army captain, a husband or a medical student, involves its incumbent in an array of roles and role relationships, each with their own sets of expectations and obligations. Thus, 'a person in the status of medical student plays not only the role of student vis-à-vis the correlative status of his teachers, but also an array of other roles relating him diversely to others in the system: other students, physicians, nurses, social workers, medical technicians, and the like'.*[6] *The distinctive problem this image generates for sociological enquiry is that of identifying the social mechanisms that allow the medical student to fulfil the expectations of all those with whom he has role relationships. It directs us to ask how, in particular sociohistorical circumstances, she can sustain all these diverse role expectations without undue stress and conflicts between the different roles that make up the role-set. This is a question informed by functional analysis. It is asking about the reproduction of certain social functions and capacities. In line with Merton's general approach, it is open-ended. While we have just posed it in* functional *terms, asking about how stresses and strains are avoided in order to reproduce a smoothly functioning role-set, it is just as possible to reverse the emphasis. So, the question can just as well be posed in terms of whether there are any social mechanisms that are* dysfunctional, *which fail to operate to sustain the stability of role-sets, 'with resulting inefficiency, confusion, and conflict'.*[7] *There is no assumption, says Merton, 'that role-sets operate with substantial efficiency. For this middle-range theory is not concerned with the historical generalization that a degree of social order or conflict prevails in society but with the analytical problem of identifying the social mechanisms which produce a greater degree of order or less conflict than would obtain if these mechanisms were not called into play.'*[8]

As a propaedeutic to this heterodox way of understanding Merton's special place in the history of contemporary theory, it might be useful to recall some 'textual history'. In 1949, still just 39, Merton pointedly distinguished his goals as a theorist and scientific researcher from those of the artist, writing a passage on 'paradigms' (anticipating Kuhn's usage) that has become famous among his many readers:

> Contributing to the tendency for sociological exposition to become lengthy rather than lucid is the tradition – inherited slightly from philosophy, substantially from history, and greatly from literature – of writing sociological accounts vividly and intensely to convey all the rich fullness of the human scene. The sociologist who does not disavow this handsome but alien heritage becomes intent on searching for the exceptional constellation of words that will best express the *particularity* of the sociological case in hand, rather than on seeking out the objective, generalizable concepts and relationships it exemplifies – the

> core of a science as distinct from the arts. Too often, this misplaced use of genuine artistic skills is encouraged by the plaudits of a lay public, gratefully assuring the sociologist that he writes like a novelist and not like an overly domesticated and academically henpecked Ph.D. Not infrequently, the sociologist pays for this popular applause, for the closer one approaches eloquence, the farther one retreats from methodical sense ... If true art consists in concealing all signs of art, true science consists in revealing its scaffolding as well as its finished structure.[9]

For my purposes, the most intriguing and telling words in this bold passage disclose Merton's belief that sociologists who embrace 'this handsome *but alien* heritage' (my emphases) – springing, as it does, from artistically inspired prose – run the serious risk of losing their credentials as 'scientists' in search of 'objective, generalizable concepts'. And yet Merton's very name has become synonymous with unrivalled sociological prose. It is around this apparent contradiction that what follows is composed, in an effort to illuminate part of Merton's continuing appeal and importance for devout students of social thought, on the one hand, and social researchers, on the other.

The Uniqueness of Merton's Sociology

It would be hard to compose a better summary tribute to Robert K. Merton's 60-year record as a sociologist and social theorist than that provided by Piotr Sztompka, one of Merton's most informed expositors, in his opening paragraph to the latest collection of the latter's work:

> Rarely has the heritage of sociology been so deeply savored and dramatically enriched as in the life and work of Robert K. Merton. Nourished by a bountiful range of classical authors and guided by a succession of remarkable mentors, Merton opened up fruitful areas of inquiry along lines that he and generations of others would pursue for decades. The self-fulfilling prophecy, focussed interview (whence 'focus groups'), opportunity structure, middle-range theory, manifest and latent function, role-sets and status-sets, social dysfunctions, locals and cosmopolitans, scientific paradigms, the Matthew effect, accumulation of advantage and disadvantage, self-exemplification of sociological ideas, strategic research site, reconceptualization, and the serendipity pattern in research are some of his ingenious generative concepts. Some of these concepts in turn have proved so useful that, once adopted in sociology, they have then entered the common parlance in ways that obscure their origins, a process Merton describes colourfully as 'obliteration by incorporation'.[10]

Among the most famous and thoroughly 'obliterated' of all Merton's analytic expressions – having been successively reduced, in unacknowledged form, from scientific prose into journalistic cant – is 'the unanticipated consequences of social action'. It began as the inspired notion of a 26-year-old graduate student at Harvard, who had the wit to crystallize this widespread sociocultural process in the first volume of the *American Sociological Review*, which has since become the top journal in the discipline.[11]

Merton has always been extremely wise, as well as fortunate, in his timing, professional affiliations and the corresponding reception of his ideas. Along with the journal article just mentioned, he also produced several brief, pithy 'classics' – a weary word nowadays, to be sure, but one well earned in this case – before he reached his thirtieth year. These included one that elaborated Durkheim's theory of anomie, reprinted 28 times before 1975,[12] and another on bureaucratic personality, which was reproduced in 19 subsequent loci after its initial appearance.[13] When one adds to this a masterful dissertation that became a foundational work in the sociology of science,[14] an additional 15 well-received articles and book chapters, plus 50 or so book reviews, all in print before 1940 when Merton turned 30, a sociological virtuoso (in **Weber**'s sense) was obviously in the making.

Thus, it can truly be said, amplifying Sztompka's remarks, that if any single scholar personifies the best about American sociology during its most optimistic period of intellectual and professional development (roughly 1937 until 1970),[15] this person would be Merton. There are many reasons for this, as many psychological as sociological, historical as well as political. But a key identifying characteristic, something uniquely his own, that has granted Merton's work its singular durability and appeal over the past 60 years, for social scientists of all types, concerns the quality not only of his analysis and sheer knowledge, but of his extraordinary attention to questions of language. Because so many sociologists of his generation and after chose to emphasize the 'scientific' nature of their enterprise, they slighted prose in order to accentuate their skill with enumeration. Merton, as much a historian and linguist as sociologist, never took that route, which gave him the opportunity to speak far beyond the perimeters of sociology, and directly to the concerns of scholars who normally regard his discipline with hostility or dismissal. Merton's induction into honorary scholarly societies worldwide has as much to do with his cultivated gracefulness, in thought and word, as with what might in a simpler writer be termed 'his ideas per se'. Somehow this hackneyed phrase jangles even louder than usual when applied to him.

The way that Merton transferred to students his great regard for the language and practices of systematic discovery was well remembered by the mathematical sociologist, James S. Coleman, nearly 40 years later: 'Merton was not content to develop his theoretical categories and show us their meaning', but also put them directly to analytic and empirical use.[16] In addition, and under the lifelong inspiration of his teacher at Harvard, George Sarton, Merton directed sociology graduate students in Coleman's cohort at Columbia to work their way through studies of scientific discovery and the maturation of various fields, in order to understand where exactly on the disciplinary continuum sociology lay. Sarton's legendary rigour as a historian of science gave Merton licence to expect similar dedication from his charges. Yet at the same time he asked them to march through Parsons' newly published *The Social System* with a level of hermeneutic care which at the time was scarce in American sociology, and has only rarely occurred since. Modern sociologists had not, until Merton's arrival, normally aspired to become great readers of difficult texts; 'close reading' did not appear in their methodology handbooks. Among the many innovations Merton can fairly claim vis-à-vis the role of language in social theory is this insistence upon vigorous hermeneutic practices within an influential graduate programme. Interestingly, the obvious connection between Merton's innovative pedagogy at Columbia and the venerable hermeneutic tradition, hundreds of years old, has seldom been noted as such.

One could go on interminably about Merton's lifelong love affair with linguistic innovation and creativity (most famously documented in his book best known to non-sociologists, *On the Shoulders of Giants*).[17] What was said 40 years ago about the great popular historian of the Middle Ages, Henry Osborn Taylor – who also taught, although briefly, at Columbia – applies equally well to Merton:

> He was a literary craftsman. The times change, of course, and new historical evidence requires new syntheses. Grace of style is not enough in any age to give a book permanence. A book, however, which combines the gift of clear prose with a truly cultivated thoughtfulness can have a timelessness all its own.[18]

That Merton has applied throughout his career 'a truly cultivated thoughtfulness' in combination with prose of memorable lucidity has become almost a platitude among careful readers. Even his (relatively few) detractors admit to the seductive quality of his writings, not only on readers predisposed to agreement with him, but also upon sceptics.

Here is a sample of typical Merton prose from an important essay, one that has been fixed on graduate school reading lists for nearly 30 years:

> The same point was made recently by the physicist, A. A. Moles, who said that scientists are 'professionally trained to conceal from themselves their deepest thought' and to 'exaggerate unconsciously the rational aspect' of work done in the past. What must be emphasized here is that the practice of glossing over the

> actual course of inquiry results largely from the mores of scientific publication which call for a passive idiom and format of reporting which imply that ideas develop without benefit of human brain and that investigations are conducted without benefit of human hand.[19]

Many of what became standard aspects of Mertonian rhetoric are here: a tantalizing opening reference to an obscure foreign savant whom no one in sociology should know; ironic detachment (often noted by Merton students) in the author's attitude toward the common practices of researchers more intent on covering their tracks than giving frank self-exposure to their mental processes of discovery; clean, bracing English prose, yet within a multiclausal sentence of almost Germanic construction; and, beneath it all, the promise of revelation – what one would expect from a magician or magus – about mysteries, the existence of which most readers had not yet even noted, but which the author had identified and also begun to solve, by means of brilliant textwork and even more arresting footnotes and asides.

Great acting depends on hiding technique from the audience so that only the portrayed character is perceivable. Much the same is true of accomplished writing. Merton, writer and teacher, seemed outwardly clear and indubitable, almost serene, about his desires and discoveries. But upon closer study, the quicksilver quality of his thinking, and the writing that carried it into the public sphere, becomes maddeningly evident, so that what Merton in 'clear and distinct' fashion might mean for one earnest party – in an ironic hermeneutic twist – seems wholly wrong-headed to another. For instance, if Merton was truly serious that the history and systematics of theorizing could profitably be separated, and ultimately that the palm goes to the latter as sociology evolves towards 'real' science, why did he spend such energy pursuing historical detail, not only within sociology proper, but from a half-dozen other fields as well?[20] It is easy to see that by using him as an exemplar, his readers could become with equal pride either historians of ideas or survey researchers, while simultaneously claiming his intellectual paternity. It is this very ambiguity of message that has, in part, contributed to the Merton mystique and helped sustain his influence over the past five decades.

Merton's Genesis

It was only when he was nearly 84 that Merton sketched his early years, claiming that his memory for personally significant incident was as imprecise as his memory for scholarly detail was exacting. Born in 'the slums of South Philadelphia' on 4 July, 1910, Meyer R. Schkolnick absorbed the city's many cultural offerings within walking distance of his home, including Stokowski's world-renowned symphony orchestra and a 10,000-volume Carnegie library. Through the encouraging complicity of the resident librarians, he regarded the latter as his 'private' store of knowledge. All this and more, taken together, is what Merton has called 'public capital', a necessary ingredient in an 'opportunity structure'[21] that would emancipate himself and countless others from what was later dubbed 'the social order of the slum'.[22] His self-transformation, at 14, into Robert K. Merlin (a stage name for his developing magic act) almost immediately became 'Merton', a less predictable name for a magician, and this was how he was known when he entered Temple College (within Temple University) several years later. As with many other upwardly mobile 'ethnic' youths, an 'American-sounding' name seemed important to Merton in the 1920s, as he explains: 'Names in the performing arts were [then] routinely Americanized; that is, to say, they were transmuted into largely Anglo-American forms. For this, of course, was the era of hegemonic Americanization, generations before the emergence of anything resembling today's multiculturalism.' By now it is almost trite to observe that the improbable metamorphosis of this son of poor immigrants into the world's most respected sociologist is itself a special act of (American) magic, the generalized processes of which have occupied Merton's imagination for some years.

Merton's startling trajectory through Temple and then Harvard has been well documented and, as Sztompka noted above, he was blessed with several excellent teachers and 'role models', not to mention a stellar set of peers once he got to Harvard. His luck began with his Temple sociology teacher, George E. Simpson, who, among many kindnesses, made certain during a professional meeting that Merton would meet the head of the young sociology department at Harvard, the volcanic Pitirim Sorokin, whose monumental *Contemporary Sociological Theories* (1928) Merton had read. Sorokin's daredevil escape from Bolshevik Russia, his pronounced cosmopolitanism, and his theory book made it clear to Merton that 'plainly he was the teacher I was looking for'.[23] Miraculously, or so it seemed, Merton was granted a scholarship and he entered the enchanted and 'serendipitous environment'[24] at Harvard. Despite the fact that neither scholar gave nor asked for any quarter when it came to intellectual matters, and remembering that Sorokin was twice his student's age, their relationship bore remarkable fruit. Merton was primarily responsible for the science and technology chapters in Sorokin's masterpiece, *Social and Cultural Dynamics* (1937–1941, in four large volumes), published two articles with him (one regarding medieval Arabian intellectual development, the other about 'social time'), and along the way also copy edited Parsons' first and probably best book, *The Structure of Social Action* (1937).

Meanwhile, Merton took full advantage of the phenomenal liveliness of scholarly life in Harvard during that period, and crossed disciplinary borders without compunction. His most important deviation from sociology proper involved persuading George Sarton, olympian historian of science, to work closely with him, which included opening to this precocious young scholar the pages of *Isis*, Sarton's journal for the history of science. From him Merton learned about the human background to scientific procedure and discovery, which new knowledge helped Merton initiate 'the sociology of science' in its American version.[25] In sum, the cadre of top-flight teachers and students at Harvard during Merton's tenure there was of such unusual quality that social science began to revolve around many of them, with Merton quickly at the head of this new legion. He had, not for the last time, been at the right place at the right time, largely, one could argue, owing to his own gifts and energy, but also through the luck of fortuitous meetings, readings and writings. A more Mertonian rendering would emphasize structurally opened possibilities that transcend the merely psychological. But a number of people, it could be shown, came upon very similar lines of opportunity between 1930 and 1940, and only one became Merton. Nevertheless, of the 'serendipitous', yet no less telling, nature of certain events throughout his career – from Temple to Harvard, on to Tulane for two years, and then to Columbia for more than fifty – he became only too aware.

Merton's Ideas and their Legacy

Speaking Merton for Forty Years without Knowing it: the Plenitude of Mertonian Notions

Already 30 years ago one could hear the slightly premature remark from sociologists who thought they were 'knowing' – one of Merton's favourite adjectives – that he had become 'the victim of his own success'; that the unintended consequence of his precocious brilliance, stylistic and substantive, had led to his own premature obliteration by ingestion, as it were. In a mythic move that Merton, knowing Frazer and Freud, would have understood, the children had consumed the father along with his heritage. His manifold theoretical 'interventions' (as they might now be termed) beginning in the late 1930s, whether pertaining to the sociology of knowledge, mass communications, social psychology, sociology of science or the history of theorizing, had become by 1970 so much the coin of the realm that ever-fewer readers knew their precise origin. And since sociology was riding a popular wave of societal and collegiate enthusiasm, giving due credit did not seem as important as it would later on when the dust had begun to settle, and the contributions of Merton's generation were beginning to be evaluated more carefully.

What this now means is that every introductory sociology textbook incorporates without acknowledgement a plenitude of Mertonian notions, those specifically his own or elaborated by his students, so that, along with Molière's 'cit', Mr Jordan, one might also exclaim, 'For more than 40 years I have been talking Merton without knowing it!'[26] Worse by far, the linguistic flotsam bequeathed by journalism to the 'educated' person's vocabulary includes regular use of 'self-fulfilling prophecy' and 'dysfunction' in such diluted form that the slogan 'I'm dysfunctional, you're dysfunctional' has become a night-club joke.[27] All this suggests that Merton's contribution to sociological thought has proved so engaging that it has virtually disappeared *as such* – at least those epigrammatic aspects of it which most readily lend themselves to capsule summary and transmission.

Although theory writers today dare not invoke certain terms without a nod to proper authorities – for example **Bourdieu**'s 'cultural capital', **Giddens**' 'structuration', 'communicative competence' from **Habermas**, or **Foucault**'s 'regimes of power–knowledge–pleasure' – the same cannot be said for Merton. Since 'everyone' knows about manifest and latent functions, role-sets and functional requisites, it would now be considered pedantic – for those who do know – to acknowledge these concepts' true progenitor. As well put by a man of Merton's generation who assayed the history of American theory with unusual perspicacity,[28] Merton's

> reputation will rest not upon any general systematic theory but rather upon the many fertile expressions he has introduced into the literature – expressions such as theories of the middle range, paradigms, unanticipated consequences of purposive social action, sociological ambivalence, the role-set, manifest and latent functions, the self-fulfilling prophecy, anticipatory socialization, reference group (in fact, Herbert Hyman's term, systematized by Merton and Alice S. Rossi) and many more.[29]

In marked opposition to Sztompka, Bierstedt believes that Merton's enormous list of publications, including as it does no single *magnum opus* 'about society' as such, but, rather, scores of essays addressed to an unfettered range of theoretical and substantive topics, makes it difficult to gauge Merton's long-term significance as a theorist. As much a master prose stylist as Merton, Bierstedt summarizes his view of this unique situation in memorable imagery: 'The first merit badge to be pinned on [Merton] is precisely this almost incredible range of interests, his moving with the speed and grace of a humming bird from one blossom to the next, never still but always seemingly in flight.'[30] Sztompka, while quoting this very line from Bierstedt elsewhere, argues forcefully for a contrary position, as have others.[31]

Of course, living well into one's ninth decade does pose for an author certain 'copyright' limitations to deference practices. Yet it is possible that by the time most of these younger theorists have reached their nineties, their terminological innovations will have become 'a collection of stale creampuffs'. So Ezra Pound designated his early poems when they were reissued, 55 years after their revolutionary detonation of Edwardian stuffiness.[32] Drawing an analogy between these two linguistic innovators is not so far-fetched after one considers the unschooled rhetoric of sociology in the 1930s, and Merton's studied remove from it. Bierstedt's opinion, that Merton's 'many fertile expressions', rather than a single, embracing theory, are what will propel his reputation into the future, is on its face more plausible, at least for the non-theory specialist, than the opposing view – even if the term 'expressions' does not properly convey the analytic labours that have gone into Merton's conceptual refinement over the past five decades.

Yet, leaving terminological precision aside, a thorny issue is indeed raised by observations of this sort, concerning phenomena about which Merton is, ironically enough, the leading expert: 'OBI' (obliteration by incorporation) and eponymy (naming discoveries for their notable predecessors in a given discipline). At what point do ritual citations become little more than attempts to legitimate current research, rather than, as they should be, attentive rethinking of foundational ideas? Put more prosaically, how frequently do scholars today read with hermeneutic alertness the essays Merton composed in the 1930s, 40s and 50s to which they give automatic obeisance in their bibliographies? Although hardly peculiar to Merton's legacy, in his case these questions become more troubling than might usually be the case for the very reason that he has systematically investigated these practices *as a social and intellectual process*.

Conceptual Virtuosity and Linguistic Elegance

That said, if opinions like Bierstedt's are not entirely wrong, at least two more questions arise. They pertain to the apparent course that sociality and literacy may well take under the influence of electronic communication, and the fate of 'traditional' scholarship that must come to terms with it. In the new world of the so-called postmodern, words carry less significance than images, and exacting attention to language *as representing a consensually acceptable reality* becomes ever-rarer – or so one reads in standard analyses of postmodernity. Thus, the sort of conceptual virtuosity and nearly Aristotelian concern for categorization and fine distinction, for which Merton has long been famous, accordingly loses some of its lustre. The same, of course, applies to any number of other theorists, but is particularly apt in Merton's case for the very reason that he exercised such care when creating his works. This claim on my part is based more on a study of recent cultural theory, which claims to have knowledge of contemporary conditions that surpasses the obvious, than on any 'empirical' investigation, and should be appraised accordingly.

He often claimed in private correspondence to be a slow writer, with the implication that painstaking precision (meant literally) goes into his pronouncements. As he put it once in an influential essay from 1949: '*Too often, a single term has been used to symbolize different concepts, just as the same concept has been symbolized by different terms*. Clarity of analysis and adequacy of communication are both victims of this frivolous use of words.'[33] In a dictionary of antonyms, 'frivolous' and 'Merton' could well serve to illuminate each other. Yet just as 'the postmodern condition' emphasizes the 'play' of words and the ludicy of social life[34] in lieu of the measured and restrained, the virtues Merton already cultivated as a young author – rigour, exactness, sobriety, inclusiveness – fall to the debit side of the ledger, becoming as detractive to the contemporary ear and eye as they were seductive to those of his mentors and peers 60 years ago.

Consider, for example, this bit of regal elegance from his dissertation, composed circa 1935:

> it is evident that the formal organization of values constituted by Puritanism led to the largely unwitting furtherance of modern science. The Puritan complex of a scarcely disguished [*sic*] utilitarianism; of intramundane interests; methodical, unremitting action; thoroughgoing empiricism; of the right and even the duty of *libre examen*; of anti-traditionalism – all this was congenial to the same values in science. The happy marriage of those two movements was based on an intrinsic compatibility and even in the nineteenth century, their divorce was not yet final.[35]

Would anyone entertain or expect this kind of writing today from a 25-year-old graduate student in sociology? 'Intramundane' is a word not in my word processor's dictionary, and captures better than standard translations do Weber's idea of the Puritan's 'this-worldly orientation'; 'unremitting' is also not currently much used among 'social scientists', it being too 'hot' a term for 'cool' analysis, in McLuhan's terms; *libre examen*, of course, is approaching extinction, in word and deed; and few social scientists would now allow themselves metaphorical reference to the pained condition of 'divorce', which during Merton's youth was as rare as today it is rampant. Most importantly, the authorial voice heard loud and clear in this characteristic passage shares none of the coy hesitancy common to today's 'theoretical' or speculative dissertations of the broad gauge. In a way, reading vintage Merton is not unlike listening to Caruso on 78-rpm 'vinyl': the voice is unapologetically bold, eager to take risks and marvellously from another world.

Nor is it that with age he changed very much. In a 1970 preface to his reissued dissertation, he recalls his juvenile labours in the third person:

> The inquiry began as he was rummaging about in seventeenth-century England, trying to make some sense of the remarkable efflorescence of science at that time and place, being directed in the search by a general sociological orientation. The orientation was simple enough: various institutions in the society are variously interdependent so that what happens in the economic or religious realm is apt to have some perceptible connections with some of what happens in the realm of science, and conversely. In the course of reading the letters, diaries, memoirs and papers of seventeenth-century men of science, the author slowly noted the frequent religious commitments of scientists in this time, and even more, what seemed to be their Puritan orientation. Only then, and almost as though he had not been put through his paces during the course of graduate study, was he belatedly put in mind of that intellectual tradition, established by Max Weber, Troeltsch, Tawney, and others, which centered on the interaction between the Protestant ethic and the emergence of modern capitalism. Swiftly making amends for this temporary amnesia, the author turned to a line-by-line reading of Weber's work to see whether he had anything at all to say about the relation of Puritanism to science and technology. Of course, he had.[36]

When one considers that this entire process occurred between 1933 and 1935 – while Merton was taking classes, helping Sorokin, learning to teach at Harvard, beginning married life, and otherwise doing what graduate students during the Depression had to do to survive – his claims of 'temporary amnesia' and 'belated' self-reminder of Weber's usefulness to his thesis almost approaches false modesty. Yet again, the rhetoric of this passage, and the effort it describes – a kind of heroic hermeneutic enterprise that now seems quite impossible for one so young – 'brings into sharp relief' (a cliché of the sort Merton would not allow himself) the conditions of his intellectual labours versus those of our own time, even among the best young scholars.

Sociological Inspiration from a World Now Lost

The other intriguing question prompted by thoughts about Merton's virtuosic writing is more sociological than linguistic, and therefore more in keeping with his own preferred domain of analysis. In a passage of mature Mertonian confidence, he writes (his italics): '*The sociological theory deals with the processes through which social structures generate the circumstances in which ambivalence is embedded in particular statuses and status-sets together with their associated social roles.*'[37] If one patiently studies this sentence, and also goes down the long list of concepts Merton left in his wake, the suspicion begins to emerge, however slowly, that he was analytically inspired by a social world not precisely commensurate with today's. Would it be too much of an exaggeration to note that the world which gave birth to his congeries of concepts and definitions has begun to seem as distant from our own as Katharine Hepburn's ingénue roles in *Bringing Up Baby* (1938) or *The Philadelphia Story* (1940) are remote from the profane, armed, hard-bitten heroines of today's popular films? Whereas Hepburn's staccato banter was pure theatre, with no comma misplaced, her sentiments never allowed to slip beneath the mark of the 'lady', today's stars, when not portraying robots or space creatures, talk and behave like teamsters rather than descendants of New England Puritans. And if film reflects its context – as one would suppose based on Merton's thoughts about the sociology of knowledge and mass culture[38] – social relations today call for an analytic apparatus that might hold relatively little in common with one designed to interpret interaction during the third and fourth decades of the twentieth century.

This is a contentious set of claims, to be sure. Yet consider, by way of mental experiment, Merton's virtuosic 'Provisional List of Group-properties' from his book-within-a-book, 'Continuities in the Theory of Reference Groups and Social Structure'.[39] If one studies each of his 26 'properties' – as creative a refinement of **Simmelian** thought as one is likely to find – and then considers contemporary life in its more typical manifestations, something of a gap begins to open between 'that time' and this. Or reconsider, in this context, Merton's (and Alice Rossi's) analysis of *The American Soldier* in 1950,[40] wherein relative deprivation, reference groups' behaviour, anticipatory socialization, and related notions are developed, using the Stouffer study as 'data'. As Bierstedt points out in a detailed examination of Merton's arguments,[41] much of this work hinges on the idea that soldiers behave according to certain observable patterns, and that, furthermore, people in society at large conform to group norms, or do not, more or less in continuity with the findings in Stouffer's monumental survey of American troops. Careful reading of the two essays Merton commits to these matters illustrates that normative expectations, and the processes which created them, during and immediately after the Second World War among Americans would appear to differ significantly from those of today. Although I cannot 'prove' this here, in point of fact, the 'new' American military – which, for instance, eschews basic training drills when the temperature exceeds 90°F for fear a recruit may suffer discomfort – is so distinct in almost every dimension from the one Stouffer studied that a one-to-one comparison becomes an exercise either in historical imagining or an analytic error, depending on one's point of view. Put still another way, Merton's very language of societal dissection *might* make it harder for him to comprehend thoroughly the depths of *anomia* into which sizable portions of modern humanity have been cast. Or so it could be argued, given sufficient space, wit and observable data.

Theory and Research of the Middle Range

Another truism regarding Merton's career and cumulative achievement holds that his brief for 'middle-range' theorizing – in opposition both to Parsons' grandiose schemes as well as to interactional theories of tiny scope – brought his ideas into broad favour with researchers who might otherwise have had little regard for 'pure' theory. Thus, to understand his theories means investigating the 'substantive' studies to which he directly contributed, and also those hundreds more which sought to test his various claims by one means or another. To my knowledge, a systematic study – that is, 'Merton's influence on empirical research' – has not yet been done, although plenty of raw materials exist were someone interested in carrying it out.[42] Yet here, again, the problem would be a superabundance of riches.

It might be argued that as a peer of Merton's, Bierstedt was better positioned than I to evaluate his colleague's ultimate role in the history of social thought. Despite having some harsh things to say about the Mertonian vision of what sociology and social theory ought to be, he concludes his own exposition with two observations that bear repeating, particularly as I cannot express these sentiments any better: 'Ideas are toys for Merton, colored balls to be conjured out of nowhere, thrown in the air, and caught again with a magician's flair and finesse.' Setting aside the mixed image of juggler and magician, this is indeed an essential element of Merton's lasting importance, that he wrote so beguilingly, so convincingly, that his readers were swept away, even sometimes without understanding what exactly it was they were applauding. But more importantly, and again in Bierstedt's words, 'There is, however, a final word for Merton, and that word is quality ... He is a serious and thoughtful scholar, a superb sociologist, and one who has illuminated every subject to which he has directed his attention.'[43] In the end it may be this characteristic more than any other – the sheer intelligence and energetic application, over 60 years, of mindfulness to the disentangling of social phenomena – that guarantees Merton's place in the discipline's history. As an exemplar of theoretical brilliance and creative sociological practice, he has had no rival during his lifetime. Perhaps more importantly, the social structure of the special kind that gave rise to him – intensely literate and hopeful, despite its external lack of amenities – is gone, and one must seriously question if, considering these irreversible changes, another of his calibre is likely to appear in the foreseeable future.

FURTHER READING

In addition to Merton's own writings cited in the notes to this chapter, of which the central source must be *Social Theory and Social Structure* (1968) (rev. edn) New York: Free Press, also see the following.

Mongardini, C. and Tabboni, S. (eds) (1998) *Robert K. Merton and Contemporary Sociology*, New Brunswick, NJ: Transaction Publishers.
Crothers, C. (1987) *Robert K. Merton*, Key Sociologists Series, London: Tavistock.
Sztompka, P. (1986) *Robert K. Merton: An Intellectual Profile*, New York, St Martin's Press.

CHAPTER 9

Norbert Elias

JASON HUGHES

Driving Impulses

Norbert Elias was born into a German Jewish family in Breslau, Germany,[1] in 1897. His most important study, *The Civilizing Process* (in its English translation), was first published in Switzerland in 1939. To an outsider, the idea of a German Jew writing on the subject of 'civilization' on the eve of the Second World War may seem more than just a little unusual. Perhaps even more so when one begins to learn of Elias's life history: how, at 18, he encountered the carnage of the First World War as a soldier on the western and eastern fronts; how he was forced to flee from the Nazis into exile in 1933; how, after seeing his parents for the last time in 1938, his mother was murdered at Auschwitz. However, as one learns more of Elias's life history and his intellectual development, it becomes easier to understand why he chose the topic of civilization to be the central focus of his major work: it exemplified the balance between involvement and detachment that was to become a hallmark of his studies. It is clear that Elias was, in part, driven by the dramatic social changes that were occurring at the time he wrote. Indeed, in the introduction to *The Civilizing Process*, his 'involvement' with the subject is explicitly stated:

> The issues raised by the book have their origins less in scholarly tradition, in the narrower sense of the word, than in the experiences in whose shadow we all live, experiences of the crisis and transformation of Western civilization as it had existed hitherto, and the simple need to understand what this 'civilization' really amounts to. But I have not been guided in this study by the idea that our civilized mode of behaviour is the most advanced of all humanly possible, nor by the opinion that 'civilization' is the worst form of life and one that is doomed. All that can be seen today is that with gradual civilization a number of specific civilizational difficulties arise. But it cannot be said that we already understand why we actually torment ourselves in this way.[2]

Clearly, Elias did not view the process of civilization as 'the progressive triumph of rationality', yet he also resisted the temptation to collapse into a fatalist position. Elias's primary concern was with building an *understanding* of the long-term processes of which this 'crisis and transformation' formed a part. Moreover, in his study of *The Civilizing Process*, Elias aimed to lay the foundations for a *radically processual, relational, and developmental sociology*.[3] The study constituted both a synthesis of, and a fundamental break from, the work of Elias's many direct and indirect intellectual influences, which included, among others, the sociologists Auguste Comte, Karl Mannheim, **Karl Marx**, **Georg Simmel** and **Max Weber**; the psychoanalyst **Sigmund Freud**; the historian Johan Huizinga; and, possibly, the philosopher Ernst Cassirer.[4]

As may already be apparent, Elias's preoccupation with the three central foci of his work – relations, process and synthesis – cannot be traced to any single event, or to any single intellectual influence. However, a brief examination of the early stages of Elias's intellectual career will help to serve two interrelated purposes: first, to elucidate the motivation behind his work, and, second, to highlight some of the key themes he was to examine in his quest to develop (what has come to be known as) 'process' sociology.[5]

In line with his father's wish for him to become a doctor, and in relation to his already deep interest in philosophy, Elias enrolled to read both medicine and philosophy at Breslau University in 1918. After obtaining the equivalent of a British first MB degree, Elias dropped medicine and concentrated his efforts on philosophy. However, Elias continued to draw upon insights gained from his medical background to develop his distinctive sociological position. For example, his dissection work on the musculature of the human face made Elias acutely aware of how laughing and smiling were fundamental indicators of how humans evolved as a social species.[6] Thus, Elias observed, even the most fundamental aspects of human existence should not be taken as 'given', 'essential', 'unchanging', but rather, these should be seen as part of a set of long-term processes. In relation to this understanding, Elias became increasingly unhappy with the dichotomies he so frequently encountered in academic writing, such as those between the 'biological' and the 'social'; the 'mind' and the 'body'; the 'individual' and 'society'. In the course of his study of 'civilizing processes', Elias began to develop a sociological understanding of *why* these divisions had become so popular in academic and lay understandings, at least since the Renaissance, by examining the fundamental interrelationship between 'social' and 'psychological' development (to use Elias's terms, *sociogenesis* and *psychogenesis* respectively). In the sections that follow, we shall examine how these insights were developed in Elias's work.

Key Issues

Elias's approach to sociology was not so much to construct 'logical' arguments to demonstrate the inadequacies of other theories and the merits of his own work, but rather to formulate academic problems in such a way as to stimulate readers to be critical of the taken-for-granted assumptions and categories that are often drawn upon when approaching these problems.[7] Indeed, it is rather difficult, and highly problematic, to use Elias's work to construct purely 'rational' arguments or *abstract* theories as his work always involved a symbiosis of, or 'two-way traffic' between, 'theory' and 'research'; the central enterprise of sociology for Elias was always research-theorizing. This reorientation of the primary vehicle for sociology as Elias envisaged it was, in turn, related to his efforts to bypass the split between 'rationalist' and 'empiricist' academic poles. The five key areas of concern discussed below make use of terminology that has no direct equivalent in the conventional sociological lexicon. Again, this relates to Elias's effort to encourage a critical attitude to ingrained modes of thinking and conceptualizing on the part of the reader. His aim was to develop alternative sociological concepts that had a higher level of 'cognitive value'. Or, to put the latter statement in another way, to encourage a higher degree of congruence between (what we currently label as) 'theory' and 'research'.

Civilizing Processes

In order properly to understand Elias's work, it is crucial from the outset to recognize a key distinction between his technical term 'civilizing process' and the normative term 'civilizaton'. A parallel can be drawn here with how anthropologists have distinguished the technical concept of 'culture' from the normative term that in common English usage today expresses attributes such as 'refinement' and 'distinction'. Indeed, the often overlooked Part One of his *magnum opus*, *The Civilizing Process*, is entirely devoted to the 'Sociogenesis of the Concepts of "Civilization" and "Culture"'. Elias sought to develop a sociological analysis of the long-term processes in which the term 'civilization' came to express the self-consciousness of specific groups in the West, and thus to gain its 'progress' overtones. In short, Elias wanted precisely to understand the social conditions under which the term came to express everything that people in the West who saw themselves as 'civilized' believed distinguished and distanced them from their perceived social inferiors – those whom they understood to be 'primitive' or 'uncivilized'; how the term came to embody 'evolutionary', colonial, racist and derogatory sentiments; and, for example, how it was that England and France came to fight against Germany in the First World War in the name of 'civilization'.

At a broader sociological level, Elias's focus on civilizing processes was bound up with his endeavour to move towards a more adequate understanding of how processes of change in the human psychic structure are interrelated with processes of changing social relations. In order to investigate these processes, Elias began his analysis by examining the highly influential etiquette manual, *De civilitate morum puerilium* (On civility in children), written in 1530 by the Dutch classical scholar Desiderius Erasmus. Elias chose Erasmus precisely because he was standing at a crucial juncture in European history: between the Middle Ages and 'modernity'. Erasmus's observations referred both 'backwards' and 'forwards', revealing much not only about conduct that was typical of his time and of 'times gone by', but also about subtle, yet incremental, shifts in standards of socially acceptable behaviour. Erasmus's work, and a range of other similar sources, thus provided Elias with a rich source of data from which he was able to elucidate an overall *direction* to changes in codes of etiquette among the secular upper classes in Europe. Through examining the minutiae of behavioural expectations relating to everything from 'manners' at the dinner table, to how to approach and experience emotions and bodily functions, Elias skilfully developed a set of core ideas about the 'developmental mechanics of history' and their relation to psychical processes.[8]

Elias builds a picture of social life in the Middle Ages as characterized by conduct that, by present-day western standards, would be considered 'distasteful'. For example, Elias convincingly argues that it was common for people to urinate and defecate quite publicly during this period. Indeed, some medieval texts proposed that 'Before you sit down [for dinner], make sure your seat has not been fouled' or that 'It is impolite to greet someone who is urinating or defecating'.[9] Similarly, it was normal for people to eat from a common dish, with unwashed hands; to spit on to the floor; or to break wind at the table.[10] In prescribing what one should not do, etiquette manuals also gave a strong indication of what was commonplace. For instance, it was recommended that one should not use the tablecloth to blow one's nose.[11] Elias analyses how the restraints on behaviour that we take for granted today began to emerge over time. He observes that, gradually, an increasing range and number of aspects of human behaviour came to be regarded as 'distasteful' and were *pushed behind the scenes* of social life. Corresponding to this shift, people begin to experience an advancing threshold of repugnance and shame in relation to their bodily functions.

Elias suggests that the increasing elaboration of codes of etiquette and manners that he observed accompanied a corresponding shift in people's behaviour: for example, defecation, urination and copulation became increasingly conducted in 'private', closed-off places. Thus, he argues, a defining characteristic of civilizing processes in the West was that people gradually came to exercise higher degrees of self-restraint. This is not to say that one cannot find any evidence of self-restraint among people of the Middle Ages or earlier. Indeed, Elias found extreme forms of asceticism and renunciation in certain sectors of medieval society (such as the self-denial of monks). However, these stood in contrast 'to a no less extreme indulgence of pleasure in others, and frequently enough ... sudden switches from one attitude to the other in the life of an individual person'.[12] In short, therefore, the western civilizing process involved a gradual stabilization of human behaviour: but while the *contrasts* in human behaviour have diminished in the course of this process, the *varieties* of behaviour have increased.[13]

Sociogenesis and Psychogenesis: 'The Social Constraint towards Self-constraint'

Having given this brief outline of the concept of civilizing processes, one is still left with the question of *why* such processes have occurred, and, indeed, are continuing to occur (although not necessarily in the same direction). Elias is able to demonstrate that the changes in behaviour which have occurred as part of a civilizing process cannot be adequately explained solely in terms of 'health and hygiene', 'material reasons', or 'religion and respect'. Rather, he argues, one needs to examine the immanent dynamics of the changing social relations of which these behavioural changes formed part. To make this clearer, Elias proposes that we consider the analogy of the different road systems of medieval and contemporary societies. On the roads of medieval societies, Elias writes:

> With few exceptions, there is very little traffic; the main danger ... is attack from soldiers or thieves. When people look around them, scanning the trees and hills or the road itself, they do so primarily because they must always be prepared for armed attack, and only secondarily because they have to avoid collision. Life on the main roads of this society demands a constant readiness to fight, and free play of the emotions in defence of one's life or possessions from physical attack. Traffic on the main roads of a big city in the complex society of our time demands quite a different moulding of the psychological apparatus. Here the danger of physical attack is [comparatively] minimal. Cars are rushing in all directions; pedestrians and cyclists are trying to thread their way through the *mêlée* of cars; policemen stand at the main crossroads to regulate the traffic with varying success. But this external control is founded on the assumption that every individual is himself or herself regulating his or her behaviour with the utmost exactitude in accordance with the necessities of this network. The chief danger that people here represent for others results from someone in this bustle *losing* their self-control.[14]

Elias's analogy serves to illustrate how, in medieval western society, the type of personality that flourished was one that was always ready for attack. Threats from violent others and the environment were omnipresent, and thus emotional restraint was of little advantage. Conversely, to be able to engage in wild, unrestrained battle; positively to enjoy the annihilation of anyone or anything hostile; to be able to live out one's feelings and passions uninhibited by thought for the feelings of others, all would have proven positive advantages in the medieval West. However, as monopolies over violence and taxation began to be established, in turn related to processes of state formation and the lengthening of interdependency chains,[15] so gradually the threat that one person posed to others became 'depersonalized' and more calculable. As societies became more complex, people were compelled to regulate their conduct in an increasingly stable, differentiated, reflexive and even manner. Everyday life became freer of insecurities relating to the immediate physical threat that one person posed to another, and there were more possibilities for exercising foresight. Indeed, in the present-day West, those who are able to moderate their behaviour and demonstrate foresight are at a distinct advantage. The effort required to behave in a 'civilized' manner becomes so great that there also emerges an almost 'blindly functioning' apparatus of self-control. Social control becomes deeply entrenched in the human psychic economy; it becomes 'absorbed' to such an extent that it functions partly autonomously from one's consciousness. It is in this way, Elias argues, that the processes of sociogenesis and psychogenesis are fundamentally interrelated.

Homo Clausus versus *Homines Aperti*: A Move away from the Structure–Agency Dilemma?

Elias argues that his study of civilizing processes throws light on many contemporary debates in sociology. At its current stage of development, sociology is a highly fragmented discipline: it contains a large number of competing paradigms that can be divided, in different ways, according to variations of the 'structure–agency' dilemma. Put crudely, some perspectives, such as variants of the structuralist paradigm, focus on 'social structures' and how these are reproduced. This focus often leads to a view of 'individuals' as simply 'driven' by 'external' forces. Others, exemplified by variants of the ethnomethodological and symbolic interactionist paradigms, focus on the 'active' and 'productive' capabilities of the 'individual subject', which, they propose, are largely overlooked by the proponents of other positions. However, this focus often leads to a view of 'individuals' as existing in a vacuum or in isolation from one another. Consequently, it becomes difficult to explain how individuals are compelled to act in one way rather than another. Particularly since the 1980s, an increasing number of sociological authors have developed theories that aim to synthesize these polar extremes, perhaps most notably Anthony Giddens in his theory of 'structuration'.[16] Yet even these theories often find it difficult to move away from stressing either 'agency' at the expense of 'structure' or vice versa.

Elias's sociology offers a possible explanation of why sociologists appear to be locked into this dilemma. Let us consider once again the long-term changes in the human psychic structure that are embedded in the process of civilization. Elias writes:

> People who ate together in the way customary of the Middle Ages ... stood in a different relationship to one another than we do ... What was lacking in this ... world, or at least had not been developed to the same degree, was the *invisible wall of affects* which seems now to rise between one human body and another, repelling and separating, the wall which is often perceptible today at the mere approach of something that has been in contact with the mouth or hands of someone else, and which manifests itself as embarrassment at the mere sight of many bodily functions of others, and often at their mere mention, or as a feeling of shame when one's own functions are exposed to the gaze of others, and by no means only then.[17]

It is this 'invisible wall of affects' that leads to a common self-experience among people in the contemporary West: it is manifested in the feeling that it is almost as though there is a 'dividing line' between 'me in here' and 'society out there'.[18] Since academics themselves are not immune from the civilizing process, it is perhaps unsurprising that this experience of a dividing line is reflected in the concepts, questions and divisions of much contemporary sociology and philosophy. Indeed, throughout his work, Elias was at pains to demonstrate that the academic/conceptual splits between 'subjects' and 'objects', 'individual' and 'society', 'ontology' and 'epistemology', and, of course, 'agency' and 'structure' are in fact reifications based in the self-experience of people at a particular stage of social development. Some of the most fundamental questions asked by philosophers and sociologists can be seen to be related to this particular experience of the 'self'. For example, a theorist might ask, 'How can "I" as a single isolated thinking "subject" inside my own shell, know anything of the world "outside"?' Moreover, 'How can "I" know what anyone else (any other "I" equally sealed within its shell) is thinking?' Elias calls this view of human beings as trapped within their containers, *Homo clausus* (or, for want of less sexist language, closed 'man'). Elias proposes that we should move away from this view of humans that is so deeply embedded in our theorizing. Instead, Elias argues, sociologists should aim to view people as *Homines aperti* (open, bonded, pluralities of interdependent human beings), as this, in part, will facilitate a move away from many of the stale debates and dichotomies that currently undermine our understanding.

Power and Interdependence

As will be seen below, Elias's conception of *Homines aperti* is central to his understanding of 'power'. Elias proposes that sociologists should abandon a *Homo clausus* view of power as a 'thing' we could somehow pick up and hold within our shells towards a more fundamentally *relational and processual* understanding of power. For Elias, what we currently label as 'power' is an aspect of relationships. In fact, it is an aspect of every human relationship. It is rooted in the fact that people can withhold or monopolize what others need, for example material resources, food, love or knowledge. Except for the most marginal circumstances, where one party's 'power' is almost that of 'absolute' over the other, we always encounter power relationships, power balances, different or equal 'power ratios'.[19] 'Power' is very rarely simply a case of the one-way 'dependence' of one party on another; it almost always refers to people's *interdependence*.[20]

In order to illustrate this understanding of power, Elias proposes that we consider the analogy of 'games'. These are greatly simplified analogies, but, Elias argues, because games are themselves social processes, such models are far less dangerous than the organic or biological analogies that are frequently used in sociology.[21]

At the most simple level, Elias provides the model of a two-person game; it may help the reader to think of a game of chess. Imagine that player A is a very strong player, and player B is much weaker. The stronger player A can force B to play certain moves, and, in direct relation to this capacity, can very largely steer the course of the game. While A has a high degree of control over B's moves, B is not completely 'powerless'. Just as B must take orientation from A's preceding moves, so must A from B's preceding moves. If B had no strength at all, there could be no game. Thus, Elias concludes from this example, in any game the players always have a degree of control over each other. They are, that is to say, always *interdependent*. However, even when only two players are involved, if their relative strengths become more equal, both players will have correspondingly less chance of controlling each other's moves or, indeed, the overall course of the game. In other words, the players become increasingly dependent on the overall process of the game, its changing course, in determining their moves. Predicting the game even a few moves in advance becomes difficult. Consequently, Elias writes, to the extent that the inequality in the strengths of the two players diminishes, there will result from the interweaving of moves of two individual people a game process *that neither of them has planned*.[22]

Elias calls this 'interwoven web' of moves that follows a largely 'blind' course, the game's *figuration*.

Figurations

To clarify the meaning and also to stress the significance of Elias's concept of figurations, consider what happens when more players are introduced into the game models.

As the number of players increases, so the game figurations become a great deal more complex. In the second game model Elias provides, a stronger player plays a number of weaker players simultaneously. While the weaker players do not communicate with one another, the stronger player's capacity to control each game may be undermined by the fact that he or she is having to conduct so many games at once. Clearly, there is a limit to the number of games that one player can effectively participate in simultaneously. Second, if the weaker players unite to form a coalition against the stronger player and they act in unison, their control over the superior player can be enhanced. However, if the coalition becomes beset by internal conflicts and tensions, they might end up at less of an advantage than they had individually.

The next model deals with two groups of almost equal strength. Here it may help the reader to think of a team sport such as football. Just as in the second case of the two-player model, neither party can fully anticipate the other's moves and tactics, and thus neither side can easily control the course of the game. It becomes impossible to understand the moves that each player makes either when considered on their own or when viewed solely in relation to the moves of the other members of their team. To understand each move properly, one must also consider each move in relation to the overall course of the game.

Elias introduces a third group of 'multi-tier' models that involve an even larger number of players. Here the models are analogous of social processes approaching in their complexity those of a modern state.[23] In relation to these models, Elias writes that as the number of players in the game increases, so the course of the game becomes more 'opaque' to each 'individual' player. Each single player, no matter how strong, is decreasingly able to control the direction of the game. From the players' perspectives, this interweaving 'mesh' of an increasing number of players' actions begins to function 'as though it had a life of its own'. Furthermore, as even more players become involved in the game, the 'individual' players become increasingly aware that they are unable to control and understand it.[24] In the absence of an overall picture of the game, players come under growing pressure to organize in a different way. They may reorganize to form smaller groups, or begin to configure more complex interdependencies, which have a number of different 'tiers' or levels. In the latter case, the moves of the group are increasingly made by people in the 'upper tiers' who have specialized functions, such as leaders, delegates or representatives. Those in the lower tiers are also involved in the moves but more through subsidiary contests with members of the upper tiers.

Elias's models here are intended to elucidate some of the changes that occur as societies become more complex, and 'chains of interdependence' lengthen (the process by which more and more people become increasingly interdependent). Of crucial importance is the tendency, which Elias highlights, to view the complex figuration that arises as 'having an existence all of its own'. When considered in conjuction with Elias's understanding of *Homo clausus*, we might begin to understand why many concepts of 'social structure' or 'social system' seem to embody a view of 'society' as somehow existing beyond the level of the 'individuals' who constitute it. According to Elias, what these concepts really refer to is

> a basic tissue resulting from many single plans and actions of people [which] can give rise to changes and patterns that no individual person has planned or created. From this interdependence of people arises an order *sui generis*, an order more compelling and stronger than the will of the individual people composing it. It is this order of interweaving human impulses and strivings, this social order, which determines the course of historical change; it underlies the civilizing process.[25]

Thus the term 'figuration' refers neither to 'metaphysical entities' nor to mere 'amalgamations' of individuals, but, rather, to shifting 'nexuses' of human interdependence.

Seeing Things Differently

I first encountered the work of Norbert Elias as an undergraduate at Leicester University. In an attempt to operationalize some of Elias's ideas, I considered the case of smoking and how it might serve as an exemplar of an 'interdependency chain'. I considered how I and the millions of other smokers across the world were interdependent with all the people who it would have taken to cultivate the tobacco, and to manufacture and transport the cigarettes I was smoking: people that I had not met, and would probably never meet. I observed that it was no accident that my cigarettes contained a specific amount of nicotine and tar, and that this was related, at least in part, to a long-term shift in the power relations between governments, tobacco producers, tobacco consumers and the medical profession. For me, Elias's work became particularly useful when I began to ask myself why I felt the 'need' to smoke, particularly when thinking or concentrating – was this simply a 'biological urge'? Or were there more 'social' or 'psychological' processes at play? Of course, in drawing upon a process sociological perspective, I became immediately suspicious of these distinctions.

As part of my subsequent doctoral research, I traced the long-term development of tobacco use in the West back to the sixteenth century, when tobacco was first introduced into many parts of Europe, and beyond, by examining tobacco use among Native American peoples. I found that among the latter, particularly prior to contact with the West, tobacco was often used in a highly ritualized way. The tobacco cultivated by Native Americans, plus the modes of consuming it, made for a more pronounced and 'stronger' range of effects that those we would associate with contemporary western cigarettes. Indeed, there is a large amount of evidence to suggest that some forms were capable of producing hallucinations.[26] Only the mildest and most palatable varieties of Native American tobacco were initially transferred to the West. Yet even these, by present-day standards, were extremely strong. Over time, the type of tobacco cultivated and used by western tobacco users became weaker and weaker. The popular medium of tobacco consumption gradually changed from the pipe, to snuff, cigars and, finally, cigarettes. The first cigarettes contained tobacco that was much milder and more palatable (to western tastes) than that of previous forms of consumption. But these, in turn, also became milder and weaker. Soon afterwards it became possible to buy filter cigarettes, and then, more recently, low tar filter cigarettes. At present in the West, with the advent of 'super' and 'ultra' 'low' brands, it is possible for smokers to select to the milligram exactly how much nicotine and tar their cigarette contains.

While the increasing dominance of biomedical understandings of tobacco use may well have influenced some of these changes, these factors alone cannot be used to explain all the changes observed. Viewed from a process sociological perspective, the changes can be seen to be related to a much broader set of processes. It is almost as if tobacco use has itself undergone a civilizing process: an increasing stabilization of the 'effects' of tobacco use that has involved 'diminishing contrasts and increasing varieties'. Put crudely, at a very general level, one can observe a move away from tobacco use to 'lose control' towards an increasing tendency towards the use of tobacco as a means of 'self-control'. One only has to think of some of the popular rationalizations among contemporary western smokers to understand the implications of this process. Many of the smokers I interviewed proposed that smoking helped them to control their 'moods', to relieve 'stress', to relieve 'boredom', to help them control their weight, to help them to 'concentrate'. To provide just one example, consider the contrast between this picture of contemporary western smoking – frequent intakes of relatively weak tobacco largely for 'control reasons' – with the account provided below of tobacco use among the Karuk Native Americans:

> He sucks in ... then quickly he shuts his mouth. For a moment he holds the smoke inside his mouth. He wants it to go in. For a moment he remains motionless holding his pipe. He shakes, he feels like he is going to faint, holding his mouth shut. It is as if he could not get enough ... He shuts his eyes, he looks kind of sleepy-like. His hand trembles, as he puts the pipe to his mouth again. Then again he smacks in [inhales]. He smokes again like he smoked before. A few or maybe four times he takes the pipe from his mouth. Then, behold, he knows he has smoked up the tobacco, there is no more inside [the pipe]. As he smokes he knows when there are only ashes inside. He just fills up the pipe once, that is enough, one pipeful.[27]

Of course, a large number of other 'factors' must be considered in order properly to understand this contrast. However, through drawing upon Elias's 'process' sociology, I sought to explore the dynamic interplay of 'social', 'cultural', 'psychological', 'biological' and 'pharmacological' processes that give rise to the distinctive patterns of tobacco use characteristic of the contemporary West.[28]

Legacies and Unfinished Business

Since his death in 1990, Norbert Elias has come to be recognized as one of the leading figures in twentieth-century sociology. To date, his work has been translated into 29 languages, and he is one of the few sociologists of the postwar era to have had a chair named in his memory (at Erasmus University, Rotterdam). He has been acknowledged as an important influence on such key sociological thinkers as **Pierre Bourdieu** and **Michel Foucault**. His work has been used to research a wide range of fields. Most notably, it has been drawn upon by Eric Dunning to study sport and leisure;[29] Johan Goudsblom to study fire and the anthroposphere;[30] Stephen Mennell to study food and, more recently, the American civilizing process;[31] and Cas Wouters, to study processes of 'informalization', female emancipation and sex. In recent years, Elias's sociology has become increasingly influential, particularly within the fields of historical criminology; the sociology of the body; the sociology of emotions; and studies of violence, genocide and war.[32] It is important to note, however, that Elias saw his work as little more than a hopeful beginning, as anything but a 'final answer'. Elias was the first to recognize that his ideas represented little more than 'small, hopeful breakthroughs in the process of growing knowledge about ourselves.'[33] A number of writers, notably Jonathan Fletcher,[34] Chris Rojek[35] and Robert van Krieken,[36] have written very much in this spirit of of extending and revising Elias's work through an ongoing critical engagement with his key ideas. Other critics, including Anton Blok,[37] Edmund Leach,[38] Derek Layder[39] and Benjo Maso,[40] have more fundamental concerns. While it is not possible to do justice to these debates here, I would like to focus on a common misunderstanding of Elias's work that is embodied in some of these critiques, and, in relation to this discussion, briefly to mention some of the ways in which his work has been extended.

As Mennell[41] has stated, a common theme in critiques of Elias's work is that changes in the twentieth century – for example, the Nazi period in Germany and the Holocaust, and, in a less dramatic way, an increasing permissiveness in the West since the 1960s – would appear to undermine the idea that the West has undergone a 'civilizing process'. On the face of it, the authors of such critiques seem to have simply misunderstood Elias's use of the concept: they do not appear to have recognized the distinction between Elias's technical use of the term and the value-laden everyday usage. However, these critiques do raise the question of whether developments of more recent years actually constitute a counter-trend to the 'direction' of change observed in *The Civilizing Process*. It is important to note at this point that Elias never saw the process of civilization in the West as a smooth unilinear transition, but rather as a change in a specific direction consisting of 'spurts' and decivilizing 'counter-spurts'. Moreover, in relation to the Holocaust in Nazi Germany, Elias did not propose that violence, killing and torture had ceased to occur in the 'civilized' West, but rather that these had become increasingly monopolized by states and deployed at an interstate level. Indeed, if anything, Elias foresaw an escalation of violence as a consequence of the struggle between hegemonial units. He writes:

> It is impossible to predict how long it will take for this struggle, with its many spurts and counter-spurts, to be finally decided … Only one thing is certain: the direction in which the integration of the modern world is veering. The competitive tension between states, given the pressures which our social structure brings with it, can be resolved only after a long series of violent or non-violent trials of strength have established monopolies of force.[42]

Robert van Krieken goes so far as to suggest that 'violence' and 'civilization' can perhaps be better understood as dialectical rather than antithetical; he proposes that a key area of development of Elias's work should reside in considering the extent to which civilizing processes actually produce their own 'dark side'.[43] Indeed, the scale and character of the mass murder of the Jews in Nazi Germany were fundamentally related to processes of civilization. As Mennell observes:

> modern social organization has vastly multiplied the technical capacity to kill. The very long chains of interdependence and 'division of social functions' which play such a part in the civilizing process were also essential to implementing the 'final solution' [in Nazi Germany]. And paradoxically, as Elias argues, 'civilized' controls in turn play their part in making possible those long chains of organized and co-ordinated activities. [44]

Similarly, as Fletcher suggests, the technology of modern warfare in many ways facilitates forms of 'killing at a distance': the pilot of a fighter jet remotely deploying an air-to-ground missile tracked on a target screen is effectively anaesthetized from the blood, the viscera, the sights, sounds and smells of the human destruction unleashed below.[45] In other words, it is quite possible to have highly 'civilized' forms of violence, torture and murder — to have 'civilized barbarism'.[46]

In relation to the increase in permissiveness or 'informalization' since the 1960s in the West, it is first important to note that a similar 'wave of informality' also occurred in the 1920s (although perhaps not to the same extent as in the 1960s and 70s).[47] Elias was, of course, fully aware of these changes when he wrote *The Civilizing Process*. In this connection, Elias gave the example of changes in bathing costumes, particularly those of women, which, at the time he wrote, were becoming increasingly revealing. Only a century previous to this, Elias observed, a woman who wore such a revealing costume publicly would have been socially ostracized.[48] However, rather than representing a counter-trend, these changes could also be understood to be characteristics of a relatively advanced stage of civilization. These developments, Elias wrote, were indicative of 'a society in which a high degree of restraint is taken for granted, and in which women are, like men, absolutely sure that each individual is curbed by self-control and a strict code of etiquette'.[49]

Elias became increasingly interested in processes of informalization in his later work. In 1967, in a joint paper with Dunning, 'The quest for excitement in leisure', Elias and Dunning summarized a number of the changes that were occurring in the 1960s in the West as 'a highly controlled decontrolling of emotional controls'.[50] Together they argued that developments in the field of leisure – changes in audience participation in sports, changes in film and other arts, changes in music – can all be understood to be complementary to the emotional control and restraint of our ordinary lives. Many of these activities provide the opportunity for compensatory 'expressive outbursts', for 'excitement' and 'emotionality'. Nonetheless, these 'are themselves tempered by civilizing restraints'.[51]

Thus, the decline of formal standards of socially acceptable behaviour marked by processes of informalization do not, for Elias, necessarily imply a corresponding decline in demands for individual self-control. Such processes might arguably also constitute an intensification of 'civilizing demands'. An example that serves to help clarify this point, both as a feature of processes of informalization and as a metaphor for the variegated demands for nuanced self-expression and control characteristic of such processes, is that of 'mufti' days at work. 'Mufti' days have become popular, particularly among large corporations in the West since the late 1980s. These are days, usually one day a week, when employees are permitted to dress 'as they wish'; they do not need to wear the corporate uniform or to dress in line with formal 'company policy'. However, rather than constituting a simple relaxation of pressures on how to dress, employees are immediately presented with another set of pressures, and these might be even more intensely felt than those arising from 'company dress code'. Employees must still dress 'appropriately'. But what is 'appropriate'? They are compelled to ask a series of questions of their clothes and appearance: Is this fashionable? Is this the right label? Is this too tarty? Does my bum look big in this? Is this too nerdy? Is this too formal? Too casual? Too stiff? Too loud? Too dull? Is this really me? Employees are compelled to dress 'correctly', not so much according to the formally defined 'external' standard of the corporation, but now according to a blend and balance of unstated 'internalized' and explicit 'external' standards and concerns: to express both their individuality and sense of belonging through a particular way of dressing. On the face of it, they are 'free' to wear a tracksuit to work, but what might 'they' think of 'me'? And what would 'we' think of those who did?

It is important to note that it was never Elias's claim that the overall direction of civilizing processes in the West was somehow fixed or inevitable. Elias did not consider it possible to predict the future on the basis of the very limited amount of knowledge that we have been able to build about ourselves. Indeed, decivilizing 'spurts' have been a recurrent feature of human history, and arguably have been in the ascendant in the West since the late 1960s. What Elias hoped was that, through laying down the foundations for a process- and relation-centred sociology, it would be possible for sociologists to develop over time more adequate understandings of these processes, and perhaps ultimately to make these more amenable to conscious control, by building growing 'islands of certainty in the vast oceans of their ignorance'.[52]

FURTHER READING

For a general introduction to Elias's work:

Mennell, S. (1992) *Norbert Elias: An Introduction*, Dublin: University College Dublin Press.

Van Krieken, R. (1998) *Norbert Elias*, London: Routledge.

Elias's most important work:

Elias, N. (1939) *The Civilizing Process*, Oxford: Blackwell, new edn 2000.

For an explication of key process sociological principles:

Elias, N. (1970) *What is Sociology?* London: Hutchinson, translated in 1978 from the original German publication.

Elias on the importance of 'process' for the sociological understanding:

Elias, N. (1987) 'The retreat of sociologists into the present', *Theory, Culture and Society*, 4: 223–47.

Elias on sociological approaches to 'method':

Elias, N. (1956) 'Problems of involvement and detachment', *British Journal of Sociology*, 7: 226–52.

A paper on sociogenesis and psychogenesis:

Elias, N. (1988) 'Violence and civilization: the state monopoly of physical violence and its infringement', in J. Keane, *Civil Society and the State*, London: Verso, pp. 177–98.

Studies which have drawn on Elias to analyse particular aspects of social life include:

Goudsblom, J. (1992) *Fire and Civilization*, London: Penguin.

Hughes, J. (2003) *Learning to Smoke: Tobacco Use in the West*, Chicago: Chicago University Press.

Mennell, S. (1985) *All Manners of Food: Eating and Taste in England and France from the Middle Ages to the Present*, London: Blackwell.

CHAPTER 10

Erving Goffman

ROBIN WILLIAMS

Driving Impulses

The complex variety of sociological theories and methods is often reduced to a series of allegedly distinctive 'schools', 'traditions', 'styles' or 'approaches' that together constitute the discipline. Some such categories have been named after individual sociologists sufficiently recognizable through fame or notoriety (for example **Marxism, Durkheimianism**). A second convention has rested on the invention of new terms signifying the distinctiveness of a particular approach (for example symbolic interactionism, structural functionalism). A third has invoked a geographical or institutional affiliation shared by at least the first generation of those associated with its type of work (for example Chicago School, West Coast School).

Throughout sociology's short and turbulent history, however, there have been scholars who have produced startlingly original and influential work, yet who have both resisted association with any existing configuration and also been unwilling to lend their names or reputations to the establishment of collective enterprises based on their own innovations.

Goffman was one such maverick scholar.[1] He became a professional sociologist shortly after the end of the Second World War in the USA, at a time when disciplinary expansion encouraged the critical development of the work of the group of founding thinkers discussed in earlier chapters of this book. From his first publication in 1952 to his death in 1983, he pursued a unique and successful programme of empirical research and conceptual development within sociology. The substance of this programme was the close analysis of the 'interaction order' – that part of social life that occurs whenever 'two or more individuals are in one another's response presence'.[2] He aimed to discover the structures and processes (the forms) exhibited in face-to-face interaction – as well as the sources of its orderliness. Goffman wanted to 'make clear what was previously unclear [to point to] the significance of things which had been regarded as of little or no consequence, and [to disentangle] what was previously an indiscriminate muddle'.[3] He single-handedly initiated and prosecuted an obstinately empirical programme driven by the impulse described above and consisting of the close analysis of what people do when they are in the company of others, and of how those doings are understood by participants. In the course of 25 years' work, he explicitly borrowed the insights, findings, concepts and vocabularies of many individuals and groups of researchers (in anthropology, social psychology, ethology, linguistics) to produce his elegant and persuasive microanalysis of a wide range of interactional phenomena. However, the impulses that really drove his work arose from his reading of classical sociological theory, especially the work of Durkheim and **Simmel**. He took ideas and interests from both, reshaped them and used them to drive forward his work in ways that were entirely novel. Three of these were particularly important: an interest in the central role of ideals and morality in social life; the attempt to formulate a fully sociological version of the individual person; and a concern to develop sociology as an empirical discipline rather than a speculative theoretical enterprise.

Both Durkheim and Simmel stressed the significance of ideals and morality for the organization of society. In Durkheim's perspective on society as a moral order, the imposition of morality through ritual and routine organization was treated as a vital element in the determination of individual conduct. Simmel's argument that society was itself a moral ideal, a necessary fiction, was essential to his focus on sociology as the study of social forms. While Goffman borrowed elements from both thinkers, he located the operation of morality and idealization not in the abstract entity of society, but in our everyday conduct in face-to-face action. The fact that our actions embody ritual concerns, that we orientate to the ideal of 'euphoria' (or 'ease' in interaction) and that a central assumption in our face-to-face dealings is an idealization of a 'working consensus' are all claims deserving of close attention and analysis.

Neither Durkheim nor Simmel thought that the organization of society could be explained as the product of individual action, yet both were concerned to understand the nature of the individual person in a way that was consistent with their respective understandings of the primacy of the social. Both developed views of the individual person as a 'social construction'. Durkheim's treatment of 'moral individualism' and Simmel's work on the personality in modernity both offer versions of the human subject as a social product in place of a view that locates the 'individual' and 'society' as opposing entities. Again, Goffman's view varies in detail from both Durkheim and Simmel while being closely related to the common intention of them both.

While there are stark contrasts between Durkheim's and Simmel's methodological preferences, Goffman's sociology seems to combine contrary impulses from both of them. Burns correctly argues that Goffman was much influenced by Durkheim's notion of social fact (defined by Durkheim as 'every way of acting, fixed or not, which is general throughout a given society, while existing in its own right, independent of its individual manifestations'), even if he restricted his search for such facts within the domain of face-to-face interaction. More obviously, Simmel's notion of social forms was immensely useful in Goffman's programme.[4] Common to both classical writers is the view that empirical sociology should be guided by an emphasis on externality and the search for recurrent patterns of action. These two features act as the driving force for Goffman's work too.

Key Issues

Goffman's substantial body of work described and analysed a large variety of actions and events that had previously failed to receive sociological attention. His analyses of this new material remain among the most elegant and exciting examples of writing within the discipline. For example, his essay 'Tie signs' offers a detailed exposé of the ways that partners in an intimate relationship exhibit public actions that provide – or conceal – evidence of that relationship.[5] Similarly, his essay 'Response cries' confounds casual reflection by showing how talking to oneself in public can provide evidence of personal competence rather than signify impropriety or carelessness in speech.

In this section, I will look at five issues concerning the substance and style of his work, beginning with a discussion of three recurrent substantive issues and concluding with a discussion of two methodological ones.

Structures of Interaction

Although much of our daily lives is spent in face-to-face interaction with other people, we usually take for granted the stability and predictability – the orderliness – of these interactions. While this reliance can sometimes catch us out (interaction can become disordered and unpredictable), these normal stable patterns arise from our orientation to a common set of rules and obligations and also from our common tacit knowledge of how to construct and recognize a range of social actions. These rules, obligations and tacit knowledge both enable and constrain what individuals can accomplish in the course of such interaction. This general approach can be seen in any of Goffman's analyses. An example is his treatment of two recurrent events within the interaction order: 'remedial interchanges' (apologies, requests and accounts); and 'supportive interchanges' (greetings, leavings and so on).[6] Both studies are demonstrations of how such ordinary actions are an essentially collaborative product of individuals who are attentive to rules, obligations and tacit knowledge. However, precisely because such sequences depend on collaborative work, he is able to show how what may happen within these interchanges from moment to moment is vulnerable to individual decision-making and choice.[7]

The interaction order is an essentially unfinished order. As Burns pointed out, 'individuals are constantly at work not only promoting, reinforcing and repairing the social order, but creating, recreating and arranging it'.[8] If such work was guided by unstated rule obligations and other presuppositions, Goffman argued that it would be possible to provide formulations of such rules following close observation of conduct. There are places in his books where he did just that (for example his formulation of the rule of 'civil inattention' in *Behaviour in Public Places*; his treatment of the rules of 'involvement' and 'misinvolvement' in several of the essays in *Interaction Ritual*). But Goffman did not stop at simply stating whatever rule he felt was at work below the surface of a number of instances of social interaction. Having offered a rule for consideration, he usually proceeded by 'uncovering, collecting, collating and interpreting all possible exceptions to a stated rule'.[9] Competent human subjects are expected to be capable of rule interpretation and manipulation, and Goffman was keen to remind his readers of that fact.

Order is not simply the result of people following rules; what rules do is permit people to enact and witness such order. As we think harder about how rules figure in our sense of the orderliness of everyday life, we are forced to consider that their application and interpretation require attention to the context in which any action might occur. A second major element in Goffman's treatment of the interaction order lies in his development of a series of concepts to express the complex array of locally relevant contexts within which action may be located. His success in this respect is witnessed by the fact that so much of his conceptual vocabulary has been used by other writers on the same topic.[10]

Structures of the Self

If the interaction order is the ongoing accomplishment of flesh and blood human subjects, how did Goffman think of these subjects and what account does he give of them in his work? His treatment of this issue generated more interest and commentary than any other area of his work. He wanted to provide what he regarded as a distinctly sociological account of the person. In doing this, he treated as irrelevant the large variety of ways that people think about their own or other people's 'inner lives'. He was not concerned with individuals in the way that psychologists or novelists are when they attempt to display the full depth of human motivation, feeling, intention, unconsciousness and so on. He was not concerned to describe or theorize the self 'in the round'.[11] To understand the self sociologically, it had to be approached as a social institution, and researched by observing and analysing externally observable forms of conduct.

His concern to establish and deploy such a rigorously sociological version of the individual has been the source of a very considerable misunderstanding of his work. He was often assumed to have denied the significance of what we take to be most important about our selves: our undeclared motivations, hidden emotions, private evaluations of our own and other people's conduct and our sense of the meaning of our lives as bound to biography and social location. In fact, it would be wrong to say that Goffman believed such matters to be unimportant as such. However, his view was that, from the standpoint of sociology, their significance was to be treated as 'virtual', as available for use rather than unavoidably used:

> My plea ... is not that one should not see that it is persons with unique biographies who do the interacting [in social situations] but that one should move on from this warming fact to try to uncover the principled ways in which such personal histories are given place and the framework of normative understanding this implies.[12]

What was the outline of his sociological perspective on the self? I think that he offers us three versions, the earlier ones in turn being incorporated into the later ones.

The first version (what Manning calls the 'two-selves' version) appears in *The Presentation of Self in Everyday Life* and in some other essays, especially in 'Where the action is' and 'On face-work'. Here Goffman describes the self as composed of two separable entities – 'character' and 'performer', but also as the combined entity of 'the self as a performed character'.[13] The organization and management of the roles (or characters) assumed by the self-as-performer are his main concern and as Burns has pointed out, his deployment of the vocabulary of drama is well suited to explore the assumptions, advantages and limitations of such a view. However, this version of the self as in contestable command of socially given roles – sometimes only by working hard – gives way to a darker version of the self offered in other books and essays.

This second version is visible in *Asylums* (and in a slightly different form in *Stigma*). In Goffman's own words, 'the self arises not merely out of its possessor's interactions with significant others, but also out of the arrangements that are evolved in an organization for its members'.[14] Here the self is seen as the product of a set of social – especially organizational – circumstances. The image veers towards social determinism except that he drew attention to the ways in which individuals resist, transgress and contest the definitions of themselves embedded and enacted through such organizational arrangements.[15] Battershill comments on such resistances, suggesting that for Goffman 'role transgression is a fundamental social requirement – an agonistic property of society arising from the weight of our manifold attachments and commitments to multi-situated social entities'.[16]

But if the two-selves version overemphasizes the scope for the performer and the socially determined version limits the scope for role choice, a third and final version abandons a description of self in terms of differing substances for a more flexible notion of self as social process. In this final version, the self 'is not an entity half-concealed behind events, but a changeable formula for managing oneself during them'.[17] **Giddens** summarizes Goffman's final version:

> The self consists in an awareness of identity which simultaneously transcends specific roles and provides an integrating means of relating them to personal biography; and furnishes a set of dispositions for managing the transactions between motives and the expectations scripted by particular roles.[18]

One final feature of Goffman's treatment of the self in sociology deserves mention. Unlike most sociologists before him, he managed to portray the self in interaction as fully embodied. In several papers he described and analysed the way that our bodies are made relevant to interaction. However, the undeniable facts of our physical being are not taken to determine who we are or even how we appear to be. As Burns has written of Goffman's argument: 'What counts in social interaction are the movements and adjustments we constantly make in order to amplify, adapt, refine and reapply the elementary functioning of what physical capabilities we have.'[19] Goffman's view of physicality as a resource rather than a constraint is perhaps best illustrated in his analyses of sex and gender in both 'The arrangement between the sexes' and in the illustrated volume *Gender Advertisements*.

Structures of Experience

A third substantive issue became the focus of Goffman's sociology in the latter part of his academic life. I have indicated that the distinctiveness of his approach to face-to-face interaction and to the individual person lay in his commitment to a fully sociological analysis of these matters. The same impulse was at work in his approach to questions of the 'meaning of social action'. The willingness to make such a question central to one's sociology is a distinctive (self-administered) mark of symbolic interactionism, phenomenology and hermeneutics – of the interpretative tradition in general. Goffman was keen to distance himself from that tradition, and he felt that it was possible to treat issues of meaning from within his preferred framework. *Frame Analysis* and his final published paper 'Felicity's condition' addressed this by considering the question of how 'what behaviour means is displayed and understood in interaction'. In pursuing this concern to look 'at how behaviour is used to display and find meaning', he managed to demystify the issue of meaning and give it a specifically sociological content. He tried to specify what common cognitive materials individuals use to determine the meaning of what they believe to be happening in any particular interaction, as well as how they assemble and use such signs and evidences in an attempt to create meanings for others. In *Frame Analysis*, Goffman argued that we use a limited number of 'frames' to determine both our sense as observers of what any particular action is and our shaping as participants of our actions as one kind rather than another.[20]

He also sought to show that underlying these strategic concerns with the shaping and interpretation of information and understanding is an even more basic social requirement for our competent participation in the interaction order. Participants have to show concern with mutual comprehension as a feature of their co-presence, and in this way, a concern with the structure of experience leads us back to a concern with the structures of interaction themselves.

I want now to turn to two final issues in Goffman's distinctive style of sociology. Both are methodological: first, his spirited advocacy of 'naturalistic observations' as the preferred source of basic sociological knowledge; and second, his use of metaphor for the development of theoretical understanding in sociology.

Naturalistic Observation and Sociological Description

Even Goffman's most critical detractors grudgingly admit that his observational capacities were extraordinarily acute. Three kinds of observational work recur throughout his work. First, there were traditional ethnographic studies of social settings (for example the hotel, cottages and farmland of the Shetland island of Unst in his Ph.D., the wards of St Elizabeth's Hospital in his book *Asylums*). Second, there were systematic naturalistic observations guided by his effort to collect and categorize the empirical variety of a chosen object of study (for example analysis of speech faults in radio broadcasts).[21] Third, there were secondary observations based on the study of a vast array of fictional and factual accounts of many different kinds of action (for example his use of detective and spy fiction in 'Strategic interaction' and his use of newspaper 'faits divers' in *Frame Analysis*).

In several public presentations, as well as in the prefaces, introductions and conclusions to his books, Goffman exhorted sociologists to cultivate such methods (although he usually stressed the importance of the first two at the expense of the third). Whichever of these three methods Goffman used, however, he never produced traditional ethnographic descriptions aimed at descriptive fidelity in their reportage of the full detail of life in the setting under study. Instead, he produced collections, categorizations and interpretations of a large range of recurrent events and sequences in social life. He often compared this to the practices of specimen or instance collection and categorization in natural science disciplines – especially botany and biology. In opposition to those who regard such activity as of limited significance, his practice of 'systematics' (as in the natural sciences) was informed by his knowledge of the importance of a strong empirical basis for disciplinary development as well as by his disdain for so much of that airy and premature theorizing in sociology that he once described as 'two thirds corn flakes, one third taffy'.

Using Metaphors Productively

It would be wrong to approach Goffman as no more than a skilled collector and arranger of sociological exhibits. His interpretative skills were unequalled and his vision of the wider significance of his findings was clear. He also worked hard to write in a way that would persuade his readers to see things his way. The main device he used to accomplish these things was that of metaphor; a number of major and minor metaphors recur throughout his work. The major metaphors of 'theatre', 'ritual', 'game' and 'frame' provided his most robust and extensive devices and while there are many minor metaphors, these four basic ones carried forward the bulk of his work.

His use of his major metaphors followed a common pattern. First he used them to portray interaction fully characterized by the vocabulary of, and understandings available from, the particular metaphor in question. The metaphor of the theatre encourages us to think about how people produce recognizable and convincing performances for others, the teamwork needed from all those involved in production, the nature of audience participation and so on. Equally, the metaphor of games was used to draw our attention to the complex sequential organization of events by means of the vocabulary of moves, tactics, strategies, gambits, stakes, players and so on.

But in addition to exploiting this literal use, Goffman probed each metaphor to find its vulnerabilities – to illusion, pretence, deception, fabrication and finally its exhaustion. Sometimes he examined a single metaphor in isolation; at other times he considered the relationship between several such metaphors.[22]

Goffman's argument was that this reflexive use of metaphors was an essential tool of sociological work. While he sometimes invoked the standard idea that such devices offer simplifications of more complex, multilayered real-world events, his practice was more subtle than this rather clichéd representation suggests. Careful attention to his texts shows (as both Burns and Manning have pointed out) that Goffman's metaphors were not simply 'employed' or 'relied on' in the course of his work. Rather, we should think of them as being 'brought into play'. It is important to understand the difference implied by this distinction – it is most visible in *Frame Analysis*. In this book, Goffman directly considered the question of what made his favoured metaphors intelligible in the first place. By asking 'what is it about games that makes them real as games?', and 'what is the nature of theatre as a social achievement?', his investigations are given an additional reflexive turn. Although in its preface, Goffman eschews an overattentiveness to methodological self-consciousness, the book can be profitably read as an extended methodological self-commentary as well as being a report of his considerations upon the organization of people's experience of the social.

Seeing Things Differently

In a review of a large range of ethnographic research on social interaction in the public realm, Lyn Lofland drew attention to the many contributions to that research that 'found their initial inspiration in the Goffmanian insight that life in the public realm is both thoroughly social and sociologically interesting'.[23] Most who work in this field accept that one of the main principles relevant for the organization and analysis of conduct in public is the way that people orientate to the 'rule of civil inattention'. In *Behaviour in Public Places*, Goffman described civil inattention as follows:

> one gives to another enough visual notice to demonstrate that one appreciates that the other is present (and that one admits openly to having seen him), while at the same moment withdrawing one's attention from him so as to express that he does not constitute a target of special curiosity or design.[24]

When following this rule, 'persons circumspectly treat each other with polite and glancing concern while each goes about his own separate business'.[25] An orientation to this rule 'makes possible co-presence without co-mingling, awareness without engrossment, courtesy without conversation. It is perhaps, the absolute *sine qua non of city life*.'[26]

There are exceptions to all such rules, these exceptions themselves being socially organized. A public setting that encouraged co-mingling, engrossment and conversation between people previously unacquainted with one another would be one that suspended or varied the operation of the rule of civil inattention. Are there such settings, and what would be the typical patterns of interactions occurring within them in conditions of the suspension of this rule? One set of answers to these questions was supplied by Sherri Cavan's study of behaviour in licensed bars.[27] Cavan's study (and its use of Goffman's original ideas) helps us convert our casual assertions about bars, pubs and other kinds of public licensed premises being places in which people are 'more sociable' into a series of focused researchable sociological issues. The increased possibilities for, and encouragement of, sociability in such settings rest on the assumption that individuals will be more open to encounters with others.[28] Suspending the rule of civil inattention allows those co-present to move from the assumption of openness into the accomplishment of talk or its non-verbal substitute. It should be easy to recognize and understand the significance of Cavan's observation that once the rule is suspended 'not only idle glances at other patrons but also idle glances at features and fixtures of the establishment all convey one's openness. There are no protective goods, no newspapers, letters and books to serve as an alternative form of involvement. If such props are used, they may themselves serve as grounds for initial overtures of sociability.'[29] We can better understand how difficult it is to resist the overtures of sociability from other users of sociability in such places by reference to variations in the operation of civil inattention and their effect on the status of participants. The same variations and effects are also relevant for understanding why the majority of verbal encounters that do occur in such settings remain momentary ones. According to Cavan, mutual openness 'shortens the life span of such interactions'. The same rules that facilitate the opening of encounters make it likely that the conversational content of such encounters will be 'tentative and superficial' and that the interaction will be difficult to maintain.[30] The normal rules that give one person rather than another control over the termination of an interaction are much looser in this context, and this makes it much easier for participants to drift into, out of and away from an encounter. Equally the open status of such conversations makes it more likely that further participants can both enter and appropriate both conversational topic and individual people.

It is difficult to convey the full complexity of the interactional structures that Cavan is able to display in the course of her work. What should be clear, even from this short account, is both the way that her observation of ordinary conduct is informed by Goffman's original vision, and the way that our own sociological understanding can be similarly developed.

Legacies and Unfinished Business

Morality, Self and Interaction

Goffman's work raised issues that lie on the border between sociology and moral philosophy. What moral stance is implied by his vision of human action? Does he license the cynical manipulation of others or is he a critic of the limits of a Machiavellian perspective on the social? Many have argued that Goffman's overall view of the self is distorted by a fascination with appearance and the neglect of deeper issues of morality and motivation.[31] A second group of commentators on Goffman's work have pointed to the emergence of a more complex view of human nature. Burns, Manning, Giddens and others have argued that he was concerned with the polarity of mistrust and trust in social encounters.[32] A third view goes further and seeks to portray Goffman's view of human nature and social order as exemplifying a strong moral commitment quite at odds with previous representations of an amoral voyeur of human conduct.[33]

Further Explorations in the Interaction Order

Goffman's commitment to the close analysis of face-to-face conduct based on a behavioural rather than interpretative programme has been taken up – and sometimes modified – by a new generation of productive scholars. One recent collection of papers includes several chapters by scholars providing more dense and subtle appreciations of the ways in which he incorporated and modified prior work as well as finer accounts of the sociohistorical contexts of his intellectual craftmanship.[34] A more critical tradition, describing their work as 'conversation analysis' or 'the analysis of talk-in-interaction', have repudiated Goffman's methods and some aspects of his overall account of social order, while still acknowledging their indebtedness to his original cultivation of a new field of sociological study.[35] Other linguistically oriented researchers outside sociology have also taken forward many of Goffman's original ideas. Recent work in anthropology, discourse analysis and pragmatics have all benefited from his vocabulary and findings.

Situating the Interaction Order

Since Goffman argued that the interaction order was one of several orders of social reality subject to sociological analysis, questions arise about how we should understand the interaction order to be related to the larger social and historical structures in which it is located. And how does the interaction order stand in relation to the biography of individuals and social groups that enliven it? Goffman's own answers continue to provoke commentary and alternative formulations. This is the final piece of unfinished business that I want to discuss in this chapter.

Goffman characterized himself as 'no rampant situationalist'.[36] He argued that it was inappropriate to treat the order of interaction as the creation of co-participants independent of wider historical and social arrangements, asserting that:

> the individuals I know don't invent the world of chess when they sit down to play, or the stock market when they buy some shares, or the pedestrian traffic system when they manoeuvre through the streets. Whatever the idiosyncrasies of their own motives and interpretations, they must gear their participation into what is available by way of standard doings and standard reasons for doing these doings.[37]

His characterization of the relationship between the interaction order and the wider social order on the one hand and to individual biographies on the other hand was in terms of ties of 'loose coupling'.[38]

A number of critics remain unconvinced by Goffman's assertion of the status of the interaction order and unsure about the 'loose coupling' by which he argues it is related to other features of the social. Both of the main alternatives to his views share an attempt to establish a more seamless unity to our view of social life. A first critique suggests that Goffman's claims for the significance of the interaction order were too timid, that he awarded too much importance to 'wider social arrangements' as exemplified by his acceptance of the significance of a micro/macro distinction for sociology. Both Rawls and Burns attack the necessity to recognize claims for the significance of an abstract (for Burns, emptily abstract) structural order seen as somehow standing above the interaction order. Burns, for example, argues that:

> social order is always, and essentially locally produced. To try to work out the connections between social interaction and a social order which prevails throughout society is not only impossibly difficult, as it has so far appeared to be, but pointless. For the immediacies and restricted dimensions of everyday interaction and social encounters are neither the elementary constituents of the larger, remote 'crystallizations' of social institutions, organizations and the like that Simmel saw in them nor the determinate outcomes of Mandelbaum's 'societal facts'.[39]

While this first critique collapses all social arrangements into the arrangements of the interaction order, a second critique collapses the interaction order into a larger set of social arrangements. Giddens, for example, is critical of the degree of independence Goffman gives to the interaction order, arguing that a false separation between the interaction and institutional order results in the diminution of the significance of Goffman's work for a unified theory of society.[40]

I am more persuaded by Goffman's own understanding of the matter, particularly because he regarded this understanding of loose coupling as no more than a guide for research. Confidence in seamless webs and unified theories does not sit comfortably alongside Goffman's drive to the close examination of human conduct, his suspicion of grand theory in sociology or his realization of the necessary arbitrariness of concept formation in the social sciences.

Goffman's work portrayed the details of face-to-face interaction in sharp sociological focus. He demonstrated a remarkable awareness of the possible scope and depth of its investigation while maintaining an awareness of the methodological complexities involved. The range of the concepts and findings he offered, his willingness to think hard about the banal as well as the exceptional, to explore the exoteric alongside the esoteric, and the extraodinary skill of his literary style: all these qualities combine to make his work one of the best introductions to the distinctiveness of the sociological imagination.

FURTHER READING

Burns, T. (1992) *Erving Goffman*, London: Routledge. A useful overview of Goffman's work.

Ditton, J. (ed.) (1980) *The View from Goffma*n, London: Macmillan– now Palgrave Macmillan. An edited volume of chapters by theorists and researchers positively influenced by Goffman's world-view.

Drew, P. and and Wootton, A. (eds) (1988) *Erving Goffman: Exploring the Interaction Order*, Cambridge: Polity Press. The idea of an interaction order is arguably the basis for a more 'structural' Goffman, and this late 1980s volume brings together some of the most interesting work on the subject.

Fine, G. and Smith, G. (eds) (2000) *Erving Goffman*, 4 vols, in Sage Masters of Modern Thought, London: Sage. This is an illuminating collection of many of the best critical reviews, commentaries and empirical applications of Goffman's insights.

Manning, P. (1992) *Erving Goffman and Modern Sociology*, Cambridge: Polity Press. An excellent, lucid, commentary which stands out, amongst other things, for the coining of the acronym SIAC to characterize the major themes in Goffman's work: Situational propriety; Involvement; Access; and Civil Inattention.

Trevino, A.J. (ed.) (2003) *Goffman's Legacy*, New York: Rowman & Littlefield. A recent lively and challenging edited volume reappraising the Goffman inheritance some 50 years after the field work on which *The Presentation of Self in Everyday Life* was carried out.

Chapter 11

David Lockwood

Nicos Mouzelis

Driving Impulses

David Lockwood began his sociological career at a time when it was **Parsonian** functionalism and its complement – what C.W. Mills called abstracted empiricism – that dominated sociology. Going against the prevailing orthodoxy, Lockwood tried to introduce into the empirically oriented sociological research issues derived from the work of **Karl Marx**, the great absentee from the early postwar sociological canon. His whole oeuvre can be seen as an imaginative and critical engagement with Marx's thought, his major aim being not a scholastic preoccupation with what the German philosopher 'really said or meant' on various issues, but creatively to use basic Marxist concepts and substantive theories in order to show the inadequacy of Parsonian conceptual tools for understanding the constitution, reproduction and transformation of modern societies; and explore empirically the social structure of modern Britain.

Whether one looks at Lockwood's theoretical contributions or his empirically oriented analyses of class, the constant, all-pervasive theme of his work is the idea that the type of **Durkheimian** sociology that Parsonian functionalism mainly represents needs to be brought nearer to a Marxist way of conceptualizing the mechanisms of social order and disorder.

Key Issues

White-collar Workers: Becoming Proletarian?

Lockwood's first major empirical contribution, *The Blackcoated Worker*, was in the sphere of white-collar work.[1] He was one of the first social scientists to show in an empirically concrete and at the same time theoretically adequate manner that, as far as the work situation is concerned, white-collar workers in our day are experiencing the type of routinization and bureaucratization of their jobs that blue-collar workers underwent during the emergence and dominance of the modern factory system. In fact, the growing importance of the large office, where a great number of employees were brought together under the same roof, had organizational effects similar to those of the factory two centuries ago. It increased the anonymity and impersonality of the employee–employer relationship, while creating favourable conditions for the development of white-collar unions.

From the above point of view, Marx was quite correct when he argued that the further development of capitalism would spread the process of proletarianization beyond the factory gates. But if in terms of the work situation, there was a certain homogenization between blue- and white-collar workers, in other respects, Lockwood pointed out, the differences between the two social categories were still significant. In terms of market chances, for instance, office workers – due to greater opportunities for promotion as well as to a variety of fringe benefits – still keep an important advantage. This in turn is one of the main reasons why, in terms of status, clerical work still entails higher prestige than manual labour.

The Affluent Worker: Becoming Middle Class?

This type of problematic was further developed by J.H. Goldthorpe et al. in the now classical study of a number of **affluent skilled manual workers** in Luton.[2] In this context, a somewhat similar issue was examined from the blue-collar perspective. Contrary to the *embourgeoisement* thesis,[3] which argued that the affluent working class was increasingly becoming middle class, Lockwood, Goldthorpe and their collaborators posited that such a notion of the assimilation of the working class into the middle class was unduly simplistic. Rather, both groups were changing in such a way that it was a particular kind of convergence rather than assimilation or merger that characterized the overall situation. For if the white-collar worker had moved from non-unionized, personal relationships between employee and employer to one of instrumental collectivism (that is, a context where white-collar workers join unions so as to promote their individual interests), the blue-collar worker was reaching the same position by a very different route. From the solidaristic collectivism of the traditional working-class community, he or she had come to view the unions in as instrumental/individualistic a manner as his or her white-collar counterpart.

According to Goldthorpe and Lockwood, what is common to both groups is *privatization*, a type of home-centred existence where the joys of consumption or newly acquired gadgets and private family life become more important than class struggles and the expression of collective sentiments and interests in the public domain.[4]

> ***The world of the affluent worker***
>
> *The interviews showed that the sample of affluent manual workers shared a predominately 'instrumental orientation' to their employment, irrespective of differences in skill, occupational status, or the technology with which they were involved. By an instrumental orientation, the authors mean that workers were attracted to their jobs because of 'extrinsic', that is, mainly economic, considerations. For example, 87 per cent of skilled men and 82 per cent of those semi-skilled explained their work attachments wholly or partly in terms of the level of pay, degree of security, or extent of the fringe benefits available. Only 29 per cent of the former and 14 per cent of the latter mentioned 'intrinsic' attractions such as job satisfaction. Consistent with this, few participated actively in work-based societies or clubs, and few were members of solidary work groups. Nor did they base their social lives outside the factory on associations with workmates. Home and factory were psychologically and socially isolated from each other. Thus, for example, 76 per cent of skilled men and 66 per cent of the semi-skilled reported they would be 'not much bothered' or 'not bothered at all' if they moved away from their present workmates to another job.*[5]

Technology, Workplace, Community, Society: A Holistic Approach

In a further creative engagement with Marxism, Lockwood and Goldthorpe have argued that if one tries to explain the two major features of the convergence trajectory, that is, instrumental collectivism and privatization, neither technology nor the organization of the workplace can provide a satisfactory answer. The workers' instrumental orientation towards their jobs (for example the fact that they are more interested in higher wages than in work satisfaction and self-fulfilment on the job) was shaped less by factors within the workplace itself and more by broader communal and societal factors.

Contrary to Robert Blauner, therefore, who was trying to establish one-to-one linkages between technology/work conditions and 'alienation' at work,[6] Goldthorpe and Lockwood argued that such rather crude technological determinism was misleading. Although subsequent studies have shown that workers' orientations are influenced by both workplace and related conditions,[7] there is no doubt that the empirical studies in Luton have shown the risk inherent in arbitrarily extracting isolated concepts (such as that of Marx's notion of work alienation) from classical theories in order to 'operationalize' them and establish correlations between so-called variables.

What is valuable and enduring in Lockwood's empirical research is that, although he is greatly influenced by Marx's writings, he takes the holistic character of Marxist theory seriously. Unlike Blauner, he does not reduce it to an aggregate of statements and disconnected hypotheses from which the modern researcher picks and chooses at will for purposes of 'operationalization' and empirical testing. In other words, whereas Blauner's excursus into classical theory was rather decorative (in the sense that he could present his research without once referring to Marx's theory of alienation), Lockwood's engagement with Marxism was and is on a more serious and fundamental level.

Social and System Integration

The same can be said of Lockwood's more theoretical writings, where the focus is less on substantive issues and more on the basic conceptual tools that *prepare the ground* for the construction of substantive theories. On this level, Lockwood, in order to show the basic differences between Marxism and Parsonian sociology, made the seminal suggestion of distinguishing between social and system integration – a distinction that came to play a leading role in various theoretical debates in the social sciences.[8]

The social/system-integration distinction makes it possible to look at a social system (whether this is a small group, a formal organization, or a whole society) from two analytically distinct but complementary perspectives. The social-integration perspective focuses on *agency*, on the way in which social actors view and relate to each other in specific social contexts. So for Lockwood, social integration refers to 'the orderly or conflictual relationships between actors'; whereas system integration focuses on the compatible or incompatible linkages between the 'parts of the social system'.[9] In this latter case, therefore, the social system and the mechanisms that integrate it are not seen from the 'inside' (not from the actors' point of view), but from the outside, so to speak, from the point of view of the system and its requirements for reproduction/survival. Given this systemic, 'externalist' perspective, the mechanisms leading to integration/disintegration are no longer those of conflict/cooperation, but those of logical compatibility/incompatibility between systemic parts.

Lockwood's Critique of Parsons: An Overemphasis on System Integration

If we look at Parsonian functionalism (which Lockwood identifies with normative functionalism) from the above perspective, systemic parts are seen to be conceptualized in institutional terms. For example, Parsons subdivides a societal system into four basic institutional subsystems: the adaptation subsystem (which refers to economic institutions), the goal-achievement subsystem (political institutions), the integration subsystem (legal and communal institutions), and the latency subsystem (kinship and religious institutions).[10] (See Chapter 7.) Since Parsons overemphasizes system and underemphasizes social integration, his only mechanisms of change are internal to the systsem and refer to incompatibilities between the social system's different subsystems. So, for example, in a late-developing country, introducing western technology and modes of management into the economic subsystem (adaptation) might render the values/norms of this subsystem logically incompatible with those still prevalent in the religious or kinship subsystem (latency).

This systemic contradiction or incompatibility between institutional subsystems constitutes the major mechanism of social transformation for Parsonian modernization theorists.[11] For Lockwood, this conceptualization of social change is misleading because of its overemphasis on system integration. Its exclusive focus on systemic incompatibilities between normative orders peripheralizes actors, and prevents one from asking who-questions about social change. For example, which specific interest groups (entrepreneurs, workers, women, priests and so on) experience the contradiction between the instrumental rationality of the economic subsystem and the 'expressive' rationality of the religious subsystem, and how do these groups deal with those incompatibilities? Are they aware of them? Do they try to set up formal organizations so as to handle the growing contradictions in one way or another? Such agency questions are peripheral or completely absent from the Parsonian analysis of the modernization process. It is as though a mysterious entity called 'society', or 'societal system', were handling the contradictions so as to bring about social change in the direction of greater differentiation and higher adaptive capacity.[12]

Advantages of Marx over Parsons

Now, according to Lockwood, if one looks at the conceptual framework underlying Marxist approaches to social change, two basic differences from Parsonian functionalism can be identified.

First, on the level of system integration, systemic parts are not only normative/institutional, but also non-normative/material. For example, the basic Marxist contradiction between *material base* (forces of production or technology in the broad sense of the term) and *institutional core* (institutions of private property) is a type of systemic incompatibility that is not found in Parsons' purely normative/institutional conceptualization of systemic subsystems.

The second major difference between Marx and Parsons is that the former (if one looks at his work as a whole) puts equal emphasis on social and system integration. Unlike Parsons, Marx does ask social-integration, who-questions, such as: What do actors do about growing systemic incompatibilities? Are they aware of the growing contradiction between the increasingly collective character of the forces of production, and the still private character of the institutions regulating the ownership of the means of production? And if so, what are the chances of building up class organizations capable of transforming the prevailing relations of production?

According to Lockwood, regardless of the fact that some of Marx's substantive theories about the development of class consciousness and class struggles in late capitalism were wrong (such as his thesis on the growing pauperization of the proletariat), the basic conceptual framework is pretty sound. It combines in a highly ingenious manner the social- with the system-integration perspective. It succeeds in viewing capitalist societies from an agency/internalist as well as a systemic/externalist perspective; both in terms of the strategies and conflicts of the main protagonists, as well as in terms of the basic incompatibilities/contradictions of a mode of production based on the private ownership of the means of production. Marx's theory raised the fundamental question that Parsonian sociology fails to raise: given growing systemic contradictions, what happens on the level of social integration, that is, on the level of actors' consciousness, strategies, struggles? How do their strategies and struggles affect systemic contradictions and vice versa?

It is precisely because it combines system and social integration more effectively that Marxism offers us tools useful for the *explanation* of both stability and change. Parson's underemphasis of social integration, his peripheralization of actors makes them appear as mere puppets of the system's requirements. In consequence, social order and disorder in normative functionalism are, at best, described, but cannot be explained.

The Dynamics of Social Change

Let us now move from Parsons to his major mentor Durkheim who, according to Lockwood, takes social integration rather more seriously. However, here again there is an interesting contrast between Durkheim's and Marx's attempts to explain social order and disorder.[13]

Durkheim views social structure in status terms. For him, social structure consists of hierarchically organized status groups whose rights and obligations are legally defined and legitimized by the prevailing societal values and norms. This type of distribution of rights and obligations Durkheim calls 'social classification', and it is social classification that confers cohesion and order on society. As for social disorder, this comes about when this hierarchical structure of normatively regulated groups is undermined by processes Durkheim defines vaguely as 'sudden changes in the economy', 'changes in wealth and power', changes in the ordering of 'men and things' and so on, changes which (when properly theorized, lead to the Marxist concepts of class structure and class struggles) disrupt the existing system of classification. They bring about 'declassification', a state of affairs characterized by such anomic phenomena as moral deregulation, egoism, social schism, moral polarization and so on.

For Lockwood, therefore, Durkheim's theory of disorder or social change is based on a notion of *discrepancy* between a status hierarchy and a vaguely defined class-power situation – the latter term referring to circumstances where 'life chances are minimally conditioned by legal status defining entitlements', and status hierarchy to circumstances where such entitlements are dominant.[14] This means that status for Durkheim entails a *de jure* distribution of rights and privileges, whereas class entails *de facto* power relationships based on the differential control of situational facilities.

According to Lockwood looking at Marx, there the situation is exactly the reverse: what is central to Durkheim becomes peripheral for Marx, and vice versa. At the centre of the Marxist view of social structure are power, rather than status, groups, that is, groups struggling over the control of the means of production and over the benefits such control bestows. From this perspective, social disorder or social transformation occurs when there is a discrepancy between class and status – status *contra* Durkheim, being defined by Marx only nebulously. For Marx, when power relations between social classes no longer correspond to the distribution of rights and obligations as defined by law, that is, when there is a discrepancy between de facto power relations and *de jure* formal arrangements, then we witness processes leading to social change. So while both Marx and Durkheim base their theories of disorder on a discrepancy between status and power relationships, the one considers as the core and conceptualizes carefully what the other considers peripheral and conceptualizes vaguely.

Marx choosing to emphasize power rather than status relations makes sense in view of the fact that his social-action schema is fundamentally utilitarian. And if in classical utilitarianism the ends of action are random, in Marxism they are 'objectively' determined by the prevailing relations of production. For example, given the fact that the worker in capitalism does not own the means of production, this situation automatically entails 'objective' interest: that is, the overthrow of an exploitative system in which the worker must sell his or her labour power in order to survive, while the capitalist, via labour-market mechanisms, profits from surplus value. Given, moreover, Marx's utilitarian assumption about the economic rationality of actors, the workers will tend to adopt revolutionary, anti-capitalist strategies. If they do not, it is because of false consciousness; because the dominant classes, by means of various ideological mechanisms, prevent them from seeing their situation objectively. According to Lockwood, the introduction of the false-consciousness argument results in Marxists veering between a positivist position (objective class locations more or less automatically bring about certain class practices), and an idealist one (whenever there is a discrepancy between objective interests and class practices, it is due to the adoption of 'false' ideas).

Linking the above considerations with an earlier critique he had developed of certain aspects of historical materialism, Lockwood stresses the fact that the positivist/idealist oscillation in Marxism is a result of it not being possible to identify 'objective interests'. Interests cannot be automatically derived from a given class position; they are constructed by processes that always entail normative considerations. For Lockwood, therefore, Marx's action schema does not seriously take into account that class interests are shaped not only by the relations of production and/or the work situation. In the workers' 'definition of the situation', extra-work and extra-class societal values and norms may, or rather do, play a crucial role.

Another major conclusion Lockwood derives from the Durkheim–Marx comparison is that the tension (or lack of it) between de facto power relations and *de jure* status is a fundamental factor for understanding social order and disorder in capitalist societies. In that sense, investigations of social change must seriously consider *both* Durkheim's theorization of status hierarchies and Marx's conceptualization of class/power.

Seeing Things Differently

Lockwood has not tried to construct a metatheory to bring together the status and power approaches, just as in his earlier work he avoided any theoretical synthesis of the social- and system-integration perspectives. However, what is crucial for empirical research is that his theoretical distinctions do clearly demonstrate the necessity of studying social stability and change in both a Durkheimian and Marxist manner, in terms of both status hierarchies and power struggles over the control of scarce resources.

Similarly, his seminal social/system-integration dichotomy encourages the study of changing social systems (micro, meso or macro) from both the systemic/functionalist perspective and that of action/agency. Any one-sided emphasis on system to the exclusion of social integration leads to teleological explanations that portray 'society' as a mysterious entity pulling all the strings behind the actors' backs. As Lockwood has shown, one finds such teleological explanations not only in Parsonian functionalism, but also in those Marxist theorists who underemphasize the voluntaristic dimension of social life (for example the **Althusserian** school).

On the other hand, overemphasis of agency at the expense of systemic considerations – as seen in the various interpretative sociologies that developed spectacularly in the 1960s and 70s – takes us from **reification** to **reductionism**: where complex macrostructural developments are reduced to interpretative understandings and actors' face-to-face interactions. Therefore, if an imbalance in favour of system integration leads to mechanistic/deterministic explanations of social order and disorder, an imbalance in favour of social integration leads to social myopia and to the elimination of crucial issues that cannot be fully accounted for by an exclusive focus on actors' orientations and definitions of the social world.[15]

> *Reification and reductionism*
>
> *Reification here refers to the way in which society, which includes people and their actions as part of its reality, can be treated as a thing without people that somehow works entirely by itself and according to goals of its own making. Reductionism here refers to the way in which society, which is more than the current actions of people today (it includes, for example, the buildings, roads, information networks, filing cabinets, energy grids and so on that were created in the past and are still here today as part of society's functioning), is treated as nothing but (reduced to) the current actions of people today.* (see p. 229 for another form of reductionism)

Legacies and Unfinished Business

Recent Attempts to Transcend the Social/System-integration Divide: Elias, Giddens, Bourdieu

I do not think it an exaggeration to claim that the neglect of the social/system-integration *balance* has been at the root of a lot of confusion and numerous false starts and sterile debates in the social sciences. The same can be said about more recent efforts to 'transcend' the social/system-integration divide. So Elias's figurational sociology,[16] **Giddens**' structuration theory[17] or **Bourdieu**'s theory of social practice[18] are all part of the repeated attempts to go beyond the agency–system or the 'subjectivist'–'objectivist' divide in the social sciences – attempts that have invariably been unsuccessful, however. Their supposed transcendence has always been rhetorical/decorative rather than substantive. They have ostensibly rejected Lockwood's more conventional way of conceptualizing the agency–system distinction, while in fact reintroducing it in a different terminological guise.

Giddens, for instance, rejects functionalism and the agency–system distinction, but brings in both by the back door, so to speak, via his distinction between institutional analysis (which is exactly what Lockwood means by the system-integration approach) and analysis in terms of strategic conduct (Lockwood's social-integration perspective). In similar fashion, Bourdieu claims that his habitus concept (see Chapter 16) transcends the objectivist–subjectivist divide, but reinstates exactly the same divide when he talks about objective locations and actors' stances or postures vis-à-vis such locations (actors' *prise de position*).[19]

Recent Attempts to Abolish the Social/System-integration Divide: Foucault, Derrida, Baudrillard

Equally unsuccessful are postmodern/poststructuralist attempts, not to transcend but simply to abolish the agency–system distinction. For postmodernists, proceeding to 'decentre' the subject, or focusing on discourses or practices rather than actors, the agency–system distinction is at best superfluous, and at worst leads to essentialist accounts of the social world.[20] This postmodernist/poststructuralist position, however, makes one view the social world reductively, as a chain of discursive practices (**Foucault**), or texts (Derrida) or signifiers (Baudrillard). From this perspective, there is no possibility of showing how practices are hierarchized and why, for instance, certain practices have greater transformational impact than others. In view of this limitation, there is a tendency in postmodern analyses to explain complex macro-phenomena simplistically in terms of signs, symbols or such 'disembodied' notions as desire, power/knowledge and so on.[21]

A Recent Confusion about Social and System Integration: Habermas

If Giddens and Bourdieu have tried to transcend the social and system-integration distinction, and postmodern theorists to abolish it, Habermas accepts its utility but incorporates it with a second distinction that ultimately cancels the heuristic utility of Lockwood's initial formulation.

More specifically, **Habermas** accepts Lockwood's position that one should look at social systems from both an agency ('internalist' in Habermas's terminology) and a systemic ('externalist') perspective; but in his later work, when Habermas uses the social/system-integration distinction, he conflates the externalist/internalist perspective with that of his system/life-world. For Habermas, in highly differentiated modern societies, *system* refers to the economic and political institutional spheres that are coordinated via the systemic media of money and power. *Life-world*, on the other hand (which Habermas identifies with social integration), refers to such institutional spheres as the family, religion, the public domain and so on, which are supposed to be integrated via non-systemic media (that is, via normative and/or communicative modes of coordination).[22]

When Habermas conflates Lockwood's *methodological* distinction (agency/internalist–systemic/externalist) with a *substantive* distinction between institutional spheres coordinated via systemic and non-systemic media, he creates confusion and counters the heuristic utility of Lockwood's initial distinction. This diverts attention from the obvious fact that one can view all social systems from an internalist and externalist perspective – whether they are embedded in the economic and political spheres (Habermas's system), or in a society's social and cultural institutional spheres.[23]

The Real Weakness in Lockwood's Conception of Social/System-integration and a Way Forward

The fact that Lockwood's social/system-integration distinction has stood the test of time so well does not, of course, mean it has no weaknesses. I think that the major one lies in the author's attempt to show that contradictions between systemic parts in Marxism are 'qualitatively' (one could say, ontologically) different from systemic contradictions in Parsonian functionalism on a material–normative continuum. To argue, as Lockwood does, that Marxist analysis, unlike normative-functionalist analysis, focuses on contradictions between a material, non-normative base (forces of production, that is, technology in the broad sense of the term) and a core *institutional* complex (institution of private ownership) implies that technology or certain aspects of the economy are not normatively regulated. This necessarily leads to a type of essentialism that is unacceptable to those who think that the social is symbolically constructed and that institutional spheres (economic, political, religious and so on) entail normative regulation.

A way out of this difficulty is for Lockwood to drop the material/normative or material/institutional distinction because in reality they are always intertwined. Social practices involve both. If we want to investigate the nature of systemic contradictions between the forces of producton and the relations of production, then we would do better to accept that both aspects of this systemic incompatibility involve both material and normative, institutional elements. It would be better to work instead a distinction between more and less *durable* institutional arrangements.[24] Marx's contradiction between forces and relations of production can then more fruitfully be conceptualized as a contradiction between more durable, hard-to-change technological structures and the more malleable institutions of private ownership of the means of production. Of course, whether the latter are more malleable than the former is an empirical question, and the degree of durability of the forces and of the relations of production can vary from one case to the next. But to replace 'materiality' with 'durability' renders the whole issue less metaphysical, more amenable to empirical research.

To conclude, Lockwood's more substantive writings on the changing class structure of modern societies, his crucial conceptualization of the social/system-integration perspectives, and his more recent theoretical analysis of the Marxist and Durkheimian sociological legacies have generated an important corpus of works attempting to criticize, reformulate or reject the author's basic insights into the mechanisms of social stability and change in modernity. The fact that the debate about the agency–system distinction is still alive, and the fact that, after a rush to transcend or simply reject the subjective/objective divide in the social sciences, this fundamental distinction is still a major organizing principle and a fruitful heuristic device in ongoing research,[25] clearly shows the importance of Lockwood's contribution.

I believe his work will become even more central in the years to come – given the sobering-up process that is gaining strength in both the UK and the USA. This consists of a growing realization that, instead of trying to transcend or abolish the agency–system divide, it might be more fruitful to try, rather more modestly, to build conceptual bridges facilitating two-way communication between the interpretative and systemic/functionalist sociologies.[26]

FURTHER READING

Goldthorpe, J.H., Lockwood, D., Bechhofer, F. and Platt, J. (1968) *The Affluent Worker: Industrial Attitudes and Behaviour*, Cambridge: Cambridge University Press. One of the most important works of post-Second World War British sociology.

Lockwood, D. (1965) 'Some remarks on the social system', *British Journal of Sociology*, 7: 134–46. This is most usefully read alongside Lockwood's 1964 article on social and system integraton, see below.

Lockwood, D. (1958) *The Blackcoated Worker*, London: Allen & Unwin. Lockwood's major analysis of the routinization and bureaucratization of white-collar jobs. Highly influential in subsequent British class analysis with its distinction between work, market and status situations.

Lockwood, D. (1964) 'Social integration and system integration', in G.K. Zollschan and W. Hirsch (eds) *Explorations in Social Change*, London: Routledge & Kegan Paul, pp. 244–57. A short but highly influential piece whose distinction between social- and system-integration has since played a major role in Habermas's *The Theory of Communicative Action*. Lockwood himself used the distinction to reject the inadequate polar extremes of the conflict and consensus approaches of the 1950s and early 1960s. The article is reproduced as an afterword in Lockwood's *Solidarity and Schism*.

Lockwood, D. (1992) *Solidarity and Schism: 'The Problem of Disorder' in Durkheimian and Marxist Sociology*, Oxford: Oxford University Press.

Mouzelis, N. (1992) 'Social and system integration: Habermas' view', *British Journal of Sociology*, **43**(2): 272–7.

Mouzelis, N. (2000) 'The subjectivist–objectivist divide against transcendence', *Sociology*, **34**(4): 741–72.

CHAPTER 12

Harold Garfinkel

JOHN HERITAGE

Driving Impulses

One of the chief sociological innovations of the postwar era has been the discovery of the world of everyday social life. This discovery was made during a period – the 1950s – in which much sociological analysis was highly abstract and divorced from real events. The sociology of that period was almost entirely concerned with the limits that social organization places on human activities, with no concern at all with how those activities were possible in the first place. Sociologists were content to sketch abstract constraints that 'box in' human action without ever addressing what actually happened in the conduct of action itself. Left out were the details of how people actually reasoned and acted, what they did inside the 'box' of constraint, indeed whether or in what sense there was a 'box' at all.

In this context, two great and original American sociologists offered massive dissent. **Erving Goffman** saw that social interaction is itself a social institution, and one that enables and mediates the operations of all the other institutions in society. Harold Garfinkel went still deeper. He argued that underlying all social institutions – including Goffman's 'interaction order' – is a still more fundamental one. This order he called 'ethnomethodological'. It concerns how persons *make sense* of their circumstances and act on them: how people analyse, understand and act in their social world.

Imagine a simple social setting, for example a medical consultation in a general practice context. The doctor and patient begin with some conversation about the patient's forthcoming holiday. Then, in response to 'What brings you here today?', the patient details some stomach problems he has been experiencing. A five-minute course of questioning ensues, followed by a physical examination and, finally, a diagnosis and a set of treatment recommendations.

Consider some questions that are absolutely central to an analysis of this encounter. How do doctor and patient understand which parts of the conversation are 'social' and which are 'medical'? In what ways and by what means does the patient understand, process and respond to the doctor's questions, and by what means does the doctor grasp the experiences and reasoning behind the patient's answers? How does the doctor reason about the patient's illness, and how is that reasoning expressed in diagnostic questioning? How much of that reasoning does the patient grasp and, more generally, how does the patient make decisions about how to answer the doctor's questions? How does each party grasp the motivations of the other at different moments in the consultation? How do the parties know 'where they are' in the consultation at any point in time? How, in short, do the doctor and patient 'make sense' of one another and their situation, and 'make sense' together? How would you go about answering these questions and analysing this encounter?

In 1950, when Harold Garfinkel was a student at Harvard University, two main approaches to understanding this interaction were available to him. One approach was to describe the value system underpinning the institution of medicine, and to illustrate the operation of this value system in the behaviours of doctor and patient.[1] The other was to describe the behaviours of the parties in terms of whether they were oriented to medical tasks or to the management of emotion, using a newly invented coding system called 'interaction process analysis'.[2] Neither of these approaches has ever offered any significant answers to our questions about sense-making in the doctor–patient encounter. Yet it is obvious that this sense-making process is foundational – for both doctor and patient – in the step-by-step unfolding of the medical encounter itself. For it is the sense-making process that is central to how doctor and patient make decisions about what to do and say next. The process of sense-making and the actions based on it make each specific medical encounter what it is.

Although Parsons and Bales were Garfinkel's teachers at Harvard in 1950, Garfinkel argued against them that what they were missing, sense-making, is the beginning of everything that is possible in the social world. Nothing can happen in society without it. Garfinkel has spent a lifetime working on how human sense-making can be analysed, and how its input into action and social structure can be grasped. Garfinkel never believed that this business of sense-making was a matter for psychology. On the contrary, he argued that people make *joint* sense of their social world *together*, and that they do so *methodically*, using social *procedures or methods* that *they* share. Because these methods are shared by the members of specific cultures and subcultures, Garfinkel called them 'ethnomethods'. And he called the sociological study of these ethnomethods 'ethnomethodology'. Ethnomethodology studies how these socially shared methods are used to understand, reason and act in the common-sense world of everyday life.

The underlying ideas with which Garfinkel began his work were conceived in a period of crisis. In the late 1930s, the philosopher Edmund Husserl contrasted the abstract mathematical rationality of science with the ordinary experiences and everyday rationality of what he called the life-world. Unconsciously echoing **Weber**, he observed that although modern science is ultimately grounded in this life-world of ordinary experience, it has become divorced from it. The result is that science has become an abstract vision of the world stripped of human value and meaning, and useless as a weapon to resist the tide of irrationality that was then engulfing Europe. Shadowed by the Nazi takeover in Germany and stalked by an illness that would be his last, Husserl described this situation in a book titled *The Crisis of European Sciences and Transcendental Phenomenology*.[3]

Harold Garfinkel came into contact with these and related writings about the life-world almost immediately. A student at the University of North Carolina in 1940, and newly in contact with another form of racism – the racial domination of the American South – he used Husserl as part of a scalding analysis of racial factors in North Carolina homicide trials.[4] During this period, he also wrote a short story, 'Color trouble',[5] which depicted the protest of an African-American woman who boarded a bus but then refused to sit at the back. Anticipating by some years the form of Rosa Parks' 1955 protest that ignited the American civil rights movement, the story embodies a vivid sense of the everyday world – Husserl's life-world of everyday experience – as the primordial site in which human values are expressed and contested.

After Garfinkel moved to Harvard in 1946 to work with **Talcott Parsons** (the dominant figure in American sociology during the ensuing 25 years), his concerns with the life-world became more theoretically focused. The sociology he encountered there had little interest in the life-world of everyday decision-making and action. Instead, it was preoccupied with how persons are motivated to conform to the demands of social structure by the impact of value systems and institutional norms.

Garfinkel vigorously disagreed with this emphasis. He insisted on the fundamental fact that for norms, values and social institutions to exist at all, the parties must somehow know what they are doing and grasp that their understanding is a joint, shared understanding. There is then this primordial social reasoning and shared sense-making that make up the vast majority of our ordinary social experience, and which inform our every move in the world of everyday life. Inspired by this conception, and drawing on Husserl and a sociological follower, Alfred Schutz,[6] for help, Garfinkel sought to develop a sociology of the common-sense world of everyday life. This sociology would focus on how meaning, understanding, knowledge and communication work in the everyday world. It would study how we use social rules and imperfect knowledge bases to achieve ordinary activities and mutual understanding in our daily lives. It would be a sociology focused on practical action, rather than one divorced from it.

Key Issues

Rules and Shared Reasoning

Garfinkel's sociology is based on the idea that common-sense reasoning is *methodical*, that is, based on methods. The methods must be social and shared, otherwise actors would not be able to reason towards the same conclusions, understand one another and act in a coordinated fashion. But how to uncover this 'methodology'? To do this, Garfinkel hit on some brilliant quasi-experimental procedures that interfere with the smooth workings of every-day actions.

One of the first of these involved violating the rules of a simple game – tick-tacktoe (British noughts and crosses).[7] The rules of ticktacktoe do two things. As *rules of action*, they define a domain of possible actions within the field of the game and they specify how those actions should occur. They specify, for example, that the players will take alternate turns, that the moves will consist of making marks within the nine cells available, that once a cell is filled it cannot be altered, that the object of the game is to get three in a row and so on.

But the rules also supply a *method of understanding* the moves in the game, and because everyone who knows how to play knows the rules, the rules supply a shared method for understanding what is going on in any state of the game. For example, the rules can let you see that in a game that has come to a situation like Figure 12.1, the person playing '0' is in a 'fork' and has no chance of winning. Or relatedly, they can be used to see (Figure 12.2) that 'X' has 'two in a row' and is threatening to beat '0'. They can also be used to see that if you 'miss' seeing that 'two in a row', you are being inattentive. When you are playing with a ten-year-old child, missing 'two in a row' can leave you open to the accusation that you are not playing properly and that 'it's not fair' because 'you're letting me win'.

X	O	X
	X	
	O	

Figure 12.1

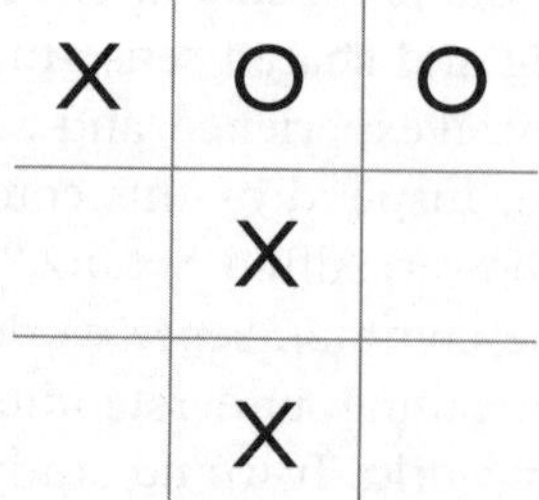

Figure 12.2

In his experiment, Garfinkel had student experimenters invite another person to play the game, and suggest that the other person make the first move (Figure 12.3). But when the subject had made that move (most subjects did so because moving first gives you an advantage in ticktacktoe), the experimenter would erase the subject's mark, move it to another cell, and then make the second move (for example Figure 12.4).

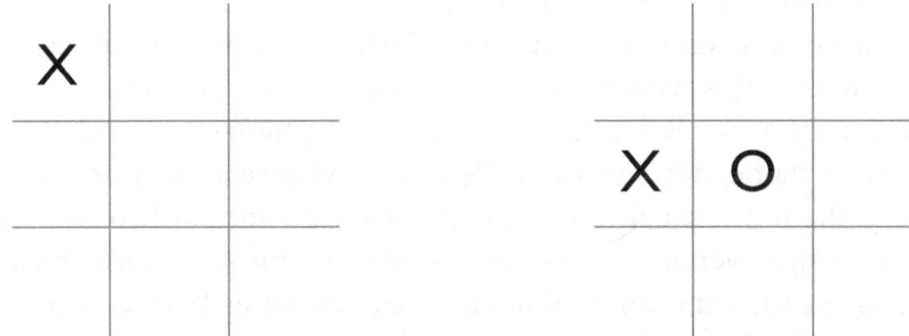

Figure 12.3 **Figure 12.4**

In over 250 trials of this procedure, Garfinkel asked the experimenters to determine the nature and strength of the subjects' reactions to what had happened; 95 per cent of the subjects reacted in some way, and over 75 per cent either objected to it strongly or demanded some kind of explanation for it. These people could not make sense of what was going on, but clung to the idea that the experimenter *ought* to be playing ticktacktoe. A small minority, however, laughed at the experimenter, or played along by erasing the experimenter's mark, moving it to another cell and then making a further move of their own. These people had obviously abandoned the idea that they were playing a traditional game of ticktacktoe, and they were able to make sense of what was going on as a joke or a 'new type of game'. Most people did not make sense of the situation in this way, and these people generally had the stronger emotional reactions to the experiment.

Garfinkel interpreted the results of this experiment in the following way. Although anger might be a natural reaction when the subjects saw that the ticktacktoe's *rules of action* had been violated, in fact not everyone became angry. The minority who did not were the ones who could continue to make sense of what was going on. Thus it was the use of ticktacktoe's rules as rules for understanding that was critical in shaping reactions. The persons who hung on to the rules as a means of making sense of the situation were confused and frustrated and angry. Those who abandoned the rules – and saw the situation as a joke or a new game – remained relaxed. In short, it was how the persons succeeded or failed to make sense of the situation that shaped whether they reacted emotionally or not.

In this simple game situation, it was clear that the participants used the rules as guidelines for action and as guidelines for understanding the meaning of what was going on. The rules of ticktacktoe were their 'ethnomethods' for operating in the game situation. These results gave rise to one of Garfinkel's core ideas: *the same set of rules and norms that guide or inform the production of action, also guide or inform reasoning about action.*

This core idea links to a second key concept in Garfinkel's work: the concept of 'accountability'. He uses this term in two senses: first, as a synonym for intelligible. In this usage, an accountable action is an intelligible action and one which we can therefore name, describe or, more generally, 'give an account of'. The second sense is the more usual moral one in which we speak of someone being 'accountable for their actions'. These two senses link back to Garfinkel's argument in the ticktacktoe experiment that rules are resources both to guide actions and to make sense of them. The notion of accountability helps to consolidate the idea that reasoning actors use rules to make sense of one another and hold one another to account. The question now becomes: What are these rules like, how do they work, what are their properties, how extensive are they?

Reasoning Using Background Knowledge

If the world was organized like the game of ticktacktoe, then it would be quite a simple matter to analyse how action, meaning and mutual understanding are achieved in everyday life. However, this is not so. There are considerable differences between games and real life. Games have a peculiar time structure, relative to most events of daily life, in that they have a determinate end point. Again, success or failure is defined inside the parameters of the game itself and is not subject to later developments outside the game. Compare this situation with President George Bush Senior and the First Gulf War (1990–91). When American armour rolled across Iraq, Bush was feted as the unchallenged victor of the Gulf War. But in the following year, when the US presidential elections were contested, Saddam Hussein's continued domination of Iraq was cited as evidence that Bush's mission had failed, and Bush lost the election. Perhaps most important, the rules of games operate independently of other features of persons – they do not alter if you are playing against a person of the opposite sex, or a movie star or whatever. In real life, by contrast, we have all kinds of *background knowledge* about people and circumstances that we employ and take account of in our dealings with them.

Garfinkel demonstrated the importance of this background knowledge using a simple two-part exercise. Undergraduate students were asked to go home and to observe what was happening under the assumption that they were just lodgers in the house and did not know the people who lived there. They had to do this for between fifteen minutes and an hour. This meant suspending their background knowledge about the identities, personalities and biographies of their own family members. They were asked to write out what they saw and to report on their own feelings while they did this. Here is the kind of thing they wrote:

> A short, stout man entered the house, kissed me on the cheek and asked 'How was school?' I answered politely. He walked into the kitchen, kissed the younger of the two women and said hello to the other. The younger woman asked me, 'What do you want for dinner honey?' I answered, 'Nothing.' She shrugged her shoulders and said no more. The older woman shuffled around the kitchen muttering. The man washed his hands, sat down at the table and picked up the paper. He read until the two women had finished putting the food on the table. The three sat down. They exchanged idle chatter about the day's events. The older woman said something in a foreign language which made the others laugh.[8]

Garfinkel notes that, once the students had adopted this attitude, they were surprised about how personal people's treatments of each other were. That, within this attitude, family news turned into trivial talk. That people who were criticized were not allowed to stand on their dignity nor to take offence. The students found that hostility and bickering became uncomfortably visible. Most of them said they were glad when the hour was up and they could go back, as they put it, 'to being the real me'. The study highlights the extent to which we all use background knowledge to 'typify' or 'normalize' our view of everyday events. The students suspended their use of these assumptions for just a few minutes and found they were 'seeing' in a dramatically different way, which they found uncomfortable and not quite 'real'.

In the second part of this experiment, Garfinkel gave the same instructions, only with the addition that the students were not just to look at the scene as lodgers, but to act in that way. Here the consequences were much more dramatic:

> Family members were stupefied. They vigorously sought to make the strange actions intelligible and to restore the situation to normal appearances. Reports were filled with accounts of astonishment, bewilderment, shock, anxiety, embarrassment and anger and with charges by various family members that the student was mean, inconsiderate, selfish, nasty or impolite.[9]

The family members also worked very hard to try to normalize and make sense of what was going on: the student was working 'too hard' at school, there had been 'another fight' with a fiancée and so on. However, they were infuriated when these explanations were not acknowledged. At all times, family members sought to restore normality by supplying some sort of routine set of background understandings that could 'make sense' of what was going on.

Garfinkel argues that we continually use this kind of background knowledge to understand everything that happens around us. His famous 'breaching experiments' demonstrated this clearly. These experiments involved demanding that people clarify the sense of their ordinary remarks. Here is the kind of thing that happened:

> On Friday night my husband and I were watching television. My husband remarked that he was tired. I asked 'How are you tired? Physically, mentally or just bored?'
>
> S: I don't know, I guess physically, mainly.
>
> E: You mean that your muscles ache or your bones?
>
> S: I guess so. Don't be so technical.
>
> *(After more watching)*
>
> S: All these old movies have the same kind of old iron bedstead in them.
>
> E: What do you mean? Do you mean all old movies, or some of them, or just the ones you have seen?
>
> S: What's the matter with you? You know what I mean.
>
> E: I wish you would be more specific.
>
> S: You know what I mean! Drop dead![10]

What has happened here? The experimenter (E) has refused to 'make sense' of what the subject (S) says, and has done so in a particular way: by refusing to use her background knowledge of the world to see how the subject's remarks 'make sense'. And when the students repeated this kind of procedure, they found that this refusal had the same effect whenever and with whomever it was used. Experiment after experiment ran off like that, with the subjects reacting with anger and outrage after extremely short periods of time. There is no quicker way, it appears, of provoking moral outrage than by not using background knowledge to make sense of other people's actions. A co-participant can become enraged in seconds – infinitely quicker than becoming angry in an argument about abortion or capital punishment or other issues that you would think have much more potential for conflict.

Let me now summarize Garfinkel's conclusions from all this. They are relatively straightforward. Much of the time we are engaged in achieving mutual understanding by using background knowledge to 'fill in' the meaning of what people say and do. This is a fundamental activity – more fundamental than anything else we do. We absolutely rely on one another's capacities and preparedness to maintain this shared universe. Garfinkel uses the term 'trust' to describe this reliance. Trust involves our expectation that others will work to see the world as we do. Garfinkel argues that, as the term implies, this expectation is a moral one. Making sense is something we morally require of one another.

Producing Sense in Context: The Documentary Method of Interpretation

If sense-making is active and uses background knowledge, how does it work? One of Garfinkel's core ideas in this regard involved a process which, following Mannheim, he called the 'documentary method of interpretation'.[11] The documentary method, Mannheim said, involves a search for an underlying pattern behind surface appearances. The method basically involves treating actual appearances as 'pointing to' or 'standing on behalf of' a presupposed underlying pattern. In it, you derive an underlying pattern from appearances. But, Garfinkel added, there is an element of circularity in this process of fitting appearances to a pattern because once you have used the appearances to decide what the underlying pattern is, you then use the pattern you have decided on to further interpret the appearances. You can see this process best with gestalt-type figures such as Figure 12.5.[12]

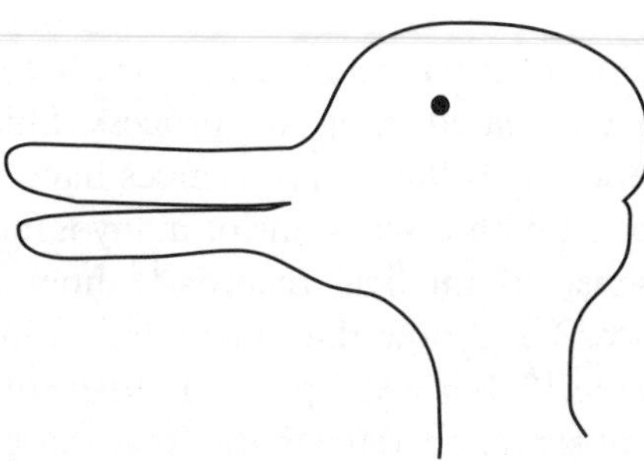

Figure 12.5

Let us assume this figure is a 'duck' and label it accordingly. We have now determined an 'underlying pattern' (the 'duck' pattern) from the appearances of the figure. Notice how this shapes (or reshapes) our view of the individual appearances: those protuberances on the left are the duck's beak, the dot in the middle is the eye, and that bump at the back of his head is an accidental dent – maybe our duck had a narrow escape! But once you construct that same dent as a 'mouth', you begin to see the 'duck' as a 'rabbit' and then you 'see' the protuberances on the left as 'ears' and so on. In each case, we draw on 'background knowledge' about the world in this circular process to fit together 'what we see' with 'what we know'.

Garfinkel argues that this process is continually used in every waking moment to make sense of the world: we recognize dogs, postmen, greetings, social class, bureaucratic red tape and 'introverted people' using this method. Most of the time, the results of the method are so 'obvious' that we do not notice how we use background knowledge to recognize things. But we become aware of the process when we are faced with ambiguous things. Max Atkinson[13] wrote about a situation in which 'a widow aged 83 was found gassed in the kitchen of her cottage, where she had lived alone since the death of her husband. Rugs and towels had been stuffed under the doors and around the window casements.' As an exercise, try working out the different ways in which your 'background knowledge' of how the world works can make sense of this situation. Use your background knowledge of human motives and physical circumstances to form a picture of how this old person died. Was it suicide, murder or accidental death? What additional information would cause you to rethink and reapply the documentary method of interpretation?

Producing Facts

To see the documentary method of interpretation at work is to realize that every 'fact' in the world has been created using this process. This very much includes the facts that the sciences and the social sciences have to deal with. Garfinkel has illustrated this point with discussions of many issues, including how social scientists make sense of medical records,[14] how astronomers discover new objects in the sky,[15] and how the police determine whether a dead person committed suicide.[16] For example, scientists often have to decide whether an important observation reflects the 'real thing' or is just a product of equipment malfunction. That decision involves making a 'judgement', and that judgement involves using the documentary method of interpretation. The situation is no different for economists evaluating employment data, or medical researchers deciding whether the evidence favours a certain treatment for cancer. Understanding that this is the case does not mean that scientists behave unscientifically and cannot get good results. As we have seen, the documentary method is not something that one can avoid using, and there is plenty of valid science out there.

In some areas though, an understanding of how facts are produced can generate a rethinking of fundamental ideas. I will illustrate this by reference to suicide analysis, which Garfinkel studied. **Durkheim**, the sociological pioneer in the study of suicide, argued that we should ignore subjective opinions and focus on social facts like the suicide rate. Garfinkel argued the reverse: that the suicide statistics are created by policemen who have opinions which, via the documentary method, feed into legal judgements. These judgements, in total, add up to the suicide statistics. The question is how are those judgements made?

Several studies have followed Garfinkel's initiative. They show that the police who investigate cases of death have to coordinate two sorts of facts: the circumstances in which the death took place and the nature of the dead persons themselves.[17] The police rank the circumstances of death into sets ranging from almost certain suicide (for example gassing or hanging) to almost certain accidents (for example car crashes). They also rank people into those who are more or less likely to commit suicide: more likely are people who are lonely, ill, or bereaved, the depressed and people who have had financial disasters. Less likely are people who have 'reasons to live' (for example people with children) or who may be frightened of perdition (for example Catholics). It is rather clear that these assumptions, when fed into actual judgements about suicide, can help to account for the distributions of suicides that Durkheim found so important. And other people who share these assumptions and are motivated to manipulate them – the deceased, the family members, coroners and other legal officials – can also strongly impact the suicide statistics.[18] Understanding that 'facts' are always socially produced and understanding how they are produced can have a major impact in grasping how everyday judgements affect large-scale societal phenomena.

Producing People and Institutions: Agnes and Gender

Earlier we saw that the notion of accountability helps to consolidate the idea that reasoning actors use rules to make sense of one another and hold one another to account. When you add in background knowledge and the documentary method of interpretation, you get a dynamic view of people and actions operating within a highly complex social framework of accountability. You also get a highly dynamic view of social institutions. Because, via frameworks of accountability, *people's actions reproduce social facts and social institutions*. Garfinkel demonstrated this in the most vivid way imaginable with the help of a transsexual called 'Agnes' who was born a boy, but who arrived in Los Angeles in search of a sex-change operation.[19] We normally think that sex and, to a lesser degree, gender are natural attributes 'ordained by nature'. Agnes knew differently. She could manipulate the appearances of sex and gender and, because of her special concerns, she became an intensely astute observer of how we manage to 'do being male' or 'do being female' in society. In the late 1950s, Garfinkel interviewed Agnes extensively about how she managed to bring off her female identity and more generally about 'doing gender'.[20] He found that she had a deep and detailed understanding about how gender shapes both the kinds of actions we can perform, and how we go about doing them and accounting for them. And she understood that to succeed it was vital to have 'female' memories, emotions and reasoning. In her dealings with Garfinkel (and the University of California, Los Angeles medical staff), Agnes always said she was 'naturally' female. She always insisted that she had 'nothing in common' with male homosexuals, transvestites or 'other' transsexuals.

In the end, Agnes got her sex-change operation and sometime later she revealed that she had been taking her mother's birth control pills (which were full of oestrogen – a female hormone) since she was 12. The revelation confirmed just how profoundly Agnes understood the significance of our claims about naturalness when we manage ourselves inside the social institution of gender. She had used that understanding to manipulate Garfinkel and the UCLA doctors into believing in her 'naturalness' as a female. For without convincing them of this, she could not have convinced them to do the sex-change operation.

Sex and gender are things that most people take for granted as natural and 'preordained' – in sociological terms an 'ascribed' characteristic. With Agnes as evidence, Garfinkel was able to show that in fact our sex and gender status is something that we achieve and reachieve, from moment to moment and day to day across our entire lifetimes. And in this same process, we all dynamically, although often in unwitting fashion, achieve and reachieve gender as a massive, omnipresent social institution. The paradox that Agnes helps us to see is that while we 'achieve' gender, we view our achievement as an 'ascribed' characteristic – a phenomenon known as 'reification'. Garfinkel's study of Agnes has inspired a great deal of subsequent thinking in this area, and it anticipated by a number of years how 'gender' is conceived in feminist studies.[21]

Seeing Things Differently

Ethnomethodology's message is: think of the social world as a production, as a 'produced world'. Think of this world as constantly produced and reproduced by sense-makers, who make decisions and act on the basis of the sense they make. Once you start to think this way, everything changes. You can see how the editing in a movie or TV show exploits your own use of the 'documentary method' to build the impression of continuity into observations that would otherwise be 'discontinuous'. You can start to see how your own ideas about people's 'characters' are constructed. You can start to see that science, music and law have their own ethnomethods, and so do police work, economic forecasting and software design.

To give you a straightforward idea of what it means to see the world as 'produced' in this way, I will draw on a study of political speeches done by Atkinson[22] a few years ago. Atkinson's focus was on how the speeches were applauded. We tend to think of applause as happening at moments when speakers say things the audience agrees with, and as being more likely to happen when the speakers are popular in the first place. Atkinson argued that these things are true, but they are not sufficient to gain audience reaction to what a speaker says. Instead, he argued that there is an ethnomethodology of audience reaction. The ethnomethods of applause arise from the situation of each individual in the audience.

Think of yourself as an audience member. You like what you are hearing and you would like to express that feeling by applauding. But that desire is matched by an anxiety: What if you are the only one to start applauding? It would be humiliating to find yourself to be that one person in a 1,000-person hall. Each audience member has that dilemma, and audiences will only applaud when speakers 'solve' that dilemma for them. Atkinson showed that politicians solve the dilemma by signalling ahead of time that there will be a place in the speech where it will be 'safe' to applaud. When everyone can anticipate that place, they will be more likely to applaud and, by a kind of self-fulfilling prophecy, everyone will be prepared to risk it. The result is a 'burst' of applause.

How do the signals work? Atkinson showed they are embedded in what the speaker is saying: safe places to applaud work by being emphatic and by being predictable. In particular, two highly predictable kinds of rhetorical statement fit this bill. One kind is the contrastive statement, such as President Kennedy's 'Ask not what your country can do for you. Ask what you can do for your country.' The other kind is the statement formatted in three's, such as Churchill's 'Never in the field of human conflict has so much been owed by so many to so few.' (Actually this statement uses contrast – between 'many' and 'few' – as well.) Statistical studies of speeches later showed that at least two-thirds of all audience reaction to political speeches is organized by this bit of speech ethnomethodology.[23]

How does this change our perception of speeches and speakers? It does not undermine the idea that audiences applaud things and speakers that they like.

But it shows that underlying this there is an ethnomethodological 'mechanics'. No matter how much you admire a person or agree with the point she or he is making, you are unlikely to applaud unless the mechanics are in place. It also turns out that 'charismatic' speakers like John F. Kennedy and Martin Luther King have intricate mastery of these methods.[24] 'Charisma' too is a 'produced' phenomenon.

Ethnomethodology's fundamental reorientation of thought about society is simply this. At the foundation of society is shared sense-making. And there can be no recognizable, shared social world independent of the use of a shared methodology – a shared set of ethnomethods – to achieve it. The production of the entire sensible social world of objects, activities and institutions is based on these ethnomethods.

Legacies and Unfinished Business

Garfinkel is very much alive and still working, so this is an interim view of his legacy. When they first came out, Garfinkel's ideas were treated as peculiar, outrageous or even scandalous. Yet his ideas have permeated almost the whole of sociological theory today. Most theories that make reference to such things as background understandings, taken-for-granted knowledge, practical reasoning, social practices, the production and reproduction of social institutions bear the marks of Garfinkel's influence. Many aspects of his approach are described in a new volume containing many practical studies.[25]

In terms of specific research, ethnomethodology has been particularly successful in areas where more traditional sociology has not done so well – in fields like science, law, music, art and so on. These are all areas of society whose members do use specific 'methodologies' to do their work. Obviously these are highly amenable to ethnomethodological study.

Another area of study where ethnomethodology has established a huge presence is the study of communication in social interaction. This field – known as 'conversation analysis' – represents a fusion between Garfinkel's ideas about the order of sense-making and Goffman's ideas about the 'interaction order'. It is now one of the pre-eminent ways of studying social interaction and language use in the world.

Not surprisingly, ethnomethodology has also established a large presence in the study of artificial intelligence, human–computer interfaces, cyberspace and the application of high-tech systems.

FURTHER READING

Cicourel, A. (1968) *The Social Organization of Juvenile Justice*, New York: Wiley. A classic study of how police beliefs about juvenile offenders are transformed into objective statistics about juvenile offences and the kind of people who commit them.

Drew, P. and Heritage, J. (eds) (1992) *Talk at Work*, Cambridge: Cambridge University Press. A set of papers using conversation analysis to study how people work in everyday and professional contexts.

Garfinkel, H. (1967) *Studies in Ethnomethodology*, Englewood Cliffs, NJ: Prentice Hall. This is a fundamental reference point. The book is complicated to read but, oddly, very clear. Bear in mind when you read it that the author was anthologized in a collection of the best American short stories of 1941: he is not a bad writer.

Garfinkel, H. (2002) *Ethnomethodology's Program: Working Out Durkheim's Aphorism*, edited and introduced by A. Warfield Rawls, Lanham, MD: Rowman & Littlefield. A collection of Garfinkel's most recent work.

Heritage, J. (1984) *Garfinkel and Ethnomethodology*, Cambridge: Polity Press. An introduction to Garfinkel's ideas.

Lynch, M. (1996) *Scientific Practice and Ordinary Action: Ethnomethodology and Social Studies of Science*, Cambridge: Cambridge University Press. A sophisticated account of ethnomethodology in relation to the analysis of science.

Pollner, M. (1987) *Mundane Reason*, Cambridge: Cambridge University Press. A beautifully written analysis of how our sense of reality is methodically sustained.

Sacks, H. (1992) *Lectures on Conversation*, Oxford: Blackwell. The originating ideas behind conversation analysis.

Schegloff, E. and Sacks, H. (1973) 'Opening up closings', *Semiotica*, 8: 289–327. A classic paper in conversation analysis. This gives a good idea of how conversation analysts reason about conversational interaction.

Finally, there are a number of sites on the internet that are devoted to ethnomethodology. A good starting point is: http://www2.fmg.uva.nl/emca/. This site carries a great deal of basic information about all aspects of contemporary work in the field.

CHAPTER 13

Louis Althusser

TED BENTON

Driving Impulses

Louis Althusser was a **Marxist** philosopher and social theorist. He was certainly the most influential Marxist thinker of his time, and one of the most influential social theorists working in any tradition. Essays written by him in the 1960s had the greatest and most long-lasting impact. He continued to publish through the 1970s, becoming increasingly explicit in his criticisms of the French Communist Party leadership. Finally, the personal turmoil and madness that had been ever present in his life led to tragedy and confinement in a psychiatric institution for much of his last decade.

Althusser was born in Algeria in 1918, moving to France with his family at the age of twelve. According to his autobiography, his childhood was very unhappy, tormented by contradictory relationships with his powerful and authoritarian but distant father, and his sexually repressed and obsessive mother, whose love he experienced as overpowering. Brought up as a Catholic, he spent much of the Second World War in a German prisoner-of-war camp. It was here that he met and was deeply impressed by a fellow prisoner – a Communist named Courrèges. After the war, Althusser returned to France and attended the Ecole Normale Supérieure in Paris as a student. The French Communists had played a crucial role in the resistance against the Nazis during the war, and were represented in the postwar government. Their influence on French public life, and on intellectuals in particular, was very great. Partly because of his wartime experience, and partly because he had been impressed by the Communists he encountered through his involvement in Catholic youth organizations, Althusser joined the Party soon after the war. However, from the beginning, he was a dissident within the organization. As an independent-minded intellectual, he found himself in frequent conflict with the Party leadership and the 'official' Party theorists.

The death of Stalin and the subsequent limited liberalization that took place in the Soviet Union under Khrushchev in the late 1950s, together with the growing split between the Soviet Union and Communist China, had their impact on left-wing circles in France. Small Communist groupings were formed, especially among students, that followed the teachings of Mao Zedong. The French Communist Party itself, as well as influential intellectuals on the left such as Sartre, Merleau-Ponty and Garaudy expressed their moral objection to Stalinism by way of a return to the 'humanist' philosophy of Marx's early writings. In those texts (most especially the famous *Economic and Philosophical Manuscripts of 1844*),[1] Marx had sketched out a brilliantly original philosophical theory, according to which human history could be seen as a long journey through which the whole species passes through a series of developmental stages on its way to a future in which all individual and collective human potential is fully realized. However, the current phase of history, for Marx, was one in which human potential was stunted and distorted by the prevailing capitalist system. Under this system, workers were 'alienated', or separated from their own autonomous life-activity, because they had to work under the control of the capitalist owners. As a result, they could not find fulfilment in work, were set into competitive relationships with other workers, and into class opposition to their employers. All the various dimensions of 'alienation' and opposition produced by capitalist property relations were to be overcome in the future Communist society, which Marx at that time described as 'the riddle of history solved'.

This framework of ideas provided a moral standard by which not only capitalist society could be measured, but also the limitations and 'errors' of the Stalinist type of 'socialism' that had developed in the Soviet Union. Althusser was strongly opposed to this 'humanist' criticism of the Soviet Union and declared himself, scandalously, to be an 'anti-humanist'. This has led to accusations that his work was just a sophisticated justification for Stalinism, and that he did not care about people. In fact, what Althusser wanted was a more deep-rooted criticism of Stalinism, and an explanation of how the great Soviet attempt at human liberation had ended in oppressive dictatorship. Mere moral condemnation was not enough – the whole terrible process had to be analysed and explained. And, for a Marxist, that meant putting Marxist theory itself to the test of explaining the consequences of the first attempt in history to put it into practice. For Althusser, the problem with the humanist interpretations of Marx was that they implicitly threw out Marx's most important theoretical breakthrough: the establishment of a 'scientific' understanding of historical processes. He thought that Khrushchev's attempt to 'deStalinize' the Communist movement had failed, and that moral criticism, while it was certainly justified, could not of itself change anything. Instead, what was needed was a careful recovery and further development of Marx's explanatory approach ('historical materialism'), and of the philosophical work that was necessary to make this recovery possible. Only this return to theory could lead to a renewal of Marxist theory and practice, after decades of distortion by the demands of obedience to the interests of the Soviet state, and unquestioning loyalty to Party bosses. As he later put it in his autobiography: 'only theoretical anti-humanism justified genuine, practical humanism'.[2]

According to Althusser's own account, French culture was very insular during the period when his own ideas were forming. He and his fellow philosophers were rather ignorant of other British and European ways of thinking – even of the work of important non-French Marxists, such as Antonio Gramsci. So, in developing his opposition to the 'humanist' takeover of Marxism, Althusser drew mainly on other influential traditions in French philosophy and social thought. First, his defence of a version of Marxism as a science involved him in a search for a theory of the nature of science: What made science different from everyday thought, or 'ideology'? How do new sciences emerge? How should change in scientific ideas be understood and explained? Althusser's most immediate influence in thinking about these issues was Georges Canguilhem.[3] Canguilhem was a historian and philosopher of science, and belonged to a distinctive French tradition of thinking about science (Alexandre Koyré and Gaston Bachelard were two other famous thinkers in this tradition). Their approach differed from the empiricist philosophy of science, which was the dominant view in Britain and America, in that the French based their view of science on careful historical study. This brought into view processes of interaction between science and the wider society, and also suggested that the criteria for what was to count as science changed as science itself changed through time.

But this French school of historians and philosophers of science had concerned themselves mainly with the natural sciences. Althusser was mainly concerned with a defence of Marxism as a social and historical science, and so he had to look for an approach in the human sciences that would provide a viable alternative to the 'humanism' of Sartre, Merleau-Ponty and the others. In this he found his main allies in the 'structuralist' approaches that were already doing battle with humanism in psychology, linguistics, anthropology and sociology. **Durkheim**'s instruction to sociologists to 'treat social facts as things', and Ferdinand de Saussure's similar view of language as a social fact, existing independently of the individual purposes of the users of language, were 'founding figures' of structuralism. The anthropologist Claude Lévi-Strauss was perhaps the best-known structuralist among Althusser's contemporaries, but Althusser himself was most influenced by the structuralist interpretation of Freudian psychoanalysis developed by Jacques Lacan. Given Althusser's personal history of recurrent depressions and crises of identity, it is perhaps not surprising that he should have developed a strong theoretical interest in psychoanalysis. Although Althusser repeatedly refused to identify himself as a structuralist, there is no mistaking the influence of structuralist themes in his reconstruction of Marx's historical materialism as a science.

Key Issues

So, armed with historical philosophy of science, and with structuralism as his ally, Althusser set out to 'rescue' the true Marx from the interpretations imposed on his work by 'humanist' philosophers. The results of this work were set out in a series of articles written between 1960 and 1965, and published together as *For Marx*,[4] and in a collaborative work with students (including Rancière and Balibar – who became important thinkers in their own right) called *Reading Capital*.[5] Given that the 'humanists' clearly had a good case for their interpretation of Marx's early works, and especially the brilliant and captivating *Manuscripts of 1844*, Althusser's task was to show that the Marx of 1844 was not yet a Marxist (even Marx himself, despairing of misinterpretations of his ideas, had insisted he was not a Marxist). The essays in *For Marx* are mainly devoted to that task, while *Reading Capital* sets out the basic concepts of 'historical materialism', as derived from the authors' reading and discussion of Marx's later writings.

The Relationship between Marx's Earlier and Later Works

First, then, the account of the relationship between Marx's earlier and later works. Althusser's approach draws upon three key ideas that he takes from Canguilhem and the historical philosophers of science. The first of these is the notion that scientific concepts are not invented one by one, but form a definite interconnected framework, or pattern of thought, each concept getting its meaning from its relationship to the others. This conceptual framework determines what questions or problems can be posed within it, and so, also, excludes the posing of questions that might arise in an alternative framework: it could be compared to the beam of a torch that illuminates everything on which it falls, but leaves everything else in shadow. This aspect of a science is called its 'problematic'.

The second idea Althusser uses is that the history of science is discontinuous. That is, a new science emerges from previous patterns of non-scientific thinking in its field by establishing a clear conceptual distance from those earlier ideas. The 'ideological' problematics that precede the emergence of a new science are often linked with the wider culture of the society, its 'common sense', or dominant ideology. This means that even after its establishment, a new science will continue to be surrounded by ways of thinking that it overthrew as part of the process whereby it came into existence. It follows that scientific problematics are discontinuous with both the patterns of ideas from which they emerged, and with the 'common sense' of the wider culture within which they continue to exist. The history of science is discontinuous in the further respect that, even when it has become established, new problems and solutions are generated, which produce subsequent restructurings of the original scientific problematic. Althusser calls the shift from prescientific ideologies to the emergent scientific problematic an 'epistemological break'. Third, Althusser follows the historical philosophers of science in recognizing that scientific work is not just a matter of gaining new knowledge. For them, ignorance is not just lack of knowledge, but, rather, powerful patterns of erroneous thinking, which are always present, invading and obstructing scientific advance: so science is a struggle to resist and overcome these invading 'epistemological obstacles'.

An example from the natural sciences might help to make it clear how these ideas work. In the late 1830s, Charles Darwin was struggling to understand how one living species gives rise to another. His notebooks reveal his realization that the new ideas he was developing called into question existing religious orthodoxy, as well as the belief that each species remained constant, which predominated among the leading scientists of the day. He knew that his ideas, which broke with previous assumptions of the special creation of each species and made humans and apes close kin (his 'epistemological break'), would create a scandal. This may be one reason why he waited 20 years before making his scientific breakthrough public. However, after the publication of his *The Origin of Species* (1859),[6] his ideas eventually became widely accepted and incorporated into a view of humans (often, in racialist versions, a view of the white European races) as at the apex of the evolutionary process – as if the evolution of life could be told as a story in which the climax is the arrival of humans (or, in the racialist versions, the 'superior' races). These ways of popularizing evolutionary biology reasserted human self-importance, implied that progress was written into nature itself, gave some ideologists a scientific backing for their belief in markets and capitalism, and were used to justify the colonization (even genocide) of non-European peoples.

In fact, however, a close reading of both the notebooks and *The Origin of Species* shows that these uses of Darwin's ideas are quite inconsistent with his scientific 'problematic'. The mechanism of 'natural selection' leads, in his theory, to a gradual change in a species as it adapts, through many generations, to its local environment. On that theory, it makes no sense to talk of 'higher' and 'lower' animals, of 'primitive' and 'advanced' forms. As an organism adapted to its environment, a cat flea is no more nor less 'evolved' than the cat it lives on. In his early notebooks, Darwin even compares our treatment of other animals with slavery – to which he was passionately opposed. However, in some later writings, such as his *Descent of Man*,[7] Darwin seems to give in to this misunderstanding of evolution as progressive development, and even to the prevailing views of a hierarchy among the human races. So, evolution as progressive development, beliefs in racial superiority, and human self-importance can be seen as 'epistemological obstacles': Darwin had to struggle against them in order to establish the scientific problematic of evolutionary biology, but they persist as powerful forces in the wider culture, and even go on to 'invade' Darwin's own subsequent writings.

Parallel considerations apply to Marx's work. He had to establish his scientific breakthrough by struggling against the powerful attractions of earlier 'humanist' understandings of history. In Marx's case, these prescientific ideologies were, most importantly, Hegel's idealist view of history as a 'dialectical' process of self-development of 'Absolute Spirit', and, second, Ludwig Feuerbach's materialist 'inversion' of Hegel's philosophy. In Feuerbach's philosophy, history is understood as, again, a process of self-development, but, now, of the human species itself, not 'Absolute Spirit'. Althusser reads the early work of Marx as a further development of Feuerbach's 'problematic', which draws upon the economic theories of the time to explain the material basis for human self-alienation, and on the Communist and socialist thought of the time to provide a vision of the future full of self-realization of humanity. However, because this is merely a development of the Feuerbachian 'problematic', and because this, in turn, had only 'inverted' Hegel's philosophy, the problematic of the early Marx is still trapped within the terms of the idealist philosophy. In short, Marx has to make a break from his own earlier 'problematic', has to struggle against his own former self, in order to establish a genuinely scientific approach to the study of history and society.

This, Althusser claims, started to happen from about 1845 onwards. Of course, such a profound intellectual achievement does not take place all at once, and the actual texts written during the next few years still contain passages that can be read as continuing the 'humanist' and 'historicist' themes of the early writings. This is what fuels the humanist interpretations of Marx against which Althusser is campaigning. There certainly are passages in which Marx seems to be clearly rejecting his early philosophy, as when he denounces philosophers who 'neatly trim the epochs of history' so as to fit them into their theories, and when he insists on the necessity for empirical study for the proper understanding of history. However, Althusser does not rely on the trading of rival quotations. Instead, he makes use of the structuralist concept of a 'symptomatic' reading. According to this idea, the underlying conceptual structure or 'problematic' is not immediately obvious from the flow of words and sentences in a text. This latter can be compared to the rippling surface of a river, which is not directly determined by the underlying currents of water, but which provides clues to, or 'symptoms' of, them. Althusser's method is to analyse each text, looking for dislocations, contradictions, unresolved tensions and so on, and then to work back to the underlying problematics that generate them.

Anti-historicism

Using this method of symptomatic reading, Althusser is able to confirm the presence of an 'epistemological break' in Marx's thinking, with the emergence of a new and 'scientific' problematic from 1845 onwards. This enables Althusser to say what Marxism (or 'historical materialism') is not, as well as to begin the process of unearthing or recovering what Marxism is. We can begin with what Marxism is now understood not to be. For Althusser, of course, the important 'nots' are 'humanism' and 'historicism'. These two 'isms' are closely linked to each other, but it is convenient to consider them separately to begin with. Sometimes the word 'historicism' is used to describe all approaches that emphasize the significance of historical change. However, this is not what Althusser objects to. For him, 'historicism' refers to those accounts of historical change that represent it as a linear series of 'stages' or phases, having a direction, and with an inherent end point or 'purpose'. This way of thinking about history has many different forms, including Hegel's philosophy of history, Feuerbach's inversion of it, Marx's own early works, and, of course, the humanist interpretations of Marx against which Althusser was arguing. The progressive-evolutionist misinterpretations of Darwin are also examples of it, and it remains deeply engrained in western thinking today, in concepts such as 'modernization' and 'development'. On Althusser's reading of it, Marx's great breakthrough was to overthrow this way of thinking about history. The faith, often present in the Communist movement, that 'history is on our side', that the eventual victory of the working-class movement was somehow written into the historical process was, in Althusser's view, completely unMarxist. Historical processes were open-ended. Historical change occurred as a result of the fortuitous coming together – or 'fusion' – of numerous contradictions in society, so that revolutions, far from being inevitable consequences of capitalist 'development', should always be seen as exceptional events. In our own time, 'postmodernist' writers such as Lyotard have proclaimed the end of widespread belief in historical 'metanarratives' such as Marxism. Ironically, if Althusser's reading is correct, Marx was the first postmodernist.

Anti-humanism

Now to Althusser's criticism of Marxist 'humanism'. One problem here is that it is not always clear what is meant by 'humanism'. There are (at least) three different things that Althusser might have been objecting to in his 'anti-humanism'. One of these, as we have seen, he explicitly rejects. This is what we might call 'moral humanism': a set of values according to which the primary objects of moral concern are human beings and their welfare. Humanism in this sense is opposed to religious moralities, which put duty to God over mere human interests, and to more recent 'ecocentric' value systems, which give equal consideration to human and non-human living creatures. Althusser made it clear that he was not an 'anti-humanist' in this sense. Indeed, as a moral reaction to Stalinist 'errors and crimes', Althusser says humanism has 'a real historical sanction'.[8]

The second possible interpretation is more plausible. In this interpretation, humanism is a philosophical understanding of history as a process, which has full development of the human species as its outcome, and which thinks of humans themselves as the agents who bring about their own development – history as human self-development. Numerous philosophical views of human 'progress' take this form, and, as we have seen, it is also represented in the philosophies of Feuerbach and the young Marx himself. As Althusser points out, humanism in this sense and historicism constitute different aspects of the same 'problematic'. So, Althusser clearly is against 'humanism' in this sense.

> ***Voluntarism***
>
> *In the present context (see below), this refers to a view of human actions that tends to overestimate the amount of freedom available to a human actor to do whatever she wants to do. The other side of the same coin is that it also underplays the social influences, pressures and constraints upon the actor and her actions (including the influences of socialization that will limit quite profoundly even what it will occur to the social actor to 'want' to do). Voluntarism thus entails a view of human agency that is far too free-floating and unsociological.*

The third possible meaning of humanism is to describe those approaches that assert the primary role of the conscious agency, or choices of individual human beings (or groups of them) in sociological or historical explanation. This is the form of humanism sometimes called **voluntarism.** It took its most extreme form in Sartre's existentialism, but is still a widespread approach in mainstream economics, and in 'rational choice' approaches in political science and sociology. The view recently advocated by **Anthony Giddens** of personal identity under conditions of 'reflexive modernization' as the outcome of a 'project' of self-creation is another example. Althusser's fellow structuralists were strongly opposed to such views. Structuralist approaches are usually committed to a certain view of what an explanation should be like. For them, the surface appearance of things may be misleading as to the real structural causes that underlie them and produce them. Scientific explanation proceeds by a critical analysis of 'appearances' so as to arrive at an adequate account of underlying structures. We have already seen one example of this method in Althusser's practice of 'symptomatic' reading. This method has quite dramatic consequences if we apply it to our own experience and self-understanding. It suggests that we should be sceptical about our own experience of our selves as fully conscious (at least some of the time) choosers, and in control of our actions, direction in life and so on. On the structuralist view, the great scientific breakthroughs of the past have all dealt blows to human conceit and self-importance. Copernicus showed that the sun was at the centre of the universe, with the earth as just one of the planets spinning round it. Darwin showed that humans are not results of special creation by God, but just one outcome among millions of the random operation of environmental pressures. Even in the sphere of the human psyche itself, the structuralists recognized Freud's concept of the unconscious as a further confirmation of their method. Slips of the tongue, dreams, lapses of memory as well as neurotic and other symptoms of mental illness could all be understood as effects of deep-rooted psychological processes of which the individual remained unaware.

Structuralism, Ideology and Personal Identity

Although Althusser was wary of identifying himself too closely with structuralism, it was tempting to put Marx's scientific achievements into the same mould. There are many places in Marx's writings where he seems to be arguing that human self-identity and the 'forms of social consciousness' through which people understand and act in the social world are products of their position in the social structure: 'social being determines social consciousness'. Particular types of society give rise to particular patterns of dominant thought, or ideology (for example the link between capitalism and liberal individualism), and a particular position in the class structure will give rise to a particular kind of identity and outlook (for example members of the working class will tend to have socialist ideas and so on). This kind of approach (which can be traced back to the influence of earlier thinkers, such as Durkheim and his students) further 'decentres' the conscious human subject. Far from being in conscious control of our activity in the social world, we are subject to two levels of influence about which we are unaware – our internal 'unconscious', and the external influence of our social 'conditioning'.

Althusser's treatment of this question of the relationship between social structures and the thought and action of individual people was one of the most controversial aspects of his theory, but to see why we have to make a detour into his account of the social structure itself.

Rejection of Economic Determinism

In *Reading Capital*, Althusser and his colleagues provided an analytical account of key concepts in Marx's later view of history and society. The economic structure, or 'mode of production', was analysed as a combination of a set of 'elements' (instruments of labour, the material being worked on, the worker, and, in class societies, owners who do not work) that are bound together by two distinct sorts of relationship – relations necessary to the tasks of production, and ownership relations, through which surplus wealth is acquired by the class of owners. The different types of society that have existed in history, or are found in other parts of the world (ancient, feudal, hunter-gatherer, capitalist and so on) can be classified in terms of the different ways in which the various elements are combined together. So far, the account is little more than an attempt to make more precise the existing 'orthodox' understanding of Marx's economic thought. However, where the Althusserians parted company with many of their fellow Marxists was in their firm rejection of 'economic determinism'. That is to say, they recognized that whole societies were made up of a number of distinct 'structures' or 'practices', of which the economy was only one. These other practices included ideological, political and 'theoretical' (scientific) practices. Each of these practices has its own reality, its own 'contradictions' (for example conflict between students and university authorities, and ideological struggles conducted by social movements such as the women's movement), and so makes its own distinct contribution to the overall 'flow' of social processes.

Marx himself had drawn an analogy between the relationship of the economy to the legal and political system of a society and the relationship between the 'foundation' and the 'superstructures' of a building. Economic determinist or 'reductionist' versions of Marxism had interpreted this as implying that everything happening 'outside' the economy was a more or less direct consequence, or 'expression', of economic processes. Althusser was critical of the foundation/superstructure analogy, but he also (rightly) points out that it does not imply that nothing important goes on in the superstructures. The real problem was that Marx had not developed an adequate theory of the superstructures to compare with his economic theory. One of the most urgent jobs to be done by contemporary Marxists was to correct this weakness in Marxism by developing theories of ideology and politics. However,

Althusser does not revert to a 'pluralist' view of society in which all structures or practices are equal in their contributions to the whole. He retains the view of Marx that economic structures and practices are in some way fundamental, that is, that the 'causal weight' of the economy within the whole society is greater than that of the other social practices. In Althusser's view, implicit in Marx's way of thinking about the internal complexity of whole societies is a novel concept of causality: 'structural causality', according to which the complex whole and the substructures which make it up all influence one another, but some have more influence than others.

Ideological State Apparatuses, Reproductions and Interpellation

Althusser's most systematic treatment of the question of the 'superstructures' came in an essay written soon after the revolutionary events of Paris 1968. In this essay, called 'Ideology and ideological state apparatuses',[9] Althusser shifts from abstract analysis of the structural make-up of society to the question: How is it possible for social structures to persist through time (day to day, year by year, generation by generation)? The key concept Marxists use to think about this process is 'reproduction'. It includes the replacement of elements such as instruments of production as they wear out, workers as they retire or die and so on. But it also includes the maintenance of the structures, or persistent patterns of relationships, which make up societies. The place of the ideological and political 'superstructures' within whole societies is understood by Althusser by way of this concept of reproduction. The school and the family, for example, play their part in 'reproducing' the labour force, both biologically and in terms of preparing and distributing people to various positions in society, according to their skills, aptitudes, qualifications and so on. Also, in the case of class societies (such as capitalism), the prevailing patterns of class domination and subordination, of authority and obedience are also learned as people acquire a certain sense of their own self-identity and place in the wider society.

In developing his account of these processes, Althusser distinguishes between two types of superstructure: the 'repressive state apparatuses' (RSAs), such as the police, courts of law and the army, and the 'ideological state apparatuses' (ISAs), such as the educational system, trade unions, family, churches, sports clubs and societies, and communications media. The RSAs, as their name implies, function to maintain the social order mainly by the use of coercion (for example the use of police to break strikes or control demonstrations), while the ISAs function by securing the active consent of the majority to the existing power relations. Althusser is here following the lead of the Italian Marxist, Antonio Gramsci,[10] in recognizing that in most modern western societies the existing system of class domination is 'legitimate'. That is, most people, most of the time, are not in open revolt against the system. The force available to the state is generally kept in reserve, and only used directly when the dominant way of life is challenged by groups such as 'travellers' who can be stigmatized as 'different', or when there is a more powerful threat to the ruling class as in the case of Paris in 1968, or the 1984 miners' strike in Britain. But what Gramsci and Althusser emphasize is that this 'consent' or 'legitimacy' is not spontaneously given by the people. It requires continuous ideological work, conducted under the ideas of the ruling ideology within the institutional framework of the ISAs. As individuals pass from family to school to university or college, as they participate in the rituals of church or sporting associations, watch TV and so on, they acquire a sense of their own personal identity and place in society, which at the same time prepares them for a life of (more or less) willing obedience to the requirements and tasks allotted to them.

This process is what Althusser calls 'interpellation': the acquisition by an individual of a sense of who they are, which carries with it a set of ideas about their place in the social world, bound up with the necessary skills and attitudes to fit them for their 'destination' in work, family, leisure and so on. Now, where Althusser departs from Gramsci and previous Marxists is that he offers this as an account of all ideologies. For him, as for structuralist thinkers, and classical sociologists such as Durkheim, individuals acquire their sense of self and place in society as a result of the effects on them of their participation in pre-existing social structures and practices ('socialization'). This seems to reduce individuals to the status of mere 'puppets' of the social system, and, deeply problematic for a socialist theorist, seems to rule out the possibility that people might come to understand their own subordination and act to change things. In rejecting the 'voluntarism' of the humanists, Althusser seems to have gone over to the opposite extreme of a 'structuralist' denial of human agency. By contrast, Gramsci had recognized the capacity of oppositional groups in society to challenge the 'hegemony' of the ruling ideas through cultural struggle in favour of an alternative ethical vision and way of life. The great difficulty in Althusser's position is that only the independent development of Marxism as a 'science' can provide an alternative to the dominant ideology. As many of his critics pointed out, this carries with it the implication that intellectuals of the Marxist left, such as Althusser himself, will become a privileged 'priesthood' of the revolutionary movement. Althusser himself saw the force of this criticism, and from the beginning of the 1970s began a series of self-criticisms and revisions to his earlier thought, at the same time becoming ever more critical of the Communist Party leadership. It is not clear how far this later body of writing succeeded in resolving the tensions inherent in the earlier work, and there is little doubt that Althusser left a considerable legacy of 'unfinished business'.

Seeing Things Differently

Looking back over my own long struggle to understand Althusser's ideas, and to define my own in relation to them, I can mention a few things that I most value. One is Althusser's intense 'reflexivity' about the crucial connection in his life between his work as a social theorist and his politics. He always recognized that these two things were different, never bending his theory to political expediency. However, he always remained painfully conscious of the political responsibility of intellectuals who conduct their work in the public sphere. Although he never resolved the tensions inherent in this relationship (as with those that destroyed his personal life), his courage in recognizing and struggling with them is one from which we can learn. My engagement with Althusser's work also was genuinely 'liberating' in two further respects – one theoretical, the other political. In the realm of theory, the liberation lay in his challenge to Marxist orthodoxy, and the re-establishment of the materialist approach to history and society as an open and creative research programme. For myself, and many other social theorists of my age group, this made it possible for us to use core insights from the Marxist heritage without being constrained by every dot and comma of Marx's writings. We could address questions (such as ecology, or gender and sexuality) upon which Marx himself was of little direct help, and we could make use of non-Marxist ideas where this was of more help (as, of course, had Marx before us). The political liberation enabled by Althusser is closely connected. His critique of economic determinism, and recognition of the relatively independent role played by non-economic practices in both maintaining and changing society, opened up a new set of possible ways of thinking about how change might occur, and who might bring it about. While Althusser himself never quite broke from the 'orthodox' view of the industrial working class as the agent of revolution, his innovations in Marxist theory allow us to think of the independent role that might be played by social movements responding to 'contradictions' between capitalist development and ecological life-support systems, to gender or racial/ethnic oppression and discrimination, or to cultural exclusion. Althusser's theoretical understanding of the complexity of the whole social structure, and the multiplicity of contradictions and tensions in it, provides the theoretical basis for the sort of broad alliance between oppositional movements that Gramsci favoured. In several countries now, there are attempts to bring together diverse campaigns and movements in opposition to the prevailing global concentrations of economic, military and political power (in the UK, for example, Green Left Convergence is one attempt to do this).[11] These new alliances include people who have backgrounds in socialist, feminist, green, gay rights, civil liberties, peace and other social movements, as well as people who are coming to active politics for the first time. This sort of grass-roots coalition building is quite a long way from the traditional focus of the orthodox Communist parties on the industrial working class as the sole, or 'leading' agent of social change. So far as socialists are concerned, Althusser's work was one important way through to this new vision of political activity on the left.

Legacies and Unfinished Business

So, what remains today of the Althusserian project? For at least two decades, Althusser's recasting of Marxism as an open research programme was immensely fruitful. Scholars in many countries, working in numerous disciplinary fields in the humanities and social sciences, took off from Althusser's achievements. Anthropologists such as Emanuel Terray[12] developed new ways for Marxists to think about non-capitalist societies, while Michel Aglietta,[13] Alain Lipietz[14] and others made important contributions to the understanding of contemporary economic processes, and Pierre Macherey[15] drew on Althusser's work in his development of a new theory of 'literary production' (see also Terry Eagleton).[16] As we have seen, Althusser anticipated some themes of postmodernist and poststructuralist thought (Derrida and **Foucault** were both students of Althusser). Althusser's emphasis on the relative autonomy of ideological or 'cultural' processes made possible approaches to the study of culture that avoided the economic (and sociological) determinism that had marred previous Marxist work. The distinctive approach to cultural studies developed in the Birmingham Centre for Contemporary Cultural Studies, especially during the directorship of Stuart Hall, owed much to both Althusser and Gramsci. However, a combination of factors, including the wider crisis of Marxism and the associated turn to the study of language as a self-contained system, soon led to the study of 'culture' as something quite removed from social and economic relations – the absolute autonomy of the superstructures. Within sociology more narrowly defined, structural Marxism inspired systematic work in the sociology of class: Nicos Poulantzas[17] and Eric O. Wright;[18] feminist sociology: Michèle Barrett,[19] Mary McIntosh[20] and Juliet Mitchell;[21] urban sociology: Manuel Castells;[22] and in political and historical sociology: Perry Anderson,[23] Bob Jessop[24] and Poulantzas.[25]

The collapse of the former Soviet 'empire', the conversion of the East Asian 'Communist' regimes to capitalism, and the widespread decline of the western Communist parties can be seen as the final victory of capitalism and liberal democracy. On this sort of view, we have witnessed the end, not just of Marxism and socialism, but of all serious aspirations for a future beyond global capitalism. However, it is remarkable that Marxist thinkers, although now clearly a minority, retain footholds in most disciplinary fields. There is strong evidence of a return of interest in Althusser's own work in the wake of the excesses of post-modernism (for example Elliott,[26] Kaplan and Sprinker,[27] Resch,[28] Levine,[29] Montag,[30] Lewis[31] and Ferretter[32]). Moreover, if we remember that Althusser's revitalization of Marxism could only take place in opposition to the dogmatism of the French Communist Party leadership, with its loyalty to the Soviet state, then it is at least possible that the demise of state and party might favour a new flowering of creative socialist and even Marxist thought in the new world (dis)order. One thing does seem certain: that the terrible consequences in terms of poverty, unemployment, malnutrition, epidemic disease, social dislocation, and ecological destruction of globalizing capitalism continue to intensify. None of the issues that first gave rise to the socialist and Communist movements, and made necessary the critical theoretical work of such thinkers as Marx and Althusser has gone away. It will be depressing indeed if a new generation of sociologists continues to look the other way.

FURTHER READING

Two collections of essays by Althusser are probably the easiest way into the primary literature. His work is demanding but repays perseverance. The second of these collections contains the seminal essay, 'Ideology and Ideological State Apparatuses'.

L. Althusser (1969) *For Marx*, trans. B. Brewster, London and New York: Verso.

L. Althusser (1971) *Lenin and Philosophy, and Other Essays*, trans. B. Brewster, London: New Left Books.

More difficult, but essential reading, is L. Althusser and E. Balibar (eds) (1970) *Reading Capital*, trans. B. Brewster, London and New York: Verso.

Gregory Elliott's *Althusser: A Critical Reader*, Oxford and Cambridge, MA: Blackwell, brings together reflections on Althusser's legacy from a range of authors well versed in Marxism, structuralism and psychoanalysis. Connections, parallels and disagreements with other theorists such as Habermas, Lacan and Foucault are drawn and critically analysed.

E.P. Thompson (1978) 'The Poverty of Theory: or an Orrery of Errors', in *The Poverty of Theory and Other Essays*, London: Merlin Press, and New York: Monthly Review Press. This piece brings out the passion aroused by Althusser's 'anti-humanism' and his notion of agents as 'bearers of structures'. For a defence of Althusser against Thompson see Ted Benton (1984) *The Rise and Fall of Structural Marxism*, London: Macmillan – now Palgrave Macmillan.

On the overly neglected work of Nicos Poulantzas, heavily influenced by Althusserian structuralism and the most influential state theorist of the 1970s and 80s, see Bob Jessop's magisterial *Nicos Poulantzas: Marxist Theory and Political Strategy*, Basingstoke: Macmillan – now Palgrave Macmillan (1985).

For a recent review and appraisal of Althusser's critical Marxism see Luke Ferretter's (2006) *Louis Althusser*, London and New York: Routledge. Ferretter shows how Althusser not only revolutionized Marxist theory but also had a major impact on literary and cultural studies and feminism, an influence that has now been extended to post-colonialism and queer theory.

CHAPTER 14

Nancy J. Chodorow

KARIN A. MARTIN

Driving Impulses

The Reproduction of Mothering (1978), the work for which Nancy Chodorow is best known, seeks to explain not only why women mother, but also how gender is constructed within individuals. That is, why do we feel so deeply that we are girls/women or boys/men? How do these identities take root? And why are these identities, girl and boy, so different? Why do men and women have such different personalities? How is gender both personal and cultural?

These questions, the driving impulses[1] for Chodorow's work, emerged from several social and intellectual influences. *The Reproduction of Mothering* is a product of second-wave feminism, 'grand' theorizing about women's oppression that characterized academic feminist theory of the 1970s, Chodorow's own training in anthropology, psychoanalysis and sociology, and her experience in a mother–daughter group in graduate school.

In the 1970s, feminists were examining, critiquing and striving to change all aspects of gender inequality in social life. In particular, feminists of the 1970s, much more than feminists who came generations before them, claimed that personal, private life – marriage, love, families, sex – was political, just as public life – voting, work, education – was. Hence the famous slogan of second-wave feminism, 'the personal is political'. This claim that personal life was important to gender politics shaped many feminist theorists of the day and led to an examination of all aspects of personal life. Chodorow, herself, participated in a mother–daughter group that considered the implications of women's parenting. For Chodorow, the claim that the personal was political also supported her interest in psychoanalytic theory (see below), a theory of the most personal aspects of the self – emotions, the unconscious, fantasy – and also of the development of sex and gender within family relations.

Chodorow's theorizing was also influenced by the types of questions academic second-wave feminists were asking. Many feminists in the academy were writing 'grand theory'. They searched for a single explanation that would account for all of gender inequality. Many of these theorists were anthropologists (Michelle Rosaldo, Sherry Ortner, Gayle Rubin) who were trying to understand what they perceived to be women's universal oppression. Data from around the world seemed to suggest that women everywhere were oppressed. Such an observation called for grand theory, a theory that could explain women's oppression everywhere and could explain it with a single cause. Chodorow trained as an anthropologist as an undergraduate, asked questions about gender and searched for a single cause to explain gender inequality in this academic context.

The profound influence of psychoanalytic theory on Chodorow's thinking often seems unusual to feminist thinkers. What, many feminists ask, can we learn about women and gender from a theory that dreamed up penis envy, that said early childhood sexual abuse was fantasy, that claimed women who did not have vaginal orgasms were frigid and immature? Looking beyond and between these issues, Chodorow found much that was useful in psychoanalytic theory and in fact describes herself as 'passionately "hooked on"' psychoanalytic theory.[2] There were many aspects of psychoanalysis that Chodorow found appealing and useful for feminist theorizing. Psychoanalysis brings to the study of gender relations the understanding that 'the social and political organization of gender does not exist apart from the fact that we are all sexed and gendered in the first place'.[3] Chodorow argues that psychoanalysis, unlike many sociological theories, has always theorized about gender and sexuality, however distortedly, and if we want to understand how people become gendered and how they develop sexual identities, psychoanalysis is the best place to start. Psychoanalysis, she suggests, reveals that the social location of gender is partly in the self and partly in social relationships, that the social and psychological are intertwined. With regard to mothering, a psychoanalytic perspective suggests that mothering is not only social and cultural but also a psychological stance towards the world. Finally, Chodorow suggests that psychoanalytic theory is the only theory that provides any insight into how people give cultural phenomena, like gender, deep personal and emotional meaning.

Thus, studying psychoanalysis during second-wave feminism led Chodorow to a career of trying to understand the personal and cultural constructions of gender identity, sexuality and mothering, and the relationship between psychoanalysis and feminism.

Key Issues

Chodorow's theory asks a key sociological question: Why do women mother? In answering this question she answers many other questions as well. Her theory offers an explanation of how we acquire gender identities and gendered personalities; how we acquire sexual identity (especially heterosexuality) or object choice; adult love relationships and the reproduction of mothering; and why change in gender norms and structures is difficult but possible.

The Significance of the Question: Why do Women Mother?

In asking this question, Chodorow problematizes the one aspect of being a woman that seems most natural, biological and innate. Some critics have suggested that there is no need to even ask the question, 'Why do women mother?' These critics often argue that women mother because it is a biological fact. Women bear children and nurse them, and therefore it makes sense that they mother. Chodorow, however, suggests that this is an inadequate explanation. There is no logical reason that because women bear the baby and often nurse it that they should be the ones to do all the caring, every minute of the day. In fact, in many societies, women who are not biologically a child's mother are the ones who care for it. Similarly, there is no biological reason that fathers are incapable of caring for children. Finally, biological factors can explain little about the quality and emotional meaning of mothering or of the mother–child relationship.

Many sociological thinkers have attempted to critique Chodorow's explanation for why women mother by suggesting that there are many alternative explanations. Some theorize that women mother because of socialization. These thinkers claim that women are taught from the time they are children that they will grow up to care for children. As girls, they are given dolls to play with and learn the mothering role. Others claim that women mother for economic reasons. In order to survive in our society as a woman, such theorists argue, one must take up the position of wife and mother, which gives women their only real access to men's economic resources. Chodorow argues that these explanations are only part of the answer to why women mother. What they cannot explain, she argues, is why women want to mother. Why do women get gratification from mothering? Why do they enjoy it? Mothering, according to Chodorow, is not just an activity that is forced on women but one in which most women desire to participate. Another problem with these previous sociological explanations for why women mother is that they define mothering as a behaviour or set of behaviours. Chodorow suggests that mothering is much more than that. It is a stance in the world, empathy, a relation to an infant or child. When we define mothering this way, a much deeper, more complex explanation of women's mothering is required. Chodorow turns to psychoanalytic theory for this explanation and ultimately argues that women get this desire and ability to mother through having been mothered by women themselves.

Because Chodorow is working from a psychoanalytic account and such accounts are often developmental, the best way to understand her theory is to learn the developmental story that she tells. Bear in mind, however, that this story of intrapsychic, relational family dynamics takes place within a larger social structure where there is a gendered division of labour in which women care for infants and small children. Chodorow is not explaining the origin of this division of labour but its reproduction.

Psychoanalytic developmental stories about gender, usually cast in terms of the oedipal conflict, seek to explain how people achieve gender identity – one's sense of self as a girl or boy – and how they achieve sexual identity or object choice – do you desire men or women? Chodorow also sets out to answer these questions, but does so quite differently from **Freud** and others, as she is a different kind of psychoanalytic theorist from those with whom most of us are familiar. Chodorow is an 'object relations' theorist. Unlike traditional Freudians who think people seek to gratify drives, object relations theorists think people seek relations with 'objects'. Objects in object relations theory refer to people. Object relations theorists privilege the preoedipal period of development (as opposed to Freud's privileging of the oedipal) and object relations theorists focus on the mother as the key figure in children's development (as opposed to Freud's focus on the father). The developmental story for both girls and boys has the same beginning, both boys and girls begin life attached to their mothers.

The Development of Gender Identities and Gendered Personalities

When they are born, both girls and boys experience a oneness or symbiosis with the mother. As an infant suckling at the mother's breast, being held and cuddled by her, and simply doing what babies do, the child cannot distinguish between mother and self. To the infant, it is as if the two are physically and psychologically one. However, as both boys and girls begin to separate from their mothers and establish selves, their experience of the preoedipal phase (approximately 0–3 years) changes because mothers mother girls and boys very differently. Through mothering a girl child, a mother re-experiences herself both as mothered child and as her mother. She feels 'like' her daughter and encourages closeness and connection with her daughter. This preoedipal mother–daughter relationship continues to include many of the early mother–child issues – boundary confusion, dependence, individuation. From this relationship with mother, girls establish their gender identity. Gender identity is not difficult for girls to establish as it is built on their sense of oneness with their mothers. From the beginning, girls are attached, dependent and connected to their mothers and the mother confirms that the girl is like her. Later this relationship may become difficult, ambivalent, boundary confused as a girl tries to separate from her mother, but it is this relationship that establishes a girl's gender identity. Through her connection or what psychoanalysts would call her 'identification' with her mother, the daughter establishes a deep, unconscious, fixed sense about herself as a girl. She comes to feel deeply that she is a girl/woman. From their relationships with their mothers, girls also develop personalities that are boundary permeable, connected, relational, dependent.

Like girls, boys experience a symbiosis or feeling of oneness with the mother at birth. However, boys have a more difficult time establishing gender identity. Boys must shift their identificatory love from their mother. As boys develop, mothers encourage separation of sons and convey to boys that they are different from her. It is not that mothers love sons any less than they love daughters, but that they experience the mothering of boy children differently and treat sons differently from the way they do daughters. These differences, according to Chodorow, are subtle differences of 'nuance, tone, quality'.[4] That is, boys cannot identify with their mothers in order to establish their sense of themselves as boys, as masculine. However, because there is (usually) no father parenting (or mothering) in the same way that the mother is, no real, concrete, available masculine person for him to identify with, he forms a masculine gender identity based on being not mother, not feminine, not woman. A boy must repudiate all that is feminine. His masculine identity is based on being not a girl/woman and is filled in with cultural stories about symbols of masculinity, for example superheroes. Another outcome of this developmental route is that masculine identity is a fragile identity. Because masculine identity is based on being 'not mother, not feminine', men constantly seek to reconstruct and reconfirm their masculinity through repudiating that which is feminine. This psychological story underlies men's derogation of women. Masculinity is not all that is produced at this developmental moment. Through this process, boys also come to develop personalities that are more autonomous, independent and boundary heightened than women's.

The Development of Sexual Object Choice/Sexual Identity

While boys have a more difficult time establishing their gender identity, according to Chodorow, the establishment of sexual identity for boys is easier developmentally. Because all children are originally 'matrisexual', that is, erotically connected to their mothers, boys maintain this connection throughout their development, much in the same way that girls maintain their identifications with their mothers. Thus, in the course of oedipal development, boys eventually shift their object choice from mother specifically to women in general and become adults with heterosexual sexual identities.

However, how heterosexual sexual identity is developed for the girl is more complex in Chodorow's theory. Chodorow argues that as girls develop, their bonds with their mothers become fraught with ambivalence, boundary confusion, an unclear sense of what is 'me' and 'not me'. These feelings cause tension and anxiety and eventually cause the girl to shift her erotic ties to the father as a means of helping her to separate from her mother and easing the tension of the mother–daughter relationship. What Chodorow does not explain is exactly what changes so dramatically at this point that a girl can no longer bear this relationship with her mother without shifting some of her ties, and specifically her sexual ties, to the father (and eventually to men in general). Some critics argue that this explanation about girls' heterosexuality ignores structures such as compulsory heterosexuality that shape women's heterosexual object choice.[5]

Heterosexual Knots and the Reproduction of Mothering

As adults, these gendered psychological family dramas continue to shape lives. The interplay of gendered personalities and heterosexuality complicate adult love relationships. Men and women become tied in 'heterosexual knots', according to Chodorow. Men and women experience adult love relationships differently because of the way their identities are constructed in early childhood. Through sex with a woman, an adult man can find the connection, oneness and dependence that he had only as a very small child with his mother. However, 'women have a richer, ongoing inner world to fall back on, and … the men in their lives do not represent the intensity and exclusivity that women represent to men'.[6] Women re-create the connection they felt with their mothers in many parts of their lives, including within friendships with other women. Thus, ultimately, 'men do not become as emotionally important to women as women do to men'.[7] These differences lead to many of the difficulties we see and experience in contemporary intimate adult heterosexual relationships.

Finally, as adults, women also seek to re-create their relationships with their mothers through having children of their own. Women want to (become) mother(s) in order to re-experience the relationship they had with their own mother. Through mothering a child, a woman re-creates her deepest feelings of connection and dependency. Thus, the gender division of labour is reproduced as women come to want to mother. In short, Chodorow theorizes that women mother because women mother.

Social Change

One of the things that Chodorow's theory explains is that gender is rooted within our psyches. It is not simply an external social relation. Because gender is anchored deeply within us, it is extremely difficult to change. Chodorow suggests that social change will come partly from a change in parenting structures. If men and women both cared for children in a daily, emotional, immediate way throughout childhood, then these dynamics would be reshaped. Boys and girls would have equal opportunity to identify with both parents, and this would eliminate many gender differences in personality and would at least lessen men's denigration of women and the feminine.

Some critics have challenged Chodorow on this point of change. How, they ask, can men ever parent when Chodorow describes their adult personalities as independent, disconnected and arelational? Men, it seems, do not have the ability to mother. However, Chodorow responds to such criticisms with a reminder that men do have 'the foundations of parental (maternal) capacities and desires for primary relationships, but these have been repressed in their development'.[8] Because all people begin their relationships connected to mothers, all have some sense of these capacities. Thus, Chodorow argues that such parenting qualities are available within men. If men could use these capacities to share equally in childcare, then social change would be possible.

Seeing Things Differently

Chodorow's work can be used to understand a wide range of social phenomena from mother–daughter relationships and adult heterosexual relationships to the construction of masculinity in organizations like fraternities and the military. I find most compelling the way that Chodorow's theory helps us to understand the derisiveness and derogation that men direct at women in our society. According to Chodorow, such sentiments derive from a sense of masculinity that is based on being not like mother, not like women. Remember, masculinity is constructed psychologically as the opposite of femininity. And, according to Chodorow and other psychoanalysts, such a construction of masculinity is never complete. It must be constantly worked on and reconstructed. Such a view of masculinity is useful for understanding a variety of institutional constructions of masculine identity in contemporary society.

In her book, *Gender Differences at Work*, Christine Williams draws from Chodorow's work to explain just such an institutional construction of masculinity. Williams examines the construction of masculinity (and femininity) by marines. She finds that much of the misogyny in the marines and the purpose it serves can be explained by Chodorow's theory: 'Psychoanalysis is uniquely able to supply us with insight into the unconscious and often irrational interests served by certain socially institutionalized practices. In the case of the military, it provides us with an explanation for what is at stake in preserving masculinity.'[9] Let us examine the marines and Williams' analysis of them more closely.

Even before the moment that recruits arrive at boot camp, the understood purpose of marine training is that it will 'make a man out of them'. Such sentiments will often have been seen in advertisements recruiting the men into the military. For example, an ad for the Army National Guard said 'kiss your momma goodbye'. Boot camp, according to Williams, 'has been culturally defined as an activity only masculine males can accomplish. It unambiguously fulfills men's largely unconscious desires to prove once and for all that they are masculine.'[10] Throughout the training, new male recruits are demeaned by others as 'girls', and they march to misogynist chants ('I don't know but I've been told, Eskimo pussy is mighty cold').[11] Men also demean women through their display of pornography in their barracks and in the slang they use to refer to women. Williams, following Chodorow, suggests that such behaviour derives from the psychological construction of masculinity where women mother and boys must give up feminine identification in favour of a masculinity that is defined only as the opposite of feminine. Military training draws on this psychological construction of masculinity.

Williams finds that this construction of masculinity with its contempt for femininity is institutionalized in the military.[12] She argues that the military has invested much effort in constructing differences between men and women. Men are marines; women are women marines. Despite much evidence that women are capable of achieving the same standards as men in military training, the military continues to segregate basic training. Similarly, the military constructs gender differences, constructs masculinity as the opposite of femininity, by institutionalizing gender appearance and behaviour. Williams finds that women marines are required to wear make-up, to take etiquette classes, to wear skirts (unless it is below freezing). Williams suggests that it is 'ironic that the branch of the military most closely associated with masculinity seems most concerned with preserving women's femininity'.[13] Williams suggests that the marines' resistance to gender integration and their institutional construction of gender difference are products of the threat to men's masculinity when women enter a previously all-male institution. Williams suggests that more than economic interests are at stake because economic interests cannot explain the stridency and irrationality that accompany the marines' talk about women in the military. Chodorow's theory allows us to explain such stridency, along with the general construction of gender difference in the marines as motivated by the fragile, early childhood construction of masculinity as that which is not feminine or female.

Legacies and Unfinished Business

Chodorow's theory has been extended by a number of sociological thinkers. Carol Gilligan's famous work about moral reasoning, *In a Different Voice*,[14] has its foundation in Chodorow's theory. Gilligan argues and tries to demonstrate empirically that men and women differ in how they make moral decisions. Men make moral decisions based on the ethic of justice (abstract moral principles) and women based on the ethic of care (relational dynamics and the implications of decisions). Drawing on Chodorow, Gilligan suggests that these differences in moral reasoning are a result of women's mothering and the different gender personalities that develop from this structure.

Jessica Benjamin's work[15] also extends Chodorow's thinking about what happens to gender psychodynamically when women mother. In particular, she asks what happens to women's desire? A question that she says drops out of Chodorow's theory which depicts women as relational and caring but without any sexuality. Benjamin claims that desire is a component of personality that is quite important in traditional psychoanalytic accounts of personality and should be returned to feminist object relations accounts.

Chodorow's theory has also been critiqued somewhat for a specific set of issues concerning generalizability. Because Chodorow relies on psychoanalytic case studies and theory to develop her explanation for women's mothering, many critics have asked: To whom does this theory apply? To only nuclear families? To only white families? Can we generalize from case studies of middle-class western European clinical patients of previous generations to contemporary, non-clinical populations that are diverse not only in class and race but also culture and society? After all, Chodorow is trying to explain a universal phenomenon (women's mothering). These questions were asked of much of the grand theorizing that feminist thinking produced in the 1970s. Chodorow responds to such criticism in a variety of ways in the collection of her work *Feminism and Psychoanalysis*. She argues in part that there is more variation than her early account may have suggested, yet insists that psychoanalysis is still a useful tool for understanding the personal construction of gender. After all 'people everywhere form a psyche, self, and identity'.[16] Similarly, like many psychoanalysts, she argues that clinical data is not problematic for generalizing to non-clinical populations because 'pathology reflects normal tendencies and becomes useful sociological evidence when a number of clinical cases reveal systematic, patterned responses'.[17]

Perhaps in response to her critics but also because she is now a practising psychoanalyst, Chodorow has begun theorizing differences in individuals' constructions of gender and love and how these individual constructions are shaped by cultural constructions of gender and love. Men and women love, she argues, 'in as many different ways as there are men and women'.[18] Since

The Reproduction of Mothering, Chodorow has further developed an understanding of unconscious gender identity by documenting that gender is both a cultural and personal construction. According to Chodorow, all people have the ability to shape cultural experiences and cultural meanings emotionally and unconsciously. She writes:

> I do not mean only that people create individualized cultural and linguistic versions of meaning by drawing upon cultural or linguistic categories at hand. Rather, perception and meaning are psychologically created. As psychoanalysis documents, people use available cultural meanings and images, but they experience them emotionally and through fantasy, as well as in particular interpersonal contexts.[19]

Finally, Chodorow's most recent book, *The Power of Feelings*,[20] returns her to an engagement with cultural anthropologists and continues to pursue the personal and cultural and what these mean for understanding gender.

FURTHER READING

Benjamin, J. (1988) *The Bonds of Love*, New York: Pantheon. An extension of Chodorow's work that affords a major role to desire in the relationship between gender and the psychodynamics of mothering.

Buhle, M. (1998) *Feminism and Its Discontents: A Century of Struggle with Psychoanalysis*, Cambridge: Harvard University Press.

Chodorow, N. (1995) 'Gender as a personal and cultural construction', *Signs*, Spring, 516–44.

Chodorow, N. (1999) *The Power of Feelings*, New Haven, CT: Yale University Press.

Gilligan, C. (1982) *In a Different Voice*, Cambridge, MA: Harvard University Press. Psychoanalysis and the analysis of gender is brought into an encounter with cultural anthropology. Gilligan's seminal discussion of how boys and girls, men and women, differ in the way they make moral decisions.

Goldner, V. (1991) 'Toward a critical relational theory of gender', *Psychoanalytic Dialogues*, **1**: 249–72.

Person, E. (1981) 'Sexuality as the mainstay of identity', *Signs*, **5**(4): 605–30.

Williams, C. (1989) *Gender Differences at Work*, Berkeley, CA: University of California Press. Williams investigates the US marines as an institutional site for the unconscious and often irrational interests served by the social construction of masculinity. This is the subject of the Seeing Things Differently section of this chapter.

PART III

CONTENTS

CHAPTER 15

Jürgen Habermas

WILLIAM OUTHWAITE

Driving Impulses

The most important intellectual source of Habermas's thinking is the broad, flexible and interdisciplinary Marxist tradition that inspired what came to be called the 'Frankfurt School' of critical theory, based in the early 1930s and again from 1950 in the Institute for Social Research in Frankfurt. As Habermas showed in detail in his *Theory of Communicative Action*,[1] this tradition draws on both **Marx** and **Max Weber**, on another non-Marxist, Weber's contemporary **Georg Simmel**, and on the father of 'western Marxism', Georg Lukács. In an autobiographical interview, Habermas recalls reading Lukács for the first time with great excitement, but with a sense that his work was no longer directly relevant to postwar societies such as West Germany. His thinking remained shaped, however, by a western Marxist agenda emphasizing the interplay between capitalist exploitation and bureaucratic state rule, and their implications for individual identity and collective political autonomy. More concretely, as a member of what has been called the 'Hitler Youth generation', drawn as a child into complicity with the most appalling regime of modern times, he was horrified both by the crimes of the Third Reich and by the unwillingness of his compatriots to face up to their responsibility for what had happened.

To all this Habermas added a concern with technocracy characteristic of the mid-twentieth century. He was concerned to construct a socialist response to the technological determinism deriving from Heidegger (whose failure to confront his complicity with Nazism Habermas found particularly repugnant) and, in postwar Germany, from Arnold Gehlen and Helmut Schelsky. For Habermas, the erosion of political choice by technical means was not inevitable, as some critics of technology had argued, but it was a pervasive feature of modern societies. This anxiety has inspired much of Habermas's work, linking his critical analysis of the decline of the public sphere and the rise of technocratic politics with his critique of positivist social science. And his more positive programme of what he has called a 'theory of communicative action' and the theories of morality, law and democracy that it sustains has again the same double focus on theory and practice. In many ways, indeed, his work has come full circle, working out in detail approaches that were presented in a more intuitive manner in his earlier writing.

Instrumental reason

The form of reasoning devoted to calculating the best way of getting something, the best way of achieving a goal. The focus is on how to do something, how to achieve some goal, how to acquire some object, rather than, for example, on questions of value and worth or principle. Thus, one does not focus on why we should do that thing, why we want to achieve that goal (why it is or should be a valued goal), why it is important to acquire that object. Instrumental reason prioritizes calculation, achieving efficiency through the optimum calculation of the best 'means' for an already given end (most often 'given' already by bureaucratic or capitalistic environments whose goals are perceived as imperative and non-negotiable), and there is a tendency in modern societies for a disproportionate amount of our energies to be devoted to this form of reasoning.

Habermas's relationship to Frankfurt critical theory was somewhat indirect in the early stages of his career. Max Horkheimer's interests, like those of **Theodor Adorno**, had become increasingly philosophical, and their critique of **instrumental reason**, expressed in their *Dialectic of Enlightenment* (1947)[2] and subsequent works, increasingly despairing. Habermas felt that a revival of critical theory had once again to engage both with philosophy and with the social and human sciences. He fully shared, however, Adorno and Horkheimer's concern with the way in which enlightenment, in the form of instrumental rationality, turns from a means of liberation into a new source of enslavement. 'Already at that time' (the late 1950s), he has written, 'my problem was a theory of modernity, a theory of the pathology of modernity, from the viewpoint of the realization – the deformed realization – of reason in history'.[3] This involved a working-through of the classics: Marx and Weber, but also Kant, Fichte and Hegel – and of course ancient Greek thought. This theoretical emphasis was, however, constantly combined, as in his early volume of essays on *Theory and Practice*,[4] with a concern for the conditions of rational political discussion in modern technocratic democracies. Only the social sciences, broadly conceived, could provide the means to construct a genuinely contemporary critical theory of advanced capitalism, but their own positivistic deformation was itself part of the problem to be overcome.

Key Issues

Communication in the Public Sphere

The issue of the conditions of communication in the public sphere, the subject of Habermas's first major book, *The Structural Transformation of the Public Sphere* (1962),[5] remained central to his thinking over the following decades. Habermas's strategy in the book was to relate the concept of public opinion back to its historical roots in the idea of the public sphere or public domain, in which the literate bourgeois (and of course almost exclusively male) public of the eighteenth century in the more advanced European societies took on a political role in the evaluation of contemporary affairs and, in particular, state policy. The 'transformation' of the public sphere begins with the commercialization of the press and leads to a shift from publicity in the sense of openness or transparency to the modern sense of the term in journalism, advertising and politics. The reading public is polarized into active specialists and a merely receptive mass. The same is true of the political process, split between a small number of party activists and a basically inactive mass electorate; public opinion ceases to be a source of critical judgement and checks, and becomes a social psychological variable to be manipulated. The result is a 'gap between the constitutional fiction of public opinion and the social-psychological dissolution of its concept'.[6]

In some ways, this book recalls Horkheimer and Adorno's *Dialectic of Enlightenment*. Just as, in their argument, the enlightenment critique of tradition and authority ended up creating even more pernicious forms of domination, so, for Habermas, the bourgeois public sphere, concerned with the critical assessment of public policy in rational discussion oriented to a concept of the public interest, turns into what he calls a 'manipulated' public sphere, in which states and corporations use 'publicity' in the modern sense of the word to secure political and financial support. Habermas is, however, somewhat less pessimistic in his conclusions. In an analysis to which he has returned in his most recent work, he envisaged certain counter-tendencies to, and opportunities in, the process he described. First, the development of the liberal constitutional state into a much more pervasive welfare state means that public organizations of all kinds are opened up to scrutiny by a corresponding variety of interest groups, which link together members of the public concerned with specific aspects of welfare state provision.

And although the bureaucratization of administration seems, as Max Weber had noted in relation to parliamentary politics, to remove the activity of specialists from rational control, it might be possible, Habermas suggests, to democratize the administrative bodies themselves. In his more recent work on legal and democratic theory, Habermas has returned to this theme, stressing the interplay between law and democratic politics and the relation of both of these to more informal processes of public discussion. Just as important as the formal relations between the legal and political institutions of the constitutional state are the quality and extent of public communication. The public sphere, he writes in *Between Facts and Norms* (1992), should not be seen as an institution or organization, but as 'a network' in which 'flows of communication are filtered and synthesized in such a way that they condense into *public* opinions clustered according to themes'.[7] In the modern world, these processes of communication are increasingly mediated, in both senses of the word: they take place both at a distance and increasingly via the mass media. In other words, rational discussion of public issues is not confined to face-to-face encounters in larger or smaller assemblies, taking place in real time. Habermas's early critiques of the restriction of political discussion as a result of technocracy and the 'scientization' of politics feed into a broader critique of scientism discussed in the next section.

Methodology of the Social Sciences

Habermas's work on the methodology of the social sciences is centred on the critique of positivism, understood as involving the abandonment of philosophical reflection on knowledge and a concentration on essentially technical issues – methodology in the narrow sense of the term. Habermas participated in the famous 'positivism dispute' of the 1960s, taking up Adorno's critique of what they both saw as an overrestrictive conception of rationality in the philosophy of Karl Popper and his followers. Habermas's own alternative involved a careful and creative appropriation of models and approaches from a wide variety of human and social sciences. He focused, in particular, on three major contributions that had become prominent in the 1960s: the 'phenomenological' sociology inspired by Alfred Schutz; Peter Winch's sociological or anthropological extension of Wittgenstein's notion of language-games; and Hans-Georg Gadamer's philosophical hermeneutics, which stressed the existential quality of the 'encounter' between reader and text. These, Habermas argued, could be brought into a complementary relation with one another and could then be further complemented by a more materialist reflection on the way in which our understanding of the social world (the common theme of these three currents of thought) is systematically distorted by relations of power and exploitation.

In *Knowledge and Human Interests* (1968),[8] Habermas brilliantly showed how positivism had limited our understanding of the natural and the social world and undermined the possibility of critique; the latter, however, could be reconstructed from the work of Kant, Fichte, Hegel and Marx and shown to inspire, for example, **Freudian** psychoanalytic theory and practice. 'Critical' sciences such as psychoanalysis or the Marxist critique of ideology, governed by an emancipatory interest in overcoming causal obstacles to self-understanding, bridged the gap between the natural or empirical sciences, oriented to the prediction and control of objectified processes and the human sciences, oriented to an expansion of mutual understanding. At this time, Habermas engaged in some extended debates with other leading thinkers, notably Gadamer and the system theorist Niklas Luhmann. Against Gadamer, he argued that understanding needed to be supplemented by a materialist critique of power and exploitation, which he justified with an appeal to a notion of social theory contrasted with Luhmann's technocratic conception. In the 1970s, Habermas scaled down some of his claims for emancipatory social science and developed an idea of reconstructive science, seen as a systematic attempt to isolate the conditions and implications of practices such as linguistic communication and moral reasoning.

Crises of State Legitimacy

One of Habermas's best-known books is a short and highly compressed text called *Legitimation Crisis*.[9] Here, and in related essays, published in English under the title *Communication and the Evolution of Society*,[10] he advanced a neo-Marxist theory of historical development and a critique of contemporary advanced or 'late' capitalism. Habermas argued that historical materialist explanations of the development of the productive forces needed to be augmented by an account of the evolution of normative structures, understood in a wide sense to include, for example, family forms. In late capitalism, again, a traditional Marxist account of capitalist crisis, which focuses on the economic contradictions of the capitalist system, needs to be modified to account for the role of the modern interventionist welfare state and the resultant displacement of crisis tendencies from the economic sphere to the political and cultural domains. Instead of the economic crises that remain at the root of the problem, what we experience are incoherent state policies leading to what Habermas calls 'rationality crises' that weaken state legitimacy; these interventions also lead to an erosion of individual motivation and a loss of meaning.

Habermas's subsequent work develops both the historical thesis and the diagnosis of contemporary capitalist crises. *The Theory of Communicative Action*[11] traces the conflict between the rationalization of world-views in early modernity, expressed, for example, in secularization and formal law and the erosion of appeals to traditional authority. It also focuses on the way in which a newly attained sphere open in principle to rational debate becomes restricted as market and bureaucratic structures come to dominate the modern world. Habermas addresses, in other words, the big question of whether we could have had, or can now have, modernity without the less attractive features of capitalism and the bureaucratic nation-state. More tentatively, in *Between Facts and Norms*,[12] he has begun to reformulate elements of his model of advanced capitalist crisis in the language of his more recent theories.

Theory of Communicative Action

The centrepiece of Habermas's developed theorizing is a theory of communicative action grounded in, but spiralling off from, the analysis of linguistic communication. His basic idea is that any serious use of language to make claims about the world, as opposed, for example, to exclamations or the issuing of orders, presupposes the claims that:

1. what we say makes sense and is true
2. that we are sincere in saying it
3. that we have the right to say it.

These claims can be questioned by our hearers or readers. As Habermas shows with the homely example of a professor asking a seminar participant to fetch a glass of water, even a simple request, understood not as a mere demand but 'as a speech act carried out in an attitude oriented to understanding', raises claims to normative rightness, subjective sincerity and factual practicability that may be questioned. The addressee of the request may reject it as illegitimate ('I'm not your servant'), insincere ('You don't really want one') or mistaken about the facts of the matter (availability of a source of water).

Only a rational agreement that excluded no one and no relevant evidence or argument would provide, in the last resort, a justification of the claims we make and presuppose in our assertions. This idea gives us, Habermas claims, a theory of truth as what we would ultimately come to rationally agree about. Moreover, if he is right that moral judgements also have cognitive content and are not mere expressions of taste or disguised prescriptions, it also provides a theory of morality and legitimate political authority. Moral norms or political institutions are justified if they are what we would still uphold at the end of an ideal process of argumentation. The latter is of course an idealization; Habermas at one time called it the 'ideal speech situation'. Yet it is presupposed, he argues, by our everyday practice of communication, which is made meaningful by the theoretical prospect of ultimate agreement. This can be seen negatively in our refusal, under certain circumstances, to engage in argument at all: who, except another Nazi, would want to enter an argument with a Nazi about whether the Holocaust was justified?

The analysis of language use can be expanded into a broader theory of communicative action, defined as action oriented by and towards mutual agreement. In social–theoretical terms, this can be contrasted with the models of instrumental or strategic, self-interested action *(Homo economicus)*, normatively regulated action (functionalism, for example **Parsons**) or dramaturgical action (**Goffman, Garfinkel**). All of these, Habermas claims, can be shown to be parasitic upon communicative action, which incorporates and goes beyond each of these. The theory of communicative action then underpins a communication theory of morality, law and democracy, and it is these aspects that have dominated Habermas's most recent work.

The Politically Engaged Intellectual

I stressed at the outset of this chapter the practical and historical origins of much of Habermas's thinking, and his recent emphasis on law and democratic theory once again aligns one of the main focuses of his theoretical work with issues of current concern on which he has commented throughout his career. From an early stage, when he worked in part as a journalist, Habermas has actively pursued opportunities to intervene in the public sphere of the Federal Republic and, more recently, what he sees as an emergent globalized public sphere or civil society. These articles and other contributions, republished in successive volumes of 'political writings', stretch, as Robert Holub shows in *Jürgen Habermas: Critic in the Public Sphere*,[13] from early critiques of the political culture of postwar West Germany through to an engagement with the 1968 student movement, which was initially sympathetic, became increasingly critical and, finally, endorsed the liberalizing long-term role of the movement and its radical democratic ethos. Then, in the late 1980s, Habermas initiated what came to be known as the 'historians' dispute' *(Historikerstreit)* over what he saw as an attempt to rewrite twentieth-century German history in a rosier light to serve the interests of the conservative right. More recently, he has written and commented at length on issues of German reunification and its aftermath (1995), on European and global politics (1998) and on ethical issues raised by biotechnology (2001).

Habermas stresses the difference between political articles and interviews and his properly theoretical works, but it can be seen that such an engagement is entailed by his theoretical position and that many of his diagnoses of the present are crucially informed by, and in turn inform, his theoretical work. This is not an unmediated fusion of theoretical and practical concerns, but a sustained parallelism with numerous crossover points.

Seeing Things Differently

I have myself been most influenced by his metatheory of the sciences, but the essential point to make about Habermas is the interplay between the various elements of his work. Thus, for example, the thoroughgoing critique of positivism and ethical subjectivism feeds into an approach to legal and democratic theory that transcends conventional separations between, on the one hand, so-called positive law, where what counts is merely that it has been enacted according to due process, and, on the other hand, an individualistic morality. These are in turn internally related, he argues, to representative democracy and public communication. Whether or not Habermas is right that one can formally reconstruct theories of all these domains on the basis of an analysis of the preconditions of communication, the basic notion that communication with others is only meaningful if it is driven by the pursuit of rational agreement, and that such agreement is the only legitimate basis of morality and political authority in the modern world, would be widely shared.

I have always been attracted by Habermas's basic idea that a neo-Marxist theory of the contemporary world must attend to the distinctiveness of advanced capitalism and, in particular, to the state forms with which it coexists, and to the issues of culture and identity to which critical theory has been more sensitive than most other Marxist and non-Marxist traditions in social theory. With the eclipse, in the 1980s and 90s, of more orthodox variants of Marxism, and a certain fusion of horizons between Marxist and non-Marxist approaches in social theory, Habermas's creative synthesis seems more attractive than ever. It is worth noting also that, although Habermas did not devote much of his published work before 1989 to an analysis of state socialist societies, his approach made possible some of the most creative work in the analysis of these regimes. Thus, whereas more orthodox Marxist approaches concentrated on the issue of how state socialist modes of production should be understood, Habermas and others, such as Andrew Arato, using a Habermasian approach, put these questions in a rather broader framework. Habermas's model of the 'colonization' of the life-world by markets and/or administrative structures can be creatively used to analyse societies where markets are more or less completely replaced by centralized administrative decisions. More particularly, Habermas's model is well placed to analyse both the undermining of free and independent communication in the state socialist dictatorships and the insidious way in which, as he once put it, they simulate or 'sham' communicative relations between 'comrades' in a fantasy world of unaninimity and solidarity.[14] His own work and that of others using a Habermasian approach has also been particularly illuminating in relation to recent discussion of the post-1989 world; thinkers concerned with, for example, the political consequences of globalization for our conceptions of ethics, democracy, citizenship and (post-) national identity have drawn significantly on Habermas's insights. In particular, Habermas has popularized a concept of 'constitutional patriotism', in which citizens may move beyond the simple loyalties of 'my country, right or wrong' to a more reflective and rational identification with 'their' states.

The rise of social theory since the beginning of the 1970s, and more particularly in the 1990s, as a relatively distinct domain of activity and a source of inspiration to the social sciences as a whole has also been due in considerable part to Habermas's work. He has always been hard to place in disciplinary terms, working on the borders of social theory and philosophy and holding an appointment in both these 'subjects', and always willing to venture into new fields such as the analysis of language or law, and now even biotechnology, as required by the development of his own work. In short, he has made it possible both to see the contemporary world differently, and to rethink the relations between theories in philosophy and the social sciences that are our main resource in understanding this world.

Legacies and Unfinished Business

As noted above, Habermas's work has been influential in a whole range of fields, and has become one of the principal reference points for much discussion both in social theory and, for example, moral philosophy, legal theory and theories of international relations. Historians and theorists of culture have also increasingly been influenced by his conception of the public sphere and other elements of his thought. Critical theory, in the broadest sense, has been carried on by contemporaries such as Albrecht Wellmer and what may be called a third generation of thinkers including Axel Honneth, Hans Joas, Thomas McCarthy and Seyla Benhabib – all of whom, in different ways, have responded to issues posed by poststructuralist, postmodernist and feminist theory and shown how Habermas's approach can be usefully developed and extended.[15] Habermas's concern with historical sociology and theorizing states and social movements has been carried forward by, for example, Claus Offe and Klaus Eder.[16] Finally, his discourse ethics and his more recent theorizing about law and the state have attracted enormous interest in areas of analytic moral and legal philosophy previously untouched by Habermasian concerns. This is currently a most active area of research and Habermas has himself been working substantially in this field.

Two other areas of 'unfinished business' are his analysis of the public sphere and crisis tendencies in contemporary societies, first addressed in his books of 1962 and 1973b. He carried forward this work in *Between Facts and Norms* (1992)[17] and *The Inclusion of the Other* (1996),[18] but so far only in outline. In relation to the public sphere, as noted above, he has stressed the interplay of public communication at many different levels and the fact that public spheres in modern societies are increasingly mediated and virtual. What this might mean in practice for a political theory of communicative democracy is an issue that clearly requires further exploration. We also badly need a developed theory of economic, social and political crises in modern societies, which Habermas is extremely well placed to provide.

FURTHER READING

Dews, P. (1999) *Habermas: A Critical Reader*, Oxford: Blackwell. An invaluable collection of chapters on various aspects of Habermas's work both by those whose own work is profoundly influenced by his writings and those who are well versed but more critical.

Edgar, A. (2005) *The Philosophy of Habermas*, London: Acumen.

Finlayson, G. (2005) *Habermas: A Very Short Introduction*, Oxford: Oxford University Press.

Outhwaite, W. (1994) *Habermas. A Critical Introduction*, Cambridge: Polity Press. A concise and clear introduction to Habermas's work from his early writings on the public sphere to his more recent work on law and the state.

Outhwaite, W. (ed.) (1996) *The Habermas Reader*, Cambridge: Polity Press. A comprehensive introduction to, and selection from, Jürgen Habermas's writings from the early 1960s to the mid-1990s. The book is divided into seven sections, covering the principal areas of Habermas's work.

White, S.K. (ed.) (1994) *The Cambridge Companion to Habermas*, Cambridge: Cambridge University Press.

CHAPTER 16

Pierre Bourdieu

Loïc Wacquant

Pierre Bourdieu was born in 1930 and raised in a remote mountain village of the Pyrénées in southwestern France where his father was a sharecropper and then the postman. At the close of the 1940s, he moved to Paris to study at the prestigious Ecole normale supérieure, at a time when philosophy was the queen discipline and the obligatory vocation of any aspirant intellectual. There he quickly grew dissatisfied with the 'philosophy of the subject' exemplified by Sartrian existentialism – then the reigning doctrine – and gravitated towards the 'philosophy of the concept' associated with the works of epistemologists Gaston Bachelard, Georges Canguilhem and Jules Vuillemin, as well as towards the phenomenologies of Edmund Husserl and Maurice Merleau-Ponty. Shortly after graduation, however, Bourdieu forsook a projected study of affective life mating philosophy, medicine and biology and, as other illustrious *normaliens* such as **Emile Durkheim** and Maurice Halbwachs had done before him, he converted to social science.

Driving Impulses

This conversion was precipitated by the conjunction of two events. On a personal level, the first-hand encounter with the gruesome realities of colonial rule and war in Algeria (where he had been sent to serve his mandatory stint in the military) prompted Bourdieu to turn to ethnology and sociology in order to make sense of the social cataclysm wrought by the clash between imperial capitalism and home-grown nationalism. Thus his first books, *The Algerians*, *Work and Workers in Algeria*, and *The Uprooting: The Crisis of Traditional Agriculture in Algeria*,[1] dissected the social organization and culture of the native society and chronicled its violent disruption under the press of wage labour, urbanization and the so-called pacification policy of the French military, in an effort to illumine and assist in the painful birth of an independent Algeria. At about the same time, Bourdieu turned the new-found instruments of social science back onto his own childhood village in seeking to understand both the collapse of the European peasant society accelerating in the postwar decades and the specificity of the sociological gaze itself.[2]

These youthful inquiries bear the hallmark of Bourdieu's lifework: they are the product of an *activist science*, impervious to ideological bias yet attuned to the burning sociopolitical issues of its day and responsive to the ethical dilemmas these entail. And they translate the grand questions of classical philosophy and social theory into precise empirical experiments pursued with the full array of methods supplied by the scientific tradition and fearlessly applied to the sociologist himself.

On an intellectual level, Bourdieu's break with philosophy was made possible by the demise of existentialism and the correlative rebirth of the social sciences in France after a half-century of eclipse. Under the broad banner of 'structuralism', the Durkheimian project of a total science of society and culture was being revived and modernized by Georges Dumézil in comparative mythology, Fernand Braudel in history and Claude Lévi-Strauss in anthropology. It was now possible to fulfil lofty intellectual ambitions, and to express progressive political impulses outside the ambit of the Communist Party, by embracing the freshly reinvigorated empirical disciplines.[3] Thus Bourdieu took to re-establishing the scientific and civic legitimacy of sociology in its motherland where it had been a pariah science since the passing of Durkheim and the decimation of his students by the First World War.

In the early 1960s, Bourdieu returned from Algiers to Paris where he was nominated director of studies at the Ecole des hautes études en sciences sociales as well as director of its newly formed Centre for European Sociology. There he pursued his ethnological work on ritual, kinship and social change in Algeria (as recorded in *Outline of a Theory of Practice* and *Algeria 1960*)[4] and took to the sociology of schooling, art, intellectuals and politics. These domains attracted him because he sensed that, in the prosperous postwar societies of the West, 'cultural capital' – educational credentials and familiarity with bourgeois culture – was becoming a major determinant of life chances and that, under the cloak of individual talent and academic meritocracy, its unequal distribution was helping to conserve social hierarchies. This he demonstrated in *The Inheritors* and *Reproduction in Education, Culture, and Society*,[5] two books that impacted the scholarly and policy debate on the school system and established him as the progenitor of 'reproduction theory' (a misleading label, as shall be seen shortly).

During the 1970s, Bourdieu continued to mine a wide array of topics at the intersection of culture, class and power to teach at the Ecole, and to lead the research team that edited *Actes de la recherche en sciences sociales*, a transdisciplinary journal he founded in 1975 to disseminate the most advanced results of social research and to engage salient social issues from a rigorous scientific standpoint. In 1981, the publication of his major works *Distinction* and *The*

Logic of Practice[6] earned him the chair of sociology left vacant at the Collège de France upon Raymond Aron's retirement, as well as worldwide renown. In the 1980s, the painstaking research conducted over the previous two decades came to fruition in such acclaimed volumes as *Language and Symbolic Power, Homo Academicus, The State Nobility* and *The Rules of Art.*[7]

In the final decade of his life, Pierre Bourdieu extended his inquiries in the sociology of symbolic goods (religion, science, literature, painting and publishing) and tackled new topics, among them social suffering, masculine domination, the historical emergence and contemporary functioning of the bureaucratic state, the social bases and political construction of the economy, journalism and television, and the institutional means for creating a European social policy.[8] He restated and amplified his theory of practice in *Pascalian Meditations*,[9] his most ambitious book, in which he also offers a critique of scholastic reason and a sociological resolution to the antinomy of rationalism and historicism. He engaged in extensive dialogues with neighbouring disciplines and returned to his youthful interest in the study of science.[10]

During the same period, Bourdieu grew more visibly active on the French and European political scenes, as new forms of social inequality and conflict linked to the rising hegemony of market ideology spread that challenged the traditional goals and organization of the Left and called for novel forms of intellectual intervention. In spite of his congenital shyness and deep-seated reluctance to play the 'media game', he was soon given the mantle of master-thinker previously held by Jean-Paul Sartre and **Michel Foucault**, and became one of the world's foremost public intellectuals and best-known critic of neoliberalism.[11] This was in keeping with one of the abiding purposes animating his work, namely, to make social science into an effective *countervailing symbolic power* and the midwife of social forces dedicated to social justice and civic morality.[12] It explains why his sudden passing in January 2002 triggered a flood of homage from political leaders, trade unionists and activists, scientists and artists from across Europe and myriad messages of grief from around the world (historian Carl Schorske compared its effect on the elite of Europe to that of the death of Voltaire).

Key Issues

With 37 books and some 400 articles oft couched in a difficult technical idiom, Bourdieu's thought might seem on first look dispersed and daunting, if not intractable. But beneath the bewildering variety of empirical objects he tackled lie a small set of theoretical principles, conceptual devices and scientific-cum-political intentions that give his writings remarkable coherence and continuity. Bourdieu's sprawling oeuvre is inseparably a *science of human practice* in its most diverse manifestations and a *critique of domination* in both the Kantian and the **Marxian** senses of the term.

A Science of Practice and a Critique of Domination

Bourdieu's sociology is critical first of inherited categories and accepted ways of thinking and of the subtle forms of rule wielded by technocrats and intellectuals in the name of culture and rationality. Next, it is critical of established patterns of power and privilege as well as of the politics that supports them. Undergirding this double critique is an explanatory account of the manifold processes whereby the social order masks its arbitrariness and perpetuates itself by extorting from the subordinate practical acceptance of, if not willed consent to, its existing hierarchies. This account of *symbolic violence* – the subtle imposition of systems of meaning that legitimize and thus solidify structures of inequality – simultaneously points to the social conditions under which these hierarchies can be challenged, transformed, nay overturned.[13]

Four notations can help us gain a preliminary feel for Bourdieu's distinctive intellectual project and style. First, his conception of social action, structure and knowledge is resolutely monist or *anti-dualistic*. It strives to circumvent or dissolve the oppositions that have defined perennial lines of debate in the social sciences: between subjectivist and objectivist modes of theorizing, between the material and symbolic dimensions of social life, as well as between interpretation and explanation, synchrony and diachrony, and micro- and macro-levels of analysis.

Secondly, Bourdieu's scientific thought and practice are genuinely *synthetic* in that they simultaneously straddle disciplinary, theoretical and methodological divides. Theoretically, they stand at the confluence of intellectual streams that academic traditions have typically construed as discordant or incompatible: Marx and Mauss, Durkheim and **Weber**, but also the diverse philosophies of Cassirer, Bachelard and Wittgenstein, the phenomenologies of Merleau-Ponty and Schutz, and the theories of language of Saussure, Chomsky and Austin. Methodologically, Bourdieu's investigations typically combine statistical techniques with direct observation and the exegesis of interaction, discourse and document.[14]

Thirdly, like Max Weber, Bourdieu's vision of society is fundamentally *agonistic:* for him, the social universe is the site of endless and pitiless competition, in and through which arise the differences that are the stuff and stake of social existence. Contention, not stasis, is the ubiquitous feature of collective life that his varied inquiries aim at making at once visible and intelligible. Struggle, not 'reproduction', is the master metaphor at the core of his thought.

Lastly and relatedly, Bourdieu's philosophical anthropology rests not on the notion of interest but on that of *recognition* – and its double, misrecognition.

Contrary to a common (mis)reading of his work, his is not a utilitarian theory of social action in which individuals consciously strategize to accumulate wealth, status or power. In line with Blaise Pascal, Bourdieu holds that the ultimate spring of conduct is the thirst for dignity, which society alone can quench. For only by being granted a name, a place, a function within a group or institution can the individual hope to escape the contingency, finitude and ultimate absurdity of existence. Human beings become such by submitting to the 'judgement of others, this major principle of uncertainty and insecurity but also, and without contradiction, of certainty, assurance, consecration'.[15] Social existence thus means difference, and difference implies hierarchy, which in turn sets off the endless dialectic of distinction and pretension, recognition and misrecognition, arbitrariness and necessity.

Constructing the Sociological Object

One of the main difficulties in understanding Bourdieu resides in the fact that the philosophy of science he draws on is equally alien – and opposed – to the two epistemological traditions that have dominated Anglo-American social science and the German *Geisteswissenschaften*, namely, positivism and hermeneutics. This conception of science takes after the works of the French school of 'historical epistemology' led by philosophers Bachelard and Canguilhem (under whom Bourdieu studied), mathematician Jean Cavaillès and intellectual historian Alexandre Koyré.[16]

This school, which anticipated many of the ideas later popularized by Thomas Kuhn's theory of scientific paradigms, conceives truth as 'error rectified' in an endless effort to dissolve the prenotions born of ordinary and scholarly common sense. Equally distant from theoretical formalism as from empiricist operationalism, it teaches that facts are necessarily suffused with theory, that laws are always but 'momentarily stabilized hypotheses' (in the words of Canguilhem), and that rational knowledge progresses through a polemical process of collective argumentation and mutual control. And it insists that concepts be characterized not by static definitions but by their actual uses, interrelations and effects in the research enterprise. For science does not mirror the world: it is a material activity of production of 'purified objects' – Bachelard also calls them 'secondary objects', by opposition to the 'primary objects' that populate the realm of everyday experience.

In *The Craft of Sociology*, a primer on sociological epistemology first published in 1968, Bourdieu adapts this 'applied rationalism' to the study of society.[17] He posits that, like any scientific object, sociological facts are not given ready-made in social reality: they must be 'conquered, constructed, and constated'.[18] He reaffirms the 'epistemological hierarchy' that subordinates empirical recording to conceptual construction and conceptual construction to rupture with ordinary perception. Statistical measurement, logical and lexicological critique, and the genealogy of concepts and problematics are three choice instruments for effecting the necessary break with 'spontaneous sociology' and for actualizing the 'principle of non-consciousness', according to which the cause of social phenomena is to be found, not in the consciousness of individuals, but in the system of objective relations in which they are enmeshed.

When it comes to the most decisive operation, the construction of the object, three closely related principles guide Bourdieu. The first may be termed *methodological polytheism*: to deploy whatever procedure of observation and verification is best suited to the question at hand and continually confront the results yielded by different methods. For instance, in *The State Nobility*,[19] Bourdieu combines the results gained by tabular and factorial analyses of survey data, archival accounts of historical trends, nosography, discourse and documentary analysis, field interviews, and ethnographic depiction to uncover the part played by elite schools in stabilizing the division of labour through which the ruling class effects its domination. A second principle enjoins us to grant *equal epistemic attention to all operations*, from the recollection of sources and the design of questionnaires to the definition of populations, samples and variables, to coding instructions and the carrying out of interviews, observations and transcriptions. For every act of research, down to the most mundane and elemental, engages in full the theoretical framework that guides and commands it. This stipulates an organic relation, indeed a veritable fusion, between theory and method.

The third principle followed by Bourdieu is that of *methodological reflexivity*: the relentless self-questioning of the method itself in the very movement whereby it is implemented.[20] For, just as the three fundamental moments of social scientific reason, rupture, construction and verification, cannot be disassociated, the construction of the object is never accomplished at one stroke. Rather, the dialectic of theory and verification is endlessly reiterated at every step along the research journey. It is only by exercising such 'surveillance of the third degree', as Gaston Bachelard christened it, that the sociologist can hope to vanquish the manifold obstacles that stand in the way of a science of society.

Overcoming the Antinomy of Objectivism and Subjectivism: Habitus, Capital, Field, Doxa

Chief among these obstacles is the deep-seated opposition between two apparently antithetical theoretic stances, objectivism and subjectivism, which Bourdieu argues can and must be overcome. *Objectivism* holds that social reality consists of sets of relations and forces that impose themselves upon agents, 'irrespective of their consciousness and will' (to invoke Marx's well-known formula). From this standpoint, sociology must follow the Durkheimian precept and 'treat social facts as things' so as to uncover the objective system of relations that determine the conduct and representations of individuals. *Subjectivism*, on the contrary, takes these individual representations as its basis: with **Herbert Blumer** and **Harold Garfinkel**, it asserts that social reality is but the sum total of the innumerable acts of interpretation whereby people jointly construct meaningful lines of (inter)action.

The social world is thus liable to two seemingly antinomic readings: a 'structuralist' one that seeks out invisible relational patterns operating behind the backs of agents and a 'constructivist' one that probes the ordinary perceptions and actions of the individual. Bourdieu contends that the opposition between these two approaches is artificial and mutilating. For 'the two moments, objectivist and subjectivist, stand in dialectical relationship'.[21] On the one side, the *social structures* that the sociologist lays bare in the objectivist phase, by pushing aside the subjective representations of the agent, do mould the latter's practices by establishing constraints and prescribing possible paths. But, on the other side, these representations, and the *mental structures* that underpin them, must also be taken into account insofar as they guide the individual and collective struggles through which agents seek to conserve or transform these objective structures. What is more, social structures and mental structures are interlinked by a twofold relationship of mutual constitution and correspondence.

To effect this synthesis of objectivism and subjectivism, social physics and social phenomenology, Bourdieu forges an original conceptual arsenal anchored by the notions of 'habitus', 'capital', 'field' and 'doxa'. Habitus designates the system of durable and transposable *dispositions* through which we perceive, judge and act in the world.[22] These unconscious schemata are acquired through lasting exposure to particular social conditions and conditionings, via the internalization of external constraints and possibilities. This means that they are shared by people subjected to similar experiences even as each person has a unique individual variant of the common matrix (this is why individuals of like nationality, class, gender and so on spontaneously feel 'at home' with one another). It implies also that these systems of dispositions are malleable, since they inscribe into the body the evolving influence of the social milieu, but within the limits set by primary (or earlier) experiences, since it is habitus itself which at every moment filters such influence. Thus the layering of the schemata that together compose habitus displays varying degrees of integration (subproletarians typically have a disjointed habitus mirroring their irregular conditions of living, while persons experiencing transnational migration or undergoing great social mobility often possess segmented or conflictive dispositional sets).[23]

As the mediation between past influences and present stimuli, habitus is at once *structured*, by the patterned social forces that produced it, and *structuring*: it gives form and coherence to the various activities of an individual across the separate spheres of life. This is why Bourdieu defines it variously as 'the product of structure, producer of practice, and reproducer of structure', the 'unchosen principle of all choices', or 'the practice-unifying and practice-generating principle' that permits 'regulated improvisation' and the 'conductorless orchestration' of conduct. Habitus is also a principle of *both social continuity and discontinuity:* continuity because it stores social forces into the individual organism and transports them across time and space; discontinuity because it can be modified through the acquisition of new dispositions and because it can trigger innovation whenever it encounters a social setting discrepant with the setting from which it issues.[24]

The system of dispositions people acquire depends on the (successive) position(s) they occupy in society, that is, on their particular endowment in *capital*. For Bourdieu, a capital is any resource effective in a given social arena that enables one to appropriate the specific profits arising out of participation and contest in it.[25] Capital comes in three principal species: economic (material and financial assets), cultural (scarce symbolic goods, skills and titles) and social (resources accrued by virtue of membership in a group). A fourth species, symbolic capital, designates the effects of any form of capital when people do not perceive them as such (as when we attribute lofty moral qualities to members of the upper class as a result of their 'donating' time and money to charities). The position of any individual, group or institution in social space may thus be charted by two coordinates, the *overall volume and the composition of the capital* they detain. A third coordinate, variation over time of this volume and composition, records their *trajectory* through social space and provides invaluable clues as to their habitus by revealing the manner and path through which they reached the position they presently occupy.

But in advanced societies, people do not face an undifferentiated social space. The various spheres of life, art, science, religion, the economy, the law, politics and so on, tend to form distinct microcosms endowed with their own rules, regularities and forms of authority – what Bourdieu calls fields.[26] A field is, in the first instance, a structured space of positions, a *force field* that imposes its specific determinations upon all those who enter it. Thus she who wants to succeed as a scientist has no choice but to acquire the minimal scientific capital required and to abide by the mores and regulations enforced by the scientific milieu of that time and place. In the second instance, a field is an arena of struggle through which agents and institutions seek to preserve or overturn the existing distribution of capital (manifested, in the scientific field, by the ranking of institutions, disciplines, theories, methods, topics, journals, prizes and so on): it is a *battlefield* wherein the bases of identity and hierarchy are endlessly disputed.

It follows that fields are historical constellations that arise, grow, change shape and sometimes wane or perish over time. In this regard, a third critical property of any field is its *degree of autonomy*, that is, the capacity it has gained, in the course of its development, to insulate itself from external influences and to uphold its own criteria of evaluation over and against those of neighbouring or intruding fields (scientific originality versus commercial profit or political rectitude, for example). Every field is thus the site of an ongoing clash between those who defend autonomous principles of judgement proper to that field and those who seek to introduce heteronomous standards because they need the support of external forces to improve their dominated position in it. That autonomy is always in danger and can be curtailed is demonstrated by the evolution of the scientific field at the turn of the century, which Bourdieu saw as doubly threatened, by the reassertion of economic interests on the outside and by the 'internal denigration' of reason fostered by 'postmodern rantings' on the inside.[27]

Just as habitus informs practice from within, a field structures action and representation from without: it offers the individual a gamut of possible stances and moves that she can adopt, each with its associated profits, costs and subsequent potentialities. Also, position in the field inclines agents towards particular patterns of thought and conduct: those who occupy the dominant positions in a field tend to pursue strategies of conservation (of the existing distribution of capital), while those relegated to subordinate locations are more liable to deploy strategies of subversion. Established members have a vested interest in preserving the existing order and criteria of judgement, new entrants an interest in challenging them.

In lieu of the naive relation between the individual and society, then, Bourdieu substitutes the *constructed relationship between habitus and field(s)*, that is, between 'history incarnate in bodies' as dispositions and 'history objectified in things' in the form of systems of positions. The crucial part of this equation is 'relationship between' because neither habitus nor field has the capacity unilaterally to determine social action. It takes the *meeting* of disposition and position, the correspondence (or disjuncture) between mental structures and social structures, to generate practice.[28] This means that, to explain any social event or pattern, one must inseparably dissect both the social constitution of the agent and the makeup of the particular social universe within which she operates as well as the particular conditions under which they come to encounter and impinge upon each other. Indeed, for the constructivist or 'genetic structuralism' advocated by Bourdieu,

> the analysis of objective structures – those of the various fields – is inseparable from the analysis of the genesis within biological individuals of the mental structures which are for a part the product of the internalization of these very social structures and from the analysis of the genesis of these structures themselves.[29]

The concepts of habitus, capital and field are thus internally linked to one another as each achieves its full analytical potency only in tandem with the others. Together they enable Bourdieu to sociologize the notion of *doxa* elaborated by Edmund Husserl: first, they suggest that the 'natural attitude of everyday life', which leads us to take the world for granted, is not an existential invariant, as phenomenologists claim, but hinges on the close fit between the subjective categories of habitus and the objective structures of the social setting in which people act; second, that each relatively autonomous universe develops its own doxa as a set of shared opinions and unquestioned beliefs (such as the sacred devotion to reason among scientists) that bind participants to one another. This conceptual triad also allows us to elucidate cases of reproduction – when social and mental structures are in agreement and reinforce each other – as well as transformation – when discordances arise between habitus and field – leading to innovation, crisis and structural change, as evidenced in Bourdieu's early work on cultural disjuncture and social transformation in war-torn Algeria and rural Béarn[30] as well as in two of his major books, *Distinction* and *Homo Academicus*.

Taste, Classes and Classification

In *Distinction* and related studies of cultural practices (notably *Photography: A Middle-brow Art* and *The Love of Art: European Museums and their Public*),[31] Bourdieu offers not only a radical 'social critique of the judgement of taste' (the subtitle of the book, in reference to Immanuel Kant's famous critiques of judgement), a graphic account of the workings of culture and power in contemporary society, and a paradigmatic illustration of the uses of the conceptual triad of habitus, capital and field. He also elaborates a theory of class that fuses the Marxian insistence on economic determination with the Weberian recognition of the distinctiveness of the cultural order and the Durkheimian concern for classification.

First, Bourdieu shows that, far from expressing some unique inner sensibility of the individual, aesthetic judgement is an eminently *social faculty*, resulting from class upbringing and education. To appreciate a painting, a poem or a symphony presupposes mastery of the specialized symbolic code of which it is a materialization, which in turn requires possession of the proper kind of cultural capital. Mastery of this code can be acquired by osmosis in one's milieu of origin or by explicit teaching. When it comes through native familiarity (as with the children of cultured upper-class families), this trained capacity is experienced as an individual gift, an innate inclination testifying to spiritual worth. The Kantian theory of 'pure aesthetic', which philosophy presents as universal, is but a stylized – and mystifying – account of this particular experience of the 'love of art' that the bourgeoisie owes to its privileged social position and condition.

A second major argument of *Distinction* is that the aesthetic sense exhibited by different groups, and the lifestyles associated with them, define themselves in opposition to one another: *taste is first and foremost the distaste of the tastes of others.* This is because any cultural practice – wearing tweed or jeans, playing golf or soccer, going to museums or to auto shows, listening to jazz or watching sitcoms and so on – takes its social meaning, and its ability to signify social difference and distance, not from some intrinsic property it has but from its location in a system of like objects and activities. To uncover the social logic of consumption thus requires establishing, not a direct link between a given practice and a particular class category (for example horseback riding and the gentry), but the structural correspondences that obtain between two constellations of relations, the space of lifestyles and the space of social positions occupied by the different groups.

Bourdieu reveals that this space of social positions is organized by *two cross-cutting principles of differentiation, economic capital and cultural capital,* whose distribution defines the two oppositions that undergird major lines of cleavage and conflict in advanced society.[32] The first, vertical, division pits agents holding large volumes of either capital – the dominant class – against those deprived of both – the dominated class. The second, horizontal, opposition arises among the dominant, between those who possess much economic capital but few cultural assets (business owners and managers, who form the dominant fraction of the dominant class), and those whose capital is pre-eminently cultural (intellectuals and artists, who anchor the dominated fraction of the dominant class). Individuals and families continually strive to maintain or improve their position in social space by pursuing strategies of reconversion whereby they transmute or exchange one species of capital into another. The conversion rate between the various species of capital, set by such institutional mechanisms as the school system, the labour market and inheritance laws, turns out to be one of the central stakes of social struggles, as each class or class fraction seeks to impose the hierarchy of capital most favourable to its own endowment.

Having mapped out the structure of social space, Bourdieu demonstrates that the *hierarchy of lifestyles is the misrecognized retranslation of the hierarchy of classes.* To each major social position, bourgeois, petty bourgeois and popular, corresponds a class habitus undergirding three broad kinds of tastes. The 'sense of distinction' of the bourgeoisie is the manifestation, in the symbolic order, of the latter's distance from material necessity and long-standing monopoly over scarce cultural goods. It accords primacy to form over function, manner over matter, and celebrates the 'pure pleasure' of the mind over the 'coarse pleasure' of the senses. More importantly, bourgeois taste defines itself by negating the 'taste of necessity' of the working classes. The latter may indeed be described as an inversion of the Kantian aesthetic: it subordinates form to function and refuses to autonomize judgement from practical concerns, art from everyday life (for example, workers use photography to solemnize the high points of collective life and prefer pictures that are faithful renditions of reality over photos that pursue visual effects for their own sake). Caught in the intermediate zones of social space, the petty bourgeoisie displays a taste characterized by 'cultural goodwill': they know what the legitimate symbolic goods are but they do not know how to consume them in the proper manner – with the ease and insouciance that comes from familial habituation. They bow before the sanctity of bourgeois culture but, because they do not master its code, they are perpetually at risk of revealing their middling position in the very movement whereby they strive to hide it by aping the practices of those above them in the economic and cultural order.

But Bourdieu does not stop at drawing a map of social positions, tastes and their relationships. He shows that the *contention between groups in the space of lifestyles is a hidden, yet fundamental, dimension of class struggles*. For to impose one's art of living is to impose at the same time principles of vision of the world that legitimize inequality by making the divisions of social space appear rooted in the inclinations of individuals rather than the underlying distribution of capital. Against Marxist theory, which defines classes exclusively in the economic sphere, by their position in the relations of production, Bourdieu argues that classes arise in the conjunction of shared position in social space and shared dispositions actualized in the sphere of consumption: 'The *representations* that individuals and groups inevitably engage in their practices is part and parcel of their social reality. A class is defined as much by its *perceived being* as by its being'.[33] Insofar as they enter into the very constitution of class, social classifications are instruments of symbolic domination and constitute a central stake in the struggle between classes (and class fractions), as each tries to gain control over the classificatory schemata that command the power to conserve or change reality by preserving or altering the representation of reality.[34]

The Imperative of Reflexivity

Collective representations thus fulfil political as well as social functions: in addition to permitting the 'logical integration' of society, as Emile Durkheim proposed, classification systems serve to secure and naturalize domination. This puts intellectuals, as professional producers in authoritative visions of the social world, at the epicentre of the games of symbolic power and requires us to pay special attention to their position, strategies and civic mission.

For Bourdieu, the sociology of intellectuals is not one specialty among others but an indispensable component of the sociological method. To forge a rigorous science of society, we need to know what constraints bear upon sociologists and how the specific interests they pursue as members of the 'dominated fraction of the dominant class' and participants in the 'intellectual field' affect the knowledge they produce. This points to the single most distinctive feature of Bourdieu's social theory, namely, its obsessive insistence on *reflexivity*.[35] Reflexivity refers to the need continually to turn the instruments of social science back upon the sociologist in an effort to better control the distortions introduced in the construction of the object by three factors. The first and most obvious is the personal identity of the researcher: her gender, class, nationality, ethnicity, education and so on. Her location in the intellectual field, as distinct from social space at large, is the second: it calls for critical dissection of the concepts, methods and problematics she inherits as well as for vigilance towards the censorship exercised by disciplinary and institutional attachments.

Yet the most insidious source of bias in Bourdieu's view is the fact that, to study society, the sociologist necessarily assumes a contemplative or scholastic stance[36] that causes her to (mis)construe the social world as an interpretive puzzle to be resolved, rather than a mesh of practical tasks to be accomplished in real time and space – which is what it is for social agents. This 'scholastic fallacy' leads to disfiguring the situational, adaptive 'fuzzy logic' of practice by confounding it with the abstract logic of intellectual ratiocination. In *Pascalian Meditations*, Bourdieu argues that this 'scholastic bias' is at the root of grievous errors not only in matters of epistemology but also in aesthetics and ethics.[37] Assuming the point of view of the 'impartial spectator', standing above the world rather than being immersed in it, preoccupied by it (in both senses of the term), creates systematic distortions in our conceptions of knowledge, beauty and morality that reinforce each other and have every chance of going unnoticed inasmuch as those who produce and consume these conceptions share the same scholastic posture.

Such *epistemic reflexivity* as Bourdieu advocates is diametrically opposed to the kind of narcissistic reflexivity celebrated by some postmodern writers, for whom the analytical gaze turns back onto the private person of the analyst.[38] For its goal is to strengthen the claims of a science of society, not to undermine its foundations in a facile celebration of epistemological and political nihilism. This is most evident in Bourdieu's dissection of the structure and functioning of the academic field in *Homo Academicus*.[39]

Homo Academicus is the concrete implementation of the imperative of reflexivity. Much like Bourdieu's early paired study of kinship in Kabylia and Béarn, it is, firstly, an epistemological experiment: it seeks to prove empirically that it is possible to know scientifically the universe within which social science is made, that the sociologist can 'objectivize the point of view of objectivity' without falling into the abyss of relativism. Secondly, it maps out the contours of the academic field (a subfield within the broader intellectual field) to reveal that the university is the site of struggles whose specific dynamic mirrors the contention between economic capital and cultural capital that traverses the ruling class. Thus, on the side of the 'temporally dominant disciplines', law, medicine and business, power is rooted principally in 'academic capital', that is, control over positions and material resources inside academe, while on the side of the 'temporally dominated' disciplines, anchored by the natural sciences and the humanities, power rests essentially on 'intellectual capital', that is, scientific capacities and achievements as evaluated by peers. The position and trajectory of professors in this dualistic structure determine, through the mediation of their habitus, not only their intellectual output and professional strategies, but also their political proclivities.

This becomes fully visible during the student uprising and social crisis of May 1968, that is, in an entropic conjuncture apparently least favourable to the theory propounded by Bourdieu. Yet it is at this very moment that the behaviour and proclamations of the different species of *homo academicus gallicus* turn out to be the most predictable. Bourdieu shows how the 'structural downclassing' and collective maladjustment experienced by a generation of students and professors led them to form expectations that the university could no longer fulfil, and triggered a series of local contestations that abruptly spread from the academic field to the field of cultural production to the political field. The 'rupture of the circle of subjective aspirations and objective chances' caused diverse agents to follow homologous strategies of subversion based on affinities of dispositions and similarities of position in different fields whose evolution thereby became synchronized. Here again we discern how the same conceptual framework that served to explore reproduction in inquiries of class and taste can be employed to explain situations of rupture and transformation.[40]

Science, Politics and the Civic Mission of Intellectuals

Bourdieu insists on putting intellectuals under the sociological microscope for yet another reason. In advanced society, wherein elite schools have replaced the church as the pre-eminent instrument of legitimation of social hierarchy, reason and science are routinely invoked by rulers to justify their decisions and policies – and this is especially true of social science and its technical offshoots, public opinion polls, market studies and advertising. Intellectuals must stand up against such misuses of reason because they have inherited from history a civic mission: to promote the 'corporatism of the universal'.[41]

Based on a historical analysis of its social genesis from the Enlightenment to the Dreyfus affair, Bourdieu argues that the intellectual is a 'paradoxical, bi-dimensional, being' composed by the *unstable but necessary coupling of autonomy and engagement:* she is invested with a specific authority, granted by virtue of the hard-won independence of the intellectual field from economic and political powers; and she puts this specific authority at the service of the collectivity by investing it in political debates. Contrary to the claims of both positivism and critical theory, the autonomy of science and the engagement of the scientist are not antithetical but complementary; the former is the necessary condition for the latter. It is because she has gained recognition in the struggles of the scientific or artistic field that the intellectual can claim and exercise the right to intervene in the public sphere on matters for which she has competency. What is more, to attain its maximum efficacy, such contribution must take a collective form: for scientific autonomy cannot be secured except by the joint mobilization of all scientists against the intrusion of external powers.

Bourdieu's own political interventions have typically assumed an indirect (or sublimated) form.[42] His major scientific works have repeatedly sought to expand or alter the parameters of public discussion by debunking current social myths – be it school meritocracy, the innateness of taste, or the rationality of technocratic rule – and by spotlighting social facts and trends that belie the official vision of reality. The collective research undertaking that culminated in the book *The Weight of the World* is exemplary in this regard.[43] The avowed aim of this 1,000-page ethnographic study of social suffering in contemporary France was not only to demonstrate the potency of a distinctive kind of socioanalysis. It was also to circumvent the censorship of the political field and to compel party leaders and policy makers to acknowledge new forms of inequality and misery rendered invisible by established instruments of collective voice and claims-making.[44]

By the 1990s, however, Bourdieu felt the need to intervene directly in the political arena because he held that we were witnessing a 'conservative revolution of a new type which claims the mantle of progress, reason, and science (in particular economics) to justify restoration and which thereby tries to reject progressive thinking and action on the side of archaism'.[45] In his eyes, the recent *fin de siècle* was pregnant with the possibility of immense social regression: 'The peoples of Europe today are facing a turning point in their history because the gains of several centuries of social struggles, of intellectual and political battles for the dignity of workers and citizens, are being directly threatened' by the spread of a market ideology that – like all ruling ideologies – presents itself as the end of ideology and the inevitable end point of history.

In accordance with his view of the historic mission of intellectuals, Bourdieu put his scientific authority at the service of various social movements of the 'non-institutional Left', helping to lend public legitimacy and symbolic force to newly formed groups defending the rights of the jobless, the homeless, paperless immigrants and homosexuals. He famously clashed with Hans Tietmeyer, the president of the German Bundesbank and 'high priest of the rule of markets', to advocate the creation of a 'European welfare state' capable of resisting the onslaught of deregulation and the incipient privatization of social goods. He also intervened against the persecution of intellectuals in Algeria and elsewhere by spawning the birth of the International Parliament of Writers, and against the tolerance of western states for the banalization of prejudice and discrimination.

Pierre Bourdieu also devoted considerable energy to the creation of institutions of intellectual exchange and mobilization on a transnational scale. In 1989, he launched *Liber: The European Review of Books*, a quarterly published simultaneously in nine European countries and languages, to circumvent national censorship and facilitate the continental circulation of innovative and engaged works in the arts, humanities and social sciences. In the wake of the December 1995 mass protests against the downsizing of the French welfare state, he founded the collective *Raisons d'agir* (Reasons for Action), which brought together researchers, artists, labour officials, journalists and militants of the unorthodox Left (with branches in several European countries). In 1997, Bourdieu launched a publishing house, Raisons d'Agir Editions, that puts out short books aimed at a wide audience on topics of urgent civic interest – starting with his own biting analysis of the wilful submission of journalism to political and economic power, *On Television*.[46]

In his many interventions before fellow scientists, unionists, social activists of various stripes and in editorial pieces published in the major dailies and weeklies of France, Germany, Argentina or Greece, as well as in his ostensibly scientific works, Bourdieu doggedly pursued a single aim: to forestall or prevent abuses of power in the name of reason and to disseminate weapons for resistance to symbolic domination. If social science cannot stipulate the political goals and moral standards we should pursue, as Emile Durkheim had hoped, it can and must contribute to the elaboration of 'realistic utopias' suited to guiding collective action and to promoting the institutionalization of justice and freedom. The ultimate purpose of Bourdieu's sociology, then, is nothing other than to foster the blossoming of a new, self-critical, *Aufklärung* fit for the new millennium. By directing us to probe the foundations of knowledge, the structures of social being, and the hidden possibilities of history, it offers us instruments of individual and collective self-appropriation and thus of wisdom – it helps us pursue, as it were, the originary mission of philosophy.

FURTHER READING

Bourdieu's major writings are referenced in the chapter, and they are the best place to start, especially the two collections *In Other Words* and *Practical Reasons*. The dialogical format of Bourdieu and Wacquant makes their systematic dissection of key concepts, methological principles and core inquiries particularly accessible. Brubaker and Thompson provide astute theoretical overviews of Bourdieu through his theories of class, language and politics. Jurt, Boschetti and Charle spotlight the use of the concept of field and the place of intellectuals in monographic, historical and comparative perspectives. Boltanski and Lenoir exemplify Bourdieu's approach to symbolic power and group-making by tracing the fabrication of social collectives in the case of the middle classes and the family. Eyal, Szelenyi and Townsley extend it to the ruling elites of Eastern Europe after the fall of Communism and Ooms to caste hierarchy in feudal Japan. Sayad's study of the suffering of Algerian immigrants in France and Wacquant's 'carnal ethnography' of prizefighters in Chicago's ghetto delve into the production of social agents and uncover the sensual and moral dimensions of habitus.

Boltanski, L. (1987) *The Making of a Class: 'Cadres' in French Society*, Cambridge, Cambridge University Press.

Boschetti, A. (1988) *The Intellectual Enterprise: Sartre and 'Les Temps Modernes'*, Evanston, Northwestern University Press.

Bourdieu, P. and Wacquant, L. (1992) *An Invitation to Reflexive Sociology*, Cambridge, Polity Press.

Brubaker, R. (1985) 'Rethinking classical theory: the sociological vision of Pierre Bourdieu', *Theory and Society*, **14**: 723– 44.

Eyal, G., Szelenyi, I. and Townsley, E. (1998) *Making Capitalism without Capitalists*, London: Verso.

Jurt, J. (1995) *Das Literarische Feld. Das Konzept Pierre Bourdieus in Theorie und Praxis*, Darmstadt: Wissenchaftsliche Buchgessellschaft.

Lenoir, R. (2003) *Généalogie de la morale familiale*, Paris: Editions du Seuil.

Ooms, H. (1991) *Tokugawa Village Practice: Class, Status, Power, Law*, Berkeley: University of California Press.

Sayad, A. (2004) *The Suffering of the Immigrant*, Cambridge, Polity Press.

Thompson, J.B. (1984) 'Symbolic violence: language and power in the sociology of Pierre Bourdieu', in J.B. Thompson, *Studies in the Theory of Ideology*, Cambridge: Polity Press.

Wacquant, L. (2002) 'The sociological life of Pierre Bourdieu', *International Sociology*, 17(4): 549–56.

Wacquant, L. (2004) *Body and Soul: Notebooks of an Apprentice Boxer*, New York: Oxford University Press.

CHAPTER 17

Michel Foucault

LAWRENCE BARTH

Driving Impulses: The Enthusiasm for Experiment

What strikes one most immediately about the work of Michel Foucault is its intellectual breadth, and indeed more than one commentator paid tribute to his curiosity. The broad sweep of his work interests the sociological audience first because of the persistence with which it crosses the themes, both central and minor, of sociological teaching. From his early books on the history of madness to his last works on sexual experience among the ancient Greeks, Foucault pursued a continuous critical reflection upon 'the human subject'. His examination of the emergence of modern medical reason speaks to medical sociology; his analysis of western punitive reason touches criminology and the study of deviance; his discussion of deep shifts in the rationality of the human sciences goes to the heart of sociological thought. Yet, it is clearly not within sociology – neither in its accumulated knowledge nor with its point of view – that his writings found their coherence, and, in fact, Foucault was famous for finding no home among any of the established scholarly disciplines.[1]

Interestingly, this is the second reason Foucault has appealed to many within sociology: as with other human sciences, there is a certain value placed upon both interdisciplinary work and a self-critical awareness of the discipline's limits. Foucault's writings provide a distinct and challenging perspective on the relations between power, subjectivity and the human sciences, and while his work is noticeably unique, it can be understood as a creative response to certain intellectual legacies and political problems. Foucault was very much in the tradition of those annoyed and troubled by contemporary liberal society, but who have been horrified by the excesses of certain historical attempts to escape it: the Nazi slaughter of Jews because of 'who they are'; the Stalinist mass imprisonment and execution of dissenters on the grounds of a government's claim to 'know the truth'. These dangers – the will to define one's nature or identity, and the sovereign claim over one's life on the basis of truth –

Foucault noticed running throughout modern society, and, of course, it is easy to notice a connection between the human sciences and both these dangers.

This did not lead Foucault to renounce rationality and the human sciences, but to analyse them with an eye towards holding these dangers in check. This places Foucault in a long philosophical tradition, for the elaboration of universal limits that reason itself must observe can be found in the eighteenth-century writings of Immanuel Kant.[2] It is respect for these limits that gave the human sciences their sense of being well founded, even reliable for the purposes of government. Obviously, this combination of power and knowledge has brought western society a long way, and now our dangers appear to be different from those which troubled the eighteenth century. Foucault, like a number of others in France at the end of the Second World War, sought a philosophical countertradition critical of our faith in the foundational subject of knowledge, and potentially more sensitive to particular connections between reason and domination. Reading Friedrich Nietzsche in the 1950s had a profound and lasting impact on Foucault's work in this respect, for it was Nietzsche's **genealogical** writings which showed that even our morality had a particular history, one moreover which bore the traces of an ongoing contest of wills.[3]

Genealogy

By 'genealogy', Foucault refers to an attitude based on a rejection of an immanent direction to history and society. Following Nietzsche, it places much emphasis on the struggle for power by different forces and on the lack of a necessary order inherent in this. The methodological consequence of this attitude is that the historian should try to uncover the contingent and violent course that society has historically taken. Genealogists do not look for grand evolutionary laws or deep meanings that can provide a key to the direction of history because they do not think that such an overarching direction exists. Instead, they trace developments from 'the surfaces of events, the small details, minor shifts, and subtle contours'.[4] By uncovering and tracing the power shifts and plays of domination inscribed in societal regimes, genealogists seek to 'shatter their aura of legitimacy'.[5]

The philosophical trajectory we have traced here bears a similarity to that which influenced both **Max Weber** and the early Frankfurt School writers, **Theodor Adorno** and Max Horkheimer (see Chapter 15, **Habermas**). Unfortunately, Foucault felt, their work was little known in mid-century France. However, the Nietzschean critique of reason did appear in France in the form of a history of science. Foucault's analytical methods, the particular practical aspects of his research, owe a great deal to this tradition, and particularly to the work of Georges Canguilhem and Gaston Bachelard (see Chapter 13, **Althusser**).[6] Here, one might find an important source of

Foucault's attention to detail, to the specific techniques by which knowledge of the human is gained, and to the certain effects the deployment of that knowledge would lead to. The level and detail of his analyses suggest an important difference between Foucault's sense of our present dangers and that which one can find in Weber or the Frankfurt School: our fate is given less in the great shifts of western rationality than in the many and various practices by which we become both subjects and objects of the human sciences. It was for this reason that Foucault could give his intellectual attention to the many minor struggles he witnessed: they testified to a continuing enthusiasm for experimentation and contest. It should be noted that it is this ethos of practical experimentation which Foucault's writings can help one bring to criminology, law or social work.

Rather than distil from Foucault a few generalizations about certain socio-theoretical categories, like power, truth or the subject, we might remain closer to the spirit of Foucault's work by considering some topics that captured his analytical attention. The five central issues that follow, *discipline*, *sexuality*, *the dangerous individual*, *ethics* and the *genealogy of the present*, represent the different kinds of issues Foucault analysed, and we have, in these five respectively, a set of practices, an experience, a fear, the relationship with oneself, and a question, one he felt a philosopher must ask today. In each case, we can see something of what Foucault learned about the formation of the human subject at the intersection of knowledge and power.

Key Issues: Critiques of the Subject

Discipline

Western culture tends generally to value the humanity of each and every individual, even those judged to be criminal or deviant. One aspect of this humanity within ourselves is one's capacity for moral reform, for self-diagnosis and improvement. Our societal norms encourage us to measure and adjust our conduct; our prisons, in principle, insist upon it. In *Discipline and Punish*, Foucault analysed our pervasive and reasoned compulsion to normalize individuals, to punish and reform deviance.[7] The book opens with a historical alteration in our rationality and practices of punishment around the turn of the nineteenth century, an event that also displays certain connections we continue to make today between imprisonment as our mode of punishment, the human sciences as our source of individual standards, and the constant improvement of our individual capacities as a political goal. To highlight that historical alteration, Foucault juxtaposes an account of a mid-eighteenth-century torture and execution and an early nineteenth-century prisoners' timetable. In the 80 years separating the two, imprisonment had become the nearly universal mode of punishing criminals, and the disciplinary techniques it rested upon would also define the new humanist terrain upon which punishment, norms and politics would intersect.

The change was not on account of the value we place upon the human individual; rather, discipline made that value practicable and politically useful. Discipline refers to a series of techniques or arts for the observation, measurement, training and direction of individuals. Foucault found that these were already widely practised in the military, in schools and monasteries: places in which one's actions come under the direction of another's will. The practical knowledge of human capacities and reformability that was compiled in this sort of institution clearly displays a link between the human sciences and domination. Nevertheless, the point that Foucault emphasizes throughout is that discipline works upon one's actions, engages one's will to perform. The tortured body of the condemned is replaced in the nineteenth century by the trained and mobilized body of the disciplines. It is this which makes discipline distinctly well suited not only to the reform of criminals, but also to the education of students, the management of workers, or the training of the modern army: it is the kind of power that 'makes' the necessary individuals who will populate the western nation-states in the nineteenth and twentieth centuries.

Foucault was interested not only in analysing the problems of our contemporary prison system, but also in the practical genealogy of the moral individual upon which the rationality of prisons is based. What his historical investigation reveals is a disciplinary power that is diffused throughout society, and may even be said to work in specific institutions because of this wider generalization and acceptance. Our reliance upon and belief in norms circulates through our language and politics; deviations draw public attention and arouse concern. Nevertheless, disciplinary practices operate only in relation to a specific programme and goal, only on the basis of a certain knowledge and authority, only in a well-defined setting on a limited number of people.[8] Foucault's emphasis upon the **panopticon** – its finite architecture, its organization of the activity and observation of the few – alerts the reader to this essential point. One might say that the power to discipline depends upon the limited authority of a certain practical expertise; the power of discipline refers to our generalized concern to measure and adjust our conduct in relation to norms. It would be a mistake to understand Foucault as suggesting that western society is governed like a prison. Because of the power of discipline, our society is precisely unlike the prison.

Panopticon

Jeremy Bentham's idea of the panopticon had a great influence on the new technology of power brought into the nineteenth-century prison. Panopticon means 'all-seeing' and involved a tower situated in the middle of a courtyard from the top of which the prison guards could look down into the prisoners' cells and observe them 24 hours a day. The prisoners were aware that their 'correct behaviour' was being monitored. Even if the guards were not observing them, the prisoners did not know this because the guards could not be seen from the cells. Psychologically, the prisoners were under constant surveillance, and were aware that the guards had the power to issue punishments and rewards.

Sexuality

During the 1960s and early 1970s, the time just prior to Foucault's writing of *The History of Sexuality*, there was a tendency to imagine a general prohibition and silence concerning our sexuality. There was talk of the importance of sexual liberation; connections were drawn to the workers' struggle and the women's movement; political programmes traced its linkages to social revolution. It seemed curious to Foucault that an experience which had clearly not been denied us, which was the topic of such pervasive and endless discussion, should be imagined as having been repressed and censored. This was more the result of our misconception of power, and he proposed an alternative series of questions. How have we been led to speak endlessly of sex? Why has sexuality been so intensely pursued by western governance? Why has sex been the object of such scrutiny, the key to so many types and disorders of the personality, the occasion of so many therapies? How have we been led to experience our sexuality as the private experience of the individual, an inner truth that one must master or express? The history of sexuality suggested to Foucault that it could be mapped at the intersection of a vast array of western techniques by which we know and govern ourselves. Not surprisingly, given this scope, when *The History of Sexuality* was published, it was presented as the introduction to a projected six-volume study.[9]

In spite of the vastness of the topic, there are three important themes that can be distilled from *The History of Sexuality*. First, we learn that relations of power have affected even what we take to be our innermost experience of ourselves, our 'secret' desires. However, contrary to the repressive hypothesis, the character of this effect is not that of a prohibition, but that of a mobilization, an incitement, and an organization of our sexual experience. Foucault concedes that since the seventeenth century there has been a screening and control of statements about sex, a new decorum and propriety. However, he also discovered a massive proliferation of public discourses concerning sex:

'an institutional incitement to speak about it, and to do so more and more; a determination on the part of the agencies of power to hear it spoken about, and to cause it to speak'.[10] The effects of this public discourse are to multiply individual sexualities, perversions and aberrations, to charge parents, educators, doctors and others with a vigilance towards the 'hidden' sexual practices of children, students and patients, in short, to saturate social space, by the nineteenth century, with the powers and pleasures of sexuality.

As a second theme, Foucault traces the multitudinous practices of confession by which we have been obliged to render our desires in speech and subject ourselves to interpretation. Beginning with the early Christian monastery, and progressively dispersed throughout law, psychiatry, medicine, pedagogy, family relationships and so on, 'it is in the confession that truth and sex are joined, through the obligatory and exhaustive expression of an individual secret'.[11] Our twentieth-century calls for self-expression, liberation or fulfillment were no doubt variations on the imperative to subject ourselves to the disclosure of our inner truths. However, this endless interpretation of ourselves as subjects of desire, as though our individual truth originated in this inner nature, occludes the extent to which the very practices of self-interpretation and self-disclosure have a political history.

Finally, then, it is through a certain political history that Foucault accounts for the highly charged network of relations that enlivens and orders our western sexual experience. Beginning in the eighteenth century, 'governments perceived that they were not dealing simply with subjects, or even with a "people", but with a "population", with its specific phenomena and its peculiar variables: birth and death rates, life expectancy, fertility', and so on.[12] In this way, one may understand the importance sex has assumed in western culture over the past three centuries, for it was 'at the pivot of the two axes along which developed the entire political technology of *life*', namely, the disciplines of the body, and the regulation of populations.[13]

The Dangerous Individual

A court case in 1975 involving a serial rapist caught Foucault's attention.[14] It seems the defendant refused to speak prior to his sentencing, refused to give an account of himself. This troubled the judge, and moved a juror to blurt out to the defendant the imperative of revealing himself. Foucault wants us to notice that the law falters before punishing those whose inner truth we do not know. It is not enough to know the crime that has been committed, for it is the criminal rather than his action that is punished. The functioning of the law is linked to the question, 'Who are you?' But, surrounding this question there is a fear, now generalized in our social perceptions: that of the dangerous individual. Drawing together a number of themes from his work throughout the 1960s and 70s, Foucault presents an analysis of these connections, and points to a danger that he considers still more troubling: that of a society which links together the power to punish, a public concern with social dangers, and the various institutions arrayed to probe and define one's individual truth.[15] He asks, does this 'not give society rights over the individual based on what he is? ... on what he is by nature?'[16]

Foucault's analysis follows a subtle and complex interweaving of psychiatry and penal law during the nineteenth century, through which the former could lend its expertise in determining the motivation and responsibility of those accused before the law, and which also served the purposes of psychiatry, striving at that time to consolidate and justify its function of controlling the dangers hidden in human behaviour.[17] It is important to notice that, in spite of psychiatry's usefulness to the criminal justice system, our legal codes did not fundamentally change; they did not relinquish to the human sciences the power to judge or assess guilt. Nevertheless, Foucault asks, is not the criminal court under a certain pressure to consider the dangerousness of an individual?

The problem of the dangerous individual arose not within but at the margins of this nineteenth-century interaction of law and psychiatry, that is, at the limits of their respective capabilities. Certain cases involving violence with neither reason nor definitive signs of madness exposed the juridical difficulty of assessing one's responsibility and reformability, and hence the appropriate punishment. On the other hand, as criminal cases threatening society, they posed a question of dangerous behaviours that psychiatry might name, but was powerless to control. As one can see, a solution would lie with a psychiatric science 'advanced' enough to discover the inner truth or nature of the defendant, and make a definitive *judgement* separating the responsible from the insane in each case. Just such a science, however, might heighten pressure on the criminal system to consider, in its judgement, not only guilt or innocence but the dangerousness of an individual. While law resisted the formal pressures that came from psychiatry, Foucault points to a series of other changes in law, society and the human sciences towards the end of the nineteenth century, which served to expand and intensify this pressure, creating a public obsession with the danger of criminality.

In this context, Foucault mentions but does not elaborate, 'the intensive development of the police network, which led to a new mapping and closer surveillance of urban space'.[18] In this new field of urban dangers, did not sociology find one of its important functions, namely to assist in the adjudication of responsibilities and dangers? And this leads to a question a sociologist might often ask today: When sociology pursues the truth of a group, a community or a culture within the city, when they assign responsibility for its dangers, or even defend it against the judgements of power on the basis of that truth, is the sociologist also enlivening a terrain obsessed with the fear of the dangerous individual?

Ethics

Running throughout Foucault's work, through his analyses of discipline, sexuality, and the many interactions of law and medicine, is the understanding that we are subjects who may resist power, may refuse to confess an inner truth, indeed, may make a difference. Of course, this would depend upon the subject having certain inner resources, the capacity for a relationship with oneself in excess of that drawn from us by power. It is this relationship with oneself that Foucault calls 'ethics'; it makes possible the cultivation of one's life as distinctive. In the half-decade before his death, Foucault increasingly turned his attention to the question of ethics and the practices by which we become the subjects of our actions. In his lecture courses at the Collège de France from 1980 onwards, he explored ancient Greek and Roman texts on a broad range of what he would call 'techniques of the self', focusing most persistently on an analysis of the problems one's sexual conduct posed for the ancient Greeks.[19] Their writings on the topic indicated four kinds of relationship – that with the body, with one's wife, with boys, and with truth – in which one's sexual practices occasioned consideration, reflection and debate. Interestingly, however, in none of these relationships did the sexual practices of Greek men meet with a prohibition imposed by power or a moral code. Nevertheless, their writings discussed and prescribed the cultivation of oneself in such a way as to meet the moral concerns and problems that arose around their sexual practices.

So, when Foucault asked how sexual behaviour came to be conceived as a domain of moral experience – and this was the central problem addressed in his last two books – his questions were directed to a particular instance of the broad terrain on which we encounter the practical matters of one's relationship with oneself, such that one could experience moral choices and actions as one's own. Between a moral code, handed down over time, and a moral action, there are many different ways of conducting oneself. These differences depend upon, for example, what aspect of oneself is to be, say, promoted, restrained or shaped; or upon the exercises that will make one capable of complying; or upon the goal promised by a life of compliance. By focusing his analysis at this level of the relationship to oneself, Foucault noticed something he considered very important: although we share with the ancient Greeks certain moral themes – the importance of conjugal fidelity, prohibition of incest, recommendations against excess – the Greeks practised and experienced a very different sexual life. This realization opened up a domain of analysis in which politics and ethics are drawn closely together in what we might call 'practices of freedom'.

Precisely because their sexual ethics emerged around issues that were neither prohibited by moral precept nor governed by law, they demonstrate a historical example of practices of freedom. For the Greeks, acts associated with intense pleasure were meant to be regulated, not by universal legislation or morality, but by a cultivated personal art, which involved both one's judgement and one's knowledge, and entailed one's dominion over oneself.[20] Also, this cultivation of oneself was not in opposition to an active or political life, nor was it connected either to an individualism or a positive valuation of private life, family or domesticity.[21]

It is important to note that Foucault's writings do not present a nostalgia for the Greeks and their sexual practices. In interviews, he repeated often that it cannot be a question of returning to an ancient experience, and, for that matter, he did not find the Greeks admirable. What one learns from these writings is that it has been possible to experiment upon, consider, reflect upon one's relationship to the self without the imposition of law or recourse to a universal morality. Foucault hoped to highlight the burden of thought that must confront the challenges of freedom. It was not a matter of establishing a new ethical norm or common position, but to show how curiosity and care are linked through our actions.

The Genealogy of the Present

We can see from these examples that Foucault's writings draw upon issues both near at hand and from the occasionally quite distant past. It is in the particular way that a question of the present is defined and then illuminated by the materials of the past that we can see the distinctive manner in which Foucault's historical analyses, his politics and his intellectual ethics link together. The present-day contestations he noticed around prison reform, in the experience of our sexuality, or in a courtroom story drew Foucault's attention because collectively these and others indicated a certain alteration in our history, a new challenge to the ways in which power and subjectivity are intertwined. Importantly, it is the fact of contestation itself that highlights a problem for our contemporary thought, for it demonstrates the will to make a difference. This is the impulse that drives both the philosophical question of the present and the *practical* critique of our subjectivity.[22]

Additionally, Foucault felt that this impulse was experienced today in terms of specific problems and goals, that these contests were directed towards the achievement of immediate ends, rather than towards broad social transformation. They were contests around the particular and local status of the subject. Nevertheless, the three great modes of social critique, namely Marxism, feminism and psychoanalysis, had shown themselves to be less than attentive to the particularity of these local contests, leaving the practical critique of our subjectivity at an impasse. It was this present impasse in the intellectual practice of critique that compelled Foucault to reflect upon the particular philosophical terrain which linked critique to universal foundations and an ideal of total transformation.

Again, it is Kant whom Foucault takes as the originator of this way of thinking about the present, when the former characterized the Enlightenment – his present – as the 'way out' of people's self-imposed acceptance of another's authority: 'both as a process in which men participate collectively and as an act of courage to be accomplished personally'.[23] Kant is here formulating the question of the present as one which includes another within its frame: Who are we today, such that we might fulfil this present promise? Foucault could recognize his own project in this aspect of Kant's critique of the present, but recognized he would have to avoid its further ties to 'programmes for a new man', which link the practice of critique both to universal knowlege of the human subject and to ideals of total transformation. In place of Kant's universal foundations for the human sciences, Foucault proposes we ask different questions: 'In what is given to us as universal, necessary, obligatory, what place is occupied by whatever is singular, contingent, and the product of arbitrary constraints?'[24] Foucault's realignment of critique is directed against both our present normalization of the human subject and the traditions of total critique connected to it.

Foucault's research on madness, medical reason, discipline and sexuality collectively presented examples of a form of critique that assessed the costs of our practical knowledge of the human subject, and yet also avoided treating that knowledge as false, ideological, or repressive of the 'true' human subject. These studies of the practical elaborations of western knowledge about ourselves forced one to reflect upon those critical understandings of power that rendered it alternately as that which repressed or falsified the true human subject. One of Foucault's gifts to sociological study is the recognition that it will always be a mistake to isolate the theory of what power is from the analysis of how it works.[25] What is at stake in the historical analyses Foucault pursued is the extent to which a different thought and a different conduct might be introduced into the present, that is, the extent to which the growth of our human capabilities can 'be disconnected from the intensification of power relations'.[26] The signs around us today suggest that this requires a rather different critique of the subject than that which Kant employed to challenge monarchy.

Seeing Things Differently

Foucault's research into ethical practices among the ancient Greeks revealed the constitution of a domain of moral experience that could be referred neither to a fundamental human nature nor to the imposition of law or a moral code. This made it possible to construe 'personal life' as having a history, but one nevertheless different from those which derive from prevailing conceptions of the private self. Against a libertarian perspective that conceives one's private life as a domain of moral autonomy, Foucault was able to present the cultivation of one's ethical self as the practical response to particular problems in the domain of shared experience. Against certain versions of feminism that understand the private sphere as both false and repressive, Foucault described an ethics that was both a practice of freedom and a cultivated relationship with knowledge. Understood as a domain of experience and conduct, the question of the subject could be opened to genealogical research that avoids the absolute polarization of public and private life, and yet without collapsing the distinction into a ruse of power. One of the most important effects of Foucault's research into the constitution of the moral subject has emerged in a reconceptualization of the family in its relation to both public and private life.

Jacques Donzelot's *The Policing of Families* is perhaps the earliest and one of the most important books to have taken up Foucault's lead and investigated the network of relations by which the family became linked over the course of the nineteenth century to the development of liberal governance.[27] Of course, from the liberal point of view, the family is by nature an enclosed and private domain of sentiment, care and nurture. The impulse towards these affective family relationships is taken to reside within the timelessness of one's soul or inner self. Instead, Donzelot is able to show how the family was reconstructed during the early nineteenth century as an intimate environment emphasizing the bonds of marriage and the parental care of children. Furthermore, these family relationships were overseen and evaluated by an extensive 'tutelary complex' involving educators, doctors, psychiatrists, social workers and philanthropists. Rather than supposing the 'private' family to have succumbed to such intrusions by the state, the autonomy of the family was promoted as an instrument in relation to the wider mobilization and normalization of social life.

This latter point must be further emphasized, for a number of critical perspectives on the family imagine it to be simply or primarily a domain subject to the repressions and oppressions of patriarchy or capitalism. Donzelot agrees that the nineteenth-century mobilization of the family involves both a differentiation of gender roles within the family, and a differential deployment of the tutelary complex in relation to class. However, his version of the family's role in the socialization process does not conform to an understanding of the family as essentially constraining the potentials of one's personal life. Instead, Donzelot tells us:

> It could even be said that this familial mechanism is effective only to the extent that the family does not reproduce the established order, to the extent that its juridical rigidity or the imposition of state norms do not freeze the aspirations it entertains, the interplay of internal and external pressures and pulls that make of it a locus of possible or imagined transformations.[28]

The family, then, describes a domain of personal and social relationships organized to provide a certain dynamism within liberal governance. Within liberalism, that is, the family becomes the practical and privileged domain not only of moral regulation, but also for the pursuit of that personal growth, freedom and fulfilment so valuable for capitalism.

Donzelot's account of the nineteenth-century assemblage of the family has been further developed for the twentieth century in Nikolas Rose's *Governing the Soul*, in which he traces a virtual explosion of psychological knowledge and its implantation within the networks governing the conduct of our personal lives.[29] One of the key pursuits of psychological research has been the development of visible, normative standards for the evaluation of child development. These standards were widely disseminated among all who were in a position of responsibility or authority towards children, such as teachers, health workers, parents and so on. The result was a kind of continuous and intensified reflection on the care of children: 'In the space between the behaviours of actual children and the ideals of the norm, new desires and expectations, and new fears and anxieties could be inspired in parents, new administrative and reformatory aspirations awakened in professionals.'[30]

These and other similar developments in psychological knowledge encouraged the design and implementation of governmental programmes directed towards the scrutiny, evaluation and reform of the family. Importantly, however, the outcome of this extensive deployment of new rationalities of conduct was not the erosion of family autonomy, but its reaffirmation; nor was it the repression of the field of personal desires, but their intensification.

> The modern private family remains intensively governed, it is linked in so many ways with social, economic, and political objectives. But government here acts not through mechanisms of social control and subordination of the will, but through the promotion of subjectivities, the construction of pleasures and ambitions, and the activation of guilt, anxiety, envy, and disappointment.[31]

Since the nineteenth century, one's ethical and personal life, tightly bound to family relationships, has become the instrument and target of an ever-changing and proliferating set of governmental practices: not a repression, but an expanding incitement to be better than we are.

Legacies and Unfinished Business: Governmentality and Conflict

As Gilles Deleuze has suggested, 'the study of the variations in the process of subjectification seems to be one of the fundamental tasks which Foucault left to those who would follow him'.[32] One must agree with Deleuze's further point that this sketches a particularly 'fecund' area of research extending well beyond the analytical histories of private life discussed above. 'Subjectification' refers to what we might think of as the formation of a thoughtful life of action – how we are positioned to respond to the ethical and political issues of our time. As we have seen, it is possible to research these processes in a variety of ways, and Foucault ultimately began to push this research towards the intersection of ethics and governmental reason.[33] In a lecture at the beginning of 1976, Foucault indicated that he was dissatisfied with the ways in which he had formulated this research up to that time.[34] With regard to the conceptualization of power, the main target of his critique had been what he might call the 'contract-oppression' schema, through which we conceptualize power as being like sovereignty. When the legitimate limits of sovereign power are exceeded, we feel ourselves oppressed as individuals and we may even be led to repress our true nature and desires. As we have seen in Foucault's explorations of discipline and sexuality, he viewed the more interesting aspects of power to function differently. Power worked in multifaceted and multidirectional ways to mobilize subjects of action, always in relation to local techniques of domination. This model of power was one based on permanent conflict – like a continuous war in pursuit of multiple adversaries. By 1976, he had come to doubt this second schema, as well, and devoted his research for that year's lectures to understanding how our politics had come to be seen as perpetual struggle and conflict.[35]

In these lectures, Foucault describes how a discourse of war emerged in the late sixteenth and early seventeenth centuries and was pervasively deployed to analyse the politics and history of nations. States came to be seen as internally divided, and the resultant antagonisms were seen to drive history and the development of populations. These studies give us a clear insight into patterns of western political thought, revealing the history of our tendency to see politics as a continuous struggle between races and classes, and accounting for a persistent fear and hatred of the other in our political motivations.

Clearly, this model of politics as war had left Foucault at an impasse, not least because it tended to leave the subject as a distillate of political forces, free only to choose sides as a relatively well-defined actor in the maelstrom of historical conflicts. Was there an alternative model supporting a politics of action and experimentation? In his lectures two years later, in 1978, Foucault was able to report on another discourse that also emerged in the sixteenth century, which focused on the art of government and explored how people might be led to conduct themselves towards positive political goals, such as prosperity, vitality, security and so on.[36] This discursive terrain, for which Foucault often used the neologism, 'governmentality', presents itself as a domain of reasoned practices, as we have seen in the foregoing examples of research into the government of the family. Government consists of the various instruments and rationalities assembled to link the power of the state, the regulation of populations, and a 'pastoral' power that addressed itself to the conduct of those who recognized themselves as subjects. This raises the genealogical question of an art of government directed towards the conduct of each and all, in their individuality and uniformity, and which furthermore emphasizes the freedom of the subject as a central part of that art. In this way, governmentality could be explored as the strategic terrain of subjectification. In his courses and a number of lectures, Foucault sketched the outlines of such a genealogy, although this was never developed in book form.[37]

Foucault's governmentality lectures have obviously presented a rich legacy for further research, as indicated by the number of books and articles that have taken these lectures as their point of departure.[38] Common to most of this recent research is an intention to flesh out Foucault's bare but suggestive outlines of a liberal art of government emerging in the nineteenth century, and in particular to clarify the changes in our twentieth-century rationalities and practices of government, which are manifested in the particular problems one faces today. The key question still confronting the future of this research concerns the extent to which it will introduce creative responses to those areas of social life characterized by conflict and opposition, such as problems of racism, religion and sexual choice. Regarding the latter, Foucault consistently used interviews to sharpen the point that it was neither a matter of opposing gay identity to a 'global' homophobic power, nor of simply securing legal rights protecting homosexual practice, but much more a question of using gay life to explore and experiment in the valorization of friendship and the constitution of new social relationships.[39]

This point connects to another line of unfinished business, suggestions of which appear throughout Foucault's work and which also seems to have been indicated in those lectures of 1976 when he looked for ways to extricate his own political ethics from the schemas of identity and perpetual struggle. At the beginning of those lectures, he notes that the application of a discourse of war to political history begins in the sixteenth century and dissipates around the end of the nineteenth century. Towards the end of the lecture series, he came increasingly to focus attention on a series of writings that took what Foucault called a more 'civil' perspective towards politics – a perspective rooted not in polarization but in a more pluralist approach to the strategies of government and the writing of history.[40] He mentions consistently that these were the discourses that emerged from the governmental rationality of the cities and towns – rather than from the perspectives of the nobility or monarchy – and we might easily recognize that the end of the nineteenth century marks the contemporaneous rise of sociology, urbanism and urban society. Foucault died in 1984, just as his studies of ethics and subjectivity were hitting their stride. Had he lived, might he have returned to the task of characterizing the strategic field of ethical and political action – and then perhaps in more distinctively urban terms? The strategic terrain of the urban subject is characterized by questions that diverge from those of domination – questions such as the securing of autonomy, the acceptance of difference, association, usurpation and reconciliation. These are themes one finds running through the work of those great sociological writers of the end of the nineteenth century and beginning of the twentieth – **Durkheim, Simmel,** and Weber. Might a reconsideration of Foucault's trajectory lead us back to these writers through an urban political field?

FURTHER READING

Foucault's own writings are broad ranging and accessible. The various stages of his work are laid out clearly in this chapter (see particularly pages 286–88) and the pieces suggested below should be approached within this frame.

Foucault, M. (1978) *The History of Sexuality: An Introduction*, Harmondsworth: Penguin.

Foucault, M. (1984) 'What is enlightenment?', in P. Rabinow (ed.) *The Foucault Reader*, New York: Pantheon Books, pp. 32–50.

Foucault, M. (1988) *Politics, Philosophy, Culture: Interviews and Other Writings, 1977–1984*, L. Kritzman (ed.) New York: Routledge.

Foucault, M. (1991)'Governmentality' in G. Burchell, C. Gordon and P. Miller (eds), *The Foucault Effect: Studies in Governmentality*, London: Harvester Wheatsheaf, pp. 87–104.

Foucault, M. (1992) *Discipline and Punish: The Birth of the Prison*, Cambridge: Polity Press.

Foucault, M. (1997) *Ethics: Subjectivity and Truth – The Essential Works of Michel Foucault*, 1954–1984, Vol. 1, P. Rabinow (ed.) New York: The New Press.

CHAPTER 18

Stuart Hall

MICHÈLE BARRETT

Key Sociologist?

Stuart Hall certainly is a key figure in contemporary sociology, but he was not trained in the discipline and his preoccupations are very different from those of mainstream sociology. Much of his work has been directed towards the development of 'cultural studies', which is now (largely through his efforts) widely recognized as an independent discipline. It is a sign of the current pluralism within sociology, and an indicator of the interdisciplinarity of the subject in its present form in Britain, that Hall is such an influential figure.

Stuart Hall was born and raised in Jamaica; in 1951 he came to study English at Oxford. At Oxford he was identified with the politics of the West Indies, and of colonialism in general; also with the development of the 'New Left' in Britain. In 1956, he abandoned the thesis he was writing on Henry James – a figure he was interested in as the last novelist before the dissolution of the 'narrative "I"' in the modernist literary revolution. Why in 1956? Because that was the year Soviet tanks rolled into Hungary, provoking anger and dissent among his colleagues and friends.

Stuart Hall married the historian Catherine Hall and settled in Britain. The 1950s were a formative period for him: they marked a complete break with traditionalist notions of culture and literature and his move towards a view of culture that binds it indissolubly to politics. The exploration of culture and power, much of it filtered through the lens of a socialism that rejected Stalinism, that turned to Marx only in a spirit of criticism and contestation, was to exercise him for many years.

He is best known for his work at the Centre for Contemporary Cultural Studies in Birmingham, indeed, for many people, Stuart Hall was the CCCS, which in turn is now an international phenomenon called 'British cultural studies'. This period (1964–79) saw an incredible production of work, much of it collectively produced by staff and students at the Centre, on issues of theory, popular culture, class and resistance. The fluency of that output was disrupted, no doubt beneficially but also traumatically, by the challenges of feminist and black students, both of whom insisted on a different agenda of work.

In 1979 Stuart Hall moved to the Open University, with the project of making the ideas of cultural studies, and its radical politics, meaningful to a much wider range of students. He turned out to be a natural TV communicator. From this time, his writing became more 'teacherly' – he typically now addresses his readers as 'you'. At the OU he revolutionized the sociology curriculum twice over: by junking the 'founding fathers' and reconceptualizing the mainstream of the subject in terms of the historical rise and decline of western modernity, and by introducing major courses in cultural studies, whose focus is 'representation', '**signification**', 'identity' and '**cultural difference**'. His time at the OU saw – outside the academic world – the establishment of a reputation as a political analyst of great perception, which was triggered by his prescient insights into the phenomenon of 'Thatcherism'.

Signification

Used by structuralists and poststructuralists, signification refers to the way in which meanings are created by a double action. This double action involves, first, written or spoken words, or images – an advertisement, fashionable clothes, or whatever – that provide us with a kind of raw material for our senses. Second, we now have to interpret or understand this raw material – these script marks, sounds, arrangements of colours and shades – as meaning something. Usually we do this automatically, routinely, without giving it a second thought, with the meanings appearing as natural and inevitable. The meanings seem to press themselves on us, and they seem to be stuck with superglue to the raw material of these words, these sounds and these images. The term 'signification' tells us that the bond between raw material (the 'signifier') and meaning (the 'signified') is much weaker than it seems, and that they are pasted together in different ways at different times by different societies, cultures and subcultures. Signification, thus, draws our attention to the cultural process by which the lines on a page, sounds in the air, a certain length and cut of cloth become meaningful in very precise ways to people within particular social contexts.

Cultural difference

Cultural difference is related to signification. It refers to the way that in particular societies and cultures, at particular times, some groups of people come to be seen as 'different'. The Nazis, to take an extreme example, singled out Jews, Gypsies and gays as 'different' in a radically discriminatory and negative manner. Poststructuralist thought highlights the many ways in which groups can be picked out, and 'signified' as different – it shows the cultural processes at work – and, in a definitely positive manner, it wishes to safeguard the rights of people to be 'different'. The main indicators of difference discussed in this literature tend to be those associated with differences of gender, ethnicity, race, age, religion, class, sexual orientation and language. The emphasis on such cultural differences often goes along with a political commitment to a radical pluralism.

In recent years, he has returned to the themes of colonialism and identity that preoccupied him earlier, this new work enriched through what he might describe as a 'necessary detour' through the study of class, power and culture. He has been able to settle personal accounts between Jamaica and England, and to explore the more general construction of what he has coined 'the West and the rest'. Migration is not only his own experience, it is the significant experience of the twentieth century. Thus Stuart Hall's identity as a 'diasporic intellectual' stands in for a more general experience in the postmodern, decolonizing world. His interest in identity is rooted in a passionate, if melancholy, sense of the structural power of social relations. Colonial culture can and does destroy you subjectively, he says, in an interview that is the nearest we have to an autobiography.[1] There is no separation between power, culture and the self.

Key Issues

Cultural Circuitry

It would be a mistake to push the electrical metaphor too far, since this is a model with some dud connections and fuses that can blow at any time. The central idea is that there is a circuit that is completed between the production and consumption of culture. The function of the circuit metaphor is to emphasize that for cultural meaning to be established, it has to be received as well as sent. The question is not only what meaning did the producer intend to convey, but what meaning actually was conveyed? In other words, the audience is not a passive recipient but an active participant in the creation of meaning. The classic statement of this argument is found in one of Stuart Hall's most cited and reprinted papers, entitled 'Encoding/decoding'.[2]

Hall argues that if we are interested in televisual meaning, for example, we should not be working with a simple model of a message and an audience. Meanings are more complexly 'coded', through conventions that may be arbitrary – just as language codes are arbitrary rather than derived from their referents – but nonetheless powerful. We may not notice these codes in situations where we are decoding them automatically – we can say that in these cases they have become 'naturalized'. Hall is using here the basic principle of Saussurean linguistics – that signification works through a set of conventions causing signifiers (sounds or images) to indicate the concepts that are being signified. He indicates that a second basic argument from semiotics – that we should distinguish between literal (denotative) and associational (connotative) meaning – is more complex. Simple denotative meaning is possible in the abstract, but in practice is normally compounded with associations. Furthermore, these connotative codes are not equal, they often form part of a much wider cultural meaning and they relate to ranked hierarchies of understanding: the way that 'our society' sees things has power.

This is the context in which a television programme is produced. There are institutional relations at play in its production, there is a technical infrastructure, and there are frameworks of knowledge in which it takes place. None of these are necessarily determining, but they set the boundaries on the meanings that can be produced, or encoded, into the broadcast. All the factors affecting the moment of encoding can be seen to be related to power, what Hall calls power 'in dominance' (that is, not comprehensive and inclusive, but exerting a push in one direction), and this leads to the encoding of what Hall terms a 'preferred reading' of the meaning. But the preferred reading is only one possible way of understanding the broadcast – Hall suggests we might have an 'oppositional' reading in which we reject its message, or a 'negotiated' one in which we only accept it in part. We might accept the general argument, but see how it affects particular groups differently. Let us take a simple example, a news item reporting a government decision to ban the export of land mines. It might be framed as 'the government today took a moral stand on the export of land mines that kill innocent children', or it might be framed as 'the government today put British industry in jeopardy by banning the production of land mines'. Depending on our views, we will 'read' the meaning with agreement or disagreement. We can take the dominant or preferred reading, accepting the item within the frame of what it takes for granted. Or we can oppose it, recognizing and rejecting its assumptions about what is right. Or we might say, well that is a good thing for children in Angola but a bad thing for my uncle who earns a living from making the mines (a 'negotiated' response).

The point is that a meaning has been encoded into the terms in which the item is framed – it is constructed as a discourse with assumptions about what is important and right. Hall's paper has been so influential because it offers a more complex model of meaning than that of a simple message and a passive audience. It presents meaning in terms of an ineradicable link between cultural production and consumption. It constructs meaning as a two-way process and in this it is more similar to a 'hermeneutic' approach that focuses on understanding, than to any of the models characterizing sociology of the media. Most importantly, it locates meaning within a context of power and domination. It holds in suspension questions about the technical and aesthetic properties of cultural works, locating them in reference to an analysis of ideology and cultural hegemony. Finally, the case of television broadcasting is an example of Hall's general focus on popular culture – a choice that rejects traditional distinctions between 'high' art and 'mass' culture. In all these respects, 'Encoding/decoding' can be read not only as an argument about interpreting television, it is also an indicator of the defining elements of the approach that has become 'cultural studies'.

The encoding/decoding model was put forward as a political one in two senses. The model inscribes power at the heart of the media, emphasizing the degree to which media output is formed within the institutions and discourses of power. It was also a political intervention in the field of media studies, which Hall regarded as dominated by a bland positivism typified by the approach of the Mass Communications Centre at Leicester. In a subsequent interview, he candidly described the motivation for the paper in unusually militaristic terms: 'Who I had in my sights was the Centre for Mass Communications Research, that was who I was trying to blow out of the water.'[3]

Stuart Hall's idea of a cultural circuit has taken hold as a better paradigm for cultural studies than the model previously dominant in media studies, which had tended to separate the message from the audience and studied them independently. Of course, the circuit itself can be conceived in different ways, and in Hall's own work we can find different ways of distinguishing the elements of it. The earlier work invokes Marxist categories of production and consumption, later formulations tend towards including regulation and identity; the key point is that the underlying dynamic model of a circuit remains a constant in Hall's way of approaching culture.

Hall's new paradigm solved more than the methodological problems of media studies. It also radically resolved a theoretical stalemate in the field known as 'sociology of art and literature'. This subfield of sociology had been dominated by an approach that we might call 'reductionist' or 'reflectionist': influenced by the work of Marxists such as Lukács, it tended to interpret art as the expression of changing historical class forces. As we shall see later, the fundamental problem was that of 'determination'. This problem was posed in terms of explaining art as the superstructural reflection of more important factors – themselves understood rather narrowly as the economics of class relations. Sociology of art and literature was primarily concerned with explicating the 'class content' of the classical canon of western culture and its rigid formulations were beginning to disintegrate as the cultural studies approach came along.

Hall's emphasis on the circular character of cultural processes in society was thus well placed, and well timed, to offer an alternative to both the mechanistic descriptiveness of media studies and the narrow reflectionism of sociology of art and literature. It is no exaggeration to conclude that cultural studies as a discipline – now far more influential than sociology's attempts to study either art or the media – was definitively established in the encoding/decoding model.

Cultural Politics: Thatcherism and After

Stuart Hall's insistence on power as a central element of culture is complemented by his insistence on culture as a crucial element of power. Indeed, this has proved particularly indigestible to those on the Left who see power as essentially driven by economic interests, and who persist in the view that cultural processes are somehow superficial in comparison with these 'structural' determinants. Stuart Hall has annoyed many of them by claiming that the study of cultural meaning is not a leisure activity, but the bread and butter of sociological work.

This theme in his work could be described, in the manner of a musical attribution, as 'Antonio Gramsci (*arr.* S. Hall)'. The Marxist tradition is classically divided between those who take an economic determinist position and those who see cultural and ideological practice as important in determining (rather than simply reflecting) political change. Gramscian Marxism, perhaps the most obvious and abiding theoretical influence on Hall's work, offers the strongest statement of the 'culturalist' position in this debate. It is, however, a debate of much more general significance than an internecine struggle within Marxist theory: contemporary sociology's unease about the place of cultural and media studies reflects a widespread disagreement within social and political analysis. This is why what is called the **'linguistic turn'**, the 'cultural turn' and the emphasis on 'discourse' in poststructuralist thought has provoked such controversy in disciplines ranging from anthropology to urban studies. Philosophical materialism – the idea that material being is theoretically more important than culture or consciousness – is not simply a doctrine that underpins classical Marxism, it is a founding assumption of the social sciences.

> ***Linguistic turn***
> *This refers to the widespread influence on philosophy, the humanities and the social sciences of structuralism and poststructuralism's insights into the processes of 'signification' (see above). It attempts to capture the significantly increased emphasis that these disciplines consequently placed upon the role played by language in the construction of social meanings and practices, cultural differences and also upon scholarly attempts to 'represent' the world and what goes on in it.*

The orientation and insights of Gramsci's work can be traced throughout Hall's writing. He has himself documented the ways in which his thinking on race – about which Gramsci did not write – has been influenced by his reading of Gramsci.[4] It is, however, in Hall's analysis of Thatcherism that we find the most effective application of Gramscian ideas to a new political situation in Britain. In January 1979, before the election that was to be the start of 18 years of Conservative government, Hall published an analysis of 'The great moving Right show' in the magazine *Marxism Today*. The article laid out the terms of his position on Thatcherism, and its wider political implications, particularly for the cherished assumptions – or the rigid and irrelevant certainties – of a puzzled and rudderless Left.

Hall argued that Mrs Thatcher's political programme represented more than the usual pendulum swing between Labour and Conservative popularity – it was a decisive and irreversible shift to the Right. He characteristically began by insisting that it was a fundamental mistake to see and discount these changes as mere ideology: reversing the usual chain of determinism, he made the claim that 'the ideology of the radical Right is less an "expression" of economic recession than the recession's condition of existence'. So the first move against the doxa of the Left was to make the contentious theoretical point that Mrs Thatcher's political and economic programme was based on, drew its strength from, an ideological force – not vice versa.

To understand what was happening, Hall invoked the ideas of Gramsci. Considering that in the years to follow, Hall has often been accused of pessimism, it is perhaps appropriate that he cited Gramsci's slogan: 'pessimism of the intelligence, optimism of the will'. He argued that the crisis was an *organic* one, not merely *conjunctural*; it was *formative* of a new *historic bloc* that was emerging to construct a new settlement. The Thatcher programme had succeeded in translating a theoretical *ideology* into a popular *idiom*, with a language of moralism. Hall summarized the programme as a rich mix, combining 'the resonant themes of organic Toryism – nation, family, duty, authority, standards, traditionalism – with the aggressive themes of a revived neoliberalism – self-interest, competitive individualism, anti-statism'. These elements were the building blocks of a new *hegemonic* project – the key feature of Hall's analysis. Gramsci's concept of hegemony (the securing of consent) allows us to see Thatcherism for what it was, a project to change the way in which people live out social and political conflict. In this, the popular appeal of an authoritarian language was crucial. Hall concludes that only by understanding the deep nature of the shift towards *authoritarianism* at a *popular* level, could the Left begin to think about challenging the Thatcher project.

The history of British politics since 1979 has borne out Hall's analysis. The reluctance of the Left to accept the seriousness of the popular shift rightwards played a large part in the successive failures of any Labour electoral challenge to Conservative government. The successful Blair project of what we might call 'free-market Christian populism' was only explicable, only conceivable, as a successor to the hegemonic penetration of Thatcherism. It relied explicitly on common sense and the mobilization of popular sentiment. Stuart Hall's timely and incisive dissection of the politics of Thatcherism was contentious for the Left, mainly because it assigned such an important political role to ideology – which traditionally the Left had been rather dismissive of. That events should have proved him right has certainly strengthened Hall's own standing and reputation as a political commentator. Perhaps more importantly, it has brought us a new understanding of politics – not so much a rational choice between clearly defined programmes but an attempt to capture people's lived experience and how they make sense of it.

Colonialism and Cultural Difference

Stuart Hall's recent work has revolved around three interlocked themes: colonialism and its role in the formation of modern western society; the question of identity in a social world characterized by migration and diaspora; and the issue of 'race' in cultural representation. These three themes can be separated out in his work, but it is more useful to consider them in conjunction with each other.

This new work differs from the Thatcherism project, where Hall spoke as a freelance intellectual, in being firmly related to a teaching project. At the Open University, Stuart Hall pioneered a new definition of the sociology core curriculum, focusing on the questions of what makes modern societies 'modern', and where are they going; he has complemented this by developing a group of courses on 'media, culture and identities'. These courses may be directed to students, but they carry the unmistakeable imprint of Hall's current theoretical priorities. Although this recent work still bears traces of the Gramscian Marxism that was so explicit in his earlier work, it is centred on some much newer theoretical debates: **Foucault**, psychoanalysis, poststructuralism and postmodernism. Before considering the implications of this change of emphasis in Hall's theoretical approach, I want to illustrate these new themes in his work.

We can best explore his approach to colonialism by starting with 'the West and the rest', a formulation that has already become standard phraseology. Hall reads the history of colonialism as not only about the impact of imperialism on colonized peoples, but as an account that shows how the emerging character of western modernity was constituted through its difference from the colonial 'other'. He uses Foucault's concept of discourse, and its illustration in Said's account of 'orientalism', to analyse this process.

Hall's own account examines representations by Europeans of their encounters with indigenous peoples, drawing out their failure to recognize human difference, the explicit sexual fantasies, their constructions of barbarism, cannibalism and so on. The European discourse was predicated on power – they 'had outsailed, outshot and outwitted peoples who had no wish to be "explored", no need to be "discovered" and no desire to be "exploited"'. This power influenced what they saw, how they saw it, and what they did not see.[5]

Hall concludes that these representations of the barbarous 'other' played not just an important part, but an essential part, in the definition of the West as 'developed, industrialized, urbanized, capitalist, secular, and modern'. The West would have been unable to define itself as enlightened *without* such an 'other', whose function was to represent the opposite of what 'the West' stood for. Stuart Hall has subsequently expressed this in a specific theoretical vocabulary. Colonization does not signify simply imperial conquest, it refers to the process that 'constituted the "outer face", the constitutive outside' of western modernity.[6]

Alongside this analysis of colonialism, Stuart Hall has been developing an account of identity in the contemporary world, which – whether or not we use the vexed descriptor of 'postcolonial' – is dominated by the effects of migration and the dispersal of peoples. Migration, he has argued, is the typical twentieth-century, indeed postmodern, experience, and it leads to a relative destabilization of the self. Diasporic cultures produce an acute awareness of cultural difference and have fostered the development of 'hybridity' – a key term in postmodern debates about identity and culture. Hall's approach to identity uses a historical, sociological understanding of the global context in which we fashion our identities, and is critical of the claims that national identities are – ever were – unified and integrated. The idea of a national culture, he suggests, is a *discursive device* that enables us to represent as a unified entity that which is in reality fragmented and differentiated – rather as Lacanian psychoanalysis sees the self to be 'misrecognized' as whole.[7] Hall's work on identity draws more explicitly on psychoanalytic ideas than this parenthetical reference to Lacan would suggest. In a recent essay on this question, he argues that the insights of Freud and others on *identification* should not be imported wholesale into thinking on cultural identity, which would lead to psychoanalytic reductionism, but nevertheless can help us to theorize identity in terms that are 'strategic' and 'positional' rather than essentialist.[8]

There is another important current in Hall's thinking on identity, and this is Foucault's work on the technology of the self. Although he is critical of the place of the body as a kind of residual 'transcendental signifier' in Foucault's work (and in that of those influenced by his approach), Hall is nonetheless engaged by Foucault's attempts to describe *performative* practices of self-production. In Hall's most recent discussions of these questions, he looks to Judith Butler's work as a source of productive exploration of the tension between Foucauldian and psychoanalytic accounts of the self.

If all this takes us to the heart of the contemporary 'poststructuralist' theory of the subject, Stuart Hall has simultaneously been examining the more concrete question of race and ethnic identity in the here and now. His paper entitled 'New ethnicities' can be singled out as marking – both noting and contributing to – a decisive shift on this issue. Hall argues that the category of 'the black subject' can no longer serve as a basis for identity politics: there is no guarantee, from nature or from experience, to justify it. Hence a new politics of the representation of ethnic difference is emerging, operating within the hybrid modalities of diaspora experience. In the British context, where white Englishness has dominated national identity, there are newly contested meanings around what it means to be black British.[9]

Hall's recent work on identity in relation to race and ethnicity is inflected by his personal interest in the cultural output of black film-makers and photographers, with whose projects he has for some time been associated. It is, then, not surprising that he has recently brought together several of his theoretical and political concerns in an analysis of what he terms a 'racialized regime of representation'. The focus here is on the politics of representation, and Hall examines some difficult images in the sorry parade of racial stereotyping as well as casting light on the visual staging of racial difference.[10] Hall's analysis of the 'spectacle of the other' reminds us again of the importance of one of the moments in the cultural circuit – representation – with which he has always been concerned.

Seeing Things Differently

One of Stuart Hall's recent books gives the following as a description of the author: 'His work has had a profound influence on cultural studies and on the rethinking of the sociological understanding of contemporary societies.' This is an understatement. Stuart Hall has had more than a profound influence on cultural studies, he virtually is cultural studies. As well as his intellectual influence, which has brought a 'political' version of cultural studies to the fore around the world, he has done more than anyone to establish cultural studies as an academic discipline in Britain. Cultural studies has tended to operate in academia as a satellite of either English literature or sociology, with the attendant disadvantages of each, but has now been accepted (for example for purposes of research assessment) as an independent discipline. This obviously brings its own problems, in terms of the institutionalization of disciplinary assumptions and histories, but is nonetheless worth noting.

Hall's influence on sociology is more complex, as his work both contributes to and has to be seen in the context of what is known as the 'cultural turn'. This 'turn' has both theoretical and empirical aspects. It reflects an awareness that the study of culture has been marginalized, and that classical sociological orthodoxies, such as those canonized in the 'founding fathers' Marx, **Weber** and **Durkheim**, gave us an inadequate account of it. There has been a long-running attempt to right this theoretical wrong. In this, Hall's theoretical polemic has been an important voice. Morley and Chen summarize his position in an epigrammatic way: 'culture thus lies *beneath* the "bottom line" of economics'.[11]

The 'cultural turn' has another dimension too, a more historically specific one. This is the recognition that, in the early twenty-first century, technological and social changes have made the media and culture more important, more necessary, for sociologists to study. As I have already indicated, Stuart Hall has made a specific and important contribution to this, in his insistence that new patterns of migration and 'diasporaization', and the development of global information and media systems, have effects on cultural difference and cultural identity.

One could also add that Stuart Hall's work does, literally rather than metaphorically, cause us to 'see' things differently. The study of representation is his first and last love, the element of the cultural circuit that most engages him personally. It is no coincidence that he is best known from 'being on television', is most recognized visually as a communicator, and is most successful at offering a new way of looking at what is on the screen.

Legacies and Unfinished Business

This heading has an obituary ring to it, which is scarcely appropriate in the case of someone who is still thinking, writing, responding and changing their ideas. It does, however, give the opportunity to comment on some general issues in relation to Hall's work. One such comment concerns disciplinary boundaries. As I have characterized 'cultural studies', it has a distinctive focus on popular culture. Stuart Hall, having been trained in 'Eng lit', has to all appearances abandoned a detailed dialogue with the analysis of non-popular culture. As a young man he made a television programme on Blake, but these concerns are now in the archive. Yet his own participation in contemporary cultural production, with the films of Isaac Julien and Mark Nash for example, shows an enthusiasm for a style of cinema and photography that is not obviously 'popular' – it is rather avant-garde as an art form. It would be interesting to hear what he has to say about the interface between cultural studies and the study of non-popular culture.

More importantly, reviewing Hall's work over time raises the question of the theoretical vocabularies he deploys and their objectives. It is striking to compare the earlier, Marxist vocabulary with the concepts he uses in his recent work. From the 1970s to the mid-1980s the terminology is Marxist. He now, however, explains his ideas in terms such as *binary oppositions*, *the constitutive outside*, *difference*, *différance*, *discursive techniques*, *enunciative strategies*, *identification*, *irreducibility*, *iteration*, *suture* – all terms drawn from Derrida, Foucault and Lacan. Does this mean that he has rejected the Marxist paradigm and moved wholesale into a 'poststructuralist' theoretical position?

The answer is not the simple one that those who police and politicize theoretical work incline to. Certainly, this change of terminology is important, in that it signals a new set of preoccupations – particularly with the question of identity – and Hall's insistence that new concepts are needed to explore them. Stuart Hall's current appropriation of psychoanalytic and Foucauldian vocabularies is a deliberate use of perspectives that, respectively, compete with and dismiss Marxism as an interpretation of the social subject. In that sense, his work can now be described as 'post-Marxist'. Yet, important continuities remain, and they are instructive in the polarized debate that now exists in relation to the political implications of poststructuralist theory.

In the first place, Stuart Hall works at a higher level than those who simply learn a new (fashionable) vocabulary in order to participate in the current conversation, junking the old because they cannot see how to reconcile the two. His latest writings show that he is not willing to let go of 'articulation' as an organizing concept. Similarly, notions of 'overdetermination' and 'interpellation' (see **Althusser**, Chapter 13) – as well as references back to Gramsci – continue to make themselves heard in a new context. Stuart Hall has not become a convert to 'textualism' or what is disparagingly called 'idealism': he continues to insist that representation must be thought within the cultural circuit – and this includes production. He is opposed to what he calls the 'playful' variant of deconstruction, which dissolves power in its description of difference. (For the very sectarian, I might also point out that the position from which he is publicly critical of the project of 'Blairism' is a staunchly socialist one.)

Hall's recent work has certainly constituted its object of study in very different terms from his earlier work, but it retains his characteristic purpose and methodology. Let me give an example. Hall writes that:

> we cannot afford to forget the over-determining effects of the colonial moment, the 'work' which its binaries were constantly required to do to *re-present* the proliferation of cultural difference and forms of life, which were always there, within the sutured and over-determined 'unity' of that simplifying, over-arching binary, 'the West and the rest'.[12]

The logical structure of this argument is recognizable from Hall's insistence in the 1970s that we pay attention to the work that the superstructures were doing for capital. Western modernity has replaced capitalism as the object of study, but the techniques of discursive analysis are deployed (rather as the concept of hegemony was employed) to insist on the historic articulation of discourse and power.

Another way of looking at this is to argue, as many people have, that the labels 'post-Marxist' and 'poststructuralist' tell us more about the process through which these positions have emerged than they signal a definitive break. Let us give Stuart Hall the last word on this: 'So "post" means, for me, going on thinking on the ground of a set of established problems, a problematic. It doesn't mean deserting that terrain but rather, using it as one's reference point.'[13]

Afterword Second Edition

Stuart Hall retired from the Open University in 1997. For much of his retirement, he has worked towards a project that came to its grand opening in late 2006. Rivington Place, a cultural diversity arts centre in London's Shoreditch, is the first major new building of an arts project in London for more than 40 years. The project was put together, and funding of several million obtained from the lottery and elsewhere, by two organizations, both of them chaired by Stuart Hall. They are the Institute for International Visual Arts (inIVA) and Autograph, the Association of Black Photographers. Rivington Place was designed by the cutting-edge architect David Adjaye. At the ground-breaking ceremony, in November 2005, it was clear whose leadership had made it all happen: Stuart Hall, sitting on a JCB wearing a hard hat.

Hall's influential social reading of the postwar photography of *Picture Post*, in the 1980s, was merely one moment in a long and varied engagement with the medium of photography. In 1986, the Commonwealth Photography Competition was framed by his distinctive approach. Hall explained that the competition was to create an outstanding collection of images and to stimulate photography throughout the Commonwealth. Taking some distance from the cosy view that the Commonwealth represented the 'Family of Man', he located it instead in the stubborn historical facts of imperialism:

> The very arbitrariness of its formation – ancient kingdoms submerged, old civilizations broken up and dispersed, peoples forcibly united across the lines of language, culture, religion, exported to one diaspora or another, endlessly criss-crossing the globe along the migratory trails created by 'poor people on the move' – is paradigmatic of the post-colonial age, in which all of us, the over-developed and the under-developed, live.

The British Commonwealth, he argued, may be transcended in the future, but can never be forgotten.[14]

Two further examples indicate the broad range of Hall's interests in photography. In 1993 he introduced a collection of Vanley Burke's photographs of black people in Birmingham in the 1970s. These are documentary images, where the events and experiences of life were plainly recorded. The people are not engaging with the camera, and the photographer is not engaging with questions of identity and self-representation. Vanley Burke referred to the images as 'histographs', simply a visual record. Stuart Hall was not content with this mimetic or reflectionist model of photography, and he showed how these images hold *love* as well as truth – how they gave meaning to those lives, and answered Burke's own yearnings for a visual 'coming home' in Britain. In the grain of Burke's histographs, Hall suggests, is an unacknowledged figure: a desire for blackness, an imagined plenitude that confers value on these subjects.[15]

A decade later, came a very different photographic aesthetic. Hall introduced the latest work, *Beyond the Limits*, of the avant-garde photographer and film-maker, Mitra Tabrizian. Her extraordinary, carefully staged photographs are explicitly informed by concepts from Lacan, Foucault, Kristeva and others, a regime that Hall calls 'a post-structuralist visual imaginary'. Tabrizian presents us with impeccable 'suits' who appear to have no affect and no powers. They are located in a disturbing world of high production values and unremarked horror. Hall applauds her 'singular and courageous attempt to break the silence about the directions in which the contemporary post-modern corporate world is going' and admires her attempt to find a new language in which to explore a visual critique of contemporary life.[16]

Hall's interest in photography reached a high point with the publication in 2001 of a major work he compiled with Mark Sealy (the director of the Association of Black Photographers). The book, lavishly colour illustrated and produced to a high specification by art specialists Phaidon Press, was entitled *Different*[17] and contained two sections: the first on historical context and the second on contemporary photographers and black identity. This collection brings forward the many photographic traditions around the world neglected in the western canon, and decisively rejects the 'orientalist' assumption that black people were the objects rather than the makers of photographs. From America, we see work from New Orleans, South Carolina and Tennessee as well as the images of the better known Harlem Renaissance; from Africa, there is work from Sierra Leone, Liberia, Senegal and Mali as well as the more familiar work of *Drum* in South Africa; from the Indian subcontinent, there is work from the Punjab, work documenting the struggle against colonialism, and the photographic capture of the war that led to the creation of Bangladesh; from the Caribbean, we are shown new traditions of recording postwar migration to Britain, new attempts to engage with the feelings and politics of dispersal and fragmentation, new engagements with the continuing diasporic experience of peoples of African descent.

These histories were outlined in the first section of *Different* with the aim of showing that contemporary black photography 'does not emerge out of thin air, but has a set of substantial, if unwritten, histories'. They do more than this, setting the whole project beyond the western canon of photography, making the reader see the contemporary images in a context that is fresh, unguarded and newly politicized. The second, and more substantial, part of the book is made up of photographic explorations of black identity. Many of these images are 'startling', if not shocking. They explore black bodies in many registers, not often that of victimhood, but with inevitable reference to exploitation and suffering. The 'shadow' of racialized and exclusionary violence, say the authors of the book, is the 'difference' signalled in its title. These photographers share that experience, however indirectly their work may engage with it. Some of these images speak directly to the cruelty of slavery, to scarring and abjection, to exile and displacement: an example being Deborah White's *Slave Ship* of 1992. Many seek to dismantle the dominant visual regime in which the black body has been eroticized and fetishized. This section of the book opens with the arresting work of Rotimi Fani-Kayode, whose *Golden Phallus* of 1978–8 'transfigures' the degraded black male body as an object of fragile beauty, 'illuminated and bound, gilded and bandaged'.[18]

Rivington Place will provide a home for the Association of Black Photographers, but also for the Institute for International Visual Arts, a sister organization also chaired by Stuart Hall. Hall's involvement with inIVA has, during the years of his retirement, provided a context for his active engagement with the work of artists – not only photographers, but painters, sculptors, makers of installations, producers of digital art, creative artists of many kinds. Of course, this is not a new interest, but it is a newly public engagement with contemporary art practice, signalled most emphatically in the essay Hall contributed to the 2003 British entry to the Venice Biennale, Chris Ofili's *Within Reach*. (We should remark here on the importance of that moment – one entry for Britain, and an artist chosen whose work engages directly with blackness, with race, with Britain, with Africa.) Hall's 'Chris Ofili in paradise: dreaming in Afro'[19] draws on time he spent with Ofili while the artist was working on the paintings for the Venice pavilion; part of the published Ofili Biennale portfolio, it was written, he says, 'with' the work rather than 'about' it.

This is a new kind of writing for Stuart Hall: more impressionistic, more allusive, more visual in metaphor, more informal in its address to the reader than his previous work. Hall conjures up the fixed colour range of the paintings – a dramatic red, green and black – and the luxuriant shapes of a tropical jungle, where we find Ofili's 'Afro-lover figures'. The hinterland of these images takes in European art history, but the work is fully inspired by what

Hall sees as a reimagined Africa, an Africa visually recalled in the register of a dream. The images are earthy, sexy, carnal, a vision of exotic, erotic love. Ofili is also playing with the notion of the primitive here, and – as in his other work, such as *The Upper Room* – he is seriously playing with religion: 'Old Snakey', observes Hall 'is already inside the picture. Occasionally we catch a glimpse of some part of his chequered body, coiled contentedly around something.'[20]

Hall's celebration of Chris Ofili's 'Afro' painting provides a counterpoint to his recent arguments against the politics of 'heritage' in Britain. He suggests that Afro-Caribbeans are simultaneously deeply familiar to the British, 'having lived with them for so long', and 'ineradicably different' because they are black – and the 'heritage' industry never asks anyone to spare this a thought. For Hall, in the contemporary construction of a Britain that is 'post-national', the important cultural history of our time is being made by the cool avant-garde black Afro-Caribbeans: he sees them as 'cultural navigators crossing without passports', and they are now also decisively joined by the 'disorienting rhythms' of Asian youth. These cultural phenomena are important in ways that the meretricious merchants of English 'heritage' will never be. For these are cultural developments that show what stake 'the margins' have in modernity, that are pioneering what Hall calls 'a new cosmopolitan, vernacular, post-national, global sensibility'.[21]

In 2004, Hall presented some new work on modernism and the art of the black diaspora, in collaboration with the artist Maria Amidu: 'Modernity and its others: three "moments" in the post-war history of the black diaspora arts'. This took the form of a public lecture, accompanied by a projected sequence of art works synchronized with the talk, and it brought the Conway Hall audience in London to its feet. (A version has recently appeared in the *History Workshop Journal*.[22]) Hall's new project involves a radical reconceptualization of the history of modernism and the visual arts, both in Britain and beyond. In this work, Hall located the pull towards a metropolitan modernist aesthetic in artists from the Caribbean and elsewhere, and considered the exclusions they were subjected to. That first 'moment' was of artists born in the 1920s and 30s, and enabled Hall to bring forward for proper recognition the important modernist work of Ronald Moody, Frank Bowling, Aubrey Williams and many others. These artists did not see modernism as a Eurocentric trap, they saw it as an international creed, a modern consciousness that was fully consistent with an anti-colonial political agenda. They came to Britain from the 1940s to the 1960s, in the spirit in which Picasso and others had gone to Paris: 'to fulfil their artistic ambitions and to participate in the heady atmosphere of artistic innovation in the most advanced centres of art at that time'.

This generation, Hall's own, knew Britain as both the mother country, and 'the mother of all our troubles', he says. He has elsewhere provided a theoretical gloss on this movement of radical colonial artists towards the 'contested centre'.

The history of modernism has been written, in triumphalist mode, as if it was an essentially western set of artistic practices. A number of deracinated artists were drawn to it, but have not been written into its history. 'In reality', Hall argues, the world is littered with modernities, and with artists who 'never regarded modernism as the secure possession of the West'. They perceived it as a visual language that was open to them, but which they would need to change. The history of modernism, therefore, 'should now be rewritten as a set of cultural translations rather than as a universal movement which can be located securely within a culture'.[23] Another factor behind the neglect of these modernist and modernizing artistic exiles, suggests Hall in the paper, is the subsequent dominance of a 'cultural nationalist' position, or 'nativism', in which the goal was to redeem indigenous traditions as the route out of the impositions of colonialism.

Hall's second 'moment' of diaspora arts identifies a very different group of artists, born in Britain in the postwar period. The first generation to be born *in* the diaspora, they are Britons who experienced the eruption of racial politics in the 1970s, 80s and 90s. Race riots, the 'rivers of blood' speech and the 'sus laws' all contributed to a Britain in which, by the mid-1970s, 'race had finally "come home" to Britain'. Artists such as Eddie Chambers, Keith Piper and Marlene Smith used art to articulate political anger, an anger that 'literally scars, fractures, invades' the surfaces of their work. This work is polemical, graphic, sloganeering, and it carried as an iconic motif the black body; 'stretched, threatened, distorted, degraded, imprisoned, beaten and resisting'. The complex currents of the artistic work of this period, running from Afro-centred aesthetics to Rastafarian culture, to the work of independent black women artists such as Lubaina Himid and Sonia Boyce, are sketched out before Hall returns to the theme that dominated *Different*, the visual staging of the black body and its relationship to identity and the culturally contextualized self. There is, he concludes, a synergy across the diaspora arts in the present, which seems unstoppable. 'Black' may now be a fading signifier, but the diaspora arts, in a 'dangerously unequal world', are engaged, impassioned and they are *about* something that really matters.

Hall's recent work on visual art is both a departure from and a complement to his previous work on culture and colonialism. He shares with other sociological thinkers a move away from social and cultural theory, now seeking to explore the themes that have always interested him, but in a different and new register – in his case, that of the visual arts. In a lecture at the Tate in 1999, entitled 'Museums of modern art and the end of history',[24] he made a new connection, extending and updating the arguments of 'The West and the rest' in the context of a consideration of visual art. We are shifting, he argued, from the anthropological definition of culture – culture as a specific way of life – towards a view of culture as principally the realm of signification. This change he located in the point where the West began to 'universalize itself', tried to 'convert the rest of the world into a province of its own forms of life'. This attempt at closure, this 'panoptic project' is now increasingly being 'prized open'. Cultures, in this new context, are more than ever the domain of the 'meanings by which people live their lives, understand and contest where they are and develop aesthetic and artistic forms of expression'. If this is still, inevitably, in some ways an anthropological approach to culture, it is one that is now also irredeemably marked by contested significations.

Since he retired from the Open University, a number of books and papers about Hall's work have been published.[25] Most of them offer useful accounts, with the Davis book including some new interview material – and interviews with Hall are probably the nearest we will get to an autobiography. Rojek's balefully critical study appears to be motivated by two main concerns, the first that Hall has changed his ideas over time rather than said the same thing for 50 years, and is thus 'inconsistent'. A second problem for Rojek is that many people find Stuart Hall personally charming and charismatic – they like him. (Not a problem Rojek is likely to encounter, on this showing.) I fear that Stuart Hall's post-retirement interests in cultural diversity and the visual arts could trigger another round of these two complaints: he has adapted his ideas once again to the changing world he inhabits, and no doubt – in his dedicated work as Rivington Place's indefatigable 'project champion' – made many more friends.

FURTHER READING

Hall, S. (1996) 'When was the post-colonial? Thinking at the limit', in I. Chambers and L. Curti (eds) *The Post-colonial Question*, London: Routledge, pp. 242–60.

Hall, S. (1996) 'Who needs "identity"'?, in S. Hall and P. du Gay (eds) *Questions of Cultural Identity*, London: Sage.

Hall, S. (ed.) (1997) *Representation: Cultural Representations and Signifying Practices*, London: Sage.

Hall, S. and Gieben, B. (eds) (1992) *Formations of Modernity*, Cambridge: Polity Press.

Hall, S. and Jacques, M. (eds) (1983) *The Politics of Thatcherism*, London: Lawrence & Wishart.

Hall, S., Held, D. and McGrew, T. (eds) (1992) *Modernity and its Futures*, Cambridge: Polity Press.

Morley, D. and Chen, K.-H. (eds) (1996) *S. Hall: Critical Dialogues in Cultural Studies*, London: Routledge.

Osborne, P. and Segal, L. (1997) 'Culture and power: Stuart Hall interviewed', *Radical Philosophy*, **86**, 24–42.

FURTHER READING: SECOND EDITION

Davis, H. (2004) *Understanding Stuart Hall*, London: Sage.

Farred, G. (2003) *What's My Name?: Black Vernacular Intellectuals*, Minneapolis: Minnesota University Press.

CHAPTER 19

Dorothy E. Smith

KARIN WIDERBERG

Dorothy E. Smith is known for her thorough critique of the sociological traditions, for our way of 'writing the social' from a ruler's perspective.[1] And for the alternative she outlines; a sociology that starts out from where women are, that is, in the local actualities of everyday life. She advocates a sociology not about people but for people, a sociology about the workings of society that can tell us how the social is put together or comes about. In proposing such 'a method of inquiry', the role of texts as sites or starting points for investigations are underlined. By illuminating 'the workings of texts', how they can be investigated and understood, she also provides a profound sociological response to the poststructuralist challenge.[2] Smith's approach represents a fruitful path for a sociology which takes seriously the critique from **Marxism**, feminism, poststructuralism and postcolonialism.

Driving Impulses

Smith was born in 1926, in the UK. The fact that her mother was a suffragette working to mobilize women to work the land and had a small farm of her own might partly explain the integrity and feminist confidence radiating from her writings. But the experiences from attending a boarding school for girls, from training to be a secretary and a social worker – and working as such – and then later being a single mother of two children probably gave her much of the very substance of the approach she was to develop. The tools handed down to her through her academic degrees, a BSc from the London School of Economics in 1955 and a PhD from Berkeley in 1963 were, however, ill fitted. Although greatly influenced and inspired by such various theoreticians as Marx, Merleau-Ponty, Schutz, **Garfinkel**, Mead and Bakhtin, she still had to restructure their ideas so as to make them function as elements in an approach that made sense of everyday life, including her own. She has often stated[3] that it was the split in her own life, between that of a woman and mother – dominated by her body and by unmediated, local and actual activities – and that of a sociologist – dominated by text and mediated and abstract activities – that made her problematize the sociological traditions. She could not find the world she knew at home with her children in the texts of sociological discourse. The sociologies she had learned were not capable of speaking about what she knew as the very matter of her life. It was the women's movement and feminism that helped her frame this discomfort felt within academia but also at home and when moving between these two spheres. The importance of the collective enterprise of feminism for her own work is something she has stressed all along.

The preoccupation with 'ruling relations' and with the role of sociology in this perspective is the golden thread running through all her works. The 'simple' questions she poses and attempts to answer are: '*Which* reality is made into sociology and *how* is this actually done?' These questions are posed as an essential prelude to thinking through how sociology can be done differently. In her first book,[4] the emphasis is on trying to answer the first of the questions, that is, 'which' reality is made into sociology, while in her later works,[5] it is rather 'how' the social is made into texts on society (texts that include but are by no means exhausted by sociological texts) that becomes the focus. The change of emphasis – which can be seen as developing further the one and the same approach she has used all along – has had the implication that her work is now perceived, even by male sociologists, as general sociological theory.

Key Issues

The Everyday World as Problematic: A Sociology from the Standpoint of Women

In her first book, *The Everyday World as Problematic: A Feminist Sociology*, Smith presents and develops the claim that sociology as a discipline is developed from the position of men of a particular class. Class and men are understood as 'material positions', where alienation in relation to both body and actual labour are fundamental aspects. It is only from this position that society can be looked upon and conceptualized in the way that sociologists have done. And it is only from 'here' (up there) that everyday life appears to consist of only trivialities, trivialities that are being endlessly repeated in a chaotic manner. Such a characterization of everyday life, and of women's role within it, means that neither seems worthy of sociological consideration. Smith claims that the conceptual apparatus of sociology as a whole has been developed out of this position, from the position of men as rulers. Interests, perspectives and relevances have simply leaked from communities of male experiences into the externalized and objectified forms of discourse that define sociology. Sociology is their map, made by and for men, as men and rulers.

'Relations of ruling', or 'ruling relations', is a key concept in Smith's approach. It defines sites for investigation where distinctive forms of organizing contemporary capitalist society are interrelated with the patriarchal forms of our contemporary experience.[6] The purpose, then, for us as researchers is to bring into view the intersection of the institutions organizing and regulating society with their gender subtext and their bases in a gender division of labour. As such, it signals an approach to investigating power similar to the one more recently associated with the concept of 'intersectionality'.[7] Smith's approach – as will be illustrated in a later section – is, however, more systematically developed so as to offer clear guidelines as to how to go about investigating power empirically in such a way that different levels (relations and institutions) are linked together. The role of texts is emphatically underlined here, since the very practices of ruling involve the representation of the local actualities of our worlds in standardized and objectified forms of knowledge. Ruling thus involves the construction of the world as texts which, in turn, become sites of action. The globalization of the economy and administration, together with the rate of technological development, have increased the role of texts in ruling relations to the point where the *sociological* investigation of texts is an absolutely fundamental issue to Smith (see later sections).

The sharp critique of sociology for its ruler's perspective has also included its women's research. Smith has illustrated how well-intentioned feminists still more often than not end up within this restricted framework. Even though they might have insisted upon studying the areas 'defined out' by traditional sociology, their approaches are still influenced by a ruling perspective. Take, for example, women's activities in the home. These activities and their content have been made visible through such concepts as 'unpaid housework'. That is, however, a concept and a perspective that is not particularly well suited as a label for these kinds of activities in which work, spare time, love and service are so intertwined. It is little wonder we cannot agree politically when so few concepts appropriate to grasp women's activities have been developed.

The things women do, for example when 'mothering', have not been properly conceptualized within sociology. Sociology cannot supply the tools necessary to make us understand how the things women do hang together, to ourselves – as individuals – and between women, as a collective. Both reality and social scientific language – as a producer of meaning – fragment us, in relation to ourselves and in relation to each other. In this situation, Smith argues, it should be our aim as researchers to try to construct and/or reconstruct the connection that 'reality' and the language of social science have so systematically deconstructed. And in framing this kind of project, she proposes a goal and a purpose radically distinct from the poststructuralist one.

Smith wants us to take women's activities and experiences as a starting point. We are, in other words, to start where women are situated. This, however, does not imply that we are to study or understand women as 'phenomena'. The purpose is not to try to find out what women or men – or daily life, for that matter – are as such. On the contrary, Smith states that it is the structure and functioning of society that should be made visible, but from the position of everyday life. She argues in favour of a sociology that is situated in daily life but which also looks up and around, and not for a sociology from above, looking (down) at daily life. Women's standpoint is a place to begin the inquiry of the social, where the subject is located in her body and is active in her work in relation to particular others. It is here that the relations of ruling can be discovered, as they come into view from where the subject is, in the actualities of her bodily existence. As ruling relations, they of course transcend the limitations of any one embodied knower. However, to explore them from a women's standpoint is to recognize them and this is an important step in beginning to understand how they enter her experience and her practices as a knower, reader and thinker.

By taking daily life as the starting point, and by conceptualizing its relations, different analytical levels such as the macro- and micro-levels are connected. Making the relations visible enables agents to understand their own activities, and thus gives new and different meanings to them. This purpose is at the heart of Smith's approach and she demands and expects that sociology speaks to women, something that is absent from 'male-stream' sociology.

The Constitutional Principles and Procedures of Sociology

In her 1990 book *The Conceptual Practices of Power: A Feminist Sociology of Knowledge*, Smith investigates the relations of the sociological text. To be a sociologist, she argues, is to be a part of a social relation in which specialized knowledge is separated from everyday knowing. Research is made into a general capacity – everything is researchable – which only researchers, the specialists, can do. As a sociologist, one is by definition part of the ruling relations, where actual work is being separated from abstract and intellectual work and where the latter is being specialized. Smith claims that this division of labour is the foundation for the development of the sociological conventions of how the social is to be written and made into sociological texts. These sociological conventions, she argues, rely on Durkheim's rules of sociological method,[8] which still, in spite of the critique of positivism, function as foundational conventions of too much of today's sociology. Smith lists the following elements as central to this kind of hegemonic sociology: [9]

1. The subject is suspended. A new social object or unit (social fact or phenomenon) is constituted as existing externally to particular individuals. This is done through, for example, the nominalization of verbs, as in aggression and depression. A verb expressing the action of an individual is hereby made into a noun whereby the subject disappears from the text. A related way of proceeding is to construct subject states of individuals as entities in and of themselves, as, for example, with attitude, opinion, belief, interest and so on.
2. Agency is reattributed from the subject to social phenomena. It is the aggression and depression, the attitude or interest, that are now made into problematics and not the individual and her relations.
3. The sociological, through the previous steps, becomes detached from the actual. These textually constituted realities then become objects of sociological work. By subsequently privileging the order of the sociological discourse over the order of the actual, the actual is made into an expression of the discursive.
4. Subjects are reconstructed as figments of discourse. The subjects now enter the text as pseudosubjects or categories of personages to whom the objectified attributes (aggression, attitude and so on) can be assigned.

Summing up, these conventions imply that the subject is first taken out, then, after some theoretical work, is put back in again as an illustration of the theoretical arguments. The perspective of the researcher is hereby made into that of her subjects, and vice versa.

The sociological conventions are characterized by the establishing of a position within the text where the social as written is separated from the social as lived and experienced. This results in positionless accounts; all subjects are either given the same position or are absent. It is as if society could be understood in its totality and from above, from the gaze of God, or rather, from the view of a bird but without the bird. For Smith, these hegemonic conventions for 'how to do sociology' are objectifying and, as such, are profoundly inadequate. The sociological text is, however, not only to be understood as simply a *result* of social relations, that is, of ruling relations. By placing the reader in a particular relation to the reality described in the text, the text also plays an active part in the ruling process. Through the objectifying conventions, the reader takes the place of the ruler, she is offered 'the gaze of God', where local positions, perspectives and experiences are not only subordinated but also made invisible.

A similar critique of how sociologists tend to write the social is formulated by **Pierre Bourdieu.**[10] Just like Dorothy E. Smith, he demands that the position of the observer (the sociologist) should be the object of the same kind of critical analysis we employ when investigating other objects. Sociology and its praxis has to be understood, he claims, in the context of the relations and positions within the academic field as well as in relation to the wider cultural and historical context this field is a part of. Otherwise there is always the risk that, without being aware of it, we read our own position – and ways of relating to and understanding the social – into 'the object', as if it was a part of the object itself instead of a result of our relation to it. Bourdieu, like Smith, advocates that we problematize the relations in which sociology has developed and in which it is practised today. If we do not, we will most likely end up as non-reflective dealers for the ruling apparatus, translating what are actually politically defined social problems (poverty, criminality and so on) into the terms and conventions of an objectivistic sociology. They both propose that reflexivity here should involve a proper systematic method, in contrast to the kind of individualized introspection they claim dominates within the sociological self-reflective analyses of today. But, and this is important to note, while Bourdieu labels this method 'objectification', hereby implying that we must make our own relations of knowledge the object for investigation, Smith uses the same word to label the very opposite, namely the process of how the social is written from a ruling perspective.[11]

The suggestions of Dorothy E. Smith and Pierre Bourdieu on how to proceed to develop another kind of sociology are also quite different. While Bourdieu proposes and has developed theoretical concepts of substance to inform and guide empirical investigations, Smith has focused on developing a very distinctive method of inquiry.

A Method of Inquiry

So how then do we go about investigating and writing the social if we are *not* to start with an objectivistic standpoint and a focus on textually mediated discourses that find no room for the local embodied activities of women? Smith suggests that the following steps should be taken:[12]

1. The subject/knower of inquiry is to be approached as situated in the actualities of her own living, in relations with others and not as a transcendent subject.
2. Here the actual activities of particular individuals are focused on as the locus of the ongoing concerting and coordinating of individuals' activities. The concern is accordingly not just with what individuals do but

with the social aspect of their doings. The social is hereby not conceived of simply as the aggregate properties of separate individuals or as an entity separable from the actual people and the activities in which we find it. Rather, the concept of the social directs us to focus on how people's activities are coordinated.

3. Concepts to express these coordinated activities such as social relations and social organization – as with the more general notion of the social – must not be used as the kinds of discursive entities that lift the phenomena out of time and place. A social relation or social organization is not a thing to be looked at but rather the place from where to do the looking. Rather, terms like 'social relations' should direct our attention to people in a given local site and to what they are experiencing. More than this, they should direct attention to how these experiences and practices hook into sequences of action coordinating multiple other such sites.
4. By thinking of concepts, beliefs and other categories of thought and mind in terms of people's actual practices, the traditional theory/practice split is avoided. Locating the knower in her body, in a lived world in which both theory and practice go on, implies an understanding of theory itself as a practice.
5. Texts, text mediation and textuality hereby become central. The text is the bridge between the actual and the discursive, between the local actualities of our living and the ruling relations. As a material object, it can be read in many settings, and by many people, at the same time or at many different times. As such, texts are the primary basis for abstraction and hence for developing critical analyses of the actualities of living. Since text-mediated relations are increasing the forms in which power is increasingly generated in contemporary societies, the sociological investigation of texts is a means of opening up the relations of ruling to critical interrogation.
6. The politics of a method of inquiry of this kind is not to explain people's behaviour or in any other way to make them the object of research. It is instead to explain to them, and to ourselves, the socially organized powers in which our lives are embedded and to which our activities contribute.

Summing up, by starting out from our actual activities, the method of inquiry proposed by Smith makes the relational context of our daily lives visible. This is a context in which ruling relations can be found, often in text-mediated forms. The increased use and importance of texts as ruling devices has made the sociological investigations of texts a key issue to Smith. And here she gives a *sociological answer* to the challenge from the poststructuralists and their approaches to texts.[13]

Texts as Organizers of Social Relations

Printed or electronic texts are indefinitely replicable and this allows identical forms of meaning to be activated in multiple local settings. This materiality of the text, Smith argues, creates a situation in which it can seem that language, thought, culture, formal organization and so on exist independently and outside time and the actualities of people's lives. But even though texts are mediators of discourses and ruling relations, they are always also occurrences in time and space. Texts 'happen', as she puts it, they are constituents and organizers of actions, activated when read at specific times and places. The replicability that texts represent and make possible is essential to the kind of organization that is characteristic of contemporary society. We could not have the existence of corporations, for example, without replicable texts and their discourses.

The texts, accordingly, represent a possibility for sociologists to explore how the translocal and extra-local are brought into local settings where people are, into their bodies and particular activities, activities which can be connected up with each other. The fact that we are reading the same text does not mean that we all read it the same way. Smith places emphasis on the notion of the text–reader conversation, acknowledging the insights of French poststructuralism, of Roland Barthes,[14] for example, which stresses that a text only becomes what it is in the reading of it. The meaning of a text, accordingly, is not fixed. Smith's argument is that in order to establish the significance of different readings, one has to be able to recognize a text as a particular, specific text. A faithfully replicated text is identical to the text that was copied. It is identical and this fact is crucial in order to establish the significance of different readings of it. Otherwise, the idea of different readings would be of no interest. This has enabled Smith to propose that the text can be treated ethnographically. In other words, it is possible to explore the variety of ways that particular texts enter into the organizing of any corporation, university and so on.

Institutional Ethnography

The term 'institutional ethnography' was used by Smith in her early work[15] but lately she and her followers have started to use it also as a kind of research programme for sociology.[16] Here a sociology is proposed that explores the institutional order and ruling relations from the point of view of people who are in various ways implicated in it, and participating in it. It does not aim to understand the institution, organization and so on as such, as in systems theory. It only takes the social activities of the institution as a starting point. Hooking on to activities and relations, both horizontal and hierarchical, the approach is never confined just to the very institution or organization immediately under investigation. The purpose is rather to illuminate the connections between the local and the extra-local, thereby making visible the workings of the wider society as they impinge upon activities in the here and now. Conversely, exploring how texts mediate, regulate and authorize people's activities also expands the scope of ethnographic method beyond the limits of observation.

Seeing Things Differently

Dorothy E. Smith has taught me to be sceptical towards the abstract and generalized understandings of social problems presented in the media as well as in social science textbooks. Her work encourages us to bring such texts back down to earth, to ask about social life 'How is it done?' or 'How is it put together?' When doing research myself on the sociality of tiredness, I have accordingly asked how people 'do' their tiredness. That is, instead of starting out with a concept of tiredness that the subjects under investigation are to represent, the actualities of their everyday life were taken as a starting point so as to explore how tiredness in that relational context was understood and handled. This allowed me to 'hook' the local to the extra- or translocal by illuminating the role of discourse-mediated ruling perspectives, which enter into the very lives and practices of embodied individuals, structuring tiredness in specific ways (for example the ideology of the so-called 'new economy' and its concepts of freedom and flexibility). The result is an understanding of 'the time of tiredness',[17] which offers quite different solutions to the common understanding of tiredness as an individual issue where it is one's self who is to blame – for not setting the limits or not being able to master the demands of life.

Many contemporary sociologists make use of Smith's approach in one variant or the other, in a variety of fields and themes.[18] Exploring how, for example, arranged marriages are actually done[19] or how 'feeding the family'[20] is actually put together, they make us see things differently. But also journalists, at least those in the Wallraff tradition,[21] now and then give us such accounts founded on approaches similar in spirit to the ones of Dorothy E. Smith. *Nickled and Dimed: On (Not) Getting By in America* by Barbara Ehrenreich[22] is such an account. For a period of two years, she took a series of different 'unqualified' jobs; as a waitress, a domestic help, a cleaner and a saleswoman, with the determination to try to get by on the salary she earned. The poverty of 'the working poor', as they are often labelled, was to be illuminated not with the intention to try to grasp how 'poverty feels' or what it is *really* like to be poor. Rather, as Barbara Ehrenreich puts it, the goal was more uncomplicated; she just wanted to find out if she could simply break even by balancing her salary and expenses – just as poor people have to every day of their lives.

Each new job situation is described in detail, from the lengthy employment process (reading advertisements, sending in applications, turning up for interview, taking employment and drug tests and so on) which is both costly (transportation costs, for example) and humiliating, through the process of acquiring the competences needed for the job in question and then to quitting it and looking for 'a new start'. All the time, the 'ongoing concerting and coordinating' (in Smith's words) that goes on between her co-workers, bosses and herself are focused upon, giving us a picture of how it all comes together, at all levels and in each area. Having a low salary is expensive and puts you at constant risk. You cannot afford the down payment for proper housing or even to pay the monthly rent, but have to rely on paying the rent weekly or daily, which always is more expensive. And living like that, leaving aside the fear and risk of assault from living so close to so many strangers, often implies that you do not have cooking facilities and have to rely on eating out, and, even when the food is both relatively cheap and fast, it is still more expensive (not forgetting the transportation costs) than eating in. Such food also has health costs, and health insurance, medicine or sick leave from work are things one cannot afford. So you have to work even though ill, which further increases the chance of more serious illnesses that might endanger the chances for further, or alternative, employment. Due to the low salaries, many people in this kind of situation have two jobs, which, of course, considering the kinds of jobs involved, represents a further risk to health. Millions of Americans live like this, in a constant 'situation of crisis', as Ehrenreich puts it.[23] Through her detailed and analytical description, and her bottom-up approach, Barbara Ehrenreich makes us see poverty differently. We see 'how poverty is done, how it is put together' in the actualities of people's everyday life, and if we look at the work also through Smith's emphasis on the mediation of texts and discourses in the organization of poverty, we soon also see how the localities of these lives are hooked up to the extra-local and to broader ruling relations.

Legacies and Unfinished Business

Smith's language is precise and carefully chosen to express the approach she has developed. It is not that her concepts and way of expressing herself are difficult to understand in themselves, quite the opposite. Her concepts are the basic sociological ones (for example the social organization of knowledge, and the coordinating of people's activities), but they are being used to develop a method of inquiry of the social rather than to develop a theory *about* the social. Her insistence that we – as sociologists – should start out from within the social activities of people, and not in theoretical concepts, when investigating how the social comes about, so as not to read and write the social (only) through our own position (as part of the ruling relations) and its *doxa*, is actually very hard to grasp when trained to do the opposite. Therefore, Dorothy Smith is easily misread and misinterpreted, a point which the debates around her work and her own responses clearly illustrate.[24] And it might be hard to foresee the full implications of her approach if translated into actual empirical research, especially one's own. And yet, to me at least, it is when translating her approach into a research design that it clearly makes a radical difference and provides a fruitful alternative to dominant ways of doing sociological research. As a method of inquiry, it is in one way an appeal for modesty. Smith does not claim to know this or that about society, she 'only' claims a valuable way to find things out. And for those looking for grand theory, she might be overlooked or neglected, for not delivering 'the goods' (theoretical conceptual schemes). For others, though, her approach, being so radically different from so much of today's sociological practice, might seem too unconventional and difficult to try out on one's own. As such, it is far from an appeal for modesty, quite the opposite.

Approaching text with this method of inquiry implies a shift in focus from the poststructuralist stance. It is not the discourse of the text that is the starting point, or the subject who makes use of it who is focused upon. Instead, the inquiry starts out from within the social relations into which the text and its discourses have entered. The idea is to investigate the social activities the text generates in that particular relational context. It is to focus on what the text makes happen, how it is used in everyday life to coordinate social activities, as a means of social organization. This can be the specific contribution of sociologists to the illumination of the powers of texts in everyday life. And since texts are being transmitted and used translocally, they are powerful tools in organizing people's activities, across institutional and national boundaries, standardizing people's activities into the kinds of social organization that, for example, make bureaucracy possible. 'Institutional ethnography' signals an approach where the use of institutional texts in the coordinating of people's activities is being investigated, with the aim of illuminating how these are hooked up hierarchically and horizontally beyond that particular institution. It is an approach that connects or maybe rather cuts across so-called micro- and macro-levels by problematizing any view of the everyday world as simply either one or the other.

One among many challenges, or pieces of 'unfinished business' important to my own thinking, is how to relate the approach thrown up by Smith's radical method of inquiry to the perspectives of postcolonialism. Are the characteristics of ruling relations presented by Smith well suited to grasp colonial and postcolonial ruling? And can her method of inquiry be used to explore and investigate the colonial and postcolonial everyday life? In what ways could postcolonial critiques and perspectives inform the perspective and approach of Smith? That is, the gains from connecting these two approaches are yet to be discussed and explored. Although her work is mentioned and appraised by some feminist postcolonial researchers,[25] it has, so far as I know, not yet been applied by them. Why it wouldn't work, I cannot see and I single out post-colonialism because I strongly believe that such a combination would be a fruitful and productive one. But of course, we first have to explore 'how it can be put together'.

FURTHER READING

Campbell, M. and Manicom, C. (eds) (1995) *Knowledge, Experience, and Ruling Relations: Studies in the Social Organization of Knowledge*, Toronto: University of Toronto Press.

Mohanty, C.T. (2003) *Feminism without Borders*, Durham: Duke University Press. Read with reference to the points made in the final paragraph regarding possible connections between the feminist postcolonial literature and Smith's radical method of enquiry.

Signs (1997) 22(2). For debates around Smith's work and her own response. See note 24.

Smith, D. (1990) *The Conceptual Practices of Power: A Feminist Sociology of Knowledge*, Toronto: University of Toronto Press.

Smith, D. (1999) *Writing the Social: Critique, Theory and Investigations*, Toronto: University of Toronto Press.

Smith, D. (2005) *Institutional Ethnography: A Sociology for People*, Oxford: AltaMira Press.

Smith, D. (ed.) (2006) *Institutional Ethnography as Practice*, Oxford: Rowman & Littlefield.

The Sociological Quarterly (1993) 34(1).

Widerberg, K. (2006) 'Embodying modern times – investigating tiredness', *Time & Society*, 15(1): 105–20.

CHAPTER 20

Anthony Giddens

IRA J. COHEN

Driving Impulses

As if by intuition, Anthony Giddens has always gravitated to the intersecting strengths of theoretical positions. As early as *Capitalism and Social Theory*, which helped bring **Marx** into the sociological mainstream in 1971, Giddens proposed that, for all their differences, Marx, **Durkheim** and **Weber** address a common agenda of problems in the analysis of modern society.[1] More recently, as centrifugal forces have carried bits and pieces of Marx, Durkheim and Weber (and others) to far-flung extremes, Giddens has managed to write with theoretical originality as he pulls ideas out of distant orbits back to intellectual common ground. In *Beyond Left and Right*, he enlists philosophic conservatism in support of what is generally regarded as a left-wing ideological agenda.[2] In *Modernity and Self-identity*, he tempers postmodernist pessimism and cynicism with sociological realism by transposing apparently intractable philosophical dilemmas from philosophy and the arts to problems actors deal with pragmatically in their everyday lives.[3]

A theorist like Giddens who writes with a distinctive sensibility can easily assume the role of the fox, Isaiah Berlin's master metaphor for social thinkers who canvas many unrelated and even contradictory themes.[4] Stylistically, Giddens' writings appear very fox-like indeed. He shifts in and out of topics quite abruptly, as if to linger over the details of his thoughts might entrap him in a theoretical system of his own design. Yet, while he avoids the systemic trap, two very unfox-like projects provide a good deal of consistency in his work:

1. His theory of modernity to which I have already referred
2. Structuration theory, a set of basic concepts regarding the constitution of social life, which requires additional commentary here.[5]

Although the name 'structuration theory' may appear to imply an explanatory model, it qualifies as a theory only in the heuristic sense of the term. That is, it provides abstract insights into the generic characteristics of society, but explicitly excludes any explanatory or descriptive 'application' to substantive problems or historically or culturally specific events. What purpose does an abstract and generic heuristic theory serve? Just as music theorists must know the generic principles of music composition before studying any particular musical genre, so social theorists must have some idea of the generic principles of the constitution of society before social life in any historical period makes sense. Structuration theory sets out a conception of the basic possibilities or potentials of social life.[6] Substantive analyses informed by structuration theory always refer to historically delimited settings, for example particular epochs in specific cultures.

Characteristically, Giddens originates structuration theory between two positions other theorists regard as antitheses: theories of collectivities on the one hand and theories of the individual on the other. He finds common ground between them by developing structuration theory from one simple idea: everything in social life, from encompassing world systems to an individual's state of mind, originates in social praxis, that is, the skilful performance of conduct and interaction. Giddens' confidence in the centrality of praxis derives from **Harold Garfinkel** and **Erving Goffman**'s remarkably subtle examinations of interaction in everyday life. Giddens seems less aware of some remarkable parallels between his thought and early twentieth-century American pragmatic philosophy, particularly John Dewey's writings on human conduct.[7] But, unlike Dewey, Giddens frames his thinking in terms of sociological problems rather than philosophical disputes. This sociological basis also distinguishes Giddens from many European theorists who try to solve philosophical problems by sociological means.[8]

Giddens clearly has a lot riding on the significance of social praxis. But why should praxis make a difference to sociological thought? Consider what would happen to contemporary social life if we subtract just two mundane practices: the use of financial credit and telling time. Although both practices may fade into the background in everyday life, public life as we know it (and much of our private life as well) would be impossible in their absence. Individuals almost immediately would be bewildered to the point of anomie. It can be surprisingly difficult for newcomers to think of practices as the most important constituents of social life. Most of us are disposed to think that individuals and social groups exhaust the possibilities. As will be evident below, much of Giddens' originality stems from reconceiving collectivities and individuals in a novel, praxiological light.

Exaggerations are conceits that magnify the power of a theorist's sociological vision. But Giddens, as I have said, writes with an aversion to ideas carried to extremes. His emphasis on praxis reinforces this aversion. To take praxis seriously, one must accept two ideas beyond the basic insight that social life at large is produced through social practices:

1. Social practices are mutable, that is, they develop and change in different ways in different historical periods
2. The manifold consequences of social practices can never be fully plotted or controlled in advance.

To be sure, Giddens knows that conduct often is reproduced in highly routinized forms. But he also knows that perversity in praxis is a part of social life, that is, every practice includes some opportunity for innovation and every occasion of praxis has some potential to yield surprising results.

Given the mutability and perversity of praxis, it is out of the question for Giddens to insist upon the centrality of one mode of conduct (for example Marx on labour), to envision an inevitable destination for history (for example Communism, organic solidarity), or to claim that insidious practices or structures thoroughly dominate our lives (for example Weber on the 'iron cage', **Foucault** on power/knowledge, **Bourdieu** on the habitus and cultural fields). As a result, social life appears far 'messier' in Giddens' writings than in many theoretical works.

Key Issues

What is a Collectivity?

A simple question with no easy answer. In fact, there is no such thing as an abstract collectivity, only particular kinds of groups such as the Roman Empire, medieval towns, or the modern state. In structuration theory, Giddens outlines the generic qualities of collectivities by rephrasing the question. Instead of asking: What is a collectivity? Giddens asks: How are collectivities formed and structured through social praxis? The shift in question permits him to avoid misleading metaphors of biological organisms and analogies to material things that permit many collectivists (for example Durkheim) to suggest that social groups are entities *sui generis* with properties of their own. If we look past misleading figures of speech, this proposition is difficult to defend. Social groups lack genetic codes that standardize biological relations between organs, and they lack chemical bonds that fix the physical properties of material things. What makes 'thing-like' images of collectivities plausible is that, considered over long periods of time, most groups exhibit two characteristic features:

1. Enduring patterns of positions and relationships
2. Characteristic structural features (for example moral codes, types of domination, class structures).

Giddens' intention is to account for these long-lasting characteristics of groups in praxiological terms without backsliding into the language of things. He proceeds on two tracks, dealing separately with relational patterns of groups on the one hand and structural features of groups on the other.[9]

Consider, first, relational patterns. The illusory image of collectivities as objects actually obscures an observable material basis for collectivities, the performance of practices by embodied actors, that is, actors physically located in a particular material setting during a particular period of time. Now, the fact that human conduct and interaction require space and time may seem more interesting to geographers than social theorists. But Giddens builds a fresh connection between geography and social theory that leads to new vistas on collectivities here.[10]

Giddens' basic image of collective life begins with the following image: actors repeating routines and rituals (reproduced practices) across time and space over and over so that the pattern itself becomes a taken-for-granted feature of social life.[11] Social rounds in a peasant farming village provide a simple, but useful example. Each day begins with routine family activity as people arise in their dwellings. During their daily rounds, they disperse and congregate in order to perform everyday activities in fields, markets, neighbours' dwellings and so on, until, at the day's end, family members reconvene for dinner and domestic affairs. The relational pattern of the village thus takes shape in the recurrent patterns of convergence and divergence through time and space, that is, across settings of conduct throughout the day. In reality, of course, these simple social rounds are complicated by weekly market days and sabbaths, seasonal holidays and non-routine events such as disasters or wars. Complications multiply further in large, modern groups employing technology that extends group connections (the term relations now seems too robust) across vast stretches of space and time.

One more point epitomizes Giddens' sense of the 'messiness' of social life. He cautions against thinking of group boundaries as demarcations between internally coherent and self-contained entities. In fact, the intensity and duration of relations and connections across time and space can establish all kinds of boundaries in any given case.[12]

Consider now structural properties, Giddens' second aspect of collectivities. If social groups consist of relations reproduced across time and space, then the properties of social groups never exist altogether at the same time. Empirical sociologists deal with this problem by inferring collective features of groups from statistics and other data collected across time and space but analysed as if all observations were taken simultaneously. Giddens does something similar to conceive structural properties of collectivities in structuration theory.

The term 'structure', as it is typically used, is misleading here. Social groups are *structured* by commonly reproduced practices. To grasp the point, consider how a single practice is structured, for example the practice in modern business firms of hiring less qualified men in preference to more qualified women. What does the term 'structured' mean here? It means preferential hiring practices are chronically reproduced. Many thousands of personnel officers perform this practice (in a variety of specific ways) over and over in the course of doing business in various firms every year. As a result, the practice comes to seem a permanent feature of business firms. And this sense of *reproduced permanence* is what the adjectives 'structured' or 'structural' imply in structuration theory.[13]

Now, consider the broader structuring (or 'structuration') of gender relations in business firms. Here we find not only preferential hiring practices, but preferential practices in pay, promotion and job evaluation, exclusionary practices of male bonding, chronic forms of sexual harassment and more. These practices never occur all at once, and any given practice may be performed in some firms more often than others. But when all these reproduced practices are considered at large, the structured subordination of women to men is an unmistakable property of business firms.

The example deceives by its simplicity. Complexities abound in structural analysis. But one essential caveat must be registered here. Just as all social practices are subject to historical change, so are all structural properties of groups. The structural subordination of women undoubtedly looked fixed for all time to a woman attempting a business career in a modern firm *circa* 1955. Today the permanence of the subordination of women in business firms looks less certain. The future remains to be seen.

The Consciousness of the Acting Subject

For Giddens, the most basic quality of the social actor is neither motivation (as in **Freud**), nor meaning (as in Weber and Geertz), nor interests (as in theories of rational choice). Giddens' unorthodox image of the individual begins with the postulate that she *knows how to act*. From this insight, Giddens infers a hierarchy of menial activity with *discursive consciousness* at the top, *practical consciousness* in the middle, and the *unconscious* at the bottom. This hierarchy comprises the centrepiece of his theory of the acting subject.

Practical consciousness bears particularly important theoretical weight because this level refers to knowledge of how to act. Knowledge of how to act is non-verbal, tacit knowledge, which means we learn much of it without didactic instruction, and we take it for granted most of the time. All this is not as mysterious as it sounds. For example, we all know how to say hello to close friends and we know when and where to say hello too. Most of us say hello without giving these skills (the 'know-how') a second thought. Each day, we perform a myriad of other practices, some quite subtle, others more obvious, without conscious reflection. We perform so many, in fact, that our practical consciousness is almost always engaged. But the secret of practical consciousness is that it works best when we fail to notice it at all.

What, then, of fully conscious thought? For Giddens, we enter a state of discursive consciousness,[14] that is, a state of awareness of our own thoughts, when for any reason, a situation arises where we lack the taken-for-granted ability to go on. Examples range from illness or disaster that dramatically disrupt day-to-day routines, to more structured problems such as puzzle-solving or artistic creation that require a synthesis of fully conscious thought and taken-for-granted skills. Of course, actors often conduct themselves for extended periods while relying exclusively on practical consciousness. Insofar as they do, they may give no attention whatsoever to their own motivation or to the meaning of their conduct. Hence meaning and motivation in the fully conscious sense of these terms appear more episodic in Giddens' structuration theory than in many other theories of the actor.

Now, it may seem that Giddens has trapped himself into saying that unreflective conduct lacks any motivation at all. But, in a move of importance both for structuration theory and for his theory of modernity, Giddens actually claims that human conduct is always subject to a very powerful unconscious motivation, the need to maintain *ontological security*. Ontological security refers to a comfortable mental state in which actors engage in taken-for-granted activities in familiar surroundings and in the company of unthreatening others. It is, in brief, a state of mind fostered whenever actors take for granted that they know how to go on without any disruption. Should an actor altogether lose the ability to go on, as might occur in the aftermath of a socially paralysing earthquake or a physically paralysing injury, she would feel helpless, anxious and intensely anomic until she works out a comfortable modus vivendi again. But disasters are not the only threat to ontological security. Indeed, disruptions of ontological security are a chronic feature in Giddens' substantive investigations of modernity.

Modernity and Social Change

The term 'modernity' has been synonymous with social change for several centuries. But in the period Giddens terms 'late modernity' (from 1900 and primarily since the Second World War), the pace of change has intensified, its scale has expanded, and its life-altering consequences have reached into even the most intimate details of everyday life. Mainstream authors suggest a widespread public ambivalence (hope/fear, excitement/bewilderment) about the life-altering consequences of modernity.[15] Giddens concurs, finding challenging opportunities on the flip side of modern dilemmas. Above all, he resists the temptation to exaggerate alienation, or succumb to despair.

Someday, someone will write a master theory of modernity, something like a *Das Kapital* for the twenty-first century. Nothing like this has surfaced in Giddens' writings to date. Instead, all his writings implicitly respond to one big question: How are the life-altering consequences of modernity implicated in the local details of everyday life? Praxis, the hub of structuration theory, operates at the centre of his thought here again. Giddens outlines the extraordinary scale and intensity of modern change with reference to two historically unique modes of praxis, reflexivity and technologically mediated relations that enable markets, bureaucracies and cultural media to stretch across the globe and back again into our local workplaces, homes and everyday lives.[16]

'Reflexivity' refers to practices guided by observation and thought (that is, discursive consciousness). Pragmatic problem-solving in all historical settings is reflexive in this sense. But reflexivity takes on an unprecedented life-altering momentum in modernity as methodically gathered information facilitates systematic planning and organization on previously unimaginable scales. Reflexive practices abound everywhere we turn: in accounting procedures and investment planning, bureaucratic management, architectural and industrial design, military operations, medical practices, the list goes on and on. Computerized information processing produces quantum leaps in the tempo of reflexivity, but the origins of reflexivity antedate the computer by several hundred years.

Why does reflexivity continue to grow? Competition and domination in many forms undoubtedly play a part. Once someone introduces reflexive practices, it is very difficult for anyone to revert to traditional ways. But Giddens stresses this 'genie-out-of-the-bottle' effect from another point of view. Just as social life appears too 'messy' to permit overly coherent social theories, so it also appears too 'messy' to allow reflexively drafted plans to succeed very often without unintended, perverse effects. The pollution of the environment by well-planned industrial organizations is an archetypical example, so are iatrogenic diseases that turn up in even the most well-run hospitals. To mitigate unwanted side-effects of any kind, we need new reflexive planning and organization. And to mitigate the next round of side-effects that inevitably will ensue, we need more reflexivity again. And so it goes on, what Giddens terms the 'juggernaut' of modernity.[17]

Turning now to social relations at a distance: capitalist enterprises, diplomatic missions and military expeditions established long-distance lines of connection well before the advent of modernity.[18] However, long delays occasioned by slow means of transport severely limited the effectiveness of these connections. Since time and space figure prominently in structuration theory, Giddens is intellectually well positioned to appreciate the enormous difference instantaneous electronic communication and rapid transshipment have made to the globalization of many fundamental processes in social life. Every facet of everyday life, from a prosaic tuna sandwich, to the newspaper article we read with our lunch, to the pop song playing on the radio as we eat, was produced somewhere far away from where we dine.

Empowerment and Risk in Post-traditional Society

Why should ambivalence be such a common reaction to modernity? Giddens conceives the root of this ambivalence as a counterpoint between empowerment and risk.[19] On one side of the issue, modern forms of reflexivity empower social actors by undermining taken-for-granted authority and practice. New forms of knowledge enable actors to challenge taken-for-granted forms of authority everywhere, from the family, to the professions, to the state. Actors now not only have the right to decide on everything from their medical treatment to their cultural lifestyle, in many cases they are compelled to choose. As recently as the 1950s, many people in modern societies remained tradition-bound 'locals' in many respects. Today, almost everyone exercises a range of 'cosmopolitan' freedoms.

But, on the other side of the issue, this empowering reflexively produces its own set of uncomfortable side-effects. Recall here that Giddens postulates a basic human need for ontological security, a sense of well-being grounded in a taken-for-granted competence in negotiating familiar ways of life. But the life-altering dynamics of modernity challenge our competence and disturb our well-being too often to permit us to take much for granted for very long. The recurrent need to make informed decisions about uncertain events opens up everywhere from career paths, to retirement planning, to the choices parents make for their children. Trust, which is an integral feature of ontological security, cannot be taken for granted when so many weighty decisions need to be made. We confront too many situations where we risk unhappy outcomes to simply assume that what we have done in the past will work out for the best here and now once again.

Giddens' emphasis on unavoidable risk and insecure trust has the important effect I mentioned earlier of transposing the philosophical agenda of postmodernism into everyday life.[20] Giddens observes that philosophical doubts about truth and ethics that startle postmodernists are nothing new. The same doubts motivated the early modern philosophers, for example Descartes, Hume and Kant, none of whom would have bothered to write philosophy if they took truth and ethics for granted. But philosophical doubt took quite some time to migrate into daily routines. Only for the past 50 years have sociological conditions replaced trust with doubt as a widespread problem in everyday life. Of course, everyday people cope with their doubts in practice not principle, and, in the process, temper angst, which predominates in many postmodern philosophies, with hope, which is a philosophically underrated resource in everyday life.

The Politics of Modernity

Discussions of empowerment often imply that politics is a zero-sum game (that is, power-holders dominate subordinates) or else presume the potential for unrealistic degrees of empowered freedom. Before turning to the politics of modernity, it is worthwhile to have in mind Giddens' most fundamental insight into power relations in structuration theory. Although domination (and hence subordination) are inescapable facts of social life, power relations between the more and less powerful always involve a mix of autonomy and dependence. But the powerful also depend upon less powerful others to carry out certain practices (which, in given situations, may range from hard labour to simply staying out of the way). To whatever extent the powerful depend upon the less powerful, this dependence can be skilfully exploited as leverage by subordinates to open up some areas of autonomy for themselves. Strikes, violent and non-violent civil disobedience, boycotts and strategic voting in elections are all useful tactics of the less powerful, in what Giddens terms the 'dialectic of control'.[21]

In relation to modernity, Giddens defines two broad sets of power relations and, in effect, two separate dialectics of control. Inevitably, but uncharacteristically, Giddens takes a partisan stand when normative political issues are at stake. His analyses of both sets of power relations implicitly begin from the standpoint of those with less power rather than those with more.

Does this partisanship imply that Giddens has a left-wing bias in ideological terms? Yes and no. Yes, if left wing means a partisanship for those engaged in what he terms 'emancipatory politics', that is, struggles for freedom from poverty and deprivation, political oppression and social exclusion.[22] But even this partisanship is unusual, in that Giddens finds fault with the unintended side-effects of left-wing programmes in the past such as state welfare policies that trap the needy in cycles of poverty. Here Giddens points out the reasonable side of right-wing criticism of social democratic policy, albeit he does so pragmatically with the problems of the needy in mind.

But the more original aspect of Giddens' politics of modernity refers to 'life-politics', that is, the politics of how we should live our lives in a world of reflexivity and globalization, where traditions have given way and the awareness of risk continually disturbs our ontological security. Life-politics encompasses personal struggles to achieve satisfying and secure lifestyles and relationships, as well as ecological, feminist and other movements that seek new ways of life in a post-traditional world.

Giddens' commentaries on life-politics crystallize a growing sense in the post-Marxist era that the nature of radical politics has changed. But Giddens, in a characteristically unorthodox move, enlists a durable strand of conservative political thought in service to life-politics. As opposed to conventional left-wing thinkers who rarely hesitate to propose social change, many conservative political philosophers respect the security and community fostered by tradition. The challenge to radical politics, from Giddens' point of view, is to restore traditions that nurture the 'good life' without sacrificing the reflexive empowerment that fuels life-politics from the start.

Seeing Things Differently

As befits a sociologist who seeks theoretical common ground rather than radical extremes, Giddens almost never tries to falsify familiar points of view. His objectives are more subtle: both in structuration theory and, especially, in his investigations into modernity, Giddens directs us to the unseen structuring of the familiar without losing sight of what we have noticed in the past. Giddens forfeits some of the 'shock of the new' that theorists like Marx, **Foucault** and Bourdieu employ to persuade us that we misrecognize our social world. But finding the unnoticed without denying the familiar ultimately is a more demanding task.

Space permits only a brief demonstration of seeing the unnoticed in the familiar here. Recently, I have been thinking about solitude in modernity and in the process I have been observing what people do during rush hour while alone in their cars. One thing I have noticed is a good deal of personal grooming: women applying make-up, men combing their hair and so on. As recently as 1970, the practice was unconventional if not slightly bizarre. Today, auto makers have installed grooming mirrors on sun visors to meet a growing demand. Now, these drivers obviously are concerned with the presentation of self. But the fact that they are grooming themselves in their cars indicates that some of the most deep-seated aspects of modernity have silently infiltrated their solitude as they drive.

Consider the broader structuration of highway grooming. First of all, it is primarily practised by commuters. Commuting, in turn, hinges on the separation of home and workplace, and the accelerating tempo of transportation that is part of the modern attempt to overcome constraints of time and space. But, like all other aspects of modernity, the attempt to overcome constraints of time and space produces perverse effects. Specifically, as more and more drivers clog the roads during rush hour, commuters must be on their way as quickly as possible if they are to arrive at work or home on time. Hence, the driver with one hand on the steering wheel and the other on the lipstick or comb engages in practices invisibly structured by the complex time–space dynamics of modernity that dislodge grooming practices from the privacy of the bathroom to the front seat of the car.

Legacies and Unfinished Business

In 1976, Giddens published his first book on structuration theory.[23] That and subsequent works theoretically established praxis as the common ground where the actions of the individual merge with the structuration of social order. Two world-class sociologists who have embedded much of their best work in deeply theoretical empirical studies, namely **Norbert Elias** and Pierre Bourdieu, should be credited, along with Giddens, for launching what has turned out to be a consequential movement in sociology (and other disciplines).[24] The 'new institutionalism' in the study of complex organizations, 'practice theory' in anthropology, William Sewell Jr's transposition of structuration theory into historical sociology and Rob Stones' work bringing structuration theory to bear on theoretical methods illustrate the growing role of praxiological reconstructions in sociology and other disciplines today.[25]

And yet, Giddens is no exception to the perversity of praxis: which is to say that in the process of making a substantial difference to the development of social theory, Giddens, no less than any other theorist, generates implicit restrictions as a by-product of his thought. Space permits only brief mention of one restriction here.[26]

Giddens' aversion to exaggeration, his unwillingness to engage philosophical questions by sociological means and his centripetal impulse to draw disparate ideas back to common ground keep his sociological compass pointed towards social life. The same features of his thought also keep his moral compass pointed towards the 'is' more than the 'ought' in normative terms, that is, towards problems that disrupt, or threaten to disrupt, the security and satisfaction people experience in their everyday lives.[27] To be quite clear, as is evident in his analyses of 'emancipatory politics' and 'life-politics' in modernity, Giddens has no problem picking up moral themes as defined by everyday actors on their own behalf. Nor does he have any problems picking up latent tensions and seen but unnoticed dilemmas that may emerge as problems somewhere down the road. But Giddens installs no moral bearings in the fundamental conception of praxis in structuration theory, nor in his analyses of the consequences of modernity. All this works reasonably well in an era such as our own, where political movements and public policies are open to academic debate, journalistic scrutiny and some degree of political pressure from 'below' as well as 'above'. But in societies where values are less subject to debate (for example the USA in the 1950s) or where politics and moral discourse about values such as justice, freedom or democracy are altogether suppressed, as is true in most authoritarian regimes, a more normative theory is needed. Inevitably, normative theories exaggerate some aspects of social life they seek to condemn or praise. And for these purposes, Giddens' theories do not work very well.

So, like all theories, the value of Giddens' theories depends upon the context in which they appear.[28] In my view, writing as an American in 1997, social theory appears to be concluding a 30-year cycle in which some of the brightest sociological minds have invested great dedication, enthusiasm and insight in developing various denominations of normative theory. This does not seem to me to have been an era in which conflicts over values have remained latent or suppressed. If I am right about this, then perhaps the moment has arrived to stand back from debates about what 'ought' to be and pragmatically assay people's private lives and their public situations in terms of their own hopes and fears. To do this we need a lucid understanding of both the seen and the unnoticed dimensions of the social world we all help to produce every day. And to this end Giddens provides sociological theories for our times.

Appendix Second Edition – Rob Stones

Since the first edition of *Key Sociological Thinkers* in 1998, Giddens' publications have been intent on further elaborating the ideas developed in his early 1990s writings on modernity in combination with the politically focused themes of *Beyond Left and Right*. He has become a man of public affairs as much as, if not more than, a man of letters, combining his role as director of the London School of Economics and his subsequent position as a Labour peer in the House of Lords with a very well-defined role as a public intellectual, whose influence has been felt in the corridors of power from London and Washington to Seoul and Brasilia.

Giddens' writings during this period have been closely intertwined with his public role, consisting of a series of popularly targeted publications that have been translated into many languages. The first of these, *The Third Way: The Renewal of Social Democracy*,[29] began life as an attempt to give logical rigour to a series of seminars he took part in during the late 1990s that included Tony Blair, the Clintons and members of the British and American Cabinets. In 1999, he was invited to give the BBC's prestigious and highly influential Reith Lectures. These were subsequently published as *Runaway World*.[30] The focus was on globalization and three of the five broadcasts were delivered outside London, from Delhi, Hong Kong and Washington, a strategy subsequently adopted and adapted by Daniel Barenboim in the 2006 lectures. In these writings and the subsequent volumes, *The Third Way and its Critics* and *The New Egalitarianism*,[31] the latter co-edited with Patrick Diamond, then special adviser in the Prime Minister's Office, Giddens has reinforced his arguments about the outmoded nature of the old 'Left' and 'Right' distinction. As some of the titles indicate, this has been closely tied to a further argument about the need to rethink traditional social democratic politics, to invent a radically new 'Third Way' *beyond* Left and Right.

At the heart of Giddens' position is the view that globalization has reduced and reconfigured the powers available to the single nation-state. He argues that any successful political project must be able to respond to the implications of the chronically reflexive forces of globalization, which have made Keynesian economics now impossible in the face of the massive expansion of international trade, the growth and power of transnational companies, and the size, speed and sophistication of the international financial markets. He singles out the theme of risk as something that unites many otherwise disparate domains in this fundamentally altered terrain of politics. In a globalized, runaway world, an understanding of the role of the relationship between risk and reflexivity can be seen as central to any attempt to get to grips with such major issues as welfare state reform, the regulation of the world's financial markets, the rapid pace of technological change, ecological crises and the increasingly volatile demands of geopolitics. In his recent volume, *Europe in the Global Age*, Giddens draws on these and further arguments, not least those to do with social policy and cultural diversity and identity, to examine what he calls 'the struggle for Europe' – this is *both* the struggle between competing visions of what the European Union should be and *also* the struggle that Europe has to engage in 'to assert itself in a world of far-reaching transformation'.[32]

In *Over To You, Mr Brown* Giddens implores the eponymous new prime minister to develop a greater enthusiasm for Europe:

> (S)ome of the major problems that concern us today – climate change, energy security, migration, international crime, drug-running and people-trafficking – can't be resolved by individual nations. The EU is our best hope of dealing with them in our region of the world.[33]

While Giddens himself has not contributed anything further to structuration theory, there have been significant developments in the theory he crystallized in the 1970s and early 1980s. In *Structuration Theory*,[34] Rob Stones, grounding structuration in the work of both Giddens and Bourdieu, argues that structuration has by now developed as a vibrant, lively tradition in its own right, strengthened and emboldened by critique, counter-critique, diverse empirical applications and synthesis. The work of Chris Bryant and David Jary, drawing together and critically dissecting a legion of theoretical contributions and empirical studies, has played a particularly important role in these developments.[35] Other key figures, in addition to William Sewell Jr,[36] mentioned above, and the seminal contributions of Ira J. Cohen himself,[37] have been Margaret Archer,[38] Nicos Mouzelis[39] and Mustafa Emirbayer and Ann Mische.[40]

There have been a number of key moments in the more recent elaboration of structuration, all of them concerned with conceptual refinement but also much more engaged with issues of empirical application than the early philosophically oriented work of Giddens. Synthesizing much of this work, Stones has argued for a fourfold notion of the cycle of structuration in which one can distinguish between: (1) structures external to a given actor, which act as her conditions of action; (2) the actor's internal, phenomenologically inflected perceptions of the external structures. These 'internal structures', in turn, can be divided into the perception of external structures in the immediate context (conjuncturally specific internal structures) and those enduring and transposable dispositions, capacities and discourses that have been acquired from past contexts (internal structures as habitus); (3) active agency, including a range of aspects, such as creativity, improvisation and innovation, involved when actors draw upon internal structures in producing practical action; and (4) the consequences of action/praxis on external structures, internal structures and events. Each actor-in-focus needs to be situated from the start, following Cohen and Mouzelis, in fields of hierarchically and horizontally organized position–practice relations, which include many other situated and networked actors whose social practices, in turn, are each subject to the fourfold cycle of structuration.

FURTHER READING

Bryant, C. and Jary, D. (1991) 'Coming to terms with Anthony Giddens', in C. Bryant and D. Jary (eds) *Giddens' Theory of Structuration: A Critical Appreciation*, London: Routledge, pp. 1–32.

Cohen, I.J. (1989) *Structuration Theory: Anthony Giddens and the Constitution of Everyday Life*, Basingstoke: Macmillan – now Palgrave Macmillan.

Cohen, I.J. (1990) 'Structuration theory and social order: five issues in brief', in J. Clark, C. Modgil and S. Modgil, *Anthony Giddens: Consensus and Controversy*,

London: Falmer Press, Chapter 4. Reprinted in C. Bryant and D. Jary, *Anthony Giddens: Critical Assessment*, London: Routledge, 1996 selection 40.

Craib, I. (1992) *Anthony Giddens*, London: Routledge.

Giddens, A. (1984) *The Constitution of Society: Outline of the Theory of Structuration*, Cambridge: Polity Press.

Giddens, A. (1990) *The Consequences of Modernity*, Cambridge: Polity Press.

ADDITIONAL FURTHER READING: SECOND EDITION

Archer, M. (1995) *Realist Social Theory: The Morphogenetic Approach*, Cambridge: Cambridge University Press.

Archer, M. (2004) *The Internal Conversation: Mediating Between Structure and Agency*, Cambridge: Cambridge University Press.

Bryant, C. and Jary, D. (2001) *The Contemporary Giddens: Social Theory in a Globalizing Age*, Basingstoke: Palgrave Macmillan.

Emirbayer, M. and Mische, A. (1998) 'What is agency?' *American Journal of Sociology*, **103**(4): 962–1023.

Giddens, A. (1998) *The Third Way: The Renewal of Social Democracy*, Cambridge: Polity Press.

Giddens, A. (1999) *Runaway World: How Globalization is Shaping our Lives*, London: Profile Books.

Giddens, A. and Diamond, P. (eds) (2005) *The New Egalitarianism*, Cambridge: Polity Press.

Giddens, A. (2007) *Europe in the Global Age*, Cambridge: Polity Press.

Giddens, A. (2007) *Over To You, Mr Brown*, Cambridge: Polity Press.

Mouzelis, N. (1991) *Back to Sociological Theory: The Construction of Social Orders*, Basingstoke: Macmillan – now Palgrave Macmillan.

Mouzelis, N. (1995) *Sociological Theory: What Went Wrong? Diagnoses and Remedies*, London: Routledge.

Stones, R. (2005) *Structuration Theory*, Basingstoke: Palgrave Macmillan.

CHAPTER 21

Michael Mann

RALPH SCHROEDER*

Driving Impulses

Michael Mann is best known for his sociological account of the history of human societies, *The Sources of Social Power*. Two volumes have been published so far, volume 1 subtitled *A History of Power from the Beginning to 1760 AD*, and volume 2 *The Rise of Classes and Nation-States, 1760–1914*.[1] The first covers the period from the earliest civilizations up to the American and French Revolutions, and the second up to the First World War. He is currently completing this work, taking the story up to the present day. In terms of scope and ambition, this project rivals the social thought of **Marx** and **Weber**. *The Sources of Social Power* also constitutes one of the very few attempts at a general sociological history of power currently available in the social sciences. Finally, the two volumes put forward a distinctive conceptual apparatus for the analysis of power – the IEMP model – which distinguishes between ideological, economic, military and political power and treats power as a set of 'overlapping and intersecting sociospatial networks'. This model offers a toolkit not just for the periods and places covered in Mann's work, but for sociological analysis in general. In short, Mann provides a comprehensive analysis of the history of human societies and a unique approach to examining power.

Apart from *The Sources of Social Power* and many articles,[2] Mann has recently produced three books, which, even before his third volume, take his sociology into the twentieth century and current affairs. The first is a study of *Fascists*[3] with a comparative historical sociology of the six main fascist regimes. The second, *The Dark Side of Democracy: Explaining Ethnic Cleansing*,[4] is a companion volume insofar as it centrally deals with the murderous consequences of the Nazi regime. But *Dark Side of Democracy* also provides a comparative account of the main other instances of ethnic

* I would like to thank Michael Mann and Rob Stones for helpful comments on this essay, although any mistakes are my responsibility.

cleansing, including the white settler colonial regimes, Armenia, Yugoslavia and Rwanda. His third book, *Incoherent Empire*,[5] analyses America's role in the world today.

In this chapter, I will focus on Mann's conceptual apparatus as laid out in the introduction to the first volume of *The Sources of Social Power*. Apart from this, I will not deal with the bulk of the first two volumes leading up the twentieth century, but rather concentrate on how his work can be used in understanding contemporary social change. This requires a rather major caveat at the outset: Mann has not given us his definitive statement about the twentieth century – backed, as in the first two volumes, by a wealth of comparative historical evidence. Much of what will be covered here therefore represents fragments from a yet-to-be completed picture, based on Mann's forays into particular topics. Still, this may be more useful in comparing Mann's thought to other key thinkers who also address contemporary change – instead of examining earlier periods. This means that this will be a very provisional account of his work.

Before launching in, however, it is worth looking briefly at the background to Mann's thinking. The distinctive thrust of all of Mann's work is that it is impossible to examine power in human societies without analysing the interrelationships between the four separate networks from a long-term historical and comparative perspective. This way of thinking comes from the initial impulse for his grand project; a dissatisfaction with the then dominant school of thought – Marxism[6] – when he embarked on writing *The Sources of Social Power*.

In the late 1960s and 70s, the main debates in sociology (as represented in this book by **Althusser**) revolved around 'historical materialism', the idea that economic forces determined the course of history, and with it the culture or 'consciousness' of different historical periods. One implication was that if sufficient 'consciousness' could be gained about the material forces driving history, this would also reveal the possibility (or impossibility) of being able to change it. This idea now seems very outdated, partly because the pendulum has swung to the other extreme: nowadays, social theory is dominated by social or cultural 'constructionism' or 'constructivism' (represented in this book by **Foucault, Bauman** and others); the idea that culture, not material forces, determines our social life and, in freeing ourselves of this cultural framing, our 'agency' can reshape it.

As we shall see, a key aim of Mann's work is to make *political* power central to sociological analysis, in the place of the Marxist focus on economic power and the recent preoccupation with culture. This has entailed assigning an important – often autonomous role – to the main institution in modern societies, the state. For Mann, this has also meant theorizing the relations *between* states, partly by means of assigning a separate – again, often autonomous – role to military power. Interstate relations and militarism are arenas otherwise almost entirely neglected by sociology. They have been left mainly to the discipline of international relations. Sociology has thus been unable to deal with some of the main issues in contemporary social change; wars and the role of the state in a globalizing era. But, as we shall see, the role of the state in the wider global world is at the centre of Mann's concerns and this concern is likely to continue when he completes the story of *The Sources of Social Power.*

Key Issues

Networks, Organizations and the Four Types of Power

Sociology typically takes individual countries – nation-states – as the unit of analysis. Mann wants to avoid this default position in sociological and political science thinking: not all the types of power are bounded by limits of national borders. His alternative is to focus on the networks of power. The most often cited statement in his writings is that 'societies are constituted by multiple overlapping and intersecting sociospatial *networks* of power'.[7] These networks can be quite different in terms of their spatial reach, from local to global, and they span shorter and longer periods. This allows Mann to track the different sources over space and time; indeed, another of his favourite terms is the 'track laying' of the sources of power.[8]

His second major theoretical argument is that power is never free-floating, it is always contained in organizations. The organization of power takes different forms: it is not just 'distributive', the power of A over B, which is zero sum – the way power is typically conceived (following Marx and Weber). It also 'collective', whereby people cooperate to achieve power over third parties or over nature (a point that Mann takes from **Parsons**), and can therefore grow or expand without being zero sum. Further, power can be either be 'extensive', with great spatial reach, or 'intensive', more tightly organized. And finally, power can be 'authoritative', deliberate and coercive, or 'diffused', arising from similar but not explicitly commanded practices.[9]

With these three distinctions about the *forms* of power in place, Mann can elaborate the four substantive *types* of power of his IEMP model.[10] Ideological power is twofold, sociospatially 'transcendent' or 'immanent morale'. The best examples of 'transcendent' ideologies are the world religions, or political ideologies like socialism and liberalism. 'Immanent morale', on the other hand, is the solidarity of soldiers in battle or protesters in the streets. Hence, Mann can argue that, while 'immanent morale' mainly reinforces existing power organizations, 'transcendent' ideology can be more autonomous and sometimes has the capacity to transform them.

Economic power includes both production and exchange. It consists of the authoritative and intensive organization of labour on one side, and of the diffused and extensive power of market exchange on the other. We can appreciate the difference between the two if we think of how, in tightly bounded work organizations, power is typically organized vertically, with managers or supervisors exercising control over workers, whereas in markets, which are spatially more extensive, the buying and selling of goods is organized along chains of transactions without central or top-down control.

Mann argues that 'classes', groupings of economic power, should not be conceived as operating the same way throughout history. For most of history before the Industrial Revolution, classes were laterally insulated from each other without any shared organization. And even during the Industrial Revolution, when classes did for a time become more tightly organized such that the horizontal links between them as well as vertical relations of exploitation became more pronounced, there were still other power networks, such as religious ideologies and national identities, which cut across classes and prevented lateral organization across borders.

Military power, like ideological power, can be intensive or extensive. In this case, Mann calls the intensive form 'concentrated-coercive' – if we think, for example, of the disciplined ranks of soldiers on the battlefield or in military compounds. But there is also a more extensive form which can reach far in exacting compliance and threaten coercion over distance – even if cannot routinely control populations. Bombing from the air is a good example here, or colonial outposts with much firepower but little manpower. Mann argues, controversially, that even in modern states where military power is formally part of the state, military elites nevertheless retain considerable control over military power, which is thus free from political and, by implication, democratic accountability.

Political power inside a given territory rests in the state, and so is organized in a centre whose power radiates outwards. A second form, apart from the state's internal power, is 'geopolitical diplomacy', which regulates the external relations between states. But it is the conceptualization of the state's – internal – power that constitutes the most well-developed part of Mann's sociology. This type of power, he says,[11] is 'predominantly' authoritative and territorially centralized, but he also develops a fourfold typology of state power based on the distinction between 'despotic' and 'infrastructural' state power.[12] The feudal state, with decentralized 'statelets', had little of either – it could not exercise routine repressive control over a given territory, nor reach deeply down into the population to govern everyday life. Imperial states such as the Chinese empire and European absolutist kingdoms did possess despotic power, the top-down power to coerce, but again, their power did not reach deeply into their subjects' daily lives. Authoritarian states had both: the Nazi and the

Soviet states both coerced their populations *and* they were able to mobilize populations via, for example, party control that penetrated deeply and extensively into the organization of everyday life. And finally, in today's developed societies, states are still able to exercise infrastructural power, the power to organize society on an everyday level and through a myriad of associations, but they lack despotic power.

This contemporary – as he calls it, 'bureaucratic-democratic' – nation-state is curiously stable without the top-down 'despotic' power to coerce. It is also a central feature of postwar developed societies whose emergence needs to be explained. Part of the explanation is that after a turbulent history of wars and authoritarian states in the first half of the twentieth century, the state in developed societies has become rule-bound, diffusing power throughout society, subject to Democratic Party competition, and, among most northern states at least, peaceful. In other words, the state's infrastructural power has been enhanced and enough space has been created for different plural interests to rule – collectively – 'through' the state.

At the same time, the state is not, *pace* most globalization theorists, becoming less powerful: it is still, as we shall see, adding to its regulatory powers and the resources – taxes – it is extracting from society are not diminishing but at most plateauing. Nor, in the manner of Marxist theory and the economic dominance of the ruling class, or in the manner of rational choice and economic theory with its individual maximizing choices, can the state be understood in terms of reducing it to economic interests – as it is an institution and an actor in its own right. The state, as Mann puts it, has become 'polymorphous', 'crystallizing' in different shapes that are able to contain multiple power organizations in a coherent form.[13]

Different power networks overlap in Mann's sociology, and this helps him to explain, for example, a puzzle which other sociologies of developed societies have been unable to cope with; namely, how societies in the developed 'North' can be so stable and peaceful, while, globally, there is so much conflict and economic suffering in which the North is implicated. The Marxist explanation used to point to the class structure of capitalist societies, which needed to exploit the underdeveloped periphery economically to maintain their own cohesion and required violence to do so. This explanation no longer holds, and Mann[14] goes some way in agreeing with Gellner[15] that in democratic societies, legitimacy and social cohesion are maintained by the 'bribery fund' of economic growth rather than by the dominant ideology. At the same time, the North is clearly at least in good part responsible for the disorder and the disparity between wealth and poverty in the 'South', partly because it dominates the world's trade and with it the rules for participation in the world economy. The North has also supplied the South's weapons of mass destruction and – so far, more lethally – its smaller scale cheap weapons supplied to the poorest states (during the Cold War, Gellner used to refer to this as the 'drug pushing' by the two superpowers who wanted to keep their clients happily on their side).

Again, the neo-Marxist explanation for the asymmetrical power between North and South is an economic one; that developed capitalist societies need markets in the periphery to sustain capitalism. Against this, Mann points out that some developing societies are excluded from the North's trade and would dearly like to be exploited more.[16] The discipline of international relations for its part has difficulty explaining this global asymmetry and the flow of weapons since it focuses on the interests of individual states (realists) or their rule-following (liberals). But not all states 'push' arms for the sake of 'realist' interests (economic and ideological interests are involved too), and while some may follow rules, others clearly flout or rewrite them to suit their own aims.

What Mann's sociology points to then is that the military and economic powers of capitalism do not coincide. At the same time, a peaceful international order is unlikely to be produced by military power, which has, among the great powers, become 'high-tech' and devastating and is rarely used for peacekeeping, or by means of diffuse and toothless economic power. Instead, it is geopolitical diplomacy, the political power of stable and strong northern democracies, that is most likely to avert war in many instances. And to avert what are nowadays mostly civil wars in the South, what is needed is not so much market liberalization but strengthened states that have less despotic 'power over', which enables elite predation in 'gatekeeper' states[17] and causes instability, and instead more 'power through' democratic-bureaucratic structures and infrastructures. Again, the contrast with the advocates of globalization as well as the protesters against it, who see the solution and the problem in terms of economic rather than political power, could not be stronger.

Multiple Globalizations

Globalization is a bewilderingly complex topic. However, the IEMP model can cope with this complexity because it recognizes that the different networks of power do not coincide: the networks of power have different chronologies and different reaches, they differ in time and space. And although Mann has not yet analysed this in detail for the twentieth century, he has sketched the networks of power in today's world, on which this section is based.[18]

Today, militarism pits overwhelming American power, the only power with global reach, against multilateral efforts at creating an international order, and against 'weapons of the weak', the inexpensive arms that are abundant in many parts of the developing world and are causing havoc in it. America, with unrivalled air power but little stomach for committing troops on the ground (soldiers' lives in the North, with its Christian legacies, have become 'sacred', unlike in earlier periods and other places), can rain bombs down on people but it cannot pacify them. Nor can America single-handedly restore order in the many civil wars around the globe today, wars that are as frequent today as they have been throughout modern history, although they take place in the South and hardly affect the North except via the mass media.

Economic power divides the world into rich and poor, North and South. The North consists of a well-integrated and regulated capitalism, but capitalism is not singularly American; instead, it consists of at least three northern blocs (North America, Europe and the Asian 'tigers'), in which the USA is at best a first among equals rather than a hegemonic power. In the South, there are two tiers: one is a tier of economies, which Mann says are 'exploited', providing mainly raw materials and subject to loans on terms dictated by the North. A second tier consists of the poorest economies, which Mann calls 'ostracized', and again, he says that most of them, as mentioned earlier, 'would welcome more capitalist exploitation'[19] or integration into the capitalist economy.

Thus, the world economy is not global: only in financial and currency markets do major transnational flows exist, but it is doubtful if these flows confer much power on any particular economic or political institutions. Meanwhile – again, globalizers notwithstanding – trade is still overwhelmingly (80 per cent) within national borders. Furthermore, a point that links economic and political power, although the nation-states' extraction of economic resources (taxes) from its populations may have stalled, there is no sign – whatever politicians may be trumpeting during elections – that the rate of extraction is declining. Instead, the trend seems to be towards convergence on the rates of tax extraction in the developed world.[20]

States – at least in the North – thus continue to control almost half the wealth of nations. Thus, in short, economic power divides the world into two asymmetrical parts, and several regions of political economy within each of these parts. Mann points out that even if there will be more economic integration in the future, more rather than less international regulation will be needed, since a number of problems – the environment, arms proliferation and epidemics are just three – are impossible to deal with without joint state action. And again, it can be mentioned that this is territory sociologists have barely touched – they cannot, since their conceptual apparatus either stops at borders or concentrates on capitalist economic power.[21]

One of the main points that Mann makes about the present era is therefore that the state is not generally losing power: our primary social cages nowadays are nation-states. ('Caging' is another key concept for Mann, referring to the constraints that networks impose – but clearly some cages are more pleasant and leave more room to manoeuvre than others.) States, he points out, are the *only* 'authoritative' political power (whether a European 'superstate' constitutes a possible exception is too early to say). He goes further against the grain of conventional thinking when he argues that globalization continues to take place 'through' states, that is, the relation between states and globalizing processes is not zero sum; instead, layers of denser networks, including the regulations mentioned earlier as well as trade and legal agreements, are being added to transnational and international relations.

This last point ties political to ideological power, since Mann argues that recent transnational social movements with, among others, anti-consumerist and anti-capitalist ideologies also do not supersede state power. Rather, they need to go *through* states to achieve their aims and have been more effective in channelling the actions of states than in changing economic or military relations.

Ideology also relates to political power since, apart from religion, the main belief system in modern times has been the ideology that claims the state for a particular group of people – nationalism. In his recent work, Mann has done much to explain how this ideology has contributed to violence in modern societies as rival groups claim that the state should be ruled by its 'people'. In this context, it is worth pointing out again that, unlike most other sociologists, Mann wants to downplay the role of ideology in contemporary societies: nationalism continues to cause conflict in the South, among states with weak democracies and in which different ethnic groups try to claim the nation. In the North, however, national identity is well institutionalized and no longer gives rise to serious conflict, even if it continues to be the main identity among northern citizens – more important than class and religion.

This does not mean that Mann agrees with the 'end of ideology' thesis: it may be that ideological movements such as the transnational social movements play a part. However, capitalist societies, as mentioned earlier, are not held together by a dominant ideology;[22] there are many contending ideologies in contemporary societies, but very few become organized and mobilized for political contestation. Ideologies are often targeted at shaping the state, but unlike under authoritarian Fascist and Communist regimes (see below), 'bureaucratic-democratic' states must 'compromise' the interests of different ideologically driven organizations and interests.

Globalization therefore consists of several processes, not all pointing in the same direction. As we have seen, the asymmetries in economic power between North and South do not overlap with the asymmetry between US military power and that of the rest of the world. And politically, northern countries in which the state plays a variety of infrastructural roles differ from many states in the South where the state is not only infrastructurally weak, but also lacks a powerful enough container in which parties can articulate the interests of different parts of society in a routine way. Ideologically, the world is complex, but the key differences between other social thinkers and Mann are, first, that he does not want see any one ideology as being pervasive globally (with the possible exception of consumerism), and that ideologies cannot *do* anything unless they are carried in organizational forms.

The State in the Twentieth Century and its Authoritarian Excesses

As we have seen, the modern state, even in the late twentieth century, was not declining. It is responsible for providing an ever more powerful infrastructure, more extensive political representation and also more extensive and deeper citizenship rights. But the state is also responsible for some of the worst atrocities in the twentieth century. Left-wing authoritarian regimes have been analysed extensively, which is partly a reflection of the Cold War preoccupation with 'totalitarian' Communist regimes.[23] Right-wing authoritarian regimes, on the other hand, have been relatively neglected by sociology, partly because the most frequently written about and worst example, Nazi Germany, is regarded as a unique case.

Mann, however, sees both left- and right-wing authoritarian regimes as part of a larger pattern of war and state formation. According to Mann, authoritarian regimes of the Right and Left had some of the same root causes in the period up to the end of Second World War. He calls this period the 'age of class and national mobilization',[24] when the pressures for political representation, which had been building up in the nineteenth century and especially during the mass mobilizations of the First World War, had to be absorbed. In the liberal democratic and social democratic northwest of Europe and in the white settler colonies (including America and Australia), these pressures had already been stably institutionalized in democratic regimes by extending political rights to property owning males – although in the white settler colonies, this was achieved at the cost of ethnically cleansing the non-white pre-colonial populations.[25]

In Europe, made unstable by the First World War, on the other hand, and where these political rights had not had the chance to become institutionalized in democratic regimes, conditions were ripe for authoritarianism. To the instability of war, however, must be added specific conditions for particular forms of authoritarianism. One of these, according to Mann, is that the state had come to be seen as the vehicle on behalf of different moral projects (an idea he takes from Perez-Diaz).[26] On the right, Fascist authoritarians tried to repress class pressures from below and instead to channel a particular conception of 'the people' into a 'pure nation'. At its most extreme, in the Nazi regime, the state was to embody a racial conception of 'the people'.

But apart from pressure from below, we must also add the carriers of these moral projects 'above', or, as he calls them, their 'core constituencies'. Mann departs from the conventional view that economic classes were the main carriers of ideologies. Instead, for right-wing authoritarian regimes, they were 'core constituencies' whose interests coincided closely with the state, including 'soldiers and veterans above all, but also civil servants, teachers and public sector manual workers',[27] as well those living in the traditional heartland of the nation or close to threatened border areas (that is, groups where ethnicity was particularly salient). When the moral project of a racially purer nation became radicalized in conditions of war, it squeezed these 'statist' elites upwards into the tops of their national cages and instigated their suppression or murder of their 'enemies' below or turned them towards outward aggression.

This summary cannot do justice to Mann's detailed account of support for right-wing authoritarian regimes and how they escalated during the interwar period into Fascism. The main point to note here is that the core constituencies of rightist authoritarian regimes had certain elements in common with left-wing authoritarian regimes, 'statists – those socialized in or economically dependent on the state'.[28] The latter, like the former, included those whose interests coincided with the state – teachers, soldiers, bureaucrats and young intellectuals. In this case, however, 'the people' were identified with the 'proletariat'. In its milder and non-authoritarian socialist form, especially in the Nordic countries, this has meant providing a welfare state looking after (all) the people's needs. But in its revolutionary form, arising from the instability of the aftermath of the war in Stalin's Russia, this meant elevating this 'people', conceived of as the 'proletariat' (or the 'peasants' where there was no proletariat, as in China and Cambodia), above other classes, at the extreme killing the classes such as landowners that were in the way of the goal of Communism ('classicide') as well as eliminating political enemies or comrades ('politicide') who were thought to oppose this goal.[29]

As mentioned earlier when discussing the forms of political power, the authoritarian Fascist and Communist states have in common that they combine high infrastructural power with high despotic power; where they differ is in the direction in which they sought to embody their moral project in an 'organic' nation-state. This organic nature of the state meant that certain groups embodied the ideals of the state and others, ethnic or class enemies of rule by 'the people', needed to be cleansed or excluded, at its most extreme by murdering them. This is the 'dark side' of the ongoing process of democratization of contemporary societies.

This 'dark side' also points to one of the most urgent contemporary political problems, the balance between extending democratic rights and avoiding excessive state power. As Dandeker[30] has noted (drawing on Mann's work), if we want the state to guarantee us deeper rights, to empower us, for example by providing more education or health benefits or family services, universally (or for *all* the people), then we must also be prepared to grant the state greater powers, especially access to and control over personal information. But this enhances the state's capacity for surveillance, and may concentrate power in a way that constrains our freedoms.

Mann's labels for the twentieth century thus reveal how he sees the underlying pattern of social change: the first half of the century was the 'age of class and national mobilization' in which the left- and right-wing excesses of 'class' and 'nation' led to the twin disasters of mass killings under Communism and Fascism. The postwar 'age of institutionalized nation-states' means that conflict over class and nation has been stably institutionalized.[31] Again, this is not just a political or ideological development, but a military one: with the defeat of Fascism at the end of Second World War, democracy was imposed on the losers, although a 'Cold' War continued until the Communist path to incorporating 'the people' was also vanquished. Hence the state in the peaceful North has successfully absorbed mass pressures and incorporated them in a polymorphous state that can represent different interests, even though the struggle to represent wider interests more deeply continues to be perhaps *the* most important political dynamic in contemporary northern societies.

Seeing Things Differently

American Militarism

Many see America's role in the world today, and the war in Iraq in particular, as a product of economic imperialism. But *economic* interests are not central to this war or to American military adventures. The Cold War was also regarded as a defence of capitalism, but the standoff between the USA and the Soviet Union should be understood in the first instance neither in economic nor in ideological terms but in terms of military power.[32] After the Soviet Union lost this conflict and America gained military hegemony, it has been tempted to flex its geopolitical and military muscle. But the new international order cannot be explained by reference to a 'clash of civilizations'[33] since, among other things, the USA promotes the self-determination of nations regardless of faith.

If military power – rather than the capitalist interests of 'economic determinism' – is responsible for the recent US-led wars, then democratic change can also curb them. An important point is that the war in Iraq in 2003 and its aftermath was made possible by military power, but it was initiated by a small group within the US government, the neoconservatives in the foreign policy and defence establishments. In this sense, the war was not the product of underlying social forces. The implication, if war is not an inevitable outcome of US imperialism, is that political power – democratic forces – can improve the international order. Mann's penultimate sentence in *Incoherent Empire* urges: 'throw the new militarists out of office'. This view is compatible with the idea that long-term structural change is inescapable, for the final sentence adds: 'Otherwise the world will reduce Americans' powers still further'.[34]

Another point is that Mann's analysis of America's empire lends support to his analytical separation of military power: if the war is the result of a small elite, insulated from the elected government and without regard to active popular support, and made possible by a part of society (military power) whose organization is separate from and out of proportion with other parts of society, then it cannot necessarily be subsumed under political power – democratic-bureaucratic decision-making. Further, and again unlike other analyses, in this case, it is not just that the weight of US military power rests on too weak an economic base – the imperial overstretch thesis[35] – but the incoherence of this empire is also political and ideological: America cannot preach self-determination and engage in occupation at the same time. And its promotion of democracy rings hollow when it undermines multilateral peacemaking efforts, and also uses economic aid and (much more so) military aid to support 'friends' and punish 'enemies' irrespective of whether they suppress their own people.

The task for sociology in this case is to identify the dangers of an international order in which such an overwhelming military capacity is at odds with declining economic and feeble political and ideological power. The excessive reliance on military power is bound to continue to cause much instability and suffering unless it is curbed by democratic forces. But sociologists have, with very few exceptions, ignored military power, and international relations and security specialists do not bring deeper sociostructural analysis to bear on the asymmetries between the different types of power and focus instead on leadership and strategy. Militarism is thus an area where social science disciplines have had least to say and have little to say to each other – although it is most urgent that they do so.

Legacies

Beyond Liberalism and Marxism

I mentioned earlier that Mann is one of the very few theorists to tackle the relations between states. There is a 'liberal' alternative[36] to Mann's critical and left-wing analysis of the global order. Liberalism sees the world as improving with the economic growth of free markets and technological progress. The liberal vision also holds that freedom and democracy are slowly diffusing throughout the world with the spread of a rule-governed liberal international order and deepening 'civil society' institutions. This civil society, consisting of markets and bottom-up associations, provides a counterbalance against the weight of all-too powerful states, thus promoting a pluralistic space with vibrant competing ideals which are, in turn, a precondition for individuals' unfettered – free – development.

Liberalism, however, is a prescription for hope in addition to a social science perspective; it posits that this international order *will* ensure this freedom eventually, but it fails to come to grips with, among other things, the unequal *structure* of economic and military power within and between nation-states – which puts all too many restrictions on access to democratic participation and to the means for individual development in many parts of the world. Liberal social theory also overlooks the fact that there are different types of nation-state cages and thus different political options and developmental paths in different regions of the world, which persist even as capitalist economic relations have marched across the globe. And finally, liberalism puts its faith in markets and a plurality of actors, while Mann, as we have seen, focuses squarely on the capacity of states, and he can also take class into account in terms of economic power, which liberalism neglects.

Another alternative are neo-Marxist ideas about global economic imperialism, but these are difficult to maintain when America's economic power – and thus its power to 'exploit' – has been declining, and its continued consumer spending rests on the willingness of the rest of the world to subsidize it and to be governed by an American-led economic order.

Finally, postcolonial theory (arguably a continuation of Marxist 'critical' theory) posits that, by promoting formerly marginal voices, an inversion of the cultural order can take place.[37] This alternative perspective is more popular in cultural studies than in social science, but it has resonated among social thinkers who focus on the conflict between western identities and the identities of other peoples. Yet it is not clear that ideological or cultural power has played more than an adjunct role in imperialism. And even if ideologies of racial superiority were borne by the 'civilizing' mission of colonial powers, nowadays, apart from lacking the power organizations to carry them, ethnic identity and ideas about 'hybridity' or cosmopolitanism are undercut by nationalist ideology, which posits the self-determination of 'peoples' everywhere.

Again, we see that theories which put their entire weight on economic or cultural factors are unable to cope with the major forces governing the international order – the powers of states and military power. Mann's sociology thus goes to the heart of contemporary relations of power, and, at the same time, like Weber, he is committed first and foremost to value-free enquiry that is based on – and constrained by – empirical evidence.

Beyond Postmodernism and Constructivism

One reason why many might be wary of engaging with Mann's work is because it is often argued nowadays that any attempt to impose a 'grand narrative' on history or on social development is bound to mislead. Curiously, this criticism comes both from a 'relativist' Left and from an 'anti-theoretical' and thus apolitical stance, from postmodern social constructivists[38] as well as from positivists.[39] But shirking a macro-theory is counterproductive, not only for the reason given by Gellner,[40] that if we do not impose an overall view on history, we will be led astray by the implicit view of history, which inevitably creeps into the premises of our epistemologies or our research programmes (we can think of the consequences of focusing on 'rational individual action' here, or of 'anti-foundationalism'). Another reason is that *any* analysis of large-scale historical patterns or processes of social change will require a theory or concepts that can guide our enquiry, and the existence of such patterns and processes can hardly be denied on *a priori* empirical – or epistemological – grounds.

It might also be tempting to see Mann as a neo-Marxist with his focus on 'reducing' social processes to power. This is mistaken not only because the types of power are irreducibly autonomous ('primacy' in relation to history generally may be impossible, but it is possible to make 'period-specific generalizations'),[41] but also because the 'master narrative', insofar as there is one for the modern period, is not about class and economic power, but about the democratization of the nation-state. This democratization has taken place both from 'below', as when different classes pressed for citizenship rights from the French and American revolutions onwards, as well as from 'above', when ruling classes had to reward ever-wider social groups with deepening citizenship rights[42] for participation in the aftermath of wars of mass mobilization (after the First World War), or when Fascist regimes, based on a racial conception of citizenship and the state, were defeated geopolitically and other conceptions triumphed (after the Second).

A major overall pattern of modernity is thus the drive to democratize our political cage, the nation-state. This is primarily driven from below, by classes, not in the economic sense but when the political demands that are made on them (tax, conscription) push them to struggle for rights.[43] But this pressure must also be put into the context of the response from 'above' – the scope that ruling classes have for accommodating people 'in' the state.[44] In short, if anything, this is a politics, or state-centred view of modern history, although Mann insists that all four sources are needed to explain social change.

The notion that power 'cages' people follows from Mann's organizational conception of power, and it points to the constraints that social relations have over us, instead of the more fashionable approaches in social science that focus on agency and individual choices. His master narrative also, however, points to the place where social change is most open to reshaping and contestation – again, the state. And again, this viewpoint goes against the grain of the political apathy that is thought to increasingly pervade northern democracies, but going against the grain of the self-images of the age should perhaps also be a function of social science.

Unfinished Business

It would be premature, in the twentieth century, to criticize Mann's account of *The Sources of Social Power* since he has only presented parts of this picture (even though this chapter has focused on these parts). Most of the critics who have engaged with his work have focused on the two volumes of *The Sources of Social Power* and have sought mainly to refine his ideas rather than reject them.[45] Mann has drawn the harshest criticism from Laitin[46] over his link between democracy and ethnic cleansing, but this debate hinges immediately on more fundamental debates about the nature of social scientific explanation.[47]

Here I want to mention only one problem that seems to me to be fundamental, which is his treatment of ideology and culture. The common criticism here is that Mann does not pay enough attention to this source of power.[48] This is not my criticism; it seems to me that in contemporary social thought all too much attention is paid to culture or to people's beliefs.

The problem is partly terminological. Mann says he is not partial to using either 'culture' or 'ideology'; both transcend everyday and empirical experience and provide symbolic meaning and power. The use of both or either is fine, but this conception seems to leave no room to distinguish between ideological or cultural power that has an effect on larger historical changes – which, as we have seen, ideologies or cultures can do when they transcend other sources of power (as in the case of world religions) or imbue them with an immanent morale boost (in the case, for example, of troops) – as against ideology (or perhaps better at this point to say culture) that does *not* have such macro-effects and mainly provides coherence to local, everyday or individual lives. This is not to say that the role of culture in more circumscribed, intimate and private situations is less important generally, but such a separation might acknowledge that there is a gulf between *effective* ideology and culture and the rest, and thus also acknowledge that ideology and culture have to a large extent retreated from the role they once had in premodern society.[49]

So, for example, the role of the media has arguably been a major change in twentieth-century society, but this falls into two parts: the mediation of politics, which has no doubt played a major role in political change, and the growing consumption of media in everyday life, which consists of leisure and nothing more. Mann has recognized this shortcoming and now adds 'institutionalized' ideology to the 'transcendental' and 'immanent' forms.[50] Although these institutionalized ideologies offer a 'vision of a better society', there is a 'recognition that progress lies through compromise and pragmatism'. But this still confuses ideologies that promote political change with those that are simply a way of life – 'culture' in the anthropological sense.

This leaves another criticism related to ideology, which is that, in my view,[51] science is separate from both ideology and culture, in principle and as a source of power. As a source of power, the scientific revolution may have been, as Mann argues, part of the ideological networks of its time.[52] But its effect was quite different from the other sources, creating not only a cumulative body of knowledge, which transcends all ideologies, but also a more extensive range of technological artefacts, which allow us to intervene more powerfully in the environment. Thus conceived, it is possible to assign to science and technology a critical role in the industrial take-off of the West in the nineteenth century – a leap in enhancing collective power – that would be impossible to understand if they were subsumed under culture or ideology.

Apart from this role, science and technology have also created a 'cage' of knowledge that constrains us in what we can 'officially' believe, for example, and technology has extended the human footprint, putting strains on our environmental resources. This failure to distinguish science and technology will become even more important in the twenty-first century, with its massive infrastructures of transport, communication and energy and scaling up of research into a major global enterprise. Perhaps it is possible to subsume science and technology under 'culture', but in that case, it must be a part of culture that is different in kind from the rest of culture. In any case, it is difficult to see how this source of power can be ignored as an autonomous one from the nineteenth century onwards. Finally, with regard to environmental transformation, science and technology provide potential solutions (as well as creating new problems) beyond those that may be achieved by means of political will and economic growth, and so may be vital when we think about our future prospects.

Still, this is a complaint that touches only one part of Mann's social theory. The core of his sociology, his account of state formation and analysis of the relations between states on a global level, is unparalleled in contemporary sociology, and makes him – on the macro-level of relations of power – an indispensable thinker for the twenty-first century.

FURTHER READING

Mann's IEMP model is laid out in the first chapter of his *The Sources of Social Power* vol.1 (1986), but for the reader who is new to Mann's writings, it may be useful to start with the essay 'Globalizations', available on a link from his webpage (see below, n.d.). Otherwise, the reader may wish to go directly to the part of Mann's work that is relevant to their own interests, whether this is further back in history, more contemporary (as in his book on contemporary American empire), or in a particular area such as nationalism, world religions, or ethnic cleansing. Commentary on Mann's work can be found in the volume edited by Hall and Schroeder (2006).

Hall, J. A. and Schroeder, R. (eds) (2006) *An Anatomy of Power: The Social Theory of Michael Mann*, Cambridge: Cambridge University Press.

Mann, M. n.d. 'Globalizations: an introduction to the spatial and structural networks of globality', http://www.sscnet.ucla.edu/04F/soc191f-1/globalizations.pdf.

Mann, M. (1986) *The Sources of Social Power*, vol. I: *A History of Power from the Beginning to 1760 AD*, Cambridge: Cambridge University Press.

CHAPTER 22

Arlie Russell Hochschild

SIMON J. WILLIAMS

What is emotional labour, what do we do when we manage emotion, and what are the costs and benefits of doing so in public and private life? These and many other pertinent sociological questions have been centrally addressed by Arlie Russell Hochschild over the years in her pioneering work on the commercialization of human feeling and the gender division of emotional labour. In doing so, she has effectively pioneered a whole new way of seeing the world, one which not only places human feeling at the heart of the sociological enterprise, but also provides a profound critique of the problems of authenticity and estrangement in late capitalist society. It is to these central, albeit neglected, sociological issues that this chapter is devoted.

Driving Impulses

Like all key thinkers, the inspiration for Hochschild's work comes from a complex fusion of personal biography, intellectual exposure and scholarly apprenticeship. In her particular case, this stemmed – as she duly acknowledges in the Preface to *The Managed Heart*[1] – from the time her parents joined the US Foreign Service. At the tender age of 11, Hochschild found herself plunged into a world of diplomatic smiles and strategic emotional exchanges. Afterwards, she would listen attentively to her parents interpreting these gestures: gestures conveying information not simply from person to person, but from nation to nation, state to state.

As a graduate student at Berkeley some years later, Hochschild found herself captivated by another intellectual source, namely, the sociological writings of C. Wright Mills, especially his chapter in *White Collar* entitled 'The great salesroom'.[2] Mills's sociological deliberations on the self-estrangement of goods' sellers in advanced capitalist society caused her to reflect on whether this particular type of labour might, in fact, be part of a distinctly patterned, yet invisible, emotional system – one comprising individual acts of 'emotional work', 'feeling rules' and a great variety of embodied exchanges between people in private and public life.[3] These questions soon led Hochschild to **Erving Goffman**'s[4] work on the insincere art of impression management and the vicissitudes of self-presentation in everyday life. This, coupled with Freud's insights into the 'signal function' of human emotions,[5] prompted her to explore the idea that emotion functions as a messenger from the self; an agent that gives us an instant report on the connection between what we are seeing and what we expect to see, telling us in the process, what we feel ready to do about it.[6]

These ideas were developing when Hochschild went out into the field, in the late 1970s and early 1980s, in order to try and 'get behind' the eyes of flight attendants and bill collectors, as each moved through their work-a-day world. The more she saw and listened, the more she came to appreciate the dilemmas of emotion management in advanced capitalist society and the loss of authenticity this involves. It is to a fuller exposition of these central sociological themes, and the insights they afford concerning the place of emotions in contemporary social life, that we now turn in the next section of this chapter.

Key Issues

Straddling the Biology–Society Divide

A defining hallmark of Hochschild's work on emotions is the manner in which she is able to straddle, in a way that so many sociological accounts in the past have failed to do, the biology–society divide. In contrast to 'organismic' or 'social constructionist' models of emotions – models that prioritize the biological and the social respectively – Hochschild adopts instead an approach that sits in the analytical space between these two extremes.[7] For Hochschild, emotion is unique among the senses, being related not only to *action* but also to *cognition*. Emotions emerge when bodily sensations are joined with what we see or imagine – forged on the template of prior expectations – and it is on this basis that we discover our own particular view of the world and our readiness to act within it.[8]

In taking this interactional stance, Hochschild joins three intellectual currents. First, drawing on Dewey,[9] Gerth and Mills,[10] and Goffman[11] within the interactionist tradition, she explores what gets 'done' to emotions and how feelings are permeable to what gets done to them. Second, from Darwin,[12] within the organismic tradition, she is able to posit a sense of what is there, impermeable, to be 'done to' (that is, a biologically given sense, which in turn, is related to an orientation to action). Finally, through Freud's[13] work on the 'signal' function of anxiety, she is able to complete the circle working backwards from the organismic to the interactionist tradition, by tracing the way in which social factors influence what we expect and thus what these feelings actually 'signify'.[14]

In advancing this model, Hochschild's interactionist approach to emotions is a lesson to us all on the role of the biological in social explanation. For far too long now, any mention of biology has raised the spectre, in sociological minds, of crude or vulgar 'reductionism'. Yet as Hochschild rightly argues, while a sociology of emotions clearly needs to 'go beyond' the biological, this does not necessarily mean 'leaving it out altogether'. Reciprocally, incorporating the biological into social explanation does not, in fact, necessitate an overly deterministic role for the latter. Indeed, while any adequate inquiry into the sociology of emotions must confront the 'limits of the social', it nonetheless remains the case that human biology, far from being fixed and immutable, displays a high degree of plasticity in relation to broader sociocultural influences. Seen in these terms, feelings are not stored 'inside' us, as the organismic theorists would have it. Rather, in a more sophisticated interactionist model, the management of feeling may contribute to the very creation of it. In this way, Hochschild builds up a subtle and sophisticated view of human emotions, thereby effectively sidestepping the either/or (biology/society) debates of the past.

Feeling Rules and Emotion Management

Leading directly on from this first point is a second core feature of Hochschild's work, namely her ability to shuttle back and forth, in fruitful ways, between the private realm of 'personal troubles' and broader 'public issues' of social structure. In this respect, Hochschild's work is an illustration, par excellence, of what C. Wright Mills has elsewhere termed *The Sociological Imagination*.[15]

Through the concept of 'emotion management', Hochschild is able to inspect the relationship between emotional experience, feeling rules and ideology. As she explains, feeling rules are the side of ideology that deals with emotions: standards that determine what is 'rightly owed and owing in the currency of feeling'.[16] Emotion management, in contrast, is the type of work it takes to cope with these feeling rules. From this perspective, acts of emotion management are not simply private acts, rather they are used in exchanges under the 'guidance' of public feeling rules. Feeling rules, in effect, give 'social pattern' to our acts of emotion management; patterns that may be more or less equal, depending on the distribution of power and authority within any given society.

What happens, then, when there is a *transmutation* of the private ways we use feelings for commercial purposes? Answers to this question, for Hochschild, run very deep indeed, providing as they do a stunning indictment of the 'managed heart' in advanced capitalist societies. These issues, as Hochschild shows, are clearly illustrated in her empirical sociological study of flight attendants. While all of us must confront the requirements of emotional labour in some shape, sense or form, the dilemmas of the flight attendant are particularly acute in this respect. Forced to wear their 'company hearts' on their sleeve and to publicly peddle the corporate image through a pretty, continually smiling face; *'the emotional style of offering the service becomes part of the service itself'*.[17] Drawing on Goffman's earlier work on the vicissitudes of impression management, Hochschild makes a useful distinction here between what she terms 'surface' and 'deep' acting. In surface acting, we try to change how we outwardly appear through the manipulation of our body language. Deep acting, in contrast, requires a taking over of the 'levers of feeling production' in order to actually alter what we feel, for example the suppression of anger and its replacement with sympathy. It is this latter strategy of deep acting that concerns Hochschild most. To 'work on' a feeling or emotion, as she explains, is the same as to 'manage' an emotion or to do 'deep acting'. Emotion work can be done by the 'self upon the self', by the 'self upon others' or by 'others upon oneself'.[18] Whatever the result, it is the effort rather than the *outcome*, and the *context* within which this occurs, which matters. Emotion management, in short, may be an honourable theatrical art or a perilous capitalist enterprise.

In particular, Hochschild identifies three specific stances that workers may take towards their work, each with its own sort of risk. In the first, the worker identifies too wholeheartedly with the job, unable to develop appropriate depersonalizing strategies, and therefore is more likely to suffer stress and burnout. In the second, the worker clearly distinguishes between herself and her job and is less likely to suffer burnout. She may, however, blame herself for making this very distinction and denigrate herself as 'just an actor, not sincere'. In the third strategy, the worker distinguishes herself, like the second, from the act, but does not blame herself for doing so and sees the job as positively requiring the capacity to act. For this actor, however, there is, as Hochschild stresses, some risk of estrangement from acting altogether, and indeed some cynicism about it: 'We're just illusion makers.'[19]

If, in the first stance, the worker is too much present in the role, then in the third, the problem is wholly reversed. In all three, however, the essential dilemma remains, namely, 'how to adjust one's self to the role in a way that allows some flow of self into the role but minimizes the stress the role puts on the self'.[20] In each, this problem is aggravated by the lack of control the worker exerts over the conditions of work itself. As Hochschild explains, the less the influence the worker has, the more likely it is that one of two things will happen: 'Either she will over-extend herself and burn out, or she will remove herself from the job and feel bad about it.'[21]

In highlighting these emotional dilemmas of the 'managed heart', Hochschild's study points to the more general sociological point that human feeling, in late capitalist society, has become increasingly 'commoditized', thereby linking the public and private worlds through the domain of emotions. As she states:

> When deep gestures of exchange enter the market sector and are bought and sold as an aspect of labour power, feelings are commoditized. When the manager gives the company his [*sic*] enthusiastic faith, when the airline stewardess gives her passengers her psyched-up but quasi-genuine reassuring warmth, what is sold as an aspect of labour power is deep acting.[22]

Gender and Class Patterns to Emotion Work

Underpinning these issues is a third key characteristic of Hochschild's work, namely her central preoccupation with issues of gender and class. In general, as she argues, lower class and working-class people tend to work more with things, and middle-class and upper-class people tend to work more with people. This division, in turn, is overlaid by the fact that more women than men deal with people as a job – males, for example, comprise only 15 per cent of flight attendants. Thus, there are both gender- and class-related patterns to the civic and commercial use of human feelings; public patterns with private emotional costs.

This intersection of gender, class and emotions is, perhaps, most fully brought out in *The Second Shift*,[23] an empirical study of working parents and the so-called 'revolution' at home. A deeply personal, compassionate view of couples struggling to find the time and energy for jobs, children and marriage, Hochschild identifies what she sees to be a major division in gender ideology between a 'traditional ideal' of caring and another more 'egalitarian ideal'. Indeed, as she shows, a split between these two ideals seemed to run not only between social classes, but also between partners within marriages and between 'two contending voices inside the same conscience'.[24]

At the time of Hochschild's first interviews, only 18 per cent of wives were married to men who shared the second shift. Most of the rest, for a variety of reasons, did not press their husbands to change. Given these tensions and dilemmas, women usually pursued several strategies over time; first being a 'supermom', then cutting back on her hours at home, precipitating a crisis, and then either cutting back on her hours at work or further limiting her work time at home. In doing so, wives often needed to do a great deal of emotion work in order constantly to sustain the ideology or myth that the relationship was indeed 'a good one'. Within these strategies, resentment and cynicism frequently resurfaced in different areas of the relationship; emotional costs borne by husbands as well as wives.

In highlighting these gender-related issues, Hochschild is able to show how the revolution at home has influenced women faster than it has influenced men. The unevenness of this revolution has thus driven a wedge, at the present time, between husbands and wives; the home, in effect, becomes the 'shock absorber' of contradictory pressures from the outside world. Seen in these terms, women's emotion work – whether cast in terms of 'denial' or 'intuitive genius' – is often all that stands between the 'stalled (feminist) revolution on the one hand, and (a deluge of) broken marriages on the other'.[25]

Methodology and the Study of Emotions

Perhaps the fourth salient feature of Hochschild's work concerns her methodological stance on the study of emotions in social life. Within the sociology of emotions, debates continue to rage over positivism versus anti-positivism, quantitative versus qualitative methods, prediction versus description, and managing versus accounting for emotions.[26] While some sociologists, emulating the model of the natural sciences, see emotions as more or less objective phenomena that lend themselves to measurement, prediction and control, others, in contrast, stress the more subjective aspects of emotions, including forms of emotional feeling, identity and selfhood. Kemper,[27] for example, in a positivist vein, argues that social structures (power and status) give rise to specific emotions – at least modally – and that a sociology of emotions must incorporate the physiological underpinnings of emotional response. In contrast, writers such as Denzin[28] assert a vigorous anti-positivist stance, resisting efforts to quantify emotions and focusing instead on self-feeling as an ongoing structure of lived experience, including the phenomenal body and the inner moral meaning of this feeling for the self that feels the feeling.

Enough has already been said here to place Hochschild's work firmly within this latter, more qualitative or 'naturalistic' tradition of sociological research. While meta-emotional concepts such as emotion management techniques may indeed lend themselves to basic frequency counts according to factors such as class and gender,[29] Hochschild's commitment is, first and foremost, to a qualitative, anti-positivist, view of the (emotional) world. This is clearly evident, not simply in her interactional theory of emotions (described above), but also in her preferred choice of methods with which to study these issues empirically. *The Managed Heart*, for example, combines a variety of qualitative methods including observation, interviews, attendance at training sessions and so on, using flight attendants and bill collectors – 'the toe and heel of capitalism' – to illustrate two extremes of occupational demand on feeling. Similarly, *The Second Shift* involved intensive interviews with 50 couples, together with observational work in a dozen homes, using couples such as Nancy and Evan Holt, Ann and Robert Myerson, Barbara and John Livingstone, to bring the study 'to life' in an emotionally illuminating way. In doing so, Hochschild offers us deep insights into the rich, complex and contradictory nature of emotional life and gender relations in late twentieth-century society; insights lost though sole reliance on large-scale surveys and other forms of quantitative assessment devoid of qualitative context and content.

The Search for Authenticity

A fifth characteristic of Hochschild's work, one which underpins many of the previous themes and issues, is her moral stance and humanistic concern for the fate of emotions in contemporary social life. This is perhaps most clearly evident in her concern with problems of 'authenticity' and 'estrangement' in advanced capitalist society. *The Managed Heart*, for example, is replete with references to the 'human costs' of emotional labour, from 'burnout' to feeling 'phony', 'cynicism' to 'emotional deadness', 'guilt' to 'self-blame'; costs which could, she suggests, be reduced if workers felt a greater sense of control over the conditions of their working lives.

As Hochschild observes, the more our activities as individual emotion managers are managed by organizations, the more we tend to celebrate the life of 'unmanaged feeling'.[30] In this way, Hochschild, in true Goffmanesque style, champions the little ways in which the self resists the institutional pull of commoditized emotional exchange, from the circumvention of feeling rules to the wider cultural concern with so-called 'spontaneous', 'natural' or 'authentic' feeling – a development manifest in the growing popularization of 'psy' therapies, which add a new 'introspective twist' to the self-help movement begun in the last century.[31]

Yet it is precisely here, as Hochschild points out, that a central paradox emerges, namely that the more we attempt to 'get in touch with' or 'recover' our 'true feelings', the more we make feeling itself subject to command, manipulation and various forms of management.[32] In this respect, Hochschild's concern with issues of authenticity – including the inauthenticity of the search for authenticity itself – ultimately translates into a Rousseauesque concern with the noble savage. What, in this day and age, makes Rousseau's noble savage seem so noble, Hochschild argues, was his ability to feel what he felt spontaneously, unfettered by any (conventionalized or commercialized) feeling rules. He did not, in other words, 'let himself feel good', 'get in touch' with, or 'into', his emotions. Rather, what distinguishes him from his latter-day pop therapy admirers is the utter absence of any calculation, will or conscious ratiocination:[33] a truly spontaneous form of spontaneity, a deeply authentic form of authenticity, which Hochschild, like Rousseau himself, (romantically?) longs for. Seen in these terms, Hochschild's work provides a profound Rousseauesque critique of the human condition in late twentieth-century capitalist society; one which calls not simply for a practical politics of worker control, but an existential reclaiming of authentic self-feeling and a championing of the 'unmanaged heart'.

Seeing Things Differently

As I have already suggested, one of the major strengths of Hochschild's work lies in her ability to transcend many traditional boundaries and divisions within the social sciences. In this respect, like the sociology of emotions itself, her work has relevance to a broad range of issues, from organizational theory[34] through to recent work on gender and intimacy.[35] However, perhaps the area where her work has had the most personal impact on me is in the sociology of health and illness.

Hochschild's emotion management perspective has been readily translated into studies of the emotional division of labour in healthcare, particularly nursing,[36] and constitutes a rich new seam of research within the sociology of health and illness. Most importantly for me, however, alongside critical explorations of the emotional sides of health and illness,[37] including the experience of pain and suffering,[38] it has contributed to a whole new way of viewing social inequalities in health and the social causes of disease.

How, for example, does society affect the health of its members? How do the social and economic conditions in which you find yourself affect the likelihood of your suffering from mental and physical illness? What role do emotions play in the social patterning of disease? Following Freund's[39] pioneering work in this area – one which builds on the sociological insights of Goffman and Hochschild – it is possible to explore these questions more fully through a critical exploration of the interrelationship between social status, social control, emotion work and bodily states, including those that may contribute to health and disease.

For Freund, differing modes of emotional being are, in effect, different ways of feeling empowered or disempowered. These feelings of empowerment or disempowerment are, in turn, very much linked to people's material and social conditions of existence. Having one's feelings ignored or, perhaps even worse, termed irrational – what Hochschild[40] terms the absence of 'status-shields' to protect the self – is so fundamental that it is analogous to people questioning your very sense experience ('you must have imagined it'). Less powerful people face a 'structurally in-built handicap' here. Their confidence is undermined from the start when it comes to trying to manage social and emotional information and this handicap may, in turn, contribute to 'dramaturgical stress', existential fear and neurophysiological perturbation. Emotional being, social agency and structural context are therefore inextricably related, and it is this cluster that physically and emotionally seeps into the body in a range of different ways.

> *Somatic*
>
> *Somatic pertains to the cells and tissues of the body as opposed to the (reproductive) germ line. The stress of the emotion work required of a working-class woman in her daily life, for example, could lead to an overproduction of adrenalin that could, in turn, lead – slowly but surely – to damaging changes in the cells of the body. Such somatic mutations are not passed on to children, as somatic cells are non-reproductive.*

In particular, Freund argues that social relationships may engender a form of 'schizokinesis', in which a split arises between what is consciously shown and experienced, as opposed to what occurs **somatically**. It is clear that emotional and other kinds of distress alter physiological reactivity. Stress can cause neurohormonally related functions, such as blood pressure, to markedly increase even while this is not consciously experienced. Here Freund poses two extremely pertinent sociological questions. First: Just how 'deep' can the social construction of feelings go? and second: Do certain forms of emotion work leave their scars on an 'unconsciously knowing body'? The answer to the first question seems to be 'very deep indeed': society affects physiological reactivity deep within the recesses of the human body. In answering the second question, Freund's concept of schizokinesis certainly implies that the conscious mind can be damagingly unaware of the body's response. Freund notes that our position in a social hierarchy, especially if it is a less powerful one, can be a strong factor in the shaping of our emotions. There is a tendency to internalize the emotional definitions that others impose on what we are or 'should' be. The physiological aspects of such processes are of interest to those studying emotions. However, these physical aspects may also be seen as examples of ways in which social controls are sedimented and fixed in the psychosoma of the person. Physiological aspects of social activity can also act as a form of feedback that colours the tone of existence. This feedback can *indirectly* serve social control functions. For instance, conditions that create depression construct an emotional mode of being where the motivation to resist is blunted.[41]

The argument here is for a subtle and sophisticated form of 'socialized' (that is, externally 'pliable') biology rather than a reductionist sociobiology; one which accords emotional modes of being a central role in linking the health and illness of the embodied social agent to the wider structures of power and domination, civilization and control in society. In these and many other ways, the sociology of health and illness is proving a particularly fertile terrain upon which to fashion these newly evolving debates about emotions in social life.

Let me briefly, however, mention another key way in which Hochschild's work feeds into my own current sociological research on sleep. This may sound like an odd topic for sociologists to study, but sleep is far from an asocial, non-social or anti-social event. How we sleep, when we sleep, where we sleep, what meanings we make of sleep, and with whom we sleep are all important sociological matters. Sleep is also closely bound up with the doing of gender, emotion, intimacy and family life. There is indeed much 'hidden' emotion work, on both self and others, that goes into the management of sleep on a daily or nightly basis. In going to bed, for example, prior to sleep, we may mull over the emotional issues of the day or share intimate moments with our loved ones. Putting children to bed, or comforting them in the night, also of course involves a lot of hidden emotion work. Relations between sleep management and emotion management, moreover, flow both ways. If I am anxious, worried or frightened, for example, I am unlikely to be able to sleep. Reciprocally, if I do not sleep well, then I am more likely to be moody, irritable, if not downright bad-tempered. Sleep management and emotion management, then, as this suggests, are intimate bedfellows. Like the sociology of emotion, moreover, a sociology of sleep sheds important new light on the world around us, helping us to see things differently. [42]

Legacies and Unfinished Business

Legacies are often talked about posthumously. In Hochschild's particular case, however, they are thankfully both active and ongoing. Perhaps Hochschild's major contribution in this respect has been the manner in which, through her pioneering sociological work on the 'fate' of emotions in contemporary society, she has enabled us precisely to 'see' the world differently; a view as relevant to sociological practitioners themselves, as emotionally embodied agents, as it is to those they seek to study. Seen in this new, corporeally expressive light, it is emotions that inform our particular view of the world, emotions that suffuse our sense of selfhood and identity, emotions that bind members of society together, emotions that underpin our (intimate) embodied relations with others, emotions that are bought and sold in the capitalist marketplace. These insights, in turn, have been augmented and carried forward in Hochschild's more recent work, which takes a more global look at the fate of love and care in the late/postmodern era.[43] With respect to global care chains, for example, Hochschild shows how such chains connect three sets of workers – one caring for the migrants' children back home, the second caring for children of the woman who cares for the migrants' children, and a third, the migrating mother herself, who cares for the children of professionals in the first world. 'Poorer women', in other words, 'raise children for wealthier women while still poorer – or older or more rural – women raise their children'.[44] As for the different models of care evident in the US today, Hochschild delineates four main types: the *traditional model*, represented by the image of the homemaker mother; the *postmodern model*, represented by the working mother 'who does it all' with little or no help from any quarter; the *cold modern model*, represented by impersonal institutional care for the very young and old alike; and the *warm modern model*, comprising a mixture of institutional care as well as private care for the young and the elderly. Each of these, Hochschild stresses, provides a model of 'what care is', 'who should give it' and 'how much is "good enough"'.[45] In these and other ways, then, in characteristic fashion, Hochschild continues to shed important light on what is happening to love and care 'in everyday life under global capitalism'.[46]

Despite these important legacies, however, Hochschild's work is not without its critics. Not only is her analysis disappointing from a comparative historical perspective – one which reveals that 'emotion management' has, in fact, been going on for millennia – it is also limited in focusing simply on contemporary commercial constraints and operating with a problematic private/public distinction. As Wouters states, from an **Eliasian** perspective:

> Developments in standards of behaviour and feeling do not stop at the borders of either public or private life; to live up to them signifies overall demands on emotion economy, an overall pattern of self-regulation, a sort of 'overall design of emotion management'. Hochschild only deals with the process of commercialization in this century. In the more remote past she apparently visualizes a more ideal society. But such an ideal society never existed. Emotion management was never a private act, nor were rules for feeling ever only privately negotiated.[47]

Over the past 100 years, emotional exchange has become more varied and more open to idiosyncratic nuances. What Wouters refers to as a process of *informalization* can, therefore, be interpreted as a 'reversal' of a long-term trend, while being a 'continuation' as far as demands on the economy of affect and the management of drives and emotions are concerned. From this viewpoint, only stronger, more even, all-rounded self-restraints allow for a greater sensitivity and flexibility of social conduct.[48] These observations highlight the importance of comparative historical perspectives on emotion, Eliasian or otherwise.[49]

Other potential problems, however, are also evident in Hochschild's account. Barbalet notes,[50] for example, that her sociology of emotions is at one and the same time a critique of commercialization. But in this very account, Hochschild 'forgets a central aspect of emotion', which, in Barbalet's view, 'ultimately undermines' the particular critique of commercialization Hochschild provides: the importance, that is, of emotional agency. Not only is the assumption of the deleterious consequences of emotional labour problematic on this count – emotional labourers may be no more likely than other workers to experience emotional exhaustion or burnout and may indeed be more satisfied with their jobs – but emotion management, contra Hochschild, does not produce an 'object' that is a 'finished emotion'. Rather, it generates a 'stage in a process': 'Endeavours to manage an emotion lead to emotions which are reactions to the purported managed emotion. One emotion leads to another.'[51] Hochschild, nevetheless, avoids this conclusion through her supposition of a 'cognitive or cultural management of emotion'. Emotions, in short, are both 'object' and 'agent': 'Persons have feelings about their feelings.'[52]

Hochschild's own particular take or stance on the problem of 'authenticity' has also come in for criticism. Duncombe and Marsden,[53] for example, in their work on the 'doing' of intimacy in heterosexual coupledom, highlight the need to distinguish more clearly between so-called 'real' underlying feelings – which Hochschild continues to describe as 'authentic' – and individuals' sense of authenticity in relation to the core self and identity they have developed through their earlier experiences. Lacking any independent guide to truly 'authentic' emotional behaviour, we have to accept, Duncombe and Marsden argue, that some individuals derive their sense of authenticity from 'core selves' and 'core identities', which various social, cultural and psychoanalytic commentators might wish to criticize as deeply 'inauthentic'.[54]

These, to be sure, are important points. Few would disagree, nevertheless, that Hochschild's contribution to the sociology of emotions has been immense, helping spawn a whole new area of study. If the hallmark of the sociological imagination is indeed, as C.Wright Mills would have it,[55] the ability to link personal troubles to broader public issues of social structure, then Hochschild's work is an exemplar of precisely this sentiment and sensibility. Her more recent work on the fate of love and care, moreover, provides a potent and poignant reminder of the 'referred pain of unfettered global capitalism itself'.[56]

All in all, then, this suggests an exciting and challenging future for the sociology of emotions, keying in as it does to a number of critical issues and debates within sociological theory and contemporary culture, not least the emotional costs and consequences of global capitalism. Perhaps, like Hochschild herself, exposure to these sociological issues will help readers to 'see things differently' and to interpret, in a new emotional light, the smiles and expressive gestures they now see around them at eye level.

FURTHER READING

Bendelow, G. and Williams S.J. (eds) (1998) *Emotions in Social Life: Critical Themes and Contemporary Issues*, London: Routledge. A useful collection of original essays on the sociology of emotions, including chapters by Hochschild, Denzin, Duncombe and Marsden, Freund, Williams and Bendelow, and Wouters.

Fineman, S. (ed.) (2000) *Emotion in Organizations* (2nd edn) London: Sage. An updated version of the first edition, which includes a useful 'Emotional arenas revisted' opening chapter by Fineman and many interesting chapters on various aspects of emotion in organizations, including emotion metaphors of management in China; commodifying the emotionally intelligent; emotional labour and authenticity; morality and emotion in police work; and children's emotion management in schools.

Hochschild, A.R. (1983) *The Managed Heart: The Commercialization of Human Feeling*, California: University of California Press. A shorter version of her emotion management perspective can be found in A.R. Hochschild (1979) 'Emotion work, feeling rules and social structure', *American Journal of Sociology*, 85: 551–75.

Hochschild, A.R. (2003) *The Commercialization of Intimate Life: Notes from Home and Work*, Berkeley, CA: University of California Press. A stimulating collection of Hochschild's essays, both old and new, including 'Working on feeling', 'The economy of gratitude', 'The commercial spirit and the abduction of feminism', 'Emotional geography and the flight plan of capitalism' and 'The culture of politics: Traditonal, postmodern, cold modern and warm modern ideals of care'.

Stearns, P. (1994) *American Cool: Constructing a Twentieth Century American Style*, New York: New York University Press. For an interesting account of the historical and cultural construction of emotions, juxtaposing the Victorian era with contemporary America.

Williams, S.J. (2005) *Sleep and Society: Sociological Ventures into the (Un)known*, London: Routledge. A useful introduction to the sociological world of sleep and its intimate links to issues of embodiment, emotion, work and family life.

CHAPTER 23

Zygmunt Bauman

TONY BLACKSHAW

Driving Impulses

It makes little sense to ask who is *the* key sociological thinker – any number might seem to fit the bill if we are considering the sociologists who appear in this book – but there is little doubt in my mind as to who has the strongest claim to being unique. Zygmunt Bauman is that unlikely key sociological thinker who realized his hidden gifts as a result of the structuration of a succession of contingencies. As this observation suggests, this holds out the possibility that there has been more than one Zygmunt Bauman. In fact, there have been two: mark one, a quite ordinary Marxist revisionist sociologist, who died a slow death; and a second, mark two version – *the* Zygmunt Bauman – who, at the backend of a long haul of an academic career in the 1980s, suddenly recognized the story he had been repeating had run out of disguises, and what he did was start over again, but this time he wanted to make his own way of seeing the world rather than rely on someone else's vision.

Think of Saavedra Cervantes' *Don Quixote* and think of Zygmunt Bauman. From the moment of his reincarnation, he was not the kind of sociologist who was ever going to be content sitting in his rocking chair bemoaning the dullness of his *La Manche*. On the contrary, he suddenly clapped a barber's basin on his head, clambered onto the back of his faithful old plough horse and ventured forth to do great deeds.[1] This *Don Quixote* figure was to become *the* Zygmunt Bauman, no longer encumbered by Marx and now the star of his own show: the ardently stubborn and ingeniously singular developer of new ideas, and proselytizer of some of the more established ones, whose sociology was to become the fruit of his own mastermind.

To draw on an another analogy, this time from the great Argentine writer Jorge Luis Borges, Bauman was reminiscent of an ordinary member of a primitive tribe who, out of the blue, started making strange noises and in the thick of things started waving his arms about revealing some new-fangled ritual. His outlandish actions prompted his fellow tribesmen to gather round him and take a look. At first, they got fed up with his outlandishness and wandered off, but after a while they became spellbound until the ritual finished, and then took it on as a part of their tribal culture.[2]

Indeed, since the late 1980s, Zygmunt Bauman has been living the life of the hero to the letter; that is what Cervantes taught him. In the process, he has not only been consistent in weaving his own special brand of magic but has also captivated the imagination of sociology and become its brightest light, its professor of professors. To paraphrase that most attentive observer of Borgesian analogies, the literary critic John Bayley, it is because Bauman is sociology's sovereign that he has no need to be modish, nor part of any school of thought. Yet, neither is he sufficiently detached from the discursive formation known as sociology to invent a wholly individual perspective; his attraction – just like his self-motivated responsibility to his vocation – is something communal, as the Borges analogy suggests, as is the shareability of something incredible, which has radically altered our ways and means of thinking sociologically.

Key Issues

The Break with Marxism

Like several other sociologists who made their mark in the second half of the twentieth century, Bauman began his sociological career with Marxism. This was not unsurprising since the ethical basis of his sociology was from the start unambiguous and simple, epitomized in **Karl Marx**'s observation that: 'The philosophers so far have only interpreted the world in various ways; the point [of sociology] is to change it'.[3] However, in common with a number of other Marxist sociologists, he ended up becoming disillusioned with the grey in grey of its revisionism. As he recalls in a recent interview, for all the conceptual sophistication that Marxism had gained by the 1960s and 70s, it remained thoroughly 'economistic, and in most cases severely reductionist',[4] and its trademark brand of still trying to fit 'the working class' into the make-believe thematic of the soon-to-be-realized worker's paradise simply did not work anymore.

As I have pointed out elsewhere, by the 1980s Bauman had become exasperated with the 'productionist', 'workerist' and 'masculinist' orientation of Marxist revisionism, which in its various manifestations continued to emphasize *similarity* rather than *difference*, *fixity* rather than *contingency*; incongruities that were now constantly being undermined and disrupted by a modern world that had become stubbornly insistent on change and by individual men and women no longer prepared to settle for a circumscribed life.[5]

As Bauman saw it, the Marxist bubble was, by the 1980s, at bursting point because its protagonists could not get their *collective* heads around the increasingly *individualized* climatic conditions of ordinary men and women's day-to-day existences in advanced capitalism.

Unlike most other key post-Marxist thinkers whose alternative blueprints emerged in sociology and other leftist curricula during the 1980s, however, Bauman's disillusionment with Marxism was also a product of his life experiences of living with actually existing Communism. Born into a family of Jewish origin in Poznan, Poland in 1925, Bauman could have been a character in a twentieth-century novel by Borges, an epic charting the peak and decline of the 'solid' stage of modernity, that is, modernity's initial phase, what Ulrich Beck has called the 'first modernity'. As Keith Tester has pointed out, by the 'time he was twenty, Bauman had confronted anti-Semitism, Stalinism, Nazism and warfare'[6] and, despite fighting for his country against the Nazis during the Second World War, was expelled from the army in 1953 during an anti-Semitic purge. In 1968 he was also sacked from his professorship at Warsaw University and expatriated from his country during another purge of Jews from positions of power in Polish society. Bauman was now an exile who might have lost his first home, but he chose not to wander for long and found a new home in Leeds, where he became professor of sociology at the city's university at the turn of the 1970s.

The story of Bauman's biography is common to that of other intellectuals who came of age in Eastern Europe during the Second World War but his is also a Polish-Jewish story that is particular to him (and his family) and there can be no doubting that his driving impulses have their genesis in his own personal circumstances. Indeed, the point that his social identity is Jewish, Polish, British, socialist, professorial and the rest means that the contingency of his own subjectivity is couched to be crucial in a particular way, which is unique to him, and which adds to our understanding of his sociology. Yet the irony was that Bauman himself did not really consent to the full implications of these personal biographical circumstances entering his work – outwardly at least – until the genesis of his mark two alter ego. But, from that point onwards, the sociology clearly embodies **Max Weber**'s idea of sociology's 'value relevance' – the acknowledgement that a person's own world-view and values affect the questions that preoccupy her or him. But, in a way not dissimilar to a growing number of contemporary theorists touched by feminism or postmodernism, Bauman takes Weber's 'value relevance' much further, grounding it in his own embodied life positionings and experiences. To paraphrase that most incisive cultural Marxist thinker, Antonio Gramsci, Bauman had by now recognized that the starting point of his own new 'critical elaboration' of the world would be wrapped up in the consciousness of who he himself was as a product of the historical process to date, which had sedimented in him 'an infinity of traces, without leaving an inventory'. And it was through his sociology that Bauman mark two took up Gramsci's challenge that he should compile such an inventory.

From Legislating to Interpreting

Bauman was also now in a position to reread orthodox Marxism as a modern legislating theory underpinned by a naive determinism that led its key proponents down the road of believing they could explain everything in a uniform way. By the 1980s, he recognized that he had not only run out of disguises for Marxism, but that he had to abandon it because it was the only way that he could move his own ideas forward. In this respect, Bauman was by now arguing that the role of sociologists is to interpret rather than to legislate.[7] The legislative impulse is one of the distinguishing features of sociology as a product of modernity and a model of modern intellectual thought. According to Bauman, with the emergence of modernity, science replaced the subjective wisdom of God as the arbiter of truth. What this meant for the new discipline of sociology as *the* 'science of society' was that its superior knowledge could be determined objectively by universally agreed procedural rules, which in turn guaranteed the attainment of truth, obtained 'valid moral judgement' and gave it a universal authority.

As his earlier work had suggested, sociology as a legislative vocation found its fullest expression in 'Durksonian' functionalism,[8] a hybrid incorporating the sociologies of **Emile Durkheim** and **Talcott Parsons**. For Bauman, the problem with Durkheimian sociology is that it understands society *sui generis*, as merely shaped by objective 'facts' external to individuals that need to be explained with recourse to other objective 'facts' . However, by now, Bauman recognized that Marxism, too, by and large, not content with positing its own valuable contributions to sociology, tended to organize its ideas around grand, unified schemas, which tried to explain everything, contrary to the growing recognition that, by the 1980s, most people's faith in grand theory had collapsed and there was no longer any room for big ideas.[9] In the cruel way of fate, this meant the emotionally cold legislating project known as 'science' had also exhausted its use value in Bauman's eyes. But it wasn't enough to merely divorce sociology from science, since Bauman mark two recognized that what it needed was, on the one hand, a new mode of interpretation and, on the other, a new style of exposition. What this meant in a nutshell was that sociology now needed a double conjugal life: a marriage to **hermeneutics** and to literature.

Hermeneutics

Hermeneutics refers to the science and art of interpretation. Originally used in relation to the interpretation of religious texts, it is also used widely in literary studies and in sociology. Anthony Giddens, *for example, refers to structuration theory as 'a hermeneutically informed social theory'. By this he means that in order to produce meaningful research, sociologists need to understand both their own world-view and the world-views of those they are researching. The thoughts, words and actions of both researcher and researched must be interpreted through an understanding of their cultural and social contexts. A commitment to hermeneutics and interpretation typically involves a moral determination to make respect for the intrinsic value of human beings count for something in the ways in which both sociology and social life are carried out. It is important to keep this in mind when considering Bauman's distinction between the* legislators *of modernity and the* interpreters *of post- and/or liquid modernity. Tony Blackshaw emphasizes Bauman's desire not only to develop a hermeneutic approach to social phenomena, but also to make sure that this hermeneutic approach is itself grounded in the sociological imagination; an imagination that he is keen to expand and enrich.*

Sociological hermeneutics recognizes that the world as an *object* of investigation is in fact the globality made up of a countless number of worlds, cultures and communities, which, as a result of the historical process to date, appear to each other as at once familiar but also fascinatingly 'other'. If what makes this kind of sociology hermeneutic is its cosmopolitan goal of trying to establish effective channels of communication between these different worlds, cultures and communities by whatever inventive means it has at its disposal, what makes it more conventionally sociological is its ongoing commitment to 'deploying the strategy of systematic, rational discourse to the task of constructing a theoretical model of [that global world] as a system in its own right'.[10]

In making sociology hermeneutic, Bauman mark two was giving sociology an alternative 'interpreter' role, suggesting that, contrary to the attitude to doxa embedded in the scientific world-view (in which instrumental goals are underpinned by knowledge that is thought with but not about), the doxas of different cultures need to be laid bare and engaged with by sociology. It takes another culture to know another culture as well as a strong dose of empathy; the watchword for his sociological hermeneutics was to become the following:

> there is more to what you see and hear than meets the eye, that the most important part is hidden from view, and that there is a huge and dense tissue of inter-human connections below the visible tip of the iceberg. An insight that triggers imagination that, if worked on properly, sediments sociology.[11]

That the wedding ceremony was a double event meant that Bauman was now developing a sociological hermeneutics (as opposed to just a hermeneutic sociology), which also dripped creative prose, reading like a greatest hits anthology of European literature: a touch of Hesse, a taste of Balzac, a nod to Beckett, visits especially to Borges, Calvino, Kundera, Musil and Perec: the great writers whose words unravel through philosophy, politics, psychoanalysis, history and the rest – all now central to his intellectual armoury for grappling with the existential density of the human experience; where people are at, how they make sense of and live their lives.

For a sociologist less than a hero, there would have been more than enough here to make the heart of sociology start beating in a new way, but there was one more major intellectual driving impulse that would make a massive impact on Bauman's work. This came to the forefront in sociology just when he was most disillusioned with Marxism; its name was 'postmodernism' and it provided another fertile seedbed for his reinvigorated sociological imagination.

Postmodernism and Culture: Contingency and Ambivalence

Bauman's reading had always cast its net much more broadly than sociology but in the 1980s he observed that radicals in fields as diverse as architecture, historiography and philosophy were creating their own styles of intellectual exposition within postmodernism. Not only that but they were using these formulations to dismember some of the putative ideals that had prevailed in their disciplines since the Enlightenment. What fascinated Bauman was that postmodernism seemed to be transforming these disciplines into something radically different by, on the one hand, moving them away from science and more closely to art and, on the other, breaking down assumed barriers between 'higher' and 'lower' forms of culture. They did the latter by paying keen attention to the quotidian of new and alternative sociocultural developments while celebrating their plurality in the process.

What these observations also taught him was to recognize the *contingency* of culture. That is, while there are many ways of being-in-the-world, all humans share the meaning of what it means to be human – in other words, all human beings have the sense of an inevitable, universal relation but with contingency attached to the cultural form it will take. It was this key insight of the convergence of the contingent and the inevitable that alerted Bauman to the *ambivalence* of human being-in-the-world. This also sowed the seeds for his exemplary study of ***Modernity and the Holocaust***,[12] whose underlying theme was that the moral universe of modernity is not so much mapped by good and evil but by people's inability to deal with *contingency* and *ambivalence*.

Modernity and the Holocaust

In his Amalfi prizewinning book, Modernity and the Holocaust, *Bauman argued against the view that the Holocaust can be understood as an aberrant return to an uncouth barbarity rooted in the prejudices of pre-modern traditions, a peculiar deviation from the onward march of the civilizing process of modernity. On the contrary, he argued, the industrial form and scale of killing represented by the Holocaust was actually* made possible by *modernity. Modernity provided the conditions of possibility for the Holocaust. These conditions included, on the one hand, the modernist ideology of social engineering, the belief that societies could be moulded to fit someone's ideal* vision of how they should be. *Bauman used the metaphors of surgery and gardening to emphasize the implications of such ideologies for less powerful groups of people who didn't fit into such visions. They became the diseased parts to be cut out, the weeds to be eradicated, in pursuit of the vision of the healthy body, the manicured lawn. The radical anti-Semitism of the Nazi type was quintessentially modern in this respect. On the other hand, the capability to translate the ideological vision into reality was provided by the existence of a huge and efficient bureaucratic apparatus and the policies of a powerful, centralized state. All this was, in turn, facilitated further by the social suppression of moral responsibility brought about by the creation of a social and moral distance between the ideologically stigmatized victims and the bureaucrats and state officials focused on rational technical considerations as to how most efficiently to get the job done. All these factors, says Bauman, are ever-present in modernity: 'only the combination of factors is unusual and rare, not the factors that are combined'.*[13]

If much of the rest of the 1980s saw him trying to come to terms with the implications of contingency and ambivalence for sociology, what was also now more noticeable than any late emerging manner was the quickening and variety of his output. He was on a quest for his own vision and his exploded imagination needed a larger canvas; and it was an intellectual amalgam of social philosophy, hermeneutics, cultural studies, literature, poststructuralism and postmodernism that increasingly came to influence him.

From Modernity and Postmodernity to Solid Modernity and Liquid Modernity

As the late Edward Said once said, it is often the case that known authors are read according to a given interpretation, and when that happens, it often results in misunderstanding where they are coming from. And so it has been with Zygmunt Bauman. He has often been called a postmodernist. This is wrong. He may have a liking for some unreliable narrators, but his sociology is unfashionably solid and it runs counter to the ironic and trendy playfulness of postmodernism. As that most astute Bauman scholar Keith Tester[14] has pointed out:

When Bauman took up discussion about the postmodern, inevitably he shifted the context of the word. He took the aesthetics of postmodern*ism* and turned it, instead, into an inspiration and competent part of a sociology of postmodernity. In these terms, postmodern*ism* is about aesthetics and artistic production, whereas postmodernity 'refers to a distinct quality of intellectual climate, to a distinctly new meta-cultural stance, to a distinct self-awareness of the era'.[15]

The problem was that if postmodernism only had a chiming resemblance to Bauman's sociology of postmodernity, it nonetheless felt like he had spotted a niche in the sociology market, wedged himself into it with enormous energy and talent, and then found it virtually impossible to wriggle out again. By the mid-1990s, however, postmodernism had lost its magnesium flare fame in sociology and at the same time Bauman was trying to come to terms with the fact that its ostensibly dead intellectual hand was always finding ways to poke its fingers into his attempts to move the debates about modernity and postmodernity onto another level. Consequently, he decided to replace these 'negative' concepts with the more 'positive' concepts of solid modernity and liquid modernity.

The critical moment of this parallax was the publication of *Liquid Modernity*[16] in which, to use a film analogy, Bauman offered a *Full Montyish* exposition of industrial decline and personal renewal. In other words, he provided sociology with an alternative to the modernity/postmodernity dualism. This was an alternative that brought to attention the redundancy of a modernity focused on 'heavy' and 'solid' hardware with its largely 'predictable and therefore manageable' habitat. This has been replaced with a more 'light' and 'liquid' software-focused modernity, altogether more underpatterned and underdetermined than its predecessor. It is rhizomatic rather than rooted, its trains of experience are busy with unremitting new arrivals and speedy departures, and unexpected diversions, derailments and cancellations replace the secure tracks that once sustained it in its formative years.

On Rethinking Sociology for Liquid Modern Times

Writing in 1989, Bauman said that what is most wrong with sociology is that it continues to try to make sense of 'society' with the concepts that have been around since its inception, without recognizing that the trouble with these concepts is that most of them do not work as well as they once did.[17] His argument was that sociology is an anachronism with deep roots in the nineteenth century. It is an approach redolent of a world that has gone; the trouble is that sociology is not sufficiently aware that this sense of belonging to another time and place pervades its analyses. In other words, Bauman's point was that if *society* is still said to exist in the form suggested in the worn-out concepts that still fill the heads of sociologists, its members – the ordinary men and women of the *sociality* – by and large have no idea that they belong to it. It is unrecognizable to them.

If, some 16 years later, it is perhaps unfair to still call sociology 'nineteenth centuryish', it is not inaccurate to say that not only is it not heroic, but that it still operates with the conceit that there is nothing within its conceptual and methodological lexicons that needs to be surrendered to posterity. My point is that if sociology's *doxa* (the way it does what it does) was founded in its formative years, this endowment still maintains a kind of constitutional status, despite infusions of theoretical insights from a wide range of perspectives. In other words, sociology has become complacent and unimaginative, and it begs the question as to whether or not it is equipped to deal with the major social, cultural, economic and political changes that have, in the past twenty or so years, been so widespread and overwhelming. The upshot is that dated concepts in sociology – class, community, gender, 'race', society, youth and so on and so on – are now unaccompanied by actual social phenomena and new social phenomena are unaccompanied by appropriate concepts. Even some of those more imaginative sociologists, like Ulrich Beck, who have taken it upon themselves to question the self-deception of sociology's tacitly taken-for-granted conceptual lexicon and cognitive frames, have in the main not managed to come up with anything alternative other than making the point that its concepts have become zombie categories caught between death and life.[18]

Bauman knows of course that liquid modern lives are not completely free of their social class, gender and ethnic statuses, but he knows that by now these markers of identity and difference flow into each other more than they did once upon a time in the not too distant past. He also knows that today they have a more in-between, DIY, ready-made feel about them, to the extent that they are much more like individualized existences. Yet in dealing with these lives, sociology lacks the variegation, the collision of the quotidian and the conceptual found in Bauman's own sociology.

Of the range of means Bauman has for giving himself something to say, his use of juxtaposition and ideal-typical analysis have proved to be most effective. However, it is in the intensity of feeling as much as the assiduous thought that marks out his sociology as distinct from the orthodoxy, which, if it has its own brisk efficiency, is too held back, too coolly distanced. I am not for a moment suggesting that the sociological mainstream lacks anything in its concern for the continuing social inequities and injustices of the world that were, and always have been, its *raison d'être*, but I am arguing that it doesn't *feel* these in the way that Bauman's sociology does. And in refusing to allow the liquid worlds it analyses to touch it, to move it, and to animate it, sociology may well itself have fossilized into a zombie category.

The lesson that Bauman teaches sociology is that by trying to remain sociological in the same way that the founding fathers were sociological, it is merely preserving theories and concepts from the past, of which it has built up a considerable archive. In Bauman's own work, we are encouraged to think sociologically in fresh ways about the world we inhabit. We are encouraged to do this through the poetic manoeuvre of *ostranenie*, 'to produce a semantic shift which makes the habitual appear strangely unfamiliar, rather as though it were being perceived for the first time'.[19] Bauman's sociology unashamedly confronts the detachment associated with orthodox sociology in its cold pursuit of the past by interpolating passages of everyday life with the personal input of the sociologist. It is to atmosphere he turns and what brings atmosphere to his writing is metaphor.

Metaphor is the rhetorical tool that Bauman uses to enable him to *defamiliarize the familiar* and show it in a new light. And it is to hermeneutics that he turns in order to develop his own conversing tradition of *ostranenie*. In other words, Bauman recognizes that metaphor is that part of language that allows him to do hermeneutics. And it is to metaphors and the metaphoric process rather than merely analogy that he turns in order to maximize his own 'talent for speaking differently' about the worlds he makes in his sociology.[20] Bauman recognizes that metaphoricity is of vital importance for developing alternative sociological ways of seeing in the world, by providing the basis for 'new language games', in Lyotard's meaning.[21]

Seeing Things Differently

What should be patently obvious to the reader by now is that Bauman provided my own discovery of perspective and he gave me a kind of sociology I could think with. Accordingly, in my book *Leisure Life*,[22] I make full use of metaphor as well as a number of other key Bauman themes – all of which have been discussed in this chapter. The thesis is developed through a hermeneutic sociological approach to make knowable the leisure life-world of a group of working-class 'lads' with whom I had grown up. This meant that the study was about their leisure life-world, my leisure life-world, but also *our* leisure life-world. Consequently, as a researcher, I occupied a strange dual position in 'the lads'' universe – Tony Blackshaw as an insider and Tony Blackshaw the sociologist as an outsider on the inside. I used this special position to not only make sense of how the lads live their leisure lives, but also to allow the reader to know how they and we *feel* that collective experience, individually together.

The crux of my thesis is that the lads may not live in *solid modernity* but their consciousness as a collective still dwells there and the universe that is their leisure life-world, experienced collectively, is framed by a *solid modern* discourse, or so it seems. Even though the wider world they *individually* inhabit has become *liquid modern*, in their leisure lives, the lads are still animated by their belief in an older imagined community, which is perceived as the cornerstone of their shared masculine working-class existence. There is a warmth, a particular feeling of home about this leisure life-world, which offers the lads a protective cocoon where they are 'naturally' safeguarded from the uncertainties of liquid modern change. They close the shutters of their mutual home and the models of themselves they produce within it, guarding against the loss of its credibility. They maintain the intricate cogs of their modernist masculinity, prevent its parts from being damaged or lost. The leisure life-world enables them to keep their ready-made narratives alive in their collective memory, their own private gallery, which is the legacy of their youth.

My central argument is that this shared leisure life-world is given depth by a shared passion for a particular kind of solid modern world that is now missing. Sometimes, this world is resurrected proudly and determinedly, celebrated in nights out, but at others, and perhaps a good deal of the time, this world is invoked merely as a force of habit or to unload the private burdens of the increasingly individualized consciences that populate liquid modernity. Thus, Stout finds solace from individualized loneliness in the imagined community of the lads, while Sean escapes his frustration at the imposed communitarian demands of a Catholic family life he cannot believe in through this same alternative community. The book charts the lads' intermittent forays into Leeds city centre on Friday and Saturday nights, which constitute a memorable vindication of this missing world. Nights out with the lads tend to spin themselves out into a familiar web which feels like one of those reunions famous rock bands have when the group get back together after playing with other people. When the lads are on stage together once again it feels great and everything just clicks into place. They drink their beer faster than is good for them and conversation moves from subject to subject. They finish each other's sentences and communicate, more remarkably, without speaking at all. With a real affinity, and in the spirit of the communion that exists between them, they use gestures known only to them. They drink and they drink. As the evening moves on, they feel themselves become fully one, the leisure life-world's machinations are in fine fettle. However, on these nights out, the lads do not so much relive their youth as create, through their leisure, its unheroic aftermath. In truth, the leisure life-world has, to use the rock band analogy once again, been turned into a sort of heritage museum for ageing lads, which in recent years has, in some ways, become more a duty than a pleasure and whose nagging subliminal power reverberates only on the edges of individual lives lived in the main elsewhere. They desire the solidly modern leisure life, but they can no longer capture it.

Outside the leisure life-world, resignation and disillusionment are the nearest things the lads have to freedom. In the fluidity of liquid modernity, they have to watch powerless as the Other invades uninvited into their existential and material realms: women controlling their bedrooms and telling them what to do, women and black people taking their jobs, buying their houses, taking over their shops and their schools. But in the leisure life-world, the lads are in control. Here the features of the Other begin to elongate and liquefy, swell and then resolidify, like Sartre's *le visqueux*, they are transformed into the lads' own DIY, custom-made creations. Take, for example, women, who can never exist as cheerful subjects of their own lives in the leisure life-world, but are instead constituted by the lads as 'birds', 'slags' and 'fanny' living 'solidly' modern lives, excluded from this discourse which imputes identities to them, ready-made. That these characterizations are not 'real' is neither here nor there, the lads simply have to be convinced that they are. What is important for the lads is the meaning for them of these characterizations as their version of truth, which is something that enables them to form what they recognize as the world when they are at leisure together. Like the Jewish race in Bauman's *Modernity and the Holocaust*, 'real' women have to be wiped out from the lads' solid modern story in which they have no place, excluded from the leisure world that has created them. These characterizations of the Other become symbols of subjugation, power and knowledge, the luscious fruit of a *solid* leisure life lived in a solid version of truth. The 'universal' truth of the rationality that divides the lads and Others into two categories: us and them, same and Other.

In the leisure life-world, the lads have the best of both worlds: they have their myth and are able to relativize it as a *contingent* leisure experience, which has its own mono-logic. Indeed, the modus operandi of the leisure time the lads spend together always presumes this form of closure: the confirmation of hegemonic masculinity and the restoration of disrupted stability, which provide intimations of a past world of communal bliss in a protected time space in which the leisure life-world attempts to impose the fixity of a masculinist, working-class myth on to the ostensible fluidity of contemporary everyday life.

Yet the lads' apparently granite authenticity isn't all that it seems. In common with other liquid modern men and women, they find it difficult to remain authentic for long because they simply have too many other choices in their lives. The lads know that the weekend experience of this life-world is just a leisure break; they understand this and are resigned to their fate. In the event, it is only because of its own impossibility that the leisure life-world is possible at all. The lads may be figures carved in the past, but their identities are maintained in the present and, in common with other liquid modern men and women, they are *individuals* first and all the rest after. In the words of Bauman, it is this observation that represents the 'irreparable and irredeemable ambivalence' of the leisure life-world of the lads.

Legacies and Unfinished Business

Bauman's detractors tend to be of the orthodoxy, and if they are not a passionate lot, they do tend to make the same obsessive and pedestrian objection to his sociology: Why has Bauman moved from sociology's concern with the *reality* of the lives of *real* men and women to the *fictionality* of human lives *imagined*, or at the very least to a generalized rather than an empirically contextualized commentary about the quotidian? However, the attentive reader, who has closely followed the constant and often pained development of Bauman's adventure (I call it an adventure because his work has the feeling of a magical quest rather than a project as such), will have noticed the moral thread that runs through it, and might pose this question rather differently: Why should we care if Bauman chooses to deal with fact or fiction, or whether or not his sociology is generalized, when its point is to help change the world for the better, for humanity?

As I have shown above, despite their obvious lack of empirical detail, Bauman's books are always prompted by life as it is lived: something seen, something heard. Their narrative threads come from elsewhere, too; from his thoughts, interests and preoccupations. With Bauman, we are rather nudged into a fresh way of thinking sociologically about the world we inhabit. And the result is more compelling than any empirical study could offer. Bauman is not attempting to depict unembroidered truth in the pages of his books but, rather, an imaginative, but critical, exploration of everyday life and the day-to-day-doings with which ordinary men and women are confronted in liquid modernity. His critical imagination is combined with an atmosphere of ironic detachment. Developing this kind of sociology also means that Bauman is not only content to not know everything about the already existing reality, but also that he is in a strong position to dwell on ethical issues and debates about what it means today to live a moral life.

An existential narrative weaves its way through Bauman's more recent books, which sees him dealing with the day-to-day business of human encounters, not just sociologically but psychoanalytically. In this regard, let us briefly consider the argument in one of his recent books, *Identity*, which suggests that liquid modern living is just as much about trying to escape our inevitable loneliness as it is about trying to escape community obligations and relationships deemed no longer to be satisfying and fulfilling.[23] As Barbara Ellen – a newspaper columnist in the *Observer* whom Bauman admires and regularly consults in making his own existential commentaries – recently put it: the true irony and loneliness of the human experience is that 'even something as shared as a relationship is inevitably experienced alone'.[24] Beyond this, however, Bauman's ethical brilliance is in obdurately exhorting a kind of orientation to the Other that he takes from Levinas and brings into the heart of sociology. Despite the inevitability of loneliness, he insists, it is through the mundane simplicities of human kindness that men and women have the potential to build some constancy into their lives. It is the selfless opening out to the Other that can bring them closer together.

Bauman is the ethical sociologist par excellence, who, in the vein of J.M. Coetzee's returning protagonist Elizabeth Costello, uses the term *human kindness* in its most comprehensive sense, by not only insisting on our feelings, our empathy, our solidarity, our *kindness* for others – as Bauman puts it, revalorizing the wisdom of the ages, 'loving others as you love yourself'[25] – but also our acceptance that for all our cultural differences as human beings we have a responsibility for each other because we are after all one of a *kind*.[26] In insisting on our *human kindness*, Bauman is suggesting that human faces come before everything else. As he points out in his book *Postmodern Ethics*, faces are the first we see of each other.[27] And in looking into the face of the other, we are reminded that we are engaged in a human encounter, person to person, that comes with the face.

Bauman's 'moral message' can be summarized in the following way: by loving others as they love themselves *and* actively taking responsibility for this responsibility, human beings might not be able to escape from the inevitability of their individual loneliness, but they will be able to pull themselves together in such a way that if it brings some constancy to their individual lives, it will also bring them autonomy and freedom (freedom de facto rather than freedom *de jure*) as well as the opportunity to enjoy the joys of their mutual human kindness. Bauman is the sociologist-as-man-of-action and in his writings, the moral and the magical are always interconnected, may well be the same thing. At 80 years of age, his ability to ignite the sociological imagination remains undiminished, and not only that, he continues to be somebody with a marvellously acute sense of how contemporary life is lived. Indeed, his is the only sociology I know of that comes close to depicting in its pages what the complexity of the contemporary world looks *and* feels like. Bauman's work is sociology at its best. It recognizes that the everyday world, as it is lived just then, is always out of its reach, but that this should not prevent it from trying its best to make its subjects live again as well as to excite interest in their lives. It puts the meanings and what it understands about that world into discourse in ways that are convincing, responsible and ethical.

To sum up his sociology would be to say that Bauman is the only key sociological thinker to create a literary sociological hermeneutics. His sociology achieves in its pages something real and specific, something we know to have taken place, but in the process of putting it into discourse, it transcends the particulars of the what, where and who of the lives it depicts. Bauman is the master craftsman in his own particular sort of sociological magic, but his appeal is to the sociological sixth sense in all of us – that special way of seeing, whose doxa we cannot precisely put into words, but which provides us with a unique window onto the world. Some in sociology want to turn him into an ism or a brand. Like all the best brands, Bauman boasts a unique flavour. His sociology is made to the measure of the here and the now – the time he captures so evocatively in the metaphor of liquid modernity.

FURTHER READING

There is a rapidly increasing literature on Bauman and the following are the best of the introductions.

Beilharz, P. (2000) *Zygmunt Bauman: Dialectic of Modernity*, London: Sage.
Beilharz, P. (ed.) (2002) *Zygmunt Bauman, Sage Masters of Modern Social Thought*, London: Sage.
Blackshaw, T. (2005) *Zygmunt Bauman*, Abingdon: Routledge.
Tester, K. (2004) *The Social Thought of Zygmunt Bauman*, Basingstoke: Palgrave Macmillan.
Smith, D. (1999) *Zygmunt Bauman: Prophet of Postmodernity*, Cambridge: Polity Press.

See also:
Theory, Culture and Society (1998) 'Explorations in critical social science: special section on Zygmunt Bauman', **15**(1) February.
Polish Sociological Review (2006) 'Special edition on Zygmunt Bauman', 3, March.
Kilminster, R. and Varcoe, I. (eds) (1996) *Culture, Modernity and Revolution: Essays in Honour of Zygmunt Bauman*, London: Routledge.

Notes

Introduction

1. T. Blackshaw, Zygmunt Bauman, in *KST2e*, p. 372.
2. See the glossary box *Voluntarist and relativist*, in the chapter on Weber, pp. 65, which deals with the status of knowledge claims.
3. B. Jessop, 'Karl Marx', in R. Stones (ed.) *Key Sociological Thinkers*, Basingstoke: Palgrave Macmillan, 1998, p. 22.
4. See W. Pope, 'Emile Durkheim', in *Key Sociological Thinkers* (2nd edn, henceforth *KST2e*), Basingstoke: Palgrave Macmillan, 2008, pp. 75–6.
5. Z. Bauman, *Liquid Modernity*, Cambridge: Polity Press, 2000; and T. Blackshaw, 'Zygmunt Bauman' in *KST2e*, pp. 370–3.
6. P. Wagner, *A Sociology of Modernity: Liberty and Discipline*, London: Routledge, 1994.
7. R. Schroeder, 'Michael Mann', in *KST2e*, pp. 343–4.
8. Ibid. R. Schroeder, p. 340.
9. On this latter point also see J. Urry, *Sociology Beyond Societies: Mobilities for the Twenty-First Century*, London: Routledge, 2000.
10. F. Jameson, 'Postmodernism: or the cultural logic of late capitalism', *New Left Review*, **146**: 53–92, 1984; F. Jameson, 'Postmodernism and the consumer society' in H. Foster (ed.) *Postmodern Culture*, London: Pluto Press, 1985; F. Jameson, *Postmodernism, or, Cultural Logic of Late Capitalism*, Durham, NC: Duke University Press, 1991; J.-F. Lyotard, *The Postmodern Condition: A Report on Knowledge*, trans. G. Bennington and B. Massumi, Manchester: Manchester University Press. 1979/84; D. Harvey, *The Condition of Postmodernity: An Enquiry into the Origins of Social Change*, Oxford: Blackwell, 1989; J. Baudrillard, *Simulations*, trans. P. Foss, P. Patton and P. Bleitchman, New York: Semiotext(e), 1983; J. Baudrillard, *Baudrillard Live: Selected Interviews* (ed. M. Gane) London: Routledge, 1993. Also see the references for Giddens and Habermas in the relevant chapters of this volume.
11. James Fulcher and John Scott provide the following brief and clear synopsis of post-Fordism: 'The diversification of products, frequent changes of style, and a more aesthetic approach to design made the techniques of mass production with its emphasis on cheap, standard, and functional products [i.e Fordism], less appropriate. Production was reorganized to meet the requirements of quality, diversity, innovation,

and change. This involved the interrelated changes in the organization of work, personnel policies, and industrial relations, which have been described as post-Fordism. Greater skill, flexibility, and commitment were required from labour. Workers were expected to be adaptable and multi-skilled, which made trade unions organized on occupational lines less appropriate. Flexible production and quality products implied a highly motivated and highly trained labour force, a more decentralized management, and a more cooperative, less conflictual style of industrial relations.' J. Fulcher and J. Scott, *Sociology* (2nd edn) Oxford: Oxford University Press, 2003, p. 615. As the authors go on to say, there is, in fact, much debate over the extent to which the reality matches up to this ideal sketch. In any event, few would contest the point that there is a close relationship between: changes in technology and production; the greater diversity of products; and deep changes in consumption and culture. MIT Professors M.J. Piore and C.F. Sabel's *The Second Industrial Divide: Possibilities for Prosperity*, New York: Basic Books, 1984, is the classic, original source for arguments in favour of 'flexible specialization' in the face of economic crises said to be caused by an outmoded attachment to standardized mass production.

12. N. Poulantzas, *Crisis of the Dictatorships*, London: New Left Books, 1976.
13. J. Urry, 2000, op. cit.
14. See M. Barrett, 'Stuart Hall' in *KST2e*, p. 296ff.
15. Z. Bauman, *Liquid Modernity*, Cambridge: Polity Press, 2000, p. 14.
16. Ibid. p. 14.
17. Ibid. p. 12.
18. Ibid. p. 4.
19. See R. Schroeder, 'Michael Mann' in *KST2e*, pp. 344–5.
20. See Z. Bauman, *Modernity and Ambivalence*, Cambridge: Polity Press, 1991; and T. Blackshaw, 'Zygmunt Bauman', in *KST2e*, pp. 369–70.
21. Op. cit. F. Jameson, 1984, pp. 53–92.
22. Ibid. p. 119; see also F. Jameson, *Postmodernism, or, Cultural Logic of Late Capitalism*, Durham, NC: Duke University Press, 1991.
23. E. Laclau and C. Mouffe, *Hegemony and Socialist Strategy*, London: Verso, 1984.
24. See J. Hughes, 'Norbert Elias', in *KST2e*, pp. 148–9 1st edn. Hughes quotes S. Mennell, *Norbert Elias*. Oxford: Blackwell, 1989, p. 248, in making this point.
25. See the discussion of the use of the term 'iron cage' or 'steel hard casing' *(stahlhartes Gehause)* in Weber's *The Protestant Ethic and the Spirit of Capitalism*, trans. S. Kalberg, Los Angeles, CA: Roxbury Publishing [1904–5] 2002. A translation of the second edition of 1920, in Richard Swedberg, *The Max Weber Dictionary: Key Words and Concepts*, Stanford: Stanford University Press, 2005, p. 132.
26. See M. Weber, 'Science as a vocation', pp. 148, 155, cited in Chapter 2 by L. Scaff, *KST2e*, p. 64.
27. M. Weber, 'Unternehmungen der Gemeinden', in *Max Weber Gesamtausgabe I:8. Wirtschaft, Staat und Sozialpolitik. Schriften und Reden, 1900–12* (ed.) W. Schluchter, Tubingen: J.C.B. Mohr, 1998, pp. 362–63, cited in F. Ringer, *Max Weber: An Intellectual Biography*, Chicago: University of Chicago Press, 2004, p. 222.
28. Ibid. Ringer, p. 222.
29. M. Weber, *The Protestant Ethic and the Spirit of Capitalism*, trans. T. Parsons, New York: Scribner's [1904–5] 1958, p. 194, cited in L. Scaff, 'Max Weber', *KST2e*, p. 63.

30. For a resurgence of interest, research and theoretical analysis of the crucial but relatively neglected dimension of value commitments, see R. Bellah et al., *Habits of the Heart: Individualism and Commitment in American Life*, Berkeley: University of California Press, 1985; M. Lamont, *Money, Morals and Manners: The Culture of the French and the American Upper-Middle Class*, Chicago: Chicago University Press, 1992; M. Lamont, *The Dignity of Working Men: Morality and the Boundaries of Race, Class, and Immigration*, Cambridge, MA: Harvard University Press, 2000; A. Sayer, *The Moral Significance of Class*, Cambridge: Cambridge University Press, 2005; L. Boltanski and L. Thevenot, *On Justification: Economies of Worth*, trans. C. Worth, Princeton: Princeton University Press, 1991/2006.
31. A.R. Hochschild, *The Managed Heart: The Commercialization of Human Feeling*, Berkeley, CA: University of California Press, 1983.
32. S. Williams, 'Arlie Russell Hochschild', in *KST2e*, p. 360; and S. Williams, *Sleep and Society: Sociological Ventures into the (Un)known*, London: Routledge, 2005.
33. K. Widerberg, 'Dorothy Smith', in *KST2e*, p. 315. See K. Widerberg, 'Embodying modern times: investigating tiredness', *Time and Society*, **15**(1): 105–20, 2006.
34. M. O'Neill, 'Theodor Adorno' in *KST2e* p. 118.
35. P. Watier, 'Georg Simmel', in *KST2e*, p. 98.
36. K. Plummer, 'Herbert Blumer' in *KST2e* p. 111.
37. S. Lash, *Sociology of Postmodernism*, London: Routledge, 1990, pp. 11–12.
38. Op. cit. R. Swedberg, 2005, p. 286. The quotation from Weber is from H. Gerth and C. Wright Mills (eds) *From Max Weber*, New York: Oxford University Press, 1946, p. 146.
39. M. Weber, 'Science as a vocation', in P. Lassman and I. Velody, with H. Martins (eds) *Max Weber's 'Science as a Vocation'*, London: Unwin Hyman, 1919/89, p. 22.
40. Ibid. p. 288.
41. R.K. Merton, *Science, Technology and Society in Seventeenth Century England*, New York: Harper & Row [1938] 1970, p. 248; drawn from Swedberg, 2005, op.cit., p. 180.
42. R.K. Merton, *On Social Structure and Science* (ed.) P. Sztompka, Chicago: University of Chicago Press, 1996. This account of Merton's comments on value neutrality is drawn from Swedberg's discussion of objectivity in *The Max Weber Dictionary*, op. cit., p. 180.
43. M. Weber, 1968, *Economy and Society*, eds G. Roth and C. Wittich, New York: Bedminster Press (reprinted by the University of California Press, 1978) pp. 321–7; and S. Kalberg, *Max Weber: Readings and Commentary on Modernity*, Oxford: Blackwell, 2005, p. 13.
44. K. Widerberg, 'Dorothy Smith', in *KST2e*, p. 310.
45. J. Scott, 'Public sociology and the neo-liberal condition', *Sociologisk Tidsskrift*, **13**(4): 325, 2005.
46. M. Burawoy, '2004 American Sociological Association presidential address: "For public sociology"', *British Journal of Sociology*, **56**(2): 259–94, 2005.
47. J. Scott, 'Who will speak and who will listen?', *British Journal of Sociology*, **56**(3): 408, 2005.
48. Ibid. p. 408.
49. Op. cit. M. Burawoy, 2005, p. 288.
50. Op. cit. S. Kalberg, 2005 p. 36.

51. R.A. Jones, 'Emile Durkheim', in G. Ritzer (ed.) *The Blackwell Companion to Major Classical Social Theorists*, Oxford: Blackwell, 2003, pp. 209–10.
52. L.D. Kritzman, *Michel Foucault: Politics, Philosophy, Culture: Interviews and Other Writings 1977–1984*, trans. A. Sheridan and others, London: Routledge, 1990, p. xviii.
53. S. Hall, 'Popular-democratic versus authoritarian populism', in A. Hunt (ed.) *Marxism and Democracy*, London: Lawrence & Wishart, 1980; and 'Authoritarian populism: a reply', *New Left Review*, **151**: 115–24, 1985.
54. L. Wacquant, 'Pierre Bourdieu', in *KST2e*, p. 271.
55. Ibid. p. 229 1st edn.
56. M. Cladis, *A Communitarian Defense of Liberalism*, Stanford, CA: Stanford University Press, 1992.
57. Ibid. p. 227.
58. Ibid. p. 57.
59. Ibid. p. 57.
60. Ibid. p. 227.
61. R. Dworkin, *Taking Rights Seriously*. London, Duckworth, 1977, p. 241–2.
62. R. Stones, 'Rights, social theory and political philosophy: a framework for case study research', in L. Morris (ed.) *Rights: Sociological Perspectives 2006*, p.145, and Kymlicka, 1995, p. 81.
63. For a more extended account of the relationship between social theory and political philosophy, with respect to rights rather than value commitments per se, see R. Stones, 'Social theory, political philosophy and rights', in L. Morris (ed.) *Rights: Sociological Perspectives*, London: Routledge, 2005, pp. 133–51.
64. For standard classical and more recent introductory discussions of these concepts and/or the literature on them see, for example: D.D Raphael, *Problems of Political Philosophy* (rev. edn), London: Macmillan – now Palgrave Macmillan, 1976; S. Mulhall and A. Swift, *Liberals and Communitarians*, Oxford: Blackwell, 1992; C. Farrelly, *An Introduction to Contemporary Political Theory*, Sage: London, 2004. For more advanced discussions and primary sources, see A. Quinton (ed.) *Political Philosophy*, Oxford: Oxford University Press, 1967; J. Rawls, *A Theory of Justice*. Cambridge, MA: Harvard University Press, 1971; M. Sandel, *Liberalism and the Limits of Justice*, Cambridge: Cambridge University Press, 1982; J. Rawls, *Political Liberalism*, New York: Columbia University Press, 1993; W. Kymlicka, *Liberalism, Community and Culture*, Oxford: Clarendon Press, 1989; B. Parekh, *Rethinking Multiculturalism: Cultural Diversity and Political Theory*, Basingstoke: Palgrave Macmillan, 2000.
65. The innovative work of Boltanski and Thevenot, op. cit. 1991/2006, could be useful here as it provides for a deep exploration of the social and cultural concepts of values and normative deliberations not only within particular societies but also within a range of specific spheres within these. Michèle Lamont's rigorous exploration of class-based moral sensibilities in the US and France (op. cit. 1992, 2000) provides a sophisticated and invaluable example of one kind of substantive sociological study of related issues. See Andrew Sayer (op. cit. 2005) for a subtle, seminal dissection of the moral-philosophical issues directly relevant to the social sciences.
66. C. Wright Mills, *The Sociological Imagination*, Harmondsworth: Pelican, 1970 (original publication, Oxford University Press, 1959).
67. K. Plummer, 'Herbert Blumer', in *KST2e*, p. 106.

68. W. Outhwaite, 'Jurgen Habermas' in *KST2e*, p. 255.
69. See S. Avineri, *The Social and Political Thought of Karl Marx*, Cambridge: Cambridge University Press, 1968, pp. 65–77 and 134–49.
70. Max Weber, op. cit., 1919/1989, p. 27.
71. R. Merton, *Social Theory and Social Structure*, New York: The Free Press, 1968, pp. 73–138.
72. Z. Bauman, *Life in Fragments: Towards a Postmodern Morality*, Oxford: Blackwell, 1995, pp. 62–3.
73. Ibid. p. 63.
74. Ibid. p. 53.
75. Ibid. p. 50.
76. Ibid. p. 60.
77. Ibid. p. 63.
78. Ibid. pp. 64–5; and see E. Levinas, 'Language and proximity', in *Collected Philosophical Papers*, trans. Alphonso Lingis, The Hague: Martinus Nijhoff, 1987, p. 137.
79. L. Scaff, 'Max Weber', in *KST2e*, p. 62.
80. P. Bourdieu, *Outline of a Theory of Practice*, Cambridge: Cambridge University Press, trans. R. Nice, 1972/1977; and P. Bourdieu and L. Wacquant, *An Invitation to Reflexive Sociology*, Chicago: The University of Chicago Press, 1992; A. Giddens, *New Rules of Sociological Method*, London: Macmillan – now Palgrave Macmillan, 1976 (2nd edn, Polity Press, 1993) and *The Constitution of Society*, Cambridge: Polity Press, 1984; I.J. Cohen, *Structuration Theory: Anthony Giddens and the Constitution of Social Life*, Basingstoke: Macmillan – now Palgrave Macmillan, 1989; N. Mouzelis, *Back to Sociological Theory*, Basingstoke: Macmillan – now Palgrave Macmillan, 1991; J.C. Alexander, *Theoretical Logic in Sociology*, 4 vols. Berkeley: University of California Press, 1982–3, and *Action and its Environments*, New York: Colombia University Press, 1988; M. Archer, *Realist Social Theory*, Cambridge: Cambridge University Press, 1995, and *Structure, Agency and the Internal Conversation*, Cambridge: Cambridge University Press, 2003; M. Emirbayer and A. Mische, 'What is agency?', *American Journal of Sociology*, **103**(4): 962–1023, 1998; A. Sayer, *Realism and Social Science*, London: Sage, 2000, and op. cit. 2005; R. Stones, *Structuration Theory*, Basingstoke: Palgrave Macmillan, 2005.
81. For a review of developments in this field and for an attempted synthesis of different positions in the structure and agency debate, see R. Stones (ibid. 2005).
82. Op.cit. Scott, 2005, p. 331.

Chapter 1 Karl Marx

1. G. Lichtheim, 'Historical and dialectical materialism', in *Dictionary of History of Ideas*, vol. 2, New York: Charles Scribner's Sons, 1973; see also the brief history of sociology http://en.wikipedia.org/wiki/Sociology, last accessed 20 February 2006.
2. G. Therborn, *Science, Class and Society: On the Formation of Sociology and Historical Materialism*, London: New Left Books, 1976.
3. K. Marx, 'Preface' (to *A Contribution to the Critique of Political Economy*), *Marx–Engels Collected Works*, vol 28, London: Lawrence & Wishart (first published 1859) 1987, pp. 261–5.

4. Ibid.
5. See J.P. Burkett, 'Marx's concept of an economic law of motion', *History of Political Economy*, 32(2): 381–94, 2000.
6. K. Marx *Capital*, vol. 3, London: Lawrence & Wishart (first published 1894), 1971, p. 886.
7. K. Marx (1852) Letter to Joseph Weydemeyer, 5 March.
8. E. Bernstein (1961) *Evolutionary Socialism: A Criticism and Affirmation*, New York: Schocken (originally published in German, 1899).
9. K. Marx (1973) *Grundrisse: Foundations of the Critique of Political Economy* (rough draft) Harmondsworth: Penguin (first written 1857–1861).
10. K. Marx and F. Engels (1848) *Manifesto of the Communist Party*; and K. Marx, 'The Eighteenth Brumaire of Louis Bonaparte', in T. Carver (ed.) *Marx: Later Political Writings*, Cambridge: Cambridge University Press (first published 1852).
11. Karl Marx (1986) 'Civil War in France', *Marx–Engels Collected Works*, vol 22, London: Lawrence & Wishart (first published 1871), 307–57.
12. E. Mandel (1975) *Late Capitalism*, London: New Left Books (first published in German 1972); D. Bell (1973) *The Coming of the Post-Industrial Society*, London: Heinemann.
13. D. Harvey (2003) *The New Imperialism*, Oxford: Oxford University Press; M. Castells (2001) *The Network Society*, Oxford: Blackwell.
14. Marx did not simply extrapolate from trends in England; he used them to illustrate claims grounded in a more fundamental theoretical critique of capitalism.
15. See also B. Jessop (2002) *The Future of the Capitalist State*, Cambridge: Polity Press.

Chapter 2 Max Weber

1. M. Weber, '"Objectivity" in social science and social policy', in E. Shils and H. Finch (eds) *The Methodology of the Social Sciences*, New York: Free Press, 1949, pp. 68, 103.
2. 'The social psychology of the world religions', in H. Gerth and C.W. Mills (eds) *From Max Weber: Essays in Sociology*, New York: Oxford, 1946, p. 270.
3. *The Protestant Ethic and the 'Spirit' of Capitalism*, trans. T. Parsons, New York: Scribner's, 1958, p. 194.
4. Ibid. p. 17.
5. Ibid. p. 26.
6. Ibid. pp. 180–1. Talcott Parsons used 'iron cage' for Weber's phrase, recalling John Bunyan's man in the iron cage in *The Pilgrim's Progress*. New translations have proposed 'shell as hard as steel' or 'steel-hard casing': see P. Baehr and G. Wells (eds and trs.) *The Protestant Ethic and the 'Spirit' of Capitalism and Other Writings*, London: Penguin, 2002, p. 121; and S. Kalberg (trans.), *The Protestant Ethic and the 'Spirit' of Capitalism*, Los Angeles: Roxbury, 2002, p. 123.
7. 'Politics as a vocation' and 'Science as a vocation', in *From Max Weber: Essays in Sociology*, pp. 120–8, 150–6; also D. Owen and T. Strong (eds) *The Vocation Lectures*, Indianapolis: Hackett, 2004, pp. 25–31, 83–94.
8. 'Science as a vocation', p. 138.
9. '"Objectivity" in social science and social policy', p. 57 (translation modified).

10. 'Science as a vocation', pp. 148, 155.
11. '"Objectivity" in social science and social policy', p. 84; a more literal translation would read, 'For scientific truth is only what wants to be valid for all who want the truth.'
12. 'On liberty' in J. Gray (ed.) *On Liberty and Other Essays*, Oxford: Oxford University Press, 1991, p. 65.
13. G. Roth and C. Wittich (eds) *Economy and Society: An Outline of Interpretative Sociology*, New York: Bedminister, 1968, vol. 1, p. 244; Weber's original title for this unfinished work read literally, 'The Economy and the Social Orders and Powers,' and it was intended as a contribution to the *Handbook of Social Economics* for which he served as chief editor.
14. *Noise: The Political Economy of Music*, trans. B. Massumi, Minneapolis: University of Minnesota Press, 1985, pp. 3, 111, with a foreword by F. Jameson that acknowledges Weber's contribution. Another application of Weber's ideas is G. Ritzer, *The McDonaldization Thesis*, London: Sage, 1998.
15. See for example L. Greenfeld, *The Spirit of Capitalism: Nationalism and Economic Growth*, Cambridge: Harvard University Press, 2001; S.H. Kim, *Max Weber's Politics of Civil Society*, Cambridge: Cambridge University Press, 2004; P. Gorski, *The Disciplinary Revolution: Calvinism and the Rise of the State in Early Modern* Europe, Chicago: University of Chicago Press, 2003.
16. Weber's texts from 1894 and 1896 are partially translated by S. Lestition as 'Stock and Commodity Exchanges' and 'Commerce on the Stock and Commodity Exchanges', *Theory and Society*, **29**: 305–71, 2000.
17. See A. Sen, *Rationality and Freedom*, Cambridge: Harvard University Press, 2002; R. Swedberg, *Max Weber and the Idea of Economic Sociology*, Princeton: Princeton University Press, 1998, and *Principles of Economic Sociology*, Princeton: Princeton University Press, 2003.
18. Weber's untitled study, published posthumously in 1921, was translated as *The Rational and Social Foundations of Music*, trans. Martindale et al. Carbondale: Southern Illinois University Press, 1958.
19. See N. Gane, *Max Weber and Postmodern Theory: Rationalization Versus Reenchantment*, Basingstoke: Palgrave – now Palgrave Macmillan, 2002; and G. Ritzer, *Enchanting a Disenchanted World: Revolutionizing the Means of Consumption*, Thousand Oaks, CA: Pine Forge Press, 2005.

Chapter 3 Emile Durkheim

1. *The New Encyclopedia Britannica*, 15th edn, vol. 29, Chicago: Encyclopedia Britannica, p. 987.
2. S. Lukes, *Emile Durkheim*, New York: Harper & Row, 1972, p. 93.
3. Ibid. p. 80.
4. E. Durkheim, *Moral Education*, New York: Free Press, 1961, p. 101.
5. E. Durkheim, *The Division of Labor in Society*, New York: Free Press, 1984.
6. E. Durkheim, *Suicide*, Glencoe, IL: Free Press, 1951.
7. E. Durkheim, *The Elementary Forms of the Religious Life*, New York: Free Press, 1965.

8. A.R. Radcliffe-Brown, *Structure and Function in Primitive Society*, London: Cohen and West, 1952.
9. T. Parsons, *The Structure of Social Action*, New York: McGraw-Hill, 1937.
10. R.K. Merton, *Social Theory and Social Structure* (rev. and enl. edn) Glencoe, IL: Free Press, 1957, pp. 131–60.
11. E. Goffman, *Interaction Ritual*, Garden City, NY: Anchor Books, 1967, pp. 47–95.
12. R. Collins and M. Makowsky, *The Discovery of Society* (5th edn) New York: McGraw-Hill, pp. 272–9; R. Collins, 'The Durkheimian tradition in conflict sociology', Chapter 5 in J.C. Alexander (ed.) *Durkheimian Sociology*, Cambridge: Cambridge University Press, 1988, pp. 107–28.

Chapter 4 Georg Simmel

1. K. Wolff (ed.) *The Sociology of Georg Simmel*, Glencoe: Free Press, 1950; Levine, D. (1971) *Georg Simmel: Individuality and Social Forms*, Chicago, IL: Chicago University Press.
2. B. Nedelmann, 'The continuing relevance of Georg Simmel: staking out anew the field of sociology', in G. Ritzer and B. Smart (eds) *Handbook of Social Theory*, Thousand Oaks, CA: Sage, 2001, pp. 66–78.
3. Cf. L. Scaff, 'Georg Simmel', in G. Ritzer (ed.) *The Blackwell Companion to Major Classical Social Theorists*, Oxford: Blackwell, 2003, pp. 239–66.
4. G. Simmel, *Les Problèmes de la philosophie de l'histoire* (1907) Paris: PUF, 1984, pp. 99, 100.
5. G. Simmel, *Uber sociale Differenzierung*, in *Gesamtausgabe*, vol. 2, Suhrkamp: Frankfurt am Main, 1989, p. 117.
6. G. Simmel, *Soziologie, Untersuchungen über die Formen der Vergesellschaftung*, in *Gesamtausgabe*, vol. 2, Suhrkamp: Frankfurt am Main, 1992, p. 436.
7. Ibid. p. 710.
8. Ibid. p. 7.
9. C. Bouglé, 'Review of *Soziologie*', *L'Année Sociologique, vol. xi, 1906–09*, p. 18.
10. G. Simmel, *Soziologie*, p. 11. This aspect of socialization, that of groups and collectivities, has been particularly stressed by M. Maffesoli cf. notably *Au creux des apparences*, Paris: Plon, 1990.
11. G. Simmel, *Secret et société secrète*, Circé, Saulxures, 1992, p. 63.
12. Ibid., 1992, p. 23. To look at the relations between these concepts of frontiers, indiscretion and the construction of the other, cf. Exkurs über die soziale Begrenzung in *Soziologie*, pp. 698–702.
13. *Soziologie*, p. 44.
14. Ibid. p. 35.
15. A. Giddens, *The Consequences of Modernity*, Cambridge: Polity Press, 1990; A. Giddens, *Runaway World: How Globalization is Reshaping our Lives*, London: Profile Books, 1999.
16. N. Luhmann, *Risk: A Sociological Theory*, New York: De Gruyter, 1993; *Observations of Modernity*, Stanford, CA: Stanford University Press, 1998.

17. Watier, P. 'Les sentiments psychosociaux dans la sociologie de G. Simmel', in L. Deroche and P. Watier (eds) *La sociologie de G. Simmel* (1908): *Essais de modélisation sociale*, Paris: PUF, 2002, pp. 217–40.

Chapter 5 Herbert Blumer

1. T. Duster, 'Herbert Blumer: 1900–1987', *ASA Footnotes* **15**(6) (1987), 16.
2. H.S. Becker, 'Herbert Blumer's conceptual impact', *Symbolic Interaction* **11**(1) (1988), 13–21.
3. Page 20 in P. Colomy, and J.D. Brown, 'Elaboration, revision, polemic and progress in the second Chicago School', in G.A. Fine (ed.) *A Second Chicago School?*, Chicago: The University of Chicago Press, 1995, pp. 17–81.
4. H. Blumer (1969) *Symbolic Interactionism: Perspective and Method*, Englewood Cliffs, NJ: Prentice Hall.
5. L. Lofland, 'Reminiscences of classic Chicago: the Blumer–Hughes talk', *Urban Life* 9(3) (1980), 251–81, reprinted in K. Plummer, *The Chicago School*, vol. 4, London: Routledge, 1997, Ch. 45.
6. Op. cit. Becker, 1988, p. 14.
7. Op. cit. Becker, 1988, p. 14.
8. A wonderful account of this which bridges Blumer and Becker is to be found in D. Matza's *Becoming Deviant*, Englewood Cliffs, NJ: Prentice Hall, 1969; H.S. Becker, *Outsiders: Studies in the Sociology of Deviance*, Illinois: Free Press, 1963.
9. K. Plummer (ed.) *Chicago Sociology*, 4 vols, London: Routledge, 1997.
10. H. Blumer, 'Sociological implications of the thought of George Herbert Mead', *American Journal of Sociology*, **71** (March 1966), 535–44; H. Blumer, 'George Herbert Mead', in B. Rhea (ed.) *The Future of the Sociological Classics*, London: Allen & Unwin, 1979b; H. Blumer (ed. and intro by T.J. Morrione) *George Herbert Mead and Human Conduct*, New York: AltaMira Press, 2004).
11. Commented upon by Lonnie Athen as he describes 'Blumer's advance social psychology course' in *Studies in Symbolic Interaction*, **14** (1993), 156.
12. This debate can be found embodied in the controversy over the publication of J.D. Lewis and R.L. Smith's 'American Sociology and Pragmatism: Mead, Chicago Sociology and Symbolic Interactionism', Chicago: The University of Chicago Press, 1980. The debates are found in Plummer, K. (ed.) *Symbolic Interactionism: 2 vols*, Aldershot: Edward Elgar, 1991, vol. 1, pp. 227–326.
13. A. Abbott, and E. Gaziano, 'Transition and tradition: departmental faculty in the era of the second Chicago School' in G.A. Fine (ed.) *A Second Chicago School? The Development of a Postwar American Sociology*, Chicago: The University of Chicago Press, 1995, pp. 221–72.
14. Cf. M. Hammersley, *The Dilemma of Qualitative Method: Herbert Blumer and the Chicago Tradition*, London: Routledge, 1989.
15. Cf. Abbott and Gaziano 1995, p. 253.
16. Cf. P. Rock, *The Making of Symbolic Interactionism*, London: Macmillan – now Palgrave Macmillan, 1979.
17. Op. cit. Becker, 1988, p. 18.

18. D.R. Maines, 'Myth, text and interactionist complicity in the neglect of Blumer's macrosociology', *Symbolic Interaction*, **11**(1) (1988), 43–57.
19. Op. cit. Blumer, 1969, p. 49.
20. Elsewhere he suggests three basic postulates: 'that human beings act toward things on the basis of the meanings that the things have for them'; 'that the meaning of such things is derived from … the social interaction that one has with one's fellows'; and 'these meanings are handled in, and modified through, an interpretative process used by the person' (Blumer, 1969, p. 2, op. cit.). These are a rather limited and possibly even trivial set of postulates, although as he points out, such a view is 'ignored or played down in practically all contemporary social science' (p. 2).
21. Op. cit. Blumer, 1969, p. 23.
22. Cf. H.S. Becker, *Doing Things Together*, Chicago: Aldine, 1986.
23. Op. cit. Blumer, 1969, p. 85.
24. H. Blumer, 'Society as symbolic interaction' in A. Rose (ed.) *Human Behavior and Social Processes*, Boston: Houghton Mifflin, 1962.
25. For discussions of pragmatism, see Plummer (op. cit. 1997), 2.
26. Op. cit. Blumer, 1969, pp. 21–2.
27. The central location of this discussion is Blumer (op. cit. 1969), Chapter 1.
28. Op. cit. Blumer, 1979b, p. 85.
29. Op. cit. Blumer, 1979b, p. 85.
30. Op. cit. Blumer, 1979b, p. 94.
31. J. Radway, *Reading the Romance*, 1991, Chapel Hill: University of North Carolina Press.
32. H. Blumer, *Movies and Conduct*, New York: Macmillan, 1933.
33. N. Denzin (1992) *Symbolic Interactionism and Cultural Studies*, Oxford: Blackwell, p. 107.
34. P.T. Clough, *The Ends of Ethnography*, London: Sage, 1992.
35. In this he followed Mead and Dewey: For Dewey, 'Every generation has to accomplish democracy over and over again. (J. Dewey, *The Problems of Men*, New York: Philosphical Library, 1946, p. 31). 'The very idea of democracy … has to be constantly discovered, and rediscovered, remade and reorganized' (p. 47).
36. Lyman, S. and Vidich, A. (1988) *Social Order and Public Philosophy: The Analysis and Interpretation of the Work of Herbert Blumer*, Fayetteville, AR: University of Arkansas Press.
37. This quote is from Blumer (1958), reprinted in Lyman and Vidich (op. cit. 1988, p. 206). The section which follows is culled from quotes on Blumer's writings on race prejudice and I have tried to piece together a kind of systematic statement. See pp. 183–233 of Lyman and Vidich (1988) for the original statements.
38. See the last key statement in H. Blumer and T. Duster 'Theories of race and social action', in *Sociological Theories: Race and Colonialism*, Paris: UNESCO, 1980, p. 235).
39. D.R. Maines, *The Faultline of Consciousness: A View of Interactionism in Sociology*, New York: Aldine de Gruyter, 2001; Atkinson, P. and W. Housley, *Interactionism*, London: Sage, 2003.
40. Cf. K. Plummer, *Sexual Stigma*, London: Routledge, 1975; K. Plummer, *Telling Sexual Stories: Power, Change and Social Worlds*, London: Routledge, 1995.

41. J. Gagnon and W. Simon, *Sexual Conduct: The Social Sources of Human Sexuality*, Chicago: Aldine, 1973.
42. A word needs to be said about his style. In reading Blumer, one is immediately struck by the almost total lack of referencing. These days sociology books are cluttered with references, quotes from others, long bibliographies. All these are absent from Blumer. He hardly ever does any of the above. Nobody is cited, there are no references and no bibliographies. It is not that there are not many allusions to the works of others – only that they are never named. Most of his essays, and that is what they are, read like thoughtful self-reflections. His standard mould is to argue against several dominant views of the world, and then to proceed to evolve his own painstaking account of it.
43. G.A. Fine, 'Symbolic interactionism in the post-Blumerian age', in G. Ritzer (ed.) *Frontiers of Sociological Theory*, New York: Columbia University Press, 1990, pp. 117–57.
44. See, for instance, the journal, *Symbolic Interaction*; the year book, *Studies in Symbolic Interaction*; and the organization, The Society for the Study of Symbolic Interaction. Details are provided in Plummer (op. cit. 1991).
45. A. Strauss, *Continual Permutations of Action*, New York: Aldine de Gruyter, 1993; H. Joas, *The Creativity of Action*, Chicago: The University of Chicago Press, 1997.
46. Op. cit. Denzin, 1992.
47. M.J. Deegan, and M.R. Hill, (eds) *Women and Symbolic Interaction*, Boston: Allen & Unwin, 1987.
48. K. Plummer, *Telling Sexual Stories: Power, Change and Social Worlds*, London: Routledge, 1995.
49. B.B. Lal, *The Romance of Culture in an Urban Civilization*, London: Routledge, 1990.
50. H. Blumer, 'Society as symbolic interaction' in A. Rose (ed.) *Human Behavior and Social Processes*, Boston: Houghton Mifflin, 1962, p. 356.
51. Ibid. p. 359.
52. Op. cit. Denzin, 1992, p. 155.
53. Op. cit. Plummer, 1995.
54. K. Plummer, 'The gay and lesbian movement in Britain, 1965–1995: schism, solidarities and social worlds', in B. Adam, J.W. Duyvendak and A. Krouwel (eds) *The Global Emergence of Gay and Lesbian Politics* (Philadelphia: Temple University Press, 1998).
55. K. Plummer, 'Rights work: constructing lesbian, gay and sexual rights in modern times', in L. Morris (ed.) *Rights: Sociological Perspectives*, London: Routledge, 2006.
56. Op. cit. Plummer, 1995, p. 125.
57. Op. cit. Plummer, 2006, p. 157.

Chapter 6 Theodor Adorno

1. Martin Jay describes five points of light and energy that form the force field of Adorno's intellectual career: western Marxism, aesthetic modernism, Mandarin cultural conservatism, Jewish identification, and deconstructionism – see chapter 1 in Martin Jay's *Adorno* (1984) London: Fontana.

2. Ibid. p. 25.
3. Ibid. p. 27.
4. See *The Correspondence of Walter Benjamin 1910–1940* (1994) G. Scholem and T. Adorno (eds) Chicago: The University of Chicago Press.
5. Adorno, T.W 'Commitment' in *Aesthetics and Politics*, translation editor R. Taylor, London: Verso, 1997, p. 189; see also the Afterword by F. Jameson.
6. Ibid. Adorno, 1997, p. 191.
7. S. Nicholsen, 'Adorno's *Minima Moralia*: On passion, psychoanalysis and the post-emotional dilemma', from personal communication with the author; presented in shorter form in 'Psychoanalysis, passion and performance', in *The Alliance Forum on Passion*, Seattle: Washington, 2002b.
8. Op. cit. Adorno, 1997, p. 188.
9. T. Adorno, Frankel-Brunswik, E., Levinson, D. and Sanford, R. *The Authoritarian Personality*, New York: Harper, 1950.
10. D. Held, *Introduction to Critical Theory: Horkheimer to Habermas*, Berkeley: University of California Press, 1980, pp. 216–7.
11. A term coined by E. Lindner to mean equal dignity for all, see 'Humiliation in a globalizing world: does humiliation become the most disruptive force?' 2004 (http://www.humiliationstudies.org/documents/LindnerHumiliationFearGlobalizingWorld.pdf).
12. Op. cit. Nicholsen, 2002b, p. 3.
13. Op. cit. Nicholsen, 2002b, pp. 25–6.
14. T.W. Adorno, *Minima Moralia*, trans. E.F.N. Jephcott, London: Verso, 1996.
15. Op. cit. Nicholsen, 2002b, p. 3.
16. Op. cit. Adorno, 1996, pp. 25–6.
17. Op. cit. Adorno, 1996, p. 26.
18. Op. cit. Nicholsen, 2002b, p. 4.
19. Adorno, T.W. (1973) *The Jargon of Authenticity*, trans. K. Tarnowski and F. Will, London: Routledge & Kegan Paul.
20. Op. cit. Nicholsen, 2002b, p. 6.
21. S. Buchanan, Grillo, B. and Threadgold. T. *What's the Story? Results from Research into Media Coverage of Refugees and Asylum Seekers in the UK*, London: Article 19, 2002, p. 5.
22. G. Rose, (1978) *The Melancholy Science: an Introduction to the Thoughts of T.W. Adorno*, London: Routledge, Ch. 3.
23. S. Buck-Morss, *The Origin of Negative Dialectics*, Brighton: Harvester Press, 1977, pp. 36–7.
24. T.W. Adorno, *Prisms*, trans. S. Weber and S. Weber, California, MA: MIT Press, 1995, pp. 246–7.
25. To better understand this point, read Kafka's short story 'Metamorphosis'.
26. Op. cit. Adorno, 1995, p. 261.
27. Adorno, T.W. and Horkheimer, M. *Dialectic of Enlightenment*, trans. J. Cumming, New York: Continuum and London: Verso, 1995, p. 139.
28. S. Crook, (1994) *Adorno: the Stars Down to Earth*, London: Routledge. Read the 'Introduction: Adorno and authoritarian irrationalism'.
29. S. Nicholsen, *Exact Imagination, Late Work: On Adorno's Aesthetics*, Cambridge MA: MIT Press, 1997, p. 3.

30. Op. cit. Adorno, 1997, p. 237.
31. See J. Hillis-Millar (1992) *Illustration*, London: Reaktion Books. Here Hillis-Millar draws upon Walter Benjamin's work to illustrate the way works of art make culture.
32. Adorno's use of mimesis is influenced greatly by Walter Benjamin and is not to be interpreted as imitation or mimicry but rather as sensuous knowledge.
33. See J. Roberts (1982) *Walter Benjamin: Theoretical Traditions in Social Sciences*, London: Macmillan – now Palgrave Macmillan.
34. Op. cit. Adorno, 1997, p. 237.
35. Osborne, P. (1989) 'Adorno and the metaphysics of modernism: the problem of a postmodern art' in A. Benjamin (ed.) *The Problems of Modernity: Adorno and Benjamin*, London: Routledge.
36. Adorno, T.W. (1984) *Aesthetic Theory*, eds G. Adorno and R. Tiedmann, trans. C. Lendhart, London: Routledge.
37. Ibid. p. 79.
38. Op. cit. Adorno, 1995, p. 20.
39. See also Z. Bauman, (1988) 'Is there a postmodern sociology?', in *Theory, Culture and Society*, 5: 217–37.
40. O'Neill, M. in association with Giddens, S., Breatnach, P., Bagley, C., Bourne, D. and Judge, T. (2002) 'Renewed methodologies for social research: ethno-mimesis as performative praxis', *Sociological Review*, **50**(1). In coming to know the work of art, Adorno reflects upon the process of interpretation, commentary, criticism via immersion, followed by objectification and dissociation – through micrology and *Verstehen*. This describes for me the research process of immersion and connection at one and the same time as maintaining a critical distance through a process of objectification to provide as close as possible an account and interpretation of an issue.
41. Jay, M. (1993) *Force Fields: Between Intellectual History and Cultural Critique*, New York: Routledge.
42. Adorno, T.W. (1978) *Minima Moralia: Reflections from a Damaged Life*, trans. E.F.N. Jephcott, London and New York: Verso.
43. See O'Neill, M. (ed.) *Adorno, Culture and Feminism*, London: Sage, 1999. For example, contemporary feminist thought evolved out of critiques of the Enlightenment, modernism, structuralism and psychoanalysis. Key themes include the disavowal of binary oppositions, a focus upon deconstruction, anti-essentialism; a focus upon the complexity of our life-worlds and the importance of mediation in exploring social life within the context of technologization, globalization and what Piccone calls 'the permanent crisis of the totally administered society' (1993: 3) marked by 'conformist political theory … mass society, pseudo culture and new class dominations' (1993: 9).
44. Op. cit. Nicholsen (2002b).
45. The research in which this image was produced sought to develop alternative forms of representing and analysing the lived experiences of refugees and asylum seekers living in Nottingham and London. The research was conducted between 1998 and 2002 with the participation of refugees and asylum seekers from Bosnia-Herzegovina and Afghanistan. The participants were the co-creators of the research. The research was contextualized within the UK Arts Council's concept of cultural diversity and was premised upon the vital role of the arts in sociocultural

regeneration. Our project drew upon processes of participatory action research (PAR) and participatory arts (PA) as 'ethno-mimesis' to produce critical theory in practice/praxis. Praxis is understood as purposeful knowledge within the context of the need to raise awareness of the lived experiences of refugees and asylum seekers and to challenge myths and stereotypes. For example, the kind of myths created in the press referenced in the work of Article 19 and the Cardiff School of Journalism and earlier in this chapter.

46. Op. cit. Nicholsen 1997, p. 3.
47. K. Tester, *The Social Thought of Zygmunt Bauman*, Basingstoke: Palgrave Macmillan, 2004.
48. Op. cit. Nicholsen, 1997.
49. S. Nicholsen, *The Love of Nature and the End of the World*, Cambridge, MA: MIT Press, 2002a.
50. Becker-Schmidt, R. (1999) 'Critical theory as a critique of society: Theodor Adorno's significance for a feminist sociology' Chapter 5 in O'Neill, M. (ed.) *Adorno, Culture and Feminism*, London, California and New Delhi: Sage, pp. 104–18.
51. Ibid. p. 105.
52. Flower Macannel, J. (1999) 'Adorno: The riddle of femininity' Chapter 7 in O'Neill, M. (ed.) *Adorno, Culture and Feminism,* London, California and New Delhi: Sage, pp. 141–60.
53. Ibid. p. 143.
54. Ibid. p. 142.
55. Ibid. p. 144
56. Ibid. p. 144.
57. Ibid. p. 144.
58. Op. cit. Nicholsen, 2002b.
59. Meštrović, S. (1997) *Postemotional Society*, London: Sage.

Chapter 7 Talcott Parsons

1. A brief but useful biographical sketch of Parsons is available in P. Hamilton, 'Systems theory', in B.S. Turner (ed.) *The Blackwell Companion to Social Theory* (Oxford: Blackwell, 1996), pp. 151–9.
2. This cross-disciplinary engagement is reflected in T. Parsons, *The Structure of Social Action*, New York: McGraw-Hill, 1937; and T. Parsons and N. Smelser, *Economy and Society*, London: Routledge, 1956.
3. Ibid. Parsons, 1937.
4. Ibid. pp. 64–9.
5. T. Parsons, *The Social System*, Chicago: Free Press, 1951.
6. T. Parsons, 'Evolutionary universals in society', *American Sociological Review*, **29**(3) (1964), 339–57.
7. Op. cit. Parsons, 1951, pp. 58–67.
8. Derived from N. Abercrombie, S. Hill and B. Turner (eds) *The Penguin Dictionary of Sociology* (2nd edn) Harmondsworth: Penguin, 1988, p. 178, and P. Hamilton, *Talcott Parsons*, London: Ellis Horwood & Tavistock, 1983, p. 103.

9. T. Parsons, *The System of Modern Societies*, Englewood Cliffs, NJ: Prentice Hall, 1971.
10. T. Parsons, 'The professions and the social structure', *Social Forces*, **17** (1939), 457–67 and T. Parsons, 'Illness and the role of the physician: a sociological perspective', *American Journal of Orthopsychiatry*, **21** (1951), 452–60.
11. These issues are discussed in T. Parsons, 'Some comments on the sociology of Karl Marx', in T. Parsons, *Sociological Theory and Modern Society*, New York: Free Press, 1967.
12. Op. cit. Parsons, 1951, pp. 428–54.
13. M. Weber, *The Protestant Ethic and the 'Spirit' of Capitalism* (trans. T. Parsons) London: Allen & Unwin, 1930.
14. J. Habermas, *Legitimation Crisis*, Boston: Beacon Press, 1979 and J. Habermas, *The Theory of Communicative Action*, vol. 1, London: Heinemann, 1984.
15. N. Chodorow, *The Reproduction of Mothering*, Berkeley: University of California Press, 1978.
16. See, for example: C. Wright Mills, *The Sociological Imagination*, Harmondsworth: Penguin, 1959, especially Chapter 2; A. Giddens, 'Power in the recent writings of Talcott Parsons', *Sociology*, 2 (1968), 257–72; F. Parkin, *Marxism and Class Theory*, London: Tavistock, 1979.
17. Symptomized by A. Gouldner, *The Coming Crisis of Western Sociology*, London: Heinemann, 1971.
18. Key works include J.C. Alexander, *Theoretical Logic in Sociology, the Modern Reconstruction of Classical Thought: Talcott Parsons*, vol. 4, London: Routledge, 1984; and R.J. Holton and B.S. Turner, *Talcott Parsons on Economy and Society*, London: Routledge, 1986.
19. Ibid. Holton and Turner, 1986, pp. 88–90.

Chapter 8 Robert K. Merton

1. R.W. Schultz, 'The improbable adventures of an American scholar: Robert K. Merton', *The American Sociologist*, **26**(1) (1995), 68–77, at 69 (reprinted from *Temple Review* **47**(1) 1995). For a partial list of books and articles that focus on Merton's ideas, see the bibliography in R.K. Merton, *On Social Structure and Science*, P. Sztompka (ed.) Chicago: The University of Chicago Press, 1996, pp. 361–8. See also C. Mongardini and S. Tabboni (eds) *Robert K. Merton and Contemporary Sociology*, New Brunswick, NJ: Transaction Publishers, 1998. Merton's final book, *The Travels and Adventures of Serependity*, was published by Princeton University Press, 2004.
2. I.B. Cohen (ed.) *Puritanism and the Rise of Modern Science: The Merton Thesis*, New Brunswick, NJ: Rutgers University Press, 1990; see especially pp. 89–111 where Cohen lists works that analyse Merton's ideas.
3. D.L. Sills and R.K. Merton (eds) *The Macmillan Book of Social Science Quotations* (also published as vol. 19 of the *International Encylopedia of the Social Sciences*) New York: Macmillan, 1991, p. 160; the quotation originally appeared in 1949 in 'Manifest and latent functions', one of Merton's most famous essays. Inasmuch as this quotation is one of only four that Merton (presumably) selected for inclusion in this summary volume of significant remarks from the history of all the social

sciences, I am assuming from this that he puts significant store by it, and have quoted it with this self-estimate in mind.

4. R.K. Merton, *On Theoretical Sociology: Five Essays, Old and New*, New York: Free Press, 1967, p. 40.
5. Ibid.
6. Ibid. p. 42.
7. Ibid. p. 45.
8. Ibid. p. 45.
9. R.K. Merton, *Social Theory and Social Structure* (enl. edn) New York: Free Press, 1968, pp. 69–70; reprinted in *On Social Structure and Science*, pp. 57–8.
10. *On Social Structure and Science*, p. 1. It may be that Sztompka compiled this list of neologisms and conceptual distinctions after seeing Merton's own, which in part reproduces but also supplements Sztompka's; see R.K. Merton, *Social Research and the Practicing Professions*, A. Rosenblatt and T. Gieryn (eds) Cambridge, MA: Abt Books, 1982, p. 102.
11. R.K. Merton, 'The unanticipated consequences of purposive social action', *American Sociological Review*, **1** (1936), 894–904. In the vast majority of contemporary references to Merton's idea, particularly in the popular press, the phrase is changed to 'unintended consequences of social action', which somewhat alters the original meaning, carrying still further the denaturing process of 'obliteration'. Interestingly, compare Weber's more cumbersome exposition of a related process: 'The final result of political action often, no, even regularly, stands in completely inadequate and often even paradoxical relation to its original meaning. This is fundamental to all history', in Hans Gerth and C. Wright Mills (eds) *From Max Weber*, New York: Oxford University Press, 1946, p. 117.
12. R. K. Merton, 'Social structure and anomie', *American Sociological Review*, **3** (1938), 672–82. The record of reprintings was compiled by M. Wilson Miles as part of 'The writings of Robert K. Merton', in L.A. Coser (ed.) *The Idea of Social Structure: Papers in Honor of Robert K. Merton*, New York: Harcourt Brace Jovanovich, 1975, pp. 500–1.
13. R.K. Merton, 'Bureaucratic structure and personality', *Social Forces*, **18** (1939), 560–8. The reprint record is in Coser (ibid. pp. 501–2). Writings of this sort, which turned out to be his métier, he defined as 'highly condensed paradigmatic essays, typically running to few more than a dozen-or-so pages'; 'A life of learning' (1994), in Merton, *On Social Structure and Science*, p. 357.
14. R.K. Merton, 'Science, technology and society in seventeenth-century England', in *OSIRIS: Studies on the History and Philosophy of Science, and on the History of Learning and Culture*, **4**(2), G. Sarton (ed.) Bruges, Belgium: St Catherine Press, 1938, pp. 362–632. Reprinted with 'Preface: 1970', New York: Howard Fertig, 1970, New York: Harper & Row, Torchbook edn, 1970. Arranging for the publication of Merton's dissertation in this privileged venue was Sarton's 'threshold gift' to Merton, as the latter, borrowing from Lewis Hyde, eventually termed this magnanimous act; see Merton, 'A life of learning' (1994), p. 352.
15. I pick these symbolically loaded dates because of Talcott Parsons' *Structure of Social Action*, New York: McGraw-Hill, 1937 at one end, and Alvin Gouldner's *The Coming Crisis of Western Sociology*, New York: Basic Books, 1970 – largely a repudiation of Parsons' version of theorizing – on the other. Undergraduate enrolment in

sociology courses in the US also peaked just after 1970, as did the number of 'majors', thus ending a steady increase in student interest that had been growing since the end of the Second World War.

16. J.S. Coleman, 'Robert K. Merton as a teacher,' in J. Clark, C. Modgil and S. Modgil (eds) *Robert K. Merton: Consensus and Controversy*, London: Falmer Press, 1990, p. 29.
17. R.K. Merton, *On the Shoulders of Giants: A Shandean Postscript*, vicennial edition with a new Preface by the author, New York: Harcourt Brace Jovanovich, 1985; there is also a 'post-Italianate edition', Chicago: University of Chicago Press, 1993. Of the many commentaries this unique book has inspired, one of the most memorable is S.J. Gould's 'Polished pebbles, pretty shells: an appreciation of OTSOG,' in Clark et al. (ibid. pp. 35–47).
18. K.M. Setton, 'Foreword to the Torchbook edition', in H.O. Taylor, *The Emergence of Christian Culture in the West* (originally, *The Classical Heritage of the Middle Ages*) New York: Harper and Brothers, 1958, p. vii.
19. R.K. Merton, 'On the history and systematics of sociological theory' (op. cit. 1968) pp. 5–6. Earlier editions had appeared in 1949 and 1957; the quoted passage itself was added to the 1968 edition.
20. An instance of this hermeneutic tangle was recorded in a journal I once edited, *History of Sociology*, when a scholar who has since become a well-known theorist attacked Merton's putative position regarding the history of social thought and I, as editor, was called upon to 'assemble' Merton's response (with his collaboration) based on his already published statements; see S. Seidman, 'Classics and contemporaries: the history and systematics of sociology revisited' and the response, 'The historicist/presentist dilemma: a composite imputation and a foreknowing response', drawn by the editor from writings of R.K. Merton, both in *History of Sociology* **6**(1) (Fall 1985), 121–36, 137–52. I should note here that Merton and I corresponded regularly for a dozen years or more, and that he generously sent me a large amount of material from his private archives, including books, offprints, preprints, historically interesting letters from himself to other theorists and the like. I elected not to draw from this store of printed goods for reasons of privacy, and because I wanted my interpretation of Merton's importance to rely on easily accessible material rather than on the dozens of letters that passed between us. Using that material, with permission, awaits another opportunity, and would require more space than is available here.
21. R.K. Merton, 'A life of learning' (1994) The Charles Homer Haskins Lecture, delivered in Philadelphia (April, 1994) and published in Merton (op. cit. 1996) pp. 343–7.
22. G.D. Suttles, *The Social Order of the Slum: Ethnicity and Territory in the Inner City*, Chicago: University of Chicago Press, 1968, a study of Chicago slums in the 1960s, and thus a far cry from the culturally promising Jewish 'slum' of Merton's youth.
23. Merton, 'A life of learning' (1994), p. 349.
24. Ibid. p. 350.
25. It could be argued that the British sociology of science was inaugurated by J.D. Bernal's *The Social Function of Science*, London: J. Routledge & Sons, 1939, although Bernal's politicized view of the task was distinct from Merton's more dispassionate (Sartonian) approach; see Merton's generous and wise review of Bernal

in *American Journal of Sociology*, **46** (1941), 622–3 (one of the few publications that identifies him with Tulane University).

26. Because Merton himself never leaves literary reference unexplored, and for those who no longer consider seventeenth-century French drama a necessary part of their evening reading, the famous exchange comes in Act IV, Scene 6 of Molière's 'The Cit Turned Gentleman' (Le Bourgeois Gentilhomme): Philosophy-Master: Is it verse that you would write to her? Jordan: No, no, none of your verse. P.M.: You would only have prose? Jordan: No, I would neither have verse nor prose. P.M.: It must be one or t'other. Jordan: Why so? P.M.: Because, sir, there's nothing to express one's self by, but prose, or verse. Jordan: And when one talks, what may that be then? P.M.: Prose. Jordan: How? When I say, Nicola, bring me my slippers, and give me my nightcap, is that prose? P.M.: Yes, sir. Jordan: On my conscience, I have spoken prose above these forty years, without knowing anything of the matter; and I have all the obligations in the world to you, for informing me of this. (*Molière, Comédies*, vol. 2, London: J.M. Dent and Sons, 1929, p. 234.)
27. One wonders how many owners of cars who sport this slogan on their bumpers know anything of the book it parodies, *I'm OK, You're OK* by T. A. Harris, with the subtitle, *A Practical Guide to Transactional Analysis*, New York: Harper & Row, 1969. Despite its glib title, the book was widely discussed with some seriousness when it first appeared. The utterly predictable pattern within mass culture of devolution, from academic thoughtfulness to light repartee, is also something Merton has probably reflected upon regarding his own work. That this particular use of 'dysfunction' is psychological in nature and not sociologically informed, as was Merton's, may suggest that it was his own widely broadcast redefinition of the term (itself borrowed from medicine and biology) that made it available for psychologistic parlance. It is possible, however, that the psychologistic trivialization came more from the tradition of medical writing than from sociology. For clarifying details of Merton's own use, see his 'Social dysfunction' in *On Social Structure and Science*, pp. 96–100, especially note 1.
28. R. Bierstedt, *American Sociological Theory: A Critical History*, New York: Academic Press, 1981; see my review, *American Journal of Sociology*, **91** (March 1986), 1229–31.
29. R. Bierstedt, 'Merton's systematic theory,' in Clark et al. (op. cit. 1990) pp. 67–74, 76–7.
30. Op. cit. Bierstedt, 1981, p. 486.
31. P. Sztompka, 'R.K. Merton's theoretical system: an overview' in Clark et al., (op. cit. 1990) pp. 53–64, 75–6; see also C. Crothers, *Robert K. Merton*, Key Sociologists Series, London: Tavistock Publishers, 1987, pp. 64–118. Other leading Mertonians who would likely find Bierstedt's opinion contrary to observable scholarly data might include Arthur Stinchcombe, Raymond Boudon, Aage Sorenson and Neil Smelser, whose particular elaborations of Merton's work I cannot pursue here. None of these, however, seem to have given quite so much attention to Merton qua writer as has Bierstedt, which is why I call upon his testimony more often than would otherwise be justifiable.
32. E. Pound, *A Lume Spento and Other Early Poems*, New York: New Directions, 1965, from the 'Foreword 1965'.
33. Op. cit. Merton, *Social Theory and Social Structure* (1968 edn), p. 74, emphases in original.

34. For a new sociological meditation on what postmodernity means for social theorists, see C. Lemert, *The Postmodern Is Not What You Think*, Malden, MA: Blackwell, 1997, especially pp. 19–68, 132–64.
35. Op. cit. R.K. Merton (1938) p. 495, 1970, p. 136.
36. Ibid. 1970 edn, p. xvii.
37. R.K. Merton, *Sociological Ambivalence and Other Essays*, New York: Free Press, 1976, p. 7.
38. Op. cit. Merton, *Social Theory and Social Structure* (1968 edn) pp. 493–582.
39. Ibid. pp. 364–80.
40. Ibid. pp. 279–334.
41. Op. cit. Bierstedt, 1981, pp. 470–83.
42. Both Coser 1975, op. cit. and Clark et al. 1990, op. cit. have extensive bibliographies toward this end, to which could be added P. Sztompka's *Robert K. Merton: An Intellectual Profile*, New York: St Martin's Press, 1986, pp. 304–14.
43. Op. cit. Bierstedt, 1981, pp. 486, 489.

Chapter 9 Norbert Elias

1. Breslau was later to become the city of Wroclaw in Poland. However, when Elias lived there it was 'entirely German'. S. Mennell, *Norbert Elias: An Introduction*, Oxford: Blackwell, 1989, p. 5.
2. N. Elias, *The Civilizing Process*, Oxford: Blackwell (rev. edn 2000, originally published 1939) p. xiv.
3. I owe much to Eric Dunning for this interpretation of Elias's work.
4. There is considerable controversy over the extent to which Cassirer influenced Elias's work. For a comprehensive account of the debate see *Theory, Culture and Society*, 12(3) August, 1995.
5. It also came to be known as 'figurational' sociology, but Elias preferred the term 'process sociology' as it had more everyday currency.
6. Op. cit. Mennell, 1989, p. 7.
7. R. Kilminster, 'Introduction to Elias', *Theory, Culture and Society*, 4 (1987), 213–22.
8. Op. cit. Elias, 2000, p. xv.
9. Ibid p. 110.
10. Ibid. pp. 72–109.
11. Ibid. p. 122.
12. Ibid. p. 373.
13. Ibid. p. 382.
14. Ibid. p. 368.
15. The process by which more and more people become 'interdependent', this concept is explained below in relation to power.
16. A. Giddens, *The Constitution of Society*, Cambridge: Polity Press, 1984.
17. Op. cit. Elias, 2000, p. 60.
18. N. Elias, *What is Sociology?*, London: Hutchinson (translated in 1978 from the original German publication in 1970) p. 119.

19. 'Knowledge and power: an interview by Peter Ludes', in N. Stehr and V. Meja (eds) *Society and Knowledge*, London: Transaction Books, 1984, pp. 252–91.
20. To provide an example of the 'marginal circumstances' referred to above, consider the case of an unwanted newborn baby in a medieval society.
21. Perhaps the chief danger with the analogy with games is their dependence on 'rules'. Elias does not want to give the impression that rules are essential to all of social life. He thus provides the model of the 'primal contest' to demonstrate how games without rules can, nonetheless, settle into a relatively stable pattern. Elias, op. cit. 1978, pp. 73–80.
22. Ibid. p. 82.
23. Op. cit. Mennell, 1989, p. 261.
24. Op. cit. Elias, 1978, p. 85.
25. Op. cit. Elias, 2000, p. 366.
26. J. Goodman, *Tobacco in History*, London: Routledge, 1993, p. 25.
27. J. Harrington, 'Tobacco smoking among the Karuk Indians of California', *Smithsonian Institute Bureau of American Ethnology Bulletin*, **94** (1932), 193–4.
28. A line of analysis that later culminated in the publication of a book on the topic: J. Hughes (2003) *Learning to Smoke: Tobacco Use in the West*, Chicago: The Chicago University Press.
29. N. Elias and E. Dunning, *Quest for Excitement: Sport and Leisure in the Civilizing Process*, Oxford: Blackwell, 1986.
30. J. Goudsblom, *Fire and Civilization*, London: Penguin, 1992.
31. S. Mennell, *All Manners of Food: Eating and Taste in England and France from the Middle Ages to the Present*, London: Blackwell, 1985.
32. C. Wouters, 'Informalization and the civilizing process' in P.R. Gleichmann, J. Goudsblom and H. Korte (eds) *Human Figurations: Essays for Norbert Elias*, Amsterdam: Stichting Amsterdams Sociologisch Tijdschrift, 1977, pp. 437–53.
33. E. Dunning and C. Rojek (eds) *Sport and Leisure in the Civilizing Process: Critique and Counter Critique*, Basingstoke: Macmillan – now Palgrave Macmillan, 1992.
34. J. Fletcher (1997) *Violence and Civilization: Introduction to the Work of Norbert Elias*, London: Polity Press.
35. C. Rojek (1986) 'Problems of involvement and detachment in the writings of Norbert Elias', *British Journal of Sociology*, **37**(4): 585–96.
36. R. van Krieken (1998) *Norbert Elias*, London: Routledge.
37. A. Blok, 'Primitief en geciviliseerd', *Sociologisch Grids*, **29**(3/4) (1982), 197–209.
38. E. Leach, 'Violence', *London Review of Books*, October (1986).
39. D. Layder, 'Social reality as figuration: a critique of Elias's conception of sociological analysis', *Sociology*, **20**(3) (1986), 367–86.
40. B. Maso, 'Riddereer en riddermoed – ontwikkelingen van de aanvalslust in de late middeleeuwen' (Knightly honour and knightly courage: on changes in fighting spirit in the late Middle Ages), *Sociologische Gids*, **29**(3–4) (1982), 296–325.
41. Op. cit. Mennell, 1989.
42. Op. cit. Elias, 2000, p. 515.
43. R. van Krieken (1998) *Norbert Elias*, London: Routledge
44. Op. cit. Mennel, 1989, p. 248.
45. Fletcher, J. (1997) *Violence and Civilization: Introduction to the Work of Norbert Elias*, London: Polity Press.

46. Op. cit. van Krieken, 1998.
47. Op. cit. Mennell, 1989, p. 241.
48. Ibid. p. 242.
49. Op. cit. Elias, 2000, p.187, cited in Mennell, op. cit. 1989, p. 242.
50. Elias and Dunning, *Quest for Excitement*, p. 44 cited in Mennell, *Norbert Elias*, p. 242.
51. Op. cit. Elias and Dunning, 1986, p. 66.
52. Op. cit. Dunning and Rojek, 1992, p. 248.

Chapter 10 Erving Goffman

1. Goffman's distaste for treating sociology as a set of schools or perspectives is brought out very clearly in his comments on Denzin and Keller's review of *Frame Analysis*. See 'Reply to Denzin and Keller', *Contemporary Sociology – An International Journal of Reviews*, **10** (1981), 60–8.
2. See E. Goffman, 'The interaction order', *American Sociological Review*, **48** (1983), 3.
3. T. Burns, *Erving Goffman*, London: Routledge, 1992, p. 6.
4. Goffman's Ph.D. thesis begins with a long quotation from Simmel in which Simmel refers to 'an immeasurable number of less conspicuous forms of relationship and kinds of interaction' that should be of interest to sociologists alongside our interest in 'large social formations'. Simmel goes on to write: 'That people look at one another and are jealous of one another; that they exchange letters or dine together, that irrespective of all tangible interests they strike one another as pleasant and unpleasant; that gratitude for altruistic acts makes for inseparable union; that one asks another man after a certain street, and that people dress and adorn themselves for one another – the whole gamut of relations that play from one person to another and that may be momentary or permanent, conscious or unconscious, ephemeral or of grave consequence (and from which these illustrations are quite casually chosen), all these incessantly tie men together. Here are the interactions among the atoms of society. They account for all the toughness and elasticity, all the colour and consistency of social life that is so striking and yet so mysterious', G. Simmel, *The Sociology of Georg Simmel*, Glencoe, IL: Free Press, 1960, p. 10.
5. See Chapter 5 of E. Goffman, *Relations in Public*, Harmondsworth: Penguin Books, 1972.
6. See Chapters 3 and 4 of Goffman, ibid.
7. A more general account of this may be found in the essay 'Replies and responses' in E. Goffman, *Forms of Talk*, Oxford: Blackwell, 1981.
8. See Burns, op. cit. 1992, p. 82.
9. P. Manning, *Erving Goffman and Modern Sociology*, Cambridge: Polity Press, 1992.
10. I have provided an account of this vocabulary elsewhere. See R. Williams, 'Goffman's sociology of talk' in J. Ditton (ed.) *The View from Goffman*, London: Macmillan – now Palgrave Macmillan, 1980.
11. See R.J. Anderson, J.A. Hughes, and W.W. Sharrock, *The Sociology Game: An Introduction to Sociological Reasoning*, London: Longman, 1985.
12. Op. cit. Goffman, 1981, p. 62.

13. 'In this report, the individual was divided by implication into two basic parts: he was viewed as a performer, a harried fabricator of impressions involved in the all-too-human task of staging a performance; he was viewed as a character, a figure, typically a fine one, whose spirit, strength and other fine qualities the performance was intended to evoke. The attributes of a performer and the attributes of a character are of a different order, quite basically so, yet both sets have their meaning in terms of the show that must go on', E. Goffman, *Asylums: Essays on the Social Situation of Mental Hospital Patients and Other Inmates*, Harmondsworth: Penguin, 1961, p. 244.
14. Ibid.
15. See 'The underlife of a public institution', in Goffman, op. cit. 1961, pp. 157–280.
16. C. Battershill, 'Erving Goffman as a precursor to post-modern sociology', in S.H. Riggins (ed.) *Beyond Goffman: Studies on Communication, Institution and Social Interaction*, New York: Mouton de Gruyter, 1990, pp. 163–86.
17. Ibid. pp. 163–86.
18. A. Giddens, 'Erving Goffman as a systematic social theorist', in A. Giddens (ed.) *Social Theory and Modern Sociology*, Cambridge: Polity Press, 1987, p. 18.
19. Op. cit. Burns, 1992, p. 24.
20. See especially Chapters 2–4 of *Frame Analysis: An Essay on the Organization of Experience*, New York: Harper & Row, 1974.
21. 'Radio talk: the ways of our errors', in Goffman, op. cit. 1981, pp. 197–330.
22. Manning has noted the way that the metaphors of games and rituals are put against one another such that 'Games emphasise information, fatefulness, manipulation and so on, while ritual emphasises morality, concern, co-operation' in Manning, op. cit. 1992, p. 36.
23. L.H. Lofland, 'Social life in the public realm: a review', *Journal of Contemporary Ethnography*, **17** (1989), 459.
24. E. Goffman, *Relations in Public and Behaviour in Public Places: Notes on the Social Organization of Gatherings*, Glencoe: Free Press, 1963, p. 84.
25. Ibid. p. 86.
26. Op. cit. Lofland, 1989, p. 462.
27. See S. Cavan, *Liquor License*, Chicago: Aldine, 1966. While Cavan's study is now more than 30 years old and was limited to bars in the USA, her observations and analyses of the dynamics of interaction in such settings continue to offer important insights into what happens in similar places here and now.
28. This can, of course become a problem for those who want to use such settings while remaining closed to the overtures of others. Many potential solo users find the work of resisting the overtures of others to be too burdensome to allow them to remain comfortable.
29. Op. cit. Cavan, 1996, p. 50.
30. This does not mean of course that a good deal of interactional work cannot be accomplished during such superficial conversational topic exploration.
31. For example: A. MacIntyre, 'The self as a work of art', *New Statesman*, March (1969) and *After Virtue*, London: Duckworth, 1981; T.G. Miller, 'Goffman, social acting, and moral behavior', *Journal for the Theory of Social Behaviour* **14** (1984), 141–63; A. Ryan, 'Maximising, minimising, moralising', in C. Hookway and P. Pettit (eds) *Action and Interpretation*, Cambridge: Cambridge University Press,

1978, pp. 65–81; R. Sennett, *The Fall of Public Man*, Cambridge: Cambridge University Press, 1977.

32. See Manning, op. cit. 1992, p. 39; Giddens, op. cit. 1987, pp. 109–39.
33. See P. Creelan, 'The degradation of the sacred: approaches of Cooley and Goffman', *Symbolic Interaction*, **10** (1987), 29–56.
34. See A.J. Trevino (ed.) *Goffman's Legacy*, New York: Rowman & Littlefield 2003.
35. See for example: H. Sacks, *Lectures on Conversation*, Cambridge: Blackwell, 1992; H. Sacks, E.A. Schegloff and G. Jefferson, 'A simplest systematics for the organisation of turn-taking in conversation', *Language*, **50** (1974), 696–735; E.A. Schegloff, 'The routine as achievement', *Human Studies*, **9** (1986), 111–51; E.A. Schegloff, 'Between micro and macro: contexts and other connections', in *The Micro–Macro Link,* J.C. Alexander (ed.) Berkeley: California University Press, 1987, pp. 207–34; E.A. Schegloff, 'Goffman and the analysis of conversation', in *E. Goffman: Exploring the Interaction Order*, P. Drew and T. Wootton (eds) Cambridge: Polity Press, 1988, pp. 89–135; E.A. Schegloff, 'Reflections on talk and social structure', in *Talk and Social Structure: Studies in Ethnomethodology and Conversation Analysis*, D. Boden and D.H. Zimmerman (eds) Cambridge: Polity Press, 1991, pp. 44–70. But also see A. Rawls, 'Orders of interaction and intelligibility: intersections between Goffman and Garfinkel by way of Durkheim' in A.J. Trevino (ed.) *Goffman's Legacy*, New York: Rowman & Littlefield, 2003, pp. 216–253 and G.H.W. Smith, 'Ethnomethodological readings of Goffman', in A.J. Trevino (ed.) *Goffman's Legacy*, New York: Rowman & Littlefield, 2003, pp. 254–283.
36. In Goffman, op. cit. 1981, p. 4.
37. Goffman, op. cit. 1983, p. 4.
38. 'In general then (and qualifications apart), what one finds in modern societies at least is a non-exclusive linkage – a 'loose coupling' – between interactional practices and social structures, a collapsing of strata and structures into broader categories, the categories themselves not corresponding one-to-one to anything in the structural world, a gearing as it were of various structures into interactional cogs. Or, if you will, a set of transformation rules, or a membrane selecting how various externally relevant social distinctions will be managed within the interaction', Goffman, op. cit. 1983, p. 11.
39. Op. cit. Burns, 1992, p. 376.
40. See Giddens, op. cit. 1987, pp. 109–39.

Chapter 11 David Lockwood

1. D. Lockwood, *The Blackcoated Worker*, London: Allen & Unwin, 1958.
2. J.H. Goldthorpe, D. Lockwood, F. Bechhofer and J. Platt, *The Affluent Worker: Industrial Attitudes and Behaviour*, Cambridge: Cambridge University Press, 1968.
3. See F. Zweig, *The Worker in an Affluent Society*, London: Heinemann, 1961.
4. See Goldthorpe et al. op. cit 1968 and *The Affluent Worker in the Class Structure* (Cambridge: Cambridge University Press, 1969).
5. G. Marshall, *In Praise of Sociology*, London, Unwin Hyman, 1990, p. 108.
6. R. Blauner, *Alienation and Freedom*, Chicago: The University of Chicago Press, 1964.

7. D. Wedderburn and R. Crompton, *Workers' Attitudes and Technology*, Cambridge: Cambridge University Press, 1972.
8. D. Lockwood, 'Social integration and system integration', in G.K. Zollschan and W. Hirsch (eds) *Explorations in Social Change*, London: Routledge & Kegan Paul, 1964, pp. 244–57; T. Parsons, *The System of Modern Societies*, Englewood Cliffs, NJ: Prentice Hall, 1971.
9. Ibid. Lockwood, p. 244.
10. See T. Parsons and E.S. Shils (eds) *Toward a General Theory of Action*, New York: Harper & Row, 1951; Parsons, op. cit. 1971.
11. For an exposition and early critique of Parsonian-based modernization theories, see H. Bernstein, 'Modernisation theory and the sociological study of development', *Journal of Development Studies*, 7 (1971).
12. On this point, see N. Mouzelis, *Modern Greece: Facets of Underdevelopment*, London: Macmillan – now Palgrave Macmillan, 1978, Ch. 2.
13 D. Lockwood, (1992) *Solidarity and Schism: 'The Problem of Disorder' in Durkheimian and Marxist Sociology*, Oxford: Oxford University Press.
14. Ibid. p. 178.
15. For a further development of these points and their linkages with the social/system-integration distinction, see N. Mouzelis, *Back to Sociological Theory*, London: Macmillan – now Palgrave Macmillan, 1990, Chs 3–7; N. Mouzelis, *Sociological Theory: What Went Wrong? Diagnosis and Remedies*, London: Routledge, 1995, Ch. 5.
16. See N. Elias, *What is Sociology?*, London: Hutchison, 1978.
17. A. Giddens, *The Constitution of Society*, Cambridge: Polity Press, 1984.
18. P. Bourdieu, *Outline of a Theory of Action*, Cambridge: Cambridge University Press, 1977.
19. See Mouzelis, op. cit. 1995, Ch. 6. It might be useful to note here that Giddens has not only unnecessarily substituted the distinction between institutional analysis and analysis in terms of strategic conduct for the social/system-integration distinction; he has also used the social/system-integration dichotomy as a substitute for the micro–macro-integration dichotomy, so making the confusion even worse. On this point, see N. Mouzelis, 'Restructuring structuration theory', *Sociological Review*, 37(4) (1989), 617–35.
20. See for instance E. Laclau and C. Mouffe, *Hegemony and Social Strategy: Towards a Radical Democratic Politics*, London: Verso, 1985; E. Laclau, *New Reflections on the Revolution of our Time*, London: Verso, 1990.
21. For a critique of poststructuralism along such lines, see N. Mouzelis, op. cit. 1995, Ch. 3.
22. J. Habermas, *The Theory of Communicative Action*, vol. II, *Lifeworld and System*, Cambridge: Polity Press, 1987.
23. See N. Mouzelis, 'Social and system integration: Habermas' view', *British Journal of Sociology*, **43**(2) (1992), 272–7.
24. See N. Mouzelis, 'Social and system integration: Lockwood, Giddens, Habermas', *Sociological Review* May, 1997. See also my earlier critique of Lockwood's social/system-integration distinction, 'System and social integration: a reconsideration of a fundamental distinction', *British Journal of Sociology*, December, 1974.
25. For an application of the social/system-integration distinction to the analysis of political transformations in nineteenth and early twentieth-century Greece, see N.

Mouzelis, *Post-Marxist Alternatives*, Basingstoke: Macmillan – now Palgrave Macmillan, 1990), Ch. 4.

26. On this point, see D. Layder, 'Contemporary sociological theory', *Sociology* **30**(3) (1996).

Chapter 12 Harold Garfinkel

1 T. Parsons, *The Social System*, Chicago, IL: Free Press, 1951.
2. R.F. Bales, *Interaction Process Analysis: A Method for the Study of Small Groups*, Reading, MA: Addison Wesley, 1950.
3. E. Husserl, *The Crisis of European Sciences and Transcendental Phenomenology* (trans. D. Carr), Evanston, IL: Northwestern University Press, 1970.
4. H. Garfinkel, 'Research note on inter- and intra-racial homicides', *Social Forces*, 27 (1949), 370–81.
5. H. Garfinkel, 'Color trouble', *Opportunity Magazine*, May 1940. Reprinted in E.J. O'Brien (ed.) *The Best Short Stories of 1941*, pp. 97–119.
6. A. Schutz, *Collected Papers, Vol. 1: The Problem of Social Reality*, The Hague: Martinus Nijhoff, 1962.
7. H. Garfinkel, 'A conception of, and experiments with, "trust" as a condition of stable concerted actions', in O.J. Harvey (ed.) *Motivation and Social Interaction*, New York: Ronald Press, 1963.
8. H. Garfinkel, *Studies in Ethnomethodology*, Englewood Cliffs, NJ: Prentice Hall, 1967a, p. 44.
9. Ibid. p. 47.
10. Ibid. p. 42.
11. Ibid. p. 78.
12. L. Wittgenstein, *Philosophical Investigations* (2nd edn) Oxford: Basil Blackwell, 1958, p. 194.
13. J.M. Atkinson, 'Societal reactions to suicide: the role of coroners' definitions', in S. Cohen (ed.) *Images of Deviance*, Harmondsworth: Penguin, 1971, p. 181.
14. Op. cit. Garfinkel 1967a, pp. 208–61.
15. H. Garfinkel, M. Lynch, and E. Livingston, 'The work of a discovering science construed with materials from the optically discovered pulsar', *Philosophy of the Social Sciences*, **11** (1981), 131–58.
16. H. Garfinkel, 'Practical sociological reasoning: some features of the work of the Los Angeles Suicide Prevention Center', in E.S. Shneidman (ed.) *Essays in Self-destruction,* New York: International Science Press, 1967b.
17. J.M. Atkinson, *Discovering Suicide: Studies in the Social Organization of Sudden Death*, London: Macmillan – now Palgrave Macmillan, 1978; S. Taylor, *Durkheim and the Study of Suicide*, London: Macmillan – now Palgrave Macmillan, 1982.
18. J. Douglas, *The Social Meanings of Suicide*, Princeton, NJ: Princeton University Press, 1967; M.W. Atkinson, N. Kessel, and J. Dalgaard, 'The comparability of suicide rates,' *British Journal of Psychiatry* (1975) **127**; L.H. Day, 'Durkheim on religion and suicide – a demographic critique', *Sociology*, **21** (1987), 449–61.
19. Op. cit. Garfinkel, 1967a, pp. 116–85.
20. C. West, and D. Zimmerman, 'Doing gender', *Gender & Society*, **1** (1987), 125–51.

21. D.E. Smith, *The Everyday World as Problematic: A Feminist Sociology*, Boston: Northeastern University Press, 1987.
22. J.M. Atkinson, *Our Masters' Voices: The Language and Body Language of Politics*, London: Methuen, 1984.
23. J. Heritage, and D. Greatbatch, 'Generating applause: a study of rhetoric and response at party political conferences', *American Journal of Sociology*, **92** (1986), 110–57.
24. J.M. Atkinson, 'Refusing invited applause: preliminary observations from a case study of charismatic oratory', in T. van Dijk (ed.) *Handbook of Discourse Analysis, vol. 3, Discourse and Dialogue*, London: Academic Press, 1985.
25. H. Garfinkel, *Ethnomethodology's Program: Working Out Durkheim's Aphorism*, ed. and introduced by A. Warfield Rawls, Lanham, MD: Rowman and Littlefield, 2002.

Chapter 13 Louis Althusser

1. K. Marx, *Economic and Philosophical Manuscripts of 1844*, trans. M. Milligan, Moscow, 1959.
2. L. Althusser, *The Future Lasts a Long Time*, London: Chatto & Windus, 1993, p. 186.
3. G. Canguilhem, *Ideology and Rationality in the History of the Life Sciences*, Cambridge: MIT, 1988.
4. L. Althusser, *For Marx*, London: New Left Books, 1969.
5. L. Althusser, and E. Balibar (eds), *Reading Capital*, London: New Left Books, 1970.
6. C. Darwin, *The Origin of Species*, Harmondsworth: Penguin, 1968 [1859].
7. C. Darwin, *Descent of Man*, Princeton University Press: Princeton, NJ, 1981.
8. Op. cit. Althusser and Balibar, 1970, p. 119.
9. L. Althusser, *Lenin and Philosophy and Other Essays*, London: New Left Books, 1971.
10. A. Gramsci, *Selections from the Prison Notebooks*, London: Lawrence & Wishart, 1971.
11. Red-Green Study Group (R-GSG) *What on Earth is to be Done?* R-GSG: 2, Hamilton Road, Manchester, 1995.
12. E. Terray, *Marxism and 'Primitive' Societies*, New York: Monthly Review Press, 1972.
13. M. Aglietta, *A Theory of Capitalist Regulation*, London: New Left Books, 1979.
14. A. Lipietz, *Towards a New Economic Order*, Cambridge: Polity Press, 1992.
15. P. Macherey, *Theory of Literary Production*, London: Routledge & Kegan Paul, 1978.
16. T. Eagleton, *Literary Theory: An Introduction*, Minneapolis: University of Minnesota, 1983.
17. N. Poulantzas, *Political Power and Social Classes*, London: New Left Books, 1973; N. Poulantzas, *Classes in Contemporary Capitalism*, London: New Left Books, 1975.
18. E.O. Wright, *Class, Crisis, and the State*, London: New Left Books, 1978; E.O. Wright, *Classes*, London: Verso, 1985; E.O. Wright et al., *The Debate on Classes*, London: Verso, 1989.
19. M. Barratt, *Women's Oppression Today* (2nd edn), London: Verso, 1988.

20. M. McIntosh, 'The state and the oppression of women', in A. Kuhn and A-M. Wolpe (eds) *Feminism and Materialism*, London: Routledge & Kegan Paul, 1978, pp. 254–89.
21. J. Mitchell, *Psychoanalysis and Feminism*, New York: Vintage Books/Harmondsworth: Penguin, 1975.
22. M. Castells, *The Urban Question*, London: Edward Arnold, 1977.
23. P. Anderson, *Lineages of the Absolutist State*, London: New Left Books, 1974a; P. Anderson, *Passages from Antiquity to Feudalism*, London: New Left Books, 1974b.
24. B. Jessop, T*he Capitalist State*, Oxford: Martin Robertson, 1982.
25. N. Poulantzas, *State, Power, Socialism*, London: Verso, 1978.
26. G. Elliott (ed.) *Althusser:A Critical Reader*, Oxford: Blackwell, 1994.
27. E.A. Kaplan and M. Sprinker (eds) *The Althusserian Legacy*, London: Verso, 1993.
28. R. Resch, *Althusser and the Renewal of Marxist Social Theory*, Berkeley, CA: University of California, 1992.
29. A. Levine, *A Future for Marxism? Althusser, the Analytical Turn and Revival of Socialist Theory*, London: Pluto, 2003.
30. W. Montag, *Louis Althusser*, Basingstoke: Palgrave Macmillan, 2003.
31. W.S. Lewis, *Louis Althusser and the Traditions of French Marxism*, Lanham: Lexington Books, 2005.
32. L. Ferretter, *Louis Althusser*, London: Routledge, 2006.

Chapter 14 Nancy J. Chodorow

1. Throughout the writing of this chapter I could not help but think of the Freudian connotations of the heading 'Driving Impulses', that we were asked to use to introduce the influences of the sociological thinkers. Driving impulses, as you will see, are as absent from object relations theory as they are present in traditional Freudian drive theory.
2. N. Chodorow, *Feminism and Psychoanalysis*, New Haven: Yale University Press, 1989, p. 8.
3. Ibid. p. 167.
4. N. Chodorow, *The Reproduction of Mothering*, Berkeley, CA: University of California Press, 1978, p. 99.
5. In her more recent work, (*Feminities, Masculinities and Sexualities: Freud and Beyond*, London: Free Association Books, 1994) Chodorow has taken up issues of sexuality again. In particular, she investigates why psychoanalysis has so many theories about homosexuality but so few about heterosexuality. She argues that like all sexuality, heterosexuality is a 'compromise formation' or a symptom.
6. Chodorow, op. cit. 1978, p. 198.
7. Ibid.
8. N. Chodorow, 'Reply by Nancy Chodorow', *Signs*, Spring (1981), 512.
9. C. Williams, *Gender Differences at Work*, Berkeley, CA: University of California Press, 1989, p. 64.
10. Ibid. p. 66.
11. Ibid. p. 66.
12. Ibid. p. 67.

13. Ibid. p. 64.
14. C. Gilligan, *In a Different Voice*, Cambridge, MA: Harvard University Press, 1982.
15. J. Benjamin, *The Bonds of Love*, New York: Pantheon, 1988.
16. Chodorow, op. cit. 1989, p. 4.
17. Chodorow, op. cit. 1981, p. 504.
18. Chodorow, 'Individuality and difference in how men and women love', in *Femininities, Masculinities and Sexualities: Freud and Beyond*, Lexington, KY: University of Kentucky Press, 1990, pp. 70–92.
19. Chodorow, 'Gender as a personal and cultural construction', *Signs*, Spring (1995), pp. 517.
20. Chodorow, *The Power of Feelings*, New Haven: Yale University Press, 1999.

Chapter 15 Jürgen Habermas

1. J. Habermas, *Theorie des kommunikativen Handelns*, Frankfurt: Suhrkamp, 1981, trans. as *Theory of Communicative Action*, London: Heinemann, 1984 and Cambridge: Polity Press, 1987.
2. M. Horkheimer and T.W. Adorno (1947), *Dialectic of Enlightenment*, trans J. Cumming, New York: Continuum, 1995.
3. J. Habermas, *Autonomy and Solidarity* (2nd edn) (ed. P. Dews) London: Verso, 1992, p. 97.
4. J. Habermas, *Theorie und Praxis*, Neuwied/Berlin: Luchterhand, 1963, trans. as *Theory and Practice*, London: Heinemann, 1974.
5. J. Habermas, *Strukturwandel der Öffentlichkeit*, Neuwied/Berlin: Luchterhand, 1962, (2nd edn) Frankfurt: Suhrkamp, 1989, trans. T. Burger as *The Structural Transformation of the Public Sphere*, Cambridge: Polity Press, 1989.
6. Ibid. p. 244.
7. J. Habermas, *Faktizität und Geltung*, Frankfurt: Suhrkamp, 1992, trans. by W. Rehg as *Between Facts and Norms*, Cambridge: Polity Press, 1996.
8. J. Habermas, *Erkenntnis und Interesse*, Frankfurt: Suhrkamp, 1968, trans. as *Knowledge and Human Interests*, London: Heinemann, 1971.
9. J. Habermas, *Legitimationsprobleme im Spätkapitalismus*, Frankfurt: Suhrkamp, 1973, trans. as *Legitimation Crisis*, London: Heinemann, 1976.
10. J. Habermas, *Communication and the Evolution of Society*, Boston, MA: Beacon Press, 1979.
11. Op. cit. Habermas, 1981/1984.
12. Op. cit. Habermas, 1992/1996.
13. R.C. Holub, *Jürgen Habermas: Critic in the Public Sphere*, London: Routledge, 1991.
14. See, in particular, A. Arato's contribution, 'Critical theory and authoritarian state socialism', in D. Held and J. Thompson (eds) *Habermas: Critical Debates*, London: Macmillan – now Palgrave Macmillan, 1982, pp. 196–218; and Habermas, 'A reply to my critics', pp. 219–83 in the same volume. In my own occasional discussions of these issues, I have found this approach particularly useful; see, for example, 'Steering the public sphere; communication policy in state socialism and after', in B. Einhorn, M. Kaldor and Z. Kavan (eds) *Citizenship and Democratic Control*, Edward Elgar, 1996, pp. 159–72.

15. See, in particular, S. Benhabib, *Critique, Norm and Utopia*, New York: Columbia University Press, 1980; A. Honneth, *Critique of Power*, Cambridge, MA: MIT Press, 1992, first published in 1985; A. Honneth, *The Struggle for Recognition*, Cambridge: Polity Press, 1994.
16. K. Eder, *The New Politics of Class: Social Movements and Cultural Dynamics in Advanced Societies*, London: Sage, 1993; C. Offe, *Contradictions of the Welfare State*, London, Hutchinson, 1984; C. Offe, *Disorganized Capitalism*, Cambridge: Polity Press, 1985.
17. Op. cit. Habermas, 1992/1996.
18. J. Habermas, *Die Einbeziehung des Anderen*, Frankfurt: Suhrkamp, 1996, edited by C. Cronin and P. De Greiff as *The Inclusion of the Other*, Cambridge: MA: MIT, 1998.

Chapter 16 Pierre Bourdieu

1. P. Bourdieu, *The Algerians*, Boston: Beacon Press, 1958/1962; P. Bourdieu, A. Darbel, J.P. Rivet and C. Seibel *Travail et Travailleurs en Algérie*, The Hague: Mouton, 1963; P. Bourdieu and A. Sayad *Le Déracinement. La crise de l'agriculture traditionnelle en Algérie*, Paris: Editions de Minuit, 1964.
2. P. Bourdieu, *The Ball of Bachelors: The Crisis of Peasant Society in Béarn*, Chicago: University of Chicago Press, 2002/2007. 'From the outset, I had designed this research on my own region of origin as a kind of epistemological experiment: to analyze as an anthropologist, in a familiar universe … the matrimonial practices that I had studied in a far-away universe, Algerian society, was to give myself the opportunity to objectivize the act of objectivation and the objectivizing subject' (Bourdieu, 'From rules to strategies', *Cultural Anthropology*, **1–1** (1985/1986): 110–120 (reprinted in *In Other Words*, 1994 rev. ed.) 1985/1986: 112). For a discussion of the pivotal role of this 'paired ethnography' of Kabylia and Béarn in the formation of Bourdieu's intellectual project and theory as well as key texts from that period, see the special issue of *Ethnography* (2004) on 'Pierre Bourdieu in the Field', 4(4).
3. P. Bourdieu recalls that the work of Claude Lévi-Strauss 'imposed upon a whole generation a new manner of conceiving of intellectual activity' that held out the hope of 'reconciling theoretical with practical intentions, the scientific vocation with the ethical or political vocation.' (*The Logic of Practice*, Cambridge: Polity Press, 1980/1990: 8).
4. P. Bourdieu, *Outline of a Theory of Practice*, Cambridge: Cambridge University Press, 1972/1977; Bourdieu, *Algeria 1960*, Cambridge: Cambridge University Press, 1976/1977.
5. P. Bourdieu and J.-C. Passeron *The Inheritors: Students and their Culture*, Chicago: The University of Chicago Press, 1964/1979; P. Bourdieu and J.-C. Passeron, *Reproduction in Education, Culture, and Society*, London: Sage, 1970/1977.
6. P. Bourdieu, *Distinction: A Social Critique of the Judgement of Taste*, London: Routledge, 1979/1984; Bourdieu, *The Logic of Practice*, 1980/1990.
7. P. Bourdieu, *Language and Symbolic Power*, ed. and intro by J.B. Thompson, Cambridge: Polity Press, 1982/1990; Bourdieu, *Homo Academicus*, Cambridge: Polity Press, 1984/1988; Bourdieu, *The State Nobility: Elite Schools in the Field of*

Power, Cambridge: Polity Press, 1989/1997; and Bourdieu, *The Rules of Art: Genesis and Structure of the Artistic Field*, Cambridge: Polity Press, 1992/1997.

8. P. Bourdieu et al., *The Weight of the World: Social Suffering in Contemporary Society*, Cambridge: Polity Press, 1993/1998; Bourdieu, *On Television and Journalism*, London: Pluto Press, 1996/1998; Bourdieu, *Masculine Domination*, Cambridge: Polity Press, 1998/2001; and Bourdieu, *The Social Structures of the Economy*, Cambridge: Polity Press, 2001/2005.
9. P. Bourdieu, *Pascalian Meditations*, Cambridge: Polity Press, 1997/2000.
10. P. Bourdieu, *Science of Science and Reflexivity*, Chicago: The University of Chicago Press, 2001/2004.
11. Both Bourdieu's coyness and his wide public impact are deftly captured in the documentary movie by Pierre Carles, *Sociology is a Martial Art* (2000).
12. L. Wacquant (ed.) *Pierre Bourdieu and Democratic Politics: The Mystery of Ministry*, Cambridge: Polity Press, 2005.
13. Bourdieu (*Masculine Domination,* op. cit.) sees masculine domination as the paradigm of symbolic violence, 'this soft violence, indetectible and invisible to its very victims, which is wielded essentially through purely symbolic channels or, more precisely, through recognition and misrecognition, or even through sentiment', insofar as women perceive themselves through a web of homological categories that operate to naturalize their subordinate relations to men. The family, the church, the school, and the state (as 'public patriarchy') work in tandem to effect the 'historical labor of dehistoricization' that effaces the arbitrariness of the masculine vision of the world inculcated to men and women alike.
14. Unlike most scholars of like stature, Pierre Bourdieu conducted much of the primary data collection and analysis for his research himself. This constant contact with the mundane practicalities of the research routine helped shelter him from the conceptual reification and dessication that often affects the work of social theorists.
15. Bourdieu *Pascalian Meditations,* op. cit., p. 237.
16. Michel Foucault's work is also rooted in, and an extension of, this school of 'historicist rationalism'. Many of the affinities or convergences between Bourdieu and Foucault can be traced back to this common epistemological mooring.
17. P. Bourdieu, J.-C. Passeron and J.-C. Chamboredon *The Craft of Sociology: Epistemological Preliminaries*, Berlin: Aldine de Gruyter, 1968/1979. This is particularly visible in the selection of texts in the philosophy of science that make up the second part of the book and illustrate its core propositions: of the 45 selections, five are by Bachelard and four by Canguilhem (as against six by Durkheim, three by Weber and two by Marx).
18. Ibid. p. 24.
19. Bourdieu *The State Nobility,* op. cit.
20. Bourdieu *Homo Academicus,* op. cit., Chapter 1, 'A book for burning?'
21. P. Bourdieu, *In Other Words: Essays Towards a Reflexive Sociology*, Cambridge: Polity Press, rev. ed., 1987/1994, p. 125.
22. Habitus is an old philosophical concept, used intermittently by Aristotle (under the term *hexis*), Thomas Aquinas, Hegel, Weber, Durkheim, Mauss and Husserl, among others. Bourdieu retrieved it in a 1967 reinterpretation of art historian Erwin Panofsky's analysis of the connection between scholastic thought and gothic architecture in the medieval era and refined it afterwards, both empirically and theoret-

ically, in each of his major works. His most sophisticated explication of the concept is in *Pascalian Meditations* (op. cit., esp. 131–46 and 208–37).

23. This was the case of Bourdieu himself, who acknowledges having 'a cleft habitus' in the sketch for a self-socioanalysis offered in *Science of Science and Reflexivity*. (Bourdieu 2001/2004: 111)
24. For an empirical illustration and conceptual elaboration setting the theory of habitus against structuralism, rational choice and symbolic interaction, see Wacquant's study of prizefighting as embodied practical reason, (*Body and Soul: Notebooks of An Apprentice Boxer*, New York: Oxford University Press, 2000/2004: esp. 77–99).
25. P. Bourdieu, 'The forms of capital', in J.G. Richarson (ed.), *Handbook of Theory and Research for the Sociology of Education*, New York: Greenwood Press, 1986, pp. 241–58.
26. The concept of field *(champ)* was coined by Bourdieu in the mid-1960s for purposes of empirical inquiry into the historical genesis and transformation of the worlds of art and literature. It was later extensively modified and elaborated, by Bourdieu and his associates, in the course of studies of the intellectual, philosophical, scientific, religious, academic, poetic, publishing, political, juridical, economic, sporting, bureaucratic and journalistic fields. The most accessible and compact source on the uses and effects of the concept is the collection of essays entitled *The Field of Cultural Production* (New York: Columbia University Press, 1993) (esp. Part II, 'Flaubert and the French literary field').
27. Bourdieu *Science of Science*, op. cit.
28. The two most common misinterpretations of Bourdieu's theory of practice are those that omit either term of the equation, and thus their varied relationship: the 'structuralist' misreading overlooks habitus and deducts conduct mechanically from social structure while the 'utilitarian' misreading misses field and condemns itself to construe action as the purposeful pursuit of the agent's interest (ironically, the very philosophy of action against which Bourdieu deployed the concept of habitus).
29. P. Bourdieu, 'Social space and symbolic power', *Sociological Theory*, **7–1** (1988/1989): 18–26 (reprinted in *In Other Words*, 1994, rev. edn).
30. *Ethnography* special issue, 'Pierre Bourdieu in the Field', **4**(4), December 2004.
31. P. Bourdieu, L. Boltanski, R. Castel, J.-C. Chamboredon and D. Schnapper (1965/1990), *Photography: A Middlebrow Art*, Cambridge: Polity Press; P. Bourdieu and A. Darbel, with D. Schnapper (1966/1991), *The Love of Art: European Art Museums and their Public*, Cambridge: Polity Press.
32. While Bourdieu's demonstration is carried out with French materials, his theoretical claims apply to all differentiated societies. For pointers on how to extract general propositions from his specific findings on France and to adapt his models to other countries and epochs, see Bourdieu, 'Social space and symbolic space: Introduction to a Japanese reading of *Distinction*', *Poetics Today*, **12–4** (1990/1991): 627–38 (reprinted in *Practical Reason*, 1998), pp. 627–38 and the Preface to the English translation of *The State Nobility* (Bourdieu 1989/1996).
33. Bourdieu *Distinction*, op. cit., p. 564.
34. P. Bourdieu, 'Social space and the genesis of groups', *Theory and Society*, **14**(6) (1984/1985), 723–44.
35. This insistence finds a paradigmatic (and dramatic) illustration in Bourdieu's inaugural lecture at the Collège de France. In this 'Lecture on the lecture', the

freshly consecrated professor dissects 'the act of delegation whereby the new master is authorized to speak with authority' so as to emphasize this fundamental property of sociology as he conceives it: 'Every proposition that this science formulates can and must apply to the subject who produces it' (Bourdieu, *Leçon sur la leçon*, Paris: Editions de Minuit (reprinted as closing chapter in 1987/1991) 1982, p. 8). It is also actualized in Bourdieu's last lecture course at the Collège de France, in which he trained his theory of practice on his own social and intellectual making and in the 'outline of a self-socioanalysis' that grew out of it (Bourdieu, *Sketch for a Self Socioanalysis*, Chicago: The University of Chicago Press, 2004/2007).

36. P. Bourdieu, *The Scholastic Point of View*, 1990.
37. Bourdieu *Pascalian Meditations,* op. cit.
38. Bourdieu *Participant Objectivation*, 2002.
39. Bourdieu *Homo Academicus,* op. cit.
40. The theory of 'symbolic revolution' adumbrated in the closing chapter of *Homo Academicus* is fully developed in *The Rules of Art* (op. cit.), which contains both an account of the historical invention of the institution of modern literature and a sociological theory of intellectual innovation that does away with the charismatic notion of 'genius' once and for all by elucidating it.
41. P. Bourdieu, 'The corporatism of the universal: the role of intellectuals in the modern world', *Telos*, **81** (1989), 99–110.
42. For a discussion of Bourdieu's personal politics, his analyses of political institutions, and his working theory of democratic politics and their implication for contemporary civic struggles, see the essays in Wacquant (*Pierre Bourdieu and Democratic Politics*, op. cit.).
43. Bourdieu et al. *The Weight of the World*, op. cit.
44. The book had an immediate impact unmatched by any social science book in recent memory: it sold over 100,000 copies in four months and stood atop the best-seller list for months; it was extensively discussed in political circles and popular magazines alike (conservative Prime Minister Balladur publicly instructed his Cabinet members to read it); it was later adapted for the stage and is widely used by school teachers, social workers and grass-roots activists.
45. P. Bourdieu (1998/2000) *Acts of Resistance: Against the Tyranny of the Market*, Cambridge: Polity Press.
46. Bourdieu also sought to make his own theories more accessible to a broad educated public in several collections of lectures and talks, notably *Sociology in Question*, *In Other Words* and *Practical Reasons* (Bourdieu 1980/1993, 1987/1994, 1994/1998).

Chapter 17 Michel Foucault

1. Foucault's Chair at the College de France was given the special title of Chair in the History of Systems of Thought. Foucault's major books are listed in the Bibliography. In addition, the following books are particularly useful introductions: J. Rajchman, *Michel Foucault and the Freedom of Philosophy*, New York: Columbia University Press, 1985; B. Smart, *Michel Foucault*, Chichester: Ellis Horwood, 1985; and A. Sheridan, *Michel Foucault: The Will to Truth*, London: Routledge, 1990.

2. M. Foucault, *The Order of Things: An Archaeology of the Human Sciences*, New York: Vintage Books, 1973.
3. For the influence of Nietzsche on Foucault's thought, students may refer to M. Foucault, *Language, Counter-memory, Practice*, D. Bouchard (ed.) Ithaca: Cornell University Press, 1977; M. Mahon, *Foucault's Nietzschean Genealogy: Truth, Power, and the Subject*, Albany: State University of New York Press, 1992; D. Owen, *Maturity and Modernity: Nietzsche, Weber, Foucault, and the Ambivalence of Reason*, London: Routledge, 1994.
4. H. Dreyfus, and P. Rabinow, *Michel Foucault: Beyond Structuralism and Hermeneutics*, Chicago: University of Chicago Press, 1982.
5. L. McNay, *Foucault and Feminism: Power, Gender and the Self*, Cambridge: Polity Press, 1992.
6. For the influences of Canguilhem and Bachelard on Foucault, see G. Gutting, *Michel Foucault's Archaeology of Scientific Reason*, Cambridge: Cambridge University Press, 1989.
7. M. Foucault, *Discipline and Punish: The Birth of the Prison*, New York: Vintage Books, 1979.
8. These points are well captured in G. Deleuze, *Foucault*, Minneapolis: University of Minnesota Press, 1988; and T. Dumm, *Michel Foucault and the Politics of Freedom*, Thousand Oaks, CA: Sage, 1996.
9. M. Foucault, *The History of Sexuality: An Introduction, Vol. 1*, New York: Vintage Books, 1980. The following five volumes did not appear as projected, and for reasons that we will explore below, Foucault directed his research into the experience of sexuality toward the ancient Greeks. M. Foucault, *The Use of Pleasure*, New York: Pantheon Books, 1985; M. Foucault, *The Care of the Self*, New York: Pantheon Books, 1986.
10 Op. cit. M. Foucault, 1980, p. 18.
11. Ibid. p. 61.
12. Ibid. p. 25.
13. Ibid. p. 145 (emphasis added).
14. M. Foucault, 'The dangerous individual', in L. Kritzman (ed.) *Politics, Philosophy, Culture: Interviews and Other Writings, 1977–1984*, New York: Routledge, 1988.
15. In addition to the themes we have covered here, namely discipline and sexuality, Foucault was also weaving in his work on those practices through which madness was separated from reason, and on transformations in the medicalization of society. See M. Foucault, *Madness and Civilization: A History of Insanity in the Age of Reason*, London: Tavistock, 1967; and M. Foucault, *The Birth of the Clinic*, London: Tavistock, 1973.
16. Op. cit. M. Foucault, 1988, p. 150.
17. Ibid. p. 135. See also, M. Foucault, *Abnormal: Lectures at the Collège de France, 1974–1975*, ed. V. Marchetti and A. Salomoni, trans. G. Burchell, London: Verso, 2003.
18. Op. cit. Foucault, 1988, p. 142.
19. M. Foucault, *The Use of Pleasure, The Care of the Self, and The Hermeneutics of the Subject: Lectures at the Collège de France, 1981–82*, ed. F. Gros, trans. G. Burchell, Basingstoke: Palgrave Macmillan, 2005.

20. M. Foucault, *The Use of Pleasure*, p. 91.
21. M. Foucault, *The Care of the Self*, pp. 86–9; p. 42.
22. The issues in this section may be pursued more closely in the following essays: M. Foucault, 'Afterword: The subject and power', in H. Dreyfus and P. Rabinow (eds) *Michel Foucault: Beyond Structuralism and Hermeneutics*, Chicago: University of Chicago Press, 1982; 'Kant on enlightenment and revolution', *Economy and Society*, 15(1)(1986), 88–96; and 'What is enlightenment?', in P. Rabinow (ed.) *The Foucault Reader*, New York: Pantheon Books, 1984.
23. M. Foucault, 'What is enlightenment?', pp. 34, 35.
24. Ibid. p. 45.
25. For a particularly useful elaboration of Foucault's approach to power, see J. Ransom, *Foucault's Discipline: The Politics of Subjectivity*, Durham: Duke University Press, 1997.
26. M. Foucault, 'What is enlightenment?', p. 48.
27. J. Donzelot, *The Policing of Families*, Baltimore: Johns Hopkins University Press, 1979.
28. Ibid. p. 94.
29. N. Rose, *Governing the Soul: The Shaping of the Private Self*, London: Routledge, 1989.
30. Ibid. pp. 149–50.
31. Ibid. p. 208.
32. G. Deleuze, 'What is a *dispositif*?', T. Armstrong (trans.) *Michel Foucault: Philosopher*, London: Harvester Wheatsheaf, 1992, p. 162.
33. These themes may be explored in M. Foucault, *Ethics: Subjectivity and Truth*, P. Rabinow (ed.) New York: The New Press, 1997.
34. M. Foucault, *Society Must Be Defended: Lectures at the Collège de France, 1975–1976*, M. Bertani and A. Fontana (eds) trans. D. Macey, New York: Picador, 2003; and 'Two lectures', in C. Gordon (ed.) *Power/Knowledge: Selected Interviews and Other Writings, 1972–1977*, New York: Pantheon Books, 1980.
35. These themes may be followed in M. Foucault, 'Politics and reason', in L. Kritzman (ed.) *Politics, Philosophy, Culture: Interviews and Other Writings, 1977–1984*, New York: Routledge, 1988; and 'Governmentality' in G. Burchell, C. Gordon, and P. Miller (eds) *The Foucault Effect: Studies in Governmentality*, London: Harvester Wheatsheaf, 1991, pp. 87–104.
36. See Burchell et al. op. cit. Especially useful for clarifying the connection between subjectification and governmentality is G. Burchell, 'Peculiar interests: civil society and governing the "system of natural liberty"', pp. 119–50.
37. See Burchell et al. op. cit. For Foucault's course summaries and other materials, see M. Foucault, *Ethics: Subjectivity and Truth*, P. Rabinow (ed.) New York: The New Press, 1997. See also M. Foucault, *Power – Essential Works of Foucault*, vol. 3, London: Penguin Books, 2002.
38. See Burchell et al. op. cit. and A. Barry, T. Osborne, and N. Rose, *Foucault and Political Reason: Liberalism, Neo-liberalism and Rationalities of Government*, London: UCL Press, 1996; M. Dean, *The Constitution of Poverty: Toward a Genealogy of Liberal Governance*, London: Routledge, 1991.
39. M. Foucault, 'Sexual choice, sexual act: Foucault and homosexuality', in L. Kritzman (ed.) *Politics, Philosophy, Culture: Interviews and Other Writings,*

1977–1984, New York: Routledge, 1988, pp. 286–303; M. Foucault 'Friendship as a way of life', in *Ethics: Subjectivity and Truth*, P. Rabinow (ed.) New York: The New Press, 1997.
40. M. Foucault, *Society Must Be Defended: Lectures at the Collège de France, 1975–1976*, New York: Picador, 2003.

Chapter 18 Stuart Hall

1. 'The formation of a diasporic intellectual: an interview with Stuart Hall by Kuan-Hsing Chen', in *Stuart Hall: Critical Dialogues in Cultural Studies*, D. Morley and K.-H. Chen (eds) London: Routledge, 1996, pp. 484–503.
2. 'Encoding/decoding' first published in 1977, CCCS *Working Papers in Cultural Studies*; reprinted in S. Hall (ed.) *Culture, Media, Language*, London: Unwin Hyman, 1990; in S. During (ed.) *The Cultural Studies Reader*, London: Routledge, 1993, pp. 90–103.
3. 'Reflections upon the encoding/decoding model: an interview with Stuart Hall' in J. Cruz and J. Lewis (eds) *Viewing, Reading, Listening: Audiences and Cultural Reception*, Boulder, CO: Westview Press, 1993, pp. 253–74.
4. 'Gramsci's relevance for the study of race and ethnicity', in Morley and Chen 1996, op. cit. pp. 411–40.
5. 'The West and the rest: discourse and power', in S. Hall and B. Gieben (eds) *Formations of Modernity*, Cambridge: Polity Press, 1992, p. 294.
6. 'When was "the post-colonial"? Thinking at the limits', in I. Chambers and L. Curti (eds) *The Post-colonial Question*, London: Routledge, 1996, pp. 242–60.
7. 'The question of cultural identity', in S. Hall, D. Held and T. McGrew (eds) *Modernity and its Futures*, Cambridge: Polity Press, 1992, p. 297.
8. 'Who needs identity?', in S. Hall and P. du Gay (eds) *Questions of Cultural Identity*, London: Sage, 1996.
9. 'New ethnicities', in Morley and Chen 1996, op. cit. pp. 441–9.
10. 'The spectacle of the "Other"', in S. Hall (ed.) *Representation: Cultural Representations and Signifying Practices*, London: Sage, 1997, pp. 223–90.
11. Op. cit. Morley and Chen 1996, p. 16.
12. Op. cit. Chambers and Curti 1996, p. 249.
13. 'On postmodernism and articulation' (an interview with Lawrence Grossberg) in Morley and Chen 1996, op. cit. p. 149.
14. N. Goodman and S. Hall, *Pictures of Everyday Life: The People, Places and Cultures of the Commonwealth*, London: Comedia, 1987.
15. Op. cit. Hall 1993.
16. S. Hall, 'The way we live now', in M. Tabrizian, *Beyond the Limits*, Germany: Steidl, 2004.
17. S. Hall, and M. Sealy, *Different: A Historical Context: Contemporary Photographers and Black Identity*, New York: Phaidon Press, 2001.
18. Ibid.
19. S. Hall, 'Chris Ofili in paradise: dreaming in Afro', in C. Ofili, *Within Reach* (British Pavilion, 50th Venice Biennale, vol. 1) London: Chris Ofili and Victoria Miro Gallery, 2003.

20. Ibid.
21. S. Hall, 'Whose heritage? Unsettling "the heritage": re-imagining the post-nation', in *Inclusive Europe? Horizon 2020*, Y. R. Isar (ed.) Budapest: Kulturpont Iroda, 2005.
22. S. Hall, 'Modernity and its others: three "moments" in the post-war history of the black diaspora arts', *History Workshop Journal*, spring 2006.
23. S. Hall, 'Museums of modern art and the end of history', in *Annotations 6: Modernity and Difference: Stuart Hall and Sarat Maharaj*, London: InIVA, 2001.
24. Ibid.
25. G. Farred, *What's My Name?: Black Vernacular Intellectuals*, Minneapolis: Minnesota University Press, 2003; J. Procter, *Stuart Hall*, London: Routledge, 2004; C. Rojek, *Stuart Hall*, Cambridge: Polity Press, 2003; H. Davis, *Understanding Stuart Hall*, London: Sage, 2004.

Chapter 19 Dorothy E. Smith

1. Although expressed in most of her works, this dimension is explored in depth most in her books; D.E. Smith, *The Everyday World as Problematic. A Feminist Sociology*, Boston: Northeastern University Press, 1987; Smith, *The Conceptual Practices of Power: A Feminist Sociology of Knowledge*, Toronto: University of Toronto Press, 1990; Smith, *Texts, Facts, and Femininity: Exploring the Relations of Ruling*, London: Routledge 1990; Smith, *Writing the Social: Critique, Theory and Investigations*, Toronto: University of Toronto Press 1999; Smith, *Institutional Ethnography: A Sociology for People*, New York: AltaMira Press 2005.
2. This issue is adressed especially in Smith's article 'Telling the truth after postmodernism', *Studies in Symbolic Interaction* (1996) **19**(3).
3. For example in Smith, 1987 op. cit., Smith, 1999 op. cit. and in her article 'Writing women's experiences into social science', *Feminism & Psychology* (1991) **1**(1): 156–7.
4. Op. cit. Smith, 1987.
5. For example in her books, Smith, op. cit. 1990, 1999, and in an article, op. cit. 1991.
6. See for example Smith, op. cit. 1987, p. 3 and 1999, p. 77–80
7. K. Crenshaw, N. Gotanda, G. Peller and K. Thomas (eds) *Critical Race Theory: The Key Writings that formed the Movement*, New York: New York Press, 1995.
8. E. Durkheim, *The Rules of Sociological Method*, New York: Free Press, 1964 in Smith, op. cit. 1991.
9. Op. cit. Smith, 1999, pp. 54–62.
10. See for example P. Bourdieu, *In Other Words*, London: Polity Press, 1990.
11. 'Objectivism' is the term used by Bourdieu to refer disapprovingly to accounts that fail to respect the participating actors.
12. D. Smith, 'Sociology from women's experience: a reaffirmation', *Sociological Theory*, (1992) **10**(1): 91–4; Smith, op. cit. 1999, pp. 5–8.
13. In her article, op. cit. 1996, 'Telling the truth after postmodernism', Smith develops in detail both her critique of the poststructuralist approach to texts as well as an alternative sociological understanding and approach.
14. R. Barthes, 'From work to text', in *Image–music–text: Essays*, Glasgow: Fontana Collins, 1977.
15. Op. cit. Smith, 1987.

16. In her article 'Texts and the ontology of organizations and institutions', *Studies in Cultures, Organizations and Societies* (2001) 7:159–198, Smith develops the perspective of institutional ethnography as well as giving empirical illustrations of its use. It is the very topic of her latest book, *Institutional Ethnography: A Sociology for People*, New York: AltaMira Press 2005.
17. The time of tiredness is also the title of the book; U.-B. Lilleaas and K. Widerberg, *Trøtthetens tid*, published in Norwegian, Oslo: Pax, 2001, in which we present our research findings. Some of its findings have so far been presented in English in two articles; K. Widerberg, 'Embodied gender talks: the gendered discourse on tiredness', in D. Morgan, B. Brandth and E. Kvande (eds) *Gender, Bodies and Work*, London: Ashgate, 2005, and K. Widerberg, 'Embodying modern times: investigating tiredness', *Time and Society* (2006) **15**(1): 105–20.
18. See for example M. Campbell and A. Manicom (eds) *Knowledge, Experience, and Ruling Relations: Studies in the Social Organization of Knowledge*, Toronto: University of Toronto Press, 1995. Also see D. Smith (ed.) *Institutional Ethnography as Practice*, Oxford: Rowman & Littlefield, 2006.
19. Anja Bredal has used Smith's approach in her Ph.D. dissertation on arranged marriages, A. Bredal, *Vi er jo en familie*, Dept of Sociology and Human Geography, University of Oslo, 2004.
20. *Feeding the Family* is also the title of a book by M.L. DeVault, Chicago: The University of Chicago Press 1994, which makes use of Smith's approach.
21. Günter Wallraff is a German journalist who became well known in the 1970s and 80s for his books on the life and situation of people living at the bottom of the social ladder, for example G. Wallraff *Ihr da oben-wir da unten*, Köln: Kiepenheuer & Witsch, 1973. He lived, for a while, as they lived, for example as a 'guest-worker', in disguise, and managed to give vivid descriptions of how they were treated. His method of dismantling and laying bare the pretensions of the German welfare society has been both appraised and criticized but his influence on investigative journalism hereafter is unquestionable. The term 'Wallraff tradition' is still common currency in the European context.
22. B. Ehrenreich, *Nickel and Dimed: On (Not) Getting By in America*, New York: Owl Books, 2001.
23. Ibid. p 187.
24. See for example *Signs* (1997) **22**(2) and *The Sociological Quarterly* (1993) **34**(1).
25. For example by C.T. Mohanty, *Feminism without Borders*, Durham: Duke University Press, 2003.

Chapter 20 Anthony Giddens

1. A. Giddens, *Capitalism and Modern Social Theory: An Analysis of the Writings of Marx, Durkheim and Max Weber*, Cambridge: Cambridge University Press, 1971, p. 224 passim.
2. A. Giddens, *Beyond Left and Right: The Future of Radical Politics*, Cambridge: Polity Press, 1994, see especially Ch. 1.

3. A. Giddens, *Modernity and Self-identity: Self and Society in the Late Modern Age*, Cambridge: Polity Press, 1991. See also A. Giddens, *The Consequences of Modernity*, Cambridge: Polity Press, 1990, p. 150.
4. I. Berlin, *The Hedgehog and the Fox: An Essay on Tolstoy's View of History*, London: Wiedenfeld & Nicolson, 1953, pp. 1–2. In social theory Berlin's sensibility of the fox corresponds in salient respects to what Robert Merton terms 'sociological ambivalence'. Insofar as Giddens consistently works at two projects of his own, he is not sociologically ambivalent in Merton's sense of the term. See R. Merton (with E. Barber) 'Sociological ambivalence', in *Sociological Ambivalence and Other Essays*, New York: Free Press, 1976 1963, Ch. 1.
5. Giddens' most extensive exposition of structuration theory appears in *The Constitution of Society: Outline of the Theory of Structuration*, Cambridge: Polity Press, 1984.
6. For a technical discussion of the 'ontology of potentials' in structuration theory, see I.J. Cohen, *Structuration Theory: Anthony Giddens and the Constitution of Social Life*, London: Macmillan – now Palgrave Macmillan, 1989, pp. 12–18 passim.
7. For some brief comparisons between Giddens and Dewey on social practices, see I.J. Cohen, 'Theories of action and praxis', in B.S. Turner (ed.) *The Blackwell Companion to Social Theory*, Oxford: Basil Blackwell, 1996, pp. 131, 134–5.
8. Giddens has maintained a distinction between philosophy and social theory from the beginning of his career, see Giddens op. cit. 1971, p. x; A. Giddens, 'The social sciences and philosophy: trends in recent social theory', in *Social Theory and Modern Sociology*, Cambridge: Polity Press, 1987, p. 72 passim.
9. For a somewhat more extensive summary of these issues, see I.J. Cohen, 'Structuration and social order: five issues in brief', in J. Clark, C. Modgil and S. Modgil, *Anthony Giddens: Consensus and Controversy*, London: Falmer Press, 1990, Ch. 4, reprinted in C.G.A. Bryant and D. Jary, *Anthony Giddens: Critical Assessments*, London: Routledge, 1996, selection 40.
10. See Giddens, op. cit. 1984, Ch. 3. Giddens acknowledges important debts to Torsten Hägerstrand, Derek Gregory, Nigel Thrift and other innovators in time-geography.
11. As I stress below, this image of repetitive routines in no way denies the potential for change that remains open in every instance of praxis.
12. Giddens converges with network analysis on the uneven strength and weakness of boundaries. For extensive commentary on the foundations of network analysis and other morphological theories from a structurational point of view, see Cohen, op. cit. 1989, Ch. 2.
13. I omit a discussion of Giddens' technical concept of the duality of structure here. I also omit Giddens' template of structural properties. Interested readers should consult A. Giddens, *Central Problems in Social Theory: Action, Structure and Contradiction in Social Analysis*, London: Macmillan – now Palgrave Macmillan, 1979, Chs 1, 3 and op. cit. 1984, pp. 16–34.
14. The adjective 'discursive' implies that our fully conscious thoughts are structured by the patterns of language (both grammar and semantics) we commonly employ. The philosophical precedents for this position begin with various American pragmatists and the later philosophy of Ludwig Wittgenstein.

15. See R. Rosenblatt, 'No escaping modern times', *U.S. News & World Report* October 2, 1989, pp. 10–11 for an exceptional example of commentary on modernity in the popular press. Rosenblatt may have been influenced by Marshall Berman's evocative literary study of ambivalence towards modernity in *All That is Solid Melts into Air: The Experience of Modernity*, New York: Simon & Schuster, 1982, see especially Ch. 1. I have found Rosenblatt's brief but elegant essay exceptionally useful in teaching courses on modernity.
16. In *Consequences of Modernity*, Giddens outlines his basic views on reflexivity in modernity. He carries these themes forward in *Modernity and Self-identity* and *Beyond Left and Right*. For his most recent account, this time in relation to the problem of culture, see 'Living in a post-traditional society' in U. Beck, A. Giddens and S. Lash, *Reflexive Modernization: Politics, Tradition, and Aesthetics in the Modern Social Order*, Cambridge: Polity Press, 1994, Ch. 2; reprinted in A. Giddens, *In Defence of Sociology*, Cambridge: Polity Press, 1996, Ch. 1.
17. On Giddens' image of the juggernaut see *The Consequences of Modernity*, op. cit. 1990, Ch. 5.
18. See A. Giddens, *A Contemporary Critique of Historical Materialism, vol. 1, Power, Property and the State*, London: Macmillan – now Palgrave Macmillan, 1981, Ch. 4; Giddens, *The National-State and Violence*, London: Macmillan – now Palgrave Macmillan, 1985, Ch. 7 passim.
19. On risk and empowerment, see Giddens, op. cit. 1990, 1991.
20. See citations at note 3 above.
21. On the dialectic of control and Giddens' theory of power in structuration theory, which is developed in bits and pieces throughout many of his works, see Cohen, op. cit. 1989, Ch. 5.
22. On emancipatory and life politics, see *Beyond Left and Right*, op. cit. 1994. For a briefer statement, see *Modernity and Self-identity*, op. cit. 1991, Ch. 7.
23. A. Giddens, *New Rules of Sociological Method: A Positive Critique of Interpretive Sociologies*, London: Hutchinson, 1976.
24. For commentary and bibliography on Elias, see S. Mennell, *Norbert Elias: Civilization and the Human Self-image*, Oxford: Basil Blackwell, 1989. For commentary and bibliography on (and by) Bourdieu, see P. Bourdieu and L.J.D. Wacquant, *An Invitation to Reflexive Sociology*, Chicago: University of Chicago Press, 1992.
25. On the 'new institutionalism', see W.W. Powell and P.J. DiMaggio, 'Introduction', in *The New Institutionalism in Organizational Analysis*, Chicago: University of Chicago Press, 1991, pp. 1–38. On 'practice theory' in anthropology, see P.B. Roscoe, 'Practice and centralisation: a new approach to political evolution', *Current Anthropology* 13(2) (1993), 111–40. William Sewell Jr's historical sociological work appears in his essay 'A theory of structure: duality, agency, and transformation: dialectic and history', *American Journal of Sociology* **98**(1) (July 1992), 1–29. Rob Stones' recent book on theoretical method is *Sociological Reasoning: Towards a Past-modern Sociology*, Basingstoke: Macmillan – now Palgrave Macmillan, 1996).
26. In a more extensive account, I would include a critique of what I judge to be Giddens' excessive reliance on ontological security as the basis of consciousness. This is one of the few reductionist tendencies in Giddens' work, but its conseq-

uences colour a great deal of his thought, including his normative limitations, which I briefly summarize below. I hope to write more on this theme in future works.

27. To be clear, I make no claim here that Giddens is 'objective' or 'value-free'. In fact, whenever Giddens or any other sociologist exposes any unfamiliar aspect of everyday life, that revelation challenges ordinary moral interpretations of everyday life, albeit to a greater extent in some cases than in others. My main point here is that Giddens does not make a normative vision or an ethical principle the keystone of his thought.
28. See Giddens' defence of his normative position in 'A reply to my critics' in D. Held and J.B. Thompson, *Social Theory of Modern Societies: Anthony Giddens and His Critics*, Cambridge: Cambridge University Press, 1989, pp. 288–93.
29. A. Giddens, *The Third Way: The Renewal of Social Democracy*, Cambridge: Polity Press, 1998.
30. A. Giddens, *Runaway World: How Globalization is Shaping our Lives*, London: Profile Books, 1999.
31. A. Giddens, *The Third Way and its Critics*, Cambridge: Polity Press, 2000; A. Giddens, and P. Diamond, (eds) *The New Egalitarianism*, Cambridge: Polity Press, 2005.
32. A. Giddens, *Europe in the Global Age*, Cambridge: Polity Press, 2007, p. ix.
33. A. Giddens, *Over To You, Mr Brown: How Labour Can Win Again*, Cambridge: Polity Press, 2007, p. 12.
34. R. Stones, *Structuration Theory*, Basingstoke: Palgrave Macmillan, 2005.
35. C. Bryant, and D. Jary, 'Coming to terms with Anthony Giddens', in Giddens' *Theory of Structuration: A Critical Appreciation*, London: Routledge, 1991; C. Bryant, and D. Jary (eds) *Anthony Giddens: Critical Assessment*, 4 vols, London: Routledge, 1997; C. Bryant, and D. Jary, *The Contemporary Giddens: Social Theory in a Globalizing Age*, Basingstoke: Palgrave Macmillan, 2001.
36. Op. cit. note 25.
37. Op. cit. Cohen, 1989.
38. M. Archer, *Realist Social Theory*, Cambridge: Cambridge University Press, 1995.
39. N. Mouzelis, *Back to Sociological Theory: The Construction of Social Orders*, Basingstoke: Macmillan – now Palgrave Macmillan, 1991; N. Mouzelis, *Sociological Theory: What Went Wrong?* London: Routledge, 1995.
40. M. Emirbayer, and A. Mische, 'What is agency?' *American Journal of Sociology*, **103**(4): 962–1023, 1998.

Chapter 21 Michael Mann

1. M. Mann, *The Sources of Social Power*, vol. I: *A History of Power from the Beginning to 1760 AD*, Cambridge: Cambridge University Press, 1986; M. Mann, *The Sources of Social Power*, vol. II: *The Rise of Classes and Nation-States, 1760–1914*, Cambridge: Cambridge University Press, 1993.
2. See the bibliography in J.A. Hall and R. Schroeder (eds) *An Anatomy of Power: The Social Theory of Michael Mann*, Cambridge: Cambridge University Press, 2006.
3. M. Mann, *Fascists*, Cambridge: Cambridge University Press, 2004.

4. M. Mann, *The Dark Side of Democracy: Explaining Ethnic Cleansing*, Cambridge: Cambridge University Press, 2005.
5. M. Mann, *Incoherent Empire*, London: Verso, 2003.
6. An engagement with Marxism and alternative analyses of history was also a running theme of a seminar called 'Patterns of History' that Mann organized together with Ernest Gellner and John Hall, whom we shall encounter later in this chapter, at the LSE in the 1980s (which the author of this chapter also attended as a Ph.D. student). At the time, Mann taught sociology at the LSE, but his career took him to the US and UCLA (in 1987), where he has since been professor of sociology. (For this background, see Hall and Schroeder 2006, op. cit.)
7. Op. cit. Mann 1986, p. 1.
8. Op. cit. Mann 1986, p. 28.
9. Op. cit. Mann 1986, pp. 6–10.
10. Op. cit. Mann 1986, pp. 22–32.
11. Op. cit. Mann 1986, p. 27.
12. Op. cit. Mann 1993, especially pp. 54–63.
13. Op. cit. Mann 1993, pp. 75–87.
14. M. Mann, 'The social cohesion of liberal democracy', *American Sociological Review*, 35: 423–39, 1970.
15. E. Gellner, 'A social contract in search of an idiom: the demise of the Danegeld state', in E. Gellner, *Spectacles and Predicaments: Essays in Social Theory*, Cambridge: Cambridge University Press, 1979, pp. 277–306.
16. M. Mann, 'Globalizations: an introduction to the spatial and structural networks of globality', http://www.sscnet.ucla.edu/04F/soc191f-1/globalizations.pdf.
17. M. Mann, 'The sources of social power revisited: A response to criticism', in J.A. Hall and R. Schroeder (eds) *An Anatomy of Power: The Social Theory of Michael Mann*, Cambridge: Cambridge University Press, 2006, pp. 343–96; F. Cooper, *Africa Since 1940: The Past of the Present*, Cambridge: Cambridge University Press, 2002.
18. Op. cit. Mann n.d.
19. Op. cit. Mann n.d. p. 10.
20. J.M. Hobson, 'Disappearing taxes or the "race to the middle"? Fiscal policy in the OECD', in L.Weiss (ed.) *States in the Global Economy: Bringing Domestic Institutions Back In*, Cambridge: Cambridge University Press, 2003, pp. 37–57.
21. But see A.-M. Slaughter, *A New World Order*, Princeton: Princeton University Press, 2004.
22. Op. cit. Mann 1970.
23. See S. Courtois, N. Werth, J.-L. Panne et al., *The Black Book of Communism: Crimes, Terror, Repression*, Cambridge, MA: Harvard University Press, 1999.
24. M. Mann, 'As the twentieth century ages', *New Left Review*, **214**:104–24, 1995.
25. Op. cit. Mann 2005, pp. 70–110.
26. V. Perez-Diaz, *The Return of Civil Society*, Cambridge, MA: Harvard University Press, 1993, pp. 66–9.
27. Op. cit. Mann 2004, p. 27.
28. Op. cit. Mann 2005, p. 506.
29. Op. cit. Mann 2005, pp. 318–52.
30. C. Dandeker, *Surveillance, Power and Modernity*, Cambridge: Polity Press, 1990.
31. Op. cit. Mann 1995.

32. M. Mann, 'The roots and contradictions of modern militarism', in M. Mann, *States, War and Capitalism*, Oxford: Basil Blackwell, pp. 166–87, 1988a.
33. S. Huntington, *The Clash of Civilizations and the Remaking of the World Order*, New York: Simon & Schuster, 1996.
34. Op. cit. Mann 2003, p. 266.
35. P. Kennedy, *The Rise and Fall of the Great Powers*, New York: Random House, 1987; N. Ferguson, *Colossus: The Rise and Fall of the American Empire*, London: Allen Lane, 2004.
36. J.A. Hall, *Powers and Liberties*, Harmondsworth: Penguin, 1986; J.A. Hall, *International Orders*, Cambridge: Polity Press, 1996; E. Gellner, *Plough, Sword and Book: The Structure of Human History*, London: Collins Harvill, 1986; E. Gellner, *Conditions of Liberty: Civil Society and its Rivals*, London: Hamish Hamilton, 1994.
37. R. Young, *Postcolonialism: A Very Short Introduction*, Oxford: Oxford University Press, 2003.
38. J.M. Hobson, 'Mann, the state and war', in J.A. Hall and R. Schroeder (eds) *An Anatomy of Power: The Social Theory of Michael Mann*, Cambridge: Cambridge University Press, 2006, pp.150–66; C. Reus-Smit, 'The idea of history and history with ideas', in S. Hobden and J.M. Hobson (eds) *Historical Sociology of International Relations*, Cambridge: Cambridge University Press, 2002, pp. 120–40.
39. J. Golthorpe, 'The uses of history in sociology: reflections on some recent tendencies', *British Journal of Sociology*, **42**(2): 211–30, 1991.
40. Op. cit. Gellner 1986, pp. 11–15.
41. Op. cit. Mann 2006, p. 385.
42. M. Mann, 'Ruling class strategies and citizenship', in M. Mann, *States, War and Capitalism*, Oxford: Basil Blackwell, pp.188–209, 1988b.
43. R. Collins, 'Maturation of the state-centered theory of revolution and ideology', *Sociological Theory*, **11**, 1993; R. Collins. 'Mann's transformation of the classic sociological traditions', in Hall and Schroeder, op. cit. 2006, pp. 19–32.
44. Op. cit. Mann 1988b.
45. See the chapters in Hall and Schroeder 2006, op. cit.
46. D. Laitin, 'Mann's dark side: linking democracy and genocide', in Hall and Schroeder op. cit. 2006, pp. 328–40.
47. Op. cit. Mann 2006, pp. 358–65; see also J. Snyder, *From Voting to Violence: Democratization and Nationalist Conflict*, New York: W.W. Norton, 2000, for an account of the link between ethnic cleansing and democracy that offers a different explanation.
48. See the contributions by Gorski, Bryant, and Snyder in Hall and Schroeder 2006, op. cit.
49. Op. cit. Gellner 1986.
50. Op. cit. Mann 2006, p. 348.
51. Schroeder, R., 'Introduction: The IEMP model and its critics', in Hall and Schroeder 2006, op. cit. pp. 1–16; J. Goldstone, 2006. 'A historical, not comparative method: breakthroughs and limitations in the theory and methodology of Michael Mann's analysis of power', in Hall and Schroeder 2006, op. cit. pp. 263–82.
52. Op. cit. Mann 2006, pp. 375–8.

Chapter 22 Arlie Russell Hochschild

1. A.R. Hochschild, *The Managed Heart: The Commercialization of Human Feeling*, Berkeley, CA: University of California Press, 1983.
2. C. Wright Mills, *White Collar*, New York: Oxford University Press, 1956.
3. Op. cit. Hochschild, 1983, pp. ix–x.
4. E. Goffman, *The Presentation of Self in Everyday Life*, New York: Doubleday Anchor, 1959.
5. S. Freud, 'The ego and the id', in S. Freud, *On Metapsychology*, Harmondsworth: Penguin, 1923/1982, pp. 357–66.
6. Op. cit. Hochschild, 1983, p. x.
7. For a detailed account of this perspective, see Appendix A in Hochschild, 1983, op. cit.
8. Ibid. p. 17.
9. J. Dewey, *Human Nature and Conduct: An Introduction to Social Psychology*, New York: Holt, 1922.
10. H. Gerth, and C.W. Mills, *Character and Social Structure: The Psychology of Social Institutions*, New York: Harcourt, Brace and World, 1964.
11. Op. cit. Goffman, 1959.
12. C. Darwin, *The Expression of Emotion in Man and Animals*, New York: Philosophical Library, 1955.
13. Op. cit. Freud, 1923/1982.
14. Op. cit. Hochschild, 1983, p. 222.
15. C.W Mills, *The Sociological Imagination*, New York: Oxford University Press, 1959.
16. Op. cit. Hochschild, 1983, p. 18.
17. Ibid. p. 5.
18. A.R. Hochschild, 'Emotion work, feeling rules and social structure', *American Journal of Sociology* 85 (1979), 561–2.
19. Op. cit. Hochschild, 1983, p. 187.
20. Ibid. p. 188.
21. Ibid. p. 189.
22. Op. cit. Hochschild, 1979, p. 569.
23. A.R. Hochschild with A. Machung, *The Second Shift: Working Parents and the Revolution at Home*, London: Piatkus, 1990. See also A.R. Hochschild, *The Time Bind: When Work Becomes Home and Home Becomes Work*, New York: Metropolitan Books, 1997.
24. Ibid. pp. 188–9.
25. Ibid. pp. 46.
26. T.J. Kemper, 'Themes and variations in the sociology of emotions', in T.J. Kemper (ed.) *Research Agendas in the Sociology of Emotions*, New York: University of New York Press, 1990.
27. T.J. Kemper, 'Social relations and emotions: a structural approach', in Kemper 1990 ibid.
28. N.K. Denzin, *On Understanding Emotion*, San Francisco: Jossey-Bass, 1984. See also N.K. Denzin, 'On understanding emotion: the interpretive–cultural agenda', in Kemper, 1990 op. cit. pp. 73–85.

29. P.A. Thoits, 'Emotional deviance: research agendas', in Kemper 1990, op. cit. pp. 135–52.
30. Op. cit. Hochschild, 1983, p. 190.
31. Ibid. pp. 192–3.
32. Ibid. p. 193.
33. Ibid. pp. 192–4.
34. S. Fineman, *Emotions and Organisations*, London: Sage, 1993.
35. J. Duncombe and D. Marsden, 'Love and intimacy: the gender division of emotion work', *Sociology*, 27(2) (1993), 221–41. See also J. Duncombe and D. Marsden, '"Stepford wives" and "hollow men": doing emotion work, doing gender and "authenticity" in intimate heterosexual relationships', in G. Bendelow and S.J. Williams (eds) *Emotions in Social Life: Critical Themes and Contemporary Issues*, London: Routledge, 1998, pp. 211–27.
36. See for example, N. James, 'Emotional labour: skill and work in the social regulation of feelings', *Sociological Review*, **37**(1) (1989), 15–42; N. James, 'Care = organisation + physical labour + emotional labour', *Sociology of Health and Illness*, **14**(4) (1992), 488–509; V. James and J. Gabe (eds) *Health and the Sociology of Emotions*, Oxford: Blackwell, 1996; J. Lawler, *Behind the Screens: Nursing, Somology and the Problem of the Body*, Edinburgh: Churchill Livingstone, 1991; P. Smith, *The Emotional Division of Labour in Nursing*, Basingstoke: Macmillan – now Palgrave Macmillan, 1992; S. Bolton, 'Changing faces: nurses as emotional jugglers'. *Sociology of Health and Illness*, **23**, 1: 85–100, 2001.
37. S.J. Williams and G. Bendelow, 'Emotions, health and illness: the "missing link" in medical sociology?', in James and Gabe 1996 op. cit. pp. 25–54.
38. S.J. Williams and G. Bendelow, 'Transcending the dualisms: towards a sociology of pain', *Sociology of Health and Illness*, **17**(2) (1995), 139–165; G. Bendelow and S.J. Williams, 'Pain and the mind–body dualism: a sociological approach, *Body and Society* **1**(2) (1995), 82–103; and G. Bendelow, 'Pain perceptions, gender and emotion', *Sociology of Health and Illness*, **15**(3) (1993), 273–94.
39. P. Freund, 'The expressive body: a common ground for the sociology of emotions and health and illness', *Sociology of Health and Illness*, **12**(4) (1990), 452–77; P. Freund, 'Social performances and their discontents: reflections on the biosocial psychology of role-playing', in G. Bendelow and S.J. Williams (eds), *Emotions in Social Life: Critical Themes and Contemporary Issues*, London: Routledge, 1998, pp. 268–94.
40. Op. cit. Hochschild, 1983, pp. 174–81.
41. Op. cit. Freund, 1990, p. 470.
42. For a fuller sociological account and exploration of these issues, see S.J. Williams, *Sleep and Society: Sociological Ventures into the (Un)Known*, London: Routledge, 2005.
43. See, for example, A.R. Hochschild, 'The global chains of care and emotional surplus value', in W. Hutton and A. Giddens (eds) *On the Edge: Living with Global Capitalism*, London: Vintage, 1999; and A.R. Hochschild, *The Commercialization of Intimacy: Notes from Home and Work*, Berkeley, CA: University of California Press, 2003.
44. Op. cit. Hochschild, 1999, p. 136.
45. Op. cit. Hochschild, 2003, p. 214.
46. Ibid. p. 9.

47. C. Wouters, 'The sociology of emotions and flight attendants: Hochschild's *The Managed Heart*', *Theory, Culture and Society*, **6**(1) (1989), 104–5.
48. Ibid. pp. 105–6. See also A.R. Hochschild, 'Reply to Cas Wouter's review essay on *The Managed Heart*', *Theory, Culture and Society*, **6**(3) (1989), 439–45; and C. Wouters, 'Response to Hochschild's reply', *Theory, Culture and Society*, **6**(3) (1989), 447–50.
49. For other historical accounts/approaches to emotions, see N. Elias, *The Civilizing Process*, vols I and II, Oxford: Basil Blackwell, 1978, 1982; N. Elias, 'On human beings and their emotions: a process-sociological essay', in M. Featherstone, M. Hepworth and B.S. Turner (eds) *The Body: Social Process and Cultural Theory*, London: Sage, 1991, pp. 103–25; P. Stearns, *American Cool: Constructing a Twentieth-Century American Style*, New York: New York University Press, 1994; and C.Z. Stearns and P. Stearns, *Emotions and Social Change*, New York: Holmes and Meier, 1988.
50. J. Barbalet, *Emotions, Social Theory and Social Structure*, Cambridge: University of Cambridge Press, 1999.
51. Ibid. Barbalet, 1999, p. 181.
52. Ibid. Barbalet, 1999, p. 182.
53. Op. cit. Duncombe and Marsden, 1998.
54. See also B.E. Ashforth and M.A. Tomiuk, 'Emotional labour and authencity: views from service agents', in S. Fineman (ed.) *Emotion in Organizations*, London: Sage, 2000.
55. Op. cit. C.W. Mills, 1959.
56. Op. cit. A.R. Hochschild, 2003, p. 9.

Chapter 23 Zygmunt Bauman

1. Cervantes' classic novel parodies the romantic deeds associated with chivalry. In his own words, Miguel de Cervantes Saavedra (*The Adventures of Don Quixote*, trans. J.M. Cohen, Harmondsworth: Penguin, 1950, p. 35) says Don Quixote 'armed himself completely, mounted Rocinante, put on his badly-mended headpiece, slung on his shield, seized his lance and went out into the plain through the back gate of his yard, pleased and delighted to see with what ease he had started on his fair design'. My own interpretation is indebted to J.M. Coetzee's apposite adaptation, which appears in John Lanchester's review of his recent novel *Slow Man* in *The New York Review of Books* (2005) 52(18) 4–6.
2. I have borrowed this observation from J. Bayley, 'Moral magic', in *London Review of Books*, 1979, reprinted in J. Bayley, *The Power of Delight*, London: Duckworth, 2005, pp. 621–5.
3. From K. Marx, *Theses on Feuerbach* (1888) p. xi, quoted in the 3rd edition of the *Oxford Dictionary of Quotations*, Oxford: Oxford University Press, 1979.
4. Z. Bauman, *Identity: Conversations with Bendetto Vecchi*, Cambridge: Polity Press, 2004, p. 32.
5. T. Blackshaw, *Zygmunt Bauman*, Abingdon: Routledge, 2005.
6. K. Tester, *The Social Thought of Zygmunt Bauman*, Basingstoke: Palgrave Macmillan, 2004, p. 1.

7. Z. Bauman, *Legislators and Interpreters: On Modernity, Post-Modernity and Intellectuals*, Cambridge: Polity Press, 1987.
8. Z. Bauman, *Towards a Critical Sociology: An Essay on Common Sense and Emancipation*, London: RKP, 1976.
9. J.-F. Lyotard, *The Postmodern Condition:A Report On Knowledge*, Minneapolis, MN: University of Minneapolis Press, 1984.
10. Z. Bauman, *Intimations of Postmodernity*, London: Routledge, 1992, p. 65.
11. T. Blackshaw, 'Interview with Zygmunt Bauman', *Network: Newsletter of the British Sociological Association*, 2002, p. 119.
12. Z. Bauman, *Modernity and the Holocaust*, Cambridge: Polity Press, 1989.
13. Ibid. p. 94.
14. Op. cit. K. Tester, 2004, p.137.
15. Op. cit. Z. Bauman, 1987, p. 119.
16. Z. Bauman, *Liquid Modernity*, Cambridge: Polity Press, 2000.
17. Z. Bauman, 'Hermeneutics and modern social theory' in D. Held and J.B. Thompson (eds) *Social Theory and Modern Societies: Anthony Giddens and His Critics*, Cambridge: Cambridge University Press, 1989.
18. U. Beck, 'Zombie categories: interview with Ulrich Beck', in U. Beck and E. Beck-Gernsheim, *Individualization*, London: Sage, 2002, pp. 202–13.
19. D. Macey, '*Ostranenie*' in *The Penguin Dictionary of Critical Theory*, London: Penguin, 2000, p. 284. As Macey points out, *ostranenie* is a Russian term that can be translated as 'making strange' or 'defamiliarization' and is associated with the work of the Russian formalist Viktor Shklovsky.
20. Where the use of analogy merely asks the reader to think about a particular theme or issue 'as if' or 'as though', Bauman's use of metaphor has a transformative capacity that involves 'seeing as' and in effect forces the reader to defamiliarize the familiar.
21. Op. cit. J.-F. Lyotard, 1984.
22. T. Blackshaw, *Leisure Life: Myth, Masculinity and Modernity*, London: Routledge, 2003.
23. Op. cit Z. Bauman, 2004.
24. B. Ellen, 'We're told we live in a confessional age. But when a relationship ends, there can be more than one truth', in *Observer* Magazine, 2005, 6 November.
25. Z. Bauman, in Orlando Radice, 'Ziggy Stardust' in *New Humanist*, 2004, 5 January.
26. In developing this particular argument and indeed this whole section of the chapter, I am indebted to J.M. Coetzee and John Lanchester's astute review of his recent novel *Slow Man*.
27. Z. Bauman, *Postmodern Ethics*, Oxford: Blackwell, 1993.

Bibliography

Abbott, A. and Gaziano, E. (1995) 'Transition and tradition: departmental faculty in the era of the second Chicago School', in G.A. Fine (ed.) *A Second Chicago School? The Development of a Postwar American Sociology*, Chicago: University of Chicago Press, pp. 221–72.

Adorno, T.W. (1973) *The Jargon of Authenticity*, trans. K. Tarnowski and F. Will, London: Routledge & Kegan Paul.

Adorno, T.W. (1973) *Negative Dialectics*, trans. E.B. Ashton, London: Routledge & Kegan Paul.

Adorno, T.W. (1978) *Minima Moralia: Reflections from a Damaged Life*, trans. E.F.N. Jephcott, London and New York: Verso.

Adorno, T.W. (1980 [1977]) 'Commitment', in *Aesthetics and Politics* (trans. and ed. R. Taylor) London: Verso.

Adorno, T.W. (1984) *Aesthetic Theory*, eds G. Adorno and R Tiedmann, trans. C. Lendhart, London: Routledge.

Adorno, T.W. (1995) *Prisms* (trans. S. Weber and S. Weber) California, MA: MIT Press.

Adorno, T.W. (1996) *Minima Moralia* (trans. E.F.N. Jephcott) London: Verso.

Adorno, T.W. (1997) *Aesthetic Theory* (trans. R. Hullot-Kentor) Minneapolis: University of Minnesota Press.

Adorno, T.W. and Horkheimer, M. (1995 [1972]) *Dialectic of Enlightenment* (trans. J. Cumming) New York: Continuum and London: Verso, 1995.

Adorno, T., Frankel-Brunswik, E., Levinson, D. and Sanford, R. (1950) *The Authoritarian Personality*, New York: Harper.

Aglietta, M.A. (1979) *Theory of Capitalist Regulation*, London: New Left Books.

Alexander, J.C. (1982) *Theoretical Logic in the Social Sciences*, vol. 2, *The Antinomies of Classical Thought: Marx and Durkheim*, Berkeley, CA: University of California Press.

Alexander, J.C. (1982–3) *Theoretical Logic in Sociology*, 4 vols, Berkeley: University of California Press.

Alexander, J.C. (1984) *Theoretical Logic in Sociology, the Modern Reconstruction of Classical Thought: Talcott Parsons*, vol. 4, London: Routledge.

Alexander, J.C. (1988) *Action and its Environments*, New York: Colombia University Press.

Alexander, J.C. (1988) *Durkheimian Sociology: Cultural Studies*, Cambridge: Cambridge University Press.

Alexander, J. and Smith, P. (eds) (2005) *Cambridge Companion to Durkheim* Cambridge, Cambridge University Press.
Althusser, L. (1971) *Lenin and Philosophy and Other Essays*, London: New Left Books.
Althusser, L. (1976) *Essays in Self-Criticism*, London: New Left Books.
Althusser, L. (1990) *Philosophy and the Spontaneous Philosophy of the Scientists and Other Essays*, London: Verso.
Althusser, L. (1993) *The Future Lasts a Long Time*, London: Chatto & Windus.
Althusser, L. (2003) *The Humanist Controversy*, London: Verso.
Althusser, L. (2006) *For Marx*, London: New Left Books, 1969, London: Verso.
Althusser, L. and Balibar, E. (1970) (eds) *Reading Capital*, London: New Left Books.
Anderson, P. (1974) *Lineages of the Absolutist State*, London: New Left Books.
Anderson, P. (1974) *Passages from Antiquity to Feudalism*, London: New Left Books.
Anderson, P. (1976) *Considerations on Western Marxism*, London: New Left Books.
Anderson, R.J., Hughes, J.A. and Sharrock, W.W. (1985) *The Sociology Game: An Introduction to Sociological Reasoning*, London: Longman.
Archer, M. (1995) *Realist Social Theory*, Cambridge: Cambridge University Press.
Archer, M. (1996) *Realist Social Theory: The Morphogenetic Approach*, Cambridge: Cambridge University Press.
Archer, M. (2003) *Structure, Agency and the Internal Conversation*, Cambridge: Cambridge University Press.
Archer, M. (2004) *The Internal Conversation: Mediating Between Structure and Agency* Cambridge: Cambridge University Press.
Armstrong, T. (1992) (trans.) *Michel Foucault: Philosopher*, London: Harvester Wheatsheaf.
Ashforth, B.E. and Tomiuk, M.A. (2000) 'Emotional labour and authencity: views from service agents', in S. Fineman (ed.) *Emotion in Organizations*, London: Sage.
Atkinson, J.M. (1971) 'Societal reactions to suicide: the role of coroners' definitions', in S. Cohen (ed.) *Images of Deviance*, Harmondsworth: Penguin.
Atkinson, J.M. (1978) *Discovering Suicide: Studies in the Social Organization of Sudden Death*, London: Macmillan – now Palgrave Macmillan.
Atkinson, J.M. (1984) *Our Masters' Voices: The Language and Body Language of Politics* London: Methuen.
Atkinson, J.M. (1985) 'Refusing invited applause: preliminary observations from a case study of charismatic oratory', in T. van Dijk (ed.) *Handbook of Discourse Analysis, vol. 3, Discourse and Dialogue*, London: Academic Press.
Atkinson, M.W., Kessel, N. and Dalgaard, J. (1975) 'The comparability of suicide rates', *British Journal of Psychiatry*, 127.
Atkinson, P. and Housley, W. (2003) *Interactionism*, London: Sage.
Attali, J. (1985) *Noise: The Political Economy of Music* (trans. B. Massumi) Minneapolis: University of Minnesota Press.
Avineri, S. (1968) *The Social and Political Thought of Karl Marx*, Cambridge: Cambridge University Press.
Bales, R.F. (1950) *Interaction Process Analysis: A Method for the Study of Small Groups* Reading, MA: Addison Wesley.
Barbalet, J. (1999) *Emotions, Social Theory and Social Structure*, Cambridge: University of Cambridge Press.
Barratt, M. (1988) *Women's Oppression Today* (2nd edn) London: Verso.

Barry, A., Osborne, T. and Rose, N. (1996) *Foucault and Political Reason: Liberalism, Neo-liberalism and Rationalities of Government*, London: UCL Press.

Barthes, R. (1977) 'From work to text', in *Image-music-text: Essays*, Glasgow: Fontana Collins.

Battersby, C. (1998) *The Phenomenal Woman: Feminist Metaphysics and the Pattern of Identity*, Cambridge: Polity Press.

Battershill, C. (1990) 'Erving Goffman as a precursor to post-modern sociology', in S.H. Riggins (ed.) *Beyond Goffman: Studies on Communication, Institution and Social Interaction*, New York: Mouton de Gruyter, pp. 163–86.

Baudrillard, J. (1983) *Simulations* (trans. P. Foss, P. Patton and P. Bleitchman) New York: Semiotext(e).

Baudrillard, J. (1993) *Baudrillard Live: Selected Interviews* (ed. M. Gane) London: Routledge.

Bauman, Z. (1976) *Towards a Critical Sociology: an Essay on Common Sense and Emancipation*, London: RKP.

Bauman, Z. (1987) *Legislators and Interpreters: On Modernity, Post-Modernity and Intellectuals*, Cambridge: Polity Press.

Bauman, Z. (1988) 'Is there a postmodern sociology?' *Theory, Culture and Society*, 5: 217–37.

Bauman, Z. (1989) 'Hermeneutics and modern social theory', in D. Held and J. B. Thompson (eds) *Social Theory and Modern Societies: Anthony Giddens and His Critics*, Cambridge: Cambridge University Press.

Bauman, Z. (1989) *Modernity and the Holocaust*, Cambridge: Polity Press.

Bauman, Z. (1993) *Postmodern Ethics*, Cambridge: Polity Press.

Bauman, Z. (1995) *Life in Fragments: Towards a Postmodern Morality*, Oxford: Blackwell.

Bauman, Z. (2000) *Liquid Modernity*, Cambridge: Polity Press.

Bauman, Z. (2004) *Identity: Conversations with Bendetto Vecchi*, Cambridge: Polity Press.

Bayley, J. (2005) *The Power of Delight*, London: Duckworth.

Beck, U. (1989) 'Zombie categories: interview with Ulrich Beck', in U. Beck and E. Beck-Gernsheim, *Individualization*, London: Sage, pp. 202–13.

Beck, U. (1992) *The Risk Society: Towards a New Modernity*, London: Sage.

Becker, H.S. (1963) *Outsiders: Studies in the Sociology of Deviance*, Illinois: Free Press.

Becker, H.S. (1986) *Doing Things Together*, Chicago: Aldine.

Becker, H.S. (1988) 'Herbert Blumer's conceptual impact', *Symbolic Interaction*, **11**(1): 13–21.

Becker-Schmidt, R. (1999) 'Critical Theory as a Critique of Society: Theodor Adorno's Significance for a Feminist Sociology' Chapter 5 in O'Neill, M. (ed.) *Adorno, Culture and Feminism*, London, California and New Delhi: Sage, pp. 104–18.

Beilharz, P. (2000) *Zygmunt Bauman: Dialectic of Modernity*, London: Sage.

Beilharz, P. (ed.) (2002) *Zygmunt Bauman: Sage Masters of Modern Social Thought*, London: Sage.

Bell, D. (1973) *The Coming of Post-industrial Society*, London: Heinemann.

Bell, D. (1993) *Communitarianism and its Critics*, Oxford: Oxford University Press.

Bellah, R., Madsen, R., Sullivan, W.M., Swidler, A. and Tipton, S. (1985) *Habits of the Heart: Individualism and Commitment in American Life*, Berkeley: University of California Press.

Bendelow, G. (1993) 'Pain perceptions, gender and emotion', *Sociology of Health and Illness*, **15**(3): 273–94.

Bendelow, G. and Williams, S.J. (1995) 'Transcending the dualisms: towards a sociology of pain', *Sociology of Health and Illness*, **17**(2): 139–65.

Bendelow, G. and Williams, S.J. (1995) 'Pain and the mind–body dualism: a sociological approach', *Body and Society*, **1**(2): 82–103.

Bendelow, G. and Williams, S.J. (eds) (1998) *Emotions in Social Life: Critical Themes and Contemporary Issues*, London: Routledge.

Benjamin, A. (1989) *The Problem of Modernity: Adorno and Benjamin*, London: Verso.

Benjamin, J. (1988) *The Bonds of Love*, New York: Pantheon.

Benjamin, W. (1973) *Charles Baudelaire: A Lyric Poet in the Era of High Capitalism*, London: New Left Books.

Benton, T. (1984) *The Rise and Fall of Structural Marxism*, Basingstoke: Macmillan – now Palgrave Macmillan.

Benton, T. (1991) 'Biology and social science: why the return of the repressed should be given a (cautious) welcome', *Sociology*, **25**(1): 1–29.

Benton, T. (1994) 'Biology and social theory in the environmental debate', in M. Redclift and T. Benton (eds) *Social Theory and the Global Environment*, London: Routledge, pp. 28–50.

Berlin, I. (1953) *The Hedgehog and the Fox: An Essay on Tolstoy's View of History*, London: Wiedenfeld & Nicolson.

Berman, M. (1982) *All That is Solid Melts into Air: The Experience of Modernity*, New York: Simon & Schuster.

Bernal, J.D. (1939) *The Social Function of Science*, London: J. Routledge & Sons.

Bernstein, E. (1961) *Evolutionary Socialism: A Criticism and Affirmation*, New York: Schocken.

Bernstein, H. (1971) 'Modernisation theory and the sociological study of development', *Journal of Development Studies*, 7.

Bhaskar, R. (1978) *A Realist Theory of Science*, Hassocks: Harvester Press.

Bierstedt, R. (1990) 'Robert Merton's systematic theory', in J. Clark, C. Modgil, and S. Modgil (eds) *Robert K. Merton: Consensus and Controversy*, London, Falmer Press.

Bierstedt, R.(1981) *American Sociological Theory: A Critical History*, New York: Academic Press.

Blackshaw, T. (2002) 'Interview with Zygmunt Bauman', *Network*, newsletter of the British Sociological Association, p. 119.

Blackshaw, T. (2003) *Leisure Life: Myth Masculinity and Modernity*, London: Routledge.

Blackshaw, T. (2005) *Zygmunt Bauman*, Abingdon: Routledge.

Blauner, R. (1964) *Alienation and Freedom*, Chicago: University of Chicago Press.

Blok, A. (1982) 'Primitief en geciviliseerd', *Sociologisch Gids*, **29**(3/4): 197–209.

Blumer, H. (1933) *Movies and Conduct*, New York: Macmillan.

Blumer, H. (1962) 'Society as symbolic interaction', in A. Rose (ed.) *Human Behavior and Social Processes*, Boston: Houghton Mifflin.

Blumer, H. (1966) 'Sociological implications of the thought of George Herbert Mead', *American Journal of Sociology*, **71**: 535–44.

Blumer, H. (1969) *Symbolic Interactionism: Perspective and Method*, Englewood Cliffs, NJ: Prentice Hall.

Blumer, H. (1979) *The Critique of the Polish Peasant* (rev. edn) New Jersey: Transaction Books.

Blumer, H. (1979) 'George Herbert Mead', in B. Rhea (ed.) *The Future of the Sociological Classics*, London: Allen & Unwin.

Blumer, H. (1990) *Industrialization as an Agent of Social Change: A Critical Analysis* (ed. and intro D.R. Maines and T.J. Morrione) New York: Aldine de Gruyter.

Blumer, H. (2004) *George Herbert Mead and Human Conduct* (ed. and intro T.J. Morrione) New York: AltaMira Press.

Blumer, H. and Duster, T. (1980) 'Theories of race and social action', in *Sociological Theories: Race and Colonialism*, Paris: UNESCO, pp. 211–38.

Bocock, R. (1976) *Freud and Modern Society*, Walton-on-Thames, Surrey: Nelson.

Boltanski, L. (1987) *The Making of a Class: 'Cadres' in French Society*, Cambridge: Cambridge University Press.

Boltanski, L. and Thevenot, L. (1991/2006) *On Justification: Economies of Worth* (trans. C. Worth) Princeton: Princeton University Press.

Bolton, S. (2001) 'Changing faces: nurses as emotional jugglers', *Sociology of Health and Illness*, **23**(1): 85–100.

Boschetti, A. (1988) *The Intellectual Enterprise: Sartre and 'Les Temps Modernes'*, Evanston: Northwestern University Press.

Bouglé, C. (1906–09) 'Review of Soziologie', *L'Année Sociologique*, xi.

Bourdieu, P. (1958/1962) *The Algerians*, Boston: Beacon Press.

Bourdieu, P. (1972/1977) *Outline of a Theory of Practice*, Cambridge: Cambridge University Press.

Bourdieu, P. (1976/1977) *Algeria 1960*, Cambridge: Cambridge University Press.

Bourdieu, P. (1979/1984) *Distinction: A Social Critique of the Judgement of Taste*, London: Routledge.

Bourdieu, P. (1980/1990) *The Logic of Practice*, Cambridge: Polity Press.

Bourdieu, P. (1980/1993) *Sociology in Question*, London: Sage.

Bourdieu, P. (1982/1990) *Language and Symbolic Power*, edited by J.B. Thompson, Cambridge: Polity Press.

Bourdieu, P. (1982/1991) *Leçon sur la leçon*, Paris: Editions de Minuit. (Reprinted in 1987/1994)

Bourdieu, P. (1984/1988) *Homo Academicus*, Cambridge: Polity Press.

Bourdieu, P. (1984/1985) 'Social space and the genesis of groups', *Theory and Society*, **14**(6): 723–44.

Bourdieu, P. (1985/1986) 'From rules to strategies', *Cultural Anthropology*, **1**(1): 110–20.

Bourdieu, P. (1986) 'The forms of capital', in J.G. Richarson (ed.) *Handbook of Theory and Research for the Sociology of Education*, New York: Greenwood Press, pp. 241–58.

Bourdieu, P. (1987/1994) *In Other Words: Essays Towards a Reflexive Sociology*, Cambridge: Polity Press.

Bourdieu, P. (1989/1997) *The State Nobility: Elite Schools in the Field of Power*, Cambridge: Polity Press.

Bourdieu, P. (1989a) 'Social space and symbolic power', *Sociological Theory*, 7(1): 18–26.

Bourdieu, P. (1989b) 'The corporatism of the universal: the role of intellectuals in the modern world', *Telos*, **81**: 99–110.

Bourdieu, P. (1990) 'The scholastic point of view', *Cultural Anthropology*, 5(4): 380–91 (reprinted in *Practical Reason*, 1998).

Bourdieu, P. (1990/1991) 'Social space and symbolic space: Introduction to a Japanese reading of Distinction', *Poetics Today*, **12**(4): 627–38.

Bourdieu, P. (1992/1997) *The Rules of Art: Genesis and Structure of the Artistic Field*, Cambridge: Polity Press.

Bourdieu, P. (1993) *The Field of Cultural Production*, New York: Columbia University Press.

Bourdieu, P. (1994/1998) *Practical Reason: On the Theory of Action*, Cambridge: Polity Press.

Bourdieu, P. (1996/1998) *On Television and Journalism*, London: Pluto Press.

Bourdieu, P. (1997/2000) *Pascalian Meditations*, Cambridge: Polity Press.

Bourdieu, P. (1998/2000) *Acts of Resistance: Against the Tyranny of the Market*, Cambridge: Polity Press.

Bourdieu, P. (1998/2001) *Masculine Domination*, Cambridge: Polity Press.

Bourdieu, P. (2001/2004) *Science of Science and Reflexivity*, Chicago: The University of Chicago Press.

Bourdieu, P. (2001/2005) *The Social Structures of the Economy*, Cambridge: Polity Press.

Bourdieu, P. (2002/2007) *The Ball of Bachelors: The Crisis of Peasant Society in Béarn*, Chicago: The University of Chicago Press.

Bourdieu, P. (2003) 'Participant objectivation: the Huxley medal lecture', *Journal of the Royal Anthropological Institute*, **9**(2): 281–94.

Bourdieu, P. (2004/2008) *Sketch for a Self Socioanalysis*, Chicago: The University of Chicago Press.

Bourdieu, P., A. Darbel, J.P. Rivet and C. Seibel (1963) *Travail et Travailleurs en Algérie*, The Hague: Mouton.

Bourdieu, P. and A. Sayad (1964) *Le Déracinement. La crise de l'agriculture traditionnelle en Algérie*, Paris: Editions de Minuit.

Bourdieu, P. and J.-C. Passeron (1964/1979) *The Inheritors: Students and their Culture*, Chicago: The University of Chicago Press.

Bourdieu, P. and J.-C. Passeron (1970/1977) *Reproduction in Education*, Culture, and Society, London: Sage.

Bourdieu, P., J.-C.Passeron and J.-C. Chamboredon (1968/1979) *The Craft of Sociology: Epistemological Preliminaries*, New York: Aldine de Gruyter.

Bourdieu, P. and L. Wacquant (1992) *An Invitation to Reflexive Sociology*, Chicago: The University of Chicago Press.

Bourdieu, P. et al. (1993/1998) *The Weight of the World: Social Suffering in Contemporary Society*, Cambridge: Polity Press.

Bourdieu, P. with L. Boltanski, R. Castel, J.-C. Chamboredon and D. Schnapper (1990) *Photography: A Middle-Brow Art*, Cambridge: Polity Press.

Bourdieu, P. and A. Darbel, with D. Schnapper (1991) *The Love of Art: European Art Museums and their Public*, Cambridge: Polity Press.

Braun, C. (1992) *Max Weber's 'Musiksoziologie'*, Laaber: Laaber-Verlag.

Breiner, P. (1996) *Max Weber and Democratic Politics*, Ithaca: Cornell University Press.

Brubaker, R. (1985) 'Rethinking classical theory: the sociological vision of Pierre Bourdieu', *Theory and Society*, **14**: 723–44.

Bryant, C. and Jary, D. (1991) 'Coming to terms with Anthony Giddens', in C. Bryant and D. Jary, *Giddens' Theory of Structuration: A Critical Appreciation*, London: Routledge.

Bryant, C. and Jary, D. (2001) *The Contemporary Giddens: Social Theory in a Globalizing Age*, Basingstoke: Palgrave Macmillan.

Bryant, C. and Jary, D. (eds) (1997) *Anthony Giddens: Critical Assessment*, 4 vols, London: Routledge.

Buck-Morss, S. (1977) *The Origin of Negative Dialectics*, Brighton: Harvester Press.

Burawoy, M. (2005) '2004 American Sociological Association Presidential address: For public sociology', *British Journal of Sociology*, **56**(2): 259–94.

Burchell, G. (1991) 'Peculiar interests: civil society and governing the "system of natural liberty"', in G. Burchell, C. Gordon and P. Miller (eds) *The Foucault Effect: Studies in Governmentality*, London: Harvester Wheatsheaf, pp. 119–50.

Burchell, G., Gordon, C. and Miller, P. (eds) (1991) 'Governmentality', in G. Burchell, C, Gordon and P. Miller, *The Foucault Effect: Studies in Governmentality*, London: Harvester Wheatsheaf, pp. 87–104.

Burchell, G., Gordon, C. and Miller, P. (eds) (1991) *The Foucault Effect: Studies in Governmentality*, London: Harvester Wheatsheaf.

Burkett, J.P. (2000) 'Marx's concept of an economic law of motion', *History of Political Economy*, **32**(2): 381–94.

Burns, T. (1992) *Erving Goffman*, London: Routledge.

Callinicos, A. (1976) *Althusser's Marxism*, London: Pluto.

Campbell, M. and Manicom, A. (eds) (1995) *Knowledge, Experience, and Ruling Relations: Studies in the Social Organization of Knowledge*, Toronto; University of Toronto Press.

Campbell, T. (2001) *Justice* (2nd edn) Basingstoke: Macmillan – now Palgrave Macmillan.

Canguilhem, G. (1988) *Ideology and Rationality in the History of the Life Sciences*, Cambridge: MIT.

Castells, M. (1977) *The Urban Question*, London: Edward Arnold.

Castells, M. (2001) *The Network Society*, Oxford: Blackwell.

Cavan, S. (1966) *Liquor License*, Chicago: Aldine.

Cervantes Saavedra, M. de (1950) *The Adventures of Don Quixote* (trans. J.M. Cohen) Harmondsworth: Penguin.

Chambers, I. and Curti, L. (1996) 'When was the "post-colonial"? Thinking at the limits', in I. Chambers, *The Post-colonial Question*, London: Routledge.

Charle, C. (1996) *Les Intellectuels en Europe au XIXè siècle. Essai d'histoire comparée.* Paris: Editions du Seuil.

Chodorow, N. (1978) *The Reproduction of Mothering*, Berkeley: University of California Press.

Chodorow, N. (1981) 'Reply by Nancy Chodorow', *Signs*, spring.

Chodorow, N. (1989) *Feminism and Psychoanalysis*, New Haven: Yale University Press.

Chodorow, N. (1994) *Feminities, Masculinities and Sexualities: Freud and Beyond*, London: Free Association Books.

Chodorow, N. (1995) 'Gender as a personal and cultural construction', *Signs*, spring, 516–44.

Chodorow, N. (1999) *The Power of Feelings*, New Haven: Yale University Press.

Cicourel, A. (1968) *The Social Organization of Juvenile Justice*, New York: Wiley.

Cladis, M. A (1992) *Communitarian Defence of Liberalism: Émile Durkheim and Contemporary Social Theory*, Stanford: Stanford University Press.

Clough, P.T. (1992) *The Ends of Ethnography*, London: Sage.

Cohen, I.B. (ed.) (1990) *Puritanism and the Rise of Modern Science: the Merton Thesis*, New Brunswick, NJ: Rutgers University Press.

Cohen, I.J. (1989) *Structuration Theory: Anthony Giddens and the Constitution of Social Life*, London, Macmillan – now Palgrave Macmillan.

Cohen, I.J. (1990) 'Structuration and social order: five issues in brief', in J. Clark, C. Modgil and S. Modgil, *Anthony Giddens: Consensus and Controversy*, London: Falmer Press, Ch. 4, reprinted in C.G.A. Bryant and D. Jary, *Anthony Giddens: Critical Assessments*, London: Routledge, 1996, Selection 40.

Cohen, I.J. (1996) 'Theories of action and praxis', in B.S. Turner (ed.) *The Blackwell Companion to Social Theory*, Oxford: Basil Blackwell, pp. 111–42.

Coleman, J.S. (1990) 'Robert K. Merton as a teacher', in J. Clark, C. Modgil and S. Modgil (eds) *Robert K. Merton: Consensus and Controversy*, London: Falmer Press.

Collins, R. (1986) *Weberian Sociological Theory*, London: Cambridge University Press.

Collins, R. (1988) 'The Durkheimian tradition in conflict sociology', in J.C. Alexander (ed.) *Durkheimian Sociology*, Cambridge: Cambridge University Press, pp. 107–28.

Collins, R. (1993) Maturation of the state-centered theory of revolution and ideology, *Sociological Theory*, **11**.

Collins, R. (2006) 'Mann's transformation of the classic sociological traditions', in J.A. Hall and R. Schroeder (eds) *An Anatomy of Power: The Social Theory of Michael Mann*, Cambridge: Cambridge University Press, pp. 19–32.

Collins, R. and Makowsky, M. (1993) *The Discovery of Society* (5th edn) New York: McGraw-Hill.

Colomy, P. and Brown, J.D. (1995) 'Elaboration, revision, polemic and progress in the second Chicago School', in G.A. Fine (ed.) *A Second Chicago School?*, Chicago: University of Chicago Press, pp. 17–81.

Cooper, F. (2002) *Africa Since 1940: The Past of the Present*, Cambridge: Cambridge University Press.

Coser, L. (ed.) (1975) *The Idea of Social Structure: Papers in Honour of Robert K. Merton*, New York: Harcourt Brace Jovanovich.

Courtois, S., Werth, N., Panne, J.-L. et al. (1999) *The Black Book of Communism: Crimes, Terror, Repression*, Cambridge, MA: Harvard University Press.

Craib, I. (1989) *Psychoanalysis and Social Theory*, Brighton: Harvester Wheatsheaf.

Craib, I. (1992) *Anthony Giddens*, London: Routledge.

Craib, I. (1994) *The Importance of Disappointment*, London: Routledge.

Creelan, P. (1987) 'The degradation of the sacred: approaches of Cooley and Goffman', *Symbolic Interaction*, **10**: 29–56.

Crenshaw, K., Gotanda, N., Peller, G. and Thomas, K. (eds) (1995) *Critical Race Theory. The Key Writings that Formed the Movement*, New York: New York Press.

Crook, S. (1994) *Adorno: the Stars Down to Earth*, London: Routledge.

Crothers, C. (1987) *Robert K. Merton, Key Sociologists Series*, London: Tavistock.

Cruz, J. and Lewis, J. (eds) (1994) 'Reflections upon the encoding/decoding model: an interview with Stuart Hall', *Viewing, Reading Listening: Audiences and Cultural Reception*, Boulder, CO: Westview Press.

Dandeker, C. (1990) *Surveillance, Power and Modernity*, Cambridge: Polity Press.

Darwin, C. (1955) *The Expression of Emotion in Man and Animals*, New York: Philosophical Library.

Darwin, C. (1968 [1859]) *The Origin of Species*, Harmondsworth: Penguin.
Davis, H. (2004) *Understanding Stuart Hall*, London: Sage.
Day, L.H. (1987) 'Durkheim on religion and suicide: a demographic critique', *Sociology*, 21: 449–61.
Dean, M. (1991) *The Constitution of Poverty: Toward a Genealogy of Liberal Governance*, London: Routledge.
Deegan, M.J. and Hill, M.R. (eds) (1987) *Women and Symbolic Interaction*, Boston: Allen & Unwin.
Deleuze, G. (1988) *Foucault*, Minneapolis: University of Minnesota Press.
Denzin, N.K. (1984) *On Understanding Emotion*, San Francisco: Jossey-Bass.
Denzin, N.K. (1990) 'On understanding emotion: the interpretive-cultural agenda', in T.J. Kemper (ed.) *Research Agendas in the Sociology of Emotions*, New York: University of New York Press, pp. 73–85.
Denzin, N.K. (1992) *Symbolic Interactionism and Cultural Studies*, Oxford: Blackwell.
DeVault, M.L. (1994) *Feeding the Family*, Chicago: University of Chicago Press.
Dewey, J. (1922) *Human Nature and Conduct: An Introduction to Social Psychology*, New York: Holt.
Dewey, J. (1946) *The Problems of Men*, New York: Philosphical Library.
Dews, P. (ed.) (1992) *Habermas: Autonomy and Solidarity* (2nd edn) London: Verso.
Ditton, J. (ed.) (1980) *The View from Goffman*, London: Macmillan – now Palgrave Macmillan.
Donzelot, J. (1979) *The Policing of Families*, Baltimore, MD: Johns Hopkins University Press.
Douglas, J. (1967) *The Social Meanings of Suicide*, Princeton, NJ: Princeton University Press.
Draghici, S. (2001) *The Pauper/Georg Simmel*, Washington DC: Plutarch.
Drew, P. and Heritage, J. (eds) (1992) *Talk at Work*, Cambridge: Cambridge University Press.
Drew, P. and Wootton, A. (eds) (1988) *Erving Goffman: Exploring the Interaction Order*, Cambridge: Polity Press.
Dreyfus, H. and Rabinow, P. (1982) *Michel Foucault: Beyond Structuralism and Hermeneutics*, Chicago: University of Chicago Press.
Dumm, T. (1996) *Michel Foucault and the Politics of Freedom*, Thousand Oaks, CA: Sage.
Duncombe, J. and Marsden, D. (1993) 'Love and intimacy: the gender division of emotion work', *Sociology*, 27(2): 221–41.
Duncombe, J. and Marsden, D. (1997) '"Stepford wives" and "Hollow men": doing emotion work, doing gender and "authenticity" in intimate heterosexual relationships', in G. Bendelow and S.J. Williams (eds) *Emotions in Social Life: Critical Themes and Contemporary Issues*, London: Routledge, pp. 211–27.
Dunning, E. and Rojek, C. (eds) (1992) *Sport and Leisure in the Civilizing Process: Critique and Counter Critique*, Basingstoke: Macmillan – now Palgrave Macmillan.
Durkheim, E. (1951) *Suicide*, Glencoe, IL: Free Press.
Durkheim, E. (1961) *Moral Education*, New York: Free Press.
Durkheim, E. (1964) *The Rules of Sociological Method*, New York: Free Press.
Durkheim, E. (1965) *The Elementary Forms of the Religious Life*, New York: Free Press.

Durkheim, E. (1973) 'The dualism of human nature and its social conditions', *Emile Durkheim on Morality and Society*, Chicago: University of Chicago Press, pp. 149–63.
Durkheim, E. (1984) *The Division of Labor in Society*, New York: Free Press.
Duster, T. (1987) 'Herbert Blumer: 1900–1987', *ASA Footnotes*, **15**(6): 16.
Dworkin, R. (1977) *Taking Rights Seriously*, London: Duckworth.
Eagleton, T. (1983) *Literary Theory: An Introduction*, Minneapolis: University of Minnesota Press.
Ehrenreich, B. (2001) *Nickel and Dimed. On (Not) Getting By in America*, New York: Owl Books.
Elias, N. (1956) 'Problems of involvement and detachment', *British Journal of Sociology*, 7: 226–52.
Elias, N. (1978) *The Civilising Process: A History of Manners*, vol. 1, Oxford: Basil Blackwell.
Elias, N. (1978) *What is Sociology?*, London: Hutchinson.
Elias, N. (1982) *State Formation and the Civilising Process*, vol. 2, Oxford: Basil Blackwell.
Elias, N. (1984) 'Knowledge and power: an interview by Peter Ludes', in N. Stehr and V. Meja (eds) *Society and Knowledge*, London: Transaction Books, pp. 252–91.
Elias, N. (1987) 'The retreat of sociologists into the present', *Theory, Culture and Society*, 4: 223–47.
Elias, N. (1988) 'Violence and civilization: the state monopoly of physical violence and its infringement', in J. Keane, *Civil Society and the State*, London: Verso, pp. 177–98.
Elias, N. (1991) 'On human beings and their emotions: a process-sociological essay', in M. Featherstone, M. Hepworth and B. Turner (eds) *The Body: Social Process and Cultural Theory*, London: Sage, pp. 103–25.
Elias, N. (1994) *The Civilizing Process*, Oxford: Blackwell.
Elias, N. and Dunning, E. (1986) *Quest for Excitement: Sport and Leisure in the Civilizing Process*, Oxford: Blackwell.
Ellen, B. (2005) 'We're told we live in a confessional age. But when a relationship ends, there can be more than one truth', in *Observer Magazine*, 6 November.
Elliott, G. (1987) *Althusser: The Detour of Theory*, London: Verso.
Elliott, G. (ed.) (1994) *Althusser: A Critical Reader*, Oxford: Blackwell.
Emirbayer, M. (ed.) (2003) *Emile Durkheim: Sociologist of Modernity*, Oxford, Blackwell.
Emirbayer, M. and Mische, A. (1998) 'What is agency?', *American Journal of Sociology*, **103**(4): 962–1023.
Ethnography (2004) Special issue, 'Pierre Bourdieu in the field', **4**(4), December.
Evans, P.B., Rueschemeyer, D. and Skocpol, T. (eds) (1985) *Bringing the State Back In*, Cambridge: Cambridge University Press.
Eyal, G., Szelenyi, I. and Townsley, E. (1998) *Making Capitalism without Capitalists*, London, Verso.
Farred, G. (2003) *What's My Name: Black Vernacular Intellectuals*, Minneapolis: Minnesota University Press.
Farrelly, C. (2004) *An Introduction to Contemporary Political Theory*, London: Sage.
Featherstone, M. and Frisby, D. (1997) *Simmel on Culture*, London: Sage.
Ferguson, N. (2004) *Colossus: The Rise and Fall of the American Empire*, London: Allen Lane.

Ferretter, L. (2006) *Louis Althusser*, London: Routledge.
Fine, G. and Smith, G. (eds) (2000) *Erving Goffman*, 4 vols in Sage Masters of Modern Thought, London: Sage.
Fine, G.A. (1990) 'Symbolic interactionism in the Post-Blumerian age', in G. Ritzer (ed.) *Frontiers of Sociological Theory*, New York: Columbia University Press, pp. 117–57.
Fine, G.A. (ed.) (1988) Special issue on Herbert Blumer's legacy, *Symbolic Interaction,* **11**(1).
Fineman, S. (1993) *Emotion in Organisations*, London: Sage.
Firestone, S. (1970) *The Dialectic of Sex*, New York: Bantam Books.
Fish, J.S. (2005) *Defending the Durkheimian Tradition: Religion, Emotion and Morality*, Aldershot, Ashgate.
Flanagan, K. and Jupp, P.C. (2001) *Virtue Ethics and Sociology: Issues of Modernity and Religion*, Basingstoke: Palgrave Macmillan.
Fletcher, J. (1997) *Violence and Civilization: Introduction to the Work of Norbert Elias*, London: Polity Press.
Flower Macannel, J. (1999) 'Adorno: The Riddle of Femininity' Chapter 7 in (O'Neill, M. (ed.) *Adorno, Culture and Feminism*, London, California and New Delhi: Sage, pp. 141–60.
Foucault, M. (1967) *Madness and Civilization: A History of Insanity in the Age of Reason*, London: Tavistock.
Foucault, M. (1972) *The Archaeology of Knowledge and the Discourse on Language*, London: Tavistock.
Foucault, M. (1973) *The Birth of the Clinic*, London: Tavistock.
Foucault, M. (1973) *The Order of Things: An Archaeology of the Human Sciences*, New York: Vintage Books.
Foucault, M. (1977) *Language, Counter-memory, Practice* (ed. D. Bouchard) Ithaca: Cornell University Press.
Foucault, M. (1979) *Discipline and Punish: The Birth of the Prison*, New York: Vintage Books.
Foucault, M. (1980) *Power/Knowledge: Selected Interviews and Other Writings 1972–1977* (ed. C. Gordon) New York: Pantheon Books.
Foucault, M. (1980) *The History of Sexuality, vol. 1, An Introduction*, New York: Vintage Books.
Foucault, M. (1982) 'Afterword: the subject and power', in H. Dreyfus, and P. Rabinow *Michel Foucault: Beyond Structuralism and Hermeneutics*, Chicago: University of Chicago Press, pp. 208–26.
Foucault, M. (1984) *The Foucault Reader* (ed. P. Rabinow) New York: Pantheon Books.
Foucault, M. (1985) *The Use of Pleasure, vol. 2 of The History of Sexuality*, New York: Pantheon Books.
Foucault, M. (1986) 'Kant on enlightenment and revolution', *Economy and Society*, **15**(1): 88–96.
Foucault, M. (1986) The Care of the Self, New York: Pantheon Books.
Foucault, M. (1988) 'Politics and reason', in L. Kritzman (ed.) *Politics, Philosophy, Culture: Interviews and Other Writings, 1977–1984*, New York: Routledge.
Foucault, M. (1988) 'Sexual choice, sexual act: Foucault and homosexuality', in L. Kritzman (ed.) *Politics, Philosophy, Culture: Interviews and Other Writings, 1977–1984*, New York: Routledge, pp. 286–303.

Foucault, M. (1988) *Politics, Philosophy, Culture: Interviews and Other Writings, 1977–1984* (ed. L. Kritzman) New York: Routledge.

Foucault, M. (1991) 'Governmentality', in G. Burchell, C. Gordon and P. Miller (eds) *The Foucault Effect: Studies in Governmentality*, London: Harvester Wheatsheaf, pp. 87–104.

Foucault, M. (1997) 'Friendship as a way of life', in *Ethics: Subjectivity and Truth* (ed. P. Rabinow) New York: The New Press.

Foucault, M. (1997) *Ethics: Subjectivity and Truth* (ed. P. Rabinow) New York: The New Press.

Foucault, M. (2002) *Power: Essential Works of Foucault*, vol. 3, London: Penguin Books.

Foucault, M. (2003) *Society Must Be Defended: Lectures at the Collège de France, 1975–1976*, New York: Picador.

Freud, S. (1923/1982) 'The ego and the id', in S. Freud, *On Metapsychology*, Harmondsworth: Penguin.

Freund, P. (1990) 'The expressive body: a common ground for the sociology of emotions and health and illness,' *Sociology of Health and Illness*, **12**(4): 452–77.

Freund, P. (1997) 'Social performances and their discontents: reflections on the biosocial psychology of role-playing', in G.A. Bendelow and S.J. Williams (eds) *Emotions in Social Life: Critical Themes and Contemporary Issues*, London: Routledge, pp. 268–94.

Friedman, D.J. (1974) 'Marx's perspective on the objective class structure', *Polity*, **6**.

Frisby, D. (1991) *Simmel and Since: Essays on Georg Simmel's Social Theory*, London: Routledge & Kegan Paul.

Fulcher, J, and Scott, J. (2003) *Sociology* (2nd edn) Oxford: Oxford University Press.

Gagnon, J. and Simon, W. (1973) *Sexual Conduct: The Social Sources of Human Sexuality*, Chicago: Aldine.

Garfinkel, H. (1940) 'Color trouble', *Opportunity* magazine, reprinted in E.J. O'Brien (ed.) *The Best Short Stories of 1941*, Boston MA: Houghton Mifflin, pp. 97–119.

Garfinkel, H. (1949) 'Research note on inter- and intra-racial homicides,' *Social Forces*, 27: 370–81.

Garfinkel, H. (1963) 'A conception of, and experiments with, "trust" as a condition of stable concerted actions', in O.J. Harvey (ed.) *Motivation and Social Interaction*, New York: Ronald Press.

Garfinkel, H. (1967) *Studies in Ethnomethodology*, Englewood Cliffs, NJ: Prentice Hall.

Garfinkel, H. (1967) 'Practical sociological reasoning: some features of the work of the Los Angeles Suicide Prevention Center', in E.S. Shneidman (ed.) *Essays in Self-destruction*, New York: International Science Press.

Garfinkel, H. (2002) *Ethnomethodology's Program: Working Out Durkheim's Aphorism* (ed. and intro by A. Warfield Rawls) Lanham, MD: Rowman & Littlefield.

Garfinkel, H., Lynch, M. and Livingston, E. (1981) 'The work of a discovering science construed with materials from the optically discovered pulsar', *Philosophy of the Social Sciences*, **11**: 131–58.

Gellner, E. (1979) 'A social contract in search of an idiom: the demise of the Danegeld state', in E. Gellner, *Spectacles and Predicaments: Essays in Social Theory*, Cambridge: Cambridge University Press, pp. 277–306.

Gellner, E. (1986) *Plough, Sword and Book: The Structure of Human History*, London: Collins Harvill.

Gellner, E. (1994) *Conditions of Liberty: Civil Society and Its Rivals*, London: Hamish Hamilton.

Gerth, H. and Mills, C.W. (1964) *Character and Social Structure: The Psychology of Social Institutions*, New York: Harcourt, Brace.
Gerth, H. and Mills, C.W. (eds) (1946) *From Max Weber*, New York: Oxford University Press.
Gerth, H. and Mills, C.W. (eds) (1946) *From Max Weber: Essays in Sociology*, New York: Oxford University Press.
Giddens, A. (1968) 'Power in the recent writings of Talcott Parsons', *Sociology*, 2: 257–72.
Giddens, A. (1971) *Capitalism and Modern Social Theory: an Analysis of the Writings of Marx, Durkheim and Max Weber*, Cambridge: Cambridge University Press.
Giddens, A. (1976) *New Rules of Sociological Method: A Positive Critique of Interpretive Sociologies*, London: Hutchinson.
Giddens, A. (1979) *Central Problems in Social Theory: Action, Structure and Contradiction in Social Analysis*, Basingstoke: Macmillan – now Palgrave Macmillan.
Giddens, A. (1981) *Contemporary Critique of Historical Materialism*, vol. 1, *Power, Property and the State*, Basingstoke: Macmillan – now Palgrave Macmillan.
Giddens, A. (1984) *The Constitution of Society: Outline of the Theory of Structuration*, Cambridge: Polity Press.
Giddens, A. (1985) *The Nation-state and Violence*, Basingstoke: Macmillan – now Palgrave Macmillan.
Giddens, A. (1987) 'Erving Goffman as a systematic social theorist', in A. Giddens (ed.) *Social Theory and Modern Sociology*, Cambridge: Polity Press, pp. 109–39.
Giddens, A. (1987) *Social Theory and Modern Sociology*, Cambridge: Polity Press.
Giddens, A. (1989) ' A reply to my critics', in D. Held and J.B. Thompson, *Social Theory of Modern Societies: Anthony Giddens and His Critics*, Cambridge: Cambridge University Press, pp. 249–301.
Giddens, A. (1990) *The Consequences of Modernity*, Cambridge: Polity Press.
Giddens, A. (1991) *Modernity and Self-identity: Self and Society in the Late Modern Age*, Cambridge: Polity Press.
Giddens, A. (1992) *The Transformation of Intimacy*, Cambridge: Polity Press.
Giddens, A. (1993) *New Rules of Sociological Method* (2nd edn) Cambridge: Polity Press.
Giddens, A. (1994) 'Living in a post-traditional society', in U. Beck, A. Giddens and S. Lash, *Reflexive Modernization: Politics, Tradition and Aesthetics in the Modern Social Order*, Cambridge: Polity Press, Ch. 2; reprinted in A. Giddens, *In Defence of Sociology*, Cambridge: Polity Press, 1996, Ch. 1.
Giddens, A. (1994) *Beyond Left and Right: The Future of Radical Politics*, Cambridge: Polity Press.
Giddens, A. (1998) *The Third Way: The Renewal of Social Democracy*, Cambridge: Polity Press.
Giddens, A. (1999) *Runaway World: How Globalization is Shaping our Lives*, London: Profile Books.
Giddens, A. (2000) *The Third Way and its Critics*, Cambridge: Polity Press.
Giddens, A. (2007) *Europe in the Global Age*, Cambridge: Polity Press.
Giddens, A. (2007) *Over To You, Mr Brown: How Labour Can Win Again*, Cambridge: Polity Press, p. 12.
Giddens, A. and Diamond, P. (eds) (2005) *The New Egalitarianism*, Cambridge: Polity Press.

Gilligan, C. (1982) *In a Different Voice*, Cambridge: Harvard University Press.

Goffman, E. (1953) 'Communication conduct in an island community', dissertation, University of Chicago.

Goffman, E. (1959) *The Presentation of Self in Everyday Life*, New York: Doubleday Anchor.

Goffman, E. (1961) *Asylums: Essays on the Social Situation of Mental Hospital Patients and Other Inmates*, Harmondsworth: Penguin.

Goffman, E. (1963) *Behaviour in Public Places: Notes on the Social Organization of Gatherings*, Glencoe: Free Press.

Goffman, E. (1964) *Stigma: Notes on the Management of Spoiled Identity*, Englewood Cliffs, NJ: Prentice Hall.

Goffman, E. (1967) *Interaction Ritual*, Garden City, NY: Anchor.

Goffman, E. (1972) *Relations in Public*, Harmondsworth: Penguin.

Goffman, E. (1974) *Frame Analysis: An Essay on the Organization of Experience*, New York: Harper & Row.

Goffman, E. (1977) 'The arrangement between the sexes', *Theory and Society*, **4**: 301–32.

Goffman, E. (1979) *Gender Advertisments*, London: Macmillan – now Palgrave Macmillan.

Goffman, E. (1981) 'Reply to Denzin and Keller', *Contemporary Sociology: An International Journal of Reviews*, **10**: 60–8.

Goffman, E. (1981) *Forms of Talk*, Oxford: Blackwell.

Goffman, E. (1983) 'Felicity's condition', *American Journal of Sociology*, **89**: 1–53.

Goffman, E. (1983) 'The interaction order', *American Sociological Review*, **48**: 1–17.

Goffman, E. (1989) 'Erving Goffman's sociology', special issue of *Human Studies*, **12**(1/2).

Goldner, V. (1991) 'Toward a critical relational theory of gender', *Psychoanalytic Dialogues*, **1**: 249–72.

Goldstone, J. (2006) 'A historical, not comparative method: breakthroughs and limitations in the theory and methodology of Michael Mann's analysis of power', in J.A. Hall and R. Schroeder (eds) *An Anatomy of Power: The Social Theory of Michael Mann*, Cambridge: Cambridge University Press, pp. 263–82.

Goldthorpe, J.H., Lockwood, D., Bechhofer, F. and Platt, J. (1968) *The Affluent Worker: Industrial Attitudes and Behaviour*, Cambridge: Cambridge University Press.

Goldthorpe, J.H., Lockwood, D., Bechhofer, F. and Platt, J. (1969) *The Affluent Worker in the Class Structure*, Cambridge: Cambridge University Press.

Golthorpe, J. (1991) 'The uses of history in sociology: reflections on some recent tendencies', *British Journal of Sociology*, 42(2): 211–30.

Goodman, J. (1993) *Tobacco in History*, London: Routledge.

Goodman, N. and Hall, S. (1987) *Pictures of Everyday Life: The People, Places and Cultures of the Commonwealth*, Comedia: London.

Gordon, C. (1991) 'Governmental rationality: an introduction', in G. Burchell, C. Gordon and P. Miller (eds) *The Foucault Effect: Studies in Governmentality*, London: Harvester Wheatsheaf, pp. 1–51.

Gordon, C. (ed.) (1980) 'Two lectures', in *Power/Knowledge: Selected Interviews and Other Writings, 1972–1977*, New York: Pantheon Books.

Goudsblom, J. (1992) *Fire and Civilization*, London: Penguin.

Goudsblom, J. (1995) 'Elias and Cassirer, sociology and philosophy', *Theory, Culture and Society*, 12: 121–6.

Gould, S.J. (1990) 'Polished pebbles, pretty shells: an appreciation of OTSOG', in J. Clark, C. Modgil and S. Modgil (eds) *Robert K. Merton: Consensus and Controversy*, London: Falmer Press.

Gouldner, A. (1971) *The Coming Crisis of Western Sociology*, London: Heinemann.

Gramsci, A. (1971) *Selections from the Prison Notebooks*, London: Lawrence & Wishart.

Gutting, G. (1989) *Michel Foucault's Archaeology of Scientific Reason*, Cambridge: Cambridge University Press.

Habermas, J. (1962) *Strukturwandel der Öffentlichkeit, Neuwied/Berlin: Luchterhand* (2nd edn) Frankfurt: Suhrkamp, trans. T. Burger as *The Structural Transformation of the Public Sphere*, Cambridge: Polity Press, 1989.

Habermas, J. (1963) *Theorie und Praxis, Neuwied/Berlin: Luchterhand*, trans. as *Theory and Practice*, London: Heinemann, 1974.

Habermas, J. (1968) *Erkenntnis und Interesse*, Frankfurt: Suhrkamp, trans. as *Knowledge and Human Interests*, London: Heinemann, 1971.

Habermas, J. (1968) *Technik und Wissenschaft als Ideologie*, Frankfurt: Suhrkamp, part trans. in J. Habermas, *Toward a Rational Society*, London: Heinemann, 1971.

Habermas, J. (1971) *Zur Logik der Sozialwissenschaften* (2nd edn) trans. as *On the Logic of the Social Sciences*, Cambridge: MIT Press, 1988.

Habermas, J. (1973) 'What does a crisis mean today?', *Social Research*, winter, reprinted in P. Connerton (ed.) *Critical Sociology*, London: Penguin, 1976.

Habermas, J. (1973) *Legitimationsprobleme im Spätkapitalismus*, Frankfurt: Suhrkamp, trans. as *Legitimation Crisis*, London: Heinemann, 1976.

Habermas, J. (1976) *Zur Rekonstruktion des historischen Materialismus*, Frankfurt: Suhrkamp, part trans. in *Communication and the Evolution of Society*, Boston: Beacon Press, 1979.

Habermas, J. (1979) *Legitimation Crisis*, Boston: Beacon Press.

Habermas, J. (1981) *Theorie des kommunikativen Handelns*, Frankfurt: Suhrkamp, trans. as *Theory of Communicative Action*, London: Heinemann, 1984 and Cambridge: Polity Press, 1987.

Habermas, J. (1982) 'The entwinement of myth and enlightenment', *New German Critique*, 26: 13–20.

Habermas, J. (1983) *Moralbewußtsein und kommunikatives Handeln*, Frankfurt: Suhrkamp, trans. as *Moral Consciousness and Communicative Action*, Cambridge, MA: MIT Press, 1989.

Habermas, J. (1984) *The Theory of Communicative Action*, vol. 1, London: Heinemann.

Habermas, J. (1985) 'Modernity: an incomplete project', reprinted in H. Foster (ed.) *Postmodern Culture*, London: Pluto Press.

Habermas, J. (1985) *Der Philosophische Diskurs der Moderne*, Frankfurt: Suhrkamp, trans. as *The Philosophical Discourse of Modernity*, Cambridge, MA: MIT Press, 1987b.

Habermas, J. (1985) *Die neue Unübersichtlichkeit*, Frankfurt: Suhrkamp, trans. as *The New Conservatism*, Cambridge: Polity Press, 1989.

Habermas, J. (1987) *The Theory of Communicative Action*, vol. 2, *Lifeworld and System: A Critique of Functionalist Reason*, Cambridge: Polity Press.

Habermas, J. (1988) *Nachmetaphysisches Denken*, Frankfurt: Suhrkamp, trans. as *Postmetaphysical Thinking*, Cambridge: Polity Press, 1992.

Habermas, J. (1990) *Moral Consciousness and Communicative Action*, Cambridge: Polity Press.

Habermas, J. (1991) *Erläuterungen zur Diskursethik*, Frankfurt: Suhrkamp, trans. as *Justification and Application*, Cambridge: MIT Press, 1993.

Habermas, J. (1991) *The Theory of Communicative Action, vol. 1, Reason and the Rationalisation of Society*, Cambridge: Polity Press.

Habermas, J. (1991) *Vergangenheit als Zukunft* (ed. M. Heller) Zürich: Pendo, trans. as *The Past as Future*, Lincoln: University of Nebraska Press, 1994.

Habermas, J. (1992) *Faktizität und Geltung*, Frankfurt: Suhrkamp, trans. W. Rehg as *Between Facts and Norms*, Cambridge: Polity Press, 1996.

Habermas, J. (1995) *Die Normalität einer Berliner Republik*, Suhrkamp Verlag, Frankfurt am Main. J. Habermas (1998) *A Berlin Republic: Writings on Germany*, trans. Steven Rendall, Cambridge: Polity Press.

Habermas, J. (1996) *Die Einbeziehung des Anderen*, Frankfurt: Suhrkamp, ed. C. Cronin and P. De Greiff as *The Inclusion of the Other*, Cambridge: MA: MIT Press, 1998.

Habermas, J. (1996) *Vom sinnlichen Eindruck zum symbolischen Ausdruck*, Philosophische Essays, Frankfurt: Suhrkamp, trans P. Dews as *The Liberating Power of Symbols*, Cambridge, MA: MIT Press, 2001.

Habermas, J. (1998) *Die postnationale Konstellation: Politische Essays*, Frankfurt: Suhrkamp, trans. and ed. Max Pensky as *The Postnational Constellation*, Cambridge: Polity Press, 2001.

Habermas, J. (1999) *Wahrheit und Rechtfertigung*, Frankfurt: Suhrkamp, trans. as *Truth and Justification*, Cambridge: Polity Press, 2003.

Habermas, J. (2001) *Die Zukunft der menschlichen Natur. Auf dem Weg zu einer liberalen Eugenik?* Frankfurt: Suhrkamp, trans. Max Pensky, Hella Beister and William Rehg as *The Future of Human Nature*, Cambridge: Polity Press, 2003.

Habermas, J. (2002) *Religion and Rationality* (ed. E. Mendieta) Cambridge: Polity Press.

Habermas, J. (2005) *Zwischen Naturalismus und Religion. Philosophische Aufsätze*, Frankfurt: Suhrkamp.

Hall, J.A. (1986) *Powers and Liberties*, Harmondsworth: Penguin.

Hall, J.A. (1996) *International Orders*, Cambridge: Polity Press.

Hall, J.A. (2006) 'Political questions', in J.A. Hall and R. Schroeder (eds) *An Anatomy of Power: The Social Theory of Michael Mann*, Cambridge: Cambridge University Press, pp. 33–55.

Hall, J.A. and Schroeder, R. (eds) (2006) *An Anatomy of Power: The Social Theory of Michael Mann*, Cambridge: Cambridge University Press.

Hall, S. (1980) 'Popular-democratic versus authoritarian populism', in A. Hunt (ed.) *Marxism and Democracy*, London: Lawrence & Wishart.

Hall, S. (1985) 'Authoritarian populism: a reply', *New Left Review*, **151**: 115–24.

Hall, S. (1990) 'Encoding/decoding', CCCS Working Papers in Cultural Studies, reprinted in S. Hall (ed.) *Culture, Media, Language*, London: Unwin Hyman, in S. During (ed.) *The Cultural Studies Reader*, London: Routledge, 1993, pp. 90–103.

Hall, S. (1992) 'The west and the rest: discourse and power', in S. Hall and B. Gieben (eds) *Formations of Modernity*, Cambridge: Polity Press, pp. 275–320.

Hall, S. (1993) 'Vanley Burke and the "desire for blackness"', in M. Sealy (ed.) *Vanley Burke: A Retrospective*, Lawrence & Wishart: London.

Hall, S. (1996) 'When was the post-colonial? Thinking at the limit', in I. Chambers and L. Curti (eds) *The Post-Colonial Question*, London: Routledge.

Hall, S. (1997) 'The spectacle of the "other"', in S. Hall (ed.) *Representation: Cultural Representations and Signifying Practices*, London: Sage.

Hall, S. (2001) 'Museums of modern art and the end of history', in Annotations 6: *Modernity and Difference: Stuart Hall and Sarat Maharaj*, InIVA: London.

Hall, S. (2003) 'Chris Ofili in paradise: dreaming in Afro', in C. Ofili, *Within Reach*, London: C. Ofili and Victoria Miro Gallery.

Hall, S. (2004) 'The way we live now', in M. Tabrizian, *Beyond the Limits*, Gottingen: Steidl.

Hall, S. (2005) 'Whose heritage? Unsettling 'the heritage': re-imagining the post-nation', in *Inclusive Europe? Horizon 2020*, Y.R. Isar (ed.) Budapest: Kulturpont Iroda.

Hall, S. (2006) 'Modernity and its others: three "moments" in the post-war history of the black diaspora arts', *History Workshop Journal*, spring.

Hall, S. and du Gay, P. (eds) (1996) 'Who needs identity', in S. Hall and P. du Gay (eds) *Questions of Cultural Identity*, London: Sage.

Hall, S. and Jacques M. (eds) (1983) *The Politics of Thatcherism*, London: Lawrence & Wishart.

Hall, S. and Sealy, M. (2001) *Different: A Historical Context: Contemporary Photographers and Black Identity*, Phaidon Press: New York.

Hall, S., Held, D. and McGrew, T. (eds) (1992) *Modernity and its Futures*, Cambridge: Polity Press.

Hall, S., Hobson, D., Lowe, A. and Willis, P. (1980) *Culture, Media, Language*, London: Hutchinson.

Hamilton, P. (1983) *Talcott Parsons*, London: Tavistock.

Hamilton, P. (1996) 'Systems theory', in B.S. Turner (ed.) *The Blackwell Companion to Social Theory*, Oxford: Blackwell, pp. 151–9.

Hamilton, P. (ed.) (1992) *Talcott Parsons: Critical Assessments*, 4 vols, London: Routledge.

Hammersley, M. (1989) *The Dilemma of Qualitative Method: Herbert Blumer and the Chicago Tradition*, London: Routledge.

Haraway, D. (1989) *Primate Visions: Gender, Race and Nature in the World of Modern Science*, New York: Routledge.

Harding, S. (1986) *The Science Question in Feminism*, Ithaca: Cornell University Press.

Harrington, J. (1932) 'Tobacco smoking among the Karuk Indians of California', *Smithsonian Institute Bureau of American Ethnology*, **94**: 193–4.

Harvey, D. (1989) *The Condition of Postmodernity: An Enquiry into the Origins of Social Change*, Oxford: Blackwell.

Harvey, D. (2003) *The New Imperialism*, Oxford: Oxford University Press.

Held, D. and Thompson J. (eds) (1982) *Habermas: Critical Debates*, Basingstoke: Macmillan – now Palgrave Macmillan

Heritage, J. (1984) *Garfinkel and Ethnomethodology*, Cambridge, Polity Press.

Heritage, J. and Greatbatch, D. (1986) 'Generating applause: a study of rhetoric and response at party political conferences', *American Journal of Sociology*, **92**: 110–57.

Heynon, H. (1992) 'Architecture between modernity and dwelling:reflections on Adorno's aesthetic theory', *Assemblage*, **17**: 78–91

Hill Collins, P. (1989) 'The social construction of black feminist thought', *Signs*, **14**(4): 745–73.

Hillis-Millar, J. (1992) *Illustration*, London: Reaktion Books.

Hobsbawm, E. (1984) 'Marx and history', *New Left Review*, **143**: 39–50.

Hobson, J.M. (2003) 'Disappearing taxes or the "race to the middle"? Fiscal policy in the OECD', in L. Weiss (ed.) *States in the Global Economy: Bringing Domestic Institutions Back In*, Cambridge: Cambridge University Press, pp. 37–57.

Hobson, J.M. (2006) 'Mann, the state and war', in J.A. Hall and R. Schroeder (eds) *An Anatomy of Power: The Social Theory of Michael Mann*, Cambridge: Cambridge University Press, pp. 150–66.

Hochschild, A.R. (1979) 'Emotion work, feeling rules and social structure', *American Journal of Sociology*, **85**: 551–75.

Hochschild, A.R. (1983) *The Managed Heart: The Commercialization of Human Feeling*, Berkeley, CA: University of California Press.

Hochschild, A.R. (1989) 'Reply to Cas Wouter's review essay on The Managed Heart', *Theory, Culture and Society*, **6**(3): 439–45.

Hochschild, A.R. (1997) *The Time Bind: When Work Becomes Home and Home Becomes Work*, New York: Metropolitan Press.

Hochschild, A.R. (1999) 'The global chains of care and emotional surplus value', in W. Hutton and A. Giddens (eds) *On the Edge: Living with Global Capitalism*, London: Vintage.

Hochschild, A.R. (2003) *The Commercialization of Intimate Life: Notes from Home and Work*, Berkeley, CA: University of California Press.

Hochschild, A.R. with Machung, A. (1990) *The Second Shift: Working Parents and the Revolution at Home*, London: Piatkus.

Hoffman, J. and Graham, P. (2006) *Introduction to Political Theory*, Harlow: Pearson Education.

Holton, R. (1991) 'Talcott Parsons and the integration of economic and sociological theory', *Sociological Inquiry*, **61**(1): 102–14.

Holton, R.J. and Turner, B.S. (1986) *Talcott Parsons on Economy and Society*, London: Routledge.

Holub, R.C. (1991) *Jürgen Habermas: Critic in the Public Sphere*, London: Routledge.

Honneth, A. and Joas, H. (eds) (1991) *Communicative Action*, Cambridge: Polity Press.

Hughes, J. (2003) *Learning to Smoke: Tobacco Use in the West*, Chicago: Chicago University Press.

Huntington, S. (1996) *The Clash of Civilizations and the Remaking of the World Order*, New York: Simon & Schuster.

Husserl, E. (1970) *The Crisis of European Sciences and Transcendental Phenomenology* (trans. D. Carr) Evanston, IL: Northwestern University Press.

James, N. (1989) 'Emotional labour: skill and work in the social regulation of feelings', *Sociological Review*, **37**(1): 15–42.

James, N. (1992), 'Care = organization + physical labour + emotional labour', *Sociology of Health and Illness*, **14**(4): 488–509.

James, V. and Gabe, J. (eds) (1996) *Health and the Sociology of Emotions*, Oxford: Blackwell.

Jameson, F. (1984) 'Postmodernism: or the cultural logic of late capitalism', *New Left Review*, **146**: 53–92.

Jameson, F. (1985) 'Postmodernism and the consumer society', in H. Foster (ed.) *Postmodern Culture*, London: Pluto Press.

Jameson, F. (1991) *Postmodernism, or, Cultural Logic of Late Capitalism*, Durham, NC: Duke University Press.

Jay, M. (1984) *Adorno*, London: Fontana

Jay, M. (1993) *Force Fields: Between Intellectual History and Cultural Critique*, New York: Routledge.

Jessop, B. (1982) *The Capitalist State*, Oxford: Martin Robertson.

Jessop, B. (2002) *The Future of the Capitalist State*, Cambridge: Polity Press.

Joas, H. (1997) *The Creativity of Action*, Chicago: University of Chicago Press.

Jones, R.A. (2003) 'Emile Durkheim', in G. Ritzer (ed.) *The Blackwell Companion to Major Classical Social Theorists*, Oxford: Blackwell, pp. 209–10.

Jurt, J. (1995) *Das Literarische Feld: Das Koncept Pierre Bourdieus in Theorie und Praxis*, Darmstadt: Wissenchaftsliche Buchgessellschaft.

Kahlberg, S. (1994) *Max Weber's Comparative-Historical Sociology*, Cambridge: Polity Press.

Kalberg, S. (2005) *Max Weber: Readings and Commentary on Modernity*, Oxford: Blackwell, p. 13.

Kaplan, E.A. and Sprinker, M. (eds) (1993) *The Althusserian Legacy*, London: Verso.

Käsler, D. (1988) *Max Weber: An Introduction to his Life and Work* (trans. P. Hurd) Chicago: University of Chicago Press.

Kemper, T.J. (1990) 'Social relations and emotions: a structural approach', in T.J. Kemper (ed.) *Research Agendas in the Sociology of Emotions*, New York: University of New York Press, pp. 207–37.

Kemper, T.J. (1990) 'Themes and variations in the sociology of emotions', in T.J. Kemper (ed.) *Research Agendas in the Sociology of Emotions*, New York: University of New York Press.

Kennedy, P. (1987) *The Rise and Fall of the Great Powers*, New York: Random House.

Kilminster, R. 1987 'Introduction to Elias', *Theory, Culture and Society*, 4: 213–22.

Kilminster, R. and Varcoe, I. (eds) (1996) *Culture, Modernity and Revolution: Essays in Honour of Zygmunt Bauman*, London: Routledge.

Kilminster, R. and Wouters, C. (1995) 'From philosophy to sociology: Elias and the neo-Kantians (a response to Benjo Maso)', *Theory, Culture and Society*, 12: 81–120.

Krieken, R. van, (1998) *Norbert Elias*, London: Routledge.

Kritzman, L.D. (1990) *Michel Foucault: Politics, Philosophy, Culture: Interviews and Other Writings 1977–1984* (trans. A. Sheridan and others) London: Routledge.

Kymlicka, W. (1989) *Liberalism, Community and Culture*, Oxford: Clarendon Press.

Laclau, E. (1990) *New Reflections on the Revolution of Our Time*, London: Verso.

Laclau, E. and Mouffe, C. (1985) *Hegemony and Social Strategy: Towards a Radical Democratic Politics*, London: Verso.

Laitin, D. (2006) 'Mann's dark side: linking democracy and genocide', in J.A. Hall and R. Schroeder (eds) *An Anatomy of Power: The Social Theory of Michael Mann*. Cambridge: Cambridge University Press, pp. 328–40.

Lal, B.B. (1990) *The Romance of Culture in an Urban Civilization*, London: Routledge.

Lamont, M. (1992) *Money, Morals and Manners: The Culture of the French and the American Upper-middle Class*, Chicago: Chicago University Press.

Lamont, M. (2000) *The Dignity of Working Men: Morality and the Boundaries of Race, Class, and Immigration*, Cambridge, MA.: Harvard University Press.

Lanchester, J. (2005) 'Review of J.M. Coetzee's Slow Man', *New York Review of Books*, 52(18): 4–6.

Lasch, C. (1980) *The Culture of Narcissism*, London: Sphere Books.

Lawler, J. (1991) *Behind the Screens: Nursing, Somology and the Problem of the Body*, Edinburgh: Churchill Livingstone.

Layder, D. (1986) 'Social reality as figuration: a critique of Elias's conception of sociological analysis', *Sociology*, **20**(3): 367–86.

Layder, D. (1996) 'Contemporary sociological theory', *Sociology*, **30**(3): 601–8.

Leach, E. (1986) 'Violence', *London Review of Books*, October.

Lemert, C. (1997) *The Postmodern Is Not What You Think*, Malden, MA: Blackwell.

Lenoir, R. (2003) *Généalogie de la morale familiale*, Paris, Editions du Seuil.

Levinas, E. (1987) 'Language and proximity', in *Collected Philosophical Papers* (trans. A. Lingis) The Hague: Martinus Nijhoff.

Levine, A. A. (2003) *Future for Marxism? Althusser, the Analytical Turn and Revival of Socialist Theory*, London: Pluto.

Levine, D. (1971) *Georg Simmel: Individuality and Social Forms*, Chicago, IL: Chicago University Press.

Lewis, J.D. and Smith, R.L. (1980) *American Sociology and Pragmatism: Mead, Chicago Sociology and Symbolic Interactionism*, Chicago: University of Chicago Press.

Lewis, W.S. (2005) *Louis Althusser and the Traditions of French Marxism*, Lanham: Lexington.

Lichtheim, G. (1973) 'Historical and dialectical materialism', in *Dictionary of History of Ideas*, vol. 2, New York: Charles Scribner's Sons.

Lilleaas, U.-B. and Widerberg, K. (2001) *Time of Tiredness* (Trøtthetens tid) Oslo: Pax.

Lipietz, A. (1992) *Towards a New Economic Order*, Cambridge: Polity Press.

Lockwood, D. (1956) 'Some remarks on the social system', *British Journal of Sociology*.

Lockwood, D. (1958) *The Blackcoated Worker*, London: Allen & Unwin.

Lockwood, D. (1964) 'Social integration and system integration', in G.K. Zollschan and W. Hirsch (eds) *Explorations in Social Change*, London: Routledge & Kegan Paul, pp. 244–57.

Lockwood, D. (1992) *Solidarity and Schism: 'The Problem of Disorder' in Durkheimian and Marxist Sociology*, Oxford: Oxford University Press.

Lofland, L. (1980) 'Reminiscences of classic Chicago: the Blumer–Hughes talk', *Urban Life*, **9**(3): 251–81, reprinted in K. Plummer, *The Chicago School*, vol. 4, London: Routledge, 1997, Ch. 45.

Lofland, L.H. (1989) 'Social life in the public realm: a review', *Journal of Contemporary Ethnography*, **17**: 453–82.

Luhmann, N. (1993) *Risk: A Sociological Theory*, New York: de Gruyter.

Luhmann, N. (1998) *Observations of Modernity*, Stanford, CA:Stanford University Press.

Lukes, S. (1972) *Emile Durkheim*, New York: Harper & Row.

Lyman, S. and Vidich, A. (1988) *Social Order and Public Philosophy: The Analysis and Interpretation of the Work of Herbert Blumer*, Fayetteville, AR: University of Arkansas Press.

Lynch, M. (1996) *Scientific Practice and Ordinary Action: Ethnomethodology and Social Studies of Science*, Cambridge: Cambridge University Press.

Lyotard, J.-F. (1984) *The Postmodern Condition: A Report On Knowledge*, Minneapolis, University of Minneapolis Press.

Macey, D. (1994) *The Lives of Michel Foucault*, London: Vintage.

Macey, D. (2000) 'Ostranenie', in *The Penguin Dictionary of Critical Theory*, London: Penguin, p. 284.

Macherey, P. (1978) *Theory of Literary Production*, London: Routledge & Kegan Paul.

MacIntyre, A. (1969) 'The self as a work of art', *New Statesman*, March.

MacIntyre, A. (1981) *After Virtue*, London: Duckworth.

Maffesoli, M. (1990) Au Creux Des Apparences, Paris: Plon.

Mahon, M. (1992) *Foucault's Nietzschean Genealogy: Truth, Power, and the Subject*, Albany: University of New York Press.

Maines, D.R. (1988) 'Myth, text and interactionist complicity in the neglect of Blumer's macrosicology', *Symbolic Interaction*, **11**(1): 43–57.

Maines, D.R. (2001) *The Faultline of Consciousness: A View of Interactionism in Sociology*, New York: de Gruyter.

Mandel, E. (1975) *Late Capitalism*, London: New Left Books.

Mann, M. (1970) 'The social cohesion of liberal democracy', *American Sociological Review*, **35**: 423–39.

Mann, M. (1986) *The Sources of Social Power*, vol. I, *A History of Power from the Beginning to 1760 AD*, Cambridge: Cambridge University Press.

Mann, M. (1988a) 'The roots and contradictions of modern militarism', in M. Mann, *States, War and Capitalism*, Oxford: Basil Blackwell, pp. 166–87.

Mann, M. (1988b) 'Ruling class strategies and citizenship', in M. Mann, *States, War and Capitalism*, Oxford: Basil Blackwell, pp. 188–209.

Mann, M. (1993) *The Sources of Social Power*, vol. II, *The Rise of Classes and Nation-States, 1760–1914*, Cambridge: Cambridge University Press.

Mann, M. (1995) 'As the twentieth century ages', *New Left Review*, **214**: 104–24.

Mann, M. (1997) 'Has globalization ended the rise and rise of the nation-state?', *Review of International Political Economy*, **4**(3).

Mann, M. (2004) *Fascists*, Cambridge: Cambridge University Press.

Mann, M. (2005) *The Dark Side of Democracy: Explaining Ethnic Cleansing*, Cambridge: Cambridge University Press.

Mann, M. (2006) 'The sources of social power revisited: A response to criticism', in J.A. Hall and R. Schroeder (eds) *An Anatomy of Power: The Social Theory of Michael Mann*, Cambridge: Cambridge University Press, pp. 343–96.

Mann, M. n.d. 'Globalizations: an introduction to the spatial and structural networks of globality', http://www.sscnet.ucla.edu/04F/soc191f-1/globalizations.pdf.

Manning, P. (1992) *Erving Goffman and Modern Sociology*, Cambridge: Polity Press.

Marcuse, H. (1969) *Eros and Civilisation*, London: Sphere Books.

Marks, E. and de Courtivron, I. (eds) (1981) *New French Feminisms*, Brighton: Harvester.

Marx, K. (1852) Letter to Joseph Weydemeyer, March 5.

Marx, K. (1959) *Economic and Philosophical Manuscripts of 1844* (trans. M. Milligan) Moscow.

Marx, K. (1963) *Early Writings* (ed. T. Bottomore) London.

Marx, K. (1973) 'Introduction to a contribution to the critique of political economy' (1857), in M. Nicolaus (ed.) *Grundrisse*, Harmondsworth: Penguin.

Marx, K. (1973) *Grundrisse: Foundations of the Critique of Political Economy* (Rough Draft), Harmondsworth: Penguin (first written 1857–61).

Marx, K. (1976) *Capital*, vols 1–3, London: Lawrence & Wishart.

Marx, K. (1979) 'Theses of Feuerbach' (1888) p. xi, quoted in 3rd edition of *Oxford Dictionary of Quotations*, Oxford: Oxford University Press.

Marx, K. (1986) 'Civil war in France', *Marx–Engels Collected Works*, vol. 22, London: Lawrence & Wishart (first published 1871), 307–57.

Marx, K. (1987) 'Preface' (to the Contribution to the Critique of Political Economy), *Marx–Engels Collected Works*, vol. 28, London: Lawrence & Wishart) (first published 1859), 261–5.

Marx, K. (1996) 'The Eighteenth Brumaire of Louis Bonaparte', in T. Carver (ed.) *Marx: Later Political Writings*, Cambridge: Cambridge University Press, (first published 1852), 31–27.

Marx, K. and Engels, F. (1975) Manifesto of the Communist Party, *Marx and Engels' Collected Works 6*.

Maso, B. (1982) 'Riddereer en riddermoed – ontwikkelingen van de aanvalslust in de late middeleeuwen' (Knightly honour and knightly courage: on changes in fighting spirit in the late Middle Ages), *Sociologische Gids*, **29**(3/4): 296–325.

Maso, B. (1995) 'Elias and the neo-Kantians: intellectual backgrounds to the civilizing process', *Theory, Culture and Society*, **12**: 43–79.

Maso, B. (1995) 'The different theoretical layers of the civilizing process: a response to Goudsblom and Kilminster and Wouters', *Theory, Culture and Society*, **12**: 127–45.

McIntosh, M. (1978) 'The state and the oppression of women', in A. Kuhn and A.-M. Wolpe (eds) *Feminism and Materialism*, London: Routledge & Kegan Paul, pp. 254–89.

McLellan, D. (1974) *Karl Marx: His Life and Thought*, Basingstoke: Macmillan – now Palgrave Macmillan.

Mead, G.H. (1934) *Mind, Self and Society*, Chicago, IL: Chicago University Press.

Mennell, S. (1985) *All Manners of Food: Eating and Taste in England and France from the Middle Ages to the Present*, London: Blackwell.

Mennell, S. (1989) *Norbert Elias: An Introduction*, Oxford: Blackwell.

Mennell, S. (1989) *Norbert Elias: Civilization and the Human Self-image*, Oxford: Basil Blackwell.

Merton, R. (1970) *Science, Technology and Society in Seventeenth Century England*, New York: Harper & Row [1938].

Merton, R.K. (1936) 'The unanticipated consequences of purposive social action', *American Sociological Review*, **1**: 894–904.

Merton, R.K. (1938) 'Science, technology and society in seventeenth century England', in *OSIRIS: Studies on the History and Philosophy of Science, History of Learning and Culture*, vol. 4, part 2 (ed. G. Sarton) Bruges: St Catherine Press, pp. 362–632.

Merton, R.K. (1938) 'Social structure and anomie', *American Sociological Review*, **3**: 672–82.

Merton, R.K. (1939) 'Bureaucratic structure and personality', *Social Forces*, **18**: 560–8.

Merton, R.K. (1941) 'Review of Bernal', *American Journal of Sociology*, **46**.

Merton, R.K. (1957) *Social Theory and Social Structure*, Glencoe, IL: Free Press.

Merton, R.K. (1968) 'On the history and systematics of sociological theory', in *Social Theory and Social Structure*, New York: Free Press.

Merton, R.K. (1968) *Social Theory and Social Structure*, New York: Free Press.
Merton, R.K. (1976) *Sociological Ambivalence and Other Essays*, New York: Free Press.
Merton, R.K. (1982) *Social Research and the Practising Professions* (eds A. Rosenblatt and T. Gieryn) Cambridge, MA: Abt Books.
Merton, R.K. (1985) *On the Shoulders of Giants: A Shandean Postcript* (vicennial edn) New York: Harcourt Brace Jovanovich, and 'post-Italianate edn', Chicago, IL: University of Chicago Press, 1993.
Merton, R.K. (1996) *On Social Structure and Science* (ed. P. Sztompka) Chicago, IL: University of Chicago Press.
Merton, R.K. and Barber, E. (2004) *The Travels and Adventures of Serependity: A Study in Sociological Semantics and the Sociology of Science*, Princeton: Princeton University Press.
Merton, R.K. with Barber, E. (1976) 'Sociological ambivalence' in R.K. Merton with E. Barber, *Sociological Ambivalence and Other Essays*, New York: Free Press.
Meštrović, S. (1997) *Postemotional Society*, London: Sage.
Miles, M.W. (1975) 'The writings of Robert K. Merton', in L.A. Coser (ed.) *The Idea of Social Structure: Papers in Honor of Robert K. Merton*, New York: Harcourt Brace Jovanovich.
Miliband, R. (1965) 'Marx and the State', *Social Register*, London: Merlin Press.
Mill, J.S. (1970) *On the Subjection of Women*, London: Dent.
Mill, J.S. (1982) *On Liberty* (ed. G. Himmelfarb) Harmondsworth: Penguin.
Mill, J.S. (1991) *On Liberty and Other Essays* (ed. J. Gray) Oxford: Oxford University Press.
Miller, T.G. (1984) 'Goffman, social acting, and moral behavior', *Journal for the Theory of Social Behaviour*, **14**: 141–63.
Millett, K. (1977) *Sexual Politics*, London: Virago.
Mills, C.W. (1956) *White Collar*, New York: Oxford University Press.
Mills, C.W. (1959) *The Sociological Imagination*, New York and Oxford: Oxford University Press.
Mitchell, J. (1975) *Psychoanalysis and Feminism*, New York: Vintage Books.
Mohanty, C.T. (2003) *Feminism without Borders*, Durham: Duke University Press.
Molière, (1929) *Comedies*, vol. 2, London: J.M. Dent and Sons.
Mongardini, C. and Tabboni, S. (eds) (1998) *Robert K. Merton and Contemporary Sociology*, New Brunswick, NJ: Transaction.
Montage, W. (2003) *Louis Althusser*, Basingstoke: Palgrave Macmillan.
Morley, D. and Chen, K.-H. (eds) (1996) *Stuart Hall: Critical Dialogues in Cultural Studies*, London: Routledge.
Morris, L (ed.) (2006) *Rights: Sociological Perspectives*, London: Routledge.
Mouzelis, N. 'Social and system integration: Lockwood, Giddens, Habermas', *Sociology* (forthcoming).
Mouzelis, N. (1974) 'System and social integration: a reconsideration of a fundamental distinction', *British Journal of Sociology*, December.
Mouzelis, N. (1978) *Modern Greece: Facets of Underdevelopment*, Basingstoke: Macmillan – now Palgrave Macmillan.
Mouzelis, N. (1990) *Post-Marxist Alternatives*, Basingstoke: Macmillan – now Palgrave Macmillan.
Mouzelis, N. (1991) *Back to Sociological Theory: The Construction of Social Orders*, Basingstoke: Macmillan – now Palgrave Macmillan.

Mouzelis, N. (1992) 'Social and system integration: Habermas' view', *British Journal of Sociology*, **43**(2): 272–7.

Mouzelis, N. (1992) 'The subjectivist–objectivist divide against transcendence', *Sociology*, **34**(4): 741–62.

Mouzelis, N. (1995) *Sociological Theory: What Went Wrong?*, London: Routledge.

Mulhall, S. and Swift, A. (1992) *Liberals and Communitarians*, Oxford: Blackwell.

Nedelmann, B. (2001) 'The continuing relevance of Georg Simmel: staking out anew the field of sociology', in G. Ritzer and B. Smart (eds) *Handbook of Social Theory*, Thousand Oaks, CA: Sage, pp. 66–78.

Nicholsen, S. (1997) *Exact Imagination, Late Work: On Adorno's Aesthetics*, Cambridge MA: MIT Press.

Nicholsen, S. (2002) *The Love of Nature and the End of the World*, Cambridge, Ma: MIT Press.

O'Neill, M. (2004) 'Global refugees (human) rights, citizenship and the law' in S. Cheng, (ed.) *Law, Justice and Power*, California: Stanford University Press.

O'Neill, M. (ed.) (1999) *Adorno, Culture and Feminism*, London: Sage.

O'Neill, M. with Giddens, S., Breatnach, P., Bagley, C., Bourne, D. and Judge, T. (2002) 'Renewed methodologies for social research: ethno-mimesis as performative praxis', *Sociological Review*, **50**(1).

Oakes, G. (1980) *Essays on Interpretation in the Social Sciences*, Totowa, NJ: Rowman & Littlefield.

Ooms, H. (1991) *Tokugawa Village Practice: Class, Status, Power, Law*, Berkeley: University of California Press.

Osborne, P. (1989) 'Adorno and the metaphysics of modernism: the problem of a post-modern art' in A. Benjamin (ed.) *The Problems of Modernity: Adorno and Benjamin*, London: Routledge.

Osborne, P. and Segal, L. (1997) 'Culture and power: Stuart Hall interview', *Radical Philosophy*, **86**.

Outhwaite, W. (1996) *Habermas: A Critical Introduction*, Cambridge: Cambridge University Press.

Outhwaite, W. (ed.) (1994) *The Habermas Reader*, Cambridge: Polity Press.

Owen, D. (1994) *Maturity and Modernity: Nietzsche, Weber, Foucault, and the Ambivalence of Reason*, London: Routledge.

Parekh, B. (2000) *Rethinking Multiculturalism: Cultural Diversity and Political Theory*, Basingstoke: Palgrave Macmillan.

Parkin, F. (1979) *Marxism and Class Theory*, London: Tavistock.

Parsons, T. (1937) *Structure of Social Action*, New York: McGraw-Hill.

Parsons, T. (1939) 'The professions and the social structure', *Social Forces*, **17**: 457–67.

Parsons, T. (1949) *The Structure of Social Action* (2nd edn) Glencoe, IL: Free Press.

Parsons, T. (1951) 'Social structure and dynamic process: the case of modern medical practice', in T. Parsons, *The Social System*, New York: Free Press.

Parsons, T. (1951) *The Social System*, Chicago, IL: Free Press.

Parsons, T. (1957) 'Illness and the role of the physician: a sociological perspective', *American Journal of Orthopsychiatry*, 2: 452–60.

Parsons, T. (1964) 'Evolutionary universals in society', *American Sociological Review*, **29**(3): 339–57.

Parsons, T. (1967) 'Some comments on the sociology of Karl Marx', in T. Parsons, *Sociological Theory and Modern Society*, New York: Free Press.

Parsons, T. (1971) *The System of Modern Societies*, Englewood Cliffs, NJ: Prentice Hall.

Parsons, T. (1973) 'The superego and the theory of the social system', in P. Roazen (ed.) *Sigmund Freud*, Englewood Cliffs, NJ: Prentice Hall.

Parsons, T. and Shils, E.A. (eds) (1951) *Toward a General Theory of Action*, New York: Harper & Row.

Parsons, T. and Smelser, N. (1956) *Economy and Society*, London: Routledge.

Parsons, T., Bales, R.F. and Shils, E.A. (1953) Working Papers in the Theory of Action, New York: Free Press.

Perez-Diaz, V. (1993) *The Return of Civil Society*, Cambridge, MA: Harvard University Press.

Person, E. (1981) 'Sexuality as the mainstay of identity', *Signs*, 5(4): 605–30

Piccone, P. (1993) 'Beyond pseudo-culture? Reconstituting fundamental political concepts', *Telos*, 95.

Piore, M.J. and Sabel, C.F. (1984) *The Second Industrial Divide: Possibilities for Prosperity*, New York: Basic Books.

Plath, S. (1963) *The Bell Jar*, London: Faber.

Plummer, K. (1975) *Sexual Stigma*, London: Routledge.

Plummer, K. (1995) *Telling Sexual Stories: Power, Change and Social Worlds*, London: Routledge.

Plummer, K. (1998) 'The gay and lesbian movement in Britain, 1965–1995: schism, solidarities and social worlds', in B. Adam, J.W. Duyvendak and A. Krouwel (eds) *The Global Emergence of Gay and Lesbian Politics*, Philadelphia: Temple University Press.

Plummer, K. (2006) 'Rights work: constructing lesbian, gay and sexual rights in modern times', in L. Morris (ed.) *Rights: Sociological Perspectives*, London: Routledge.

Plummer, K. (ed.) (1991) *Symbolic Interactionism*, 2 vols, Aldershot: Edward Elgar.

Plummer, K. (ed.) (1997) *Chicago Sociology*, 4 vols, London: Routledge.

Polish Sociological Review 'Special edition on Zygmunt Bauman', 3, March 2006.

Pollner, M. (1987) *Mundane Reason*, Cambridge: Cambridge University Press.

Pope, W. (1976) *Durkheim's 'Suicide'*, Chicago: The University of Chicago Press.

Poulantzas, N. (1973) *Political Power and Social Classes*, London: New Left Books.

Poulantzas, N. (1975) *Classes in Contemporary Capitalism*, London: New Left Books.

Poulantzas, N. (1976) *Crisis of the Dictatorships*, London: New Left Books.

Poulantzas, N. (1978) *State, Power, Socialism*, London: Verso.

Pound, E. A. (1965) *Lume Spento and Other Early Poems*, New York: New Directions.

Powell, W.W. and DiMaggio, P. (1991) 'Introduction', in W.W. Powell and P. DiMaggio (eds) *The New Institutionalism in Organizational Analysis*, Chicago: University of Chicago Press, pp. 1–38.

Procter, J. (2004) *Stuart Hall*, London: Routledge.

Quinton, A. (ed.) (1967) *Political Philosophy*, Oxford: Oxford University Press.

Radcliffe-Brown, A.R. (1952) *Structure and Function in Primitive Society*, London: Cohen and West.

Rademacher, L.M. (2002) *Structuralism versus Humanism in the Formation of the Political Self: The Philosphy of Politics of Jean-Paul Sarte and Louis Althusser*, New York: Edwin Mellen.

Radway, J. (1991) *Reading the Romance*, Chapel Hill: University of North Carolina Press.

Rajchman, J. (1985) *Michel Foucault: The Freedom of Philosophy*, New York: Columbia University Press.

Ransom, J. (1997) *Foucault's Discipline: The Politics of Subjectivity*, Durham: Duke University Press.

Raphael, D.D. (1976) *Problems of Political Philosophy* (rev. edn) London: Macmillan – now Palgrave Macmillan.

Rawls, A. (2003) 'Orders of interaction and intelligibility: intersections between Goffman and Garfinkel by way of Durkheim', in A.J. Trevino (ed.) *Goffman's Legacy*, New York: Rowman & Littlefield, pp. 216–53.

Rawls, J. (1971) *A Theory of Justice*, Cambridge, MA: Harvard University Press.

Rawls, J. (1993) *Political Liberalism*, New York: Columbia University Press.

Red-Green Study Group (R-GSG) (1995) What on earth is to be done? *R-GSG*, 2, Hamilton Road, Manchester.

Reich, W. (1957) *The Sexual Revolution*, London: Vision Press.

Resch, R.P. (1992) *Althusser and the Renewal of Marxist Social Theory*, Berkeley, Los Angeles: University of California.

Reus-Smit, C. (2002) 'The idea of history and history with ideas', in S. Hobden and J.M. Hobson (eds) *Historical Sociology of International Relations*, Cambridge: Cambridge University Press, pp. 120–40.

Rice, O. (2004) 'Ziggy Stardust', *New Humanist*, 5 January.

Rich, A. (1977) *Of Women Born*, London: Virago.

Ringer, F. (2004) *Max Weber: An Intellectual Biography*, Chicago: University of Chicago Press.

Roberts, J. (1982) *Walter Benjamin: Theoretical Traditions in Social Sciences*, London: Macmillan – now Palgrave Macmillan.

Robertson, R. and Turner, B.S. (eds) (1991) *Talcott Parsons: Theorist of Modernity*, London: Sage.

Rock, P. (1979) *The Making of Symbolic Interactionism*, London: Macmillan – now Palgrave Macmillan.

Rojek, C. (2003) *Stuart Hall*, Cambridge: Polity Press.

Roscoe, P.B. (1993) 'Practice and centralisation: a new approach to political evolution', *Current Anthropology*, **14**(2): 111–40.

Rose, G. (1978) *The Melancholy Science: an Introduction to the Thoughts of T.W. Adorno*, London: Routledge.

Rose, N. (1989) *Governing the Soul: The Shaping of the Private Self*, London: Routledge.

Rosenblatt, R. (1989) 'No escaping modern times,' *US News and World Report*, October 2, pp. 10–11.

Ryan, A. (1978) 'Maximising, minimising, moralising', in C. Hookway and P. Pettit (eds) *Action and Interpretation*, Cambridge: Cambridge University Press.

Sacks, H. (1992) *Lectures on Conversation*, Oxford: Blackwell.

Sacks, H., Schegloff, E.A. and Jefferson, G. (1974) 'A simplest systematics for the organisation of turn-taking in conversation', *Language*, **50**: 696–735.

Sandel, M. (1982) *Liberalism and the Limits of Justice*, Cambridge: Cambridge University Press.

Sartre, J.-P. (1992) *Witness to My Life*, London: Hamish Hamilton.

Sayad, A. (2004) *The Suffering of the Immigrant*, Cambridge, Polity Press.

Sayer, A. (1984) *Method in Social Science*, London: Hutchinson.

Sayer, A. (2000) *Realism and Social Science*, London: Sage.

Sayer, A. (2005) *The Moral Significance of Class*, Cambridge: Cambridge University Press.

Scaff, L. (1989) *Fleeing the Iron Cage: Culture, Politics and Modernity in The Thought of Max Weber*, Berkeley, CA: University of California Press.

Scaff, L. (2003) 'Georg Simmel', in G. Ritzer (ed.) *The Blackwell Companion to Major Classical Social Theorists*, Oxford: Blackwell, pp. 239–66.

Schegloff, E.A. (1986) 'The routine as achievement', *Human Studies*, **9**: 111–51.

Schegloff, E.A. (1987) 'Between micro and macro: contexts and other connections', in J.C. Alexander (ed.) *The Micro-Macro Link*, Berkeley, CA: California University Press, pp. 207–34.

Schegloff, E.A. (1988) 'Goffman and the analysis of conversation', in P. Drew and T. Wootton (eds) *Erving Goffman: Exploring the Interaction Order*, Cambridge: Polity Press.

Schegloff, E.A. (1991) 'Reflections on talk and social structure', in D. Boden and D.H. Zimmerman (eds) *Talk and Social Structure: Studies in Ethnomethodology and Conversation Analysis*, Cambridge: Polity Press, pp. 44–70.

Schegloff, E.A. and Sacks. H. (1973) 'Opening up closings', *Semiotica*, **8**.

Scholem, G. and Adorno. T. (eds) (1994) *The Correspondence of Walter Benjamin 1910–1940*, Chicago: University of Chicago Press.

Schroeder, R. (1998) From Weber's political sociology to contemporary liberal democracy, in R. Schroeder (ed.) *Max Weber, Democracy and Modernization*, Basingstoke: Macmillan – now Palgrave Macmillan.

Schroeder, R. (2006) 'Introduction: The IEMP model and its critics', in J.A. and R. Schroeder (eds) *An Anatomy of Power: The Social Theory of Michael Mann*, Cambridge: Cambridge University Press, pp. 1–16.

Schultz, R.W. (1995) 'The improbable adventures of an American scholar: Robert K. Merton,' *The American Sociologist*, **26**(1): 68–77.

Schutz, A. (1962) *Collected Papers, vol. 1, The Problem of Social Reality*, The Hague: Martinus Nijhoff.

Scott, J. 'Who will speak and who will listen?', *British Journal of Sociology*, **56**(3): 405–9.

Scott, J. (2005) 'Public sociology and the neo-liberal condition', *Sociologisk Tidsskrift*, **13**(4): 324–34.

Seidman, S. (1985) 'Classics and contemporaries: the history and systematics of sociology revisited' and the response 'The historicist/presentist dilemma: a composite imputation and a foreknowing response', drawn from writings of R.K. Merton, *History of Sociology*, **6**(1): 121–36, 137–52.

Sennett, R. (1977) *The Fall of Public Man*, Cambridge: Cambridge University Press.

Setton, K.M. (1958) 'Foreword to the Torchbook edition', in H.O. Taylor, *The Emergence of Christian Culture in the West* (originally, *The Classical Heritage of the Middle Ages*) New York: Harper & Brothers.

Sewell, W.H. Jr (1992) 'A theory of structure: duality, agency, and transformation: dialectic, and history', *American Journal of Sociology*, **98**(1): 1–29.

Shalin, D.N. (1988) 'G.H. Mead, socialism and the progressive agenda', *American Journal of Sociology*, **93**(4): 913–52.

Sheridan, A. (1990) *Michel Foucault: The Will To Truth*, London: Routledge.

Sica, A. (1986) 'Review of R. Bierstedt's "American sociological theory: a critical history"', *American Journal of Sociology*, **91**: 1229–31.

Sills, D.L. and Merton, R.K. (eds) (1991) *The Macmillan Book of Social Science Quotations* (also published as vol. 19 of the *International Encyclopaedia of the Social Sciences*) New York: Macmillan.

Simmel, G. (1907) *Les Problèmes de la Philosophie de L'Histoire*, Paris: PUF, 1984.

Simmel, G. (1955) *Conflict and the Web of Group Affiliations*, Glencoe, IL: The Free Press.

Simmel, G. (1971) 'The metropolis and mental life', in D. Levine (ed.) *Georg Simmel on Individuality and Social Forms*, Chicago: Chicago University Press, pp. 324–39.

Simmel, G. (1989) 'Uber sociale differenzierung', Gesamtausgabe 2 Suhrkamp: Frankfurt am Main.

Simmel, G. (1992) 'Secret et société secrète', Saulxures: Circé.

Simmel, G. (1992) 'Soziologie: untersuchungen über die formen der vergesellschaftung', in Gesamtausgabe 11 Suhrkamp, Frankfurt am Main.

Slaughter, A.-M. (2004) *A New World Order*, Princeton: Princeton University Press.

Smart, B. (1985) *Michel Foucault*, Chichester: Ellis Horwood.

Smelser, N.J. and Swedberg, R. (1994) 'The sociological perspective on the economy,' in N. Smelser and R. Swedberg (eds) *The Handbook of Economic Sociology*, Princeton: Princeton University Press, pp. 3–26.

Smith, D.E. (1987) *The Everyday World as Problematic: A Feminist Sociology*, Boston: Northeastern University Press.

Smith, D.E. (1990) *Texts, Facts, and Femininity: Exploring the Relations of Ruling*, London: Routledge.

Smith, D.E. (1990) *The Conceptual Practices of Power: A Feminist Sociology of Knowledge*, Toronto: University of Toronto Press.

Smith, D.E. (1991) 'Writing women's experiences into social science', *Feminism & Psychology*, **1**(1): 156–7.

Smith, D.E. (1992) 'Sociology from women's experience: a reaffirmation', *Sociological Theory*, **10**(1): 91–4.

Smith, D.E. (1996) 'Telling the truth after postmodernism', *Studies in Symbolic Interaction*, **19**(3).

Smith, D.E. (1999) *Writing the Social: Critique, Theory and Investigations*, Toronto: University of Toronto Press.

Smith, D.E. (1999) *Zygmunt Bauman: Prophet of Postmodernity*, Cambridge: Polity Press.

Smith, D.E. (2001) 'Texts and the ontology of organizations and institutions', *Studies in Cultures, Organizations and Societies*,7: 159–98.

Smith, D.E. (2005) *Institutional Ethnography: A Sociology for People*, New York: AltaMira Press.

Smith, D.E. (ed.) (2006) *Institutional Ethnography as Practice*, Oxford: Rowman & Littlefield.

Smith, G.H.W. (2003) 'Ethnomethodological readings of Goffman', in A.J. Trevino (ed.) *Goffman's Legacy*, New York: Rowman & Littlefield, pp. 254–83.

Smith, P. (1992) *The Emotional Division of Labour in Nursing*, Basingstoke: Macmillan – now Palgrave Macmillan.

Snyder, J. (2000) *From Voting to Violence: Democratization and Nationalist Conflict*, New York: W.W. Norton.

Solow, R.M. (1997) 'How did economics get that way and what way did it get?', *Daedalus*, **126**: 39–58.

Stearns, C.Z. and Stearns, P. (1988) *Emotions and Social Change*, New York: Holmes & Meier.

Stearns, P. (1994) *American Cool: Constructing a Twentieth Century American Style*, New York: New York University Press.

Stedman Jones, S. and Watts Miller, W. *A Durkhiem Quest: Solidarity and the Sacred,* Basingstoke: Palgrave Macmillan, forthcoming.

Stevens, R. (ed.) (1996) *Understanding the Self*, London: Sage.

Stoler, A. (1995) *Race and the Education of Desire*, Durham: Duke University Press.

Stones, R. (1996) *Sociological Reasoning: Towards a Past-modern Sociology*, Basingstoke: Macmillan – now Palgrave Macmillan.

Stones, R. (2005) *Structuration Theory*, Basingstoke: Palgrave Macmillan.

Stones, R. (2006) 'Rights, social theory and political philosophy: a framework for case study research', in L. Morris (ed.) *Rights: Sociological Perspectives*, London: Routledge, pp. 133–51.

Strauss, A. (1993) *Continual Permutations of Action*, New York: Aldine de Gruyter.

Suttles, G.D. (1968) *The Social Order of the Slum: Ethnicity and Territory in the Inner City*, Chicago: University of Chicago Press.

Swedberg, R. (2005) *The Max Weber Dictionary: Key Words and Concepts*, Stanford: Stanford University Press.

Sztompka, P. (1986) *Robert K. Merton: An Intellectual Profile*, New York: St Martin's Press.

Sztompka, P. (1990) 'R.K. Merton's theoretical system: an overview', in J. Clark, C. Modgil and S. Modgil (eds) *Robert K. Merton: Consensus and Controversy*, London: Falmer Press.

Taylor, S. (1982) *Durkheim and the Study of Suicide*, London: Macmillan – now Palgrave Macmillan.

Terray, E. (1972) *Marxism and 'Primitive' Societies*, New York: Monthly Review.

Tester, K. (1995) *The Inhuman Condition*, London: Routledge.

Tester, K. (2004) *The Social Thought of Zygmunt Bauman*, Basingstoke: Palgrave Macmillan.

Theory, Culture and Society (1998) 'Explorations in critical social science: special section on Zygmunt Bauman', **15**(1).

Therborn, G. (1976) *Science, Class and Society: On the Formation of Sociology and Historical Materialism*, London: New Left Books.

Thoits, P.A. (1990) 'Emotional deviance: research agendas', in T.J. Kemper (ed.) *Research Agendas in the Sociology of Emotions*, New York: University of New York Press, pp. 135–52.

Thompson, J.B. (1984) 'Symbolic violence: language and power in the sociology of Pierre Bourdieu', in *Studies in the Theory of Ideology*, Cambridge: Polity Press.

Trevino, A.J. (ed.) (2003) *Goffman's Legacy*, New York: Rowman & Littlefield.

Turner, B. (1996) *The Blackwell Companion to Social Theory*, Oxford: Blackwell.

Urry, J. (2000) *Sociology Beyond Societies: Mobilities for the Twenty-First Century*, London: Routledge.

Wacquant, L. (2002) 'The sociological life of Pierre Bourdieu', *International Sociology*, **17**(4): 549–56.

Wacquant, L. (2004) *Body and Soul: Notebooks of An Apprentice Boxer*, Oxford: Oxford University Press.

Wacquant, L. (ed.) (2005) *Pierre Bourdieu and Democratic Politics: The Mystery of Ministry*, Cambridge: Polity Press.

Wagner, P. (1994) *Sociology of Modernity*, London: Routledge.

Wallraff, G. (1973) *Ihr da oben-wir da unten*, Köln: Kiepenheuer & Witsch.

Wanderer, J. (1995) 'Adventure in a theme park', in F. Dörr-Backes and L. Nieder, *Georg Simmel: Between Modernity and Postmodernity*, Wurzburg: Konigshausen & Neumann, pp. 171–88.

Watier, P. (2002) 'Les sentiments psychosociaux dans la sociologie de G. Simmel', in L. Deroche and P. Watier (eds) *La sociologie de G. Simmel (1908): Essais de modélisation sociale*, Paris: PUF, pp. 217–40.

Watier, P. (2007) 'Les resources de l'interprétation sociologique. Dans les traces de G. Simmel et M. Weber', *L'Année Sociologique*, 57(1).

Watier, P. and Markhova, I. (2004) 'Trust and psycho-sociological feelings: socialization and totalitarianism', in I. Markhova (ed.) *Trust and Democratic Transitions in Post-Communist Europe, Proceedings of the British Academy*, 119, Oxford: Oxford University Press, pp. 25–46.

Weber, M. (1946) *From Max Weber: Essays in Sociology* (ed. and trans. H. Gerth and C.W. Mills) New York: Oxford University Press.

Weber, M. (1949) *The Methodology of the Social Sciences* (ed. and trans. E. Shils and H. Finch) New York: Free Press.

Weber, M. (1958) *The Protestant Ethic and the 'Spirit' of Capitalism* (trans. T. Parsons) London: Allen & Unwin, [1930]; New York: Scribner's [1904–05].

Weber, M. (1958) *The Rational and Social Foundations of Music* (trans. Martindale et al.), Carbondale: Southern Illinois University Press.

Weber, M. (1968) *Economy and Society: An Outline of Interpretive Sociology* (ed. and trans. G. Roth and C. Wittich) New York: Bedminster Press.

Weber, M. (1978) *Economy and Society* (eds G. Roth and C. Wittich) New York: University of California Press.

Weber, M. (1989) 'Science as a vocation', in P. Lassman and I. Velody, with H. Martins (eds) *Max Weber's 'Science as a Vocation'*, London: Unwin Hyman.

Weber, M. (1998) 'Unternehmungen der Gemeinden', in Max Weber *Gesamtausgabe I:8. Wirtschaft, Staat und Sozialpolitik. Schriften und Reden, 1900–12* (ed. Wolfgang Schluchter) Tubingen: J.C.B. Mohr.

Wedderburn, D. and Crompton, R. (1972) *Workers' Attitudes and Technology*, Cambridge: Cambridge University Press.

West, C. and Zimmerman, D. (1987) 'Doing gender,' *Gender & Society*, **1**: 125–51.

White, S.K. (ed.) (1994) *The Cambridge Companion to Habermas*, Cambridge: Cambridge University Press.

Widerberg, K. (2005) 'Embodied gender talks: the gendered discourse on tiredness', in D. Morgan, Brandth, B. and Kvande, E. (eds) *Gender, Bodies and Work*, Aldershot: Ashgate.

Widerberg, K. (2006) 'Embodying modern times: investigating tiredness', *Time & Society*, **15**(1): 105–20.

Williams, C. (1989) *Gender Differences at Work*, Berkeley, CA: University of California Press.

Williams, R. (1980) 'Goffman's sociology of talk', in J. Ditton (ed.) *The View from Goffman*, London: Macmillan – now Palgrave Macmillan.

Williams, S. (2005) *Sleep and Society: Sociological Ventures into the (Un)known*, London: Routledge.

Williams, S.J and Bendelow, G. (1996) 'Emotions, health and illness: the "missing link" in medical sociology?', in V. James and J. Gabe (eds) *Health and the Sociology of Emotions*, Oxford: Blackwell, pp. 25–54.

Williams, S.J. (1998) 'Emotions, cyberspace and the "virtual" body: a critical appraisal', in G. Bendelow and S.J. Williams (eds) *Emotions in Social Life: Critical Themes and Contemporary Issues*, London: Routledge, pp. 120–32.

Witkin, R. (1998) *Adorno on Music*, London: Routledge.

Wittgenstein, L. (1958) *Philosophical Investigations* (2nd edn) Oxford: Basil Blackwell.

Wolff, K. (1950) *The Sociology of Georg Simmel*, Glencoe, IL: The Free Press.

Wollstonecraft, M. (1970) *A Vindication of the Rights of Woman*, London: Dent.

Woolf, J. (1990) 'The invisible flaneusse', in J. Woolf, *Feminine Sentences*, Cambridge: Polity Press, pp. 34–50.

Woolf, V. (1993) *The Crowded Dance of Modern Life*, London: Penguin.

Wouters, C. (1977) 'Informalization and the civilizing process', in P.R. Gleichmann, J. Goudsblom and H. Korte (eds) *Human Figurations: Essays for Norbert Elias*, Amsterdam: Stichting Amsterdams Sociologisch Tijdschrift.

Wouters, C. (1989) 'Response to Hochschild's reply', *Theory, Culture and Society*, **6**(3): 447–50.

Wouters, C. (1989) 'The sociology of emotions and flight attendants: Hochschild's Managed Heart', *Theory, Culture and Society*, **6**(1): 104–5.

Wright, E.O. (1978) *Class, Crisis, and the State*, London: New Left Books.

Wright, E.O. (1985) *Classes*, London: Verso.

Wright, E.O., U. Becker, J. Brenner et al. (1989) *The Debate on Classes*, London: Verso.

Wrong, D. (1961) 'The oversocialised conception of man in modern sociology', *American Sociological Review*, **26**: 183–93.

Young, R. (2003) *Postcolonialism: A Very Short Introduction*, Oxford: Oxford University Press.

Zweig, F. (1961) *The Worker in an Affluent Society*, London: Heinemann.

Websites

http://www2.fmg.uva.nl/emca/

http://www.humiliationstudies.org/documents/LindnerHumiliationFearGlobalizingWorld.pdf

http://en.wikipedia.org/wiki/Sociology

http://www.sscnet.ucla.edu/04F/soc191f-1/globalizations.pdf

Index

Page numbers printed in **bold type** refer to glossary boxes. *n* after a page number indicates a note number on that page

C

N

R

S

T

Z